Soho and Trafalgar Square
Pages 100–111

Bloomsbury and Fitzrovia
Pages 122–33

Covent Garden and the Strand
Pages 112–21

Holborn and the Inns of Court
Pages 134–43

Bloomsbury
and Fitzrovia

Smithfield
and
Spitalfields

Holborn and the
Inns of Court

ho and
afalgar
quare

Covent
Garden
and the
Strand

The City

RIVER THAMES

South Bank

Southwark and
Bankside

Whitehall and
Westminster

Smithfield and Spitalfields
Pages 162–73

The City
Pages 144–61

Whitehall and Westminster
Pages 70–87

Piccadilly and St James's
Pages 88–99

South Bank
Pages 186–93

Southwark and Bankside
Pages 174–85

EYEWITNESS TRAVEL

LONDON

EYEWITNESS TRAVEL

LONDON

Main Contributor **Michael Leapman**

LONDON, NEW YORK,
MELBOURNE, MUNICH AND DELHI
www.dk.com

Project Editor Jane Shaw

Art Editor Sally Ann Hibbard

Editor Tom Fraser

Designers Pippa Hurst, Robyn Tomlinson

Design Assistant Clare Sullivan

Contributors

Christopher Pick, Lindsay Hunt

Photographers

Max Alexander, Philip Enticknap,
John Heseltine, Stephen Oliver

Illustrators

Brian Delf, Trevor Hill, Robbie Polley

This book was produced with the assistance
of Websters International Publishers.

Printed and bound in China

First published in UK in 1993
by Dorling Kindersley Limited
80 Strand, London WC2R 0RL, UK

15 16 17 18 10 9 8 7 6 5 4 3 2 1

**Reprinted with revisions 1994, 1995, 1996, 1997, 1999, 2000 (twice),
2001, 2002, 2003, 2004, 2005, 2006, 2007, 2008, 2009, 2010, 2011,
2012, 2013, 2014, 2015**

A CIP catalogue record is available from the British Library.

ISBN 978-0-24100-719-8

MIX
Paper from
responsible sources
FSC
www.fsc.org   FSC™ C018179

**The information in this
DK Eyewitness Travel Guide is checked annually.**
Every effort has been made to ensure that this book is as up-to-date as possible
at the time of going to press. Some details, however, such as telephone numbers,
opening hours, prices, gallery hanging arrangements and travel information are
liable to change. The publishers cannot accept responsibility for any consequences
arising from the use of this book, nor for any material on third party websites, and
cannot guarantee that any website address in this book will be a suitable source of
travel information. We value the views and suggestions of our readers very highly.
Please write to: Publisher, DK Eyewitness Travel Guides, Dorling Kindersley,
80 Strand, London, WC2R 0RL, UK, or email: travelguides@dk.com.

Front cover main image: The Houses of Parliament and Lambeth Bridge

◀ View of St Paul's Cathedral from One New Change

Contents

How to use this Guide **6**

Portrait of Sir Walter Raleigh (1585)

Introducing London

Great Days
in London **10**

Putting London
on the Map **14**

The History of London **18**

London
at a Glance **38**

London Through
the Year **58**

A River View
of London **62**

Bedford Square doorway (1775)

London Area by Area

Whitehall and Westminster **70**

Piccadilly and St James's **88**

Soho and Trafalgar Square **100**

Covent Garden and the Strand **112**

Bandstand in St James's Park

Bloomsbury and Fitzrovia **122**

Holborn and the Inns of Court **134**

The City **144**

Smithfield and Spitalfields **162**

Southwark and Bankside **174**

South Bank **186**

Chelsea **194**

South Kensington and Knightsbridge **200**

Kensington and Holland Park **216**

The Broadwalk at Hampton Court (c.1720)

Beefeater at the Tower of London

Regent's Park and Marylebone **222**

Hampstead **230**

Greenwich and Blackheath **238**

Further Afield **246**

Six Guided Walks **264**

St Paul's Church: Covent Garden

Travellers' Needs

Where to Stay **280**

Where to Eat and Drink **288**

Shops and Markets **312**

Entertainment in London **334**

Children's London **348**

Houses of Parliament

Survival Guide

Practical Information **354**

Getting to London **364**

Getting Around London **370**

London Street Finder **378**

General Index **416**

Acknowledgments **438**

HOW TO USE THIS GUIDE

This Eyewitness Travel Guide helps you get the most from your stay in London with the minimum of practical difficulty. The opening section, *Introducing London*, locates the city geographically, sets modern London in its historical context and describes the regular highlights of the London year. *London at a Glance* is an overview of the city's specialities. *London Area by Area* takes you round the city's areas of interest. It describes all the main sights with maps, photographs and detailed illustrations. In addition, six planned walking routes take you to parts of London you might otherwise miss.

Well-researched tips on where to stay, eat, shop, and on entertainments are in *Travellers' Needs*. *Children's London* lists highlights for young visitors, and *Survival Guide* tells you how to do anything from posting a letter to using the Underground.

London Area by Area

The city has been divided into 16 sightseeing areas, each with its own section in the guide. Each section opens with a portrait of the area, summing up its character and history and listing all the sights to be covered. Sights are numbered and clearly located on an *Area Map*. After this comes a large-scale *Street-by-Street Map* focusing on the most interesting part of the area.

Finding your way about the area section is made simple by the numbering system. This refers to the order in which sights are described on the pages that complete the section.

Colour-coding on each page makes the area easy to find in the book.

A locator map shows you where you are in relation to surrounding areas. The area of the *Street-by-Street Map* is highlighted.

Numbered circles pinpoint all the listed sights on the area map. St Margaret's Church, for example, is ❻

Recommended restaurants in the area are listed and plotted on the map.

1 Area Map
For easy reference, the sights in each area are numbered and located on an *Area Map*. To help the visitor, the map also shows Underground and mainline stations.

Stars indicate the sights that no visitor should miss.

A locator map shows you where you are in relation to surrounding areas. The area of the *Street-by-Street Map* is shown in red.

A suggested route for a walk takes in the most attractive and interesting streets in the area.

2 Street-by-Street Map
This gives a bird's-eye view of the heart of each sightseeing area. The numbering of the sights ties in with the area map and the fuller descriptions on the pages that follow.

London at a Glance

Each map in this section concentrates on a specific theme: *Remarkable Londoners, Museums and Galleries, Churches, Parks and Gardens, Ceremonies.* The top sights are shown on the map; other sights are described on the following two pages.

Each sightseeing area is colour-coded.

Practical Information lists all the information you need to visit every sight, including a map reference to the *Street Finder* at the back of the book.

Numbers refer to each sight's position on the area map and its place in the chapter.

3 Detailed information on each sight
All important sights in each area are described in depth in this section. They are listed in order, following the numbering on the *Area Map*. Practical information on opening hours, telephone numbers, websites, admission charges and facilities available is given for each sight. The key to the symbols used can be found on the back flap.

The façade of each major sight is shown to help you spot it quickly.

The Visitors' Checklist provides the practical information you will need to plan your visit.

Stars indicate the most interesting architectural details of the building, and the most important works of art or exhibits on view inside.

Numbered circles point out major features of the sight listed in a key.

4 London's major sights
These are given two or more full pages in the sightseeing area in which they are found. Historic buildings are dissected to reveal their interiors; museums and galleries have colour-coded floor plans to help you find important exhibits.

INTRODUCING LONDON

Great Days in London   **10–13**

Putting London on the Map   **14–17**

The History of London   **18–37**

London at a Glance   **38–57**

London Through the Year   **58–61**

A River View of London   **62–67**

GREAT DAYS IN LONDON

For things to see and do, visitors to London are spoiled for choice. Whether here for several days, or just wanting a flavour of this great city, you need to make the most of your time. Over the following pages, you'll find itineraries for some of the best attractions London has to offer, arranged first by theme and then by length of stay. Price guides on pages 10–11 include travel on public transport, food and admission for two adults, while family prices are for two adults and two children.

Café at the National Portrait Gallery with a view of Trafalgar Square

History and Culture

Two adults
allow at least £140

- Art at the National Gallery
- Coffee with a view
- Houses of Parliament
- Buckingham Palace

Morning
Start the day by 10am in **Trafalgar Square** (see p104). This is when the **National Gallery** (see pp106–9) opens. Give yourself an hour and a half. The gallery is free, but visitors are encouraged to make a donation. After, go for a coffee at the Portrait Restaurant on the top floor of the neighbouring **National Portrait Gallery** (see p104), which has a great view over Trafalgar Square and Nelson's column. Set off down Whitehall to Parliament Square, a 15-minute walk that may be extended by the passing distractions of Horse Guard's Parade, **Banqueting House** (see p82) and **Downing Street** (see p77). See the **Houses of Parliament** (see pp74–5) before visiting the next highlight, the magnificent **Westminster Abbey** (see pp78–81). There are a number of inexpensive lunch spots around St James's Park tube station, such as Fuller's Ale and Pie House, 33 Tothill Street. Or go to the more pricey but attractive Inn the Park (book ahead; 020 7451 9999) by the lake in **St James's Park** (see p95).

Afternoon
On the far side of St James's Park is **Buckingham Palace** (see pp96–7). The Queen's Gallery has changing exhibitions and you can buy regal souvenirs in its shop. For tea, head up past St James's Palace to Piccadilly. You may not feel you can afford £47 per person for tea at the Palm Court at the **Ritz** (see p93) but there are several cafés and patisseries nearby, such as Richoux at 172 Piccadilly. For the best evening entertainment, get tickets for a West End play or show. These should be booked in advance (see p335), although last-minute tickets are sometimes on sale at the theatre box offices.

Shopping in Style

Two adults
allow at least £55

- St James's – shopping with history
- Old Bond Street for style
- Browse in trendy Covent Garden and the Piazza

Morning
Start in Piccadilly and **St James's Street**, (see pp90–91), home of suppliers to royalty and historic fashion leaders: John Lobb, the bootmaker is at No. 88 and Lock the hatter at 6. Turn right into Jermyn Street for high-class men's tailors such as Turnbull & Asser and New Lingwood, outfitters to Eton College. Floris the perfumer at 89 was founded in 1730 and the cheese shop Paxton & Whitfield at 93 has been here since 1740. Walk through Piccadilly Arcade to **Fortnum & Mason** (see p304), where the Fountain Tea Room can provide refreshment before buying souvenirs. Stop in at

Historic shopping mall at the Burlington Arcade, Piccadilly

◀ The Thames from Somerset House Terrace towards the City (c.1750–51) by Canaletto

The Queen's House, Greenwich

The Royal Academy (see p92) and the **Burlington Arcade** (see p93), before heading up **Old** and **New Bond** streets (see p315), the smartest shopping address in town, with art galleries, antiques and designer shops. Try South Molton Street for women's fashion and Oxford Street for **Selfridges** department store (see p313).

Afternoon
Head to **Covent Garden** (see p116). Take a look around **London's Transport Museum** (see p116), then wander the Piazza and streets to the north; Floral Street is renowned for high fashion. Check out alternative lifestyles in **Neal's Yard** (see p117). Stop for tea in Paul bakery and café at 29 Bedford Street.

The Great Outdoors

Two adults
allow at least £100
- **Sail to the Cutty Sark**
- **Ponds and a memorial in the Palace gardens**
- **Tea at Kensington Palace**

Morning
Take a 1-hour boat trip from Westminster Millennium Pier to **Greenwich** (see pp240–45). A morning is easily passed at this UNESCO World Heritage Site. There's the Maritime Museum, Royal Observatory, Queen's House, and Cutty Sark.

Have a snack lunch overlooking the river at the historic **Trafalgar Tavern** (see p244).

Afternoon
Return by boat and head to **Kensington Gardens** (see p210). Admire the boats on the Round Pond, and see what's on at the **Serpentine Gallery** (see p210). To the east is the Princess Diana Memorial Fountain. By the Long Water is the delightful statue of Peter Pan. Visit **Kensington Palace** (see p210), Princess Diana's former home. Have tea in the Palace's Orangery Tea Room.

A Family Fun Day

Family of Four
allow at least £250
- **Take the kids to the Tower**
- **Lunch at St Katharine's Dock**
- **Enjoy the undersea world**
- **Explore Chinatown**

Morning
Head to the **Tower of London** (see pp156–9), London's top visitor attraction and an established family favourite. Book tickets to avoid the queue. The fascinating castle and Crown Jewels will take at least a couple of hours to explore. For lunch, head across the road to **St Katharine's Dock** (see p160) where, among an eclectic collection of yachts and pleasure cruisers, there are several good places to eat.

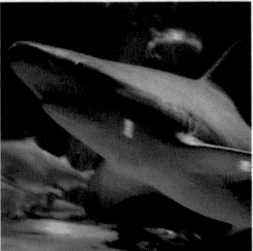

Predators at the London Aquarium

Afternoon
The **London Eye** is a thrilling trip above the city on the South Bank (see p191; online bookings can be made at www.london eye.com).

Vertigo sufferers need not panic – there is plenty of entertainment at and below ground level to choose from, especially in **County Hall** (see p190), which was the seat of London's local government for more than 60 years. This leisure complex is home to the Sea Life London Aquarium and The London Dungeon. Older children will enjoy the video games and simulators, bowling alley and bumper cars in the Namco Station. Afterwards, head to **Chinatown** (see p110), situated in and around Gerrard Street, which has many superb restaurants, colourful shops and a vibrant streetlife. Go for an early Chinese supper of *dim sum* or small dishes. If the kids are still going strong, end the day with a film at one of the many cinemas in **Leicester Square** (see p105).

View of the Houses of Parliament from the London Eye, South Bank

2 days in London

- Enjoy a panoramic spin on the London Eye
- Admire Wren's masterpiece, St Paul's Cathedral
- Take a Beefeater tour of the Tower of London

Naval gunship HMS *Belfast* moored in front of Tower Bridge

Day 1

Morning Start off by examining monuments to England's kings and queens on a self-guided tour of **Westminster Abbey** *(pp78–81)*. Don't miss the intricate Lady Chapel and peaceful cloisters. Next, wander through **Parliament Square** *(p76)* into idyllic **St James's Park** *(p95)*, with its pelicans and black swans, reaching **Buckingham Palace** *(p96–7)* in time for some pomp and circumstance at the 11:30am Changing of the Guard ceremony. If it's autumn or winter try **Horse Guards Parade** *(p82)* instead. Then walk through stately **Trafalgar Square** *(p104)* into the West End. Buy theatre tickets for the evening at bargain prices from the official cut-price booth on **Leicester Square** *(p105)*.

Afternoon Head to **Chinatown** *(p110)* for *dim sum*, then spend an hour or two admiring works by Van Eyck, Van Gogh and Constable at the **National Gallery** *(pp106–109)*. If there's time before the show, head to Covent Garden's **Piazza and Central Market** *(p116)* to watch the street performers.

Day 2

Morning The **Tower of London** *(pp156–9)* is a must-see. Two hours is enough time to join an entertaining Beefeater tour and inspect the murderous-looking Tudor weaponry in the White Tower. Afterwards, head to the **Monument** *(p154)*, Sir Christopher Wren's splendid 17th-century column built to commemorate the Great Fire of London. Climb its spiral staircase for a spectacular view that takes in landmarks old and new. Next, walk to Wren's glorious masterpiece, **St Paul's Cathedral**

(pp150–53). Highlights include the Whispering Gallery, the spectacular dome and the crypt.
Afternoon Cross the Millennium Bridge to Bankside, taking in views of **Tower Bridge** *(p155)*. Grab lunch from one of the artisan food stalls or cafés at **Borough Market** *(p178)*, then stroll to **Shakespeare's Globe** *(p179)* for an enthralling auditorium tour. Next door is **Tate Modern** *(pp180–83)*, housing paintings and art installations on a magnificent scale. End the day with a ride on the **London Eye** *(p191)*, timing it as the sun sets over the city.

3 days in London

- Uncover England's history at Westminster Abbey and the Houses of Parliament
- View contemporary art at Tate Modern
- Meet the Old Masters at the National Gallery

Day 1

Morning Visit the **Tower of London** *(pp156–9)*: explore the armoury, infiltrate the torture chambers and admire the Crown Jewels. Afterwards, have a drink by the colourful quayside at **St Katharine's Dock** *(p160)*, then cross **Tower Bridge** *(p155)* to Shad Thames: its scrubbed-up dockside warehouses are now pricey pent-houses. The white building houses the **Design Museum** *(p185)*, which hosts ever-changing exhibitions on furniture and fashion.

Afternoon Walk along the riverside and stop off to look around

HMS *Belfast* *(p185)*, now a floating naval museum, before detouring into **Southwark** *(pp176–7)* for one of London's most macabre attractions: the **Old Operating Theatre** *(pp178–9)*. Located in St Thomas' church, the surgery dates from before anaesthetics.

Day 2

Morning Get to **Westminster Abbey** *pp78–81)* early to explore its royal memorials. Nearby rise the Neo-Gothic **Houses of Parliament** *(pp74–5)* and **Big Ben** *(p76)*. Cross the river and head for the **Southbank Centre** *(pp188–9)*, which offers diversions for every taste. As well as the **London Eye** *(p191)*, there's the aquarium at **County Hall** *(p190)*, the **Hayward Gallery** *(p190)* and the **Royal Festival Hall** *(p190)*.

Afternoon Wander the huge galleries of **Tate Modern** *(pp180–83)*. Then walk over the Millennium Bridge for views of **Shakespeare's Globe** *(p179)* and **Tower Bridge** *(p155)*, reaching **St Paul's**

A performance in progress at Shakespeare's Globe in Southwark

Cathedral (pp150–53) in time for Choral Evensong.

Day 3
Morning Start at Covent Garden's **Piazza and Central Market** (p116), then join a tour of the **Royal Opera House** (p117). If time allows cross the cobbled piazza and pop into the **London Transport Museum** (p116). Next, browse the quirky designer shops on **Neal Street** and colourful **Neal's Yard** (p117).

Afternoon Head to Leicester **Square** (p105) for cheap theatre tickets, then walk to **Trafalgar Square** (p104) and spend a few hours at the **National Gallery** (pp106–9) for world-famous art, and the adjacent **National Portrait Gallery** (pp104–5) for paintings of royalty and celebrities. Later meander in **St James's Park** (p95) and a peek at **Buckingham Palace** (p96–7) before the theatre.

Day 1
Morning Begin at the **Design Museum** (p185) for avant-garde exhibits. Then walk over **Tower Bridge** (p155), from where you can see one of Britain's great battle-ships, **HMS Belfast** (p185). Next, spend two hours at the **Tower of London** (pp156–9) and have lunch at **St Katharine's Dock** (p160).

Afternoon Allow time to see two of Sir Christopher Wren's works of art, **St Paul's Cathedral** (pp150–53) and the **Monument** (p154), before heading to **Southwark** (pp176–7). Explore the intriguing **Old Operating Theatre** (p178–9) and view

contemporary art at **Tate Modern** (p180–83). End the day with a play (Apr–Oct) at **Shakespeare's Globe** (p179).

Day 2
Morning Soak up the ambience of the West End with a visit to its heart, **Leicester Square** (p105). Take in some culture at the **National Gallery** (pp106–9) and the **National Portrait Gallery** (pp104–5), which showcases a fascinating collection of paintings and photographs, before stopping for lunch in **Chinatown** (p110).

Afternoon Walk to **Covent Garden** (pp114–15) and take a back-stage tour of the **Royal Opera House** (p117), then climb aboard old trams at the **London Transport Museum** (p116). After- wards, peruse the trendy shops along **Neal Street** (p117).

Day 3
Morning Start the day at the **British Museum** (pp126–29), a treasure trove charting two million years of human civilization. Don't miss the Ancient Egyptian mummies and the Rosetta Stone.

Afternoon Head to Trafalgar **Square** (p104), then stroll along **The Mall** (p95) to **Buckingham Palace** (p96–7), to visit the State Rooms (Jul–Sep). End the day by relaxing in **St James's Park** (p95).

Day 4
Morning Start with a spin on the **London Eye** (p191), then

Assembled crowds watch a daredevil street performer in Covent Garden's piazza

Al fresco eating and drinking at bohemian Gabriel's Wharf

head to **Westminster Abbey** (pp78–81). This incredible building has witnessed royal weddings and coronations. If it's summer, book a tour of the **Houses of Parliament** (pp74–5), or at other times queue up to see the Lords and Commons in action. As you leave, look up at the clock tower of **Big Ben** (p76).

Afternoon Make your way to the **Imperial War Museum** (pp192–3), with its poignant exhibition on the Holocaust. For something lighter, walk through the vibrant **Southbank Centre** (pp188–9) to the boutiques and cafés of **Gabriel's Wharf** (p193).

Day 5
Morning Start in **Notting Hill** (p221), with a turn around **Portobello Road** (p221). If it's a Saturday, the bric-a-brac market enlivens this desirable neighbourhood. From here, wander into **Kensington Gardens** (p210) for a view of the palace and the Peter Pan statue.

Afternoon Exit into South Kensington's museum quarter. With three world-class museums, there's something for everyone. Choose between the **Science Museum** (pp208–9), with its hands-on experiments and aircraft simulators, the **Natural History Museum** (pp204–5) for animatronic dinosaurs and touch-screen creepy-crawlies, or the **Victoria and Albert Museum** (pp212–15), for one of the world's finest collections of decorative art.

Putting London on the Map

London, the capital of the United Kingdom, is a city of over seven million people covering 620 sq miles (1,606 sq km) of southeast England. It is built on the River Thames and is at the centre of the UK road and rail networks. From London visitors can easily reach the UK's other main tourist attractions.

Western Europe

NORWAY

SWEDEN

North Sea

DENMARK

UNITED KINGDOM

REP. OF IRELAND

NETHERLANDS

POLAND

GERMANY

London

BELGIUM

CZECH REPUBLIC

SLOVAKIA

Atlantic Ocean

FRANCE

SWITZ.

AUSTRIA

HUNGARY

SLOV.

CROATIA

BOSNIA HERZ.

SERBIA

ITALY

MONTEN.

KOS.

ALBANIA

MAC.

PORTUGAL

SPAIN

GREECE

Chesterfield

Mansfield

A1

Newark-on-Trent

M1

Nottingham

Derby

A52

Loughborough

Coalville

Leicester

A444

Nuneaton

A6

Co

M6

Coventry

A14

Ketterin

A46

Warwick

Wellingborou

A40

A423

Northampton

M1

Stratford-on-Avon

A429

Banbury

A43

Milto Keyne

Evenlode

A44

A34

A41

Gloucester

Cotswolds

A40

Aylesbury

Abergavenny

A465

A48

Stroud

Oxford

A449

M5

Cirencester

Thames

Abingdon

A40

Pontypool

Severn

A420

High Wycomb

A429

A419

Henley-on-Thames

Newport

Swindon

A34

M4

Bristol

M4

A350

Reading

Cardiff

A38

Chippenham

Kennet

M4

Newbury

Barry

Bath

Kennet and Avon Canal

Camberl

Weston-super-Mare

A37

A36

A34

Basingstoke

Aldersho

A39

Frome

Salisbury Plain

Andover

Farnham

M5

A303

Test

A31

Bridgwater

A303

M3

Taunton

A358

Winchester

Petersfield

M5

Yeovil

Salisbury

A36

A3

A303

Avon

Itchen

Waterlooville

Honiton

A37

A31

Southampton

Havant

A35

North Dorset Downs

Stour

New Forest

M27

Portsmouth

A31

Ringwood

Dorchester

Poole

Christchurch

Frome

Bournemouth

Isle of Wight

Weymouth

Purbeck Hills

Poole Bay

Weymouth Bay

Channel Islands, St Malo

Cherbourg

Bilbao, Santander

Le Havre, Caen, St Malo, Cherbourg

Greater London

Watford
Edgware
Harrow
Hampstead
Ealing
See next page
Enfield
Ilford
Romford
London City Airport
Heathrow Airport
Richmond
Greenwich
Dartford
Kingston
Croydon
Bromley
Thames

0 kilometres 10
0 miles 5

Lincoln
Boston
The Wash
Spalding
The Fens
Wisbech
Peterborough
March
Bedford
Letchworth
Luton
Luton Airport
St. Albans
Cambridge
Haverhill
Sudbury
Stevenage
Stansted Airport
Braintree
Colchester
Harlow
Chelmsford
See inset map above
Brentwood
Rayleigh
Basildon
Southend-on-Sea
Grays
Thames
Gravesend
Sheerness
London City Airport
LONDON
Heathrow Airport
Guildford
Gatwick Airport
Horsham
Crawley
Uckfield
The Weald
Royal Tunbridge Wells
Worthing
Brighton
Newhaven
South Downs
Hailsham
Bexhill
Hastings
Eastbourne
Bognor Regis

Ipswich
Stour
Harwich
Clacton-on-Sea
Blackwater
North Sea
Hook of Holland, Esbjerg

Gillingham
Sittingbourne
Herne Bay
Canterbury
Margate
Ramsgate
Deal
North Downs
Maidstone
Medway
Ashford
Dover
Folkestone
Channel Tunnel
Calais
Oostende
Rother
Strait of Dover
Boulogne-sur-Mer
FRANCE
le Touquet-Paris-Plage

English Channel
Dieppe

Key
— Motorway
— Dual carriageway
— A road
— Railway
  Urban area

0 kilometres 25
0 miles 15

Central London

Most of the sights described in this book lie within 14 areas of central London, plus two outlying districts of Hampstead and Greenwich. Each area has its own chapter. If time is short, you may decide to restrict yourself to the five areas that contain most of London's famous sights: Whitehall and Westminster, The City, Bloomsbury and Fitzrovia, Soho and Trafalgar Square, and South Kensington.

Tower of London
For much of its 900-year history the Tower was an object of fear. Its bloody past and the Crown Jewels make it a major attraction (*see pp156–9*).

National Gallery
This gallery has over 2,300 paintings, and the collection is particularly strong on Dutch, early Renaissance Italian and 17th-century Spanish painting (*see pp106–9*).

Natural History Museum
Life on Earth and the Earth itself are vividly explored at the museum, through a combination of interactive techniques and traditional displays (*see pp204–5*).

For key to symbols *see back flap*

0 kilometres 1
0 miles 0.5

Buckingham Palace
The office and home of the monarchy, the palace is also used for state occasions. The State Rooms open to the public in the summer *(see pp96–7)*.

Museum of London
This museum, on the edge of the Barbican complex in the City, provides a lively account of London life from prehistoric times to the present day *(see pp168–9)*.

Houses of Parliament
The Palace of Westminster has been the seat of the two Houses of Parliament, called the Lords and the Commons, since 1512 *(see pp74–5)*.

THE HISTORY OF LONDON

In 55 BC, Julius Caesar's Roman army invaded England, landed in Kent, and marched north-west until it reached the broad River Thames at what is now Southwark. There were a few tribesmen living on the opposite bank but no major settlement. However, by the time of the second Roman invasion 88 years later, a small port and mercantile community had been established here. The Romans bridged the river and built their administrative headquarters on the north bank, calling it Londinium – a version of its old Celtic name.

London as Capital

London was soon the largest city in England and, by the time of the Norman Conquest in 1066, it was the obvious choice for national capital.

Settlement slowly spread beyond the original walled city, which was virtually wiped out by the Great Fire of 1666. The post-Fire rebuilding formed the basis of the area we know today as the City but, by the 18th century, London enveloped the settlements around it. These included the royal city of Westminster which had long been London's religious and political center. The explosive growth of commerce and industry during the 18th and 19th centuries made London the biggest and wealthiest city in the world, creating a prosperous middle class who built the fine houses that still grace parts of the capital. The prospect of riches also lured millions of the dispossessed from the countryside and from abroad. They crowded into insanitary dwellings, many just east of the City, where docks provided employment.

By the end of the 19th century, 4.5 million people lived in inner London and another 4 million in its immediate vicinity. Bombing in World War II devastated many central areas and led to substantial rebuilding in the second half of the 20th century, when the docks and other Victorian industries disappeared.

The following pages illustrate London's history by giving snapshots of significant periods in its evolution.

A map of 1580 showing the City of London and, near the lower left corner, the City of Westminster

◀ A 15th-century manuscript showing the Tower of London with London Bridge in the background

Roman London

When the Romans invaded Britain in the 1st century AD, they already controlled vast areas of the Mediterranean, but fierce opposition from local tribes (such as Queen Boudicca's Iceni) made Britain difficult to control. The Romans persevered however, and had consolidated their power by the end of the century. Londinium, with its port, developed into a capital city; by the 3rd century, there were some 50,000 people living here. But, as the Roman Empire crumbled in the 5th century, the garrison pulled out, leaving the city to the Saxons.

Extent of the City
☐ 125 AD   ▆ Today

Public Baths
Bathing was an important part of Roman life. This pocket-sized personal hygiene kit (including a nail pick) and bronze pouring dish date from the 1st century.

Site of present-day Museum of London

Roman fort

Site of present-day St Paul's

Temple of Mithras
Mithras protected the good from evil. This 2nd-century head was in his temple.

Forum

Basilica

Londinium
Roman London was an important centre on the site of the present-day City (see pp144–61). On the Thames, it was in a good position to trade with the rest of the Empire.

Forum and Basilica
About 200 m (600 ft) from London Bridge was the forum (the chief market and meeting place) and the basilica (the town hall and court of justice).

55 BC Julius Caesar invades Britain

AD 61 Boudicca attacks

200 City wall built

410 Roman troops begin to leave

| 100 | 200 | 300 | 400 | 500 |

AD 43 Claudius establishes Roman London and builds the first bridge

London Wall
The tombstone of a Roman legionnaire was built into the city wall. The writing tablets in his left hand suggest he did clerical work.

Amphitheatre
Entertainment was brutal. A popular spectacle was gladiators, dressed like this figurine, fighting to the death.

Roman basilica and forum

Old London Bridge

Site of present-day Tower of London

Roman governor's palace

Where to See Roman London

Most traces of the Roman occupation are in the City (see pp144–61) and Southwark (see pp174–85). The Museum of London (see pp168–9) and the British Museum (see pp126–9) have extensive collections of Roman finds. There's a Roman pavement in the crypt of All Hallows by the Tower (see p155), and in the 1990s an amphitheatre was found below the Guildhall (see p161). The foundations of the Temple of Mithras are on view near the site on Queen Victoria St.

This section of the Roman wall, built in the 3rd century to defend the city, can be seen from the Museum of London.

London's best Roman mosaic is this 2nd-century pavement, found in 1869 in the City, now in the Museum of London.

604 King Ethelbert builds first St Paul's

834 First Viking raids

600	700	800	1000

871 Alfred the Great becomes king of Wessex

1014 Norse invader Olaf pulls down London Bridge to take the city

Medieval London

The historic division between London's centres of commerce (the City) and government (Westminster) started in the mid-11th century when Edward the Confessor established his court and sited his abbey *(see pp78–81)* at Westminster. Meanwhile, in the City, tradesmen set up their own institutions and guilds, and London appointed its first mayor. Disease was rife and the population never rose much above its Roman peak of 50,000. The Black Death (1348) reduced the population by half.

Extent of the City
☐ 1200   ▨ Today

St Thomas à Becket
As Archbishop of Canterbury he was murdered in 1170, at the prompting of Henry II with whom he was quarrelling. Thomas was made a saint and pilgrims visited his Canterbury shrine.

London Bridge

The first stone bridge was built in 1209 and lasted 600 years. It was the only bridge across the Thames in London until Westminster Bridge (1750).

Houses and shops projected over both sides of the bridge. Shopkeepers made their own merchandise on the premises and lived above their shops. Apprentices did the selling.

The Chapel of St Thomas, erected the year the bridge was completed, was one of its first buildings.

Iron railings

The piers were made from wooden stakes rammed into the river bed and filled with rubble.

Dick Whittington
The 15th-century trader was thrice mayor of London *(see p41)*.

Stag Hunting
Such sports were the chief recreation of wealthy landowners.

The arches ranged from 4.5 m (15 ft) to 10 m (35 ft) in width.

1042 Edward the Confessor becomes king

1086 Domesday Book, England's first survey, published

1191 Henry Fitzalwin becomes London's first mayor

1050	1100	1150	1200	1250

1066 William I crowned in Abbey

1065 Westminster Abbey completed

1176 Work starts on the first stone London Bridge

1215 King John's Magna Carta gives City more powers

1240 First parliament sits at Westminster

Chivalry
Medieval knights were idealized for their courage and honour. Edward Burne-Jones (1833–98) painted George, patron saint of England, rescuing a maiden from this dragon.

Geoffrey Chaucer
The poet and customs controller (see p41), is best remembered for his *Canterbury Tales* which creates a rich picture of 14th-century England.

Where to See Medieval London

There were only a few survivors of the Great Fire of 1666 (see pp26–7) – the Tower (see pp156–9), Westminster Hall (see p74) and Westminster Abbey (see pp78–81), and a few churches (see p48). The Museum of London (see pp168–9) has artifacts, while Tate Britain (see pp84–7) and the National Gallery (see pp106–9) have paintings. Manuscripts, including the Domesday Book, are found at the British Library (see p127).

The Tower of London was started in 1078 and became one of the few centres of royal power in the largely self-governing City.

A 14th-century rose window is all that remains of Winchester Palace near the Clink on Bankside (see p184).

Plan of the Bridge
The bridge had 19 arches to span the river making it, for many years, the longest stone bridge in England.

Many 13th-century pilgrims went to Canterbury.

	1348 Black Death kills thousands	**1394** Westminster Hall remodelled by Henry Yevele	*The Great Seal of Richard I, who spent most of his 10-year reign fighting abroad.*
1350		**1400**	**1450**
	1381 Peasants' Revolt defeated	**1397** Richard Whittington becomes mayor	**1476** William Caxton sets up first printing press at Westminster

Elizabethan London

In the 16th century the monarchy was stronger than ever before. The Tudors established peace throughout England, allowing art and commerce to flourish. This renaissance reached its zenith under Elizabeth I as explorers opened up the New World, and English theatre, the nation's most lasting contribution to world culture, was born.

Curtain

Shakespeare's Globe

Elizabethan theatres were built of wood and only half covered; performances took place in summer.

A balcony on the stage was part of the scenery.

The thrust stage had a trap door for special effects.

Extent of the City
☐ 1561   ■ Today

Death at the Stake
The Tudors dealt harshly with social and religious dissent. Here Bishops Latimer and Ridley die for so-called heresy in 1555, when Elizabeth's sister, Mary I, was queen. Traitors could expect to be hung, drawn and quartered.

In the yard, below the level of the stage, commoners stood to watch the play.

Hunting and Hawking
Popular 16th-century pastimes are shown on this cushion cover.

1536 Henry VIII's second wife, Anne Boleyn, executed

1535 Sir Thomas More executed for treason

1553 Edward dies, succeeded by his sister Mary I

1530   **1540**   **1550**

Rat catchers, and other pest controllers, could not prevent epidemics of plague.

1547 Henry dies, succeeded by his son Edward VI

1534 Henry VIII breaks with the Roman Catholic church

The galleries were for rich theatre-goers who could watch from the comfort of seats.

Elizabeth I
The "Virgin Queen" sat for this portrait to celebrate victory over the Spanish in 1588.

Tilting Spurs
The aim of this high-speed sport, popular among noblemen, was to knock opponents off their horses.

Steps allowed tiered seating.

Astronomical Clock
Made in 1540 at Hampton Court, it shows the sun moving round the earth.

Audience entrance

Where to See Elizabethan London

The Great Fire of 1666 wiped out the City. Fortunately, Middle Temple Hall (see p141), Staple Inn (see p143) and the Lady Chapel inside Westminster Abbey (see pp78–81) were beyond its reach. The Museum of London (see pp168–9), Victoria and Albert (see pp212–15), and Geffrye Museums (see p250) have fine furniture and artefacts. Further afield are Hampton Court (see pp256–9) and Sutton House (see p250).

Elizabeth I watched *Twelfth Night* by Shakespeare under the hammerbeam roof of Middle Temple Hall in 1603.

The Parr Pot, now in the Museum of London, was made by Venetian craftsmen in London in 1547.

1563 Plague sweeps Europe

1558 Mary I's death makes Elizabeth queen

1560	1570	1580	1590

1570 Francis Drake makes first voyage to the West Indies

Gloves made from imported silk and velvet

1584 Walter Raleigh's first attempt to colonize America

1588 Drake defeats Spanish Armada

1591 First play by Shakespeare produced

1603 Elizabeth dies, James I accedes

Restoration London

Civil War had broken out in 1642 when the mercantile class demanded that some of the monarch's power be passed to Parliament. The subsequent Commonwealth was dominated by Puritans under Oliver Cromwell. The Puritans outlawed simple pleasures, such as dancing and theatre, so it was small wonder that the restoration of the monarchy under Charles II in 1660 was greeted with rejoicing and the release of pent-up creative energies. The period was, however, also marked with two major tragedies: the Plague (1665) and the Great Fire (1666).

Extent of the City

☐ 1680 ■ Today

St Paul's was destroyed in the fire that raged as far west as Fetter Lane *(map 14 E1)*.

London Bridge itself survived, but many of the buildings on it were burned down.

Oliver Cromwell He led the Parliamentarian army and was Lord Protector of the Realm from 1653 until his death in 1658. At the Restoration, his body was dug up and hung from the gallows at Tyburn, near Hyde Park *(see p213)*.

Charles I's Death The king was beheaded for tyranny on a freezing day (30 January 1649) outside Banqueting House *(see p82)*.

Charles I His belief in the Divine Right of Kings angered Parliament and was one of the causes of civil war.

1623 Shakespeare's First Folio published

1625 James I dies, succeeded by his son Charles I

1642 Civil war starts when Parliament defies king

| 1620 | 1630 | 1640 | 165● |

Feathered helmet worn by Royalist cavaliers.

1605 Guy Fawkes leads failed attempt to blow up the King and Parliament

1649 Charles I executed, Commonwealth established

Newton's Telescope
Physicist and astronomer
Sir Isaac Newton
(1642–1727)
discovered the
law of gravity.

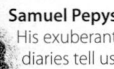

Samuel Pepys
His exuberant
diaries tell us
much about
courtly life
of the time.

The Tower of London
was just out of the
fire's reach.

Where to See Restoration London

Wren's churches and his St Paul's Cathedral *(see p49 and pp150–3)* are, with Inigo Jones's Banqueting House *(see p82)*, London's most famous 17th-century buildings. Other fine examples are Lincoln's Inn *(see p138)* and Cloth Fair *(see p167)*. The Museum of London *(see pp168–9)* has a period interior. The British Museum *(see pp126–9)* and the V&A *(see pp212–15)* have numerous pottery, silver and textile collections.

Ham House *(p254)* was built in 1610 but much enlarged later in the century. It has the finest interior of its time in England.

The Great Fire of 1666

An unidentified Dutch artist painted this view of the fire that burned for five days, destroying 13,000 houses.

The Plague
During 1665, carts
collected the dead
and took them to
communal graves
outside the city.

Peter Paul Rubens painted the ceiling in 1636 for Inigo Jones's Banqueting House *(p82)*. This is one of its panels.

1664–5 Plague kills 100,000

1685 Charles II dies, Catholic James II becomes king

1692 First insurance market opens at Lloyd's

1666 Great Fire

1660

1670

1680

1690

1660 Monarchy restored under Charles II

A barber's bowl made by London potters in 1681.

1688 James ousted in favour of Protestant William of Orange

1694 First Bank of England set up by William Paterson

Georgian London

The foundation of the Bank of England in 1694 spurred the growth of London and, by the time George I came to the throne in 1714, it had become an important financial and commercial centre. Aristocrats with West End estates began laying out elegant squares and terraces to house newly-rich merchants. Architects such as the Adam brothers, John Soane and John Nash developed stylish medium-scale housing. They drew inspiration from the great European capitals, as did English painters, sculptors, composers and craftsmen.

Extent of the City
☐ 1810   ☐ Today

Portman Square was on the town's outskirts when it was started in 1764.

Manchester Square was laid out in 1776–8.

Great Cumberland Place
Built in 1790, it was named after a royal duke and military commander.

Grosvenor Square
Few of the original houses remain on one of the oldest and largest Mayfair squares (1720).

Docks
Purpose-built docks handled the growth in world trade.

1714 George I becomes king

1727 George II becomes king

1717 Hanover Square built, start of West End development

1729 John Wesley (1703–91) founds the Methodist Church

1759 Kew Gardens established

1760 George III becomes king

1768 Royal Academy of Art established

1720   **1740**   **1760**   **1770**

John Nash
Stylish Nash shaped 18th-century London with variations on Classical themes, such as this archway in Cumberland Terrace, near Regent's Park.

Where to See Georgian London

The portico of the Theatre Royal Haymarket *(see pp336–7)* gives a taste of the style of fashionable London in the 1820s. In Pall Mall *(see p94)* Charles Barry's Reform and Travellers' Clubs are equally evocative. Most West End squares have some Georgian buildings, while Fournier Street *(see p172)* has good small-scale domestic architecture. The Victoria and Albert Museum *(V&A, see pp212–15)* has silver, as do the London Silver Vaults *(see p143)*, where it is for sale. Hogarth's pictures, at Tate Britain *(see pp84–7)* and Sir John Soane's Museum *(see pp138–9)*, show the social conditions.

This English long-case clock (1725), made of oak and pine with Chinese designs, is in the V&A.

Georgian London
The layout of much of London's West End has remained very similar to how it was in 1828, when this map was published.

Berkeley Square
Built in the 1730s and 1740s in the grounds of the former Berkeley House, several characteristic original houses remain on its west side.

Ironwork
Crafts flourished. This ornate railing is on Manchester Square.

Captain Cook
This Yorkshire-born explorer discovered Australia during a voyage round the world in 1768–71.

Signatories of the American Declaration of Independence

1802 Stock Exchange formally established

1820 George III dies, Prince Regent becomes George IV

1830 George IV dies, brother William IV is king

| 1790 | 1800 | 1810 | 1820 | 1830 |

1776 Britain loses American colonies with Declaration of Independence

1811 George III goes mad, his son George is made Regent

1829 London's first horse bus

Victorian London

Much of London today is Victorian. Until the early 19th century, the capital had been confined to the original Roman city, plus Westminster and Mayfair to the west, ringed by fields and villages such as Brompton, Islington and Battersea. From the 1820s, these green spaces filled rapidly with terraces of houses for the growing numbers attracted to London by industrialization. Rapid expansion brought challenges to the city. The first cholera epidemic broke out in 1832, and in 1858 came the Great Stink, when the smell from the Thames became so bad that Parliament had to go into recess. But Joseph Bazalgette's sewerage system (1875), involving banking both sides of the Thames, eased the problem.

Extent of the City
☐ 1900   ▨ Today

Pantomime
The traditional family Christmas entertainment – still popular today *(see p336)* – started in the 19th century.

Nearly 14,000 exhibitors came from all over the world, bringing more than 100,000 exhibits.

The building was 560 m (1,850 ft) long and 33 m (110 ft) high.

Soldiers marched and jumped on the floor to test its strength before the exhibition opened.

Massive elm trees growing in Hyde Park were left standing and the exhibition was erected around them.

The Crystal Fountain was 8 m (27 ft) high.

Carpets and stained glass were hung from the galleries.

1836 First London rail terminus opens at London Bridge

1837 Victoria becomes queen

1851 Great Exhibition

A Wedgwood plate in typically florid Victorian style

1861 Prince Albert dies

1840

1850

1860

1840 Rowland Hill introduces the Penny Post

Season ticket for Great Exhibition

1863 Metropolitan Railway, world's first underground system, is opened

Railways
By 1900 fast trains, such as this Scotch *Express*, were crossing the country.

Where to See Victorian London

Grandiose buildings best reflect the spirit of the age, notably the rail termini, the Kensington Museums *(see pp200–15)* and the Royal Albert Hall *(see p207)*. Leighton House *(see p220)* has a well-preserved interior. Pottery and fabrics are in the Victoria and Albert Museum, and London's Transport Museum *(see p116)* has buses, trams and trains.

Crystal Palace
Between May and October 1851, 6 million people visited Joseph Paxton's superb feat of engineering. In 1852, it was dismantled and reassembled in south London, where it remained until destroyed by fire in 1936.

Formal Dress Under Victoria, elaborate men's attire was replaced by more restrained evening wear.

The Victorian Gothic style suited buildings like the Public Record Office in Chancery Lane.

The Great Exhibition of 1851
The exhibition, held in the Crystal Palace in Hyde Park, celebrated industry, technology and the expanding British Empire.

Telegraph
Newly invented communications technology, like this telegraph from 1840, made business expansion easier.

1870 First Peabody Buildings, to house the poor, built in Blackfriars Road

1890 First electric Underground line, from Bank to Stockwell, opens

1891 First LCC public housing built, in Shoreditch

1901 Queen Victoria dies, Edward VII accedes

70 — 1880 — 1890 — 1900

A special box for carrying top hats

1889 London County Council (LCC) established

1899 First motor buses introduced

Commemorative fan for the Boer War, which ended in 1903

London Between the World Wars

The society that emerged from World War I grasped eagerly at the innovations of early 20th-century London – the motor car, the telephone, commuter transport. The cinema brought transatlantic culture, especially jazz and swing music. Victorian social restraints were discarded as people flocked to dance in restaurants, clubs and dance halls. Many left the crowded inner city for new suburban estates. Then came the 1930s global Depression, whose effects had barely worn off when World War II began.

Extent of the City
☐ 1938   ☐ Today

Commuting
London's new outer suburbs were made popular by the underground railway. In the north was "Metroland", named after the Metropolitan line which penetrated Hertfordshire.

Communications
The radio provided home entertainment and information. This is a 1933 model.

High Fashion
The sleek flowing new styles contrasted with the fussy elaboration of the Victorians and Edwardians. This tea gown is from the 1920s.

Formal evening wear, including hats for both sexes, was still compulsory when going to smart West End night spots.

A London Street Scene
Maurice Greiflenhagen's painting (1926) captures the bustle of London after dark.

Medals, like this from 1914, were struck during the campaign for women's votes.

1910

1920

1921 North Circular Road links northern suburbs

1910 George V succeeds Edward VII

Cavalry was still used in the Middle Eastern battles of World War I (1914–18).

1922 First BBC national radio broadcast

Early Cinema
London-born Charlie Chaplin (1889–1977), seen here in *City Lights*, was a popular star of both silent and talking pictures.

George VI
Oswald Birley painted this portrait of the king who became a model for wartime resistance and unity.

Seven new theatres were built in central London from 1924 to 1931.

Early motor buses had open tops, like the old horse-drawn buses.

Throughout the period newspaper circulations increased massively. In 1930 *The Daily Herald* sold 2 million copies a day.

World War II and The Blitz

World War II saw large-scale civilian bombing for the first time, bringing the horror of war to Londoners' doorsteps. Thousands were killed in their homes. Many people took refuge in Underground stations and children were evacuated to the safety of the country.

WOMEN OF BRITAIN
COME INTO THE FACTORIES

As in World War I, women were recruited for factory work formerly done by men who were away fighting.

Bombing raids in 1940 and 1941 (the Blitz) caused devastation all over the city.

1929 US stock market crash brings world Depression

1939 World War II begins

25 | 1930

1927 First talking pictures

1936 Edward VIII abdicates to marry US divorcée Wallis Simpson. George VI accedes

1940 Winston Churchill becomes Prime Minister

Postwar London

Much of London was flattened by World War II bombs.
Afterwards, the chance for imaginative rebuilding was missed –
some badly designed postwar developments are already being
razed. But, by the 1960s, London was such a dynamic world
leader in fashion and popular music that *Time* magazine dubbed
it "swinging London". Skyscrapers sprang up, but some stayed
empty as 1980s boom gave way to 1990s recession.

Extent of the City
☐ 1959   ▨ Today

The Beatles
The Liverpool pop group, pictured in 1965,
had rocketed to stardom two years earlier with
songs of appealing freshness and directness.
The group symbolized carefree 1960s London.

Festival of Britain
After wartime,
the city's morale
was lifted by the
Festival, marking
the 1851 Great
Exhibition's
centenary
(see pp30–31).

Margaret Thatcher
Britain's first woman
Prime Minister (1979–90)
promoted the market-
led policies that fuelled
the 1980s boom.

The Royal Festival Hall (1951)
was the Festival's centrepiece and
is still a landmark *(see p190).*

Telecom Tower (1964), at
189 m (620 ft) high, dominates
the Fitzrovia skyline.

The Lloyd's Building (1986) is
Richard Rogers' Post-Modernist
emblem *(see p161).*

OLYMPIC GAMES
OFFICIAL SOUVENIR

1948 Olympic Games
held in London

1952 George VI
dies; his daughter
Elizabeth II accedes

*Minis became a symbol of the 1960s; small
and manoeuvrable, they typified the
go-as-you-please mood of the decade.*

1977 Queen's Silver Jubilee; work
starts on Jubilee line underground

| 1945 | 1950 | 1955 | 1960 | 1965 | 1970 | 1975 | 1980 |

1951 Festival
of Britain

1945
End of World War II

1954
Food rationing,
introduced
during World
War II, abolished

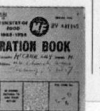

RATION BOOK

1963
National Theatre
founded at the Old Vic

1971 New London
Bridge built

1982
Last of the London
docks closes

Docklands Light Railway
In the 1980s, new, driverless trains started to transport people to the developing Docklands.

Post-Modern Architecture

Since the 1980s, architects have reacted against the stark shapes of the Modernists. Landmarks like the "Gherkin" by Norman Foster and "The Shard" by Renzo Piano now dominate the skyline. Architect Richard Rogers emphasizes structural features; others, like Terry Farrell, adopt a more playful approach using pastiches of Classical features.

Youth Culture

With their new mobility and spending power, young people began to influence the development of British popular culture in the years after World War II. Music, fashion and design were increasingly geared to their rapidly changing tastes.

Punks were a phenomenon of the 1970s and 1980s. Their clothes, music, hair and habits were designed to shock.

The Prince of Wales
As heir to the throne, he is outspokenly critical of much of London's modern architecture. He prefers more traditional styles.

Canada Tower (1991) in Canary Wharf *(see p251)* was designed by César Pelli.

Charing Cross (1991) has Terry Farrell's glasshouse on top of the Victorian station *(see p121)*.

1984 Thames Barrier completed

1986 Greater London Council abolished

1992 Canary Wharf development opens

2000 Ken Livingstone becomes London's first directly elected mayor

The observation wheel, the London Eye, was raised during the spring of 2000.

2011 Prince William marries Catherine Middleton at Westminster Abbey

| 1985 | 1990 | 1995 | 2000 | 2005 | 2010 | 2015 | 2020 |

1985 Ethiopian famine leads to Live Aid relief campaign

Vivienne Westwood's clothes won prizes in the 1980s and 1990s.

1997 Princess Diana's funeral procession brings London to a halt

2005 London shaken by bombs on the public transport system

2013 Birth of Prince George to William and Catherine

2012 London hosts the Olympic games

Kings and Queens in London

London has been the royal capital of England since 1066, when William the Conqueror began a tradition of holding coronations in Westminster Abbey. Since then, successive kings and queens have left their mark on London and many of the places described in this book have royal associations: Henry VIII hunted at Richmond, Charles I was executed on Whitehall and the young Queen Victoria rode on Queensway. Royalty is also celebrated in many of London's traditional ceremonies – for more details on these turn to pages 54–7.

1413–22 Henry V

1509–47 Henry VIII

1399–1413 Henry IV

1485–1509 Henry VII

1553–8 Mary I

1483–5 Richard III

1066–87 William the Conqueror

1087–1100 William II

1100–35 Henry I

1135–54 Stephen

1327–77 Edward III

1050	1100	1150	1200	1250	1300	1350	1400	1450	1500	
Norman		Plantagenet					Lancaster	York	Tudor	
1050	1100	1150	1200	1250	1300	1350	1400	1450	1500	

1154–89 Henry II

1189–99 Richard I

1199–1216 John

1216–72 Henry III

1307–27 Edward II

1272–1307 Edward I

1461–70 and 1471–83 Edward IV

1547–53 Edward VI

1422–61 and 1470–1 Henry VI

1377–99 Richard II

Matthew Paris's 13th-century chronicle showing Kings Richard I, Henry II, John and Henry III.

1483 Edward V

1901–10
Edward VII

1936 Edward VIII

1689–1702
William and Mary

1685–8 James II

1702–14
Anne

1660–85
Charles II

1714 27
George I

1603–25
James I

1837–1901
Victoria

1727–60
George II

1952– Elizabeth II

1600	1650	1700	1750	1800	1850	1900	1950	2000	2050
Stuart		Hanover				Windsor			
1600	1650	1700	1750	1800	1850	1900	1950	2000	2050

1830–37
William IV

1649–60 The Commonwealth,
established by Oliver Cromwell

1820–30
George IV

1936–52 George VI shown
on the George Medal

1910–36
George V

1625–49 Charles I

1558–1603
Elizabeth I

1760–1820 George III

LONDON AT A GLANCE

There are nearly 300 places of interest described in the Area by Area section of this book. These range from the magnificent National Gallery *(see pp106–9)* to gruesome Old St Thomas' Operating Theatre *(see p178)*, and from ancient Charterhouse *(see p166)* to modern Canary Wharf *(see p251)*. To help you make the most of your stay, the following 18 pages are a time-saving guide to the best London has to offer. Museums and galleries, churches, and parks and gardens each have a section, and there are guides to remarkable Londoners and ceremonies in London. Each sight mentioned is cross-referenced to its own full entry. Below are the ten top tourist attractions to start you off.

London's Top Ten Tourist Attractions

St Paul's
See pp150–53.

National Gallery
See pp106–9.

Changing of the Guard
Buckingham Palace, see pp96–7.

London Eye
See p191.

Hampton Court
See pp256–9.

Westminster Abbey
See pp78–81.

British Museum
See pp126–9.

Houses of Parliament
See pp74–5.

Tower of London
See pp156–9.

Victoria and Albert Museum
See pp212–15.

◀ The spectacular Great Court at the British Museum

Remarkable Londoners

London has always been a gathering place for the most prominent and influential people of their times. Some of these figures have come to London from other parts of Britain or from countries further afield; others have been Londoners, born and bred. All of them have left their mark on London, by designing great and lasting buildings, establishing institutions and traditions, and by writing about or painting the city they knew. Most of them have also had an influence on their times that spread out from London to the rest of the world.

Venus Venticordia by Dante Gabriel Rossetti

John Nash's Theatre Royal Haymarket (1821)

Architects and Engineers

A number of people who built London still have works standing. Inigo Jones (1573–1652), London-born, was the father of English Renaissance architecture. He lived and worked at Great Scotland Yard, Whitehall, then the residence of the royal architect – he was later succeeded by Sir Christopher Wren (1632–1723).

Wren's successors as the prime architects of London were his protégé Nicholas Hawksmoor (1661–1736)

and James Gibbs (1682–1754). Succeeding generations each produced architects who were to stamp their genius on the city: the brothers Robert (1728–92) and James Adam (1730–94), then John Nash (1752–1835), Sir Charles Barry (1795–1860), Decimus Burton (1800–81), Alfred Waterhouse (1830–1905), Norman Shaw (1831–1912), and Sir George Gilbert Scott (1811–78). Sir Joseph Bazalgette (1819–91) built London's sewer system and the Thames Embankment. More recently, Sir Norman Foster (1935–) has left

his mark with such iconic buildings as 30 St Mary Axe, known as "the Gherkin".

Artists

Painters in London, as elsewhere, often lived in enclaves, for mutual support and because they shared common priorities. During the 18th century, artists clustered around the court at St James's to be near their patrons. Thus both William Hogarth (1697–1764) and Sir Joshua Reynolds (1723–92) lived and worked in Leicester Square, while Thomas Gainsborough (1727–88) lived in Pall Mall. (Hogarth's Chiswick house was his place in the country.)

Later, Cheyne Walk in Chelsea, with its river views, became popular with artists, including the masters J M W Turner (1775–1851), James McNeill Whistler (1834–1903), Dante Gabriel Rossetti (1828–82), Philip Wilson Steer (1860–1942) and the sculptor Sir Jacob Epstein (1880–1959). Augustus John (1879–1961) and John

Historic London Homes

Four writers' homes that have been recreated are those of the romantic poet **John Keats** (1795–1821); the historian **Thomas Carlyle** (1795–1881); the lexicographer **Dr Samuel Johnson** (1709–84); and the prolific and popular novelist **Charles Dickens** (1812–70). The house that the architect **Sir John Soane** (1753–1837) designed for himself remains largely as it was when he died, as does the house where the psychiatrist **Sigmund Freud** (1856–1939) settled after fleeing from the Nazis before World War II.

Apsley House, on Hyde Park Corner, was the residence of the **Duke of Wellington** (1769–1852), hero of the Battle of Waterloo. The life and music of Baroque composer **George Frideric Handel** (1685–1759) are on show at his former home in Mayfair. Finally, the rooms of Sir Arthur Conan Doyle's fictional detective **Sherlock Holmes** have been created in Baker Street.

Carlyle's House

Plaques

All over London, the former homes of well-known figures are marked by plaques. Look out for these, especially in Chelsea, Kensington, and Mayfair, and see how many names you recognize.

No. 3 Sussex Square, Kensington

No. 27b Canonbury Square, Islington

No. 56 Oakley Street, Chelsea

Singer Sargent (1856–1925) had studios in Tite Street. John Constable (1776–1837) is best known as a Suffolk painter but lived for a while at Hampstead, from where he painted many fine views of the heath.

Writers

Geoffrey Chaucer (c.1345–1400), author of *The Canterbury Tales,* was born in Upper Thames Street, the son of an innkeeper. William Shakespeare (1564–1616) and Christopher Marlowe (1564–93) were both associated with the theatres in Southwark, and may have lived nearby.

The poets John Donne (1572–1631) and John Milton (1608–74) were both born in Bread Street in the City. Donne, after a profligate youth, became Dean of St Paul's. The diarist Samuel Pepys (1633–1703) was born off Fleet Street.

The young novelist Jane Austen (1775–1817) lived briefly off Sloane Street, near the Cadogan Hotel, where the flamboyant Oscar Wilde (1854–1900) was arrested in 1895 for homosexuality. Playwright George Bernard Shaw (1856–1950) lived at No. 29 Fitzroy Square in Bloomsbury. Later the same house was home to Virginia Woolf (1882–1941) and became a meeting place for the Bloomsbury Group, which included Vanessa Bell, John Maynard Keynes, E M Forster,

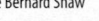

George Bernard Shaw

Roger Fry and Duncan Grant. Current authors with works set in London include Monica Ali and Ian McEwan.

Leaders

In legend, a penniless boy named Dick Whittington came to London with his cat seeking streets paved with gold, and later became Lord Mayor. In fact, Richard Whittington (1360?–1423), Lord Mayor three times between 1397 and 1420 and one of London's most celebrated early politicians, was the son of a noble. Sir Thomas More (1478–1535), a Chelsea resident, was Henry VIII's chancellor until they quarreled over the king's break with the Catholic church and Henry ordered More's execution. More was canonized in 1935. Sir Thomas Gresham (1519?–79) founded the Royal Exchange. Sir Robert Peel (1788–1850) started the London police force, who were known as "bobbies" after him.

Actors

Nell Gwynne (1650–87) won more fame as King Charles II's mistress than as an actress. However, she did appear on stage at Drury Lane Theatre; she also sold oranges there. The Shakespearean actor Edmund Kean (1789–1833) and the great tragic actress

Sarah Siddons (1755–1831) were more distinguished players at Drury Lane. So were Henry Irving (1838–1905) and Ellen Terry (1847–1928), whose stage partnership lasted 24 years. Charlie Chaplin (1889–1977), born in Kennington, had a poverty-stricken childhood in the slums of London.

In the 20th century, a school of fine actors blossomed at the Old Vic, including Sir John Gielgud (1904–2001), Sir Ralph Richardson (1902–83), Dame Peggy Ashcroft (1907–91), and Laurence (later Lord) Olivier (1907–89), who was appointed the first director of the National Theatre.

Laurence Olivier

Where to Find Historic London Homes

Thomas Carlyle *p198*
Charles Dickens *p131*
Sigmund Freud *p248*
George Frideric Handel *p341*
William Hogarth *p261*
Sherlock Holmes *p228*
Dr Samuel Johnson *p142*
John Keats *p235*
Sir John Soane *p138*
The Duke of Wellington *p99*

London's Best: Museums and Galleries

London's museums are filled with an astonishing diversity of treasures from all over the world. This map highlights 15 of the city's most important galleries and museums, whose exhibits cater to most interests. Some of these collections started from the legacies of 18th- and 19th-century explorers, traders and collectors. Others specialize in one aspect of art, history, science or technology. A more detailed overview of London's museums and galleries is on pages 44–5.

British Museum
This Anglo-Saxon helmet is part of a massive collection of antiquities.

Wallace Collection
Frans Hals's *Laughing Cavalier* is a star attraction in this museum of art, furniture, armour and *objets d'art*.

Royal Academy of Arts
Major international art exhibitions are held here, and the renowned Summer Exhibition, when works are on sale, takes place every year.

Regent's Park and Marylebone

Kensington and Holland Park

South Kensington and Knightsbridge

Piccadi and S James

Natural History Museum
All of life is here, with vivid displays on everything from dinosaurs (like this Triceratops skull) to butterflies.

Chelsea

Science Museum
Newcomen's steam engine of 1712 is just one of many exhibits that cater for both novice and expert.

Victoria and Albert Museum
It is the world's largest museum of decorative arts. This Indian vase is from the 18th century.

National Portrait Gallery
Important British figures are documented in paintings and photographs. This is Vivien Leigh, by Angus McBean (1954).

National Gallery
The world-famous paintings in its collection are mainly European and date from the 15th to the 19th centuries.

Museum of London
London's history is told through fascinating objects such as this 15th-century reliquary.

Tower of London
The Crown Jewels and a vast collection of arms and armour are here. This armour was worn by a 14th-century Italian knight.

British Museum

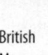

National Portrait Gallery

Bloomsbury and Fitzrovia

Smithfield and Spitalfields

Holborn and the Inns of Court

Design Museum
The changing exhibitions here showcase all aspects of design, from household prototypes to high fashion garments.

oho and rafalgar Square

Covent Garden and the Strand

The City

Southwark and Bankside

South Bank

Whitehall and Westminster

RIVER THAMES

0 kilometres 1
0 miles 0.5

Tate Modern
Works of the 20th century, such as Dali's *Lobster Telephone*, are celebrated here.

Tate Britain
Formerly the Tate Gallery, this museum showcases an outstanding collection of British art covering the 16th century to the present.

Imperial War Museum
It uses displays, film and special effects to recreate 20th-century battles. This is one of the earliest tanks.

Courtauld Gallery
Well-known works, such as Manet's *A Bar at the Folies-Bergère*, line its galleries.

Exploring Museums and Galleries

London boasts an astonishingly rich and diverse collection of museums. The city's position for centuries at the hub of world-wide trade has been partly responsible for this extraordinarily rich cultural heritage. Britain's rule of a far-flung empire has also played its part. The world-renowned collections are impressive, but find time for the city's range of smaller museums, which are often more peaceful than their grander counterparts. Brimming with character, they cover every imaginable theme from buses and toys to electricity and water power.

Geffrye Museum: Art Nouveau Room

Antiquities and Archaeology

Some of the most celebrated artifacts of ancient Asia, Egypt, Greece and Rome are housed in the **British Museum** fine collection. Other antiquities, including books, manuscripts, paintings, busts and gems, are displayed in **Sir John Soane's Museum**, which is one of the most idiosyncratic to be found in London.

The **Museum of London** contains much of archaeological interest from all periods of the city's history.

Eclectic collection at Sir John Soane's Museum

Furniture and Interiors

The Museum of London recreates typical domestic and commercial interiors from the Roman period right up to the present day. The **Victoria and Albert Museum** (or V&A) contains complete rooms rescued from now vanished buildings, plus a magnificent collection of furniture ranging from the 16th century to work by

Design Museum display of chairs

contemporary designers. On a more modest scale, the **Geffrye Museum** consists of fully-furnished period rooms dating from 1600 to the 1990s. Writers' houses, such as the **Freud Museum**, give insights into the furniture of specific periods, while the **Linley Sambourne House** offers visitors a perfectly preserved example of a late Victorian interior.

Costume and Jewellery

The **V&A's** vast collections include English and European clothes of the last 400 years, and some stunning jewellery from China, India and Japan. The priceless Crown Jewels, at the **Tower of London**, should not be missed. Here you can also see the world's largest cut diamond, Cullinan I, set in the Sovereign's Sceptre. **Kensington Palace's** Court Dress Collection opens a window on Court uniforms and protocol from about 1750. The **British Museum** displays ancient Aztec, Mayan and African costume.

Crafts and Design

Once again, the **Victoria and Albert Museum** (V&A) is the essential first port of call; its collections in these fields remain unrivalled. The **William Morris Gallery** shows every aspect of the 19th-century designer's work within the Arts and Crafts movement. The **Design Museum** focuses on modern design including products and fashion, while the **Crafts Council Gallery** displays (and sometimes sells) contemporary British craftwork.

Military Artifacts

The **National Army Museum** uses vivid models and displays to narrate the history of the British Army from the reign of Henry VII to the present. The crack regiments of Foot Guards, who are the elite of the British Army, are the main focus of the **Guards Museum**. The **Tower of London** holds part of the national collection of arms and armour; the **Wallace Collection** also has a large and impressive display. The **Imperial War Museum** has recreations of World War I trenches and the 1940 Blitz. The **Florence Nightingale Museum** illustrates the hardships of 19th-century warfare.

Imperial War Museum

Toys and Childhood

Teddy bears, toy soldiers and dolls' houses are some of the toys that can be seen in **Pollock's Toy Museum**. The collection includes Eric, "the oldest known teddy-bear". The **V&A Museum of Childhood** and the **Museum of London** are a little more formal, but still fun, and illustrate aspects of the social history of childhood, with both offering some interesting children's activities.

Science and Natural History

Computers, electricity, space exploration, industrial processes and transport can all be studied at the **Science Museum**. Transport enthusiasts are also catered for at the **London Transport Museum**. There are

other specialized museums such as the **Faraday Museum** concerning the development of electricity, and the **Kew Bridge Steam Museum**, focusing on water power. The **National Maritime Museum** and the **Royal Observatory** in Greenwich chart both maritime history and the creation of GMT, by which the world still sets its clocks. The **Natural History Museum** mixes displays of animal and bird life with ecological exhibits. The **Museum of Garden History** is devoted to the favourite British pastime.

Visual Arts

The particular strengths of the **National Gallery** are early Renaissance Italian and 17th-century Spanish painting and a wonderful collection of Dutch masters. **Tate Britain** specializes in British paintings spanning all periods, while **Tate Modern** has displays of international modern art from 1900 to the present day. The **V&A** is strong on European art from 1500–1900 and British art of 1700–1900. The **Royal Academy** and the **Hayward Gallery** specialize in major temporary exhibitions. The **Courtauld Institute of Art Gallery** contains Impressionist and Post-Impressionist works, while the **Wallace Collection** has 17th-century Dutch and 18th-century French paintings. The **Dulwich Picture Gallery** includes works by Rembrandt, Rubens, Poussin and Gainsborough, while **Kenwood House** is home

Samson and Delilah (1620) by Van Dyck at the Dulwich Picture Gallery

to paintings by Reynolds, Gainsborough and Rubens in fine Adam interiors. The **Saatchi Gallery** is devoted to contemporary, mainly British, art.

Where to Find the Collections

British Museum *pp126–9*
Courtauld Institute of Art Gallery *p119*
Crafts Council Gallery *p249*
Design Museum *p185*
Dulwich Picture Gallery *p252*
Faraday Museum *p99*
Florence Nightingale Museum *p192*
Freud Museum *p248*
Geffrye Museum *p250*
Guards Museum *p83*
Hayward Gallery *p190*
Imperial War Museum *p192*
Kensington Palace *p212*
Kenwood House *p236*
Kew Bridge Steam Museum *p260*
Linley Sambourne House *p220*
London's Transport Museum *p116*
Museum of Garden History *p192*
Museum of London *pp168–9*
National Army Museum *p199*
National Gallery *pp106–9*
National Maritime Museum *p242*
Natural History Museum *pp204–5*
Pollock's Toy Museum *p133*
Royal Academy of Arts *p92*
Saatchi Gallery *p199*
Science Museum *pp208–9*
Sir John Soane's Museum *p138*
Tate Britain *pp84–7*
Tate Modern *pp180–83*
Tower of London *pp156–9*
Victoria and Albert Museum *pp212–15*
Victoria and Albert Museum of Childhood *p250*
Wallace Collection *p228*
William Morris Gallery *p251*

Ornate Drawing Room at the Wallace Collection

London's Best: Churches

It is worth stopping to look at London's churches and going in, if they are open. They have a special atmosphere unmatched elsewhere in the city, and they can often yield an intimate glimpse of the past. Many churches have replaced earlier buildings in a steady succession, dating back to pre-Christian times. Some began life in outlying villages beyond London's fortified centre, and were absorbed into suburbs when the city expanded in the 18th century. The memorials in the capital's churches and churchyards are a fascinating record of local life, liberally peppered with famous names. A more detailed overview of London churches is on pages 48–9.

All Souls
This plaque comes from a tomb in John Nash's Regency church of 1824.

Bloomsbury and Fitzrovia

St Paul's Covent Garden
Inigo Jones's Classical church was known as "the handsomest barn in England."

Regent's Park and Marylebone

Soho and Trafalgar Square

St Martin-in-the-Fields
James Gibbs's church of 1722 –6 was originally thought "too gay" for Protestant worship.

South Kensington and Knightsbridge

Piccadilly and St James's

Whitehall and Westminster

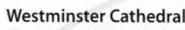

0 kilometres   1
0 miles   0.5

Westminster Cathedral
The Italian-Byzantine Catholic cathedral's red-and-white brick exterior conceals a rich interior of multicoloured marbles.

Brompton Oratory
This sumptuous Baroque church was decorated with works by Italian artists.

Westminster Abbey
The famous abbey has the most glorious medieval architecture in London, and highly impressive tombs and monuments.

St Mary-le-Strand
Now on a traffic island, this ship-like church was built by
James Gibbs in 1714–17 to a lively Baroque design.
Featuring high windows and rich interior detailing, it was
made solid enough to keep out the noise from the street.

Smithfield and
Spitalfields

Holborn and
the Inns of
Court

Covent
Garden
and the
Strand

The City

St Mary Woolnoth
The jewel-like interior of Nicholas
Hawksmoor's small Baroque
church (1716–27) appears larger
than the outside.

South
Bank

Southwark
and
Bankside

St Stephen Walbrook
Wren was at his best with this
domed interior of 1672–7. Its
carvings include Henry Moore's
austere modern altar.

St Paul's
At 110 m (360 ft) high,
the dome of Wren's
cathedral is the world's
second largest after
St Peter's in Rome.

Temple Church
Built in the 12th and 13th centuries
for the Knights Templar, this is one
of the few circular churches to
survive in England.

Southwark Cathedral
This largely 13th-century priory
church was not designated a
cathedral until 1905. It has a
fine medieval choir.

RIVER THAMES

Exploring Churches

The church spires that puncture London's skyline span nearly a thousand years of the city's history. They form an index to many of the events that have shaped the city – the Norman Conquest (1066); the Great Fire of London (1666); the great restoration, led by Wren, that followed it; the Regency period; the confidence of the Victorian era; and the devastation of World War II. Each has had its effect on the churches, many designed by the most influential architects of their times.

St Paul's, Covent Garden

Medieval Churches

The most famous old church to survive the Great Fire of 1666 is the superb 13th-century **Westminster Abbey,** the church of the Coronation, with its tombs of British monarchs and heroes. Less well known are the well-hidden Norman church of **St Bartholomew-the-Great**, London's oldest church (1123), the circular **Temple Church**, founded in 1160 by the Knights Templar, and **Southwark Cathedral**, set amid Victorian railway lines and warehouses. **Chelsea Old Church** is a charming village church near the river.

Churches by Jones

Inigo Jones (1573–1652) was Shakespeare's contemporary, and his works were almost as revolutionary as the great dramatist's. Jones's Classical churches of the 1620s and 1630s shocked a public used to conservative Gothic finery. By far the best-known is **St Paul's Church** of the 1630s, the centrepiece of Jones's Italian-style piazza in Covent Garden. **Queen's Chapel, St James's** was built in 1623 for Queen Henrietta Maria, the Catholic wife of Charles I. It was the first Classical church in England and has a magnificent interior but is, unfortunately, usually closed to the public.

Churches by Hawksmoor

Nicholas Hawksmoor (1661–1736) was Wren's most talented pupil, and his

Spires

Look out for London's richly decorated church steeples. Here are four of the city's most distinctive to get you started.

St Martin-in-the-Fields, by James Gibbs, is in a prominent position grandly overlooking Trafalgar Square.

Clock dating from 1758

St Mary-le-Bow, by Christopher Wren, has a copper dragon weathervane on top of its fine steeple.

Graceful bow arches

St Bride's has Wren's tallest steeple. Originally 234 ft (71m) high, 8 ft (2.5 m) were lost in a thunderstorm in 1764.

Four octagonal tiers

St George's Bloomsbury by Nicholas Hawksmoor, is topped by George I in a Roman toga.

Steeple rising in steps

churches are among the finest Baroque buildings to be found in Britain.

St George's, Bloomsbury (1716–31) has an unusual centralized plan and a pyramid steeple topped by a statue of King George I. **St Mary Woolnoth** is a tiny jewel of 1716–27, and further east **Christ Church, Spitalfields** is a Baroque tour-de-force of 1714–29, now being restored.

Among Hawksmoor's East End churches are the stunning **St Anne's, Limehouse** and **St Alfege**, of 1714–17, which is across the river in Greenwich. The tower on this temple-like church was added later by John James in 1730.

Christopher Wren

Sir Christopher Wren (1632–1723) was leader among the many architects who helped restore London after the Great Fire of London. He devised a new city plan, replacing the narrow streets with wide avenues radiating from piazzas. His plan was rejected, but he was commissioned to build 52 new churches; 31 have survived various threats of demolition and the bombs of World War II, although six are shells. Wren's great masterpiece is the massive **St Paul's**, while nearby is splendid **St Stephen Walbrook**, his domed church of 1672–7. Other landmarks are **St Bride's**, off Fleet Street, said to have inspired the traditional shape of wedding cakes, **St Mary-le-Bow** in Cheapside and **St Magnus the Martyr** in Lower Thames Street. Wren's own favourite was **St James's, Piccadilly** (1683–4). Smaller gems are **St Clement Danes**, Strand (1680–82) and **St James, Garlickhythe** (1674–87).

St Anne's, Limehouse

Churches by Gibbs

James Gibbs (1682–1754) was more conservative than his Baroque contemporaries such as Hawksmoor, and he also kept his distance from the Neo-Classical trend so popular after 1720. His idiosyncratic London churches were enormously influential. **St Mary-le-Strand** (1714–17) is an island church which appears to be sailing down the Strand. The radical design of **St Martin-in-the-Fields** (1722–6) predates its setting, Trafalgar Square, by a hundred years.

Regency Churches

The end of the Napoleonic Wars in 1815 brought a flurry of church building. The need for churches in London's new suburbs fused with a Greek Revival. The results may lack the exuberance of Hawksmoor, but they have an austere elegance of their own. **All Souls, Langham Place** (1822–4), at the north end of Regent Street, was built by the Prince Regent's favourite, John Nash, who was ridiculed at the time for its unusual combination of design styles. Also worth visiting is **St Pancras**, Greek Revival church of 1819–22, which is typical of the period.

Victorian Churches

London has some of the finest 19th-century churches in Europe. Grand and colourful, their riotous decoration is in marked contrast to the chaste Neo-Classicism of the preceding Regency era. Perhaps the best of the capital's late Victorian churches is

Westminster Cathedral, a stunningly rich, Italianate Catholic cathedral built in 1895–1903, with architecture by J F Bentley and *Stations of the Cross* reliefs by Eric Gill. **Brompton Oratory** is a grand Baroque revival, based on a church in Rome and filled with magnificent furnishings from all over Catholic Europe.

Where to find the Churches

All Souls, Langham Place *p227*
Brompton Oratory *p206*
Chelsea Old Church *p198*
Christ Church, Spitalfields *p172*
Queen's Chapel *p95*
St Alfege *p242*
St Anne's, Limehouse *p251*
St Bartholomew-the-Great *p167*
St Bride's *p141*
St Clement Danes *p140*
St George's, Bloomsbury *p130*
St James, Garlickhythe *p146*
St James's, Piccadilly *p92*
St Magnus the Martyr *p154*
St Martin-in-the-Fields *p104*
St Mary-le-Bow *p149*
St Mary-le-Strand *p120*
St Mary Woolnoth *p147*
St Pancras *p132*
St Paul's Cathedral *pp150–53*
St Paul's Church *p116*
St Stephen Walbrook *p148*
Southwark Cathedral *p178*
Temple Church *p141*
Westminster Abbey *pp78–81*
Westminster Cathedral *p83*

Brompton Oratory

London's Best: Parks and Gardens

Since medieval times London has had large expanses of green. Some of these, such as Hampstead Heath, were originally common land, where smallholders could graze their animals. Others, such as Richmond Park and Holland Park, were royal hunting grounds or the gardens of large houses; several still have formal features dating from those times. Today you can cross much of central London by walking from St James's Park in the east to Kensington Gardens in the west. Purpose-built parks, like Battersea, and botanical gardens, like Kew, appeared later.

Hamps

Hyde Park
The Serpentine is one of the highlights of a park which also boasts restaurants, an art gallery and Speakers' Corner.

Hampstead Heath
This breezy, open space is located in the midst of north London. Nearby Parliament Hill offers views of St Paul's, the City and the West End.

Kensington and Holland Park

South Kensington an Knightsbridge

Kew Gardens
The world's premier botanic garden is a must for anyone with an interest in plants, exotic or mundane.

Kensington Gardens
This plaque is from the Italian Garden, one of the features of this elegant park.

Holland Park
The former grounds of one of London's grandest homes are now its most romantic park.

0 km 1
0 miles 0.5

Richmond Park
The biggest Royal Park in London remains largely unspoiled, with deer and magnificent river views.

Regent's Park
In this civilized Park, surrounded by fine
Regency buildings, you can stroll around
the rose garden, visit the open-air theatre,
or simply sit and admire the view.

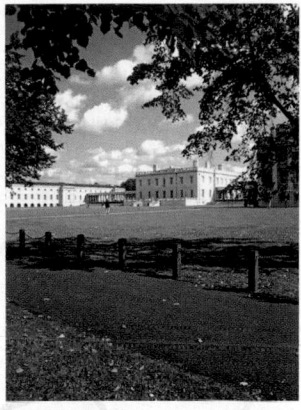

Greenwich Park
Its focal point is the National
Maritime Museum, well worth a visit
for its architecture as well as its
exhibits. There are also fine views.

Bloomsbury
and Fitzrovia

gent's
k and
lebone

Smithfield
and
Spitalfields

Holborn
and the Inns
of Court

Soho and
Trafalgar
Square

The City

T H A M E S

Piccadilly

South
Bank

Southwark
and Bankside

R I V E R

Whitehall
and
Westminster

sea

Green Park
Its leafy paths are favoured by early-
morning joggers from the Mayfair hotels.

Greenwich and
Blackheath

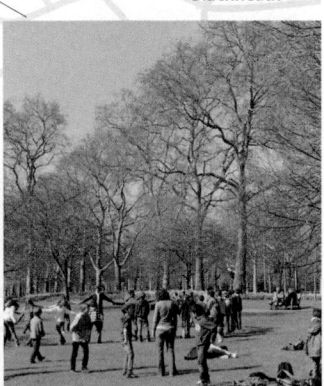

Battersea Park
Visitors can hire a rowing boat for the best view
of the Victorian landscaping around the lake.

St James's Park
Located in the heart of the city, this park
is a popular escape for office workers. It is
also a reserve for wildfowl.

Exploring Parks and Gardens

London has one of the the world's greenest city centres, full of tree-filled squares and grassy parks. From the intimacy of the Chelsea Physic Garden to the wild, open spaces of Hampstead Heath, every London park has its own charm and character. For those looking for a specific outdoor attraction – such as sports, wildlife or flowers – here are some of the most interesting London parks.

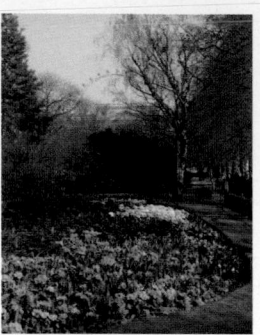

Flower Gardens

The British are famed for their gardens and love of flowers and this is reflected in several of London's parks. Really keen gardeners will find all they ever wanted to know at **Kew Gardens** and the **Chelsea Physic Garden**, which is especially strong on herbs. Closer to the centre of town, **St James's Park** boasts some spectacular flower beds, filled with bulbs and bedding plants, which are changed every season. **Hyde Park** sports a magnificent show of daffodils and crocuses in the spring and London's best rose garden is Queen Mary's in **Regent's Park**.

Kensington Gardens' flower walk has an exemplary English mixed border, and there is also a delightful small 17th-century garden at the **Museum of Garden History**.

    Battersea Park also has a charming flower garden, and indoor gardeners should head to the **Barbican Centre's** well-stocked conservatory.

Colourful flower beds at St James's Park

Formal Gardens

The most spectacular formal garden is at **Hampton Court**, which has a network of gardens from different periods, starting with Tudor. The gardens at **Chiswick House** remain dotted with their

18th-century statuary and pavilions. Other restored gardens include 17th-century **Ham House**, and **Osterley Park**, whose 18th-century layout was retraced through the art of dowsing. **Fenton House** has a really fine walled garden; **Kenwood** is less formal, with its woodland area. **The Hill** is great in summer. The sunken garden at **Kensington Palace** has a formal layout and **Holland Park** has flowers around its statues.

Restful Corners

London's squares are cool, shady retreats but, sadly, many are reserved for key-holders, usually residents of the surrounding houses. Of those open to all, **Russell Square** is the largest and most secluded. **Berkeley Square** is open but barren. **Green Park** offers shady trees and deck chairs, right in central London. The Inns of Court provide some pleasant havens: **Gray's Inn** gardens, **Middle Temple** gardens and **Lincoln's Inn Fields**. **Grovesnor Square** is one of London's

Sunken garden at Kensington Palace

Green London

In Greater London, there are 1,700 parks covering a total of 67 sq miles (174 sq km). This land is home to some 2,000 types of plant and 100 bird species that breed in the trees. Trees help the city to breathe, manufacturing oxygen from the polluted air. Here are some of the species you are most likely to see in London.

The London plane, now the most common tree in London, grows along many streets.

The English oak grows all over Europe. The Royal Navy used to build ships from it.

oldest Georgian squares, while **Soho Square**, surrounded by streets, is more urban.

Music in Summer

Stretching out on the grass or in a deck chair to listen to a band is a British tradition. Military and other bands give regular concerts throughout the summer at **St James's** and **Regent's Parks** and also at **Parliament Hill Fields**. The concert schedule will usually be found posted up close to the bandstand in the park.

Open-air festivals of classical music are held in the summer in several parks *(see p341).*

Wildlife

There is a large and well-fed collection of ducks and other water birds, even including a few pelicans, in **St James's Park**. Duck lovers will also appreciate **Regent's, Hyde** and **Battersea Parks,** as well as **Hampstead Heath**. Deer roam in **Richmond** and **Greenwich Parks**. For a wide variety of captive animals, **London Zoo** is in **Regent's Park** and there are aviaries or aquariums at several parks and gardens, including **Kew Gardens** and **Syon House**.

Geese in St James's Park

Historic Cemeteries

In the late 1830s, private cemeteries were established around London to ease the pressure on the overcrowded and unhealthy burial grounds of the inner city. Today some of these, notably **Highgate Cemetery**, **Kensal Green Cemetery** (Harrow Road, W10) and **Brompton Cemetery** (Fulham Road, SW10), are worth visiting for their Victorian monuments. **Bunhill Fields** is earlier; it was first used during the plague of 1665.

Kensal Green cemetery

Boating pond at Regent's Park

Sports

Cycling is not universally encouraged in London's parks, and footpaths tend to be too bumpy to allow much rollerskating. However, most parks have tennis courts, which normally have to be reserved in advance with the attendant. Rowing boats may be hired at **Hyde**, **Regent's** and **Battersea Parks**, among others. Athletics tracks are at both Battersea Park and also **Parliament Hill**. The public may swim at the ponds on **Hampstead Heath** and in the Serpentine in Hyde Park. Hampstead Heath is also ideal kite-flying territory.

Where to Find the Parks

Barbican Centre *p167*
Battersea Park *p253*
Berkeley Square *p273*
Bunhill Fields *p170*
Chelsea Physic Garden *p199*
Chiswick House *pp260–61*
Fenton House *p235*
Gray's Inn *p143*
Green Park *p99*
Greenwich Park *p245*
Ham House *p254*
Hampstead Heath *p236*
Hampton Court *pp256–9*
Highgate Cemetery *p248*
The Hill *p237*
Holland Park *p220*
Hyde Park *p217*
Kensington Gardens *pp210–11*
Kensington Palace *p210*
Kenwood House *pp236–7*
Kew Gardens *pp262–3*
Lincoln's Inn Fields *p139*
London Zoo *p229*
Middle Temple *p141*
Museum of Garden History *p192*
Osterley Park *p255*
Parliament Hill Fields *pp236–7*
Regent's Park *p226*
Richmond Park *p254*
Russell Square *p130*
St James's Park *p95*
Soho Square *p110*
Syon House *p255*

The common beech has a close relation, the copper beech, with reddish purple leaves.

The horse chestnut's hard round fruits are used by children for a game called conkers.

London's Best: Ceremonies

Much of London's rich inheritance of tradition and ceremony centres on royalty. Faithfully enacted today, some of these ceremonies date back to the Middle Ages, when the ruling monarch had absolute power and had to be protected from opponents. This map shows the venues for some of the most important ceremonies in London. For more details on these and other ceremonies please turn to pages 56–7; information on all sorts of events taking place in London throughout the year can be found on pages 58–61.

St James's Palace and Buckingham Palace
Members of the Queen's Life Guard stand at the gates of these two palaces.

Bloomsbury and Fitzrovia

Soho and Trafalgar Square

South Kensington and Knightsbridge

Piccadilly and St James's

Hyde Park
Royal Salutes are fired by guns of the King's Troop Royal Horse Artillery on royal anniversaries and ceremonial occasions.

Whitehall and Westminster

Chelsea

Chelsea Hospital
In 1651 Charles II hid from parliamentary forces in an oak tree. On Oak Apple Day, Chelsea Pensioners decorate his statue with oak leaves and branches.

Horse Guards
At Trooping the Colour, the most elaborate of London's royal ceremonies, the Queen salutes as a battalion of Foot Guards parades its colours before her.

The City and Embankment
At the Lord Mayor's Show, pikemen and musketeers escort the newly elected Lord Mayor through the City in a gold state coach.

Smithfield and
Spitalfields

Holborn and the
Inns of Court

Covent
arden and
ne Strand

The City

0 kilometres   1

0 miles   0.5

R I V E R   T H A M E S

Southwark
and Bankside

South Bank

Tower of London
In the nightly Ceremony of the Keys, a Yeoman Warder locks the gates. A military escort ensures the keys are not stolen.

Houses of Parliament
Each autumn the Queen goes to Parliament in the Irish State Coach to open the new parliamentary session.

The Cenotaph
On Remembrance Sunday the Queen pays homage to the nation's war dead.

Attending London's Ceremonies

Royalty and commerce provide the two principal sources of London's rich calendar of ceremonial events. Quaint and old-fashioned these events may be, but what may seem arcane ritual has real historical meaning – many of the capital's ceremonies originated in the Middle Ages.

Royal Ceremonies

Although the Queen's role is now largely symbolic, the Guard at Buckingham Palace still patrols the palace grounds. The impressive ceremony of the **Changing of the Guard** – dazzling uniforms, shouted commands, military music – consists of the Old Guard, which forms up in the palace forecourt, going off duty and handing over to the New Guard. The Guard consists of three officers and 40 men when the Queen is in residence, but only three officers and 31 men when she is away. The ceremony takes place in front of the palace. In another changeover ceremony, the Queen's Life Guards travel daily from Hyde Park Barracks to Horse Guards' Parade.

The **Ceremony of the Keys** at the Tower of London is one of the capital's most timeless ceremonies. After each of the Tower gates has been locked, the last post is sounded by a trumpeter before the keys are secured in the Queen's House.

The Tower of London and Hyde Park are also the scene of **Royal Salutes** which take place on birthdays and other occasions throughout the year. At such times 41 rounds are fired in Hyde Park at noon, and 62 rounds at the Tower at 1pm. The spectacle in Hyde Park is a stirring one as 71 horses and six 13-pounder cannons swirl into place and the roar of the guns begins.

The combination of pageantry, colour and music makes the annual **Trooping the Colour** the high point of London's ceremonial year. The Queen takes the Royal Salute, and after her troops have marched past, she leads them to Buckingham Palace where a second march past takes place. The best place to watch this spectacle is from the Horse Guards Parade side of St James's Park. Bands of the Household Cavalry and the Foot Guards stage the ceremony

of **Beating the Retreat** at Horse Guards Parade. This takes place on two successive evenings a year, in June, leading up to Trooping the Colour. The spectacular **State Opening of Parliament**, when the Queen opens the annual parliamentary session in the House of Lords – usually in November – is not open to the general public, although it is now televised. The huge royal procession, which moves from Buckingham Palace to Westminster, is, however, a magnificent sight, with the Queen travelling in the highly ornate Irish State Coach drawn by four horses.

A Queen's Guard in winter

Military Ceremonies

The Cenotaph in Whitehall is the setting for a ceremony held on **Remembrance Sunday**, to give thanks to those who died fighting in any conflict from World War I onwards.

National **Navy Day** is commemorated by a parade down the Mall, followed by a service held at Nelson's Column in Trafalgar Square.

One of the Queen's Life Guards

Royal salute, Tower of London

Trooping the Colour

Silent Change ceremony at Guildhall for the new Lord Mayor

Ceremonies in the City

November is the focus of the City of London's ceremonial year. At the **Silent Change** in Guildhall, the outgoing Lord Mayor hands over symbols of office to the new Mayor in a virtually wordless ceremony. The following day sees the rumbustious **Lord Mayor's Show**. Accompanying the Lord Mayor in his gold state coach a procession of bands, decorated floats, and military detachments makes its way through the City from Guildhall past the Mansion House to the Law Courts, and back again along the Embankment.

Many of the ceremonies that take place in the City are linked to the activities of the Livery Companies. These include the Worshipful Companies of **Vintners' and Distillers'** annual celebration of the wine harvest and the Stationers' **Cakes and Ale Sermon**, held in St Paul's. Cakes and ale are provided according to the will of a 17th-century stationer.

Lord Mayor's chain of office

Name-Day Ceremonies

Every 21 May **King Henry VI**, who was murdered in the Tower of London in 1471, is still remembered by the members of his two famous foundations, Eton College and King's College, Cambridge, who meet for a ceremony at the Wakefield Tower where he was killed. **Oak Apple Day** commemorates King Charles II's lucky escape from the Parliamentary forces of Oliver Cromwell in 1651. The King managed to conceal himself in a hollow oak tree, and today Chelsea Pensioners honor his memory by decorating his statue at Chelsea Royal Hospital with oak leaves and branches. On 18 December, the lexicographer **Dr Johnson** is commemorated in an annual service held at Westminster Abbey.

Informal Ceremonies

Each July, six guildsmen from the Company of Watermen compete for the prize in **Doggett's Coat and Badge Race**. In autumn, the **Pearly Kings and Queens**, representatives of east London's traders, meet at St Mary-le-Bow. In March children are given oranges and lemons at the **Oranges and Lemons service** at St Clement Danes church. In February, clowns take part in a service for **Joseph Grimaldi** (1779–1837) at the Holy Trinity Church in Dalston, E8.

Pearly Queen

Where to Find the Ceremonies

Beating the Retreat
Horse Guards *p82*, two successive evenings in June.

Cakes and Ale Sermon
St Paul's *pp150–53*, Ash Wed.

Ceremony of the Keys
Tower of London *pp156–9*, 9:30pm daily. Tickets from the Tower, but book well in advance.

Changing of the Guard
Buckingham Palace *pp96–7*, May–Jul: 11:30am daily; Aug–Apr: alternate days. Horse Guards, Whitehall *p82*, 11am Mon–Sat, 10am Sun. For details, call the London Tourist Board Information Line on 0906 201 5151.

Doggett's Coat and Badge Race
From London Bridge to Cadogan Pier, Chelsea *pp194–9*, July.

Dr Johnson Memorial
Westminster Abbey *pp78–81*, 18 Dec.

Joseph Grimaldi Memorial
Holy Trinity Church, Dalston E8, 7 Feb.

King Henry VI Memorial
Wakefield Tower, Tower of London *pp156–9*, 21 May.

Lord Mayor's Show
The City *pp144–61*, second Sat Nov.

Navy Day
Trafalgar Sq *p104*, 21 Oct.

Oak Apple Day
Royal Hospital *p199*, Thu after 29 May.

Oranges and Lemons Service
St Clement Danes *p140*, March.

Pearly Kings and Queens Harvest Festival
St Mary-le-Bow *p149*, autumn.

Remembrance Sunday
Cenotaph *p76*, Sun nearest 11 Nov.

Royal Salutes
Hyde Park *p217*, royal anniversaries and other state occasions.

Silent Change
Guildhall *p161*, second Fri Nov.

State Opening of Parliament
Houses of Parliament *pp74–5*, Oct–Nov. Procession from Buckingham Palace to Westminster.

Trooping the Colour
Horse Guards *p82*, 2nd Sat Jun. (rehearsals on previous two Sats). Tickets from Household Division, Horse Guards.

Vintners' and Distillers' Wine Harvest
St Olave's Church, Hart St EC3, second Tue Oct.

LONDON THROUGH THE YEAR

Springtime in London carries an almost tangible air of a city waking up to longer days and outdoor pursuits. The cheerful yellow of daffodils studs the parks, and less hardy Londoners turn out for their first jog of the year to find themselves puffing in the wake of serious runners training for the Marathon. As spring turns into summer, the royal parks reach their full glory, and in Kensington Gardens nannies gather to chat under venerable chestnut trees. As autumn takes hold, these same trees are ablaze with red and gold, and Londoners' thoughts turn to afternoons in museums, followed by tea in a café. The year closes with Guy Fawkes and Christmas shopping. The official visitor organization, Visit London, www.visitlondon.com *(p354),* and the listings magazines *(p334)* have details of seasonal events.

Spring

The weather during the spring months may be raw, and an umbrella is a necessary precaution. Druids celebrate the Spring Equinox in a subdued ceremony on Tower Hill. Painters compete to have their works accepted by the Royal Academy. Footballers close their season in May with the FA Cup Final, while cricketers don their sweaters to begin theirs. Oxford and Cambridge Universities row their annual boat race along the Thames, and Marathon runners pound the streets.

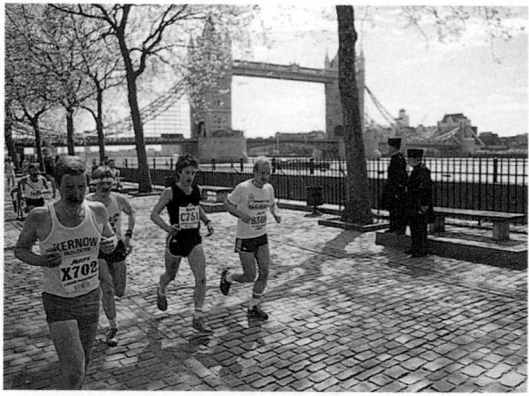

Runners in the London Marathon passing Tower Bridge

March

Chelsea Antiques Fair *(week varies, also Sep),* Chelsea Old Town Hall, King's Rd SW3. **Ideal Home Show** *(17 days from mid-Mar),* Earl's Court, Warwick Rd SW5. It is a long-established show with the latest in domestic gadgetry and state-of-the-art technology. **Oranges and Lemons Service** *(3rd Thu in Mar),* St Clement Danes *(see p57).* Service for school children; each child is given an orange and a lemon. **Oxford and Cambridge boat race** *(late Mar or early Apr),* Putney to Mortlake *(see p347).* **Spring Equinox celebration** *(21 Mar),* Tower Hill EC3. Historic pagan ceremony with modern-day druids. **London Festival of Railway Modelling** *(late Mar),* Alexandra Palace. Of real interest to people of all ages, and held in a gorgeous Victorian setting.

Easter

Good Friday and **Easter Monday** are public holidays. **Easter parades**, Battersea Park *(see p253).* **Easter Kite Festival**, Hampstead Heath *(see p236).* **Easter procession and hymns** *(Easter Mon),* Westminster Abbey *(see pp78–81).* **London Harness Horse Parade** *(Easter Mon),*

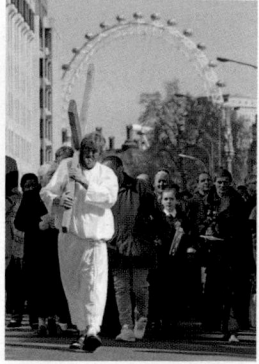

The Holy Cross being carried through the streets during the Good Friday procession

Battersea Park *(see p253).* **April Head of the River Race** *(early Apr),* more than 400 teams row from Mortlake to Putney. **Queen's Birthday gun salutes** *(21 Apr),* Hyde Park, Tower of London *(see p56).* **London Marathon** *(Sun in Apr or May),* champions and novices run from Greenwich to Westminster *(see p347).*

May

First and last Mon are public holidays. **FA Cup Final**, football season's climax *(see p346).* **Beating the Bounds** *(Ascension Day),* throughout the City. Young boys from the City parish beat buildings that mark the parish boundaries. **Oak Apple Day** *(29 May),* Royal Hospital, Chelsea *(see p57).* **Covent Garden May Fayre and Puppet Festival** *(mid-May),* St Paul's Church, Covent Garden *(see p116).* **Chelsea Flower Show** *(late May),* Royal Hospital, Chelsea.

Average Daily Hours of Sunshine

Sunshine Chart
London's longest and hottest days fall between May and August. In the height of summer, daylight hours can extend from well before 5am to after 9pm. Daytime is much shorter in the winter, but London can be stunning in the winter sunshine.

Summer

London's summer season is packed full of indoor and outdoor events. The weather is unreliable, even at the height of summer, but unless you are notably unlucky there should be enough fine days to sample what is on offer.

The selection includes many traditional events, such as the Wimbledon tennis championships and the cricket test matches at Lord's and the Oval. Well out of view from the general public and prying photographers, the Queen holds garden parties for favoured subjects in the splendid grounds of Buckingham Palace. The summer public holiday is also marked with funfairs in some of London's parks.

June

Beating the Retreat (see p56) **Coronation Day gun salutes** (2 Jun), Hyde Park and Tower of London (see p56). **Art Antiques London** (mid-Jun), Kensington Gardens W8. The world's top dealers gather in a purpose-built pavilion opposite the Royal Albert Hall (see p207) **Trooping the Colour**, Horse Guards Parade (see p56). **Duke of Edinburgh's Birthday gun salutes** (10 Jun), Hyde Park and Tower of London (see p56). **Wimbledon Lawn Tennis Championships** (two weeks in late Jun) (see p346). **Cricket test match**, Lord's Cricket Ground (see p346). **Open-air theatre season** (throughout the summer), stages in Regent's Park and Holland Park.

Revellers at Notting Hill Carnival

Shakespeare, Shaw and others offer the perfect opportunity for a picnic with a cultural flavour (see p336). **Open-air concerts**, Kenwood, Hampstead Heath, Crystal Palace, Marble Hill, St James's Park (see p341). **Summer festivals** (late Jun), Spitalfields and Primrose Hill. Contact Visit London (see p354) or see the listings magazines (see p334) for times and venues of all these events and see July, below. **City of London Festival** (late Jun–mid-July), various City venues (see p145). Arts and music festival with concerts taking place in some of London's most beautiful historic churches.

July

Summer festivals, Greenwich and Docklands, Regent's Park, Richmond and Soho. **Sales**, mid-year price reductions across London's

shops (see p313). **Hampton Court Flower Show**, Hampton Court Palace (see pp256–9). **Henry Wood Promenade Concerts (The Proms)** (late Jul–Sep), Royal Albert Hall (see p207). **Royal Academy of Arts Summer Exhibition** (Jun–Aug), Piccadilly (see p92). **Doggett's Coat and Badge Race**, a historic river-rowing contest between Thames watermen (see p65).

August

Last Monday in August is a public holiday. **Notting Hill Carnival** (late Aug holiday weekend). An internationally famous and well attended Caribbean carnival organized by the area's various ethnic communities (see p221). **Funfairs** (Aug holiday). Throughout London's parks in the summer.

Regimental band, St James's Park

Average Monthly Rainfall

MM												Inches
64												2.5
48												2
32												1.5
16												1
												0.5
0												0
Jan	Feb	Mar	Apr	May	Jun	Jul	Aug	Sep	Oct	Nov	Dec	

Rainfall Chart
London's average monthly rainfall remains much the same throughout the year. July and August, the capital's warmest months, are also two of its wettest. Rain is less likely in spring, but visitors should be prepared for a shower at any time of year.

Autumn

There is a sense of purpose about London in autumn. The build-up to the busiest shopping season, the start of the academic year, and the new parliamentary session, opened by the Queen, inject some life into the colder months. The cricket season ends in mid-September, while food-lovers may be interested in the spectacular displays of fresh fish that are laid out in the vestry of St Mary-at-Hill, celebrating the harvest of this island nation.

Memories of a more turbulent opening of Parliament are revived on 5 November. Bonfires and fireworks across the country commemorate the failed conspiracy, led by Guy Fawkes in 1605, to blow up the Palace of Westminster. A few days later, the dead of any conflict, from World War I onwards, are honoured at a ceremony held in Whitehall.

Pearly Kings gathering for the harvest festival at St Mary-le-Bow

September
The Mayor's Thames Festival, *(mid-Sep)*. Entertainment by and on the river between Westminster Bridge and Southwark Cathedral. **Great River Race**, Thames. **Last Night of the Proms** *(mid-Sep)*, Royal Albert Hall *(see p207)*. Entertaining the masses with rousing classical hits and favourite British patriotic pieces.

October
Pearly Harvest Festival *(first Sun)*. The Festival begins at Guildhall Yard, from where a parade of Pearly Kings and Queens makes its way to St-Mary-le-Bow Church for the Harvest Festival service *(see p149)*. **Harvest of the Sea** *(second Sun)*, St Mary-at-Hill Church *(see p154)*. **Vintners' and Distillers' Wine Harvest** *(see p57)*. **Navy Day** *(see p56)*.

November
State Opening of Parliament *(see p56)*. **Guy Fawkes Night** *(5 Nov)*. Listings magazines give details of firework displays *(see p334)*. **Remembrance Day Service** *(see p56)*. **Silent Change** *(see p57)*. **Lord Mayor's Show** *(see p57)*. **London to Brighton** veteran car rally *(first Sun)*. **Christmas lights** *(late Nov– 6 Jan)*. The West End *(see p315)*, especially Regent's Street, lights up for the festive season.

London-to-Brighton veteran car run

Fireworks explode during Guy Fawkes Night

Average Monthly Temperature

Temperature Chart
The chart shows the average minimum and maximum temperatures for each month. Top temperatures averaging 22° C (75° F) belie London's reputation for year-round chilliness, although November through to February can be extremely cold and icy.

Winter

Some of the most striking images of London are drawn from winter: paintings of frost fairs in the 17th and 18th centuries, when the River Thames froze over completely; and Claude Monet's views of the river and its bridges.

For centuries thick "pea-souper" fogs were an inevitable part of winter, until the Clean Air Act of 1956 barred coal-burning in open grates.

Christmas trees and lights twinkle everywhere – from the West End shopping streets to construction sites. The scent of roasting chestnuts pervades as street pedlars sell them from glowing mobile braziers.

Seasonal menus feature roast turkey, mince pies and Christmas pudding. Traditional fare in theatres includes colourful family pantomimes (where the customary cross-dressing between the sexes baffles many visitors – p336) and popular ballets such as Swan Lake or The Nutcracker.

Skaters use open-air ice rinks at Canada Square, Greenwich, Hyde Park, Hampton Court and at Somerset House (see p119). It is rarely safe to use the parks' frozen lakes.

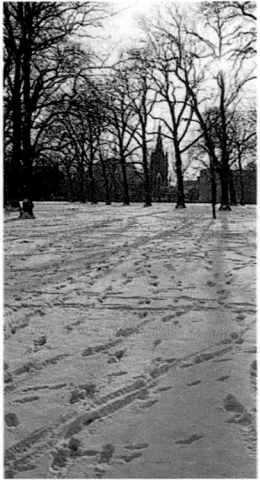

Winter in the picturesque gardens of Kensington Palace

December

Oxford v Cambridge rugby union match Twickenham (see p347). **Spitalfields Music Winter Festival** (mid-Dec), Old Spitalfields Market (see p172). **London International Horse Show** (late Dec), Olympia. Equestrian competition.

Christmas, New Year

25–26 Dec and **1 Jan** are public hols. There is no train service on Christmas Day.

Carol services (leading up to Christmas), Trafalgar Square (see p104), St Paul's (see pp150–53), Westminster Abbey (see pp78–81) and many other churches. **Turkey auction** (24 Dec), Smithfield Market (see p166). **Christmas Day swim** Serpentine, Hyde Park (see p213). **New Year's Eve celebrations** (31 Dec), Trafalgar Square, St Paul's.

January

Sales (see p313). **New Year's Day Parade** starts at Parliament Sq (see p76). **London Boat Show**, ExCel London, Docklands E16. **International Mime Festival** (mid-Jan–early Feb), various venues. **Charles I Commemoration** (last Sun), procession from St James's Palace (see p93) to Banqueting House (see p82). **Chinese New Year** (late Jan–mid-Feb), Chinatown (see p110) and Soho (see p111).

February

Queen's Accession gun salutes (6 Feb), 41-gun salute Hyde Park; 62-gun salute Tower of London (see p56). **Pancake races** (Shrove Tue), Lincoln's Inn Fields (see p139) and Covent Garden (see p114).

Public Holidays

New Year's Day (1 Jan); **Good Friday; Easter Monday;** **May Day** (first Monday in May); **Whit Monday** (last Monday in May); **August Bank Holiday** (last Monday in Aug); **Christmas Day and Boxing Day** (25–26 Dec).

Christmas illuminations in Trafalgar Square

A River View of London

Cruising down the Thames is one of the most interesting ways to experience London. As the country's main commercial artery from the Roman invasion to well into the 1950s, the river is packed with historical references, including the reconstruction of the Elizabethan Globe Theatre, royal palaces and parks, numerous storied bridges and decommissioned power stations. Now the river is the city's foremost leisure amenity, with the banks accessible via the Thames Path, numerous riverside pubs and commuters as well as tourists sailing the river.

Passenger boat services cover about 50 kilometres (30 miles) of the Thames, from Hampton Court in the west to the Thames Barrier in the east. The most popular and best served section runs through the heart of the city from Westminster to Tower Bridge. Often accompanied by interesting and witty commentary, a cruise along this fascinating stretch of the Thames should not be missed.

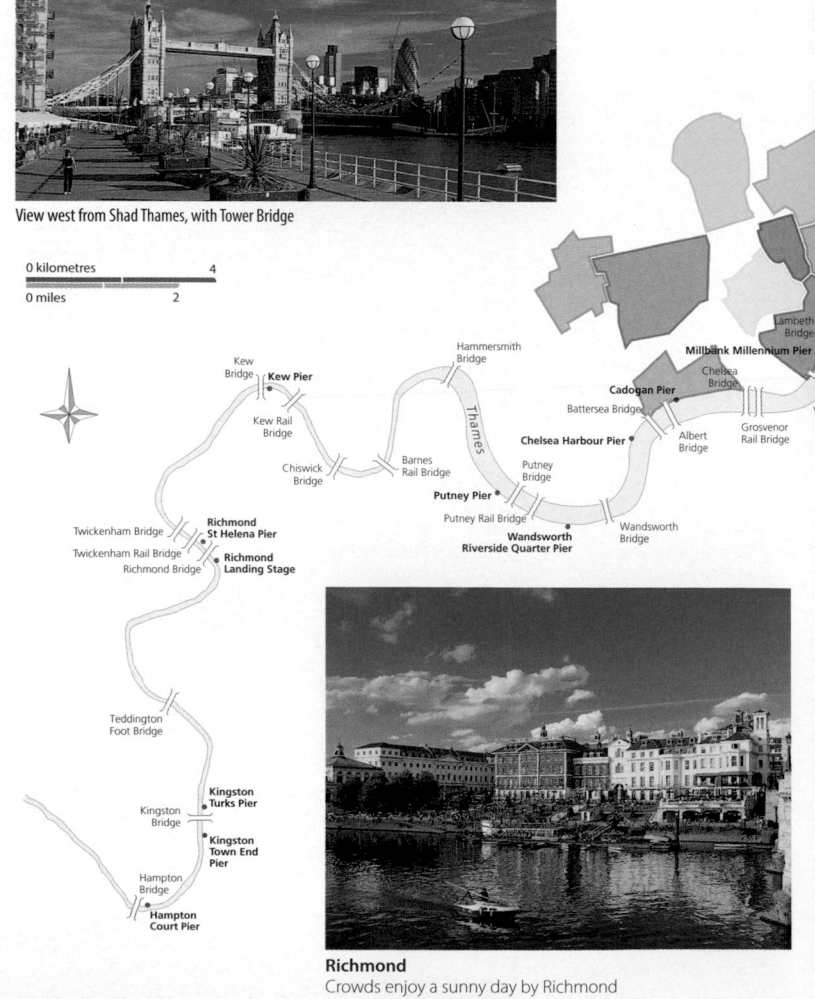

View west from Shad Thames, with Tower Bridge

0 kilometres 4
0 miles 2

Kew Bridge
Kew Pier
Kew Rail Bridge
Chiswick Bridge
Barnes Rail Bridge
Hammersmith Bridge
Thames
Millbank Millennium Pier
Lambeth Bridge
Chelsea Bridge
Cadogan Pier
Battersea Bridge
Chelsea Harbour Pier
Albert Bridge
Grosvenor Rail Bridge
Va Br
Putney Bridge
Putney Pier
Putney Rail Bridge
Wandsworth Riverside Quarter Pier
Wandsworth Bridge
Twickenham Bridge
Richmond St Helena Pier
Twickenham Rail Bridge
Richmond Bridge
Richmond Landing Stage
Teddington Foot Bridge
Kingston Turks Pier
Kingston Bridge
Kingston Town End Pier
Hampton Bridge
Hampton Court Pier

Richmond
Crowds enjoy a sunny day by Richmond St Helena Pier in this west London village.

The Thames Barrier
Completed in 1982, the world's second largest moveable flood barrier protects London from rising water levels. The massive steel gates have been raised over 100 times.

Riverside pubs
Beautifully preserved pubs, such as the Prospect of Whitby in Wapping, hug the river's banks.

See pp66–7

See pp64–5

Rotherhithe Tunnel

Hilton Docklands Pier

Greenland Pier

Canary Wharf Pier

Masthouse Terrace Pier

Greenwich Foot Tunnel

Greenwich Pier

Blackwall Tunnel

North Greenwich Pier

Thames

Thames Barrier

Barrier Gardens Pier

Cruise Operators

**Bateaux London/
Catamaran Cruisers**
Tel 020 7695 1800.
W bateauxlondon.com

City Cruises
Tel 020 7740 0400.
W citycruises.com

Crown River Cruises
Tel 020 7936 2033.
W crownriver.com

Thames Clippers
Tel 0870 781 5049.
W thamesclippers.com

**Thames Executive
Charters**
Tel 01342 820600.
W thamesexecutive
charters.com

Thames River Services
Tel 020 7930 4097.
W thamesriverservices.
co.uk

Turks Launches
Tel 020 8546 2434.
W turks.co.uk

**Westminster Passenger
Service Association
(Upriver) Ltd**
Tel 020 7930 2062
W wpsa.co.uk

Cruise Highlights

Most regular services run from April through September, with some routes having winter schedules. During the summer, sailing times are frequent from Westminster and Embankment to Greenwich, with a boat arriving between every half hour and every hour. Commuter river services link Canary Wharf and Chelsea Harbour with some of the city's main termini. Numerous operators cover a variety of routes and a River Thames Boat Service Guide is available at tube stations. Most operators give a third off the ticket price to Travelcard holders (see p370).

Greenwich (see pp238–45)
Blessed with frequent service, accessing this area steeped in shipping lore by boat gives a day trip a fitting nautical spin.
Operators: Bateaux London/ Catamaran Cruisers, City Cruises, Thames River Services.
Piers: Westminster, Waterloo, Embankment, Bankside, Tower.
Duration: 1 hr (Westminster).
Thames Barrier (see p251) Sail between the nine massive piers that raise the steel gates. Cruises to the barrier also pass the O2 Arena, formerly the Millennium Dome.
Operator: Thames River Services.
Piers: Westminster, Greenwich.
Duration: 30 mins (Greenwich).

Kew (see pp262–3) A cruise to Kew leaves the city behind after passing the Battersea Power Station and sailing through Hammersmith.
Operator: WPSA (upriver only).
Piers: Westminster.
Duration: 1.5 hrs (Westminster).
Hampton Court (see pp256–9) Arrive at Hampton Court in regal style, but be aware that the round trip from Westminster can take up to eight hours. Consider sailing from one of the piers upriver.
Operator: WPSA (upriver only), Turks Launches.
Piers: Kew, all Richmond and Kingston piers.
Duration: 2 hrs (Kew).

Westminster Bridge to Blackfriars Bridge

Until World War II, this stretch of the Thames marked the division between rich and poor London. On the north bank were the offices, shops, luxury hotels and apartments of Whitehall and the Strand, the Inns of Court and the newspaper district. To the south were smoky factories and slum dwellings. After the war, the Festival of Britain in 1951 started the revival of the South Bank (see pp186–93), which now has some of the capital's most interesting modern buildings.

Savoy Hotel
This hotel is on the site of a medieval palace (see p118).

Somerset House, built in 1786, houses an art gallery (see p119).

Shell Mex House
Once offices for the oil company, they were built in 1931 on the site of the vast Cecil Hotel.

Embankment Gardens is the site of many open-air concerts held in the bandstand during summer (see p120).

Cleopatra's Needle was made in ancient Egypt and given to London in 1819 (see p120).

Waterloo Bridge

🚇 Charing
🚈 Cross

Festival Pier

🚇 Embankment
🚈 Embankment Pier

The South Bank was the site of the 1951 Festival of Britain and is London's most important arts complex. It is dominated by the Royal Festival Hall, the National Theatre and the Hayward Gallery (see pp186–93).

Charing Cross
The rail terminus is encased in a Post-Modernist office complex (see p121).

London Eye Pier

Jubilee Gardens

The London Eye offers incredible views over London (see p191).

Hungerford Railway Bridge and Golden Jubilee Footbridges

The Banqueting House is one of Inigo Jones's finest works, built as part of Whitehall Palace (see p82).

The Ministry of Defence is a bulky white fortress completed in the 1950s.

Westminster Pier

Westminster

Westminster Bridge

County Hall
This is home to the state-of-the-art London Aquarium and its 350 species of fish.

Temple and the Inns of Court
These historic buildings have been the offices of lawyers and barristers for over 500 years *(see pp138–41)*.

St Paul's
Christopher Wren's masterwork, finished in 1708, formerly dominated the London skyline *(see pp150–53)*.

Blackfriars

Blackfriars Millennium Pier

Blackfriars Bridge

Millennium Bridge

Tate Modern is located in the old Bankside power station *(see pp180–83)*.

Gabriel's Wharf
A lively craft market operates where once there were warehouses *(see p193)*.

Doggett's Coat and Badge
The modern pub here is named after a river race in which boatmen compete for this huge badge.

Blackfriars Bridge
The logo of a former railway company adorns the bridge.

OXO Tower
The windows were designed to spell the brand name of a popular meat extract.

St Paul's
The cathedral dominates views from the South Bank.

For key to symbols *see back flap*

Southwark Bridge to St Katharine's Dock

For centuries the stretch just east of London Bridge was the busiest part of the Thames, with ships of all sizes jostling for position to unload at the wharves on both banks. Then, in the 19th century, the construction of the docks to the east eased congestion. Today most landmarks on this section hark back to that commercial past.

Old Billingsgate
Note the flying fish weather vanes on what was London's main fish market (p154).

Fishmongers' Hall
The hall (1834) of this ancient City guild dominates the view north from London Bridge (p154).

A Custom House
has been here since 1272. This version dates from 1825.

Monument
The Great Fire of 1666 started near this spot (p154).

Cannon Street

Monument

Southwark Bridge

Bankside Pier

Cannon Street Railway Bridge

London Bridge

London Bridge City Pier

The Shard is a 306-m (1,004-ft) glass spire of apartments, offices, a hotel, restaurants, and, of course, The View.

London Bridge

The Globe Theatre
This replica Elizabethan theatre was built to recreate the experience of the way Shakespeare's plays were first performed (p179).

St Olave's House
A fine Art Deco building shows its best face to the river.

Southwark Cathedral
Parts of this building date from the 12th century. It contains memorials to Shakespeare (p178).

Hay's Galleria
Once a wharf for unloading food, it has been covered to house shops and restaurants.

Southwark Wharves
Now there are walkways with river views where ships used to dock.

Tower of London
Look out for Traitors' Gate, where prisoners would be taken into the Tower by boat *(pp156–9)*.

Tower Bridge
It still opens to let tall ships pass, but not as often as it did when cargo vessels came through *(p155)*.

St Katharine's Dock
The former dock is now a lively attraction for visitors. Its yacht marina is a highlight *(p160)*.

Tower Millennium Pier

Tower Bridge

St Katharine's Pier

The stunning City Hall
houses the Mayor and the governing offices.

HMS Belfast
This World War II cruiser has been a museum since 1971 *(p185)*.

Victorian warehouses
on Butlers Wharf have been converted into apartments.

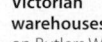

Design Museum
Opened in 1989, this ship-like building is a shining example of Docklands' renaissance *(p185)*.

Arial view of the City of London by night ▶

LONDON AREA BY AREA

Whitehall and Westminster	**70–87**
Piccadilly and St James's	**88–99**
Soho and Trafalgar Square	**100–111**
Covent Garden and The Strand	**112–121**
Bloomsbury and Fitzrovia	**122–133**
Holborn and The Inns of Court	**134–143**
The City	**144–161**
Smithfield and Spitalfields	**162–173**
Southwark and Bankside	**174–185**
South Bank	**186–193**
Chelsea	**194–199**
South Kensington and Knightsbridge	**200–215**
Kensington and Holland Park	**216–221**
Regent's Park and Marylebone	**222–229**
Hampstead	**230–237**
Greenwich and Blackheath	**238–245**
Further Afield	**246–263**
Six Guided Walks	**264–277**

WHITEHALL AND WESTMINSTER

Whitehall and Westminster have been at the centre of political and religious power in England for a thousand years. King Canute, who ruled at the beginning of the 11th century, was the first monarch to have a palace on what was then an island in the swampy meeting point of the Thames and its vanished tributary, the Tyburn. Canute built his palace beside the church that, some 50 years later,

Edward the Confessor would enlarge into England's greatest abbey, giving the area its name (a minster is an abbey church). Over the following centuries the offices of state were established in the vicinity. All this is still reflected in Whitehall's heroic statues and massive government buildings. But, to its north, Trafalgar Square marks the start of the West End entertainment district.

Sights at a Glance

Historic Streets and Buildings
1 Houses of Parliament pp74–5
2 Big Ben
3 Jewel Tower
5 Dean's Yard
7 Parliament Square
9 Downing Street
10 Cabinet War Rooms and Churchill Museum
11 Banqueting House
12 Horse Guards Parade
14 Queen Anne's Gate
16 St James's Park Station
17 Blewcoat School

Churches, Abbeys and Cathedrals
4 Westminster Abbey pp78–81
6 St Margaret's Church
18 Westminster Cathedral
19 St John's, Smith Square

Museums and Galleries
15 Guards' Museum
20 Tate Britain pp84–7

Theatres
13 Trafalgar Studios

Monuments
8 Cenotaph

Street Finder, maps 13, 20, 21

0 metres 500
0 yards 500

Restaurants see pp292–295
1 Cinnamon Club
2 Regency Café

◀ The clock face on the Houses of Parliament

For keys to symbols see back flap

Street-by-Street: Whitehall and Westminster

Compared with many capital cities, London has little monumental architecture designed to overawe with pomp. Here, at the historic seat both of the government and of the established church, it most closely approaches the broad, stately avenues of Paris, Rome and Madrid. On weekdays the streets are crowded with members of the civil service, as most of their work is based in this area. At weekends, however, it is popular with tourists visiting some of London's most famous sights.

🔟 ★ **Cabinet War Rooms and Churchill Museum**
The War Rooms were Winston Churchill's World War II headquarters.

The Treasury is where the nation's finances are administered.

Central Hall is a florid example of the Beaux Arts style, built in 1911 as a Methodist meeting hall. In 1946 the first General Assembly of the United Nations was held here.

❹ ★ **Westminster Abbey**
The Abbey is London's oldest and most important church.

❼ **Parliament Square**
Statues of famous statesmen, such as Benjamin Disraeli, Sir Winston Churchill and Nelson Mandela, stand here.

The Sanctuary was a medieval safe place for those escaping the law.

❻ **St Margaret's Church**
Society weddings often take place here, in Parliament's church.

❺ **Dean's Yard**
Westminster School was founded here in 1540.

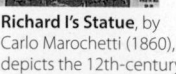

Richard I's Statue, by Carlo Marochetti (1860), depicts the 12th-century *Coeur de Lion* (Lionheart).

❸ **Jewel Tower**
Kings once stored their most valuable possessions here.

The Burghers of Calais is a cast of Auguste Rodin's original in Paris.

To Trafalgar Square

12 Horse Guards
A mounted guard is ceremonially changed here twice a day.

Dover House, a stately mansion dating from 1787, now houses the Scottish Office.

WHITEHALL

Earl Haig, the British World War I chief, was sculpted by Alfred Hardiman in 1936.

9 Downing Street
British Prime Ministers have lived here since 1732.

RICHMOND TERRACE

8 Cenotaph
Edwin Lutyens's war memorial dates from 1920.

Richmond House is William Whitfield's prize-winning 1980s building for the Department of Health.

VICTORIA EMBANKMENT

Westminster station

Westminster Pier is a starting point for river excursions.

Portcullis House provides offices for Members of Parliament.

Boudicca, the British queen who resisted the Romans, was portrayed by Thomas Thornycroft in the 1850s.

Locator Map
See Central London Map pp14–15

PICCADILLY & ST JAMES'S / SOUTH BANK / Thames / WHITEHALL & WESTMINSTER / Victoria / Lambeth

11 ★ Banqueting House
Inigo Jones designed this elegant building, which has a Rubens ceiling, in 1622.

1 2 ★ Houses of Parliament and Big Ben
These were designed by Barry in 1834 when the Palace of Westminster burned down.

0 metres   100
0 yards   100

Key
— Suggested route

❶ Houses of Parliament

For over 500 years the Palace of Westminster has been the seat of the two Houses of Parliament, called the Lords and the Commons. The Commons is made up of elected Members of Parliament (MPs) of different political parties; the party – or coalition of parties – with the most MPs forms the Government, and its leader becomes Prime Minister. MPs from other parties make up the Opposition. Commons' debates can become heated and are impartially chaired by an MP designated as Speaker. The Government formulates legislation which must be agreed to in both Houses before becoming law.

★ **Commons' Chamber**
The room is upholstered in green. The Government sits on the left, the Opposition on the right, and the Speaker presides from a chair between them.

The mock-Gothic building was designed by Victorian architect Sir Charles Barry. Victoria Tower, on the left, contains over 3 million parliamentary records, including every Act of Parliament passed since 1497.

Big Ben
The vast bell was hung in 1858 and chimes on the hour; four smaller ones ring on the quarter hours *(see p76)*.

Members' entrance

KEY

① **Peers** are members of the House of Lords. They come from many walks of life and bring experience and knowledge from a wide range of professions. This is their lobby.

② **Royal Gallery** is used for quiet work by members of the Lords, and occasional special events.

★ **Westminster Hall**
The only surviving part of the original Palace of Westminster, it dates from 1097; its hammerbeam roof is 14th century.

Central Lobby
People who come to meet their MP wait here under a ceiling of rich mosaics.

Peers' entrance

Cromwell Green entrance

★ **Lords' Chamber**
The room is upholstered in red and is similar in layout to the Commons, but has crossbenchers (non-party-political members). The Lord Speaker sits on the Woolsack.

1042 Work starts on first palace for Edward the Confessor

1550 St Stephen's chapel becomes first Chamber of the House of Commons

1834 Palace destroyed by fire; only Westminster Hall and the Jewel Tower survive

1870 Present building completed

1000	1200	1400	1600	1800	2000

1097–99 Westminster Hall built

1512 After a fire, palace stops being a royal residence

The Mace: symbol of royal authority in the Commons and Lords.

1605 Guy Fawkes and others try to blow up the king and Houses of Parliament

1642 Charles I tries to arrest five MPs but is forced to withdraw by the Speaker

1941 Chamber of House of Commons destroyed by World War II bomb

The world's most famous clock tower that houses Big Ben

❷ Big Ben

Bridge St SW1. **Map** 13 C5. 🚇 Westminster. 📷 9am, 11am & 2pm Mon–Fri (also May–Sep: 4pm Tue–Thu), except bank hols.

Big Ben is not the name of the world-famous four-faced clock in the 96-m (315-ft) tower that rises above the Houses of Parliament, but of the resonant 14-tonne bell on which the hours are struck, thought to be named after the Chief Commissioner of Works Sir Benjamin Hall, in 1858. Cast at Whitechapel, it was the second giant bell made for the clock, the first having become cracked during a test ringing. The clock is the largest in Britain, its four dials 7.5 m (23 ft) in diameter and the minute hand 4.25 m (14 ft) long, made in hollow copper for lightness. It has kept exact time for the nation more or less continuously since it was first set in motion in May 1859, and has become a symbol of Britain the world over. The tower itself was renamed the Elizabeth Tower in 2012 in honour of Queen Elizabeth II in her Diamond Jubilee Year.

❸ Jewel Tower

Abingdon St SW1. **Map** 13 B5.
Tel 020 7222 2219. 🚇 Westminster.
Open Apr–Oct: 10am–5pm daily; Nov–Mar: 10am–4pm Sat & Sun.
Closed 24–26 Dec, 1 Jan. 🅿️
♿ ground floor only. 📷
🅦 **english-heritage.org.uk**

This and Westminster Hall (*see p74*) are the only vestiges of the old Palace of Westminster. The tower was built in 1365 as a stronghold for Edward III's treasure and today houses a fascinating exhibition, *Parliament Past and Present*, that relates the history of Parliament. It includes a display devoted to the history of the Jewel Tower itself.

The tower served as the weights and measures office from 1869 until 1938 and another small display relates to that era. Alongside are the remains of the moat and a medieval quay.

❹ Westminster Abbey

See pp78–81.

❺ Dean's Yard

Broad Sanctuary SW1. **Map** 13 B5.
🚇 Westminster. Buildings **Closed** to the public.

An arch near the west door of the Abbey leads into this secluded grassy square, surrounded by a jumble of buildings from many different periods. A medieval house on the east side has a distinctive dormer window and backs

Entrance to the Abbey and cloisters from Dean's Yard

on to Little Dean's Yard, where the monks' living quarters used to be. Dean's Yard is private property. It belongs to the Dean and Chapter of Westminster and is close to Westminster School, whose famous former pupils include poet John Dryden and playwright Ben Jonson. Scholars are, by tradition, the first to acknowledge a new monarch.

❻ St Margaret's Church

Parliament Sq SW1. **Map** 13 B5.
Tel 020 7654 4840. 🚇 Westminster.
Open 9:30am–3:30pm Mon–Fri, 9:30am–1:30pm Sat, 2–4:30pm Sun.
✝️ 11am Sun. 📷 ♿ via North Door 🅦
westminster-abbey.org/st-margarets

Overshadowed by the Abbey, this late-15th-century church has long been a favoured venue for political and society weddings, such as Winston and Clementine Churchill's. Although much restored, the church retains some Tudor features, notably a stained-glass window commemorating the marriage of King Henry VIII and his first wife, Catherine of Aragon.

❼ Parliament Square

SW1. **Map** 13 B5. 🚇 Westminster.

Laid out in the 1840s to provide a more open aspect for the new Houses of Parliament, the square became Britain's first official roundabout in 1926. Today it is hemmed in by heavy traffic. Statues of statesmen and soldiers are dominated by Winston Churchill in his greatcoat, glowering at the House of Commons. On the north side, Abraham Lincoln sits in front of the mock-Gothic Middlesex Guildhall, completed in 1913.

❽ Cenotaph

Whitehall SW1. **Map** 13 B4.
🚇 Westminster.

This suitably bleak and pale monument, completed in 1920 by Sir Edwin Lutyens to commemorate the dead of

World War I, stands in the middle of Whitehall. On Remembrance Day every year – the Sunday nearest 11 November – the monarch and other dignitaries place wreaths of red poppies on the Cenotaph. This solemn ceremony, commemorating the 1918 armistice, honours the victims of World Wars I and II *(see pp56–7)*.

The Cenotaph

🔟 Churchill Museum and Cabinet War Rooms

Clive Steps, King Charles St SW1. **Map** 13 B5. **Tel** 020 7930 6961. ☻ Westminster. **Open** 9:30am–6pm daily (last adm: 5pm). **Closed** 24–26 Dec. 🦽♿🖻📷 **w** iwm.org.uk/cabinet

This intriguing slice of 20th-century history is a warren of rooms below the Government Office Building north of Parliament Square. It is where the War Cabinet – first under Neville Chamberlain, then Winston Churchill – met during World War II when German bombs were falling on London. The War Rooms include living quarters for key ministers and military leaders

Telephones in the Map Room of the Cabinet War Rooms

and a Cabinet Room, where many strategic decisions were taken. They are laid out as they were when the war ended, complete with period furniture, including Churchill's desk, communications equipment and maps for plotting military strategy. The Churchill Museum is a multimedia exhibit recording Churchill's life and career.

🔟 Downing Street

SW1. **Map** 13 B4. ☻ Westminster. **Closed** to the public.

Sir George Downing (1623–84) spent part of his youth in the American colonies. He was the second graduate from the nascent Harvard College before returning to fight for the Parliamentarians in the English Civil War. In 1680, he bought

some land near Whitehall Palace and built a street of houses. Four of these survive, though they are much altered. George II gave No. 10 to Sir Robert Walpole in 1732. Since then it has been the official residence of the Prime Minister and contains offices as well as a private apartment. In 1989, for security reasons, iron gates were erected at the Whitehall end.

The famous front door of No. 10

No. 12, the Whips' Office, is where Party campaigns are organized.

Government policy is decided in the Cabinet Room at No. 10.

No. 11 is the Chancellor of the Exchequer's official residence.

No. 10 is the official home of the Prime Minister.

The Prime Minister entertains official guests in the State Dining Room.

❹ Westminster Abbey

The Abbey is world-famous as the resting-place of Britain's monarchs, and as the setting for coronations and other great pageants, such as the marriage of Prince William in 2011. Within its walls can be seen some of the most glorious examples of medieval architecture in London. It also contains one of the most impressive collections of tombs and monuments in the world. Half national church, half national museum, the Abbey is part of British national consciousness.

★ **Flying Buttresses**
The massive flying buttresses help transfer the great weight of the 31-m (102-ft) high nave.

North/Main Entrance
The stonework here, like this carving of a dragon, is Victorian.

★ **West Front Towers**
These towers, completed in 1745, were designed by Nicholas Hawksmoor.

KEY

① **The North Transept** has three chapels on the east side containing some of the Abbey's finest monuments.

② **St Edward's Chapel** houses Edward the Confessor's shrine and the tombs of other English medieval monarchs.

③ **The South Transept** contains "Poets' Corner", where memorials to famous literary figures can be seen.

④ **Museum**

⑤ **The Cloisters**, built mainly in the 13th and 14th centuries, link the Abbey church with the other buildings.

★ **The Nave viewed from the West End**
At 10 m (35 ft) wide, the nave is comparatively narrow, but it is the highest in England.

★ The Lady Chapel
The chapel, consecrated in 1516, has a superb vaulted ceiling and choir stalls dating from 1512.

★ Chapter House
This octagonal structure is worth seeing for its 13th-century tiles.

13th-century tile from the Chapter House

1050 New Benedictine abbey church begun by Edward the Confessor

1376 Henry Yevele begins rebuilding the nave

1838 Queen Victoria's coronation

2011 Prince William and Catherine Middleton's wedding

1000	1200	1400	1600	1800	2000

1245 New church begun to the designs of Henry of Reyns

1269 Body of Edward the Confessor moved to new shrine in the Abbey

1540 Monastery dissolved

1745 West towers completed

1953 Most recent coronation in the Abbey: Elizabeth II's

A Guided Tour of Westminster Abbey

The abbey's interior presents an exceptionally diverse array of architectural and sculptural styles. These range from the austere French Gothic of the nave to the stunning complexity of Henry VII's Tudor chapel and the riotous invention of the later 18th-century monuments. Many British monarchs were buried here; some of their tombs are deliberately plain, while others are lavishly decorated. At the same time, there are monuments to a number of Britain's greatest public figures – ranging from politicians to poets – crowded into the aisles and transepts.

② **Grave of the Unknown Warrior**
The body of an unknown soldier was brought from the battlefields of World War I and buried here in 1920. His grave commemorates all who have lost their lives in war.

Historical Plan of the Abbey

The first Abbey church was established as early as the 10th century, when St Dunstan brought a group of Benedictine monks to the area. The present structure dates largely from the 13th century; the new, French-influenced design was begun in 1245 at the behest of Henry III. Because of its unique role as the royal coronation church, the Abbey survived Henry VIII's mid-16th-century onslaught on Britain's monastic buildings.

Key

☐ Built between 1055–1350
▨ Added from 1350–1420
☐ Built between 1500–1512
☐ Towers completed 1745
☐ Restored after 1850

Main entrance

The Choir houses a gilded 1840s screen, which contains remnants of the 13th-century original.

The Jericho Parlour, added in the early 16th century, contains some fine panelling. It is closed to the public.

The Jerusalem Chamber has a 17th-century fireplace, fine tapestries and an interesting painted ceiling. It is closed to the public.

The Deanery, home of the Dean of Westminster, was once the monastic abbot's house. It is closed to the public.

① **Coronation Chair**
Constructed in 1301, this chair has been used at every coronation since 1308.

Coronation

The abbey has been the fittingly sumptuous setting for all royal coronations since 1066. The last occupant of the Coronation Chair was the present monarch, Elizabeth II. She was crowned in 1953 in the first televised coronation.

The Chapel of St John the Baptist is full of tombs dating from the 14th to the 19th centuries.

St Faith Chapel contains works of art that date back to the 13th century.

The Pyx Chamber's gaunt columns date from the 11th century. This is where the coinage was tested in medieval times.

③ The Nave
The nave is 10.5 m (35 ft) wide and 31 m (102 ft) high. It took 150 years to build.

④ Nightingale Memorial
The North Transept chapels contain some of the Abbey's finest monuments – this one, by Roubiliac, is for Lady Elizabeth Nightingale (1761).

⑤ Tomb of Elizabeth I
Inside the Lady Chapel you will find Elizabeth I's (reigned 1558–1603) huge tomb. It also houses the body of her sister, "Bloody" Mary I.

⑥ The Lady Chapel
The undersides of the choir stalls, dating from 1512, are beautifully carved with exotic and fantastic creatures.

⑦ The Chapel of St Edward the Confessor
The shrine of the Saxon king Edward the Confessor and the tombs of many medieval monarchs are here.

Key
— Tour route

Dean's Yard entrance

⑧ Poets' Corner
Take time to explore the memorials to countless literary giants, such as Shakespeare and Dickens, which are gathered here.

⓫ Banqueting House

Whitehall SW1. **Map** 13 B4. **Tel** 0844 482 7777 (UK) or 020 3166 6000 (outside UK; possible closures – call ahead). ⊖ Charing Cross, Embankment, Westminster. **Open** 10am–5pm daily (last adm 4:15pm). **Closed** Sun, public hols, 24 Dec–1 Jan; for functions (phone first). 🔗 🏛 📷 🌐 **hrp.org.uk**

This delightful building is of great architectural importance. It was the first in central London to embody the Classical Palladian style that designer Inigo Jones brought back from his travels in Italy. Completed in 1622, its disciplined stone façade marked a startling change from the Elizabethans' fussy turrets and unrestrained external decoration. It was the sole survivor of the fire that destroyed most of the old Whitehall Palace in 1698.

The ceiling paintings by Rubens, a complex allegory on the exaltation of James I, were commissioned by his son, Charles I, in 1630. This blatant glorification of royalty was despised by Oliver Cromwell and the Parliamentarians, who executed King Charles I on a scaffold outside Banqueting House in 1649. Ironically, Charles II celebrated his restoration to the throne here 11 years later. The building is used for official functions.

Mounted sentries stationed outside Horse Guards Parade

⓬ Horse Guards Parade

Whitehall SW1. **Map** 13 B4. **Tel** 020 7766 7300. ⊖ Westminster, Charing Cross, Embankment. **Open** 8am–6pm daily. Changing the Guard May–Jul: 11:30am daily; Aug–April: 11:30am Sun (phone first). Dismounting Ceremony 4pm daily. Times for both are subject to change (phone for details). Trooping the Colour *see Ceremonies pp54–7.*

Once Henry VIII's tiltyard (tournament ground), nowadays the Changing of the Guard takes place here every morning. The elegant buildings, completed in 1755, were designed by William Kent. On the left is the Old

Treasury, also by Kent, and Dover House, completed in 1758 and now used as the Scottish Office. Nearby is a trace of the "real tennis" court where Henry VIII is said to have played the ancient precursor of modern lawn tennis. On the opposite side, the view is dominated by the ivy-covered Citadel. This is a bomb-proof structure that was erected in 1940 beside the Admiralty. During World War II, it was used as a communications headquarters by the Navy.

⓭ Trafalgar Studios

14 Whitehall SW1. **Map** 13 B3. **Tel** 0844 871 7627. ⊖ Charing Cross. **Open** for performances only. *See Entertainment pp336–7.*

Formerly the Whitehall Theatre and built in 1930, the plain white front seems to emulate the Cenotaph *(see p76)* at the other end of the street but, inside, the theatre boasts fine Art Deco detailing. The studios comprise two intimate spaces.

⓮ Queen Anne's Gate

SW1. **Map** 13 A5. ⊖ St James's Park.

The spacious terraced houses at the west end of this well-preserved enclave date from 1704 and are notable for the ornate canopies over their front doors. At the other end are houses built some 70 years later, sporting blue plaques that record former residents, such as Lord Palmerston, the Victorian Prime Minister. It is rumoured that the British Secret Service, MI5, was formerly based in this unlikely spot. A small statue of Queen Anne stands in front of the wall separating Nos. 13 and 15. To the west, situated at the corner of Petty France, Sir Basil Spence's Home Office building (1976) is an architectural incongruity. Cockpit Steps, leading down to Birdcage Walk, mark the site of a 17th-century venue for the popular, yet blood-thirsty, sport of cockfighting.

Panels from the Rubens ceiling, Banqueting House

⓯ Guards Museum

Birdcage Walk SW1. **Map** 13 A5.
Tel 020 7414 3428. ⓔ St James's Park.
Open 10am–4pm daily (last adm:
3:30pm). **Closed** Christmas, ceremonies. 🏛 (free for under-16s). 🏛 ♿
🏛 🌐 theguardsmuseum.com

Entered from Birdcage Walk, the
museum is under the parade
ground of Wellington Barracks,
headquarters of the five Guards
regiments. A must for military
buffs, the museum uses
tableaux and dioramas to
illustrate various battles in
which the Guards have taken
part, from the English Civil War
(1642–8) to the present.
Weapons and row after row of
colourful uniforms are on
display, as well as a fascinating
collection of models.

⓰ St James's Park Station

55 Broadway SW1. **Map** 13 A5.
ⓔ St James's Park.

The station is built into
Broadway House, Charles
Holden's 1929 headquarters for
London Transport. It is notable
for its sculptures by Jacob
Epstein and reliefs by Henry
Moore and Eric Gill.

⓱ Blewcoat School

23 Caxton St SW1. **Map** 13 A5.
Tel 020 7222 2877. ⓔ St James's Park.
Closed to public.

A red-brick gem hemmed in
by the office towers of Victoria
Street, it was built in 1709 as a
charity school to teach pupils

Statue of a Blewcoat pupil above the
Caxton Street entrance

Baroque interior of St John's, Smith Square

how to "read, write, cast accounts
and the catechism". All pupils
were boys until 1713, when
girls were admitted. The
attendance of girls was
discontinued in1876. In 1899, it
passed to Christchurch National
Schools. It remained as a school
until 1939, becoming an army
store during World War II, and
was bought by the National
Trust in 1954.

⓲ Westminster Cathedral

Ashley Place SW1. **Map** 20 F1.
Tel 020 7798 9055. ⓔ Victoria.
Open 7am–7pm Mon–Fri,
8am–7pm Sat & Sun. 🏛 for bell
tower lift (9:30am–5pm Mon–Fri,
9:30am–6pm Sat & Sun). ✝ Check
website for details of Mass and
services. ♿ 🏛 🏛
🌐 westminstercathedral.org.uk

One of London's rare Byzantine
buildings, it was designed by
John Francis Bentley for the
Catholic diocese and completed
in 1903 on the site of a former
prison. Its 87-m (285-ft) high,
red-brick tower, with horizontal
stripes of white stone, stands
out on the skyline in sharp
contrast to the Abbey nearby.
A restful piazza on the north side
provides a good view of the
cathedral from Victoria Street.
The rich interior decoration,
with marble of varying colours
and intricate mosaics, makes
the domes above the nave

seem incongruous. They were
left bare because the project
ran out of money.
   Eric Gill's dramatic reliefs of
the 14 Stations of the Cross,
created during World War I,
adorn the pier of the nave,
which is the widest in Britain.
The organ is one of the finest
in Europe, and there are often
free recitals on Sunday
afternoons at 4:45pm.

⓳ St John's, Smith Square

Smith Sq SW1. **Map** 21 B1. **Tel** 020
7222 1061. ⓔ Westminster. Box office
Open 10am–5pm Mon–Fri. **Closed** to
public except for concerts. 🏛 ♿
phone first. 🏛 🌐 sjss.org.uk

Described by artist and art
historian Sir Hugh Casson as one
of the masterpieces of English
Baroque architecture, Thomas
Archer's plump church, with its
turrets at each corner, looks as if
it is trying to burst from the
confines of the square, and
rather overpowers the pleasing
18th-century houses on its
north side. Today it is principally
a concert hall. It has an accident-
prone history: completed in
1728, it was burned down in 1742,
struck by lightning in 1773 and
destroyed by a World War II bomb
in 1941. There is a reasonably
priced basement restaurant that
is open daily for lunch and on
concert evenings.

⑳ Tate Britain

Tate Britain displays the world's largest collection of British art from the 16th to the 21st century. In the Clore Galleries are works from the magnificent Turner Bequest, left to the nation by the great landscape artist J M W Turner in 1851. The Clore Galleries have their own entrance, giving direct access to the Turner Collection and allowing a full appreciation of Sir James Stirling's Post-Modernist design for the building. The Tate often loans out, or removes works for restoration so exhibits described here may not always be on display.

Gallery Cafe

Main floor

Lower floor

Manton entrance

★ **Three Studies for Figures at the Base of a Crucifixion** (c.1944, detail) Francis Bacon's famous triptych encapsulates an anguished vision of human existence. When first displayed, its savagery deeply shocked audiences.

Gallery Guide

Tate Britain has undergone a restoration and expansion creating new spaces for displays and educational activities. Highlights from the collection are displayed chronologically around the outer perimeter of the galleries. More focused displays, "BP Spotlights", offer a more detailed look at specific artists or themes. The Duveen Galleries showcase the work of contemporary sculptors. Tate Britain also exhibits the annual Turner Prize nominees.

★ **Ophelia** (1851–2) Taken from Shakespeare's play *Hamlet*, the scene of the drowning of Ophelia by Pre-Raphaelite John Everett Millais is one of the most famous – and popular – paintings at Tate Britain.

The Saltonstall Family (c.1637)
David Des Granges's life-size family portrait includes the dead first Lady Saltonstall as the second shows off her new baby.

Henry Moore Galleries
This permanent display holds valuable works by the famous sculptor.

Entrance to Clore Galleries

Rotunda

Stairs to lower floor
🚻 ✎ ✏ 🎨 🅲 📞

★ Peace – Burial at Sea (1842)
This is J M W Turner's tribute to his friend and rival David Wilkie. It was painted in 1842, the year after Wilkie died at sea.

Millbank entrance

Key to Floorplan
- BP Walk Through British Art
- Duveen Galleries
- Clore Galleries
- Loan Exhibitions
- Non-exhibition space
- BP Spotlights
- Permanent displays

The Art of Good Food

The lower floor of Tate Britain boasts a café and an espresso bar, as well as a restaurant. Celebrated murals by Rex Whistler adorn the walls of the restaurant, telling the tale of the mythical inhabitants of Epicuriana and their expedition in search of rare foods. The extensive wine list has won awards. Open for lunch, weekend brunch and afternoon tea.

Exploring Tate Britain

Tate Britain draws its displays from the massive Tate Collection. The variety of works on show, combined with a rigorous programme of loan exhibitions and career retrospectives of British artists results in a selection to suit all tastes – from Elizabethan portraiture to cutting-edge installation. The displays are changed frequently to explore many different aspects of the history and art of Britain from 1500 to the present day.

The Cholmondeley Ladies (c.1600–10), British School

BP Walk Through British Art

The national collection of British art has been rehung in a continuous chronological display from the 1500s to the present day. This presentation allows viewers to observe a range of art from any one historical moment and see how British art has changed over the last five hundred years. The walk comprises around 500 artworks in some 20 galleries, and covers a period of dramatic change in British history, from the Tudors and Stuarts through to the age of Thomas Gainsborough.

Included are important works by one of Britain's greatest painters, William Hogarth, known for his biting satire on the lifestyle and beliefs of his contemporaries. His *Marriage à la Mode* series satirised the marriage contracts of the upper classes. In contrast are the dramatic large-scale paintings in an idealised style by artists such as Benjamin West and Joshua Reynolds, the head of the newly established Royal Academy. Landscape painting lies at the heart of the revolution in British painting during the 19th century, when

images of the countryside changed ideas not only about art, but about what it means to be British. Works by the poet and artist William Blake reveal him as a seminal figure of the Romantic Age, though largely unrecognized in his lifetime.

The first half of the 19th century saw dramatic expansion and change in the arts in Britain. New themes began to emerge, and artists started working on a much larger scale as they competed for attention on the walls of public exhibitions. Monumental canvases by John Martin, Thomas Lawrence and William Etty, as well as celebrated works by David Wilkie are evidence of this. Storytelling was at the heart of Victorian art; the Victorians' belief in the power of art to convey moral messages produced such important works as Augustus Egg's series *Past and Present*. Pre-Raphaelite and Idealist works are perhaps the most popular works at Tate Britain; key examples are John Everett Millais's *Ophelia* and William Holman Hunt's *Awakening Conscience*. Painting and sculpture from the late Victorian period includes John Singer Sargent's haunting *Carnation, Lily, Lily, Rose.*

Modern British Art

The modern section of the gallery begins with the early 20th century. "Modern Figures" looks at artists' fascination with modern cities: cosmopolitan, noisy places with crowded streets, continually changing architecture and fast, mechanized transport, as well as new places of entertainment. It includes Jacob Epstein's *Torso in Metal from "The Rock Drill"*, a machine-like robot, visored and menacing, that became a symbol of the new age, as well as the work of Wyndham Lewis and his Vorticist group, who saw the artist at the still centre of the vortex of modern life.

Work by celebrated British sculptors, such as Barbara Hepworth and Henry Moore, can also be seen in this section. Paintings by two of the most famous, and disturbing, modern British artists are also on display here: Francis Bacon, whose *Three Studies for Figures at the Base of a Crucifixion* (c.1944) depicts three mutant organisms in agony, confined in an apparently hostile and godless world; and Lucian Freud, whose expressive nudes are on display.

From the 1960s, Tate's funding for the purchase of works began to increase substantially, while artistic activity continued to pick up speed, encouraged by public funding. As a result, the Tate Collection is particularly rich on this time period, which means that the frequent rotation of displays is necessary.

There is, however, one room devoted to "Pop", one of the liveliest developments of British art in the 1960s, which focuses in particular on the beginnings of the movement through iconic works by artists such as Sir Peter Blake, Richard Hamilton, the early work of David Hockney, and Gerald Laing, deriving his inspiration for *Skydiver VI* (1964) from mass produced images of the 1960s. A revolt against this movement took place at the end of the 1960s, with the emergence of Conceptual artists such as Gilbert & George, known as the

Self-Portait with Knickers (2000) by Sarah Lucas

Living Sculptures, and Richard Long, who created a whole new approach to landscape painting by importing the land itself into the gallery.

Conceptual art in turn was rejected at the start of the 1980s by the School of London painters, including Howard Hodgkin, Frank Auerbach and R B Kitaj, while Tony Cragg, Richard Deacon and Antony Gormley pioneered a new kind of sculpture.

The 1990s saw a new surge in British art. Most recent British movements are well represented at Tate Britain. These include the work of the so-called Young British Artists (YBAs), who include Damien Hirst, perhaps the most notorious, as well as the controversial installations and photographic work of Tracey Emin and Sarah Lucas, exhibiting both individually and as a collective. Other contemporary artists, who have their work displayed at Tate Britain include Lucian Freud, Barbara Hepworth, David Hockney, Howard Hodgkin, Damien Hirst, Phyllida Barlow, Mona Hatoum and Chris Ofili.

The frequently changing displays at Tate Britain include wider surveys as well as rooms devoted to single artists, and feature important newly acquired works. The Contemporary British Art galleries reflect current developments in British art and are devoted to work by the latest up-and-coming artists.

The gallery also organizes the prestigious annual Turner Prize, which is presented to a British visual artist. Representing all sections of the art world, artists are selected on the basis of their work over the course of the preceding year. Works by all the artists shortlisted are showcased at Tate Britain, before a judging panel decides the winner.

Previous winners include Yoko Ono and British painter Howard Hodgkin. In the past winners have often been surrounded by controversy including Damien Hirst's *The Physical Impossibility of Death in the Mind of Someone* *Living* (1991), which consists of a shark preserved in formaldehyde, and British artist Tracey Emin's *My Bed* (1998), which comprises a dishevelled bed.

Clore Galleries

The Turner Bequest comprises some 300 oil paintings, 300 sketchbooks, and about 20,000 watercolours and drawings received by the nation from the great landscape painter J M W Turner after his death in 1851. Turner's will had specified that a gallery be built to house his pictures and this was finally done in 1987 with the opening of the Clore Galleries. Most of the oil paintings are on view in the main galleries, while the watercolours are the subject of changing displays.

Kids at the Tate

To encourage art appreciation from a young age, under 12s can visit any special exhibition at Tate Britain for free (when accompanied by an adult). Family-friendly events are held most weekends and during school holidays, including Open Studio, where families can get hands-on and creative; and the Families Welcome Area, with activities encouraging exploration of concepts such as scale, space and architecture.

Shipping at the Mouth of the Thames (c.1806–7) by J M W Turner

PICCADILLY AND ST JAMES'S

Piccadilly is the main artery of the West End. Once called Portugal Street, it acquired its present name from the ruffs, or pickadills, worn by 17th-century dandies. St James's still bears traces of the 18th century, when it surrounded the royal residences, and denizens of the court and society shopped and disported themselves here. Two shops in St James's Street – James Lock the hatter and Berry Bros. & Rudd vintners – recall that era. Fortnum and Mason, on Piccadilly, has served high-quality food for nearly 300 years. Mayfair to the north is still the most fashionable address in London, while Piccadilly Circus marks the start of Soho.

Sights at a Glance

Historic Streets and Buildings
1. Piccadilly Circus
3. Albany
5. Burlington Arcade
6. Ritz Hotel
7. Spencer House
8. St James's Palace
9. St James's Square
10. Royal Opera Arcade
11. Pall Mall
14. The Mall
15. Marlborough House
17. Clarence House
18. Lancaster House
19. Buckingham Palace pp96–7
22. Wellington Arch
24. Shepherd Market

Museums and Galleries
4. Royal Academy of Arts
12. Institute of Contemporary Arts
20. The Queen's Gallery
21. Royal Mews
23. Apsley House
26. Faraday Museum

Churches
2. St James's Church
16. Queen's Chapel

Parks and Gardens
13. St James's Park
25. Green Park

Restaurants see pp292–5
1. Al Duca
2. Apsleys
3. Bentley's Oyster Bar and Grill
4. Le Caprice
5. Cecconi's
6. Cut at 45 Park Lane
7. El Pirata
8. Hard Rock Café
9. Murano
10. Nobu
11. Noura
12. The Ritz Restaurant
13. Veeraswamy
14. The Wolseley

Street Finder, maps 12, 13

◀ Soldier at the Changing of the Royal Guard

For keys to symbols see back flap

Street-by-Street: Piccadilly and St James's

As soon as Henry VIII built St James's Palace in the 1530s, the area around it became the centre of fashionable London, and it has remained so ever since. The most influential people in the land strut importantly along its historic streets as they press on with the vital business of lunching in their clubs, discussing matters of pith and moment and brandishing their gold cards in the capital's most exclusive stores, or paying a visit to one of the many art galleries.

❸ Albany
This has been one of London's smartest addresses since it opened in 1803.

❹ ★ Royal Academy of Arts
Sir Joshua Reynolds founded the Academy in 1768. Now it mounts large popular exhibitions.

Fortnum and Mason
was founded in 1707 by one of Queen Anne's footmen *(see p313)*.

❺ ★ Burlington Arcade
Uniformed beadles discourage unruly behaviour in this 19th-century mall.

❻ Ritz Hotel
Named after César Ritz, and opened in 1906, it still lives up to his name.

❼ Spencer House
An ancestor of Princess Diana built this house in 1766.

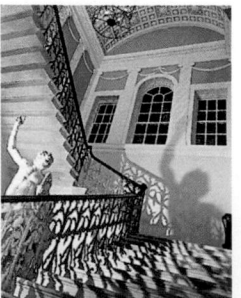

❽ St James's Palace
This Tudor palace is still the Court's official headquarters.

To The Mall

Jermyn Street is one of London's most elegant streets, lined with shops for style-conscious men *(see p316)*.

Piccadilly station

Locator Map
See Central London Map pp16–17

❶ ★ **Piccadilly Circus**
The crowds and dazzling neon lights make Piccadilly Circus the West End's focal point.

❷ ★ **St James's Church**
The organ in Christopher Wren's favourite church was brought here from Whitehall Palace in 1691.

❶ **Pall Mall**
Its famous clubs provide a haven for businessmen (and a few women).

❾ **St James's Square**
William III's statue dominates the square.

King Street is lined with art galleries, including Christie's, St James's.

Key

━ Suggested route

| 0 metres | 100 |
| 0 yards | 100 |

Alfred Gilbert's statue of *Eros*

❶ Piccadilly Circus

W1. **Map** 13 A3. 🚇 Piccadilly Circus.

For years people have congregated beneath the symbolic figure of Eros, originally intended as an angel of mercy but renamed after the Greek god of love. Poised delicately with his bow, Eros has become almost a trademark for the capital. It was erected in 1892 as a memorial to the Earl of Shaftesbury, the Victorian philanthropist. Part of Nash's master plan for Regent Street, Piccadilly Circus has been considerably altered over the years and consists for the most part of shops. One shopping mall can be found behind the façade of the London Pavilion (1885), once a popular music hall. The circus has London's gaudiest array of neon advertising signs marking the entrance to the city's lively entertainment district with cinemas, theatres, nightclubs, restaurants and pubs.

❷ St James's Church

197 Piccadilly W1. **Map** 13 A3. **Tel** 020 7734 4511. 🚇 Piccadilly Circus. **Open** 8am–6:30pm daily. Craft market 10am–6pm Wed–Sat, antiques market 10am–6pm Tue. ♿ 🖥 Concerts, talks, events. 🇼 sjp.org.uk

Among the many churches Wren designed *(see p49)*, this is said to be one of his favourites. It has been altered over the years and was half-wrecked by a bomb in 1940, but it maintains its essential features from 1684 – the tall, arched windows, thin spire (a 1966 replica of the original) and a light, dignified interior. The ornate screen behind the altar is one of the finest works of the 17th-century master carver Grinling Gibbons, who also made the exquisite marble font, with a scene depicting Adam and Eve standing by the Tree of Life. Artist and poet William Blake and Prime Minister Pitt the Elder were both baptized here. More of Gibbons's carvings can be seen above the grandiose organ, made for Whitehall Palace chapel but installed here in 1691. The church now has a full calendar of events, and houses a popular café.

❸ Albany

Albany Court Yard, Piccadilly W1. **Map** 12 F3. 🚇 Green Park, Piccadilly Circus. **Closed** to the public.

These desirable and discreet bachelor apartments, half hidden through an entrance off Piccadilly, were built in 1803 by Henry Holland. Notable residents have included the poet Lord Byron, novelist Graham Greene, two Prime Ministers (William Gladstone and Edward Heath) and the actor Terence Stamp. Married men were admitted in 1878 but could not bring their wives to live with them until 1919. Women are now allowed to live here in their own right.

Byron lived in Albany

Michelangelo's *Madonnna and Child*

❹ Royal Academy of Arts

Burlington House, Piccadilly W1. **Map** 12 F3. **Tel** 020 7300 8000. 🚇 Piccadilly Circus, Green Park. **Open** 10am–6pm Sat–Thu, 10am–10pm Fri. **Closed** Good Fri, 24–26 Dec. ♿ Adm charge some exhibitions. 🖥 ♿ 📷 🇼 royalacademy.org.uk

The courtyard in front of Burlington House, one of the West End's few surviving mansions from the early 18th century, is often crammed with people waiting to get into one of the prestigious visiting art exhibitions on show at the Royal Academy (founded 1768). The famous annual summer exhibition, which has now been held for over 200 years, comprises around 1,200 new works by both established and unknown artists. Any artist, established or unknown, may submit work.

The airy Sackler Galleries (1991), designed by Norman Foster, show visiting exhibitions. There are permanent items in the sculpture promenade outside the galleries, notably a Michelangelo relief of the *Madonna and Child* (1505). The exceptional permanent collection (not all on display) includes one work by each current and former Academician; the highlights are displayed in the Madejski Rooms. Two shops adjacent to the gallery exits sell merchandise inspired by the current exhibitions, as well as a great range of art books.

❺ Burlington Arcade

Piccadilly W1. **Map** 12 F3. 🚇 Green Park, Piccadilly Circus.

This is one of four 19th-century arcades of small shops that sell traditional British luxuries. (The Princes and Piccadilly Arcades are on the south side of Piccadilly, while the Royal Opera Arcade is off Pall Mall.) It was built for Lord Cavendish in 1819 to stop rubbish being thrown into his garden. The arcade is still patrolled by beadles who make sure an atmosphere of refinement is maintained. They have authority to eject anyone who sings, whistles, runs or opens an umbrella; those powers are infrequently invoked now, perhaps because the dictates of commerce take precedence over those of decorum.

❻ Ritz Hotel

Piccadilly W1. **Map** 12 F3. **Tel** 020 7493 8181. 🚇 Green Park. **Open** to non-residents for tea or restaurant (book ahead). ♿ *(See p284).* 🌐 **theritzlondon.com**

Cesar Ritz, the famed Swiss hotelier who inspired the adjective "ritzy", had virtually retired by the time this hotel was built and named after him in 1906. The colonnaded frontal aspect of the imposing château-style building was meant to suggest Paris, where the very grandest and most fashionable hotels

The exquisite Palm Room of Spencer House

were to be found around the turn of the century. It maintains its Edwardian air of opulence and is a popular stop, among those who are suitably dressed (no jeans or trainers; jacket and tie for men), for afternoon tea, with daily servings in the Palm Court at 11:30am, 1:30, 3:30 and 5:30pm. Champagne tea is served at 7:30pm.

❼ Spencer House

27 St James's Pl SW1. **Map** 12 F4. **Tel** 020 7514 1958 (Mon–Fri). 🚇 Green Park. **Open** 10:30am–5:45pm Sun (last adm: 4:45pm). Garden: **Open** in spring and summer; call 020 7499 8620 to check dates. **Closed** Jan & Aug. No children under 10. 🚫 ✉ ♿ 📷 compulsory. 🌐 **spencerhouse.co.uk**

This Palladian palace, built in 1766 for the first Earl Spencer, an ancestor of the late Princess of Wales, has been completely restored to its 18th-century

splendour (thanks to an £18 million renovation project). It contains some wonderful paintings and contemporary furniture; one of the highlights is the beautifully decorated Painted Room. The house is open to the public for guided tours, receptions and meetings.

St James's Tudor gatehouse

❽ St James's Palace

Pall Mall SW1. **Map** 12 F4. 🚇 Green Park. **Closed** to the public. 🌐 **royal.gov.uk**

Built by Henry VIII in the late 1530s on the site of a former leper hospital, it was a primary royal residence only briefly, mainly during the reign of Elizabeth I and during the late 17th and early 18th centuries. In 1952, Queen Elizabeth II made her first speech as queen here, and foreign ambassadors are still officially accredited to the Court of St James's. Its northern gatehouse, seen from St James's Street, is one of London's great Tudor landmarks. The palace buildings are now occupied by privileged Crown servants.

Afternoon tea served in the opulent Palm Court of the Ritz

Royal Opera Arcade

❾ St James's Square

SW1. **Map** 13 A3. 🔁 Green Park,
Piccadilly Circus.

One of London's earliest squares,
it was laid out in the 1670s and
lined by exclusive houses for
those whose business made
it vital for them to live near
St James's Palace. Many of the
buildings date from the 18th
and 19th centuries and have
had many illustrious residents.
During World War II, Generals
Eisenhower and de Gaulle both
had headquarters here.

Today No. 10 on the north
side is Chatham House (1736),
home of the Royal Institute for
International Affairs and, in the
northwest corner, can be found
the London Library (1896), a
private lending library founded
in 1841 by historian Thomas
Carlyle *(see p198)* and others.
The lovely gardens in the middle
contain an equestrian statue of
William III, here since 1808.

❿ Royal Opera Arcade

SW1. **Map** 13 A3. 🔁 Piccadilly Circus.

London's first shopping arcade
was designed by John Nash and
completed in 1818, behind the
Haymarket Opera House (now
called Her Majesty's Theatre).
It beat the Burlington Arcade
(see p93) by a year or so. The
traditional shops that once used
to be based here have since
moved on: Farlows, selling

shooting and fishing
equipment, and the famous
Hunter's green Wellington
boots, are now nearby, at
No. 9 Pall Mall.

The Duke of Wellington (1842): a frequent
visitor to Pall Mall

⓫ Pall Mall

SW1. **Map** 13 A4. 🔁 Charing Cross,
Green Park, Piccadilly Circus.

This dignified street is named
from the game of palle-maille –
a cross between croquet and
golf – which was played here in
the 17th century. For more than
150 years, Pall Mall has been at
the heart of London's clubland.
Here, exclusive gentlemen's
clubs were formed to provide
members with a refuge from
their womenfolk.

The clubhouses now amount
to a text book of the most
fashionable architects of the era.
From the east end, on the left is
the colonnaded entrance to
No. 116, Nash's United Services
Club (1827). This was the
favourite club of the Duke of

Wellington and now houses the
Institute of Directors. Facing it,
on the other side of Waterloo
Place, is the Athenaeum
(No. 107), designed three years
later by Decimus Burton, and
long the power house of the
British establishment. Next door
are two clubs by Sir Charles
Barry, architect of the Houses of
Parliament *(see pp74–5)*; the
Travellers' is at No. 106 and the
Reform at No. 104. The clubs'
stately interiors are well
preserved but only members
and their guests are admitted.

⓬ Institute of Contemporary Arts

The Mall SW1. **Map** 13 B3.
Tel 020 7930 3647. 🔁 Charing Cross,
Piccadilly Circus. **Open** 11am–11pm
Tue–Sun. (Exhibition space closes
6pm, 9pm Thu, bookshop 9pm.)
Closed 1 Jan, 24–26, 31 Dec, public
hols. 🎦 ♿ (cinema and lower
gallery) phone first. 📱 🖊 📷
Concerts, theatre, dance, lectures,
films, exhibitions. *See Entertainment
pp342–3.* 🔳 ica.org.uk

The Institute (ICA) was
established in 1947 in an effort
to offer British artists some of
the facilities which were
available to artists at The
Museum of Modern Art in New
York. Originally on Dover Street,
it has been situated in John
Nash's Classical Carlton House
Terrace (1833) since 1968. With
its entrance on The Mall, this
extensive warren contains a
cinema, auditorium, bookshop,
art gallery, bar and restaurant.
It also offers plays, concerts
and lectures. Non-members
pay a charge.

Institute of Contemporary Arts, Carlton
House Terrace

⓭ St James's Park

SW1. **Map** 13 A4. **Tel** 0300 061 2350.
🚇 St James's Park. **Open** 5am–
midnight daily. 🚲 **Open** daily.
♿ Concerts twice daily on summer
weekends in good weather.
🌐 **royalparks.org.uk**

In summer, office workers
sunbathe between the dazzling
flower beds of the capital's most
ornamental park. In winter,
overcoated civil servants discuss
affairs of state as they stroll by
the lake and eye its ducks, geese
and pelicans (who are fed at
1:30pm daily). Originally a
marsh, the park was drained by
Henry VIII and incorporated into
his hunting grounds. Charles II
redesigned it for pedestrian
pleasures, with an aviary along
its southern edge (hence
Birdcage Walk, the street where
the aviary was). It is still a
popular place to take the air,
with an appealing view of
Whitehall rooftops. In the
summer, there are concerts
on the bandstand.

⓮ The Mall

SW1. **Map** 13 A4. 🚇 Charing Cross,
Green Park, Piccadilly Circus.

This broad triumphal approach
to Buckingham Palace was
created by Aston Webb when
he redesigned the front of the
palace and the Victoria Monument in 1911 *(see picture p98)*.
It follows the course of the old
path at the edge of St James's
Park, laid out in the reign of
Charles II when it became
London's most fashionable
promenade. On the flagpoles
down both sides of The Mall fly
national flags of foreign heads
of state during official visits.

⓯ Marlborough House

Pall Mall SW1. **Map** 13 A4. **Tel** 020
7747 6491. 🚇 St James's Park, Green
Park. **Open** Tue am tours subject to
availability. 🎧 group tours by appt.

Marlborough House was
designed by Christopher Wren
(see p49) for the Duchess of
Marlborough, and finished in
1711. It was substantially
enlarged in the 19th century
and used by members of the
Royal Family. From 1863 until
he became Edward VII in 1901,
it was the home of the Prince
and Princess of Wales and the
social centre of London.
An Art Nouveau memorial in
the Marlborough Road wall of
the house commemorates
Edward's queen, Alexandra.
The building now houses the
Commonwealth Secretariat.

Queen's Chapel

⓰ Queen's Chapel

Marlborough Rd SW1. **Map** 13 A4.
Tel 020 7930 4832. 🚇 Green Park.
Open during services only. ✝ Oct–
Jul: 8:30am & 11:15am Sun.

This exquisite work of the
architect Inigo Jones was built
for Charles I's French wife,
Henrietta Maria, in 1627, and
was the first Classical church in
England. It was initially intended
to be part of St James's Palace
but is now separated from it by
Marlborough Gate. George III
married his queen, Charlotte of
Mecklenburg-Strelitz (who was
to bear him 15 children), here in
1761. The interior of the chapel,
with its wonderful Annibale
Carracci altarpiece and glorious
17th-century fittings is open to
both regular worshippers and
visitors during the spring and
early summer.

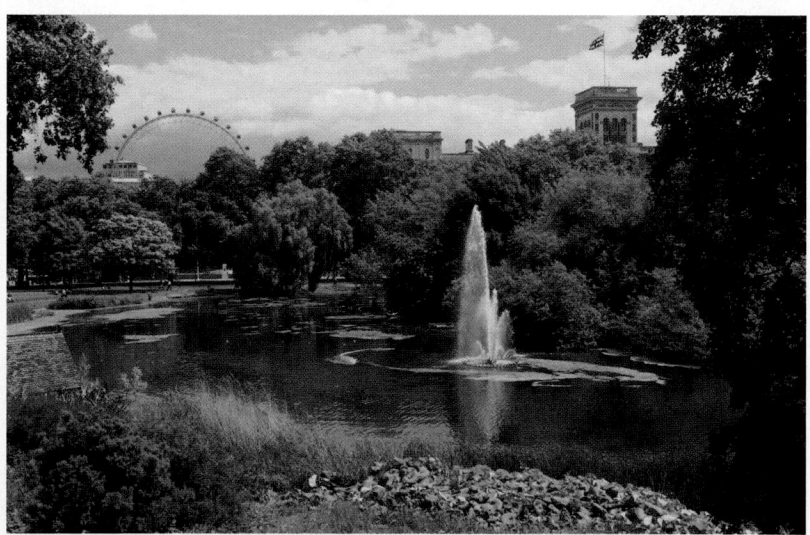
The lake in St James's Park with the London Eye in the background

⑲ Buckingham Palace

Buckingham Palace is both office and official London residence of the British monarchy. It is also used for ceremonial state occasions such as banquets for visiting heads of state. About 500 people work at the palace, including officers of the Royal Household and domestic staff.

John Nash converted the original Buckingham House into a palace for George IV (reigned 1820–30). Both he and his brother, William IV (reigned 1830–37), died before work was completed, and Queen Victoria was the first monarch to live at the palace. The present east front, facing The Mall, was added to Nash's conversion in 1913. The State Rooms are open to the public in summer.

Music Room
State guests are presented and royal christenings take place in this room, which boasts a beautiful, original parquet floor by Nash.

The Ballroom
The Victorian ballroom is used for state banquets and investitures.

The Queen's Gallery
Artworks from the Royal Collection *(see p98)*, such as Canaletto's *Rome: The Pantheon*, are often on display.

KEY

① **The State Dining Room** is where meals that are less formal than state banquets are held.

② **Blue Drawing Room** is decorated with imitation onyx columns, created by John Nash.

③ **The White Drawing Room** is where the Royal Family assemble before passing into the State Dining Room or Ballroom.

④ **The Green Drawing Room** is the first of the large and magnificent state rooms entered by guests of the Queen at royal functions.

⑤ **The Royal Standard** flies when the Queen is in residence.

Changing of the Guard
Visitors can witness the Buckingham Palace grounds guard handing over duty regularly throughout the year in a colourful and musical royal military ceremony *(see pp54–7)*.

Who Lives in Buckingham Palace?

The palace is the London residence of the Queen and her husband, the Duke of Edinburgh. The Princess Royal, the Duke of York and the Earl of Wessex also have apartments here. About 50 domestic staff have rooms in the palace. There are more staff homes situated in the Royal Mews *(see p98)*.

VISITORS' CHECKLIST

Practical Information
SW1.
Map 12 F5.
Tel 020 7766 7300.
W **royalcollection.org.uk**
State rooms **Open** end Jul–end Sep:
daily (see website as timings vary).
Changing of the Guard: May–Jul:
11:30am daily; Aug–Apr: alternate
days. Tickets not required.

Transport
St James's Park, Victoria.
2R, 11, 16, 24, 25, 36, 38, 52, 73,
135, C1. Victoria.

The Throne Room
In a room lit by seven magnificent chandeliers sit the thrones used by the Queen and the Duke of Edinburgh during her coronation.

The garden is a haven for wildlife and is overlooked by most of the lavishly decorated state rooms at the back of the palace. It is also the venue for Royal Garden Parties, where guests enjoy tea and cakes.

View over The Mall
Traditionally, the Royal Family waves to crowds from the balcony.

⑰ Clarence House

Stable Yard SW1. **Map** 12 F4. **Tel** 020 7766 7303. ⊖ Green Park, St James's Park. **Open** call or check website for opening times and dates. & ⚑ ☑ mandatory. **W** royalcollection.org.uk

Designed by John Nash for William IV in 1827, this is Prince Charles's London home. Once a year, the public can visit the opulent ground floor.

Lancaster House

⑱ Lancaster House

Stable Yard SW1. **Map** 12 F4. ⊖ Green Park, St James's Park. **Closed** to the public.

This royal residence was built for the Duke of York by Benjamin Wyatt, architect of Apsley House, in 1825. In 1848, Chopin played here for Queen Victoria, Prince Albert and the Duke of Wellington. It is now a conference centre.

⑲ Buckingham Palace

See pp96–7.

⑳ The Queen's Gallery

Buckingham Palace Rd SW1. **Map** 12 F5. **Tel** 020 7766 7301. ⊖ St James's Park, Victoria. **Open** 10am–5:30pm daily (Aug & Sep: 9:30am–5:30pm). **Closed** dates vary; call or check website. ⚑ & ☒ **W** royalcollection.org.uk

The Royal Family possesses one of the finest and most valuable art collections in the world, rich in the work of Old Masters, including Vermeer and Leonardo. In 2002, the galleries were expanded in the most extensive addition to Buckingham Palace in 150 years, resulting in three and a half times more display space and an impressive entrance gallery with a striking columned portico.

The gallery has seven rooms, which host a rolling programme of the royal collection's masterpieces. No items are on permanent display and changing exhibitions include fine art, jewels, porcelain, furniture and manuscripts.

㉑ Royal Mews

Buckingham Palace Rd SW1. **Map** 12 E5. **Tel** 020 7766 7302. ⊖ St James's Park, Victoria. **Open** Apr–Oct: 10am–5pm daily; Nov, Feb–Mar: 10am–4pm Mon–Sat. Subject to closure at short notice (phone first). **Closed** Dec–Jan. ⚑ & ☒ **W** royalcollection.org.uk

The Mews is worth catching for all lovers of horses and of royal pomp. The stables and coach houses, designed by Nash in 1825, accommodate the horses and coaches used by the Royal Family on state occasions. The star exhibit is the gold state coach, built for George III in 1761, with fine

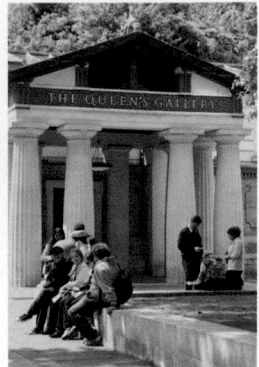

The Queens Gallery at Buckingham Palace

panels by Giovanni Cipriani. Among the other vehicles are the Irish state coach, bought by Queen Victoria for the State Opening of Parliament; the open-topped royal landau; and the glass coach, which was used for royal weddings and for transporting foreign ambassadors. The elaborate horses' harnesses are also on display, and so are some of the fine animals that wear them. Visitors may see carriages being prepared for use or limousines in action. A guided route around the mews includes a chance to view the 18th-century riding school where the horses are put through their paces. There is also a shop here selling royal souvenirs, open daily from 9:30am until 5pm.

The Victoria Monument outside Buckingham Palace

㉒ Wellington Arch

Hyde Park Corner SW1. **Map** 12 D4.
Tel 020 7930 2726. 🚇 Hyde Park
Corner. **Open** call or check website
for times and dates. **Closed** 1 Jan,
Good Friday, 24–26 & 31 Dec.
🎫 joint ticket with Apsley House
available. 🚻 limited. 📷
W english-heritage.org.uk

After nearly a century of
debate about what to do with
the patch of land in front of
Apsley House, Wellington
Arch, designed by Decimus
Burton, was erected in 1828.
The sculpture, by Adrian Jones,
was added in 1912. Before it
was installed Jones seated
three people for dinner in the
body of one of the horses.

The public now has access to
exhibitions in the inner rooms
of the arch. A viewing platform
beneath the sculpture has great
views over London.

Wellington Arch

㉓ Apsley House

Hyde Park Corner W1. **Map** 12 D4.
Tel 020 7499 5676. 🚇 Hyde Park
Corner. **Open** call or check website
for opening times and dates.
Closed 24–26 Dec, 1 Jan. 🎫 joint
ticket with Wellington Arch available.
🔊 📷 pre-booked only. 📷
W english-heritage.org.uk

Apsley House, or Number One
London, as it is also known, on
the south-east corner of Hyde
Park, was completed by Robert
Adam for Baron Apsley in 1778.
Fifty years later it was enlarged
and altered by the architect
Benjamin Dean Wyatt, to
provide a grand home for the
Duke of Wellington. His dual
career as soldier and politician
brought him victory against

Interior of Apsley House

Napoleon at Waterloo (1815),
and two terms as prime minister
(1828–30, 1834). Against a
sumptuous background of silk
hangings and gilt decoration
hangs the duke's art collection.
Paintings by Goya, Velázquez,
Brueghel and Rubens stand
alongside displays of porcelain,
silver and furniture. The duke's
memorabilia include swords
and medals, but are dominated
by Canova's colossal statue of
Napoleon, who was Wellington's
arch-enemy.

㉔ Shepherd Market

W1. **Map** 12 E4. 🚇 Green Park.

This attractive and bijou
pedestrianized enclave of small
shops, restaurants, and outdoor
cafés, between Piccadilly and
Curzon Street, was named
after Edward Shepherd, who
built it in the middle of the
18th century. During the
17th century, the annual 15-day
May Fair (from which the name
of the area is derived) took place
on this site, and today Shepherd
Market is still very much the
centre of Mayfair.

㉕ Green Park

SW1. **Map** 12 E4. **Tel** 0300 061 2350.
🚇 Green Park, Hyde Park Corner.
Open all day, year-round.
W royalparks.org.uk

Once part of Henry VIII's hunting
ground, it was, like St James's
Park, adapted for public use by
Charles II in the 1660s and is a
natural, undulating landscape of
grass and trees (with a good
spring show of daffodils). It was
a favourite site for duels during
the 18th century; in 1771 the
poet Alfieri was wounded here
by his mistress's husband,
Viscount Ligonier, but then
rushed back to the Haymarket
Theatre in time to catch the
last act of a play. Today the
park is popular with guests
staying at the Mayfair hotels
as a place to jog.

㉖ Faraday Museum

The Royal Institution, 21 Albemarle St
W1. **Map** 12 F3. **Tel** 020 7409 2992.
🚇 Green Park. **Open** 9am–6pm Mon–
Fri. **Closed** 24 Dec–3 Jan. 🔊 🎫 📷
📷 phone first. Lectures. **W** rigb.org

Michael Faraday was a
19th-century pioneer of the
uses of electricity. The collections
in the Michael Faraday Museum
include some of his scientific
apparatus and personal effects,
as well as the work of other
great scientists across the lower
three floors.

Michael Faraday

SOHO AND TRAFALGAR SQUARE

Soho has been renowned for pleasures of the table, the flesh and the intellect ever since it was first developed in the late 17th century. For its first century the area was one of London's most fashionable, and Soho residents of the time have gone down in history for their extravagant parties.

During the later part of the 20th century, Soho consolidated its reputation as a centre for entertainment. With a cosmopolitan mix

of people, visitors here enjoy the many pleasant bars, restaurants and cafés – popular with everyone from tourists to locals, office workers and London's gay community.

Soho is one of London's most multi-cultural districts. The first immigrants were 18th-century Huguenots from France (see Christ Church, Spitalfields p172). Soho is also famous as a Chinatown; Gerrard Street is lined with Chinese restaurants.

Sights at a Glance

Historic Streets and Buildings
1 Trafalgar Square
2 Admiralty Arch
6 Leicester Square
8 Shaftesbury Avenue
9 Chinatown
10 Charing Cross Road
12 Soho Square
14 Carnaby Street

Shops and Markets
13 Berwick Street Market
15 Liberty

Churches
4 St Martin-in-the-Fields

Museums and Galleries
3 National Gallery pp106–9
5 National Portrait Gallery
16 Photographers' Gallery

Theatres
7 Theatre Royal Haymarket
11 Palace Theatre

Restaurants see pp292–5
1 Andrew Edmunds
2 Asia de Cuba
3 Barrafina
4 Bocca di Lupo
5 Dehesa
6 Gopals of Soho
7 Haozhan
8 Inamo
9 Kulu Kulu Sushi
10 Mildred's
11 Nopi
12 Patara
13 Princi
14 The Portrait
15 Refuel
16 Soho Joe
17 Tokyo Diner
18 Vasco and Piero's Pavilion
19 Yalla Yalla
20 Yauatcha

0 metres 250
0 yards 250

Street Finder, maps 11, 12, 13

◄ Chinatown, Soho

For keys to symbols see back flap

Street-by-Street: Trafalgar Square

This area buzzes both day and night with crowds enjoying the numerous restaurants, cinemas and nightclubs. Broad avenues lined with regal office buildings converge at Trafalgar Square. Some of the roads that ring the square have now been pedestrianized, making this already popular meeting place far more accessible.

⑩ Charing Cross Road
Famous for specialist and second-hand bookshops.

⑧ Shaftesbury Avenue
Theatreland's main artery is lined with announcements for current shows.

⑨ ★ Chinatown
An area of Chinese restaurants and shops, this is home to many Chinese-speaking people.

Notre Dame, once a theatre, was converted into a church in 1855. The Jean Cocteau murals inside date from 1960.

To Tottenham Court Road station

W Hotel, perfectly situated in the heart of London, has a very glamorous bar where you can enjoy evening cocktails.

The Blue Posts pub stands on the site of a pick-up point for sedan chairs in the 18th century.

⑥ Leicester Square
A 19th-century statue of William Shakespeare stands in the traffic-free square.

⑦ Theatre Royal Haymarket
It is graced by a John Nash portico.

Key

— Suggested route

| 0 metres | 100 |
| 0 yards | 100 |

The Hippodrome, a former nightclub, was once a variety theatre and is now a cabaret venue.

Cecil Court is lined with shops selling old books and prints.

Leicester Square station

Locator Map
See Central London Map pp14–15

BLOOMSBURY & FITZROVIA

HOLBORN & THE INNS OF COURT

SOHO & TRAFALGAR SQUARE

COVENT GARDEN & THE STRAND

Thames

PICCADILLY & ST JAMES'S

WHITEHALL & WESTMINSTER

SOUTH BANK

❹ ★ St Martin-in-the-Fields
James Gibbs's masterpiece set the US "colonial" style.

❺ ★ National Portrait Gallery
Portraits of prominent Britons from Tudor times to the present-day adorn the walls here.

DUNCANNON ST

Charing Cross station

STRAND

❸ ★ National Gallery
The national collection of art is housed in these buildings.

NORTHUMBERLAND AVE

TRAFALGAR SQUARE

CHARING CROSS

COCKSPUR STREET

MALL EAST

Nelson's Column

❷ Admiralty Arch
The entrance to the Mall was designed in 1911.

❶ ★ Trafalgar Square
Millions of tourists come here to admire the statues and the fountains.

❶ Trafalgar Square

WC2. **Map** 13 B3. ⊖ Charing Cross.

London's main venue for rallies and outdoor public meetings was conceived by John Nash and was mostly constructed during the 1830s. The 50-m (165-ft) column commemorates Admiral Lord Nelson, Britain's most famous sea lord, who died heroically at the Battle of Trafalgar against Napoleon in 1805. It dates from 1842; 14 stonemasons held a dinner on its flat top before the statue of Nelson was finally installed. Edwin Landseer's four lions were added to guard its base 25 years later. The north side of the square is now taken up by the National Gallery and its annexe *(see pp106–9)*, with Canada House on the west side, and South Africa House on the east. The restored Grand Buildings on the south side, with their fine arcade, were built in 1880 as the Grand Hotel. The square was partially pedestrianized in 2003, with other refurbishments including an enlarged central staircase descending from the National Gallery.

Nelson's statue
overlooking the square

❷ Admiralty Arch

The Mall SW1. **Map** 13 B3. ⊖ Charing Cross.

Designed in 1911, this triple archway was part of Aston Webb's scheme to rebuild The Mall as a grand processional route honouring Queen Victoria. The arch effectively seals the eastern end of The Mall, although traffic passes through the smaller side gates, and separates courtly London from the hurly-burly of Trafalgar Square. The central gate is opened only for royal processions. There are plans to turn the Grade I listed building into a five-star hotel.

Filming *Howard's End* at Admiralty Arch

❸ National Gallery

See pp106–9.

❹ St Martin-in-the-Fields

Trafalgar Sq WC2. **Map** 13 B3. **Tel** 020 7766 1100. ⊖ Charing Cross. **Open** daily. ✝ throughout the day; check website for details as times vary. ♿ 🔊 🖥 📷 London Brass Rubbing Centre **Tel** 020 7766 1122 (leave a message with contact details). **Open** 10am–6pm Mon–Wed, 10am–8pm Thu–Sat, 11:30am–5pm Sun (last brass rubbing entry 1 hr before close). Concerts: *See Entertainment pp340–41.* 🆆 **smitf.org**

There has been a church on this site since the 13th century. Many famous people were buried here, including Charles II's mistress, Nell Gwynne, and the painters William Hogarth and Joshua Reynolds. The present church was designed by James Gibbs and completed in 1726. In architectural terms it was one of the most influential ever built; it was much copied in the United States, where it became a model for the Colonial style of church-building. An unusual feature of St Martin's spacious interior is the royal box at gallery level on the left of the altar.

From 1914 until 1927 the crypt was used as a shelter for homeless soldiers and down-and-outs; during World War II it was an air-raid shelter. Today it helps the homeless by providing a lunchtime soup kitchen for them. It also has a café in the crypt, and a religious bookshop as well as the London Brass Rubbing Centre. Lunchtime and evening concerts are held in the church and in the café.

❺ National Portrait Gallery

2 St Martin's Place WC2. **Map** 13 B3. **Tel** 020 7306 0055. ⊖ Leicester Sq, Charing Cross. **Open** 10am–6pm Sat–Wed, 10am–9pm Thu–Fri. **Closed** 24–26 Dec. ✉ ♿ Orange St entrance. 🔊 🚫 🖥 📷 Lectures. 🆆 **npg.org.uk**

Too often ignored in favour of the National Gallery next door, this fascinating museum recounts Britain's development through portraits of its main characters, giving faces to names, which are familiar from the history books. There are pictures of kings, queens, poets, musicians, artists, thinkers, heroes and villains from all periods since the late 14th century. The oldest

William Shakespeare portrait on display in the Ondaatje Wing

works, on the fourth floor, include a Hans Holbein cartoon of Henry VIII and paintings of some of his wives.

The National Portrait Gallery's millennium development project, the Ondaatje Wing, opened in May 2000, allowing it 50 per cent more exhibition and public space. It includes a Tudor Gallery, displaying some of the earliest and most important paintings, including one of Shakespeare (by John Taylor in 1651), and the Ditchley portrait of Elizabeth I. A balcony provides an extra display area for portraits from the 1960s to the 1990s.

The gallery has a rooftop restaurant, and the spacious lecture theatre in the basement, which is also used for drama and film events.

The gallery also houses temporary exhibitions and has an excellent shop selling books on art and literature, as well as an extensive range of cards, prints and posters featuring pictures from the main collection.

❻ Leicester Square

WC2. **Map** 13 B2. ⊖ Leicester Sq, Piccadilly Circus.

It is hard to imagine that this, the perpetually animated heart of the West End entertainment district, was once a fashionable place to live. Laid out in 1670 south of Leicester House, a long-gone royal residence, the square's occupants included the scientist Isaac Newton and the artists Joshua Reynolds and William Hogarth. Reynolds made his fortune painting high society in his elegant salon at No. 46. Hogarth's house, in the south-east corner, became the Hôtel de la Sablionère in 1801, probably the area's first public restaurant.

In Victorian times several popular music halls were established here, including the Empire (today the cinema on the same site perpetuates the name) and the Alhambra, replaced in 1937 by the Art Deco Odeon. A booth selling cut-price theatre tickets

(see p336) sits in the square. There is also a statue of Charlie Chaplin, which was unveiled in 1981. The Shakespeare fountain dates from 1874.

Regeneration of the south-west corner of the square was completed in 2012, increasing public space and including cafés, restaurants and a state-of-the-art cinema.

❼ Theatre Royal Haymarket

Haymarket SW1. **Map** 13 A3. **Tel** 020 7930 8800. ⊖ Piccadilly Circus. **Open** performances and guided tours (phone to check). ♿ 🖥 **trh.co.uk**

The fine frontage of this theatre, with its portico of six Corinthian columns, dates from 1821, when John Nash designed it as part of his plan for a stately route from Carlton House to Regent's Park. The interior is equally grand.

❽ Shaftesbury Avenue

W1. **Map** 13 A2. ⊖ Piccadilly Circus, Leicester Sq.

The main artery of London's theatreland, Shaftesbury Avenue has six theatres and two cinemas, all on its north side. This street was cut through an area of terrible slums between 1877 and 1886 in order to improve communications across the city's busy West End; it follows the route of a much earlier highway. It is named after the Earl of Shaftesbury (1801–85), whose attempts to improve housing conditions had helped some of the local poor. (The Earl is also commemorated by the Eros statue in Piccadilly Circus – see p92.) The Lyric Theatre, which was designed by C J Phipps, has been open for almost the same length of time as the avenue.

London's West End: the façade of the Gielgud Theatre

❸ National Gallery

Trafalgar Square façade

The National Gallery has flourished since its inception in the early 19th century. In 1824 the House of Commons was persuaded to buy 38 major paintings, including works by Raphael and Rubens, and these became the start of a national collection. Contributions by rich benefactors have today resulted in a collection of some 2,300 Western European paintings. The main gallery building was designed in Greek Revival style by William Wilkins and built in 1833–8. To its left lies the Sainsbury Wing, financed by the grocery family and completed in 1991.

★ The Burlington House Cartoon (c.1500)
The genius of Leonardo da Vinci glows through this chalk drawing of the Virgin and Child with St Anne and St John the Baptist.

Pigott Education Centre entrance 🛗

Stairs to lower floor 🛗 🚻

Stairs and lift to lower galleries

Link to main building

Stairs to lower floors
🖥 🛗 🚹 🚺 ℹ 🚪

Doge Leonardo Loredan (1501–2)
Giovanni Bellini portrays this Venetian head of state as a serene father figure.

★ The Baptism of Christ
Piero della Francesca painted this tranquil masterpiece (1450s) of early Renaissance perspective for a church in his native Umbria.

Entrance to Sainsbury Wing 🛗

★ **Philip IV of Spain** (1631–2) One of Diego Velázquez's few signed paintings and the principal portrait of the king of that period.

★ **The Hay Wain** (1821) John Constable brilliantly caught the effect of distance and the changing light and shadow of a typically English cloudy summer day in this famous classic.

VISITORS' CHECKLIST

Practical Information
Trafalgar Sq WC2.
Map 13 B3.
Tel 020 7747 2885.
w nationalgallery.org.uk
Open 10am–6pm daily (9pm Fri).
Closed 24–26 Dec, 1 Jan. 🅿️ ♿
Sainsbury Wing and Getty
entrances. 🎒 📷 💻 ✏️ 🍴 🎁
🖼️ Major temporary exhibitions.
Lectures, film presentations,
exhibitions, special events.

Transport
🚇 Charing Cross, Leicester Sq,
Piccadilly Circus. 🚌 3, 6, 9, 11,
12, 13, 15, 23, 24, 29, 88, 91,
139, 159, 176, 453. 🚆 Charing
Cross.

Central Hall

Getty entrance ♿

Trafalgar Square entrance

At the Theatre (1876–7) Renoir was one of the greatest painters of the Impressionist movement. The theatre was a popular subject among artists of the time.

★ **The Ambassadors** The strange shape in the foreground of this Hans Holbein portrait (1533) is an anamorphic or distorted skull, a symbol of mortality.

Key to Floorplan
- 🟦 13th- to 15th-century
- 🟫 16th-century
- ⬜ 17th-century
- ⬜ 18th- to early 20th-century
- ⬛ Special exhibitions
- 🟦 Non-exhibition space

Gallery Guide

Most of the collection is housed on one floor divided into four wings. The paintings hang chronologically, with the earliest works (1250–1500) in the Sainsbury Wing. The North, West and East Wings cover 1500–1600, 1600–1700 and 1700–1900. Lesser paintings of all periods are on the lower floor.

Exploring the National Gallery

The National Gallery has over 2,300 paintings, most kept on permanent display. The collection ranges from early works by Cimabue, in the 13th century, to 19th-century Impressionists, but its particular strengths are in Dutch, early Renaissance Italian and 17th-century Spanish painting. The bulk of the British collections are housed in Tate Britain *(see pp84–7)* while Tate Modern specializes in international modern art *(pp180–83)*.

The Adoration of The Kings (1564) by Pieter Bruegel the Elder

Early Renaissance (1250–1500): Italian and Northern European Painting

Three lustrous panels from the *Maestà*, Duccio's great altarpiece in Siena cathedral, are among the earliest paintings here. Other Italian works of the period include his outstanding Madonna.

The fine *Wilton Diptych* portraying England's Richard II is probably by a French artist. It displays the lyrical elegance of the International Gothic style that swept Europe.

Italian masters of this style include Pisanello and Gentile da Fabriano, whose *Madonna* often hangs beside another, by Masaccio – both date from 1425. Also shown are works by Masaccio's pupil, Fra Filippo Lippi, as well as Botticelli and Uccello. Umbrian paintings include Piero della Francesca's *Nativity* and *Baptism*, and there is an excellent collection of Mantegna, Bellini and other works from the Venetian and Ferrarese schools. Antonello da Messina's *St Jerome in his Study* has been mistaken for a van Eyck; it is not hard to see why, when you compare it with van Eyck's *Arnolfini Portrait*.

Important Netherlandish pictures, including some by Rogier van der Weyden and his followers, are also here, in the Sainsbury Wing.

St Jerome in his Study by Antonello da Messina (c.1475)

High Renaissance (1500–1600): Italian, Netherlandish and German Painting

Sebastiano del Piombo's *The Raising of Lazarus* was painted, with Michelangelo's assistance, to rival Raphael's great *Transfiguration*, which hangs in the Vatican in Rome. These and other well-known names of the High (or Late) Renaissance are extremely well represented, often with massive works. Look out for Parmigianino's *Madonna and Child with Saints*, Leonardo da Vinci's charcoal cartoon of the *Virgin and Child* (a full-sized drawing used for copying as a painting), and his second version of the *Virgin of the Rocks*. There are also tender and amusing works by Piero di Cosimo, and several Titians, including *Bacchus and Ariadne* – which the public found too bright and garish when it was first cleaned by the gallery in the 1840s.

The Netherlandish and German collections are weaker. Even so, they include *The Ambassadors*, a fine double portrait by Holbein; and Altdorfer's superb *Christ Taking Leave of his Mother*, bought by the gallery in 1980. There is also an Hieronymus Bosch of *Christ Mocked* (sometimes known as *The Crowning with Thorns*), and an excellent Brueghel, *The Adoration of the Kings*.

The Annunciation (c.early 1450s) by Fra Filippo Lippi

The Sainsbury Wing

Plans for the Sainsbury Wing, opened in 1991, provoked a storm of dissent. An incensed Prince Charles dubbed an early design "a monstrous carbuncle on the face of a much-loved friend". The final building, by Venturi, has drawn criticism from other quarters for being a derivative compromise.

Major temporary exhibitions are held here – check the gallery's website for details. Visitors can also find permanent collections on the Italian Renaissance.

Dutch, Italian, French and Spanish Painting (1600–1700)

The superb Dutch collection gives two entire rooms to Rembrandt. There are also works by Vermeer, Van Dyck (among them his equestrian portrait of King Charles I) and Rubens (including the popular *Chapeau de Paille*).

From Italy, the works of Carracci and Caravaggio are strongly represented, and Salvatore Rosa has a glowering self-portrait.

French works on show include a magnificent portrait of Cardinal Richelieu by Philippe de Champaigne. Claude's seascape, *Seaport with the Embarkation of the Queen of Sheba*, hangs beside Turner's rival painting *Dido Building Carthage*, as Turner himself had instructed.

The Spanish school has works by Murillo, Velázquez, Zurbarán and others.

The Scale of Love (1715–18) by Jean-Antoine Watteau

Venetian, French and English Painting (1700–1800)

One of the gallery's most famous 18th-century works is Canaletto's *The Stonemason's Yard*. Other Venetians here are Longhi and Tiepolo.

The French collection includes Rococo masters such as Chardin, Watteau and Boucher, as well as landscapists and portraitists.

Gainsborough's early work *Mr and Mrs Andrews* and *The Morning Walk* are favourites with visitors; his rival, Sir Joshua Reynolds, is represented by some of his most Classical work and by more informal portraits.

English, French and German Painting (1800–1900)

The great age of 19th-century landscape painting is amply represented here, with fine works by Constable and Turner, including Constable's *The Hay Wain* and Turner's *The Fighting Temeraire*, as well as works by the French artists Corot and Daubigny.

Of Romantic art, there is Géricault's vivid work, *Horse Frightened by Lightning*, and several interesting paintings by Delacroix. In contrast, the society portrait of *Madame Moitessier* by Ingres, though still Romantic, is more restrained and Classical.

Impressionists and other French avant-garde artists are well represented. Among the highlights are *The Water-Lily Pond* by Monet, Renoir's *At the Theatre*, Van Gogh's *Sunflowers*, not to mention one of Rousseau's famous jungle scenes, *Surprised!*, in which a tiger hunts explorers. In Seurat's *Bathers at Asnières* he did not originally use the pointillist technique he was later to invent, but subsequently reworked areas of the picture using dots of colour.

Young Woman Standing at a Virginal (1670–72) by Jan Vermeer

Sunflowers (1888) by Vincent Van Gogh

❾ Chinatown

Streets around Gerrard St W1. **Map** 13 A2. 🚇 Leicester Sq, Piccadilly Circus.

There has been a Chinese community in London since the 19th century. Originally it was concentrated around the East End docks at Limehouse, where the opium dens of Victorian melodrama were sited. As the number of immigrants increased in the 1950s, many moved into Soho where they created an ever-expanding Chinatown. It contains scores of restaurants, and mysterious aroma-filled shops selling oriental produce. Three Chinese arches straddle Gerrard Street, where a vibrant, colourful street festival, held in late January, celebrates Chinese New Year *(see p61)*.

Rows of jars containing Chinese sweets in Chinatown

❿ Charing Cross Road

WC2. **Map** 13 B2. 🚇 Leicester Sq. *See Shops and Markets pp312–13.*

Once a mecca for book lovers, with a clutch of shops that were able to supply just about any recent volume, many independent bookshops at Charring Cross Road have been forced to shut due to rising rents. However, bibliophiles can head to the nearby Cecil Court for smaller, second-hand bookstores. Visit the giants: a huge Foyle's and the specialist shops: try Francis Edwards *(see p322)* for travel and art. At the junction with New Oxford Street rises the 1960s tower, Centrepoint. It lay empty for ten years after it was built, its owners finding this more profitable than renting it out.

At the Palace Theatre in 1898

⓫ Palace Theatre

Shaftesbury Ave W1. **Map** 13 B2. **Tel** Box office 0844 412 4656. 🚇 Leicester Sq. **Open** for performances only. *See Entertainment pp336–7.* ⓦ nimaxtheatres.com/palace-theatre

Most West End theatres are disappointingly unassertive. This one, which dominates the west side of Cambridge Circus, is a splendid exception, with its sparkling terracotta exterior and opulent furnishings. Completed as an opera house in 1891, it became a music hall the following year. The ballerina Anna Pavlova made her London debut here in 1910. Now the theatre, owned by Andrew Lloyd Webber whose own musicals are all over London, stages hit shows such as *Spamalot*.

⓬ Soho Square

W1. **Map** 13 A1. 🚇 Tottenham Court Rd.

Soon after it was laid out in 1681 this Square enjoyed a brief reign as the most fashionable address in London. Originally it was called King Square, after Charles II, whose statue was erected in the middle. The square went out of fashion by the late 18th century and is now surrounded by bland office buildings. The mock-Tudor garden shed in the centre was added much later in Victorian times.

⓭ Berwick Street Market

W1. **Map** 13 A1. 🚇 Piccadilly Circus. **Open** 9am–6pm Mon–Sat. *See Shops and Markets p331.*

There has been a market here since the 1840s. Berwick Street trader Jack Smith introduced grapefruit to London in 1890. Today this is the West End's best street market, at its cheeriest and most crowded during the lunch hour. The freshest and least expensive produce for miles around is to be had here. There are also some interesting shops, including Borovick's, which sells extraordinary fabrics, and a growing number of cafés and restaurants. At its southern end the street narrows into an alley on which Raymond's Revue Bar (the comparatively respectable face of Soho sleaze) has presented its festival of erotica since 1958.

Some of London's cheapest produce at Berwick Street Market

⓮ Carnaby Street

W1. **Map** 12 F2. ⊖ Oxford Circus.

During the 1960s this street was so much the hub of swinging London that the Oxford English Dictionary recognized the term "Carnaby Street" as meaning "fashionable clothing for young people". Today fashion shops can be found on nearby streets such as Kingly Court and Fouberts Place.

⓯ Liberty

Regent St W1. **Map** 12 F2. ⊖ Oxford Circus. *See Shops and Markets p313.* ⓦ liberty.co.uk

Arthur Lasenby Liberty opened his first shop, selling oriental silks, on Regent Street in 1875.

Liberty's mock-Tudor façade

Among his first customers were the artists Ruskin and Rossetti. Soon Liberty prints and designs, by artists such as William Morris, epitomized the Arts and Crafts movement of the late 19th and early 20th centuries. They are still fashionable today.

The present mock-Tudor building with its country-house feel dates from 1925, and was built specifically to house the store.

Today the shop maintains its strong links with top quality craftmanship of all kinds.

⓰ Photographers' Gallery

16-18 Ramillies St W1. **Map** 12 F1. ⊖ Oxford Circus. **Tel** 020 7087 9300. **Open** 10am–6pm Mon–Sat (till 8pm Thu), 11:30am–6pm Sun. ⓦ **photonet.org.uk**

Dedicated to photography, this gallery exhibits work from both new and more renowned artists, as well as putting on regular talks and events. The bookshop also sells cameras and prints.

The Heart of Soho

Old Compton Street is Soho's High Street. Its shops and restaurants reflect the variety of people who have lived in the area over the centuries. These include many great artists, writers and musicians.

Maison Bertaux is known for producing delicious croissants and coffee and wonderful cakes as good as those found in Paris.

Ronnie Scott's opened in 1959, and nearly all the big names of jazz have played here *(see pp343–5)*.

Bar Italia is a coffee shop situated under the room where John Logie Baird first demonstrated television in 1926. As a child, Mozart stayed next door with his family in 1764 and 1765.

The Coach and Horses pub has been a centre of bohemian Soho since the 1950s and is still popular.

Algerian Coffee Stores is one of Soho's oldest shops. Delicious aromas of the world's coffees fill the shop.

GREEK STREET

MOOR ST

FRITH STREET

DEAN STREET

OLD COMPTON STREET

WARDOUR STREET

ROMILLY STREET

Patisserie Valerie is a Hungarian-owned café serving delicious pastries *(see pp304–7)*.

St Anne's Church Tower is all that remains after a bomb destroyed the church in 1940.

The French House was frequented by Maurice Chevalier and General de Gaulle.

The Palace Theatre has hosted many successful musicals.

COVENT GARDEN AND THE STRAND

The open-air cafés, street entertainers, stylish shops, and markets make this area a magnet for visitors. At its centre is the Piazza, site of a wholesale market until 1974. Since then, the Georgian and Victorian buildings here and in the surrounding streets have been converted into one of the city's liveliest districts. In medieval times the area was occupied by a convent garden that supplied Westminster Abbey with produce. Then in the 1630s, Inigo Jones laid out the Piazza as London's first square, with its west side dominated by his St Paul's Church.

The Piazza was commissioned as a residential development by the Earl of Bedford, owner of one of the mansions that lined the Strand. Before the Embankment was built, the Strand ran along the river.

Sights at a Glance

Historic Streets and Buildings
1 The Piazza and Central Market
7 Neal Street and Neal's Yard
12 Savoy Hotel
14 Somerset House
16 Roman Bath
17 Bush House
20 Adelphi
21 Charing Cross

Museums and Galleries
3 London's Transport Museum

Churches
2 St Paul's Church
13 Savoy Chapel
15 St Mary-le-Strand

Monuments and Statues
9 Seven Dials
18 Cleopatra's Needle

Famous Theatres
5 Theatre Royal Drury Lane
6 Royal Opera House
11 Adelphi Theatre
22 The London Coliseum
10 Wyndham's Theatre
22 Parks and Garden
19 Victoria Embankment Gardens

Historic Pubs and Shopping Arcades
4 Lamb and Flag
8 Thomas Neal's

☐ Restaurants see pp292–5
1 Atelier de Joël Robuchon
2 Belgo Centraal
3 Clos Maggiore
4 Le Deuxieme
5 Food for Thought
6 J Sheekey
7 Porter's English
8 Rules
9 Sagar
10 The Ten Cases
11 Terroirs
12 Thai Pot
13 Wahaca

Street Finder, maps 13, 14

0 metres   500
0 yards   500

◀ Enzo Piazotta's statue *The Young Dancer* (1988), Covent Garden

For keys to symbols *see back flap*

Street-by-Street: Covent Garden

Once an area of decaying streets and warehouses, Covent Garden came alive only after dark when the fruit and vegetable market traders went about their business. Now it is completely revitalized. Day and night, visitors, residents and street-entertainers of every vocation throng the Piazza, much as they would have done several centuries ago.

❼ ★ Neal Street and Neal's Yard Shops line this traffic-free area.

Covent Garden station

❽ Thomas Neal's This airy complex is full of designer shops and cafés.

❾ Seven Dials A replica of a 17th-century monument marks the crossroads.

Ching Court is a Post-Modernist courtyard by architect Terry Farrell.

St Martin's Theatre is home to the world's longest-running play: *The Mousetrap*.

Stanfords, established in 1852, is the largest map and guide retailer in the world *(see pp322–3)*.

❹ Lamb and Flag Parts of this pub, one of London's oldest, date from 1623.

The Garrick Club is London's literary club.

New Row is lined with little shops and cafés.

Goodwin's Court was inhabited by a colony of tailors in the 18th century.

❶ ★ The Piazza and Central Market
Performers of all kinds – jugglers, clowns, acrobats and musicians – entertain the crowds in the square.

Locator Map
See Central London Map pp16–17

❻ Royal Opera House
Most of the world's greatest singers and dancers have appeared on its stage.

Bow Street Police Station housed London's first police force, the Bow Street Runners, in the 18th century. It closed in 1992.

❺ ★ Theatre Royal Drury Lane
A theatre has stood on this site since 1663, making it London's oldest theatre. The present theatre was built in 1812. It is owned by composer Andrew Lloyd Webber and stages popular musicals.

Boswells, now a coffee house, is where Dr Johnson first met his biographer, Boswell.

❸ ★ London Transport Museum
The history of the city's Tube and buses is brought to life in this museum.

Jubilee Market sells clothes and bric-ac-brac.

Key

— Suggested route

0 metres	100
0 yards	100

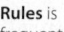

Rules is frequented by the rich and famous for its typically English food.

❷ ★ St Paul's Church
Despite appearances, Inigo Jones's church faces away from the Piazza – the entrance is through the churchyard.

❶ The Piazza and Central Market

Covent Garden WC2. **Map** 13 C2.
🚇 Covent Garden. 🅰 but cobbled streets. Street performers 10am–dusk daily. *See Shops and Markets p315.*
🌐 coventgardenlondonuk.com

West entrance to St Paul's

The 17th-century architect Inigo Jones originally planned this area to be an elegant residential square, modelled on the piazza at Livorno, northern Italy. Today the buildings on and around the Piazza are almost entirely Victorian. The covered central market was designed by Charles Fowler in 1833 for fruit and vegetable wholesalers, the glass and iron roof anticipating the giant rail termini built later in the century – for instance, St Pancras *(see p132)* and Waterloo *(see p193).* It now makes a magnificent shell for an array of small shops selling designer clothes, books, arts, crafts, decorative items and antiques, surrounded by bustling market stalls that continue south in the neighbouring Jubilee Hall, which was built in 1903.

The colonnade Bedford Chambers, on the north side, give a hint of Inigo Jones's plan, although even they are not original: they were rebuilt and partially modified in 1879.

Street entertainment is a well-loved and now expected tradition of the area; in 1662, diarist Samuel Pepys wrote of watching a Punch and Judy show under the portico of St Paul's Church.

❷ St Paul's Church

Bedford St WC2. **Map** 13 C2.
Tel 020 7836 5221. 🚇 Covent Garden. **Open** 8:30am–5pm Mon–Fri, 9am–1pm Sun. ✝ 11am Sun, 2nd Sun of the month 4pm evensong.
🅰 🌐 actorschurch.org

Inigo Jones built this church (completed in 1633) with the altar at the west end, so as to allow his grand portico, with its two square and two round columns, to face east into the Piazza. Clerics objected to this unorthodox arrangement, and the altar was moved to its conventional position at the east end. Jones went ahead with his original exterior design. Thus the church is entered from the west, and the east portico is a fake door, used now as an impromptu stage for street entertainers. In 1795, the interior was destroyed by fire but was rebuilt in Jones's airy, uncompli-cated style. Today the church is all that is left of Jones's original plan for the Piazza. St Paul's is known as "The Actors' Church" and plaques commemorate

Punch and Judy performer

distinguished men and women of the theatre. A 17th-century carving by Grinling Gibbons, on the west screen, is a memorial to the architect.

❸ London Transport Museum

The Piazza WC2. **Map** 13 C2. **Tel** 020 7379 6344 or 020 7565 7299 (24 hour infoline). 🚇 Covent Garden. **Open** 10am–6pm Sat–Thu, 11am–6pm Fri (last adm: 5:15pm). 🔲 🖥 📷 🅰 🎫 book ahead.
🌐 ltmuseum.co.uk

You do not have to be a train spotter or a collector of bus numbers to enjoy this museum. The intriguing collection is housed in the picturesque Victorian Flower Market, which was built in 1872, and features public transport from the past and present.

The history of London's transport is in essence a social history of the capital. Bus, tram and underground route patterns first reflected the city's growth and then promoted it; the northern and western suburbs began to develop only after their tube connections were built. The museum houses a fine collection of 20th-century commercial art. London's bus and train companies have been, and still are, prolific patrons of contemporary artists, and copies of some of the finest posters on display can be bought at the well-stocked museum shop. They include the innovative Art Deco designs of E McKnight Kauffer, as well as work by renowned artists of the 1930s, such as Graham Sutherland and Paul Nash.

A mid-18th-century view of the Piazza

This museum is excellent for children. There are plenty of hands-on exhibits, and these include the opportunity for children to put themselves in the driver's seat of a London bus, or a train from the underground system.

❹ Lamb and Flag

33 Rose St WC2. **Map** 13 B2. **Tel** 020 7497 9504. Covent Garden, Leicester Sq. **Open** 11am–11pm Mon–Sat, noon–10:30pm Sun. *See Pubs and Bars p308.*

There has been an inn here since the 16th century, making the Lamb and Flag the oldest tavern in Covent Garden. Tucked away next to a narrow alleyway linking Garrick Street with Floral Street, the cramped bars are still largely unmodernized. A plaque concerns satirist John Dryden, attacked in the alley outside in 1679. He was set upon by hooligans sent by Charles II to uphold the honour of the Duchess of Portsmouth, one of his mistresses. Dryden had lampooned her in some of his verse. The upstairs bar is also named after Dryden.

The pub is popular with both city centre workers and in-the-know tourists, who spill out into the courtyard.

❺ Theatre Royal Drury Lane

Catherine St WC2. **Map** 13 C2. **Tel** 0844 871 8810. Covent Garden, Holborn. **Open** for tours and performances. *See Entertainment p336* theatreroyaldrurylane.co.uk

The first theatre on this site was built in 1663 as one of only two venues in London where drama could legally be staged. Nell Gwynne acted here. Three of the theatres built here since then burned down, including one designed by Sir Christopher Wren (*see p49*). The present one, by Benjamin Wyatt, was completed in 1812 and has one of the city's largest auditoriums. In the 1800s, it was famous for pantomimes – now it stages blockbuster musicals. It is called

The glass Floral Hall, part of the Royal Opera House

the Theatre Royal Drury Lane even though its entrance is on Catherine Street.

❻ Royal Opera House

Covent Garden WC2. **Map** 13 C2. **Tel** 020 7304 4000. Covent Garden. **Open** for tours and performances (phone to check). *See Entertainment p340.* roh.org.uk

Built in 1732, the first theatre on this site staged more spoken drama than music drama, although many of Handel's operas and oratorios were premiered here. Like its neighbour the Theatre Royal Drury Lane, the building proved prone to fire and was destroyed in 1808 and again in 1856. The present opera house was designed in 1858 by E M Barry. John Flaxman's portico frieze, depicting tragedy and comedy, survived from the previous building of 1809.

The Opera House has had both high and low points during its history. In 1892, the first British performance of Wagner's Ring was conducted here by Gustav Mahler. Later, during World War I, the building was used as a storehouse by the government. Today, it is home to the Royal Opera and Royal Ballet Companies – the best tickets can cost over £100. An extensive renovation project, completed in 1999, added a

second auditorium, along with rehearsal rooms for the Royal Opera and Royal Ballet companies. Backstage tours are available, and once a month visitors can watch the Royal Ballet attending its daily class.

❼ Neal Street and Neal's Yard

Covent Garden WC2. **Map** 13 B1. Covent Garden. *See Shops and Markets p315.*

In this attractive street, former warehouses from the 19th century can be identified by the hoisting mechanisms high on their exterior walls. The buildings have been converted into shops, art galleries and restaurants. Off Neal Street in Short's Gardens is Neal's Yard Dairy, one of London's best cheese shops, which also sells delicious breads. Brainchild of the late Nicholas Saunders, it, and Neal's Yard itself, remain an oasis of alternative values amid the growing commercialism of the area.

A specialist shop on Neal Street

Entrance to Thomas Neal's

❽ Thomas Neal's

Earlham St WC2. **Map** 13 B2.
🚇 Covent Garden, Leicester Sq.
Open 10am–7pm Mon–Sat, noon–6pm Sun. 🚹 ground floor only.

Opened in the early 1990s in an old converted banana warehouse, this upscale shopping complex offers an interesting range of shops, selling designer clothes and cosmetics, jewellery and accessories, antique clothing and lace. When it is time for a break from shopping, there is a café and restaurant on the lower floor. The Donmar Warehouse theatre *(see p338)* is also part of the complex, staging must-see productions such as *The Blue Room*.

❾ Seven Dials

Monmouth St WC2. **Map** 13 B2.
🚇 Covent Garden, Leicester Sq.

The pillar at this junction of seven streets incorporates six sundials (the central spike acted as a seventh). It was installed in 1989 and is a copy of a 17th-century monument. The original was removed in the 19th century because it had become a notorious meeting place for criminals who operated in an area that had become one of London's most infamous slums.
   Today Seven Dials is a vibrant shopping and dining area. Its streets and alleyways are known for their one-off shops, funky boutiques, holistic medicine shops, restaurants and bars.

❿ Wyndham's Theatre

32 Charing Cross Rd, WC2. **Map** 13 B2.
Tel 0871 976 0072. 🚇 Leicester Square. **Open** for performances only.
🚹 🖥 **wyndhams-theatre.com**
See Entertainment pp336–7.

The Wyndham's Theatre opened its doors in 1899 and takes its name from Charles Wyndham (1837–1919) – lauded as one of the greatest actors of his day. Designed by the architect William Sprague, the Wyndham was the first of seven theatres he completed that year.
It boasts a Portland stone exterior and a turquoise, cream and gold interior decorated in Louis XVI style, with a ceiling painted in the style of Boucher.
   Many greats in British theatre have graced the stage since Wyndham himself: Vanessa Redgrave, Sir Alec Guinness and Sir John Gielgud among them. It has also seen such talents as Dame Judi Dench in *Madame de Sade* and Jude Law as Hamlet.

⓫ Adelphi Theatre

Strand WC2. **Map** 13 C3. **Tel** 0844 412 4651. 🚇 Charing Cross, Embankment. **Open** performances only. 🚹
🖥 **adelphitheatre.co.uk**
See Entertainment pp336–7.

There has been a theatre on this site since 1806, when the Sans Pareil Theatre opened here. It was set up by John Scott, a wealthy tradesman, who was helping to launch his daughter on the stage. After several refurbishments and name changes, the current Adelphi Theatre was remodelled in 1930 in Art Deco style by Ernest Schaufelburg. His modernist "straight-line" design resulted in a building without curves. Note the highly distinctive lettering on the frontage, and the well-kept lobby and auditorium, with their stylized motifs.
   The Adelphi now stages a variety of plays from *The Bodyguard*, featuring music of the late Whitney Houstan to *One Man, Two Guvnors*, which transferred to the Theatre Royal Haymarket *(see p103)* in 2011.

⓬ Savoy Hotel

Strand WC2. **Map** 13 C2. **Tel** 020 7836 4343. 🚇 Charing Cross, Embankment.
🖥 **fairmont.com/savoy**

Pioneer of ensuite bathrooms and electric lighting, the grand Savoy was built in 1889 on the site of the medieval Savoy Palace. A £100 million lavish refurbishment took place in 2008–2010, incorporating both the original Edwardian and the later Art Deco style. The forecourt is the only street in Britain where traffic drives on the right. Attached to the hotel are the Savoy Theatre built for D'Oyly Carte opera, famed for performing the operas of Gilbert and Sullivan; and Simpson's-in-the-Strand English restaurant.

Front entrance to the Savoy Hotel

⓭ Savoy Chapel

Strand WC2. **Map** 13 C2. **Tel** 020 7836 7221. 🚇 Charing Cross, Embankment. **Open** 9am–4pm Mon–Thu, 9am–1pm Sun. **Closed** Aug–Sep. 🚹 11am Sun. 🎫 📷 phone to book. 🖥 **royalchapelsavoy.org**

The first Savoy Chapel was founded in the 16th century as the chapel for the hospital set up by Henry VII on the site of the old Savoy Palace. Parts of the outside walls date from 1512, but most of the present building dates from the mid-19th century. In 1890, it was London's first church to be electrically lit. It became the chapel of the Royal Victorian Order in 1937, and is the Queen's private chapel now. Nearby on Savoy Hill were the first studios of the BBC.

⑭ Somerset House

Strand WC2. **Map** 14 D2. **Tel** 020 7845 4600. ☺ Temple. Gallery & House **Open** 10am–6pm daily (last adm to galleries: 5:30pm). **Closed** 1 Jan, 24–26 Dec. ☑ free guided tours. Ice rink **Open** 2 months in winter. ☒ call 0844 847 1520 for tickets. ☐ Courtauld Institute of Art Gallery: ☒ ☐ ☒ & Embankment Galleries: ☒ & Tom's Kitchen: **Tel** 020 7845 4646. W **somersethouse.org.uk**

This elegant Georgian building was the creation of Sir William Chambers. It was erected in the 1770s after the first Somerset House, a Renaissance palace built for the Duke of Somerset in the mid-16th century, was pulled down following years of neglect. The replacement was the first major building to be designed for use as government offices and has served to house the Navy Board (note that the classical grandeur of the Seamen's Waiting Hall and Nelson's Staircase are not to be missed), a succession of Royal Societies and, for a substantial amount of time, the Inland Revenue. Today it is home to the Courtauld Institute of Art

Gallery. The courtyard of Somerset House was closed to the public for nearly a century, but on the Inland Revenue's departure in 1997 it was cleared, as part of a £48-million restoration scheme. This created an attractive piazza with a 55-jet fountain. Films and concerts are often staged here in the summer, and for a few weeks in winter, there is an enchanting ice rink. From the courtyard, visitors can stroll through the South Building, where the highly regarded Tom's Kitchen restaurant overlooks the Thames, on to a riverside terrace that includes an open-air summer café and a restaurant, with pedestrian access to Waterloo Bridge and the South Bank's theatres and other attractions.

Fountains at Somerset House

Located in Somerset House, but famous in its own right, is the small but spectacular **Courtauld Institute of Art Gallery**. Its exquisite collection of paintings has been displayed here since 1990 and owes its existence to the bequest of textile magnate and philanthropist Samuel Courtauld. On display are works by Botticelli, Brueghel, Bellini and Rubens (including one of his early masterpieces *The Descent from the Cross*), but it is the Courtauld's collection of Impressionist and Post-Impressionist paintings that draws the most attention. As well as works by Monet, Gauguin, Pissarro, Renoir and Modigliani, visitors can gaze captivated on Manet's *A Bar at the Folies-Bergères*, Van Gogh's *Self-Portrait with Bandaged Ear*, Cézanne's *The Card Players* and some evocative studies of dancers by Degas. In addition to its permanent collection, the Courtauld Institute now hosts a series of world-class temporary exhibitions that take place throughout the year.

A modern riverside gallery was launched within Somerset House in 2008. The **Embankment Galleries** occupy 750 square metres of exhibition space on the two lower floors of the south wing. The changing exhibition programme covers a broad range of contemporary arts, including photography, design, fashion and architecture.

Van Gogh's *Self-Portrait with Bandaged Ear* (1889) at the Courtauld

⓯ St Mary-le-Strand

Strand WC2. **Map** 14 D2. **Tel** 020 7836 3126. 🚇 Temple. **Open** 11am–4pm Tue–Thu, 10am–1pm Sun. 🕙 11am Sun, 1:05pm Thu. 📷
w stmarylestrand.org

Now beached on a road island at the east end of the Strand, this pleasing church was consecrated in 1724. It was the first public building by James Gibbs, who designed St-Martin-in-the-Fields *(see p104)*. Gibbs was influenced by Christopher Wren, but the exuberant external decorative detail here was inspired by the Baroque churches of Rome, where Gibbs studied. Its multi-arched tower is layered like a wedding cake, and culminates in a cupola and lantern. St-Mary-le-Strand is now the official church of the Women's Royal Naval Service.

St Mary-le-Strand

⓰ Roman Bath

5 Strand Lane WC2. **Map** 14 D2. **Tel** 020 7641 5264. 🚇 Temple, Embankment, Charing Cross. **Open** by appt only. 🚻 via Temple Pl.

This little bath and its surround may be seen from a full-length window on Surrey Street, by pressing a light switch on the outside wall. It is almost certainly not Roman, for there is no other evidence of Roman habitation in the immediate

Bush House from Kingsway

area. It is more likely to have been part of Arundel House, one of several palaces which stood on the Strand from Tudor times until the 17th century, when they were demolished for new building. In the 19th century the bath was open to the public for cold plunges, believed to be healthy.

⓱ Bush House

Aldwych WC2. **Map** 14 D2. 🚇 Temple, Holborn. **Closed** to the public.

Situated at the centre of the Aldwych crescent, this Neo-Classical building was first designed as manufacturers' showrooms by an American, Irving T Bush, and completed in 1935. It appears especially imposing when viewed from Kingsway, its dramatic north entrance graced with various statues symbolizing Anglo-American relations. Since 1940 it has been used as radio studios, and was the head-quarters of the BBC World Service until 2012. To most Londoners it still symbolizes the home of the BBC.

⓲ Cleopatra's Needle

Embankment WC2. **Map** 13 C3. 🚇 Embankment, Charing Cross.

Erected in Heliopolis in about 1500 BC, this incongruous pink granite monument is much older than London itself. Its inscriptions celebrate the deeds of the pharaohs of ancient Egypt. It was presented

to Britain by the then Viceroy of Egypt, Mohammed Ali, in 1819 and erected in 1878, shortly after the Embankment was built. It has a twin in New York's Central Park, behind the Metropolitan Museum of Art. The bronze sphinxes, added in 1882, are not Egyptian.

In its base is a Victorian time capsule of artifacts of the day, such as the day's newspapers, a rail timetable and photographs of 12 contemporary beauties.

⓳ Victoria Embankment Gardens

WC2. **Map** 13 C3. 🚇 Embankment, Charing Cross. **Open** 7:30am–dusk Mon–Sat, 9am–dusk Sun & public hols. 🚻 📷

This narrow sliver of a public park, created when the Embankment was built, boasts well-maintained flower beds, a clutch of statues of British worthies (including the Scottish poet Robert Burns) and, in summer, a season of concerts. Its main historical feature is the water gate at its northwest corner, which was built as a triumphal entry to the Thames for the Duke of Buckingham in 1626. It is a relic of York House, which used to stand on this site and was the home first of the Archbishops of York and then of the Duke. It is still in its original position and although the water used to lap against it, because of the Thames's Embankment the gate is now a good 100 m (330 ft) from the river's edge.

Victoria Embankment Gardens

The office block above Charing Cross station

The façade of No. 7 Adam Street

⑳ Adelphi

Strand WC2. **Map** 13 C3. 🔁 Embankment, Charing Cross. **Closed** to the public.

Adelphi is a pun on *adelphoi*, the Greek word for brothers – this area was once an elegant riverside residential development designed in 1772 by brothers Robert and John Adam. The name now refers to the Art Deco office block, its entrance adorned with N A Trent's heroic reliefs of workers at toil, which in 1938 replaced the Adams' much admired Palladian-style apartment complex. That destruction is now viewed as one of the worst acts of 20th-century official vandalism. A number of the Adams' surrounding buildings survive, notably No. 8, the ornate Royal Society for the encouragement of Arts, Manufactures & Commerce just opposite (open first Sunday of the month, 10am–12:30pm, not January; 0207 930 5115). In the same exuberant idiom are Nos. 1–4 Robert Street, where Robert Adam lived for a time, and No. 7 Adam Street.

㉑ Charing Cross

Strand WC2. **Map** 13 C3. 🔁 Charing Cross, Embankment.

The name derives from the last of the 12 crosses erected by Edward I to mark the funeral route in 1290 of his wife, Eleanor of Castile, from Nottinghamshire to Westminster Abbey. Today a 19th-century replica stands in the forecourt of Charing Cross station. Both the cross and the Charing Cross Hotel, built into the station frontage, were designed in 1863 by E M Barry, architect of the Royal Opera House *(see p117)*.

Above the station platforms has risen an assertive shopping centre and office block, completed in 1991. Designed by Terry Farrell, it resembles a giant ocean liner, with portholes looking on to Villiers Street. The building is best seen from the river, where it dominates its neighbours. The railway arches at the rear of the station have been modernized as a suite of small shops and cafés, as well as a venue for the Players Theatre, the last repository of Victorian music hall entertainment.

㉒ The London Coliseum

St Martin's Lane WC2. **Map** 13 B3. **Tel** 020 7845 9300. 🔁 Leicester Sq, Charing Cross. **Open** performances ♿ 🔲 Lectures. *See Entertainment p340.* 🆆 eno.org

London's largest theatre and one of its most elaborate, this flamboyant building, topped with a large globe, was designed in 1904 by Frank Matcham and was equipped with London's first revolving stage. It was also the first theatre in Europe to have lifts. A former variety house, today it is the home of the English National Opera, and well worth visiting, if only for the Edwardian interior with its gilded cherubs and heavy purple curtains. In 2003, the original glass roof was restored, providing dramatic views over Trafalgar Square.

London Coliseum

BLOOMSBURY AND FITZROVIA

Since the beginning of the 20th century, Bloomsbury and Fitzrovia have been synonymous with literature, art and learning. The Bloomsbury Group of writers and artists were active from the early 1900s until the 1930s; the name Fitzrovia was invented by writers such as Dylan Thomas who drank in the Fitzroy Tavern. Bloomsbury still boasts the University of London, the British Museum and many fine Georgian squares. But it is now also noted for its Charlotte Street restaurants and the furniture and competitively priced electrical shops lining Tottenham Court Road.

Sights at a Glance

Historic Streets and Buildings
2 Bloomsbury Square
4 Russell Square
5 Queen Square
8 British Library
9 St Pancras International
11 Woburn Walk
13 Fitzroy Square
15 Charlotte Street

Museums
1 British Museum pp126–9
6 Charles Dickens Museum
7 Foundling Museum
12 Wellcome Collection
16 Pollock's Toy Museum

Churches
3 St George's, Bloomsbury
10 St Pancras Parish Church

Pubs and Bars
14 Fitzroy Tavern

☐ Restaurants see pp297–8
1 Bam-Bou
2 Malabar Junction
3 Pied à Terre
4 Ragam
5 Roka
6 Salt Yard
7 Thai Metro

Street Finder, maps 4, 5, 6, 13

| 0 metres | | 500 |
| 0 yards | | 500 |

Street-by-Street: Bloomsbury

The British Museum dominates Bloomsbury. Its earnestly intellectual atmosphere spills over into the surrounding streets, and to its north lies the main campus of London University. The area has been home to writers and artists, and is a traditional centre of the book trade. Most of the publishers have left, but there are still many bookshops around.

The Senate House (1932) is the administrative headquarters of the University of London. It holds a priceless library.

Bedford Square is one of London's most complete Georgian squares. Its uniform doorways are fringed in artificial stone.

1 ★ **British Museum**
Designed in the mid-19th century, it is extremely popular and attracts some five million visitors a year.

Key

— Suggested route

0 metres 100
0 yards 100

Museum Street is lined with small cafés and shops selling old books, prints and antiques.

Pizza Express occupies a charming and little-altered Victorian dairy.

The Duke of Bedford's statue commemorates the fifth duke, Francis Russell (1765–1805). An avid farmer, he is shown with sheep and a plough.

Locator Map
See Central London Map pp16–17

④ ★ Russell Square
It was once part of the Duke of Bedford's estate, and is now a shady retreat on a hot day.

❷ Bloomsbury Square
Laid out in 1661, it is graced by a statue of statesman Charles James Fox (1749–1806).

To Holborn station

❸ St George's, Bloomsbury
The tower on this typically flamboyant Hawksmoor church is modelled on the tomb of King Mausolus.

Sicilian Avenue is a small and unexpected pedestrian precinct from 1905, where colonnades evoke Roman architecture.

❶ British Museum

The oldest public museum in the world, the British Museum was established in 1753 to house the collections of the physician Sir Hans Sloane (1660–1753), who also helped create the Chelsea Physic Garden *(see p199)*. Sloane's

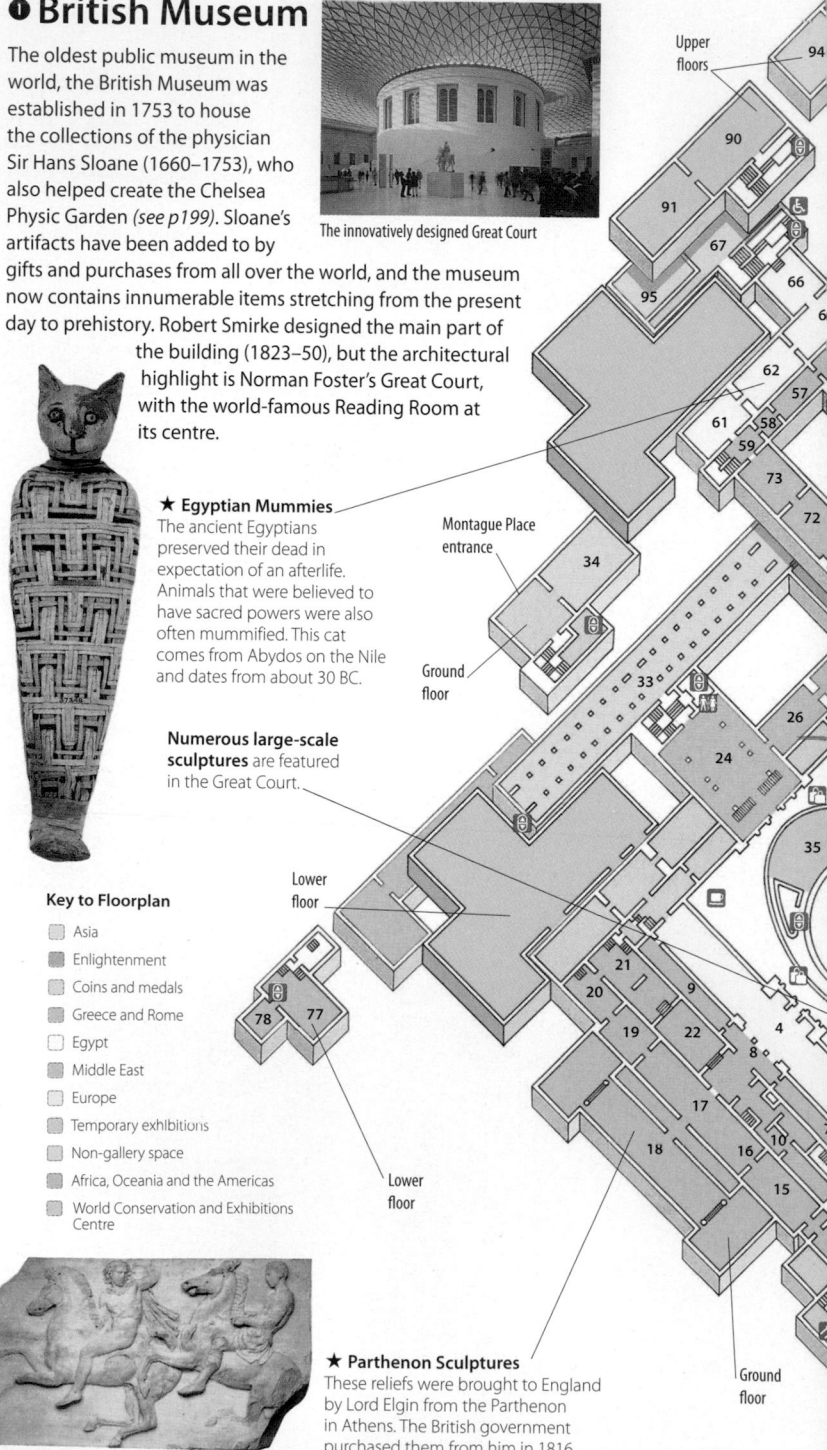

The innovatively designed Great Court

artifacts have been added to by gifts and purchases from all over the world, and the museum now contains innumerable items stretching from the present day to prehistory. Robert Smirke designed the main part of the building (1823–50), but the architectural highlight is Norman Foster's Great Court, with the world-famous Reading Room at its centre.

★ **Egyptian Mummies**
The ancient Egyptians preserved their dead in expectation of an afterlife. Animals that were believed to have sacred powers were also often mummified. This cat comes from Abydos on the Nile and dates from about 30 BC.

Numerous large-scale sculptures are featured in the Great Court.

Montague Place entrance

Ground floor

Lower floor

Key to Floorplan

- Asia
- Enlightenment
- Coins and medals
- Greece and Rome
- Egypt
- Middle East
- Europe
- Temporary exhibitions
- Non-gallery space
- Africa, Oceania and the Americas
- World Conservation and Exhibitions Centre

Upper floors

Lower floor

Ground floor

★ **Parthenon Sculptures**
These reliefs were brought to England by Lord Elgin from the Parthenon in Athens. The British government purchased them from him in 1816.

★ Lindow Man
The skin on this 2,000-year-old human body was preserved by the acids of a peat bog in Cheshire. He was probably killed in an elaborate ritual.

Two grand staircases wrap around the Reading Room and link to the upper floors via a bridge.

Upper floor

★ Sutton Hoo Treasure
Remarkably preserved, the 7th-century ship burial includes this striking helmet.

Reading Room

The Great Court

Paul Hamlyn Library

Main entrance

Portland Vase
It was made in Italy or Egypt shortly before the birth of Christ. In 1845, a visitor smashed it into 200 pieces; since then it has been reassembled.

Gallery Guide
The Greece and Rome and Middle East collections are found on all three levels of the museum, predominantly on the west side. The Africa collection is located on the lower floor, while Asia exhibits are found on the main and upper floors on the north side of the Museum. The Americas collection is located in the northeast corner of the main floor. Egyptian artifacts are found west of the Great Court and on the upper floors.

Exploring the British Museum's Collections

The Museum's immense hoard of treasure spans two million years of history and culture. The 94 galleries, which stretch 2.5 miles (4 km), cover civilisations from ancient Egypt and Assyria to modern Japan.

1st-century BC bronze helmet dredged up from the Thames

Prehistoric and Roman Britain

Relics of prehistoric Britain are on display in six separate galleries. The most impressive items include the gold "Mold Cape", a ceremonial bronze-age cape found in Wales; an antlered headdress worn by hunter-gatherers some 9000 years ago; and "Lindow Man", a 1st-century AD sacrificial victim who lay preserved in a bog until 1984. Some superb Celtic metalwork is also on show, alongside the silver Mildenhall Treasure and other Roman pieces. The Hinton St. Mary mosaic (4th century AD) features a roundel containing the earliest known British depiction of Christ.

Europe

The spectacular Sutton Hoo ship treasure, the burial hoard of a 7th-century Anglo-Saxon king, is on display in Room 41. This superb find, made in 1939, revolutionized our understanding of Anglo-Saxon life and ritual. The artifacts include a helmet and shield, Celtic hanging bowls, the remains of a lyre, and gold and garnet jewellery.

Adjacent galleries contain a collection of clocks, watches and scientific instruments. Some exquisite timepieces are on view, including a 400-year-old clock from Prague, designed as a model galleon; in its day it pitched, played music, and even fired a cannon. Also nearby are the famous 12th-century Lewis chessmen, and a gallery housing Baron Ferdinand Rothschild's (1839–98) remarkably varied treasures.

The museum's modern collection includes some Wedgwood pottery, glassware, and a series of Russian revolutionary plates.

Gilded brass late-16th-century ship clock from Prague

Ancient Near East

There are numerous galleries devoted to the Western Asian collections, covering 7,000 years of history. The most famous items are the 7th-century BC Assyrian reliefs from King Ashurbanipal's palace at Nineveh, but of equal interest are two large human-headed bulls from 7th-century BC Khorsabad, and an inscribed Black Obelisk of Assyrian King Shalmaneser III. The upper floors contain pieces from ancient Sumeria, part of the Oxus Treasure (which lay buried for over 2,000 years), and the museum's collection of clay cuneiform tablets. The earliest of these are inscribed with the oldest known pictographs (c.3300 BC). Also of interest is a skull discovered in Jericho in the 1950s; augmented with shells and lime plaster, the skull belonged to a hunter who lived in the area some 7,000 years ago.

Ornamental detail from a Sumerian Queen's lyre

Egypt

In Room 4 are Egyptian sculptures. These include a fine red granite head of a king, thought to depict Amenophis III, and a colossal statue of King Rameses II. Also on show is the Rosetta Stone, used by Jean-François Champollion (1790–1832) as a primer for deciphering Egyptian hieroglyphs. An extraordinary array of mummies, jewellery and Coptic art can also be found upstairs. The various instruments that were used by embalmers to preserve bodies before entombment are all displayed. Room 61 houses paintings from the lost tomb-chapel of Nebamun.

Part of a colossal granite statue of Rameses II, the 13th-century BC Egyptian monarch

Greece and Rome

The Greek and Roman collections include the museum's most famous treasure, the Parthenon sculptures. These 5th-century BC reliefs were once part of a marble frieze that decorated the Parthenon, Athena's temple on the Acropolis in Athens. Much of it was ruined in battle in 1687, and most of what survived was removed between 1801 and 1804 by the British diplomat Lord Elgin, and sold to the British nation. Other highlights include the Nereid Monument and sculptures and friezes from the Mausoleum at

Ancient Greek vase illustrating the mythical hero Hercules's fight with a bull

Halicarnassus. The beautiful 1st-century BC cameo-glass Portland Vase is located in the Roman Empire section.

Asia

The Chinese collection boasts fine porcelain and ancient Shang bronzes (c.1500–1050 BC). Particularly impressive are the ceremonial ancient Chinese bronze vessels, with their enigmatic animal-head shapes.

The fine Chinese ceramics range from delicate tea bowls to a model pond, which is almost a thousand years old. In the Sir Percival David gallery the Chinese ceramics date from the 10th to early 20th centuries.

Adjacent to these is one of the finest collections of Asian religious sculpture outside India. A major highlight is an assortment of sculpted reliefs, which once covered the walls of the Buddhist temple at Amaravati, and which recount stories from the life of the Buddha. A Korean section contains some gigantic works of Buddhist art.

The museum's collection of Islamic art, including a jade

Statue of the Hindu god Shiva as Nataraja, or Lord of the Dance (11th century AD)

terrapin found in a water tank, can be found in Room 34. Rooms 92 to 94 house the Japanese galleries, with a Classical teahouse in Room 92.

Africa

An interesting collection of African sculptures, textiles and graphic art can also be found in Room 25 on the lower floor of the museum. Famous bronzes from the Kingdom of Benin stand alongside modern African prints, paintings, drawings and colourful fabrics.

The Great Court and the Reading Room

Surrounding the Reading Room of the former British Library, the £100-million Great Court opened to coincide with the new millennium. Designed by Sir Norman Foster, the Court is covered by a wide-span, lightweight roof, creating London's first indoor public square. The Reading Room has been restored to its original design, so visitors can sample the atmosphere which Karl Marx, Mahatma Gandhi and George Bernard Shaw found

so agreeable. From the outside, however, it is scarcely recognizable; it is housed in a multi-level construction which partly supports the roof, and which also contains a Centre for Education, temporary exhibition galleries, bookshops, cafés and restaurants. Part of the Reading Room also serves as a study suite where those wishing to learn more about the Museum's collections have access to information.

Fine lattice roof of glass and steel

Restored decoration

❷ Bloomsbury Square

WC1. **Map** 5 C5. ⊖ Holborn.

This is the oldest of the Bloomsbury squares. It was laid out in 1661 by the fourth Earl of Southampton, who owned the land. None of the original buildings survives and its shaded garden is encircled by a busy one-way traffic system. (Unusually for central London, you can nearly always find a space in the car park under the square.)

The literary and artistic avant-garde Bloomsbury Group lived in the area during the early years of the last century. It included many prominent figures such as novelists Virginia Woolf and EM Forster, biographer Lytton Strachey and artists Vanessa Bell, Duncan Grant and Dora Carrington. Look out for their individual plaques throughout the area (see p41).

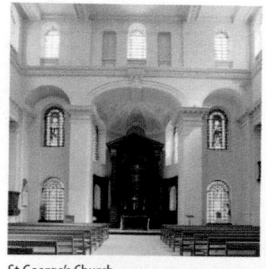

St George's Church

❸ St George's, Bloomsbury

Bloomsbury Way WC1. **Map** 13 B1. **Tel** 020 7242 1979. ⊖ Holborn, Tottenham Court Rd, Russell Sq. **Open** 1–4pm daily (times may vary – call to check). ✝ 1:10pm Wed & Fri, 10:30am Sun. Recitals. ♿ 📷 🌐 **stgeorgesbloomsbury.org.uk**

A slightly eccentric church, St George's was designed by Nicholas Hawksmoor, Wren's pupil, and completed in 1730. It was built as a place of worship for the prosperous residents of newly-developed, fashionable Bloomsbury. The layered tower, modelled on the tomb of King

The flamboyant Russell Hotel on Russell Square

Mausolus (the original mausoleum in Turkey) and topped by a statue of George I, was for a long time an object of derision – the king was thought to be presented too heroically. In 1913, the funeral of Emily Davison, the suffragette who threw herself under King George V's horse, was held here.

Restored in 2006, it is now a thriving parish church, concert venue and centre for community art.

❹ Russell Square

WC1. **Map** 5 B5. ⊖ Russell Sq. 🚻 **Open** 7:30am–10pm daily.

One of London's largest squares, Russell Square is a lively place, with a fountain, café and traffic roaring around its perimeter. The east side boasts perhaps the best of the Victorian grand hotels to survive in the capital. Charles Doll's Russell Hotel, which was opened in 1900, is a wondrous confection of red terracotta, with colonnaded balconies and

prancing cherubs beneath the main columns. The exuberance is continued in the lobby, faced with marble of many colours.

Poet T S Eliot worked at the west corner of the square, from 1925 until 1965, in what were the offices of publishers Faber and Faber.

❺ Queen Square

WC1. **Map** 5 C5. ⊖ Russell Sq.

In spite of being named after Queen Anne, this square contains a statue of Queen Charlotte. Her husband, George III, stayed at the house of a doctor here when he became ill with the hereditary disease that drove him mad before his death in 1820. Originally, the north side of the square was left open so that inhabitants had a clear view of Hampstead and Highgate. Today the square is almost completely surrounded by hospital buildings, with early Georgian houses on the west side.

Queen Charlotte's statue in Queen Square

❻ Charles Dickens Museum

48 Doughty St WC1. **Map** 6 D4.
Tel 020 7405 2127. 🚇 Chancery
Lane, Russell Sq. **Open** 10am–5pm
daily (last adm 4:30pm). 🅿️ 📷
♿ ground floor. 🛍️ 🖥️ 📷
🌐 dickensmuseum.com

The novelist Charles Dickens lived
in this early 19th-century terraced
house for three of his most
productive years (from 1837 to
1839). The popular works *Oliver
Twist* and *Nicholas Nickleby* were
entirely written here, and *Pickwick
Papers* was finished. Although
Dickens had many London
homes throughout his lifetime,
this is the only one to have
survived. In 1923, it was acquired
by the Dickens Fellowship and
it is now a well-
conceived museum
with some of the
principal rooms laid
out exactly as they
were in Dickens's
time. Others have
been adapted to
display a varied
collection of articles
associated with him. The
museum houses over 100,000
exhibits including manuscripts,
paintings and personal items;
papers and pieces of furniture
from his other homes; and first
editions of many of his
best-known works.

A £3 million
restoration project
was completed in
2011 in readiness
for the bicentenary
of Dickens' birth, in 2012.

Nautical publisher's trade sign,
Dickens Museum

❼ Foundling Museum

40 Brunswick Square WC1. **Map** 5 C4.
Tel 020 7841 3600. 🚇 Russell
Square. **Open** 10am–5pm Tue–Sat,
11am–5pm Sun. **Closed** 1 Jan, 24–26
& 31 Dec. 🅿️ 🖥️ ♿ 📷 book ahead.
🛍️ 📷 Coram's Fields: Guilford St
WC1. **Open** 9am–dusk.
🌐 foundlingmuseum.org.uk

In 1722, Captain Thomas Coram,
a retired sailor and shipbuilder
recently returned from the
Americas, vowed to establish a
refuge for abandoned children.

Portrait of Captain Coram (1740) by
William Hogarth

Horrified by the poverty on
London streets, he was
determined to alter the fate of
the city's foundlings by housing,
educating and placing them
in private homes. Assisted
by his friend, the artist
William Hogarth, and the
composer George Frederick
Handel, Coram worked
tirelessly to raise funds for
the refuge. Finally in 1739,
after much petitioning of
George II, he was granted
a Royal Charter to
establish a Foundling
Hospital. Hogarth donated
paintings to the hospital and
other artists followed suit,
creating Britain's first art
gallery. The wealthy
were encouraged to
view the works of
art and the children
at the hospital, in
the hope that they
would donate funds.

The original hospital located
at the end of Lambs Conduit
Street was demolished in the
1920s, but the interiors of two
of the 18th-century rooms were
saved and relocated to 40 Brunswick Square, the current location
of the museum. On the ground
floor, the story of the many
children who were cared for in
the Foundling Hospital is told.
The nationally important collection of 18th-century paintings,
sculpture, furniture and interiors
is displayed on the first floor.

Adjacent to the museum,
with its entrance on Guilford
Street, is **Coram's Fields**, a

unique playground for children
and young people (aged under
16). All adults, however, must
be accompanied by children.
The park is open all year round
and the entrance is free. It
includes a youth centre, a city
farm and a café.

❽ British Library

96 Euston Rd NW1. **Map** 5 B3.
Tel 01937 546 060. 🚇 King's Cross
St Pancras. Exhibition galleries
Open 9:30am–6pm Mon–Fri (8pm
Tue), 9:30am–5pm Sat, 11am–5pm
Sun. Regular events. ♿ 🖥️ 🛍️ 📷
📷 🌐 bl.uk

London's most important
building from the late 20th
century houses the national
collection of books, manuscripts
and maps, as well as the British
Library Sound Archive.
Designed in red brick by Sir
Colin St John Wilson, it opened
in 1997 after nearly 20 years
under construction, involving
controversial cost over-runs,
but is now widely admired.

A copy of nearly every printed
book in the United Kingdom is
held here – more than 14 million
– and can be consulted by those
with a reader's ticket. There are
also exhibition galleries open to
everyone. Visitors may view some
of the Library's most precious
items, including the Lindisfarne
Gospels, with the Turning the
Pages system which shows each
page on a monitor. Other
volumes include a Gutenberg
Bible and Shakespeare's First
Folio. Running through six floors
is a spectacular glass tower
holding George III's library.

Page from the Lindisfarne Gospels

The massive St Pancras Renaissance Hotel above St Pancras Station

❾ St Pancras International

Euston Rd NW1. **Map** 5 B2.
Tel 020 7843 7688. 🚇 King's Cross,
St Pancras. **Open** 24 hours.
Closed 25 Dec. *See Getting to London p364.* 🅦 stpancras.com

St Pancras is the London terminal for Eurostar services to continental Europe. It is easily the most spectacular of the three rail termini along Euston Road, thanks to the extravagant frontage, in red-brick gingerbread Gothic, of the former Midland Grand Hotel, opened in 1874 as one of the most sumptuous hotels of its time. By 1935, it was too expensive to run and became office space. Threatened with demolition in the 1960s, the poet John Betjeman

Figures on St Pancras Church

campaigned to save it (there is a statue of him on the upper level). It has since been lavishly restored as a five-star hotel, plus apartments, penthouses and Europe's longest champagne bar.

❿ St Pancras Parish Church

Euston Rd NW1. **Map** 5 B3. **Tel** 020 7388 1461. 🚇 Euston. **Open** 8am–6pm Mon–Thu, 8am–noon Fri.
✝ 8am, 10am, 6pm Sun. ♿ Recitals 1:15pm Thu. 🅦 stpancraschurch.org

This is a stately Greek revival church of 1822 designed by William Inwood and his son Henry, both great enthusiasts for Athenian architecture. The design is based on the Erectheum on the Acropolis in Athens, and even the wooden pulpit stands on miniature Ionic columns of its own. The long, galleried interior has a dramatic severity appropriate to the church's style. The female figures on the northern outer wall were originally taller than they are now; a chunk had to be taken out of the middle of each to make them fit under the roof they were meant to be supporting.

The church hosts a festival of contemporary church music in May, and art exhibitions are sometimes held in the atmospheric crypt.

⓫ Woburn Walk

WC1. **Map** 5 B4. 🚇 Euston, Euston Sq.

A well-restored street of bow-fronted shops, it was designed by Thomas Cubitt in 1822. The high pavement on the east side was to protect shop fronts from the mud thrown up by carriages. The poet W B Yeats lived at No. 5 from 1895 until 1919.

⓬ Wellcome Collection

183 Euston Rd NW1. **Map** 5 A4.
Tel 020 7611 2222. 🚇 Euston, King's Cross, Warren St. **Open** 10am–6pm Tue–Sat (to 10pm Thu), 11am–6pm Sun, noon–6pm public hols.
Closed 23 Dec–1 Jan. ♿ 🚻 📷
🅦 wellcomecollection.org

Sir Henry Wellcome was a pharmacist, entrepreneur and collector. His passionate interest in medicine and its history, as well as ethnography and archaeology, led him to gather more than one million objects from around the world. Wellcome Collection is a £30-million public venue used to house his vast collection as well as explore the connections between medicine, art and the human condition through events and exhibitions.

Exhibits range from the bizarre to the beautiful, the ancient to the futuristic. More than 900 objects are on permanent display, including a used guillotine blade and Napoleon's toothbrush. Contemporary works include a DNA sequencing robot and a sculpture exploring HIV by Mark Quinn. The Wellcome library, on the upper floors, is the world's largest devoted to the history of medicine.

⓭ Fitzroy Square

W1. **Map** 4 F4. 🚇 Warren St, Great Portland St.

Designed by Robert Adam in 1794, the square's south and east sides survive in their original form, in dignified Portland stone. Blue plaques record the homes of many artists, writers and statesmen: George Bernard Shaw and Virginia Woolf both lived at No. 29 – although not at the same time. Shaw gave money to the artist Roger Fry to establish the Omega workshop at No. 33 in 1913. Here young artists were paid a fixed wage to produce Post-Impressionist furniture, pottery, carpets and paintings for sale to the public.

No. 29 Fitzroy Square

⓮ Fitzroy Tavern

16 Charlotte St W1. **Map** 4 F5.
Tel 020 7580 3714. ⊖ Tottenham Court Rd, Goodge St. **Open** 11am–11pm Mon–Sat, noon–10:30pm Sun. ♿ *See Pubs and Bars pp308–9.*

This traditional pub was a meeting place between World Wars I and II for a group of writers and artists who dubbed the area around Fitzroy Square and Charlotte Street "Fitzrovia". A basement "Writers and Artists Bar" contains pictures of former customers, including the writers Dylan Thomas and George Orwell, and the artist Augustus John.

⓯ Charlotte Street

W1. **Map** 5 A5. ⊖ Goodge St.

As the upper classes moved west from Bloomsbury in the early 19th century, a flood of artists and European immigrants moved in, turning the area into a northern appendage to Soho *(see pp100–11)*. The artist John Constable lived and worked for many years at No. 76. Some of the new residents established small workshops to service the clothing shops on Oxford Street and the furniture stores on Tottenham Court Road. Others set up reasonably-priced restaurants. The street still boasts a great variety of eating places. It is overshadowed from the north by the 189-m (620-ft) Telecom Tower, built in 1964 as a vast TV, radio and telecommunications aerial *(see p34)*.

Telecom Tower

⓰ Pollock's Toy Museum

1 Scala St W1. **Map** 5 A5.
Tel 020 7636 3452. ⊖ Goodge St, Warren St, Tottenham Court Rd. **Open** 10am–5pm Mon–Sat. ♿ 🖼
🌐 pollockstoymuseum.com

Benjamin Pollock was a renowned maker of toy theatres in the late 19th and early 20th centuries – the novelist Robert Louis Stevenson was an enthusiastic customer. The museum opened in Monmouth Street in Covent Garden in 1956 and relocated to these premises in 1969. The final room is devoted to stages and puppets from Pollock's theatres, together with a reconstruction of his workshop. This is a child-sized museum created in two largely unaltered 18th-century houses. The small rooms have been filled with a fascinating assortment of historic toys from all over the world. There are dolls, puppets, trains, cars, construction sets, a fine rocking horse and a splendid collection of mainly Victorian doll's houses. Parents should beware – the exit leads you through a very tempting toyshop.

Pearly king and queen dolls from Pollock's Toy Museum

HOLBORN AND THE INNS OF COURT

This area is traditionally home to the legal and journalistic professions. The law is still here, in the Royal Courts of Justice and the Inns of Court, but the national newspapers left Fleet Street in the 1980s. Several buildings here predate the Great Fire of 1666 (see pp26–7). These include the superb façade of Staple Inn, Prince Henry's Room, and the interior of Middle Temple Hall. Holborn used to be one of the capital's main shopping districts. Times have changed the face of the area, but the jewellery and diamond dealers of Hatton Garden are still here, as are the London Silver Vaults.

Sights at a Glance

Historic Buildings, Sights and Streets
❷ Lincoln's Inn
❹ Old Curiosity Shop
❺ Law Society
❼ Royal Courts of Justice
❾ Fleet Street
❿ Prince Henry's Room
⓫ Temple
⓮ Dr Johnson's House
⓰ Holborn Viaduct
⓲ Hatton Garden
⓳ Staple Inn
㉑ Gray's Inn

Museums and Galleries
❶ Sir John Soane's Museum

Churches
❻ St Clement Danes
⓬ St Bride's
⓯ St Andrew, Holborn
⓱ St Etheldreda's Chapel

Monuments
❽ Temple Bar Memorial

Parks and Gardens
❸ Lincoln's Inn Fields

Pubs and Bars
⓭ Ye Olde Cheshire Cheese

Shops
⓴ London Silver Vaults

Restaurants see pp297–8
1 De Palo's
2 The Chancery
3 Vanilla Black
4 The White Swan

Street Finder, maps 6, 14

0 metres 500
0 yards 500

◀ Gothic façade of the Royal Courts of Justice

For keys to symbols see back flap

Street-by-Street: Lincoln's Inn

This is calm, dignified, legal London, packed with history and interest. Lincoln's Inn, adjoining one of the city's first residential squares, has buildings dating from the late 15th century. Dark-suited lawyers carry bundles of briefs between their offices here and the Neo-Gothic Law Courts. Nearby is the Temple, another historic legal district with a famous 13th-century round church.

① ★ Sir John Soane's Museum
The Georgian architect made this his London home and left it, with his collection, to the nation.

To Kingsway

LINCOLN'S INN FIELDS

③ ★ Lincoln's Inn Fields
The mock-Tudor archway, leading to Lincoln's Inn and built in 1845, overlooks the Fields.

Lincoln's Inn

PORTSMOUTH ST

PORTUGAL STREET

④ Old Curiosity Shop
This is a rare 16th-century, pre-Great Fire building which is now a shop.

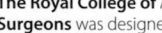

The Royal College of Surgeons was designed in 1836 by Sir Charles Barry. Inside there are laboratories for research and teaching as well as a museum of anatomical specimens.

Key

— Suggested route

0 metres	100
0 yards	100

Twinings has been selling tea here since 1706. The doorway dates from 1787 when the shop (216 Strand) was called the Golden Lion.

The Gladstone Statue was erected in 1905 to commemorate William Gladstone, the Victorian statesman who was Prime Minister four times.

2 ★ Lincoln's Inn
The Court of Chancery sat here, in Old Hall, from 1835 until 1858. Sir John Taylor Coleridge, nephew of the poet, was a well-known judge of the time.

Locator Map
See Central London Map pp16–17

7 Royal Courts of Justice
The country's main court for civil cases and appeals was built in 1882. It is made out of 35 million bricks faced with Portland stone.

5 Law Society
Look for the gold lions on the railings of this superb building.

9 Fleet Street
For two centuries this was the centre of the national press. Today the newspaper offices are gone.

El Vino is a venerable wine bar, where journalists still mingle with lawyers.

10 Prince Henry's Room
There is an authentic 17th-century room in this former gatehouse.

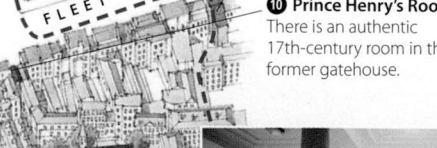

6 St Clement Danes
Designed by Wren (1679), it is the Royal Air Force church.

8 Temple Bar Memorial
A dragon marks where the City of London meets Westminster.

11 ★ Temple
It was built for the Knights Templar in the 13th century, but today lawyers stroll here.

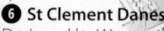

❷ Lincoln's Inn

WC2. **Map** 14 D1. **Tel** 020 7405 1393.
🚇 Holborn, Chancery Lane.
Open Chapel: 9am–5pm Mon–Fri.
Other buildings: check website.
♿ ⬤ 1st Fri of month, 2pm.
🌐 **lincolnsinn.org.uk**

Some of the buildings in
Lincoln's Inn, the best-preserved
of London's Inns of Court, go
back to the late 15th century.
The coat of arms above the arch
of the Chancery Lane gatehouse
is Henry VIII's, and the heavy oak
door is of the same vintage.
Shakespeare's contemporary,
Ben Jonson, is believed to have
laid some of the bricks of
Lincoln's Inn during the reign of
Elizabeth I. The chapel is early
17th-century Gothic. Women
were not allowed to be buried
here until 1839, when the
grieving Lord Brougham
petitioned to have the rule
changed so that his beloved
daughter could be interred in
the chapel, to wait for him
to join her.
   Lincoln's Inn has its share
of famous alumni. Oliver
Cromwell and John Donne,

The interior of the chapel in the grounds of Lincoln's Inn

❶ Sir John Soane's Museum

13 Lincoln's Inn Fields WC2. **Map** 14 D1.
Tel 0207 405 2107. 🚇 Holborn.
Open 10am–5pm Tue–Sat, 6–9pm
first Tue of month. **Closed** Sun, Mon,
bank hols & Christmas Eve. ♿ limited –
phone first. 📷 11:30am Tue & Fri,
3:30pm Wed & Thu, 11am Sat; groups
book ahead. 📷 🌐 **soane.org**

One of the most surprising
museums in London, this house
was left to the nation by Sir
John Soane in 1837, with a far-
sighted stipulation that nothing
at all should be changed. One
of Britain's leading 19th-century
architects, Soane was responsible
for designing Dulwich Picture
Gallery, still the most influential
top-lit gallery. The son of a
bricklayer, he prudently married
the niece of a wealthy builder,
whose fortune he inherited. He
bought and reconstructed No.
12 Lincoln's Inn Fields, then No.
13, which he and his wife moved
into in 1813, and later, in 1823–4,

he rebuilt No. 14, extending his
museum into the rear of this
building. Today, the collections
are much as Soane left them – an
eclectic gathering of beautiful,
peculiar and instructional objects.
   The building itself abounds
with architectural surprises and
illusions. In the main ground
floor room, with its deep red
and green colouring, cunningly
placed mirrors play tricks with
light and space. The picture
gallery is lined with layers of
folding panels to increase its
capacity. The panels open out
to reveal galleried extensions to
the room itself. Among other
works here are many of Soane's
own exotic designs, including
those for Pitzhanger Manor (see
p260) and the Bank of England
(see p149). Here also is William
Hogarth's *Rake's Progress* series.
   In the centre of the basement,
an atrium stretches up to the
roof. A glass dome lights
galleries, on every floor, that are
laden with Classical statuary.

A glass dome allows light
into the basement.

A vast sarcophagus
(1300 BC) stands on the
floor of the basement.

the 17th-century poet, were both students here, as was William Penn, founder of the US state of Pennsylvania.

❸ Lincoln's Inn Fields

WC2. **Map** 14 D1. ⊖ Holborn. **Open** dawn–dusk daily. Public tennis courts.

This used to be a public execution site. Under the Tudors and the Stuarts, many religious martyrs, and those suspected of treachery to the Crown, perished here.

When the developer William Newton wanted to build here in the 1640s, students at Lincoln's Inn and other residents made him undertake that the land in the centre would remain a public area forever. Thanks to this early protest, lawyers today play tennis here throughout the summer, or read their briefs in the fresh air. For some years, it has also been the site of an evening soup kitchen for some of London's homeless.

Old Curiosity Shop sign

❹ Old Curiosity Shop

13–14 Portsmouth St WC2. **Map** 14 D1. ⊖ Holborn.

Whether it is or is not the original for Charles Dickens's novel of the same name, this is a genuine 16th-century building and almost certainly the oldest shop in central London. With its overhanging first floor, it gives a rare impression of a London streetscape from before the Great Fire of 1666. The Old Curiosity Shop maintains its retailing tradition, and currently

operates as a handmade shoe shop. A preservation order guarantees the building's long-term future.

❺ Law Society

113 Chancery Lane WC2. **Map** 14 E1. **Tel** 020 7242 1222. ⊖ Chancery Lane. **Closed** to the public.

The headquarters of the solicitors' professional body is, architecturally, one of the most interesting buildings in the legal quarter. The main part, dominated by four Ionic columns, was completed in 1832. More significant is the northern extension, an early work of Charles Holden, an Arts and Crafts enthusiast who later made his name as a designer of London Underground stations. In his window arches the four seated figures depict truth, justice, liberty and mercy.

The building is on the corner of Carey Street, the site of the bankruptcy court whose name, corrupted to "Queer Street", entered the language to describe a state of destitution.

Every wall is covered, and every room filled, with artifacts from Soane's massive collection.

In the picture gallery, panels covered with paintings unfold to reveal more works of art behind them.

The Monk's Parlour is full of grotesque, Gothic casts.

❻ St Clement Danes

Strand WC2. **Map** 14 D2. **Tel** 020 7242 8282. Temple. **Open** 9am–4pm daily. **Closed** noon 25–27 Dec, public hols. 12:30am Wed & Fri, 11am Sun. *See Ceremonies p57.* **raf. mod.uk/stclementdanes**

Christopher Wren designed this wonderful church in 1680. Its name derives from an earlier church built here by the descendants of Danish invaders whom Alfred the Great had allowed to remain in London in the 9th century. From the 17th to 19th centuries many people were buried here, and their restplates are now in the crypt. The chain now hanging on the crypt wall was probably used to secure coffin lids against body snatchers who stole fresh corpses and sold them to the teaching hospitals.

St Clement Danes sits proudly isolated on a traffic island. It is now the Royal Air Force (RAF) church, and the interior is dominated by RAF

Clock at the Victorian law courts

symbols, memorials and monuments. Outside, to the east, is a statue (1910) of Dr Johnson *(see p142)*, who often came to services here. The church bells ring to the tune of the English nursery rhyme "Oranges and Lemons" at 9am, noon, 3pm and 6pm Mon–Sat, and there is an oranges and lemons service each March.

❼ Royal Courts of Justice (the Law Courts)

Strand WC2. **Map** 14 D2. **Tel** 020 7947 6000. Holborn, Temple, Chancery Lane. **Open** 9am–4:30pm Mon–Fri. **Closed** public hols. call ahead 077 8975 1248. **justice. gov.uk/courts**

Knots of demonstrators and television cameras can often be seen outside this sprawling and fanciful Victorian Gothic building, waiting for the result of a contentious case. These are the nation's main civil courts, dealing with such matters as divorce, libel, civil liability and appeals. Criminals are dealt with at the Old Bailey *(see p149)*, ten minutes' walk to the east. The public are admitted to all the court rooms and a list tells you which case is being heard in which court. The massive Gothic building was completed in 1882. It is said to contain 1,000 rooms and 5.6 km (3.5 miles) of corridors.

❽ Temple Bar Memorial

Fleet St EC4. **Map** 14 D2. Holborn, Temple, Chancery Lane.

The monument in the middle of Fleet Street, outside the Law Courts, dates from 1880 and marks the entrance to the City of London. On state occasions it is a long-standing tradition for the monarch to pause here and ask permission of the Lord Mayor to enter. Temple Bar, a huge archway designed by Wren, used to stand here. You can see what it used to look like from one of the four reliefs that surround the base of the present monument.

❾ Fleet Street

EC4. **Map** 14 E1. Temple, Blackfriars, St Paul's.

England's first printing press was set up here in the late 15th century by William Caxton's assistant, and Fleet Street has been a centre of London's

The dragon, symbol of the City, at the entrance to the City at Temple Bar

William Capon's engraving of Fleet Street in 1799

publishing industry ever since. Playwrights Shakespeare and Ben Jonson were patrons of the old Mitre tavern, now No. 37 Fleet Street. In 1702, the first newspaper, *The Daily Courant*, was issued from Fleet Street – conveniently placed for the City and Westminster, which were the main sources of news. Later the street became synonymous with the Press.

The printing presses underneath the newspaper offices were abandoned in 1987, when new technology made it easy to produce papers away from the centre of town in areas such as Wapping and the Docklands. Today the newspapers have left Fleet Street and the only remaining agency is the Commonwealth Broadcasting Association.

El Vino wine bar, at the western end opposite Fetter Lane, is a traditional haunt of journalists and lawyers.

Effigies in Temple Church

❿ Prince Henry's Room

17 Fleet St EC4. **Map** 14 E1.
🚇 Temple, Chancery Lane.
Closed currently but check website for news. 🌐 **cityoflondon.gov.uk**

The site itself can be traced back to the 12th century when it belonged to the Knights Templar, but this Fleet Street tavern is from 1610 and gets its name from the Prince of Wales's coat of arms and the initials PH in the ceiling, probably put there to mark the investiture as Prince of Wales of Henry, James I's eldest son who died before he became king.

The fine half-timbered front, alongside the gateway to Inner Temple, is original and so is some of the room's oak panelling.

⓫ Temple

Inner Temple, King's Bench Walk EC4. **Map** 14 E2. **Tel** 020 7797 8250. 🚇 Temple. **Open** 12:30–3pm Mon–Fri (grounds only). ♿ Middle Temple Hall, Middle Temple Lane EC4. **Tel** 020 7427 4800. **Open** 10–11:30am & 3–4pm Mon–Fri. **Closed** at short notice for functions. ♿ 📷 book ahead. ✉ Temple Church **Tel** 020 7353 8559. **Open** Wed–Fri; call for times & services. 🌐 **templechurch.com**

This embraces two of the four Inns of Court, the Middle Temple and the Inner Temple. (The other two are Lincoln's and Gray's Inns, *pp138* & *143*.) The name derives from the Knights Templar, a chivalrous order that used to protect pilgrims to the

Holy Land. The order was based here until it was suppressed by the Crown because its power was viewed as a threat. Initiations probably took place in the crypt of Temple Church and there are 13th-century effigies of Knights Templar in the nave.

Among some other ancient buildings is the Middle Temple Hall. Its fine Elizabethan interior survives – Shakespeare's *Twelfth Night* was performed here in 1601. Behind Temple, peaceful lawns stretch lazily down towards the Embankment.

⓬ St Bride's

Fleet St EC4. **Map** 14 F2. **Tel** 020 7427 0133. 🚇 Blackfriars. **Open** 9am–6pm Mon–Fri, 10am–6:30pm Sun (hours vary Sat). **Closed** public hols. ♿ 📷 🎵 11am & 6:30pm Sun. 🎵 Concerts check website for details. 🌐 **stbrides.com**

St Bride's is one of Wren's best-loved churches. Its position just off Fleet Street has made it the traditional venue for memorial services to departed journalists. Wall plaques commemorate Fleet Street journalists and printers.

The marvellous octagonal layered spire has been the model for tiered wedding cakes since shortly after it was added in 1703. Bombed in 1940, the interior was faithfully restored after World War II. The fascinating crypt contains remnants of earlier churches on the site, and a section of Roman pavement.

St Bride's, church of the Press

⓭ Ye Olde Cheshire Cheese

145 Fleet St EC4. **Map** 14 E1.
Tel 020 7353 6170. ⊖ Blackfriars.
Open 11am–11pm Mon–Fri,
noon–11pm Sat, noon–7pm Sun.
See Pubs and Bars pp308–11.

There has been an inn here for
centuries; parts of this building
date back to 1667, when the
Cheshire Cheese was rebuilt
after the Great Fire. The diarist
Samuel Pepys often drank here
in the 17th century, but it was
Dr Samuel Johnson's association
with "the Cheese" that made
it a place of pilgrimage for
19th-century literati. These
included novelists Mark Twain
and Charles Dickens.

This is one of the few pubs
to have kept the 18th-century
arrangement of small rooms
with fireplaces, tables and
benches, instead of knocking
them into larger bars.

⓮ Dr Johnson's House

17 Gough Sq EC4. **Map** 14 E1.
Tel 020 7353 3745. ⊖ Blackfriars,
Chancery Lane, Temple. **Open** May–
Sep: 11am–5:30pm Mon–Sat; Oct–
Apr: 11am–5pm Mon–Sat.
Closed 24 Dec–3 Jan & public hols.
📷 🎫 book ahead. 📱
w drjohnsonshouse.org

Dr Samuel Johnson was an
18th-century scholar famous
for the many witty (and often
contentious) remarks that his
biographer, James Boswell,
recorded and published.

Schoolgirl figure mounted on the façade of
St Andrew church

Johnson lived here from 1748
to 1759. He compiled the first
definitive English dictionary
(1755) in the attic, where six
scribes and assistants stood all
day at high desks.

The house, built before
1700, is furnished with
18th-century pieces and a small
collection of exhibits relating to
Johnson and the times in which
he lived. These include a tea set
belonging to his friend Mrs
Thrale and pictures of Johnson
and his contemporaries. It also
houses replica Georgian
costumes for children to try on.

⓯ St Andrew, Holborn

5 St Andrew St EC4. **Map** 14 E1.
Tel 020 7583 7394. ⊖ Chancery Lane.
Open 8:30am–5pm Mon–Fri. 📷 ♿
w standrewholborn.org.uk

The medieval church here
survived the Great Fire of 1666.
In 1686, Christopher Wren was,
however, asked to redesign it,
and the lower part of the tower
is virtually all that remains of the
earlier church. One of Wren's
most spacious churches, it was
gutted during World War II but
faithfully restored as the church
of the London trade guilds.
Benjamin Disraeli, the Jewish-
born Prime Minister, was
baptized here in 1817, at the
age of 12. In the 19th century,
a charity school was attached
to the church.

Civic symbol on Holborn Viaduct

⓰ Holborn Viaduct

EC1. **Map** 14 F1. ⊖ Farringdon, St
Paul's, Chancery Lane.

This piece of Victorian ironwork
was erected in the 1860s as part
of a much-needed traffic scheme.
It is best seen from Farringdon
Street, which is linked to the
bridge by a staircase. Climb up
and see the statues of City
heroes and bronze images of
Commerce, Agriculture, Science
and Fine Arts.

⓱ St Etheldreda's Chapel

14 Ely Place EC1. **Map** 6 E5.
Tel 020 7405 1061. ⊖ Farringdon.
Open 8am–5pm Mon–Sat, 8am–
12:30pm Sun. 📷 📱 noon–2pm.
w stetheldreda.com

This is a rare 13th-century
survivor, the chapel and crypt
of Ely House, where the
Bishops of Ely lived until the

Reconstructed interior of Dr Johnson's house

Reformation. Then it was acquired by an Elizabethan courtier, Sir Christopher Hatton, whose descendants demolished the house but kept the chapel and turned it into a Protestant church. It passed through various hands and, in 1874, reverted to the Catholic faith.

🔞 Hatton Garden

EC1. **Map** 6 E5. 🚇 Chancery Lane, Farringdon.

Built on land that used to be the garden of Hatton House, this is London's diamond and jewellery district. Gems ranging from the priceless to the mundane are traded from scores of small shops with sparkling window displays, and even from the pavements. The city's only pawn-broker is here – look for its traditional sign of three brass balls above the door.

🔞 Staple Inn

Holborn WC1. **Map** 14 E1. 🚇 Chancery Lane. Courtyard **Open** 9am–5pm Mon–Fri.

This building was once the wool staple, where wool was weighed and taxed. The frontage overlooks Holborn and is the only real example of Elizabethan half-timbering left in central London. Although now much restored, it would still be recognizable by someone who had known it in 1586, when it was built. The shops at street level have the feel of the 19th century, and there are some 18th-century buildings in the courtyard.

🔞 London Silver Vaults

53–64 Chancery Lane WC2. **Map** 14 D1. **Tel** 020 7242 3844. 🚇 Chancery Lane, Holborn. **Open** 9am–5:30pm Mon–Fri, 9am–1pm Sat. 🌐 **thesilvervaults.com**

These silver vaults originate from the Chancery Lane Safe Deposit Company, established in 1885. After descending a staircase you pass through

Staple Inn, a survivor from 1586

steel security doors and reach a nest of underground shops sparkling with antique and modern silverware. London silver makers have been renowned for centuries, reaching their peak in the Georgian era. The best examples sell for many thousands of pounds but most shops also offer modest pieces at realistic prices.

Coffee pot (1716): Silver Vaults

🔞 Gray's Inn

Gray's Inn Rd WC1. **Map** 6 D5. **Tel** 020 7458 7800. 🚇 Chancery Lane, Holborn. Grounds **Open** noon–2:30pm Mon–Fri. ♿ 🖥️

This ancient legal centre and law school goes back to the 14th century. Like many of the buildings in this area, it was badly damaged by World War II bombs but much of it has been rebuilt. At least one of Shakespeare's plays (*A Comedy of Errors*) was first performed in Gray's Inn hall in 1594. The hall's 16th-century interior screen still survives.

More recently, the young Charles Dickens was employed as a clerk here in 1827–8. Today the garden, once a convenient site for staging duels, is open to lunchtime strollers for part of the year, and typifies the cloistered calm of the four Inns of Court. The buildings may be visited only by prior arrangement.

THE CITY

London's financial district is built on the site of the original Roman settlement. Its full title is the City of London, but it is usually referred to as the City. Most traces of the early City were obliterated by the Great Fire of 1666 and World War II (see pp26–7, 35). Today glossy modern offices stand among a plethora of banks, with marbled halls and stately pillars. It is the contrast between dour, warren-like Victorian buildings and shiny new ones that gives the City its distinctive character. Though it hums with activity in business hours, few people have lived here since the 19th century, when it was one of London's main residential centres. Today only the churches, many of them by Christopher Wren (see p49), are a reminder of those past times.

Sights at a Glance

Historic Streets and Buildings
1 Mansion House
3 Royal Exchange
7 Old Bailey
8 Apothecaries' Hall
9 Fishmongers' Hall
16 Tower of London pp156–9
17 Tower Bridge
19 Stock Exchange
23 Lloyd's of London

Museums and Galleries
4 Bank of England Museum
24 Guildhall Art Gallery

Historic Markets
12 Old Billingsgate
22 Leadenhall Market

Monuments
11 Monument

Churches and Cathedrals
2 St Stephen Walbrook
5 St Mary-le-Bow
6 St Paul's Cathedral pp150–53
10 St Magnus the Martyr
13 St Mary-at-Hill
14 St Margaret Pattens
15 All Hallows by the Tower
20 St Helen's Bishopsgate
21 St Katharine Cree

Docks
18 St Katharine's Dock

☐ **Restaurants** see pp298–300
1 Goodman
2 Haz
3 The Restaurant at St Paul's Cathedral
4 Sauterelle

0 metres		500
0 yards		500

Street Finder, maps 14, 15, 16

◀ South side view of St Paul's Cathedral with its impressive dome

For keys to symbols see back flap

Street-by-Street: The City

This is the business centre of London, home to vast financial institutions such as the Stock Exchange and the Bank of England. But in contrast to these 19th- and 20th-century buildings are the older survivors. A walk through the City is in part a pilgrimage through the architectural visions of Christopher Wren, England's most sublime and probably most prolific architect. After the Great Fire of 1666 he supervised the rebuilding of 52 churches within the area, and enough survive to testify to his genius.

⑤ St Mary-le-Bow
Anyone born within earshot of the bells of this Wren church (the historic Bow Bells) is said to be a true Londoner or Cockney.

St Paul's station

Mansion House station

NEW CHANGE

ST PAUL'S CHURCHYARD

WATLING STREET

BREAD STREET

CANNON STREET

FRIDAY ST

QUEEN VICTOR

St Nicholas Cole Abbey was the first church Wren built in the City (in 1677). Like many others, it had to be restored after World War II bomb damage.

St James Garlickhythe contains unusual sword rests and hat stands, beneath Wren's elegant spire of 1717.

COLLEGE · OF · ARMS

The College of Arms received its royal charter in 1484 from Richard III. Still active today, it assesses who has a legitimate claim to a British family coat of arms.

⑥ ★ St Paul's
Wren's masterpiece still dominates the City skyline.

Key
— Suggested route

| 0 metres | 100 |
| 0 yards | 100 |

1 Mansion House
The official home of the City of London's Lord Mayor contains a small prison.

4 ★ Bank of England Museum
The intriguing story of England's financial system is vividly displayed here.

Bank station

Locator Map
See Central London Map pp16–17

SMITHFIELD & SPITALFIELDS

THE CITY

Thames

SOUTHWARK & BANKSIDE

KING ST

IRONMONGER LANE

OLD JEWRY

PRINCE'S STREET

THREADNEEDLE STREET

CORNHILL

LOMBARD ST

STREET

WALBROOK

ST SWITHIN'S

KING WILLIAM STREET

CANNON STREET

3 Royal Exchange
Since its foundation in Tudor times, this has been at the heart of London's commerce.

Lombard Street is named after Italian bankers who settled here from Lombardy in the 13th century. It is still a banking centre.

St Mary Woolnoth is a characteristically powerful work by Wren's pupil, Nicholas Hawksmoor.

St Mary Abchurch owes its unusually spacious feel to Wren's large dome. The altar carving is by Grinling Gibbons.

2 ★ St Stephen Walbrook
Experimenting for St Paul's, Wren created its unique dome. The interior contains original features, such as this font.

Skinners' Hall is the Italianate 18th-century guild hall for the leather trade.

❶ Mansion House

Walbrook EC4. **Map** 15 B2. **Tel** 020 7626 2500. Bank, Mansion House. **Open** to group tours only by appt or 2pm Tue on first-come-first-served basis. 1:45pm Tue (near the entrance). **cityoflondon.gov.uk**

The official residence of the Lord Mayor, it was completed in 1753 to the design of George Dance the Elder, whose work is now in John Soane's Museum *(see pp138–9)*. The Palladian front with its six Corinthian columns is one of the most familiar City landmarks. The state rooms have a dignity appropriate to the office of mayor, one of the most spectacular being the 27-m (90-ft) Egyptian Hall.

Formerly located here, and now in the Museum of London *(see pp168–9)*, were 11 holding cells, a reminder of the building's other function as a magistrate's court; the Mayor is chief magistrate of the City during his year of office. Emmeline Pankhurst, who campaigned for women's suffrage in the early 20th century, was once held here.

Egyptian Hall in Mansion House

❷ St Stephen Walbrook

39 Walbrook EC4. **Map** 15 B2. **Tel** 020 7626 9000. Bank, Cannon St. **Open** 10am–4pm Mon–Fri. 12:45pm Thu, sung Mass. Organ recitals 12:30pm Fri. **ststephenwalbrook.net**

The Lord Mayor's parish church was built by Christopher Wren in 1672–9. Architectural writers consider it to be the finest of his City churches *(see p49)*. The deep, coffered dome, with its ornate plasterwork, was a forerunner of St Paul's. St Stephen's airy columned interior comes as a surprise after its plain exterior. The font cover and pulpit canopy are decorated with exquisite carved figures that contrast strongly with the stark simplicity of Henry Moore's massive white stone altar (1987).

However, perhaps the most moving monument of all is a telephone in a glass box. This is a tribute to Rector Chad Varah who, in 1953, founded the Samaritans, a voluntarily staffed telephone helpline for people in emotional need.

The church is also the home of the London Internet Church, which brings together people from all over the world to worship and discuss Christianity.

The spire was added in 1717.

The dome makes this small church light and airy.

Wren's original altar and screen are still here.

Wren's pulpit has a delicate canopy.

Henry Moore's polished stone altar was added in 1987.

❸ Royal Exchange

EC3. **Map** 15 C2. **Tel** 020 7623 0444. 🔄 Bank. Shopping centre **Open** 10am–6pm daily.

Sir Thomas Gresham, the Elizabethan merchant and courtier, founded the Royal Exchange in 1565 as a centre for commerce of all kinds. The original building was centred on a vast courtyard where merchants and tradesmen did business. Queen Elizabeth I gave it its Royal title and it is still one of the sites from which new kings and queens are announced. Dating from 1844, this is the third splendid building on the site since Gresham's.

The building now contains a luxurious shopping centre with such designer stores as Cartier, Hermès and Paul Smith.

The façade of William Tite's Royal Exchange of 1844

The Duke of Wellington (1884) opposite the Bank of England

❹ Bank of England Museum

Bartholomew Lane EC2. **Map** 15 B1. **Tel** 020 7601 5545. 🔄 Bank. **Open** 10am–5pm Mon–Fri, Lord Mayor's Show (*p57*). **Closed** public hols. 🔄 phone first. 📷 📽 Films, lectures. 🆆 **bankofengland.co.uk/education/museum**

The Bank of England was set up in 1694 to raise money for foreign wars. It grew to become Britain's central bank, and also issues currency notes. Sir John Soane (*see pp138–9*) was the architect of the 1788 bank building on this site, but only the exterior wall of his design has survived. The rest was destroyed in the 1920s and 1930s when the Bank was enlarged. There is now a reconstruction of Soane's stock office of 1793.

Glittering gold bars, silver plated decoration and a Roman mosaic floor, discovered during the rebuilding, are among the items on display. The museum illustrates the work of the Bank and the financial system. The gift shop sells paperweights, which are made out of used banknotes.

❺ St Mary-le-Bow

(Bow Church) Cheapside EC2. **Map** 15 A2. **Tel** 020 7248 5139. 🔄 St Paul's, Mansion Hse. **Open** 7:30am–6pm Mon–Wed, 7:30am–6:30pm Thu, 7:30am–4pm Fri. 🔔 weekdays (see website for details). 🔄 by arrangement. ♿ 🚻 🆆 **stmarylebow.co.uk**

The church takes its name from the bow arches in the Norman crypt. When Wren rebuilt the church (in 1670–80) after the Great Fire, he continued this pattern through the arches on the steeple. The weathervane, dating from 1674, is an enormous dragon.

The church was bombed in 1941 leaving only the steeple and two outer walls standing. It was restored in 1956–62 when the bells were recast and rehung. Bow bells are important to Londoners; traditionally only those born within their sound can claim to be true Cockneys.

❻ St Paul's

See pp150–53.

❼ Old Bailey

EC4. **Map** 14 F1. **Tel** 020 7248 3277. 🔄 St Paul's. **Open** 10am–1pm & 2–5pm Mon–Fri (but opening hours vary from court to court). **Closed** Easter, Christmas, New Year, public hols. 📷 🆆 **cityoflondon.gov.uk**

This short street has a long association with crime and punishment. The new Central Criminal Courts opened here in 1907 on the site of the notorious and malodorous Newgate prison (on special days in the legal calendar judges still carry small posies to court as a reminder of those times). Across the road, the Magpie and Stump served "execution breakfasts" until 1868, when mass public hangings outside the prison gates were stopped.

Today, when the courts are in session, they are open to members of the public.

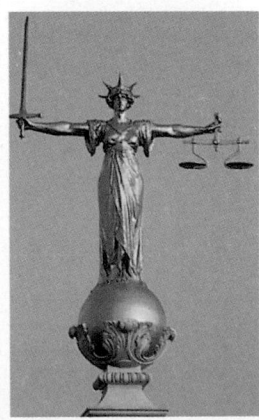
Old Bailey's rooftop Justice

⑥ St Paul's Cathedral

Following the Great Fire of London in 1666, the medieval cathedral of St Paul's was left in ruins. The authorities turned to Christopher Wren to rebuild it, but his ideas met with considerable resistance from the conservative Dean and Chapter. Wren's 1672 Great Model plan was not at all popular with them, and so a watered-down plan was finally agreed in 1675. Wren's determination paid off though, as can be witnessed from the grandeur of the present cathedral.

Stone urn outside
the South Transept

Queen Anne's Statue
An 1886 copy of Francis Bird's 1712 original now stands on the forecourt.

KEY

① **The West Porch**, approached from Ludgate Hill, is the main entrance to St Paul's.

② **The West Portico** comprises two tiers of columns rather than the single colonnade that Wren intended.

③ **The pediment** carvings, dating from 1706, show the Conversion of St Paul.

④ **The balustrade** along the top was added in 1718 against Wren's wishes.

⑤ **The lantern** weighs a massive 850 tonnes.

⑥ **The golden gallery** lies at the highest point of the dome.

⑦ **The brick cone** located inside the outer dome supports the heavy lantern.

⑧ **The oculus** is an opening through which the lantern can be seen.

⑨ **The stone gallery** offers a splendid view over London.

⑩ **The Upper screen wall** masks the flying buttresses.

⑪ **Flying buttresses** support the nave walls and the dome.

⑫ **The North and South Transepts** cross the nave in a medieval style that contrasts with Wren's original plan (see p152).

★ **The West Front and Towers**
The towers were not on Wren's original plan – he added them in 1707, when he was 75 years old. Both were designed to have clocks.

Main Entrance

★ **The Dome**
At 110 m (360 ft) high, the dome at St Paul's is the second biggest in the world after St Peter's in Rome, as spectacular from inside as outside.

VISITORS' CHECKLIST

Practical Information
Ludgate Hill EC4.
Map 15 A2.
Tel 020 7246 8357.
w stpauls.co.uk
Cathedral **Open** 8:30am–4pm Mon–Sat.
Galleries **Open** 9:30am–4:15pm Mon–Sat. Crypt & ambulatory **Open** 9:15am–4:15pm Mon–Sat.
Closed for sightseeing on Sun.
🚻 ✝ times vary. 🚾 📷 🎧 📱
📷 ♿ Concerts.

Transport
🚇 St Paul's, Mansion House.
🚌 6, 8, 11, 15, 22, 23, 25, 76.
🚆 City Thameslink.

★ **Whispering Gallery**
The unusual acoustics here cause whispers to echo around the dome.

South Porch
Wren took the idea of a semi-circular porch from a Baroque church in Rome.

604 Bishop Mellitus built the first St Paul's. It burned down in 1087

Detail on Tijou gate (see p153).

1666 St Paul's reduced to a burnt ruin after the Great Fire

1708 Wren's son Christopher lays the last stone on the lantern

2011 Extensive restorations finished

600	800	1000	1200	1400	1600	1800	2000

1087 Bishop Maurice began Old St Paul's: a Norman cathedral of stone

1675 Foundation stone of Wren's design laid

1940–1 Slight bomb damage to the cathedral

1981 Prince Charles marries Lady Diana Spencer

A Guided Tour of St Paul's

Visitors to St Paul's will be immediately impressed by its cool, beautifully ordered and extremely spacious interior. The nave, transepts and choir are arranged in the shape of a cross, as in a medieval cathedral, but Wren's Classical vision shines through this conservative floor plan, forced on him by the cathedral authorities. Aided by some of the finest craftsmen of his day, he created an interior of grand majesty and Baroque splendour, a worthy setting for the many great ceremonial events that have taken place here. These include the funeral of Winston Churchill in 1965 and the wedding of Prince Charles and Lady Diana Spencer in 1981.

The mosaics on the choir ceiling were completed in the 1890s by William Richmond.

② The North Aisle
As you walk along the North Aisle, look above: the aisles are vaulted with small domes mimicking those of the nave ceiling.

Key

— Tour route

① The Nave
Take in the full glory of the massive arches and the succession of saucer domes that open out into a huge space below the main dome.

⑨ South Aisle
From here the brave can ascend the 259 steps to the Whispering Gallery and test the acoustics.

Entrance to Whispering Gallery

Main entrances

The Geometrical Staircase is a spiral of 92 stone steps giving access to the cathedral library.

⑧ Florence Nightingale's Memorial
Famous for her pioneering work in nursing standards, Florence Nightingale was the first woman to receive the Order of Merit.

⑦ Wren's Tomb
Wren's burial place is marked by a slab. The inscription states: "Reader, if you seek a monument, look around you."

③ The Crossing
The climax of Wren's interior is this great open space. The vast dome is decorated with monochrome frescoes by Sir James Thornhill, the leading architectural painter of Wren's time.

Entrance to crypt

④ The Quire
Jean Tijou, a Huguenot refugee, created much of the cathedral's fine wrought ironwork, such as these screens in the quire aisles.

John Donne's memorial, from 1631, was the only monument to survive the Great Fire of 1666 intact. The poet posed for it in his lifetime.

⑤ The High Altar
The canopy over the altar was replaced after World War II. It is based on Wren's original Baroque drawings.

Grinling Gibbons's work can be found on the choir stalls, with typically intricate carvings of cherubs, fruits and garlands.

T E Lawrence, or Lawrence of Arabia, the British World War I hero who earned his nickname by fighting alongside Arab tribes in their resistance to Turkish rule in 1915, is commemorated by this bust in the crypt.

⑥ The Crypt
The tombs of famous figures and such popular heroes as Lord Nelson, can be seen in the crypt.

Apothecaries' Hall, rebuilt in 1670

❽ Apothecaries' Hall

Blackfriars Lane EC4. **Map** 14 F2.
Tel 020 7236 1189. 🚇 Blackfriars.
Courtyard **Open** 9am–5pm Mon–Fri.
Closed public hols, end Aug. Phone
Hall for appt to visit (groups only). ♿

London has had livery
companies, or guilds, to protect
and regulate specific trades
since early medieval times.
The Apothecaries' Society was
founded in 1617 for those who
prepared, prescribed or sold
drugs. It has some surprising
alumni, including Oliver Cromwell
and the poet John Keats.
Now nearly all the members
are physicians or surgeons.

❾ Fishmongers' Hall

London Bridge EC4. **Map** 15 B3.
Tel 020 7626 3531. 🚇 Monument.
Closed to the public. Limited tours by
appt only. 🌐 fishhall.org.uk

This is one of the oldest livery
companies, established in
1272. Lord Mayor Walworth,
a member of the Fishmongers'
Company, killed Wat Tyler,
leader of the Peasants' Revolt,
in 1381 (see p164).
Today it still fulfils its original
role; all the fish sold in the
City must be inspected by
Company officials.

❿ St Magnus the Martyr

Lower Thames St EC3. **Map** 15 C3.
Tel 020 7626 4481. 🚇 Monument.
Open 10am–4pm Tue–Fri.
🕐 12:30pm Tue–Fri, 11am Sun. ♿
🌐 stmagnusmartyr. org.uk

There has been a church here
for over 1,000 years. Its patron
saint, St Magnus, Earl of the
Orkney Islands and a renowned

Norwegian Christian leader,
was brutally murdered in 1116.
When Christopher Wren built
this church in 1671–6, it was at
the foot of old London Bridge,
until 1738 the only bridge across
the River Thames in London.
Anyone going south from the
city would have passed under
Wren's magnificent arched porch
spanning the flagstones leading
to the old bridge.
Highlights of St Magnus the
Martyr include the carved
musical instruments that decorate
the organ case. Wren's pulpit,
with its slender supporting
stem, was restored in 1924.

⓫ Monument

Monument St EC3. **Map** 15 C2.
Tel 020 7626 2717. 🚇 Monument.
Open 9:30am–5:30pm daily (6pm in
summer). **Closed** 1 Jan, 24–26 Dec.
📷 🌐 themonument.info

The column designed by
Christopher Wren to
commemorate the Great Fire
of London, which devastated
the original walled city in
September 1666, is the tallest
isolated stone column in the
world. It is 62 m (205 ft) high
and is said to be 62 m west
of where the fire started in
Pudding Lane. It was sited on
the direct approach to old
London Bridge, which was a
few steps downstream from
the present one. Reliefs around
the column's base show Charles

The altar of St Magnus the Martyr

II restoring the city. The 311
steps to the top lead to a
viewing platform. In 1842, this
was enclosed with railings
after a suicide. The views
are spectacular.

Fish weathervane at Billingsgate

⓬ Old Billingsgate

Lower Thames St EC3. **Map** 15 C3.
🚇 Monument. **Closed** to the public.

London's main fish market was
based here for 900 years, on
one of the city's earliest quays.
During the 19th and early 20th
centuries, 400 tonnes of fish
were sold here every day,
much of it delivered by boat.
It was London's noisiest
market, renowned, even in
Shakespeare's day, for foul
language. In 1982, the market
moved from this building
(1877) to the Isle of Dogs.

⓭ St Mary-at-Hill

Lovat Lane EC3. **Map** 15 C2.
Tel 020 7626 4184. 🚇 Monument.
Open 11am–4pm Tue, Wed, Thu.
🕐 1pm Wed, 1:05pm Thu. Concerts.
🌐 stmary-at-hill.org

The interior and east end of
St Mary-at-Hill were Wren's first
church designs (1670–76).
The Greek cross design was
a prototype for his St Paul's
proposals. Ironically, the
delicate plasterwork and rich
17th-century fittings, which
had survived both the Victorian
mania for refurbishment and
the bombs of World War II,

were lost in a fire in 1988. The building was then restored to its original appearance, only to be damaged again by an IRA bomb in 1992.

⓮ St Margaret Pattens

Rood Lane and Eastcheap EC3. **Map** 15 C2. **Tel** 020 7623 6630. ⊖ Monument. **Open** 7:30am–6pm Mon–Fri. **Closed** Christmas week. 🕇 1:05pm Thu. Concerts and recitals. 🚻 🖵 **stmargaretpattens.org**

Wren's church of 1684–7 was named after a type of overshoe made near here. Its rendered brickwork and Portland stone contrast with the Georgian stucco shopfront in the forecourt. It retains 17th-century canopied pews and an ornate font.

⓯ All Hallows by the Tower

Byward St EC3. **Map** 16 D3. **Tel** 020 7481 2928. ⊖ Tower Hill. **Open** 8am–5pm Mon–Fri, 10am–5pm Sat, 10am–1pm Sun. **Closed** 26 Dec–2 Jan. 🕇 11am Sun. 🚻 🖵 must book ahead. 🚻 📷 📷 undercroft museum. 🖵 **allhallowsbythetower.org.uk**

The first church on this site was Saxon. The arch in the southwest corner, which contains Roman tiles, dates from that period, as do some crosses in the crypt. There is a Roman pavement in the crypt. William Penn, founder of Pennsylvania, was baptized here in 1644. Most of the interior has been altered, but a limewood font cover, carved by Grinling Gibbons in 1682, survives. John Quincy Adams married here in

Roman tile from All Hallows

1797 before he was US president. Samuel Pepys watched the Great Fire from the church tower. There are a small museum, brass rubbing centre, concerts and a bookstall.

⓰ Tower of London

See pp156–9.

⓱ Tower Bridge

SE1. **Map** 16 D3. **Tel** 020 7403 3761. ⊖ Tower Hill. The Tower Bridge Exhibition **Open** Apr–Sep: 10am–6pm daily; Oct–Mar: 9:30am–5:30pm daily (open from noon on Jan 1). **Closed** 24–26 Dec. 📷 🚻 🚻 📷 🖵 **towerbridge.org.uk**

Completed in 1894, this flamboyant piece of Victorian engineering quickly became a symbol of London. Its pinnacled towers and linking catwalk support the mechanism for raising the roadway when big ships have to pass through, or for special and historic occasions.

The bridge now houses The Tower Bridge Exhibition, with interactive displays bringing the bridge's history to life, river views from the catwalk and a close-up look at the steam engine which powered the lifting machinery until 1976, when the system was electrified.

The walkways, which are now open to the public, afford stunning views along the river.

There are nearly 300 stairs to the top of the towers.

The Victorian winding machinery was powered by steam until 1976.

When raised, the bridge is 40 m (135 ft) high and 60 m (200 ft) wide. In its heyday, it was opened five times a day.

⑯ Tower of London

For much of its 900-year history, the Tower was an object of fear. Those who had committed treason or threatened the throne were held within its dank walls. A lucky few lived in comparative comfort, but the majority had to put up with appalling conditions. Many did not get out alive, and some were tortured before meeting violent deaths on nearby Tower Hill.

"Beefeaters"
Thirty-seven Yeoman Warders guard the Tower and live here.

★ **The Jewel House**
The magnificent Crown Jewels are housed here *(see p158)*.

Queen's House
This is the official residence of the constables.

Main entrance

KEY

① **Beauchamp Tower** was used for high-ranking prisoners, who were often allowed to keep their own retinues of servants.

② **Tower Green** was where the aristocratic prisoners were executed, away from the ghoulish crowds on Tower Hill. But while only seven people died here – including two of Henry VIII's six wives – there were hundreds of public executions on Tower Hill.

③ **Wakefield Tower**, part of the Medieval Palace, has been carefully refurbished to match its original appearance in the 13th century.

④ **The Bloody Tower** is associated with the legend of the two princes and other deaths *(see p159)*.

The Ravens

The Tower's most celebrated residents are a small colony of ravens. It is not known when they first settled here, but there is a legend that should they desert the Tower, the kingdom will fall. In fact, the birds have part of their wings trimmed on the right side, making full flight impossible. The Ravenmaster, one of the Yeoman Warders, looks after the birds.

A memorial in the moat commemorates some of the ravens who have died at the Tower since the 1950s.

★ **The White Tower**
When it was finished, c.1097, it was the tallest building in London – 30 m (90 ft) high.

VISITORS' CHECKLIST

Practical Information
Tower Hill EC3.
Map 16 D3.
Tel 0844 482 7799 (info); 0870 756 7070 (advance booking).
Ⓦ hrp.org.uk
Docklands Light Railway Tower Gateway. **Open** Mar–Oct: 9am–5:30pm Tue–Sat, 10am–5:30pm Sun & Mon; Nov–Feb: 9am–4:30pm Tue–Sat, 10am–4:30pm Sun & Mon.
Closed 1 Jan, 24–26 Dec. 🐾 Ceremony of the Keys 9:30pm daily (book ahead). *See pp54–7.*
♿ 🖊 📷 🎧

Transport
🚇 Tower Hill. 🚌 RV1, 15, X15, 25, 42, 78, 100.
🚆 Fenchurch Street.

★ **Chapel of St John**
Stone for this austerely beautiful Romanesque chapel was brought from France.

Medieval Palace
This was created by Henry III in 1220. It was enlarged by his son, Edward I, who added Traitors' Gate.

★ **Traitors' Gate**
Prisoners, many on their way to die, entered the Tower by boat here.

1536 Anne Boleyn executed

1078 White Tower started

1483 Princes probably murdered in the Tower

1553–4 Lady Jane Grey held and executed

1810–15 Mint moves from the Tower and arms stop being manufactured here

1050	1250	1450	1650	1850	1950

1066 William I erects a temporary castle

1534–5 Thomas More imprisoned and executed

1671 "Colonel Blood" tries to steal Crown Jewels

1603–16 Walter Raleigh imprisoned in Tower

1834 Menagerie moves out of Tower

1941 Rudolf Hess is the last prisoner held in Queen's House

Inside the Tower

The Tower has been a tourist attraction since the reign of Charles II (1660–85), when both the Crown Jewels and the collection of armour were first shown to the public. They remain powerful reminders of royal might and wealth.

The Orb, symbolizing the power and Empire of Christ the Redeemer

The Crown Jewels

The Crown Jewels comprise the regalia of crowns, sceptres, orbs and swords used at coronations and other state occasions. They are impossible to price but their worth is irrelevant beside their enormous significance in the historical and religious life of the kingdom. Most of the Crown Jewels date from 1661, when a new set was made for the coronation of Charles II; Parliament had destroyed the previous crowns and sceptres after the execution of Charles I in 1649. Only a few pieces survived, hidden by the clergy of Westminster Abbey until the Restoration.

The Coronation Ceremony

Many elements in this solemn and mystical ceremony date from the days of Edward the Confessor. The king or queen proceeds to Westminster Abbey, accompanied by objects of the regalia, including the State Sword which represents the monarch's own sword. He or she is then anointed with holy oil, to signify divine approval, and invested with ornaments and royal robes. Each of the jewels represents an aspect of the monarch's role as head of the state and church. The climax comes when St Edward's Crown is placed on the sovereign's head; there is a cry of "God Save the King" (or Queen), the trumpets sound, and guns at the Tower are fired. The last coronation was Elizabeth II's in 1953.

The Imperial State Crown, containing more than 2,800 diamonds, 273 pearls as well as other gems

The crowns

There are ten crowns on display at the Tower. Many of these have not been worn for years, but the Imperial State Crown is in frequent use. The Queen wears it at the Opening of Parliament *(see p56)*. The crown was made in 1937 for George VI, and is similar to the one made for Queen Victoria. The sapphire set in the cross is said to have been worn in a ring by Edward the Confessor (ruled 1042–66).

The most recent crown is not at the Tower, however. It was made for Prince Charles's investiture as Prince of Wales at Caernarvon Castle in north Wales in 1969, and is kept at the Museum of Wales in Cardiff.

The Queen Mother's crown was made for the coronation of her husband, George VI, in 1937. It is the only one to be made out of platinum – all the other crowns on display at the Tower are made of gold.

Other regalia

Apart from the crowns, there are other pieces of the Crown Jewels that are essential to coronations. Among these are three Swords of Justice, symbolizing mercy, spiritual and temporal justice. The orb is a hollow gold sphere encrusted with jewels and weighing about 1.3 kg (3 lbs). The Sceptre with the Cross contains the biggest cut diamond in the world, the 530-carat First Star of Africa. The rough stone it comes from weighed 3,106 carats.

The Sovereign's Ring, sometimes referred to as "the wedding ring of England"

Plate Collection

The Jewel House also holds a collection of elaborate gold and silver plates. The Maundy Dish is still used on Maundy Thursday when the monarch distributes money to selected old people. The Exeter Salt (a very grand salt cellar from the days when salt was a valuable commodity) was given by the citizens of Exeter, in west England, to Charles II; during the 1640s' Civil War Exeter was a Royalist stronghold.

The Sceptre with the Cross (1660), rebuilt in 1910 after Edward VII was presented with the First Star of Africa diamond

The hilt and solid-gold scabbard of the jewelled State Sword, one of the most valuable swords in the world

The White Tower

This is the oldest surviving building in the Tower of London, begun by William I in 1075 and completed before 1079. For centuries it served as an armoury, and much of the national collection of arms and armour is held here. Fit for a King showcases 500 years of royal arms and armour, while Hands on History allows visitors literally to get to grips with items of weaponry.

The Power House exhibition tells the stories of what went on behind the Tower's walls from 1100 to the present day, and the personalities that lived here are brought to life.

The Royal Castle and Armour Gallery

These two chambers on the first floor were the main ceremonial rooms of the original Norman castle. The first one, to the east, is the smaller, probably an antechamber to the Banqueting Hall beyond, and contains exhibits setting out the history of the White Tower. It adjoins St John's Chapel, a rare surviving early Norman chapel virtually intact, a powerfully solid interior with little ornamentation. Originally the two main rooms were twice their present height; a pitched roof was removed in 1490 to allow extra floors to be built on top. Suits of armour from Tudor and Stuart times are here, including three made for Henry VIII, one covering his horse as well. A suit made in Holland for Charles I is decorated in gold leaf.

Japanese armour presented to James I in 1613

The Ordnance Gallery

This and the temporary exhibition gallery next door were chambers created in 1490 when the roof was raised. They were used chiefly for storage, and in 1603 a new floor was installed to allow gunpowder to be kept here; by 1667 some 10,000 barrels of it were stored in the Tower. Among the displays are gilt panels and ornament from the barge of the Master of the Ordnance built in 1700.

The Small Armoury and Crypt

The westerly room on the ground floor may originally have been a living area, and has traces of the oldest fireplaces known in England. Pistols, muskets, swords, pikes and bayonets are mounted on the walls and panels in elaborate symmetrical patterns based on displays in the Tower armouries in the 18th and 19th centuries. They were shown in the Grand Storehouse until it burned down in 1841. A collection of weapons taken from the men who planned to assassinate William III in 1696 is on show, and a wooden block made in 1747 for the execution of Lord Lovat – the last public beheading in England – is on the third floor. The crypt now houses a shop.

The Line of Kings

The Line of Kings, ten life-size carvings of prominent English Monarchs, wearing armour and seated on horseback, originated in Tudor times, when eight such figures adorned the royal palace at Greenwich. Two more had been added by the time they first appeared in the Tower in 1660, celebrating the Restoration of Charles II. In 1688, 17 new horses and heads were commissioned, some from the great carver Grinling Gibbons (the third from the left is reputed to be his work).

Henry VIII's armour (1540)

The Princes in the Tower

Now explored in a display in the Bloody Tower, one of the Tower's darkest mysteries concerns two boy princes, sons and heirs of Edward IV. They were put into the Tower by their uncle, Richard of Gloucester, when their father died in 1483. Neither was seen again and Richard was crowned later that year. In 1674, the skeletons of two children were found nearby.

The yacht haven of the restored St Katharine's Dock

⓲ St Katharine's Dock

E1. **Map** 16 E3. **Tel** 020 7264 5312.
🚇 Tower Hill. ♿ 🚻 🖥 🏠
🌐 **skdocks.co.uk**

This most central of all London's docks was designed by Thomas Telford and opened in 1828 on the site of St Katharine's hospital. Commodities as diverse as tea, marble and live turtles (turtle soup was a Victorian delicacy) were unloaded here.

During the 19th and early 20th centuries, the docks flourished, but by the mid-20th century, cargo ships were delivering their wares in massive containers. The old docks became too small and new ones had to be built downstream. St Katharine's closed in 1968.

St Katharine's is now one of London's most successful developments, with its commercial, residential and entertainment facilities, including a hotel and a yacht haven. Old warehouse buildings have shops and restaurants on their ground floors, and offices above.

On the north side of the dock is LIFFE Commodity Products, trading in commodities such as coffee, sugar and oil. There is no public gallery but, if you ask at the door, you may be able to look down from the glass-walled reception area on to the frenzied trading floors. The dock is worth wandering through after visiting the Tower or Tower Bridge *(see pp155–9)*.

⓳ Stock Exchange

Paternoster Sq EC4. **Map** 15 A1.
🚇 Bank, Farringdon.
Closed to the public.

The first Stock Exchange was established in Threadneedle Street in 1773 by a group of stockbrokers who previously met and did business in nearby City coffee houses. By the 19th century, the rules of exchange were laid down, and for a hundred years London's was the biggest stock exchange in the world. Nevertheless, the rise of the American and Japanese economies during the 20th century gradually challenged London's dominance.

In 1986, the deregulation of the UK market, known as the "Big Bang", resulted in the computerization of trades, making the trade floor redundant and setting London's financial markets on a course of rapid growth. Today London has reclaimed its position as the market of choice for companies around the world wishing to raise capital.

⓴ St Helen's Bishopsgate

Great St Helen's EC3. **Map** 15 C1.
Tel 020 7283 2231. 🚇 Liverpool St, Bank. **Open** 9:30am–12:30pm Mon–Fri; some afternoons (phone to check).
✝ 1pm Tue & Thu, 10:30am, 6pm Sun. ♿ 🌐 **st-helens.org.uk**

The curious appearance of this 13th-century church is due to its origins as two places of worship: one a parish church, the other the chapel of a long-gone nunnery next door. (The medieval nuns of St Helen's were notorious for their "secular kissing".)

Among its monuments is the tomb of Sir Thomas Gresham, who founded the Royal Exchange *(see p149)*.

The organ at St Katharine Cree

㉑ St Katharine Cree

86 Leadenhall St EC3. **Map** 16 D1.
Tel 020 7283 5733. 🚇 Aldgate, Tower Hill. **Open** 10:30am–4pm Mon–Fri. ✝ 1:05pm Thu.
🌐 **london.anglican.org**

A rare pre-Wren 17th-century church with a medieval tower, this was one of only eight churches in the City to survive the fire of 1666. Some of the elaborate plasterwork on and beneath the high ceiling of the nave portrays the coats of arms of the guilds, with which the church has special links. The 17th-century organ, supported on magnificent carved wooden columns, was played by both Purcell and Handel.

St Helen's Bishopsgate

㉒ Leadenhall Market

Whittington Ave EC3. **Map** 15 C2.
Tel 020 7332 1523. ⊝ Bank,
Monument. **Open** 10am–6pm Mon–
Fri. *See Shops and Markets pp312–33.*
♿ ⓦ cityoflondon.gov.uk

There has been a food market
here, on the site of the Roman
forum *(see pp20–21)*, since the
Middle Ages. Its name comes
from a lead-roofed mansion
that stood nearby in the 14th
century. The ornate, Victorian
covered shopping precinct of
today was designed in 1881 by
Sir Horace Jones, the architect
of Billingsgate fish market
(see p154). Essentially a food
market, offering traditional
game, poultry, fish, and meat,
Leadenhall also has a number
of independent shops, which
offer all kinds of fare from
chocolates to wine. The area is
busiest during breakfast and
lunch hours, and is best seen at
Christmas when all the stores
are decorated. Next door is the
Lloyd's of London building.

㉓ Lloyd's of London

1 Lime St EC3. **Map** 15 C2. **Tel** 020
7327 1000. ⊝ Bank, Monument,
Liverpool St, Aldgate. **Closed** to the
public. ⓦ lloyds.com

Lloyd's was founded in the late
17th century and takes its name
from the coffee house where
underwriters and shipowners
used to meet to arrange marine
insurance contracts. Lloyd's
soon became the world's main
insurers, issuing policies on
everything from oil tankers to
Betty Grable's legs.
　The present building, by
Richard Rogers, dates from 1986
and is one of the most interesting
modern buildings in London
(see p34). Its exaggerated stainless
steel external piping and high-
tech ducts echo Rogers' forceful
Pompidou Centre in Paris.
Lloyd's is a far more elegant
building and particularly worth
seeing floodlit at night. Nearby
is 30 St Mary Axe, otherwise
known as "the Gherkin", one of
the most recognisable landmarks on the London skyline.

Leadenhall Market in 1881

㉔ Guildhall Art Gallery

Guildhall Yard EC2. **Map** 15 B1.
Tel 020 7332 3700. ⊝ St Paul's.
Open 10am–5pm Mon–Sat, noon–
4pm Sun (last adm: 30 mins prior).
Closed 1 Jan, 25 & 26 Dec. 📷 for
temporary exhibitions. 📹 ♿ 📷
Guildhall Gresham St EC2. **Tel** 020
7606 3030. **Open** phone to check.
ⓦ cityoflondon.gov.uk

The Guildhall Art Gallery was
built in 1885 to house the art
collection of the Corporation of
London, but was destroyed in
World War II. The present gallery
houses the studio collection of
20th-century artist Sir Matthew
Smith, portraits from the
16th century to the present day,
a gallery of 18th-century works,
including John Singleton
Copley's *Defeat of the Floating
Batteries at Gibraltar*, and
numerous Victorian works.
　In 1988, the foundations of a
Roman amphitheatre were
discovered beneath the gallery.
Built in 70 AD and capable of
holding about 6000 spectators,
the arena would have featured
animal hunts, executions and
gladiatorial combat. Access to
the atmospheric ruins is free.
　The adjacent Guildhall itself
has been the administrative
centre of the City for at least 800
years. For centuries the hall was
used for trials and many people
were condemned to death here,
including Henry Garnet, one of
the Gunpowder Plot conspirators
(see p26). Today, a few days
after the Lord Mayor's parade
(see p57), the Prime Minister
addresses a banquet here.

Richard Rogers' Lloyd's building illuminated at night

COLUMBIA MARKET
LONDON. E. 2

COLUMBIA MARKET
LONDON. E. 2

COLUMBIA M

BIA MARKET
NDON. E. 2

MBIA MARKET
DON

BIA M

SMITHFIELD AND SPITALFIELDS

The areas just north of the City walls have always been a refuge for those who did not want to come under its jurisdiction, or were not welcome there. These included Huguenots in the 17th century and, in later times, other immigrants from Europe and then Bengal. They founded small industries and brought with them their restaurants and places of worship. The name Spitalfields comes from the medieval priory of St Mary Spital. Middlesex Street became known as Petticoat Lane in the 16th century, for its clothing stalls; it is still the hub of a popular Sunday morning street market that spreads as far east as Brick Lane, today lined with aromatic Bengali food shops. London's meat market is at Smithfield, and nearby is the Barbican, a late 20th-century residential and arts complex.

Sights at a Glance

Historic Streets and Buildings
- 4 Charterhouse
- 5 Cloth Fair
- 7 Barbican
- 9 Whitbread's Brewery
- 11 Wesley's Chapel–Leysian Mission
- 13 Petticoat Lane
- 17 Fournier Street
- 19 Spitalfields Centre Museum of Immigration & Diversity
- 20 Brick Lane
- 21 Dennis Severs House

Museums and Galleries
- 3 Museum of London pp168–9
- 14 Whitechapel Gallery

Churches and Mosques
- 2 St Botolph, Aldersgate
- 6 St Bartholomew-the-Great
- 8 St Giles, Cripplegate
- 12 St Leonard's Church
- 16 Christ Church, Spitalfields
- 18 London Jamme Masjid

Cemeteries
- 10 Bunhill Fields

Markets
- 1 Smithfield Market
- 15 Old Spitalfields Market
- 22 Columbia Road Market

Restaurants see pp298–300
1. L'Anima
2. The Boundary
3. Café du Marché
4. Carnevale
5. Casa Negra
6. Cây Tre
7. Club Gascon
8. Galvin la chapelle
9. Hawksmoor
10. Leon Spitalfields
11. Pham Sushi
12. St John
13. Vinoteca

Street Finder, maps 6, 7, 8, 15, 16

0 metres 500
0 yards 500

◀ Columbia Road flower and plant market

For keys to symbols see back flap

Street-by-Street: Smithfield

This area is among the most historic in London. It contains one of the capital's oldest churches, some rare Jacobean houses, vestiges of the Roman wall (near the Museum of London) and central London's only surviving whole-sale food market.

Smithfield's long history is also bloody. In 1381 the rebel peasant leader Wat Tyler was killed here by an ally of Richard II as he presented the king with demands for lower taxes. Later, in the reign of Mary I (1553–8), scores of Protestant religious martyrs were burned at the stake here.

The Fox and Anchor pub is open from 7am for hearty breakfasts, washed down with ale by the market traders of Smithfield.

❶ ★ Smithfield Market
A contemporary print shows Horace Jones's stately building for the meat market when it was completed in 1867.

Key

— Suggested route

Golden Boy of Pye Corner

The Saracen's Head, a historic inn, stood on this site until the 1860s when it was demolished to make way for Holborn Viaduct (*see p142*).

CHARTERHOUSE STREET

LON

WEST SMITHFIELD

SMITHFIELD STREET

COCK LANE

SNOW HILL

GILTSPUR STREET

St Bartholomew's Hospital has stood on this site since 1123. Some of the existing buildings date from 1759.

St Bartholomew-the-Less has a 15th-century tower and vestry. Its links to the hospital are shown by this early 20th-century stained glass of a nurse, a gift of the Worshipful Company of Glaziers.

0 metres		100
0 yards		100

❹ Charterhouse
The square contains the remnants of a medieval monastery and a school where John Wesley *(see p170)* studied.

(see p170)

Locator Map
See Central London Map pp16–17

Hackney

Islington

SMITHFIELD & SPITALFIELDS

THE CITY

See Central London Map pp16–17

Barbican station

❼ ★ Barbican
World War II bombs flattened this immense site, which was rebuilt as a housing development in the 1960s. It contains the famous Barbican Centre.

CARTHUSIAN ST

BEECH STREET

ALDERSGATE STREET

LITTLE BRITAIN

❺ Cloth Fair
Two of its houses are survivors of the 1666 Great Fire.

❻ St Bartholomew-the-Great
It has the best-preserved medieval interior of any London church.

LONDON WALL

St Paul's station

MUSEUM OF LONDON

❸ ★ Museum of London
The city's history is told vividly through fascinating and colourful exhibits.

Christ Church tower is all that remains of one of Wren's most splendid churches (1704).

Smithfield Market, now officially known as London Central Markets

① Smithfield Market

Charterhouse St EC1. **Map** 6 F5.
🚇 Farringdon, Barbican. **Open** 3–9am Mon–Fri. **Closed** public hols.
🌐 **smithfieldmarket.com**

Animals have been traded here since the 12th century, but the site was granted its first official charter in 1400. In 1648, it was officially established as a cattle market and live cattle continued to be sold here until the mid-19th century. It now confines itself to wholesale trading in dead meat and poultry. It was originally sited in Smithfield outside the city walls. Although moved to its present location in Charterhouse Street in the 1850s and called the London Central Meat Market, the original name stuck. The old buildings are by Horace Jones, the Victorian architect, but there are 20th-century additions. Some pubs in the area keep market hours and, from dawn, serve hearty breakfasts. After much-needed modernisation, the market is now one of the best equipped meat markets in the world. Aim to arrive by 7am.

② St Botolph, Aldersgate

Aldersgate St EC1. **Map** 15 A1. **Tel** 020 7283 1670. 🚇 St Paul's, Barbican, Moorgate. **Open** 10am–3pm Mon–Fri (to 2pm Mon & Wed). 🕴 1pm Tue & Thu, 10:30am Sun 🌐 **stbotolphs.org. uk**. ♿

A modest late Georgian exterior (completed in the late 18th century) conceals a flamboyant, well-preserved interior that has a finely decorated plaster ceiling, a rich brown wooden organ case and galleries, and an oak pulpit resting on a carved palm tree. The original box pews have been kept in the galleries rather than in the body of the church. Some of the memorials come from a 14th-century church that originally existed on the site.

The former churchyard alongside was converted in 1880 into a relaxing green space known as Postman's Park, because it was used by workers

from the nearby Post Office headquarters. In the late 19th century, the Victorian artist G F Watts dedicated one of the walls to a quirky collection of plaques that commemorate acts of bravery and self-sacrifice by ordinary people. Some of these plaques are still here and can be viewed. There are three St Botolph churches in the City; the other two can be found at Aldgate and in Bishopsgate.

③ Museum of London

See pp168–9.

④ Charterhouse

Charterhouse Sq EC1. **Map** 6 F5.
🚇 Barbican. **Open** for 🎫 Apr–Aug: book well ahead (see website for details). 🌐 **thecharterhouse.org**

The Tudor gateway on the north side of the square leads to the site of a former Carthusian monastery, which was dissolved under Henry VIII. In 1611, the buildings were converted into a hospital for poor pensioners, and a charity school – called Charterhouse – whose pupils included John Wesley *(see p170)*, writer William Thackeray and Robert Baden-Powell, founder of the Boy Scouts. In 1872, the school, now a top boarding school, relocated to Godalming in Surrey. Part of the original site was subsequently taken over by St Bartholomew's Hospital medical school. Some of the old buildings survived. These include the chapel and part of the cloisters. Today Charterhouse is still home to more than 40 pensioners, who are supported by the charitable foundation.

Charterhouse: stone carving

❺ Cloth Fair

EC1. **Map** 6 F5. ⊖ Barbican.

This pretty street is named after the notoriously rowdy Bartholomew Fair, which was the main cloth fair in medieval and Elizabethan England, held annually at Smithfield until 1855. Nos. 41 and 42 are fine 17th-century houses and have distinctive two-storeyed wooden bay windows, although their ground floors have since been modernized. The former poet laureate John Betjeman, who died in 1984, lived in No. 43 for most of his life. It has now been turned into a wine bar named after him.

17th-century houses: Cloth Fair

❻ St Bartholomew-the-Great

West Smithfield EC1. **Map** 6 F5. **Tel** 020 7600 0440. ⊖ Barbican. **Open** 8:30am–5pm Mon–Fri, 10:30am–4pm Sat, 8:30am–8pm Sun. **Closed** Christmas week. 🕙 9am, 11am, 6:30pm Sun. 🎫 ♿ 🎟 by appt. 🎵 Concerts. 🌐 **greatstbarts.com**

One of London's oldest churches was founded in 1123 by the monk Rahere, whose tomb is inside. A courtier of Henry I, he dreamt St Bartholomew saved him from a winged monster.

The 13th-century arch used to be the door to the church until the nave of that earlier building was pulled down when Henry VIII dissolved the priory. Today the arch leads from West Smithfield to the burial ground – the gatehouse above it is from

a later period. The present building retains the crossing and chancel of the original, with its round arches and other fine Norman detailing. There are also some fine Tudor monuments. The painter William Hogarth was baptized here in 1697.

Parts of the church have been used for secular purposes. In 1725, US statesman Benjamin Franklin worked for a printer in the Lady Chapel. The church also featured in the films *Four Weddings and a Funeral*, *Shakespeare in Love* and *The Other Boleyn Girl*.

❼ Barbican

Silk St EC2. **Map** 7 A5. **Tel** 020 7638 8891. ⊖ Barbican, Moorgate. Barbican Centre **Open** 9am–11pm Mon–Sat, noon–11pm Sun, public hols. 🎫 🖥 🚫 🎧 📷 ♿ induction loop. *See Entertainment pp341–3.* 🌐 **barbican.org.uk**

An ambitious piece of 1960s city planning, this residential, commercial and arts complex was begun in 1962 on a site devastated by World War II bombs, and not completed for nearly 20 years. Residential tower blocks surround the Barbican Centre, the arts complex, which also includes an ornamental lake and fountains.

The old city wall turned a corner here and substantial remains are still clearly visible (particularly so from the Museum of London – *see pp168–9*). The word barbican means a defensive tower over a gate –

St Bartholomew's gatehouse

perhaps the architects were trying to live up to the name when they designed this self-sufficient community with formidable defences against the outside world. Obscure entrances and raised walkways remove pedestrians from the cramped bustle of the City, but, in spite of the signposts, and yellow lines on the pavement, the complex can be difficult to navigate.

As well as two theatres and a concert hall, the Barbican Centre has two cinemas, two galleries, an excellent library, and a surprising conservatory. It is home to the London Symphony Orchestra and the Guildhall School of Music and Drama.

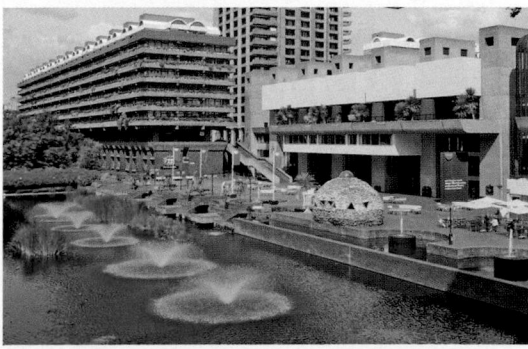

Pretty lake with fountains in the Barbican Centre

❸ Museum of London

Opened in 1976 on the edge of the Barbican, this museum provides a lively account of London life from prehistoric times to the Victorian era to the present day. Reconstructed interiors and street scenes are alternated with displays of original domestic artifacts and items found on the museum's archaeological digs. The museum underwent a huge redevelopment of its lower galleries in 2010, which opened up 25 per cent more gallery space.

★ **Marble Head of Serapis**
This statue of the Egyptian god of the underworld (2nd–3rd century) was discovered in the temple of Mithras.

Stairs to Galleries of Modern London

Oliver Cromwell's Death Mask
This plaster copy made from a wax impression acts as a permanent record of how he looked.

Boy's Leather Jerkin
This practical sleeveless jacket (c.1560), decorated with punched hearts and stars, would have been worn over a doublet for extra warmth.

Main entrance

Flint Hand Axe
Thousands of these cutting tools (c.350,000–120,000 BC) have been found in the gravels beneath modern London.

Key

- ☐ 450,000 BC–AD 50: London before London
- AD 50–410: Roman London
- AD 410–1558: Medieval London
- 1550s–1660s: War, Plague and Fire
- 1670s–1850s: Expanding City
- Victorian Walk
- Sackler Hall
- 1850s–1940s: People's City
- 1950s–Today: World City
- Inspiring London
- Linbury Gallery
- City Gallery
- Temporary Exhibitions

Gallery Guide

The galleries are laid out chronologically, starting on the entrance level with prehistory. Visitors can walk through Roman and medieval London galleries to the War, Plague and Fire gallery, which includes a special display on the Great Fire. On the lower level, they can learn about London from 1666 to the present day, and see the Lord Mayor of London's spectacular State Coach.

Tobacconist
The Victorian Walk uses several original shop fronts and objects to recreate the atmosphere of late 19th-century London.

The Expanding City Gallery explores London after the Great Fire.

Ignazio Pluchino Shoes
The Sicilian opened his shoemaking business in London in 1900. He made high quality shoes for the wealthy.

Selfridges Lift
These bronze and cast iron Brandt Edgar lifts were installed in 1928.

Beatles Dress
Made in 1964, this cotton dress is printed with the Beatles' heads alongside a guitar that features their signatures.

★ **Lord Mayor's Coach**
Finely carved and painted, this gilded coach (c.1757) is paraded once a year during the Lord Mayor's Show (see p57).

St Giles, Cripplegate

❽ St Giles, Cripplegate

Fore St EC2. **Map** 7 A5. **Tel** 020 7638 1997. 🚇 Barbican, Moorgate. **Open** 11am–4pm Mon–Fri. 🕎 8:30am Mon–Thu, 10am, 4pm Sun. 🕎 2–5pm Tue. 🚻 🅦 **stgilescripplegate.co.uk**

Completed in 1550, this church survived the ravages of the Great Fire in 1666, but was so badly damaged by a World War II bomb that only the tower survived. St Giles was refurbished during the 1950s to serve as the parish church of the Barbican, and now stands awkwardly amidst the stark modernity of the Barbican. It is one of the few UK churches to boast two complete organs.

Oliver Cromwell married Elizabeth Bourchier here in 1620 and the poet John Milton was buried here in 1674. Well-preserved remains of London's Roman and medieval walls can be seen to the south.

❾ Whitbread's Brewery

Chiswell St EC1. **Map** 7 B5. 🚇 Barbican, Moorgate. **Closed** to the public.

In 1736, when he was aged just 16, Samuel Whitbread became an apprentice brewer in Bedford. By the time of his death in 1796, his Chiswell Street brewery (which he had bought in 1750) was brewing 909,200 litres (200,000 gal) a year. The building has not been used as a brewery since 1976 when it was converted into rooms hired out for private functions – they are no longer open to the public. The Porter Tun room, which is now used as a banqueting suite, boasts the largest timber post roof in Europe, and has a huge span of 18 m (60 ft).

The street's 18th-century buildings are well-preserved examples of their period, and are worth a look from the outside. A plaque on one commemorates a visit to the brewery in 1787 by George III and Queen Charlotte.

❿ Bunhill Fields

City Rd EC1. **Map** 7 B4. **Tel** 020 7374 4127 (City Gardens). 🚇 Old St. **Open** Apr–Sep: 7:30am–7pm Mon–Fri, 9:30am–7pm Sat, Sun & public hols; Oct–Mar: 7:30am–4pm Mon–Fri; 9:30am–4pm Sat, Sun & public hols. **Closed** 1 Jan, 25 & 26 Dec. 🕎 see website for details. 🚻 phone first. 🅦 **cityoflondon.gov.uk/openspaces**

This spot was first designated a cemetery after the Great Plague of 1665 (see p27), when it was

William Blake's gravestone at Bunhill Fields

enclosed by a brick wall and gates. Twenty years later it was allocated to Non-conformists, who were banned from being buried in churchyards because of their refusal to use the Church of England prayer book. The cemetery is situated on the edge of the City, and shaded by large plane trees. There are monuments to the well-known writers Daniel Defoe, John Bunyan and William Blake, as well as to members of the Cromwell family. John Milton wrote his epic poem *Paradise Lost* while he lived in Bunhill Row, located on the west side of the cemetery. The website has further information on the burial records of Bunhill Fields.

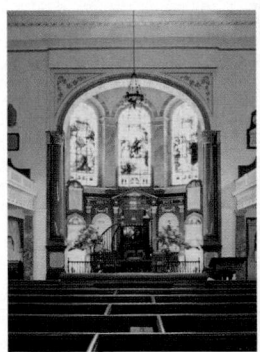
Wesley's Chapel

⓫ Wesley's Chapel–Leysian Mission

49 City Rd EC1. **Map** 7 B4. **Tel** 020 7253 2262. 🚇 Old St, Moorgate. **Open** 10am–4pm Mon–Sat, 12:30–1:45pm Sun. **Closed** between Christmas & New Year, public & bank hols (except Good Friday). 🚻 ground floor of John Wesley's house. 🕎 9:45am (not 1st Sun of month), 11am Sun, 12:45pm Wed. 🕎 groups book ahead. 🎵 Free lunchtime recitals: Tue. 🅦 **wesleyschapel.org.uk**

John Wesley, the founder of the Methodist church, laid the chapel's foundation stone in 1777. He preached here until his death in 1791, and is buried behind the chapel. Next door is the house where he lived, and today some of his furniture, books and other assorted possessions can be seen on display there.

The chapel, adorned in a spartan style, in accordance with Wesley's austere religious principles, has columns made from ships' masts. Baroness Thatcher, the first British woman Prime Minister (1979–90), was married here. Beneath it is a small museum about the history of the Methodist church.

Façade of St Leonard's Church

⑫ St Leonard's Church

Shoreditch High St F1. **Map** 8 D3. 🚇 Old Street, Liverpool Street. **Open** noon–2pm Mon–Fri. 🕐 10:30am Sun. 🎵 Concerts and theatrical performances. 🌐 spitalfieldsmusic.org.uk

Standing as it does on the spot where several major Roman roads converged, this has been a site of worship for millennia. The Norman St Leonard's was the original "actors' church" and many famous names of Tudor theatre are buried in the crypt, including Richard Burbage, who played the first Hamlet, Macbeth and Romeo, and his brother Cuthbert, founder of the Globe Theatre.

The current Palladian-style church was erected in 1736–40, making it the oldest building in Shoreditch. Its fine acoustics make it popular as a performance space with musicians.

⑬ Petticoat Lane

Middlesex St E1. **Map** 16 D1. 🚇 Aldgate East, Aldgate, Liverpool St. **Open** 10am–2:30pm Mon–Fri, 9am–2pm Sun. *See Shops and Markets p333.*

In Queen Victoria's prudish reign the name of this street, long famous for its market, was changed to the respectable but colourless Middlesex Street. That is still its official designation, but the old name, derived from the petticoats and lace sold here by the Huguenots who came from France, has stuck, and is now applied to the market held every Sunday morning in this and the surrounding streets. Numerous attempts were made to stop the market, but it was allowed by Act of Parliament in 1936. A great variety of goods is sold but there is still a bias towards clothing, especially leather coats. The atmosphere is noisy and cheerful, with Cockney stallholders making use of their wit to attract custom. There are scores of snack bars, and many of these sell traditional Jewish food such as salt beef sandwiches and bagels with smoked salmon.

Entrance to Whitechapel Gallery

⑭ Whitechapel Art Gallery

77–82 Whitechapel High St E1. **Map** 16 E1. **Tel** 020 7522 7888. 🚇 Aldgate East, Aldgate. **Open** 11am–6pm Tue–Sun, (to 9pm Thu). **Closed** 1 Jan, 25 & 26 Dec. 🎨 occasionally for exhibitions. 🦽 🎫 💻 🏛 Wide range of talks & events. 🌐 whitechapelgallery.org

A striking Art Nouveau façade by C Harrison Townsend fronts this light, airy gallery, founded in 1901 and expanded in the 1980s and again in 2007–9. Situated close to Brick Lane and the area's burgeoning art scene, this independent gallery was founded with the aim of bringing great art to the people of East London. Today it enjoys an excellent international reputation for high-quality shows of major contemporary artists. In the 1950s and 1960s, the likes of Jackson Pollock, Robert Rauschenberg, Anthony Caro and John Hoyland all displayed their work here. In 1970 David Hockney's first exhibition was held here.

The gallery has a well-stocked arts bookshop, a relaxed wholefood café and an award-winning restaurant.

Bustling Petticoat Lane Market

18th-century Fournier Street

⓯ Old Spitalfields Market

Commercial St E1. **Map** 8 D5. 🚇 Liverpool St, Aldgate. **Open** General Market Stalls: 10am–5pm Sun–Wed (from 9am Sun); Antiques & Vintage: 9am–5pm Thu; Fashion & Art: 10am–4pm Fri; Themed Market Day: 11am–5pm Sat. *See Shops and Markets p333.*
🌐 oldspitalfieldsmarket.com

One of the oldest markets in London, Spitalfields started life as a produce market in 1682, and foods such as organic greens, breads and jams can still be purchased here. It's open during the week, but it is on Sundays that crowds come in search of vintage clothing, bric-a-brac, crafts and innovative fashion.

⓰ Christ Church, Spitalfields

Commercial St E1. **Map** 8 E5. **Tel** 020 7377 6793. 🚇 Liverpool St. **Open** 10am–4pm Mon–Fri (unless in use as venue), 1–4pm Sun. 📅 1:10pm Tue; 8:30am & 10:30am Sun. Concerts ♿ 🎫 book ahead. 🌐 ccspitalfields.org

The finest of Nicholas Hawksmoor's six churches, Christ Church was commissioned by parliament in the Fifty New Churches Act of 1711, aimed at combating the threat of Non-conformism. It was intended to make a powerful statement in an area fast becoming a Huguenot stronghold. (The Protestant Huguenots had fled from persecution in Catholic France and came to Spitalfields to work in the local silkweaving

industry). Completed in 1729, the building was mauled by alterations in the 1850s. By 1960 it was derelict, narrowly escaping demolition. In 1976 the Friends of Christ Church Spitalfields was formed to restore the building to its former glory – a goal achieved in 2004. It is now used as a music venue.

Christ Church still dominates the surrounding streets. The impression of size and strength created by its portico and spire is continued inside by such features as the high ceiling and the gallery.

⓱ Fournier Street

E1. **Map** 8 E5. 🚇 Aldgate East, Liverpool Street.

The 18th-century houses on the north side of this street have attics with broad windows that were designed to give maximum light to the silkweaving French Huguenot community who lived here. Even now, the textile trade lives on, in this and nearby streets, still dependent on immigrant labour. Today it is Bengalis who toil at sewing machines in workrooms that are as cramped as they were when the Huguenots used them. Working conditions have improved, however, and many of the sweatshops have been converted into showrooms for companies which now have modern factories away from the town centre.

Christ Church, Spitalfields

Bengali sweet factory: Brick Lane

⓲ London Jamme Masjid

59 Brick Lane E1. **Map** 8 E5. 🚇 Liverpool St, Aldgate East.

Muslims now worship here, in a building whose life story as a religious site reflects the history of immigration in the area. Built in 1743 as a Huguenot chapel, it was a synagogue in the 19th century, a Methodist chapel in the early 20th century, and has been a mosque since 1976.

⓳ Spitalfields Centre Museum of Immigration & Diversity

19 Princelet St E1. **Map** 8 E5. **Tel** 020 7247 5352. 🚇 Liverpool St. **Open** some days & by appt (phone to check). 🌐 19princeletstreet.org.uk

A little Victorian synagogue hidden behind a 1719 Huguenot silk merchant's house with exhibitions celebrating the Jewish and other peoples who arrived as immigrants and settled in London's East End. This historic gem is under constant threat of closure due to lack of funding, thus donations are welcome.

⓴ Brick Lane

E1. **Map** 8 E5. 🚇 Liverpool St, Aldgate East, Shoreditch. Market **Open** dawn–noon Sun. *See Shops and Markets p331.*

Once a lane running through brickfields and the busy centre of London's Bengali district, Brick Lane is now stacked with hip

The grand bedroom of Dennis Severs House

galleries and quirky boutiques. Its shops and houses, some dating from the 18th century, have seen immigrants of many nationalities, and most now sell food, spices, silks and sarees. The first Bengalis to live here were sailors who came in the 19th century, when it was a predominantly Jewish quarter. Some Jewish shops remain, including a 24-hour bagel shop at No. 159.

On Sundays, a large market is held here and in the surrounding streets, complementing Petticoat Lane (see p171). At the northern end of Brick Lane is the former Black Eagle Brewery, a medley of 18th- and 19th-century industrial architecture, now reflected in, and set off by, a sympathetic mirror-glassed extension.

18th-century portrait: Dennis Severs House

㉑ Dennis Severs House

18 Folgate St E1. **Map** 8 D5. **Tel** 020 7247 4013. ⊖ Liverpool St. **Open** noon–4pm Sun (book ahead); noon–2pm 1st & 3rd Mon of month; for further dates see website. Private and group bookings welcome. 🖺
🌐 **dennissevershouse.co.uk**

At No. 18 Folgate Street, built in 1724, the late designer and performer Dennis Severs recreated a historical interior that takes you on a journey from the 17th to the 19th centuries. It offers what he called "an adventure of the imagination … a visit to a time-mode rather than … merely a look at a house". The rooms are like a series of tableaux vivants, as if the occupants had simply left for a moment. There is broken bread on the plates, wine in the glasses, fruit in the bowl; the candles flicker and horses' hooves clatter on the cobbles outside. This highly theatrical experience is far removed from more usual museum recreations and is not suitable for the under-12s. Praised by many, including artist David Hockney, it is truly unique. The house's motto is "you either see it or you don't". Around the corner on Elder Street are two of London's earliest surviving terraces, where many of the Georgian red-brick houses have been carefully restored.

㉒ Columbia Road Market

Columbia Rd F2. **Map** 8 D3. ⊖ Liverpool St, Old St, Bethnal Green. **Open** 8am–3pm Sun. See Shops and Markets p332.

A visit to this flower and plant market is one of the most delightful things to do on a Sunday morning in London, whether you want to take advantage of the exotic species on offer there or not. Set in a well-preserved street of small Victorian shops, it is a lively, sweet-smelling and colourful event. Apart from the stalls, there are several shops selling, among other things, home-made bread and farmhouse cheeses, antiques and interesting objects, many of them flower-related. There is also a Spanish delicatessen and an excellent snack bar that sells bagels and welcome mugs of hot chocolate on chilly winter mornings.

Columbia Road flower market

SOUTHWARK AND BANKSIDE

Southwark once offered an escape route from the City, where many forms of entertainment were banned. Borough High Street was lined with taverns: the medieval courtyards that still run off it mark where they stood. The George survives as the only galleried London inn. Among the illicit pleasures that thrived here were brothels in houses by the river, as well as theatres and bear and cock pits, which were established in the late 16th century. Shakespeare's company was based at the Globe Theatre, which has now been rebuilt close to its original site. Today the south bank of the river has undergone extensive renovation. Riverside attractions range from the Design Museum and Tate Modern, next to the Millennium Bridge, to historic pubs, Borough Market, Southwark Cathedral and London's tallest building – The Shard.

Sights at a Glance

Historic Streets and Areas
2 Hop Exchange
5 The Old Operating Theatre
7 Cardinal's Wharf
13 Bermondsey

Museums and Galleries
6 Shakespeare's Globe
8 Bankside Gallery
9 Tate Modern
11 Vinopolis
12 Clink Prison Museum
14 The Shard
15 Design Museum

Cathedrals
1 Southwark Cathedral

Pubs
4 George Inn
10 The Anchor

Markets
3 Borough Market

Historic Ships
16 HMS Belfast

Restaurants see pp300–301
1 Blueprint Café
2 Champor-Champor
3 Dim T - London Bridge
4 José
5 Roast
6 Tapas Brindisa
7 Tito's Peruvian Restaurant
8 Wright Brothers
9 Zucca

Street Finder, maps 14, 15, 16

◄ Seasonal fruit and vegetables on sale at Borough Market

For keys to symbols see back flap

Street-by-Street: Southwark

From medieval times until the 18th century, Southwark
was a venue for the pursuit of illicit pleasures; south of the
Thames, it was out of the jurisdiction of the City authorities.
The 18th and 19th centuries brought docks, warehouses and
factories. Now it is once again one of London's most exciting
boroughs, with the arrival of Tate Modern, a regenerated
Borough Market, the stunning recreation of Shakespeare's
Globe Theatre, and The Shard, soaring through the clouds.

Southwark Bridge was opened in
1912 to replace a bridge of 1819.

Millennium Bridge

Key

— Suggested route

```
0 metres        100
0 yards         100
```

9 ★ Tate Modern
The former Bankside Power Station is
now a powerhouse of contemporary
art, its spectacular open spaces
showing off exhibits to perfection.

6 ★ Shakespeare's Globe
This brilliant recreation of an
Elizabethan theatre has open-air
performances in the summer months
and an exhibition open all year round.

Southwark Quayside

Locator Map
See Central London Map pp16–17

THE CITY

Thames

SOUTHWARK &
BANKSIDE

Elephant &
Castle

❿ The Anchor
For centuries it has been
a favourite riverside pub
with fine views.

⓫ Vinopolis
This attraction is a city
of wine on the banks
of the river.

⓬ Clink Prison Museum
This museum, on the site of
the notorious old prison,
looks back at Southwark's
colourful past.

14th-century rose
window

Replica of Sir
Francis Drake's
Golden Hinde

**❶ ★ Southwark
Cathedral**
Despite major
alterations, it still
contains medieval
elements.

BANK END

CLINK STREET

PARK STREET

STONEY STREET

CATHEDRAL STREET

MONTAGUE CLOSE

LONDON BRIDGE

London Bridge, in its
various forms, was the
only river crossing in
London from Roman times
until 1750. The present
bridge, completed in 1972,
replaced the one of
1831 now in the US.

**❸ Borough
Market**
There has been a
market on or near
this site since
1276. Now it is a
flourishing fine
food market.

SOUTHWARK STREET

BOROUGH HIGH STREET

ST THOMAS STREET

The Shard

The War Memorial,
commemorating soldiers
who fell in World War I,
was erected in 1924 on
Borough High Street,
where it has become
a powerful landmark.

❹ George Inn
This is London's only
surviving traditional,
galleried inn.

THE GEORGE

❶ Southwark Cathedral

Montague Close SE1. **Map** 15 B3.
Tel 020 7367 6700. 🚇 London
Bridge. **Open** 8am–6pm Mon–Fri,
8:30am–6pm Sat & Sun. 🕆 daily
(check website). ♿ 🅿 📷 🎁
Concerts. 🆆 **cathedral.southwark.
anglican.org**

This church did not become a
cathedral until 1905. However,
some parts of it date back to the
12th century, when the building
was attached to a priory, and
many of its medieval features
remain. The memorials are
fascinating, including a late
13th-century wooden effigy
of a knight. John Harvard, the
first benefactor of Harvard
University, was baptized here
in 1607 and there is a chapel
named after him.

In 2000, the cathedral was
restored in a multi-million
pound restoration programme
including the addition of new
buildings, which house a shop
and a refectory. The exterior has
been landscaped to create a
herb garden and an attractive
Millennium Courtyard that leads
to the riverside.

Southwark Cathedral's Shakespeare Window

❷ Hop Exchange

Southwark St SE1. **Map** 15 B4. 🚇
London Bridge. **Closed** to the public.

Southwark, with its easy access
to Kent where hops are grown,
was a natural venue for brewing
beer and trading hops. In 1866,
this building was constructed as
the centre of that trade. Now a
hospitality venue, it retains its
original pediment complete

The George Inn, now owned by the National Trust

with carved scenes showing
the hop harvest, and iron gates
with a hop motif.

❸ Borough Market

8 Southwark St SE1. **Map** 15 B4.
🚇 London Bridge. Retail market:
Open 10am–5pm Wed–Thu,
10am–6pm Fri, 8am–5pm Sat.
🆆 **boroughmarket.org.uk**

Borough Market was once an
exclusively wholesale fruit and
vegetable market, which had
its origins in medieval times,
and moved to its current
atmospheric position beneath
the railway tracks in 1756.
A popular fine food market, it
sells gourmet foods from Britain
and Europe, as well as quality
fruit and vegetables, and organic
meat, fish and dairy produce.

❹ George Inn

77 Borough High St SE1. **Map** 15 B4.
Tel 020 7407 2056. 🚇 London Bridge,
Borough. **Open** 11am–11pm Mon–Sun.
📖 See Pubs and Bars pp308–11.
🆆 **nationaltrust.org.uk/george-inn**

Dating from the 17th century, this
building is the only example of a
traditional galleried coaching inn
left in London and is mentioned
by Dickens in Little Dorrit. It was
rebuilt after the Southwark fire of
1676 in a style that dates back to
the Middle Ages. Originally, there
would have been three wings
around a courtyard where plays

were staged in the 17th century.
In 1889, the north and east wings
were demolished, so there is only
one wing remaining.

The inn, now owned by the
National Trust, is still a restaurant.
Perfect on a cold wet day, the
pub has a well-worn, comfortable
atmosphere. In the summer, the
yard fills with picnic tables and
patrons are occasionally
entertained by actors and morris
dancers.

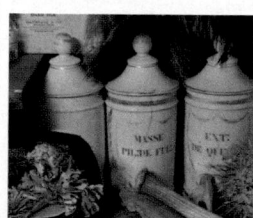

Ancient remedies, The Old Operating Theatre

❺ The Old Operating Theatre

9a St Thomas St SE1. **Map** 15 B4.
Tel 020 7188 2679. 🚇 London Bridge.
Open 10:30am–5pm daily.
Closed 15 Dec–5 Jan. 📷 🎁 ♿
limited. 🆆 **thegarret.org.uk**

Guy's & St Thomas' Hospital, one
of the oldest in Britain, stood
here from its foundation in the
12th century until it was moved
west in 1862. At this time,
nearly all of its buildings were
demolished in order to make
way for the railway. The
women's operating theatre

(The Old Operating Theatre Museum and Herb Garret) survived only because it was located away from the main buildings, in a garret over the hospital church. The UK's oldest operating theatre, it dates back to 1822, lay, bricked up and forgotten, until the 1950s. It has now been fitted out just as it would have been in the early 19th century, before the discovery of either anaesthetics or antiseptics. The display shows how patients were blindfolded, gagged and bound to the wooden operating table, while a box of sawdust underneath was used to catch the blood.

Shakespeare's Henry IV (performed at the Globe Theatre around 1600)

❻ Shakespeare's Globe

New Globe Walk SE1. **Map** 15 A3. **Tel** 020 7902 1400. Box Office: **Tel** 020 7401 9919. ⊖ Southwark, London Bridge. Exhibition open May–Sep: 9am–5:30pm; Oct–Apr: 10am–5pm daily. 🎟 🎫 every 30 mins. (Rose Theatre tours for groups of 15 or more by appt only.) Performances Apr–early Oct. ♿ 🖥 🚫 🎫
Ⓦ shakespearesglobe.com

Built on the banks of the Thames, Shakespeare's Globe is an impressive reconstruction of the Elizabethan theatre where many of his plays were first performed. The wooden, circular structure is open in the middle, leaving some of the audience exposed to the elements. Those holding seat tickets have a roof over their heads. The performances operate only in summer, and

seeing a play here is a thrilling experience, with top-quality acting. There is an informative tour for visitors, and groups may book to see the foundations of the nearby Rose Theatre. Beneath the theatre, and open all year round, is Shakespeare's Globe Exhibition, which brings his work and times to life.

❼ Cardinal's Wharf

SE1. **Map** 15 A3. ⊖ London Bridge

A small group of 17th-century houses still survives here in the shadow of Tate Modern art gallery (see pp180–83). A plaque commemorates Christopher Wren's stay here while St Paul's Cathedral (see pp150–53) was being built. He would have had a particularly fine view of the works. It is thought that the wharf got its name from Cardinal Wolsey who was Bishop of Winchester in 1529.

❽ Bankside Gallery

48 Hopton St SE1. **Map** 14 F3. **Tel** 020 7928 7521. ⊖ Blackfriars, Southwark. **Open** 11am–6pm daily. **Closed** 1 Jan, 24–26 Dec. ♿ 🖼 Lectures.
Ⓦ banksidegallery.com

This modern riverside gallery is the headquarters of two historic British societies, namely the Royal Watercolour Society and the Royal Society of Painter-Printmakers. The members of

View from the Founders' Arms

these societies are elected by their peers in a tradition that dates back over 200 years. Their work embraces both established and experimental practices. The gallery's permanent collection is not on show here, but there are constantly changing temporary displays of contemporary water colours and original artists' prints. The exhibitions feature the work of both societies and many of the pieces on display are for sale. There is also a superb specialist art shop that sells both books and materials.

There is an unparalleled view of St Paul's Cathedral from the nearby pub, the Founders' Arms – built on the site of the foundry where the cathedral's bells were cast. South of here, on Hopton Street, is a series of almshouses that date from 1752.

Row of 17th-century houses on Cardinal's Wharf

❾ Tate Modern

Looming over the southern bank of the Thames, Tate Modern occupies the converted Bankside power station, a dynamic space for one of the world's premier collections of contemporary art. Up until 2000, the Tate collection was shown at three galleries: Tate St Ives, Tate Liverpool and the former Tate Gallery, now Tate Britain *(see pp84–7)*. With the addition of Tate Modern, space was made for a growing acquisition of contemporary art. Tate Modern continually re-hangs its collection, so works and exhibitions may differ. A new extension is currently under construction.

The "light beam", a two-storey glass box, allows light to filter into the upper galleries.

A balcony gives great views of St Paul's Cathedral *(see pp150–53)* across the river.

Restaurant at Tate Modern
The restaurant on level 6 of the Tate Modern boasts a view that's a veritable work of art in its own right, with floor-to-ceiling windows overlooking the Thames and St Paul's Cathedral.

The Turbine Hall
The massive scale of this space – it covers 3,300 sq m (35,520 sq ft) – presents an unusual challenge for the artists who install pieces here.

Level 6

Level 5

Level 4

Level 3

Level 2

Level 1

♿ entrance

Level 0

West entrance

North entrance

Key to Floorplan

- ⬜ Turbine Hall
- ⬜ Transformed Visions
- ⬜ Poetry and Dream
- ⬜ Energy and Process
- ⬛ Structure and Clarity
- ⬛ Temporary exhibition space
- ⬜ Non-exhibition space

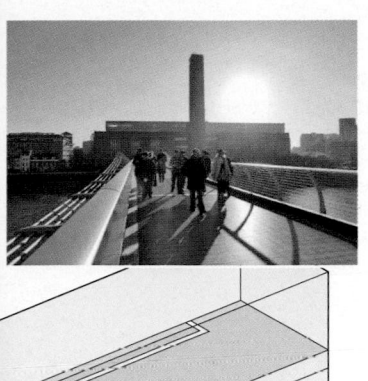

Façade of Tate Modern
The imposing former power station is a recognisable building along the river. It is the perfect space to house its vast collection of contemporary art.

VISITORS' CHECKLIST

Practical Information
Bankside, SE1
Map 14 F3, 15 A3.
Tel 020 7887 8888.
🅦 tate.org.uk
Open 10am–6pm Sun–Thu, 10am–10pm Fri–Sat.
Closed 24–26 Dec.
🏠 for special exhibitions only.
🔟 🖥 🖾 🔄 🎧 ♿ 🏠

Transport
🚇 Blackfriars, Mansion House, Southwark. 🚌 45, 63, 100, 344, 381, RV1.

Interacting with Art
Tate Modern has won awards for its handheld multimedia guides, which present audio commentary alongside images, film clips and games. The gallery's latest digital project, Bloomberg Connects, enables members of the public to actively connect with art, artists and other visitors. A digital drawing bar allows people to respond visually and see large-scale

versions of their art projected on the wall. Visitors can compose captions to artworks, bringing their own experiences to bear. Screens on the walls throughout the building display visitors' ideas and comments. Through this interactive digital space, visitors become participants and co-creators of modern art.

Quattro Stagioni
(1993–4)
Cy Twombly's four paintings depict the changes of light and colour over the seasons.

★ **Fish** (1926)
Constantin Brâncuşi attempted to portray the "spirit" of a fish in this abstract work constructed from bronze, metal and wood.

Gallery Guide
The main west entrance opens into the expansive, sloped Turbine Hall. From here, a flight of stairs leads to the café and foyer of level 1, or an escalator whisks visitors straight up to gallery level 2. Temporary exhibitions are on levels 2 and 3, while level 4 is again devoted to galleries. Level 5 is members' access only, but a superb restaurant and spectacular city views can be found on level 6.

Exploring Tate Modern

Tate Modern's displays are arranged into four thematic wings, each of which revolves around a large central room that focuses on a key period of modern art: Cubism, Surrealism; Post-war painting and sculpture; and Minimalism. Around these focal points, smaller, changing displays explore how each movement reflects earlier artistic practice or influenced subsequent developments. Works shown here are examples of what might be on display.

Transformed Visions

The Transformed Visions wing is largely devoted to works from 1945–60, which demonstrates how new forms of abstraction and expressive figuration arrived in America and Europe in the aftermath of World War II. Artists showcased in these rooms – such as Francis Bacon, Willem de Kooning and Germaine Richier – were all associated with the existentialist movement and their works deal with a new image of the human form in primitive and thought-provoking ways. Germaine Richier's *Chessboard* (1959) is one such key work on display here. This group of five sculpted and painted plaster figures is semi-abstracted, combining human and animal characteristics.

Mark Rothko's Seagram murals (1958–9) are also featured in this wing. This series of canvasses had originally been commissioned by the opulent Four Seasons restaurant, located in the Seagram building in New York. The group of paintings, entitled *Red on Maroon* and *Black on Maroon*, are of open, rectangular, window-like forms and are sombre in mood. Rothko eventually decided to withhold the murals from the restaurant as he did not want them to be a part of the privileged's environment. Rothko ultimately donated the murals to the Tate in 1970.

This wing also displays new works that focus on conflict and redemption.

Poetry and Dream

The central concept of Poetry and Dream is the process by which modern and contemporary art develops out of what has gone before, whilst also fuelling our understanding of these past movements. Poetry and Dream illustrates this primary concept using the key artists of the Surrealist movement, including Salvador Dalí, René Magritte and Pablo Picasso. After identifying key Surrealist themes, techniques and principles, the wing invites visitors to examine works by more modern figures such as Cindy Sherman, Louise Bourgeois and Francis Bacon and illustrates how these artists invoke the legacy of their Surrealist predecessors. Further rooms focus on the use of film as a Surrealist medium, Cy Twombly and Joseph Beuys, Susan Hiller and her installation piece *From the Freud Museum* (1991-6), and the survival of Realism alongside the burgeoning Surrealist movement using works by André Derain, Max Beckman and Diego Rivera.

Section of *From the Freud Museum* (1991–6) by Susan Hiller

Energy and Process

"Artists' interest in transformation and natural forces" is the concept behind this fascinating sequence of 11 rooms. Room 1 contrasts the work of painter Kazimir Malevich, a pioneer of the early-20th-century avant-garde, and contemporary

The façade, chimney, and lightbeam of Tate Modern

Bankside Power Station

This forbidding fortress was designed in 1947 by Sir Giles Gilbert Scott, the architect of Battersea Power Station, Waterloo Bridge and London's famous red telephone boxes. The power station is of a steel-framed brick skin construction, comprising over 4.2 million bricks. The Turbine Hall was designed to accommodate huge oil-burning generators and three vast oil tanks are still *in situ*, buried under the ground just south of the building. The tanks are to be employed in a future stage of Tate Modern development. The power station itself was converted by Swiss architects Herzog and de Meuron who designed the two-storey glass box, or lightbeam, which runs the length of the building. This serves to flood the upper galleries with light and also provides wonderful views of London.

sculptor Richard Serra, known for his sheet-metal assemblages. Non-traditional approaches to canvas are explored in room 2. Sculptures made from everyday materials – sometimes organic, sometimes industrial – are featured in room 3. Photography is the focus in room 4, with work from Ana Mendieta. More sculpture follows in room 5 with work by the Italian sculptor Marisa Merz, who applies craft techniques to industrial materials. Room 6 brings together three representatives of the Arte Povera school – Boetti, Fabro and Pistoletto. Magdalena Abakanowicz's striking, sculptural textiles are found in room 7. Room 8 documents artistic "interventions" in the natural landscape and room 9 highlights a video installation by Brazilian artist Lucia Nogueira. In Room 10, you can view an early video art piece – Juan Downey's *Video Trans Americas*. Finally, room 11 has an installation by artists Peter Fischli and David Weiss, whose work recreates cheap, mass-produced objects.

Dynamic Suprematism (1915 or 1916) by Kazimer Malevich

Structure and Clarity

The Structure and Clarity wing begins with two large-scale masterpieces in room 1: Henri Matisse's *Snail* (1953) and Bridget Riley's *Deny II* (1967). Both works are experiments in colour, shape and tonality. Room 2 focuses on the abstract art of the inter-war years. Following World War I, artists sought a utopian ideal

Untitled (1964) by Larry Bell

for art and society, and aimed to remove art from human conflict. This resulted in producing nonfigurative works of cool geometric compositions. The movement is represented with major works by figures such as Wassily Kandinsky and Constantin Brâncuşi, whose bronze, metal and wood sculpture *Fish*, created in 1926, is on display here.

The surrounding rooms explore the impact of abstraction on various media including film and photography with works by Werner Mantz and Sameer Makerius in room 4. Room 5 presents artists from the mid-20th century whose works dealt with form, space and movement. The minimalist art of the 1960s, which not only echoed the works of the 1920s and 1930s but also had its own distinct style, is featured in this wing

too. Works by Larry Bell, Jo Baer and Carl Andre can be found in rooms 7 and 8, including the latter's *Equivalent III* (1966) – the last in a series of *Equivalent* sculptures, each consisting of a rectangular arrangement of 120 firebricks.

Special Exhibitions

To complement its permanent collection, Tate Modern presents a programme of exhibitions including five large shows a year (retrospectives of modern masters or surveys of important movements). Smaller-scale projects are dotted around, and occasionally outside, the gallery. Once a year, Tate Modern challenges an artist to create a work capable of occupying the vast Turbine Hall. This has resulted in a spectacular display of innovative sculptures and interactive works of art.

Louise Bourgeois was the first artist to exhibit here, with works that included her sculpture *Maman* (1999), a monumental steel spider. Others have included Olafur Eliasson's *The Weather Project* (2003), which lit the Turbine Hall with a giant glowing sun. In 2010, Ai Weiwei's *Sunflower Seeds* filled the hall with 100 million hand-crafted porcelain seeds, and in 2012, Tate Modern staged its first live commission using non-actors – *These associations* created by Tino Sehgal.

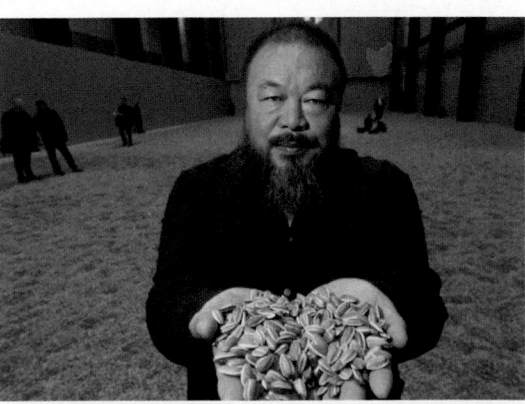

Ai Weiwei holds painted ceramic "seeds" from his *Sunflower Seeds* installation (2010)

Pub sign at the Anchor Inn

❿ The Anchor

34 Park St SE1. **Map** 15 A3. **Tel** 020 7407 1577. 🚇 London Bridge. **Open** 11am–11pm Mon–Wed, 11am–midnight Thu–Sat, noon–10:30pm Sun. ♿ ✍

This is one of London's most famous riverside pubs. It dates from after the Southwark fire of 1676, which devastated the area *(see pp26–7)*. The present building is 18th-century, but traces of much earlier hostelries have been found beneath it. The inn was once connected with a brewery across the road that belonged to Henry Thrale, a close friend of Dr Johnson *(see p142)*. When Thrale died in 1781, Johnson went to the brewery sale and encouraged the bidders with a phrase that has passed into the English language: "The potential of growing rich beyond the dreams of avarice."

⓫ Vinopolis

1 Bank End SE1. **Map** 15 B3. **Tel** 020 7940 8300. 🚇 London Bridge. **Open** phone or check website for details. **Closed** 1 Jan, 25 & 26 Dec. 🅿 ♿ ✍ 🎧 🔊 📷 W **vinopolis.co.uk**

Vinopolis is a unique attraction devoted to the enjoyment of wine. Its blend of interactive fun and educational exhibits has made it a popular destination for anyone who wishes to know more about making and drinking wine. Set within cavernous Victorian railway arches, Vinopolis explores the history of the grape from earliest times and illuminates the process of wine-making from planting the vines through to labelling the bottles. "Tasting stations" provide an opportunity to savour the subject matter along the way.

A selection of choice vintages can be purchased from the wine warehouse after the tour, while the shop has a vast assortment of wine-related merchandise. Cantina Vinopolis offers good food, great service, and, unsurprisingly, high-quality wines.

Replica of Civil War trooper's helmet made in the Clink

⓬ Clink Prison Museum

1 Clink St SE1. **Map** 15 B3. **Tel** 020 7403 0900. 🚇 London Bridge. **Open** Jul–Sep: 10am–9pm daily; Oct–Jun: 10am–6pm Mon–Fri, 10am–7:30pm Sat & Sun. **Closed** 25 Dec. 🎧 📷 ✍ for groups (phone first). W **clink.co.uk**

Now a macabre museum, the prison that was once located here first opened in the 12th century. It was owned by successive Bishops of Winchester, who lived in the adjoining palace just east of the museum, of which all that now remains is a lovely rose window. During the 15th century, the prison became known as the "Clink", and finally closed in 1780.

The museum illustrates the history of the prison. Tales of the inmates are told, including those of the numerous prostitutes, debtors and priests that were incarcerated here. Hands-on displays of instruments of torture leave little to the imagination and are not for the faint-hearted.

⓭ Bermondsey

SE1. **Map** 15 C5. 🚇 London Bridge, Borough. Market **Open** 4am–1pm Fri, starts closing noon. Fashion and Textile Museum: 83 Bermondsey St SE1. **Tel** 020 7407 8664. **Open** 11am–6pm Tue–Sat (till 8pm Thu), 11am–5pm Sun. 🎧 ♿ ✍ on request. 📷 🔊 W **ftmlondon.org**

Bermondsey's winding streets still hold traces of its historic past in the form of medieval, 18th-century and Victorian buildings. Today, it is famous for its antique market. Each Friday at dawn, seriously committed antiques dealers trade their latest acquisitions at Bermondsey. There are occasional press reports about long-lost masterpieces changing hands here for a song, and optimists are welcome to try their luck and test their judgment. However, trading starts at the crack of dawn, and the best bargains tend to go before most people are even awake. The **Fashion and Textile Museum** in Bermondsey Street combines an education, exhibition and visitor centre and is a cutting-edge creative hub for contemporary fashion, textiles and jewellery. A shop sells products by up-and-coming designers.

Antiques stall at Bermondsey Market

The Shard, London's tallest building, soaring above Tower Bridge

⑭ The Shard

London Bridge Street. **Map** 15 B4.
⊖ London Bridge. The View:
Entrance via Joiner Street. **Tel** 0844
499 7111. **Open** 10am–10pm
Thu–Sat, 10am–7pm Sun–Wed.
Closed 25 Dec. 🅿 🔥 🏠
Ⓦ **theviewfromtheshard.com**

Designed by Renzo Piano, the
Shard is the tallest building in
Western Europe and dominates
the London skyline. At 310-m
(1,016-ft) high with a crystalline
façade, the 95-storey building
houses offices, restaurants, the
five star Shangri-La hotel,
exclusive apartments and the
country's highest observation
gallery, the View. Take a high-
speed lift to the top of the
building for unobstructed views
of the capital. The public
galleries on the top four floors
have multimedia exhibits.

⑮ Design Museum

Butlers Wharf, Shad Thames SE1.
Map 16 E4. **Tel** 020 7403 6933.
⊖ Tower Hill, London Bridge.
Open 10am–5:45pm daily (last adm:
5:15pm). **Closed** 25 & 26 Dec. 🅿 🚫
Blueprint Café: **Tel** 020 7940 8785
(booking advised). 🖥 🏠 👓 🔥
Ⓦ **designmuseum.org**

This museum was the first in the
world to be devoted solely to
modern and contemporary
design when it was founded in
1989. A frequently changing
programme of exhibitions
explores landmarks in modern
design history and the most
exciting innovations in contemporary design set against the
context of social, cultural,
economic and technological

changes. The Design Museum
embraces every area of design,
from furniture and fashion, to
household products, cars,
graphics, websites and architecture in exhibitions and new
design commissions. Each spring,
the museum hosts Designer of
the Year, a national design prize,
with an exhibition at which the
public can vote for the winner.

The museum is arranged over
three floors, with major exhibitions on the first floor. There are
smaller displays on the second,
which also has an Interaction
Space, where visitors can play
vintage video games and learn
about the designers featured in
the museum in the Design at
the Design Museum online
research archive. The shop and
café are on the ground floor.
On the first floor is the **Blueprint
Café** restaurant, which has
stunning views of the Thames.

⑯ HMS Belfast

Morgan's Lane, Tooley St SE1. **Map** 16
D3. **Tel** 020 7940 6300. ⊖ London
Bridge, Tower Hill. **Open** Mar–Oct:
10am–6pm daily (last adm 5:45pm);
Nov–Feb: 10am–5pm. **Closed** 24–26
Dec. 🅿 🔥 limited. 🖥 🏠
Ⓦ **hmsbelfast.iwm.org.uk**

Originally launched in 1938 to
serve in World War II, HMS
Belfast was instrumental in the
destruction of the German
battle cruiser, *Scharnhorst*, in the
battle of North Cape, and also
played an important role in the
Normandy Landings.

After the war, the battle
cruiser, designed for offensive
action and for supporting
amphibious operations, was
sent to work for the United
Nations in Korea. The ship
remained in service with the
British navy until 1965.

Since 1971, the cruiser has
been used as a floating naval
museum. Part of it has been
recreated to show what the ship
was like in 1943, when it partici-
pated in sinking the German
battle cruiser. Other displays
portray life on board during
World War II and there are also
exhibits relating to the history
of the Royal Navy, as well as an
interactive Operations Room.

It is also possible for children
to take part in educational
activity weekends on board
the ship.

The now familiar sight of the naval gunship HMS *Belfast* on the Thames

SOUTH BANK

Following the Festival of Britain in 1951, the Southbank Centre grew up around the newly erected Royal Festival Hall. The architecture has been criticized over the years, especially the chunky concrete building that houses the Hayward Gallery, but now appears to be valued as an important part of London's river frontage. The area is popular with locals and tourists, and is crowded with culture-seekers

most evenings and afternoons. As well as the National Theatre and the Old Vic theatre, concert halls, and galleries, the South Bank has the BFI Southbank and London's most striking cinema, the BFI IMAX *(see p339)*. In keeping with Festival of Britain tradition, the South Bank was a focal point for the new millennium, with the raising of the world's highest observation wheel, the London Eye.

Sights at a Glance

Historic Streets and Buildings
9 Lambeth Palace
12 Gabriel's Wharf
13 Waterloo Station

Museums and Galleries
2 Hayward Gallery
7 Florence Nightingale Museum
8 Museum of Garden History
10 Imperial War Museum

Attractions
4 County Hall
5 London Dungeon
6 The London Eye

Theatres and Concert Halls
1 National Theatre
3 Royal Festival Hall
11 The Old Vic

☐ Restaurants *see pp300–301*
1 Anchor and Hope
2 The Laughing Gravy
3 Oxo Tower Restaurant

Street Finder, maps 13, 14, 21, 22

Street-by-Street: Southbank Centre

Originally this was an area of wharves and factories which was much damaged by bombing during World War II. It was chosen as the site of the 1951 Festival of Britain *(see p34)*, celebrating the centenary of the Great Exhibition *(see pp30–31)*. The Royal Festival Hall is the only building from 1951 to remain, but since then London's main arts centre has been created around it, including the national showplaces for theatre, music and film, and a major art gallery.

To the Strand ←

❶ ★ National Theatre
Its three auditoriums offer a choice of plays ranging from the classics to the sharpest modern writing.

BFI Southbank, previously the National Film Theatre, was established in 1953 to show historic films *(see p339)*.

Festival Pier

The Queen Elizabeth Hall stages more intimate concerts than the Festival Hall. The adjoining Purcell Room is for chamber music *(see pp340–41)*.

❷ Hayward Gallery
The concrete interior of this venue for important exhibitions is well suited to many modern works.

❸ ★ Royal Festival Hall
The London Philharmonic is one of many world-class orchestras to perform here in the focal point of the Southbank Centre.

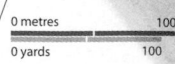

0 metres   100
0 yards   100

Hungerford Bridge was built in 1864 to carry both trains and pedestrians to Charing Cross. It now includes two footbridges, the Golden Jubilee Bridges.

❻ ★ The London Eye
The world's tallest cantilevered observation wheel offers passengers a unique view of London.

Waterloo Bridge was completed in 1945 to Sir Giles Gilbert Scott's design. It replaced Rennie's bridge of 1817.

Locator Map
See Central London Map pp16–17

The Struggle is My Life is a bronze of Nelson Mandela, the South African leader. Made by Ian Walters, it was unveiled here in 1985.

THE STRUGGLE IS MY LIFE
NELSON MANDELA

CONCERT HALL APPROACH

Southbank Centre

The Shell Building, head-quarters of the international oil company, was completed in 1963. The building has been earmarked for redevelopment.

BELVEDERE ROAD

CHICHELEY STREET

London Eye

WESTMINSTER BRIDGE ROAD

❹ **County Hall**
Home to the Sea Life London Aquarium, the London Dungeon, hotels and restaurants.

Key

— Suggested route

To Westminster station

Jubilee Gardens were laid out in 1977 to celebrate the Silver Jubilee of Queen Elizabeth II, and redesigned in 2012 in time for her Diamond Jubilee and the Olympic Games.

The façade of the Hayward Gallery

❶ National Theatre

South Bank SE1. **Map** 14 D3. **Tel** 020 7452 3000. 🚇 Waterloo. **Open** 9:30am–11pm Mon–Sat, noon–6pm Sun (performance days). **Closed** Good Fri, 24 & 25 Dec, bank hols. 🔊 during performances. 🚫 🖥 📷 🚻 🎫 Foyer concerts (free) 5:45pm Mon–Sat, 1pm Sat & Sun, exhibitions. *See Entertainment p336.* 🌐 **nationaltheatre.org.uk**

Even if you don't want to see a play, this well-appointed complex is worth a visit. Sir Denys Lasdun's building was opened in 1976 after 200 years of debate about whether there should be a national theatre and its location. The company was formed in 1963, under Laurence (later Lord) Olivier, Britain's leading 20th-century actor. The largest of the three theatres is named after him; the others are the Cottesloe and the Lyttleton.

❷ Hayward Gallery

South Bank SE1. **Map** 14 D3. **Tel** 020 7960 4200. 🚇 Waterloo. **Open** noon–6pm Mon, 10am–6pm Tue, Wed, Sat & Sun (to 8pm Thu & Fri). **Closed** 1 Jan, 24–26 Dec, between exhibitions. 📷 🚻 🖥 📷 🌐 **southbankcentre.co.uk**

The Hayward Gallery is one of London's main venues for large art exhibitions. Its slabby grey concrete exterior is too starkly modern for some tastes, but it is also considered by many as an icon of 1960s "Brutalist" architecture. The Waterloo Sunset Pavilion by Dan Graham

shows a selection of cartoons and artists' videos.

Hayward exhibitions cover classical and contemporary art, but the work of British contemporary artists is particularly well represented.

❸ Royal Festival Hall

South Bank SE1. **Map** 14 D4. **Tel** 0844 875 0073. 🚇 Waterloo. **Open** 10am–11pm daily. **Closed** 25 Dec. 🔊 during performances. 🚫 🖥 📷 🚻 Pre-concert talks, exhibitions, free concerts. *See Entertainment p340.* 🌐 **southbankcentre.co.uk**

The Royal Festival Hall was the only structure in the 1951 Festival of Britain *(see p34)* that was designed for permanence. Sir Robert Matthew and Sir Leslie Martin's concert hall was the first major public building works undertaken in London following World War II. It has stood the test of time so well that many of the capital's major arts institutions have gathered round it, and the Grade I listed building is today one of the world's leading performance venues. As well as the main auditorium, there is the Clore Ballroom, the poetry-library Spirit Level of three rooms – Blue, White and Yellow – and also a gift shop, the Riverside Terrace Cafe, Central Bar and Skylon restaurant. Skylon offers a modern European menu, with an extensive wine and cocktail list.

❹ County Hall

Westminster Bridge Rd SE1. **Map** 13 C4. Aquarium **Tel** 0871 663 1678. 🚇 Waterloo. **Open** 10am–7pm daily (aquarium). **Closed** 25 Dec. 📷 🚻 🖥 📷 🌐 **visitsealife.com/london**

Once the home of London's elected government, this imposing building now houses a leisure complex. The Sea Life London Aquarium, London Dungeons *(see below)* and *Namco Station*, a computer games hall, occupy the space alongside two hotels, several restaurants and a health club.

The Aquarium is home to hundreds of aquatic species from all over the world, including stingrays, turtles and sea scorpions. Special features include a 25-m (82-ft) glass tunnel walkway through a tropical ocean environment, and, for the brave, a Shark Walk across a suspended glass platform.

Shark in a tank at the Sea Life London Aquarium

❺ London Dungeon

Westminster Bridge Rd SE1. **Map** 13 C4. **Tel** 0871 423 2240. 🚇 Waterloo. **Open** 10am–5pm Mon–Fri (from 11am Thu), 10am–6pm Sat–Sun. Extended hours in school holidays. **Closed** 25 Dec. 📷 🚻 🖥 📷 🌐 **thedungeons.com**

This museum is a great hit with children. It illustrates the most bloodthirsty events in British history, with live actors and special effects. It is played strictly for terror, and screams abound with experiences such as Gruesome Goings-on, which includes live actors and shows; the Great Plague; and Jack the Ripper. Don't miss Henry's Wrath – cruise along a black River Thames to find out what happened to Anne Boleyn and her co-conspirators – but watch you don't get wet.

❻ The London Eye

The Energy London Eye is a 135-m (443-ft) high observation wheel. Opened in 2000 as part of London's millennium celebrations, it immediately became one of the city's most recognizable landmarks, notable not only for its size, but for its circularity amid the block-shaped buildings flanking it. Thirty-two capsules, each holding up to 25 people, take a gentle 30-minute round trip. On a clear day, the Eye affords a unique 40-km (25-mile) view, which sweeps over the capital in all directions and on to the countryside and hills beyond.

VISITORS' CHECKLIST

Practical Information
Jubilee Gardens SE1.
Map 14 D4. **Tel** 0871 781 3000 (info and 24-hour advance booking – strongly recommended).
🅦 **londoneye.com**
Open daily Apr–Jun: 10am–9pm; Jul & Aug: 10am–9:30pm, Sep–Mar: 10am–8:30pm.
Closed 25 Dec and mid-Jan for maintenance.
🎟 Pick up tickets at County Hall (adjacent to Eye) at least 30 mins before boarding time. Fast-track tickets are also available.
🖥 🎦 ♿

Transport
🚇 Waterloo, Westminster. 🚌 11, 24, 211.

Houses of Parliament
Seventeen minutes into the flight, the spectacular aerial view of Westminster should not be missed.

The glass capsules are mounted on the outside of the rim, allowing unobstructed 360-degree views.

80 spokes made from 6 km (3.7 miles) of cable hold the structure in tension, strengthening the wheel.

Battersea Power Station
After 15 minutes, the distinctive white smokestacks of this old power station are visible.

Two cables, 60 metres (197 ft) in length, support the entire structure from concrete bases in Jubilee Gardens.

The wheel rim was floated down the Thames in sections and then assembled on site.

Buckingham Palace
Ten minutes into the journey, the Queen's official residence glides into view.

The Eye turns continuously and moves slowly enough that the capsules are boarded here while moving. The wheel is halted for those requiring assistance.

❼ Florence Nightingale Museum

2 Lambeth Palace Rd SE1. **Map** 14 D5. **Tel** 020 7620 0374. 🚇 Waterloo, Westminster. **Open** 10am–5pm daily (last adm 4:30pm). **Closed** 25 Dec (and some other dates; call to check). 📷 📹 🎫 ♿ Videos, lectures. 🆆 florence-nightingale.co.uk

This determined woman captured the nation's imagination as the "Lady of the Lamp", who nursed the wounded soldiers of the Crimean War (1853–6). She also founded Britain's first school of nursing at old St Thomas' Hospital in 1860.

Obscurely sited near the entrance to St Thomas' Hospital, this museum gives an account of Nightingale's career through displays of original documents and personal memorabilia. They illustrate her life and the developments she pioneered in health care, until her death in 1910 at the age of 90.

Florence Nightingale

❽ Museum of Garden History

Lambeth Palace Rd SE1. **Map** 21 C1. **Tel** 020 7401 8865. 🚇 Waterloo, Lambeth North, Westminster. **Open** 10:30am–5pm Sun–Fri, 10:30am–4pm Sat. **Closed** 1st Mon of month; 22 Dec–1 Jan. 📷 ♿ 🎫 last Tue of month (free). 📹 📷 Library by appt, lectures, filmshows. 🆆 gardenmuseum.org.uk

The world's first museum of garden history is housed in the restored church of St Mary of Lambeth Palace, and set around a central knot garden. In the grounds are the tombs of John Tradescant, father and son who, as well as being gardeners to Charles I and Charles II, were adventurous plant hunters and collectors of curiosities. The tomb of William Bligh of *The Bounty* can also be seen here.

The museum presents a history of gardening in Britain,

illustrated by a selection of historic garden tools, artifacts and curiosities. It also runs a programme of exhibitions, events, lectures and educational activities. There is a shop offering garden-related items for freshly inspired gardeners.

❾ Lambeth Palace

SE1. **Map** 21 C1. 🚇 Lambeth North, Westminster, Waterloo, Vauxhall. **Open** for guided tours only. 🎫 Tue & Fri (booking essential). 🆆 archbishopofcanterbury.org

This palace has housed Archbishops of Canterbury since the 13th century and today remains the Archbishop's official London residence. The chapel and its undercroft contain elements from the 13th century, but a large part of the rest of the building is far more recent. It has been frequently restored, most recently by Edward Blore in 1828. The Tudor gatehouse, however, dates from 1485 and is one of London's most familiar riverside landmarks.

Until the first Westminster Bridge was built, the horse ferry that operated between here and Millbank was a principal river crossing. The revenues from it went to the Archbishop, who received compensation when the bridge opened in 1750.

The Tudor gatehouse

❿ Imperial War Museum

Lambeth Rd SE1. **Map** 22 E1. **Tel** 020 7416 5000. 🚇 Lambeth North, Elephant & Castle. **Open** 10am–6pm daily. **Closed** 24–26 Dec. ♿ 📹 📷 Filmshows, lectures. 🆆 iwm.org.uk

This museum is not just concerned with the engines of modern warfare. Massive tanks, artillery, bombs and aircraft are on show, yet some of the most fascinating exhibits in the museum relate more to the impact on the lives of people at home than to the business of fighting. There are displays about food rationing, air raid precautions, censorship and morale-boosting.

Extracts from wartime films, radio programmes and literature are shown alongside hundreds of photographs, paintings by John Singer Sargent, Graham Sutherland and Paul Nash, and sculpture by Jacob Epstein. Henry Moore did some evocative drawings of life during the Blitz of 1940, when many Londoners slept in Underground stations to protect themselves from falling

The machinery of war through the ages

bombs. There is also a library with a fascinating archive. Major permanent displays include the Holocaust exhibition, which tells the story of Nazi persecution of Jews before and during the World War II; Secret War, which reveals the covert world of espionage, secret operations and the work of Britain's Special Forces. The museum is housed in part of what used to be the Bethlehem Royal Hospital for the Insane ("Bedlam"), built in 1811. Visitors would come for the afternoon to enjoy the antics of the patients. The hospital moved out to new premises in Surrey in 1930, leaving this vast building empty. Its two large flanking wings were pulled down and this central block converted into the museum which moved here from its former South Kensington site in 1936.

To mark the centenary of World War I in 2014, the museum has rebuilt its First World War Galleries and Atrium, improving visitor facilities.

The Old Vic's façade from 1816

⓫ The Old Vic

Waterloo Rd SE1. **Map** 14 E4. **Tel** 0844 871 7628. 🚇 Waterloo. **Open** for performances only. ♿ 🚻 *See Entertainment pp336–8.* 🌐 **oldvictheatre.com**

This splendid building dates back to 1818, when it was opened as the Royal Coburg Theatre. In 1833, the name was changed to the Royal Victoria, in honour of the future queen. Shortly after this the theatre became a centre for "music hall", the immensely popular Victorian entertainment, which included singers, comedians

The memorial to the dead of World War I at Waterloo Station

and other acts. In 1912, Lillian Baylis became manager and from 1914 to 1923 she staged all of Shakespeare's plays here. In the 1960s, the National Theatre *(see p190)* was founded and based at this site.

In 1997, Sally Greene, with the director Stephen Daldry and others, set up a charitable trust to secure the theatre's future. The Trust set up The Old Vic Theatre Company as a resident company in 2003, with Kevin Spacey as Artistic Director. There are cheap seats for younger people and pantomimes at Christmas.

⓬ Gabriel's Wharf

56 Upper Ground SE1. **Map** 14 E3. 🚇 Waterloo. *See Shops and Markets pp312–33.*

This pleasant enclave of boutiques, craft shops and cafés was the product of a long and stormy debate over the future of what was once an industrial riverside area. Residents of Waterloo strongly opposed various schemes for office developments before a community association was able to acquire the site in 1984 and build co-operative housing around the wharf.

Adjoining the market is a small garden and a riverside walkway with marvellous views to the north of the City. The OXO Tower to the east, built in 1928 to surreptitiously advertise a meat extract by means of its window shapes, is now the setting for a fine restaurant *(see p301).*

⓭ Waterloo Station

York Rd SE1. **Map** 14 D4. **Tel** 08457 484950. 🚇 Waterloo. *See Getting to London p364.*

The terminus for trains to southwest England, Waterloo station was originally built in 1848 but completely remodelled in the early 20th century, with the addition of a grand formal entrance on the northeast corner. Today the spacious concourse, lined with shops, cafés and bars, makes it one of the most practical of the London rail terminals.

Towards the end of the 20th century the station was enlarged again to serve as London's first Channel Tunnel rail link to Europe. In autumn 2007, the Eurostar terminal moved from Waterloo station to its present home at St Pancras International *(see p132).*

The area around Waterloo has a great community feel and it is worth passing down Lower Marsh with its shops, eateries and street market.

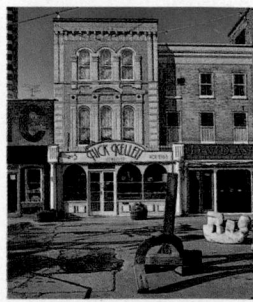

Illusionistic painting on the buildings around Gabriel's Wharf

CHELSEA

The showy young shoppers who paraded along the King's Road from the 1960s until the 1980s have more or less gone, along with Chelsea's reputation for extreme behaviour established by the bohemian Chelsea Set of writers and artists in the 19th century. Formerly a riverside village, Chelsea became fashionable in Tudor times. Henry VIII liked it so much that he built a small palace (long vanished) here. Artists, including Turner, Whistler and Rossetti, were attracted by the river views from Cheyne Walk. The historian Thomas Carlyle and the essayist Leigh Hunt arrived in the 1830s and began a literary tradition continued by writers such as the poet Swinburne. Yet Chelsea has always had a raffish element, too: in the 18th century the pleasure gardens were noted for beautiful courtesans and the Chelsea Arts Club has held riotous balls for nearly a century. The Chelsea of today is home to expensive boutique shops, up-market restaurants and exclusive residential areas.

Sights at a Glance

Historic Streets and Buildings
1 King's Road
2 Carlyle's House
5 Cheyne Walk
8 Royal Hospital
10 Sloane Square

Museums
7 National Army Museum
9 Saatchi Gallery

Churches
3 Chelsea Old Church

Gardens
4 Roper's Garden
6 Chelsea Physic Garden

Restaurants *see pp295–7*
1 Buona Sera Jam
2 Caraffini
3 Gallery Mess
4 Gordon Ramsay

Street Finder, maps 19, 20

For keys to symbols *see back flap*

Street-by-Street: Chelsea

Once a peaceful riverside village, Chelsea has been
fashionable since Tudor times when Sir Thomas
More, Henry VIII's Lord Chancellor, lived here.
Artists, including Turner, Whistler and Rossetti, were
attracted by the views from Cheyne Walk, before a
busy main road disturbed its peace. Chelsea's artistic
connection was maintained by upscale galleries
and antique shops, many of which have closed
due to a rise in rents. Enclaves of 18th-century
houses preserve a genteel atmosphere.

❶ King's Road
In the 1960s and
1970s it was the
boutique-lined
centre of fashionable
London, and is still
a main shopping
street.

❷ Carlyle's House
The historian and
philosopher lived here from
1834 until his death in 1882.

The Old Dairy, at 46 Old
Church Street, was built
in 1796, when cows still
grazed in the surrounding
fields. The tiling is original.

To King's
Road

❸ Chelsea Old Church
Although severely damaged
during World War II, it still holds
some fine Tudor monuments.

❹ Roper's Garden
It includes a sculpture
by Jacob Epstein who
had a studio here

Thomas More, sculpted
in 1969 by L Cubitt Bevis,
gazes calmly across the
river near where he lived.

Key

━ Suggested route

| 0 metres | | 100 |
| 0 yards | | 100 |

To Sloane
Square station

Chelsea Old Town Hall was built in the late 19th century and now hosts exhibitions and antique fairs.

Locator Map
See Central London Map pp16–17

SOUTH KENSINGTON & KNIGHTSBRIDGE

Brompton

Belgravia

CHELSEA

Thames

Battersea

❻ ★ Chelsea Physic Garden
The statue is of Sir Hans Sloane, benefactor of this historic herb garden.

Cadogan Pier

Albert Bridge, completed in 1873, is the most elegant of the Thames Bridges, especially at night when it is illuminated by hundreds of light bulbs.

Boy and Dolphin, the vigorous sculpture (1975) by David Wynne, enlivens the Albert Bridge junction.

❺ Cheyne Walk
Once favoured by artists, it boasts some of London's finest houses and has had many famous residents. Look out for the plaques.

The Pheasantry, King's Road

❶ King's Road

SW3 and SW10. **Map** 19 B3.
🚇 Sloane Square. *See Shops and Markets pp312–33.*

This is Chelsea's central artery, with its wealth of small fashion shops packed with young people looking for designer fashions. The mini-skirt revolution of the 1960s began here and so have many subsequent style trends, perhaps the most famous of them being punk.

Look out for the Pheasantry at No. 152, with its columns and statuary. It was built in 1881 as the shop-front of a furniture maker's premises but now conceals a modern restaurant.

Once also a vibrant area for antiques, most of the Kings Road's merchants have packed up shop. Nearby Kensington Church Street is where to go to find high-quality art and antiques today.

❷ Carlyle's House

24 Cheyne Row SW3. **Map** 19 B4.
Tel 020 7352 7087. 🚇 Sloane Sq, South Kensington. **Open** Mar–Oct: 11am–5pm Wed–Sun (last adm: 4:30pm). 🦽 ♿ 📷 tours 11am–12:30pm Wed–Fri (by appt).
🌐 **nationaltrust.org.uk/carlyleshouse**

The historian and founder of the London Library *(see St James's Square p94)*, Thomas Carlyle moved into this modest 18th-century house in 1834, and wrote many of his best-

known books here, notably *The French Revolution* and *Frederick the Great*. His presence made Chelsea more fashionable and the house became a mecca for some great literary figures. The novelists Charles Dickens and William Thackeray, poet Alfred Lord Tennyson and naturalist Charles Darwin were all regular visitors here. The house has been restored and looks as it did during Carlyle's lifetime.

Chelsea Old Church in 1860

❸ Chelsea Old Church

64 Cheyne Walk SW3. **Map** 19 A4.
Tel 020 7795 1019. 🚇 Sloane Sq, South Kensington. **Open** 2–4pm Tue–Thu. 🦽 📷 by appt. ✝ 8am Thu, 8am, 10am, 11am, 12:15pm, 6pm Sun.
🌐 **chelseaoldchurch.org.uk**

Rebuilt after World War II, this square-towered building does not look old from the outside. However, early prints confirm that it is a careful replica of the medieval church that was largely destroyed by World War II bombs.

The glory of this church is its Tudor monuments. One to Sir Thomas More, who built a chapel here in 1528, contains an inscription he wrote (in Latin), asking to be buried next to his wife. Among other monuments is a chapel to Sir Thomas Lawrence, who was an Elizabethan merchant, and a 17th-century memorial to Lady Jane Cheyne, after whose husband Cheyne Walk was named. Outside the church is a statue in memory of Sir Thomas More, "statesman, scholar, saint", gazing piously across the river.

❹ Roper's Garden

Cheyne Walk SW3. **Map** 19 A4.
🚇 Sloane Square, South Kensington.

This is a small park outside Chelsea Old Church. It is named after Margaret Roper, Thomas More's daughter, and her husband William, who wrote More's biography. The sculptor Jacob Epstein worked at a studio on the site between 1909 and 1914, and there is a stone carving by him commemorating the fact. The park also contains a figure of a nude woman by Gilbert Carter.

❺ Cheyne Walk

SW3. **Map** 19 B4. 🚇 Sloane Square, South Kensington.

Until Chelsea Embankment was constructed in 1874, Cheyne Walk was a pleasant riverside promenade. Now it overlooks a busy road that has destroyed much of its charm. Many of the 18th-century houses remain, though, bristling with blue plaques celebrating some of the famous people who have lived in them. Most were writers and artists, including J M W Turner who lived incognito at No. 119, George Eliot who died at No. 4 and a clutch of writers (Henry James, T S Eliot and Ian Fleming) in Carlyle Mansions.

Thomas More on Cheyne Walk

❻ Chelsea Physic Garden

66 Royal Hospital Road SW3. **Map** 19 C4. **Tel** 020 7352 5646. 🚇 Sloane Square. **Open** 1st week Feb; Apr–Oct: 11am–6pm Sun–Fri, occasional late openings. 🅿 ♿ call in advance. 📷 💻 🏛 Gardening school. 🆆 chelseaphysicgarden.co.uk

Established by the Society of Apothecaries in 1673 to study plants for medicinal use, this garden was saved from closure in 1722 by a gift from Sir Hans Sloane, whose statue adorns it. Many new varieties have been nurtured in its glasshouses, including cotton sent to the plantations of the southern United States. Visitors to London's oldest botanic garden can see ancient trees and one of Britain's first rock gardens, installed in 1772.

❼ National Army Museum

Royal Hospital Rd SW3. **Map** 19 C4. **Tel** 020 7730 0717. 🚇 Sloane Square. **Open** 10am– 5:30pm daily; see website for celebrity speaker programme (closed for redevelopment). **Closed** 1 Jan, 24–26 Dec. ♿ 📷 🏛 🆆 nam.ac.uk

A lively account of the history of British land forces from 1485 to the present can be found here. Tableaux, dioramas, archive film and interactive displays illustrate major engagements and give a taste of life behind the lines. There are fine paintings of battle scenes and portraits of soldiers. The shop sells a range of books and model soldiers.

❽ Royal Hospital

Royal Hospital Rd SW3. **Map** 20 D3. **Tel** 020 7881 5516. 🚇 Sloane Sq. **Open** museum: 10am–noon & 2–4pm Mon–Fri. **Closed** Sun Oct–Mar, public hols, functions (check first). 📷 10am & 1:30pm Mon–Fri, book in advance. 🏛 🆆 chelsea-pensioners.co.uk

This graceful complex was commissioned by Charles II

Chelsea Physic Garden in autumn

A Chelsea Pensioner in uniform

from Christopher Wren in 1682 as a retirement home for old or wounded soldiers, who have been known as Chelsea Pensioners ever since. The hospital opened ten years later and is still home to about 330 retired soldiers, whose distinctive uniforms of scarlet coats and tricorne hats date from the 17th century. Flanking the northern entrance are Wren's two main public rooms: the chapel, notable for its wonderful simplicity, and the panelled Great Hall, still used as the dining room. A small museum explains the history of the Pensioners.

A statue of Charles II by Grinling Gibbons is to be found on the terrace outside, and there is a fine view of the remains of Battersea Power Station across the river.

❾ Saatchi Gallery

Duke of York's HQ, King's Road, Chelsea. **Map** 19 C2. 🚇 Sloane Square. **Open** 10am–6pm daily. **Closed** for private events. ♿ call in advance 020 7811 3085. 📷 💻 🆆 saatchi-gallery.co.uk

The Saatchi Gallery is famous for presenting the best in contemporary art and showcasing talent from the UK and international art world. The gallery now receives over 600,000 visitors each year.

Many of the featured artists are unknown when first exhibited at the gallery but often rise to fame as a result. Relocated from its original site on the South Bank, the Saatchi Gallery's present home at the Duke of York's HQ offers an ideal environment in which to view contemporary art. Admire pieces by established names such as Tracy Emin and Jenny Saville while also keeping an eye open for up-and-coming talent.

Sloane Square fountain

❿ Sloane Square

SW1. **Map** 20 D2. 🚇 Sloane Square.

This pleasant small square (rectangle to be precise) has a paved centre with a flower stall and fountain depicting Venus. Laid out in the late 18th century, it was named after Sir Hans Sloane, the wealthy physician and collector who bought the manor of Chelsea in 1712. Opposite Peter Jones, the 1936 department store on the square's west side, is the Royal Court Theatre, which for over a century has fostered new drama.

SOUTH KENSINGTON AND KNIGHTSBRIDGE

Bristling with embassies and consulates, South Kensington and Knightsbridge are among London's most desirable, and expensive, areas. With Kensington Palace being a royal residence, the surrounding area has remained fairly unchanged.

The prestigious shops of Knightsbridge serve their wealthy residents. With Hyde Park to the north, and museums that celebrate Victorian learning at its heart, visitors to this part of London can expect to find a unique combination of the serene and the grandiose.

Sights at a Glance

Historic Streets and Buildings
- ⑤ Royal College of Music
- ⑦ Royal College of Art
- ⑩ Kensington Palace
- ⑬ Speakers' Corner

Churches
- ④ Brompton Oratory

Museums and Galleries
- ① *Natural History Museum pp204–5*
- ② *Science Museum pp208–9*
- ③ *Victoria and Albert Museum pp212–15*
- ⑨ Serpentine Gallery

Parks and Gardens
- ⑪ Kensington Gardens
- ⑫ Hyde Park

Monuments
- ⑧ Albert Memorial
- ⑭ Marble Arch

Concert Halls
- ⑥ Royal Albert Hall

Shops
- ⑮ Harrods

Restaurants *see pp295–7*
1. Bar Boulud
2. Dinner
3. Zuma

Street Finder, maps 10, 11, 19

◀ The Royal Albert Hall and the Albert Memorial

For keys to symbols *see back flap*

Street-by-Street: South Kensington

A clutch of museums and colleges provide this area with its dignified character. The Great Exhibition of 1851 in Hyde Park was so successful that in the following years smaller exhibitions were held here, just to its south. By the end of the 19th century some of these had become permanent museums, housed in grandiose buildings celebrating Victorian self-confidence.

7 Royal College of Art
David Hockney and Peter Blake are among the great artists who trained here.

The Royal College of Organists was decorated by F W Moody in 1876.

6 ★ Royal Albert Hall
Opened in 1870, the Hall was partly funded by selling seats on a 999-year lease.

5 Royal College of Music
Historic musical instruments are exhibited here.

1 ★ Natural History Museum
The dinosaur exhibits are one of the museum's most popular attractions.

Key

— Suggested route

0 metres   100
0 yards   100

2 ★ Science Museum
Visitors here can experiment with the interactive displays.

The Albert Hall Mansions, built by Norman Shaw in 1879, started a fashion for red brick.

Locator Map
See Central London Map pp16–17

❽ **Albert Memorial**
This memorial was built to commemorate Queen Victoria's consort.

The Royal Geographical Society was founded in 1830. Scottish missionary and explorer David Livingstone (1813–73) was a member.

Imperial College, part of London University, is one of the country's leading scientific institutions.

❸ ★ **Victoria and Albert Museum**
A range of objects and a stunning photo gallery illustrate the nation's history of design and decoration.

Holy Trinity church dates from the 19th century and is located in a calm backwater among cottages.

❹ **Brompton Oratory**
The Oratory was built during the 19th-century Catholic revival.

Brompton Square, begun in 1821, established this as a fashionable residential area.

To Knightsbridge station

❶ Natural History Museum

Life on Earth and the Earth itself are vividly explained at the Natural History Museum. Using the latest interactive techniques and traditional displays, exhibits tackle such issues as how human beings evolved and how we can safeguard our planet. The Images of Nature exhibit showcases 350 years of wildlife artwork and photography. The vast museum building is a masterpiece in itself. It opened in 1881 and was designed by Alfred Waterhouse using revolutionary Victorian building techniques. It is built on an iron and steel framework concealed behind arches and columns, richly decorated with sculptures of plants and animals.

★ Mammals
The life-sized model of a blue whale dwarfs everything else in this vast gallery.

The Darwin Centre features a futuristic cocoon in a glass atrium. It is home to 20 million insect and plant specimens and a research centre.

Ground floor

Grand staircase

Cromwell Road entrance

Access to basement

★ Dinosaurs
T Rex, one of the museum's impressively life-like animatronic models, lurches and roars in this hugely popular gallery. More traditional exhibits of fossilized skeletons and eggs are also on display.

Gallery Guide

The museum is divided into four sections: the Blue Zone, the Green Zone, the Red Zone and the Orange Zone.

A 26-m (85-ft) skeleton of the dinosaur Diplodocus dominates Hintze Hall. Beyond – in the Blue Zone – Human Biology, together with Mammals, Dinosaurs and the Images of Nature are to the left, while Creepy Crawlies and Ecology are to the right. On the first floor are found Our Place in Evolution and The Vault.

The giant escalator in Visions of Earth leads through a stunning globe to Red Zone highlights The Power Within and Earth's Treasury.

Creepy Crawlies
This popular gallery celebrates arthropods – insects, crustaceans, centipedes and spiders, such as this tarantula.

Key to Floorplan
- ▇ Blue Zone
- ▇ Green Zone
- ▇ Red Zone
- ▇ Orange Zone

The Vault
The Vault contains a dazzling collection of the finest gems, crystals, meteorites and metals from around the world, such as this Latrobe gold nugget.

Treasures is a showcase for the best of the museum's collections.

Second floor

Second floor Red Zone

First floor Red Zone

First floor

Access to Red Zone

Exhibition Road entrance – Earth Galleries

Volcanoes and Earthquakes has an earthquake simulator that is very popular.

Earth's Treasury gallery glitters with thousands of gems, rocks and minerals, including some of the Earth's rarest products.

Birds
This traditional display, with many species in Victorian glass cases, includes a model of the legendary dodo. A flightless bird from Mauritius, it was extinct by the mid-1600s, a potent symbol of human impact on nature.

★ **Visions of Earth**
Specimens are recessed into the etched slate walls of this beautiful gallery. Access to the rest of the Red Zone is via an escalator that runs through a massive model of the Earth.

VISITORS' CHECKLIST

Practical Information
Cromwell Rd SW7.
Map 19 A1.
Tel 020 7942 5000.
W nhm.ac.uk
Open 10am–5:50pm daily
(to 10:30pm last Fri of month) –
last admission 5:30pm.
Closed 24–26 Dec. ♿ 🎒 📷
💻 🎭 Lectures, workshops for adults and children, film presentations.

Transport
⊖ South Kensington. 🚌 14, 49, 70, 74, 345, 360, 414, C1.

❷ Science Museum

See pp208–9.

Kids captivated by the exhibits on display in the Science Museum

❸ Victoria and Albert Museum

See pp212–15.

❹ Brompton Oratory

Brompton Rd SW7. **Map** 19 A1. **Tel** 020 7808 0900. 🚇 South Kensington. **Open** 6am–8pm daily. 🕇 11am Sun sung Latin Mass (see website for other times). 🚻 📷 **W** bromptonoratory.com

The Italianate Oratory is a rich (some think a little too rich) monument to the English Catholic revival of the late 19th century. The Oratory was established by John Henry Newman (who later became Cardinal Newman). Father Frederick William Faber (1814–63) had already founded a London community of priests at Charing Cross. The group had moved to Brompton, then an outlying London district, and this was to be its oratory. Newman and Faber (both Anglican converts to Catholicism) were following the example of St Philip Neri, who set up a community of city-based secular priests living without vows.

The present church was opened in 1884. Its façade and dome were added in the 1890s, and the interior has been progressively enriched ever since. Herbert Gribble, the architect, who was also a Catholic convert, was only 29 when he triumphed in the highly prestigious competition to design it. Inside, all the most eye-catching treasures predate the church – many of them were transported here from Italian churches. Giuseppe Mazzuoli carved the huge marble figures of the 12 apostles for Siena Cathedral in the late 17th century. The beautiful Lady Altar was originally created in 1693 for the Dominican church in Brescia, and the 18th-century altar in St Wilfrid's Chapel was actually imported from a church in Rochefort, Belgium.

The Oratory has always been famous for its splendid musical tradition.

❺ Royal College of Music

Prince Consort Rd SW7. **Map** 10 F5. **Tel** 020 7591 4300. 🚇 Knightsbridge, South Kensington. Museum of Instruments: **Tel** 020 7591 4842. **Open** 2–4:30pm Tue–Fri in term-time or by appointment. 🚻 call 020 7591 4322 before visit. 📷 📱 **W** rcm.ac.uk

17th-century viol at the Royal College of Music

Sir Arthur Blomfield designed the turreted Gothic palace, with Bavarian overtones, that has housed this distinguished institution since 1894.

The college was founded in 1882 by George Grove, who also compiled the famous *Dictionary of Music*; pupils have included English composers Benjamin Britten and Ralph Vaughan Williams. The **Museum of Musical Instruments** has limited opening hours; if you do manage to get inside, you will see instruments from the earliest times and from many parts of the world. Some of the exhibits were played by such greats as Handel and Haydn.

The sumptuous interior of Brompton Oratory

Joseph Durham's statue of Prince Albert (1858) by the Royal Albert Hall

❻ Royal Albert Hall

Kensington Gore SW7. **Map** 10 F5.
Tel 020 7589 8212. ⊖ High St
Kensington, South Kensington.
Open for performances. 📷 📹 to
book call 0845 401 5045; charge for
tour. ♿ 📹 🖥 *See Entertainment
pp340–41.* 🅦 **royalalberthall.com**

Designed by an engineer,
Francis Fowke, and completed
in 1871, this huge concert hall
was modelled on Roman
amphitheatres and is easier on
the eye than most Victorian
structures. On the red-brick
exterior the only ostentation is a
pretty frieze symbolizing the
triumph of arts and science. In
plans, the building was called
the Hall of Arts and Science but
Queen Victoria changed it to
the Royal Albert Hall, in memory
of her husband, when she laid
the foundation stone in 1868.
    The hall is often used for
Classical concerts, most
famously the "Proms", but it

also accommodates other large
gatherings, such as tennis
matches, comedy shows, rock
concerts, circus shows and
major business conferences.

❼ Royal College of Art

Kensington Gore SW7. **Map** 10 F5.
Tel 020 7590 4444. ⊖ High St
Kensington, South Kensington.
Open 10am–5:30pm daily (phone
first). ♿ 🖥 📷 Lectures, events,
film presentations, exhibitions.
🅦 **rca.ac.uk**

Sir Hugh Casson's mainly glass-
fronted building (1962) is in
stark contrast to the Victoriana
around it. The college was
founded in 1837 as a school
of design and practical art for
the manufacturing industries.
It became noted for modern art
in the 1950s and 1960s when
David Hockney, Peter Blake and
Eduardo Paolozzi were there.

❾ Albert Memorial

South Carriage Drive, Kensington
Gdns SW7. **Map** 10 F5. ⊖ High St
Kensington, South Kensington.

This grandiose but dignified
memorial to Queen Victoria's
beloved consort was completed
in 1876, 15 years after his death.
Albert was a German prince and
a cousin of Queen Victoria's.
When he died from typhoid in
1861, he was only 41 and they
had been happily married for 21
years, producing nine children.
It is fitting that the monument is
near the site of the 1851 Exhibition *(see pp30–31)*, for Prince
Albert was closely identified
with the Exhibition itself and
with the scientific advances it
celebrated. The larger than life
statue, by John Foley, shows
him with an exhibition
catalogue on his knee.
    The desolate Queen chose
Sir George Gilbert Scott to
design the monument that
stands 55 m (175 ft) high. It is
loosely based on a medieval
market cross – although many
times more elaborate, with a
black and gilded spire, multicoloured marble canopy, stones,
mosaics, enamels, wrought iron
and nearly 200 sculpted figures.
In October 1998, the re-gilded
statue was unveiled by Elizabeth
II; it had not been gilded since
1915 when it was painted black
to avoid attracting attention
during World War I.

Victoria and Albert at the Great
Exhibition opening (1851)

❷ Science Museum

Centuries of continuing scientific and technological development lie at the heart of the Science Museum's massive collections. The variety of objects displayed is magnificent: from steam engines to aeroengines; spacecraft to the first mechanical computers. Equally important is the social context of science – what discoveries and inventions mean for day-to-day life – and the process of discovery itself. The high-tech Wellcome Wing has interactive displays, an IMAX Cinema, a 4D theatre and galleries devoted to new advances in science.

★ Science and Art of Medicine
A 17th-century Italian vase for storing snake bite treatment is part of this interesting collection.

Science in the 18th Century
The original orrery, a mechanical model of the solar system, is one of many beautiful scientific instruments in this gallery.

Computing
Babbage's Difference Engine No. 1 (1832), the first automatic calculator and a magnificent example of precision engineering, is a highlight of this gallery.

Energy: Fuelling the Future
explores how energy powers every aspect of our lives.

Media Space
looks at relationships between photography, science, art and technology.

★ The Energy Hall
Dedicated to steam power, this gallery includes the still-operational Harle Syke Mill Engine (1903).

Key to Floorplan

- Basement
- Ground floor
- First floor
- Second floor
- Third floor
- Fourth floor
- Fifth floor
- Wellcome Wing

Stairs to lower level

Exploring Space
Rockets, satellites, space probes, landers and more.

Main entrance

★ Flight
This gallery is packed with early flying contraptions, fighter planes and aeroengines, many of them suspended as if in mid-flight.

VISITORS' CHECKLIST

Practical Information
Exhibition Rd SW7
Map 19 A1.
Tel 0870 870 4868.
w **sciencemuseum.org.uk**
Open 10am–6pm daily.
Closed 24–26 Dec. some exhibitions & IMAX Cinema. Lectures, films, workshops.

Transport
South Kensington. 9, 10, 14, 49, 52, 70, 74, 345, 360, 414, 430, 452, C1.

Atmosphere
This interactive gallery allows visitors to explore the science behind our changing climate – how it works, why it changes and what might happen in the future.

Escalator to Imax Cinema

★ Who Am I?
Find out what makes you unique and explore the science of being human. The exhibition utilizes intriguing objects, displays and hands-on exhibits.

★ Making the Modern World
Apollo 10 took US astronauts around the moon in May 1969, and now forms part of this stunning gallery of museum highlights.

The hands-on galleries, including The Garden, prove very popular with children.

Gallery Guide

The Science Museum is spread over seven floors, balconies and mezzanine levels. The Wellcome Wing, offering four floors of interactive technology, is at the west end of the museum and is accessible from the ground floor and third floor of the main building. Power dominates the ground floor; here too are Exploring Space and Making the Modern World. The first floor has Challenge of Materials, Agriculture as well as the brand new Information Age galleries. On the second floor, a range of diverse galleries look at energy, mathematics and computing. The third floor includes Flight, Health Matters and Launchpad. The fourth and fifth floors (accessible by only one of the lifts) house the medical history galleries.

Statue of young Queen Victoria by her daughter Princess Louise outside Kensington Palace

❾ Serpentine Gallery

Kensington Gdns W2. **Map** 11 A4.
Tel 020 7402 6075. 🚇 Lancaster Gate,
South Kensington. **Open** 10am–6pm
Tue–Sun. **Closed** 1 Jan, 24–26, 31 Dec
& between exhibitions. Lectures. 🚻
📷 summer only. 📖 art bookshop.
🌐 **serpentinegallery.org**

The Serpentine Gallery houses
temporary exhibitions of major
contemporary artists' work.
Past exhibitors include Gilbert &
George, Rachel Whiteread
and Felix Gonzalez-Torres.
This exciting gallery transforms
its space to suit the exhibits,
sometimes spilling out into
the park. Every summer, a
temporary pavilion (open daily)
is commissioned from a major
architect; this is where you
will find the café.

❿ Kensington Palace

Kensington Palace Gdns W8. **Map** 10
D4. **Tel** 0844 482 7777. 🚇 High St
Kensington, Queensway, Notting Hill
Gate. **Open** Mar–Oct: 10am–6pm
daily; Nov–Feb: 10am–5pm daily (last
adm: 1 hr earlier). **Closed** 24–26 Dec.
🔊 📷 🚫 📖 🚻 Exhibitions.
🌐 **hrp.org.uk**

Half of this spacious palace is
used as royal apartments; the
other half, which includes
the 18th-century state rooms,
is open to the public. When
William III and his wife Mary
came to the throne in 1689,

they bought a mansion, dating
from 1605, and commissioned
Christopher Wren to convert it
into a royal palace. He created
separate suites of rooms for
the king and queen.

The palace has seen some
important royal events. In 1714,
Queen Anne died here from a
fit of apoplexy brought on by
over-eating and, on 20 June
1837, Princess Victoria of Kent
was woken at 5am to be told
that her uncle William IV had
died and she was now queen –
the start of her 64-year reign.
After the death in 1997 of
Diana, Princess of Wales, the
gold gates south of the palace
became a focal point for
mourners in their thousands,
who turned the surrounding
area into a field of bouquets.

A £12 million renovation
project has seen the palace
gardens connected to
Kensington Gardens for the
first time since the 19th
century. The palace interior
has been rearranged into
four "story zones" focusing
on the lives of William and
Mary; George II; Victoria's
Story, told in her own
words; and Margaret
and Diana, some
of whose dresses
are on display.
Visitors can try to
master the games
of the royal
court in the
King's State
Apartments.

⓫ Kensington Gardens

W8. **Map** 10 E4. **Tel** 0300 061 2000.
🚇 Bayswater, High St Kensington,
Queensway, Lancaster Gate.
Open 6am–dusk daily. 📷
🌐 **royalparks.gov.uk**

The former grounds of
Kensington Palace became a
public park in 1841. A small part
of it has been dedicated as a
memorial playground to Diana,
Princess of Wales (see p221). The
gardens are full of charm, starting
with Sir George Frampton's
statue (1912) of J M Barrie's
fictional Peter Pan, the boy who
never grew up, playing his pipes
to the bronze fairies and animals
that cling to the column below.
Often surrounded by parents,
nannies and their charges, the
statue stands near the west
bank of the Serpentine, not far
from where Harriet, wife of the
poet Percy Bysshe Shelley,
drowned herself in 1816.
Just north of here (in Hyde
Park) are the ornamental
fountains and statues,
including Jacob Epstein's
Rima, at the lake's head.
George Frederick Watts's
statue of a muscular
horse and rider, *Physical
Energy*, stands to the
south. Not far away
is a summer house
designed by
William Kent in
1735, and the
Serpentine
Gallery. The Round

Detail of the Coalbrookdale gate,
Kensington Gardens

Pond, created in 1728 just east of the palace, is often packed with model boats navigated by children and older enthusiasts. In winter it is occasionally fit for skating. In the north, near Lancaster Gate, is a dogs' cemetery, started in 1880 by the Duke of Cambridge while mourning one of his pets.

Riding on Rotten Row, Hyde Park

⑫ Hyde Park

W2. **Map** 11 B3. **Tel** 0300 061 2000. ⊖ Hyde Park Corner, Knightsbridge, Lancaster Gate, Marble Arch. **Open** 5am–midnight daily. 🏃 Sporting facilities. 🅦 **royalparks.gov.uk**

The ancient manor of Hyde was part of the lands of Westminster Abbey seized by Henry VIII at the Dissolution of the Monasteries in 1536. It has remained a royal park ever since. Henry used it for hunting but James I opened it to the public in the early 17th century. The Serpentine, an artificial lake used for boating and bathing, was created when Caroline, George II's queen, dammed the flow of the Westbourne River in 1730.

In its time, the park has been a venue for duelling, horse racing, highwaymen, demonstrations and music. The 1851 Exhibition was held here in a vast glass palace *(see pp30–1)*. The Princess Diana Memorial fountain is to the south of the Serpentine. Hyde Park is the setting for one of the UK's largest Christmas markets, complete with an ice rink and funfair.

⑬ Speakers' Corner

Hyde Park W2. Map 11 C2. ⊖ Marble Arch.

An 1872 law made it legal to assemble an audience and address them on whatever topic you chose; since then this corner of Hyde Park has become the established venue for budding orators and a fair number of eccentrics. It is well worth spending time here on a Sunday: speakers from fringe groups and one-member political parties reveal their plans for the betterment of mankind while the assembled onlookers heckle them without mercy.

⑭ Marble Arch

Park Lane W1. **Map** 11 C2. ⊖ Marble Arch.

John Nash designed the arch in 1827 as the main entrance to Buckingham Palace. It was, however, too narrow for the grandest coaches and was moved here in 1851. Historically, only senior members of the Royal Family and one of the royal artillery regiments are allowed to pass under it.

The arch stands near the site of the old Tyburn gallows (marked by a plaque), where until 1783 the city's most notorious criminals were hanged in front of crowds of bloodthirsty spectators.

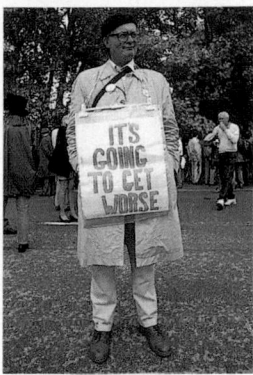

An orator at Speakers' Corner

⑮ Harrods

Knightsbridge SW1. **Map** 11 C5. **Tel** 020 7730 1234. ⊖ Knightsbridge. **Open** 10am–8pm Mon–Sat, 11:30am–6pm Sun. 🈳 ⊘ 💻 ♿ *See Shops and Markets p313.* 🅦 **harrods.com**

London's most famous department store began in 1849 when Henry Charles Harrod opened a small grocery shop nearby on Brompton Road. By concentrating on good quality and impeccable service, the store was soon popular enough to expand.

It used to be claimed that Harrods could supply anything from a packet of pins to an elephant – not quite true today, but the range of stock is still vast. A dress code applies so shorts, bare midrifs and flip-flops are not permitted.

Harrods at night, lit by 11,500 lights

❸ Victoria and Albert Museum

The Victoria and Albert Museum (the V&A) contains one of the world's widest collections of art and design, ranging from early Christian devotional objects to cutting-edge furniture design. Originally founded in 1852 as the Museum of Manufactures to inspire design students, it was renamed by Queen Victoria in 1899 in memory of Prince Albert. The museum is undergoing a dramatic redisplay of some of its collection, including work on a number of galleries and the Sackler Education Centre. To find out if a particular gallery is open, call the bookings office on 020 7942 2211.

British Galleries (1760–1900)
This charming sweet box (1770) is one of many pieces on display that were crafted in the workshops of Britain.

Silver Galleries
Radiant pieces such as the Burgess Cup (Britain, 1863) fill these stunning galleries.

★ **British Galleries (1500–1760)**
Displays of evocative objects, such as this writing desk from King Henry VIII's court, illustrate Britain's fascinating history.

★ **Fashion Gallery**
European fashion, fabrics and accessories from 1750 to the present day are on display, including these floral 1920s Lilley & Skinner shoes.

Exhibition Road entrance

Gallery Guide

The V&A has a 7-mile (11-km) layout spread over six levels, and the museum incorporates approximately 150 different galleries. The main floor, level 1, houses the China, Japan and South Asia Galleries, as well as the Fashion Gallery and the Cast Courts. The British Galleries are on levels 2 and 4. Level 3 contains the 20th Century Galleries and displays of silver, ironwork, paintings, photography and design works. The glass display is also on level 4. The Ceramics Galleries and Furniture are on level 6. The Henry Cole Wing houses the Sackler Education Centre, RIBA Architecture Study Rooms and the Prints and Drawings Study Rooms.

Key to Floorplan

- Level 0
- Level 1
- Level 2
- Level 3
- Level 4
- Level 6
- Henry Cole Wing
- Non-exhibition space

★ **Architecture Gallery**
This features highlights from the world-class collection of drawings, models, photographs and architectural fragments from the V&A and RIBA collections.

★ **Medieval and Renaissance Galleries**
The stunning Burghley Nef (France, 1527) is one of the many treasures in rooms 62–64.

China Gallery
This magnificent ancestor portrait is among the many exquisite pieces on show in this gallery.

The John Madejski Garden

Islamic Middle East Gallery
On display are fantastic objects representing the finest in Islamic art and design, such as this 16th-century table from the Ottoman Empire.

Aston Webb's façade (1909) is decorated with 32 sculptures of English craftsmen and designers.

Main entrance

Exploring the V&A's Collections

The sheer size of the V&A means you should plan your visit carefully to avoid missing a highlight or an area of particular interest. The following sections offer highlights but are by no means exhaustive. Be sure to visit the museum's original refreshment rooms off room 16a (one of which was designed by William Morris), now being used again as a café. If the weather is good, don't miss the John Madejski Garden. The Photographs galleries (rooms 38a and 100) display a changing selection of 300,000 photographs from 1856 to the present.

Covering the millennia from 3000 BC to the present, the impressive collection includes a giant Buddha's head from 700–900 AD, a huge yet elegant Ming canopied bed, and rare jade and ceramics.

Japanese art is concentrated in the Japan gallery in room 45, and is particularly notable for lacquer, Samurai armour and woodblock prints.

British Galleries

A sequence of grand rooms starting on level 2 and continuing on level 4 are devoted to the luxurious British Galleries. By presenting design and decorative arts from 1500 to 1900, the galleries chart Britain's rise from obscure island to "workshop of the world". The galleries present the evolution of British high design and the numerous influences, whether technological or aesthetic, absorbed from all over the world.

Beautiful textiles, furniture, costumes and household objects illustrate the tastes and lifestyles of Britain's ruling classes. Among the highlights are James II's wedding suit, the opulent State Bed from Melville House, and a number of carefully preserved period rooms, including the stunning Rococo Norfolk House Music Room. Discovery Areas give visitors a chance to delve even deeper into the past

Waistcoat (1734) in room 52b

by sporting a Tudor ruff or viewing 3-D images through a Victorian stereoscope.

China, Japan and South Asia

The Jameel Gallery of Islamic Art was opened in July 2006 and houses a significant collection of more than 400 objects including ceramics, textiles, carpets, metalwork, glass and woodwork. The exhibits date from the great days of the Islamic caliphate of the 8th and 9th centuries through to the years preceding the First World War.

Middle Eastern art from Syria, Iraq, Iran, Turkey and Egypt is found in room 42. Beautifully crafted textiles and ceramics illustrate the Islamic influence on fine and decorative arts. A dramatic arc of burnished steel fins, representing the spine of a Chinese dragon, spans the China gallery (room 44).

Gilt copper ice chest (Qing Dynasty 1700s), room 44

Architecture Gallery

The Architecture Gallery features highlights from the world-class collections of drawings, models, photographs and architectural fragments of the V&A and the Royal Institute of British Architects (RIBA).

The gallery explores the architecture that shapes our world through five themes. "The Art of Architecture" explores the history and ideas behind architectural styles. A superb collection of artifacts and illustrations is on display, grouped by period and spanning world cultures, including Asian, Spanish Islamic, Classical, Gothic and Modernist. "The Function of Buildings" looks at the way in

The Great Bed of Ware

Made in about 1590 of oak with inlaid and painted decoration, the Great Bed of Ware measures some 3.6 by 3.6 m (12 by 12 ft) and is 2.6 m (8 ft 9 inches) high. It is the V&A's most celebrated piece of furniture. Elaborately carved and decorated, the bed is a superb example of the art of the English woodworker. Its name derives from the town of Ware in Hertfordshire, about a day's ride north of London, where it resided in a number of inns. The Great Bed's enormous size made it an early tourist attraction, and no doubt interest was boosted by Shakespeare's reference to it in *Twelfth Night*, which he wrote in 1601.

Redecorated and refurbished, the bed is located in room 57.

Detail of the Ardabil Carpet (c. 1539–40) from the Jameel Gallery of Islamic Art

which the design of a building is informed not only by its function but also by the demands of climate.

"Architects and Architecture" examines the team effort involved in designing a building, and how this has evolved over the centuries. A huge range of sketches, models and drawings used by architects supports the theme.

"Structures" examines the different structures needed to create different buildings, from chunky low-rise to tall buildings.

"Buildings in Context" takes a look at the construction of London's Trafalgar Square, from the original maps in 1730 to the present day, in order to explore the relationship that exists between a building and its surroundings.

Medieval and Renaissance

Ten galleries, occupying an entire wing of the museum, house some of the world's greatest treasures of this era. Among the many remarkable exhibits are the notebooks of Leonardo da Vinci; sculptures by Italian masters such as Donatello and Giambologna, some in a Renaissance courtyard garden setting; the fine enamel Becket Casket (c.1180); and the reconstructed Santa Chiara Chapel, the only one of its kind outside Italy.

Textiles and Fashion

The popular Fashion Gallery displays items from the largest and most comprehensive collection of dress in the world. Around 100 exhibits, spanning over three centuries, are arranged chronologically. They include a magnificent mantua from the 1760s; an 1850s wedding dress with veil and shoes; a Schiaparelli evening coat embroidered with a design by Jean Cocteau; as well as a punk outfit designed by Vivienne Westwood. The equally fine Textiles collection is currently featured in galleries across the museum, but there are plans for a purpose-built, dedicated gallery.

Ruby glass flagon (c. 1858–9)

Metalwork

This group of galleries is located on level 3. In the Silver Galleries, 3500 pieces from 1400 to the present day are displayed in the beautifully refurbished Victorian rooms 65 to 69. Arms and armour, European metalwork from the 1500s to the present, and Islamic brass and bronze can be found in rooms 81, 82 and 87 to 89.

The Sacred Silver and Stained Glass galleries in rooms 83 and 84 display devotional treasures. The highlight of the ironwork galleries, which are located in rooms 113 to 114e, is the dazzling Hereford Screen designed by Sir George Gilbert Scott in 1862, and displayed at the International Exhibition of that year. The screen became the V&A's largest conservation project.

The Gilbert Collection of gold, silver, micromosaics and gold boxes, formerly housed at Somerset House, re-opened here in 2009.

Glass and Ceramics

Examples of 2,000 years of glass are exhibited across galleries on level 4. These contain superb porcelain from European china factories and a stunning balustrade by glass artist Danny Lane in room 131. Displays of international contemporary glass are on display in this room as well as in room 129.

The museum holds the world's largest and most comprehensive collection of ceramics. The introductory gallery presents the history and development of ceramics across the world.

Stained glass roundel entitled *Susanna Accused by the Elders* (c.1520)

KENSINGTON AND HOLLAND PARK

The western and northern perimeters of Kensington Gardens are a rich residential area and include many foreign embassies. The shops on Kensington High Street are almost as smart as those in Knightsbridge, and Kensington Church Street is a good source of quality antiques. Around Holland Park are some magnificent late Victorian houses, two of them open to the public. But as you cross into Bayswater and Notting Hill, you enter a more vibrant, cosmopolitan part of London. Its stucco terraces are lined with medium-priced hotels and inexpensive restaurants.

Westbourne Grove has become increasingly popular with the young, designer-clad crowd. Whiteleys, in Queensway, is one of the many historic buildings in the area. Built in 1912 by Belcher and Joass as a fashionable department store, it was converted in the 1980s into a vibrant shopping centre. To the west, Portobello Road is a popular street market selling anything from food to antiques. Notting Hill is known for its flamboyant Caribbean carnival, which took to the streets in 1966 and has been staged every year since, on the last weekend in August (see p59).

Sights at a Glance

Historic Streets and Buildings
❷ Holland House
❸ Leighton House
❹ Linley Sambourne House
❻ Kensington Square
❼ Kensington Palace Gardens
❾ Queensway

Parks and Gardens
❶ Holland Park
❺ Kensington Roof Gardens
❽ The Diana, Princess of Wales Memorial Playground

Markets
❿ Portobello Road

Historic Areas
⓫ Notting Hill

Street Finder, maps 9, 10, 17

☐ **Restaurants** *see pp295–7*
1 Assaggi
2 Babylon at the Roof Garden
3 The Belvedere
4 Byron
5 Kensington Place
6 Kitchen W8

0 metres   500
0 yards   500

Street-by-Street: Kensington and Holland Park

Although now part of central London, as recently as the 1830s this was a country village of market gardens and mansions. Outstanding among these was Holland House; part of its grounds are now Holland Park. The area grew up rapidly in the mid-19th century and most of its buildings date from then – mainly expensive apartments, mansion flats and fashionable shops.

② Holland House
The rambling Jacobean mansion, started in 1605 and pictured here in 1795, was largely demolished in the 1950s.

① ★ Holland Park
Parts of the old formal gardens of Holland House have been retained to grace this delightful public park.

The Orangery, now a restaurant has parts that date from the 1630s when it was within the grounds of Holland House.

Melbury Road is lined with large, Victorian houses. Many were built for fashionable artists of the time.

The Victorian letter box on the High Street is one of the oldest in London.

③ ★ Leighton House
It is preserved as it was when the Victorian painter, Lord Leighton, lived here. He had a passion for Middle Eastern tiles.

No. 16 Phillimore Place was home to the author of the children's classic *The Wind in the Willows*, from 1901 until 1908.

KENNETH GRAHAME 1859–1932 Author of "THE WIND IN THE WILLOWS" lived here 1901–8

Church Walk leads to Church Street, which is lined with antique shops *(see p323).*

Locator Map
See Central London Map pp16–17

Notting Hill

Shepherd's Bush

SOUTH KENSINGTON & KNIGHTSBRIDGE

KENSINGTON & HOLLAND PARK

West Kensington

Earl's Court

Kensington High Street station

Key

— Suggested route

Kensington Civic Centre, an assertive modern building by Sir Basil Spence, was completed in 1976.

0 metres 100
0 yards 100

❹ **Linley Sambourne House** Its carefully preserved late Victorian interior remains intact, complete with original furnishings and draperies.

Sticky Fingers, a lively café on the corner of Phillimore Gardens, is owned by Bill Wyman, former guitarist of the *Rolling Stones*.

Drayson Mews is one of the quaint alleys that were built behind large town houses for the stabling of horses and coaches. Today most have been converted into small houses.

The café in Holland Park

❶ Holland Park

Abbotsbury Rd W14. **Map** 9 B5.
Tel 020 7602 2226 to book facilities.
🚇 Holland Park, High St Kensington,
Notting Hill Gate. **Open** 7:30am–dusk
daily (hours are flexible depending on
light). **Closed** 25 Dec. 🚫 🚽 Open-air
opera, theatre, dance. Information:
Tel 020 7361 3570. Art exhibitions
Apr–Oct. *See Entertainment pp336–7.*
🇼 **rbkc.gov.uk**

This small but delightful park,
more wooded and intimate
than the large royal parks to its
east (Hyde Park and Kensington
Gardens, *see pp210–11*), was
opened in 1952 on what
remained of the grounds of
Holland House – the rest had
been sold off in the late 19th
century for the construction of
large houses and terraces to
the north and west. The park
still contains some of the formal
gardens, laid out in the early
19th century for Holland House.
There is also a Japanese garden,
created for the 1991 London
Festival of Japan. The park has
an abundance of wildlife,
including peacocks.

❷ Holland House

Holland Park W8. **Map** 9 B5. Youth
Hostel **Tel** 020 7937 0748. 🚇 Holland
Park, High Street Kensington.

During its heyday in the 19th
century, this was a noted centre
of social and political intrigue.
Statesmen such as Lord
Palmerston mixed here with
the likes of the poet Byron.

The remains of the house are
now used as a youth hostel.
    The outhouses are put to
various uses: exhibitions are
held in the orangery and the
ice house (a forerunner of
the fridge), and the old Garden
Ballroom is now a restaurant.

❸ Leighton House

12 Holland Park Rd W14. **Map** 17 B1.
Tel 020 7602 3316. 🚇 High St Kensington. **Open** 10am–5:30pm Wed–
Mon. **Closed** 1 Jan, 25 Dec.
🚫 🎫 3pm Wed & Sun or by
appt for groups. 🎵 Concerts,
exhibitions. 🇼 **rbkc.gov.uk/
leightonhousemuseum**

Built for respected Victorian
painter Lord Leighton in 1864–79,
the house has been preserved
with its opulent decoration as an
extraordinary monument to
Victorian aesthetics. The highlight
is the Arab hall, added in 1879 to
house Leighton's collection of
Islamic tiles, some of which are
inscribed with pieces from the
Koran. The best paintings include
some by Edward Burne-Jones,
John Millais, G F Watts and many
works by Leighton himself.

Original tiling in Holland House

❹ Linley Sambourne House

18 Stafford Terrace W8. **Map** 9 C5.
Tel 020 7602 3316 Mon–Fri; 020 7938
1295 Sat & Sun. 🚇 High St
Kensington. **Open** for guided tours
only: 11:15am & 2:15pm Wed; 11:15am
Sat & Sun; costumed tours 1pm,
2:15pm & 3:30pm Sat & Sun; phone to
book. 🚫 🎫 🇼 **rbkc.gov.uk/
linleysambournehouse**

The house, built in about 1870,
has undergone a major
renovation, but remains much as
Linley Sambourne furnished it, in
the Victorian manner, with china
ornaments and heavy velvet
drapes. Sambourne was a
cartoonist for the satirical
magazine *Punch*; drawings cram
the walls of the house. Some
rooms are decorated with William
Morris wallpaper *(see p251)*.

❺ Kensington Roof Gardens

99 Kensington High Street W8
(entrance in Derry Street). **Map** 10 D5.
Tel 020 7937 7994. **Open** 9am–5pm
daily (but call ahead, as sometimes
closed for private functions). 🚫
🇼 **roofgardens.virgin.com**

High above the bustle of
Kensington High Street is one
of London's best-kept secrets –
a 6,000-sq m (1.5-acre)-roof
garden. First planted in the
1930s by the owners of Derry &
Toms department store below
(now houses many different
stores), the themed gardens are
a lavish flight of fancy and

feature a woodland garden, a Spanish garden (with palm trees) and a formal English garden (with a pond, live ducks and a pair of pink flamingos). Best of all, it's free to wander round, though there is no access when the gardens have been booked for events.

❻ Kensington Square

W8. **Map** 10 D5. ⊖ High St Kensington.

This is one of London's oldest squares. It was laid out in the 1680s, and a few early 18th-century houses still remain. (Nos. 11 and 12 are the oldest.) The renowned philosopher John Stuart Mill lived at No. 18, and the Pre-Raphaelite painter and illustrator Edward Burne-Jones at No. 41.

❼ Kensington Palace Gardens

W8. **Map** 10 D3. ⊖ High St Kensington, Notting Hill Gate, Queensway.

This private road of luxury mansions occupies the site of the former kitchen gardens of Kensington Palace *(see p210)*. It changes its name half-way down; the southern part is known as Palace Green. It is open to pedestrians but closed to cars, unless they have specific business here. Most of the houses are occupied by embassies and their staff. At cocktail hour, you can watch black limousines with diplomatic number plates sweep beneath the raised barriers at each end of the road.

Queensway shop front

❽ The Diana, Princess of Wales Memorial Playground

Kensington Gardens. **Map** 10 E3. **Tel** 0300 061 2001. ⊖ Bayswater, Queensway. **Open** daily, Feb & Oct: 10am–4:45pm; Mar: 10am–5:45pm; Apr & Sep: 10am–6:45pm; May–Aug: 10am–7:45pm; Nov–Jan: 10am–3:45pm. **Closed** 25 Dec. 🚻 ♿
🌐 royalparks.org.uk

The newest of Kensington Gardens' three playgrounds was opened in 2000. Dedicated to the memory of the late Princess Diana, it is located close to the Bayswater Road, on the site of an earlier playground funded by Peter Pan's creator, J M Barrie. Diana's innovative adventure playground takes the boy who didn't want to grow up as its theme and is packed with novel ideas and activities including a beach cove with a 50-ft pirates' galleon, a tree house with walkways and ramps and a mermaid's fountain with a half-submerged slumbering crocodile (careful not to rouse him!). Though all children up to the age of 12 must be accompanied by an adult, staff are on hand to make sure the children are safe. Many features of the playground are accessible to children with special needs.

❾ Queensway

W2. **Map** 10 D2. ⊖ Queensway, Bayswater.

One of London's most cosmopolitan streets, Queensway has the heaviest concentration of eating places outside Soho. Newsagents are abundantly stocked with foreign newspapers. At the northern end is Whiteley's shopping centre. Founded by William Whiteley, who was born in Yorkshire in 1863, it was probably the world's first

Antique shop on Portobello Road

department store. The present building dates from 1911.

The street is named after Queen Victoria, who rode here as a princess.

❿ Portobello Road

W11. **Map** 9 C3. ⊖ Notting Hill Gate, Ladbroke Grove. Antiques market **Open** 9:30am–4pm Fri, 8am–5pm Sat. *See also Shops and Markets p333.*

There has been a market here since 1837. These days the southern end consists almost exclusively of stalls that sell antiques, jewellery, souvenirs and many other collectables. The market is extremely popular with tourists and tends to be very crowded on summer weekends. However, it is well worth visiting just to experience its bustling and cheerful atmosphere even if you don't intend to buy anything. If you do decide to buy, be warned – you are unlikely to get a real bargain, since the stallholders have a sound idea of the value of what they are selling.

⓫ Notting Hill

W11. **Map** 9 C3. ⊖ Notting Hill Gate.

Now the home of Europe's biggest street carnival, most of this area was farmland until the 19th century.

In the 1950s and 1960s, Notting Hill became a centre for the Caribbean community, many of whom lived here when they first arrived in Britain. The carnival started in 1966 and takes over the area every August over the bank holiday weekend *(see p59)* when costumed parades flood through the streets.

REGENT'S PARK AND MARYLEBONE

The area south of Regent's Park, incorporating the medieval village of Marylebone, has London's highest concentration of quality Georgian housing. It was developed by Robert Harley, Earl of Oxford, as London shifted west in the 18th century. Terraces by John Nash adorn the southern edge of Regent's Park, the busiest of the Royal Parks, while to its northwest lies St John's Wood, a smart inner suburb.

Sights at a Glance

Historic Streets and Buildings
④ Harley Street
⑤ Portland Place
⑥ Broadcasting House
⑮ Cumberland Terrace

Museums and Galleries
⑩ Wallace Collection
⑪ Sherlock Holmes Museum

Churches and Mosques
③ St Marylebone Parish Church
⑦ All Souls, Langham Place
⑫ London Central Mosque

Parks and Gardens
② Regent's Park

Entertainment
① Madame Tussauds
⑨ Wigmore Hall
⑭ London Zoo

Historic Hotels
⑧ Langham Hotel

Historic Waterways
⑬ Regent's Canal

Street Finder, maps 3, 4, 12

☐ Restaurants see pp297–8
1 Galvin Bistrot de Luxe
2 Golden Hind
3 Orrery
4 The Providores and Tapa Room
5 Texture

| 0 metres | 500 |
| 0 yards | 500 |

◀ Georgian-style architecture, Regent's Park

For keys to symbols *see back flap*

Street-by-Street: Marylebone

South of Regent's Park lies the medieval village of
Marylebone (originally Maryburne, the stream by St Mary's
church). Until the 18th century it was surrounded by fields,
but these were built over as fashionable London drifted west.
In the mid-19th century, professional people, especially
doctors, used the spacious houses to receive wealthy clients.
The area has maintained both its medical connections and its
elegance. Marylebone High Street is full of interesting, high-
quality food and clothes shops, bookshops and cafés.

❷ ★ Regent's Park
John Nash laid out the royal
park in 1812 as a setting for
classically designed villas
and terraces.

**The Royal Academy of
Music**, England's first
music academy, was
founded in 1774. The
present brick building,
with its own concert
hall, is from 1911.

❶ ★ Madame Tussauds
The wax museum of famous people,
historical and contemporary, has been
in business since 1835 and remains one
of London's most popular attractions. It
moved to its present location in 1884.

To Regent's
Park

**❸ St Marylebone
Parish Church**
Poets Robert Browning
and Elizabeth Barrett
married in this church.

Key

— Suggested route

0 metres   100
0 yards   100

Baker Street
station

Park Crescent's
breathtaking façades by Nash have
been preserved, although the
interiors were rebuilt as offices in
the 1960s. The crescent seals the
north end of Nash's ceremonial
route from St James's to Regent's
Park, via Regent Street and
Portland Place.

Locator Map
See Central London Map pp16–17

The London Clinic is one of the
best-known private hospitals in
this medical district.

Regent's Park station

❺ Portland Place
In the centre of this broad street
stands a statue of Field Marshal Sir
George Stuart White, who won
the Victoria Cross for gallantry
in the Afghan War of 1879.

The Royal Institute of British Architects
is housed in a striking Art Deco building
designed by Grey Wornum in 1934.

❹ Harley Street
Consulting rooms of
eminent medical
specialists have been
located here for more
than a century.

❶ Madame Tussauds

Marylebone Rd NW1. **Map** 4 D5. **Tel** 0871 894 3000. ⊖ Baker St. **Open** 9:30am–5:30pm Mon–Fri, 9am–6pm Sat & Sun (Aug: 9am–6pm daily). **Closed** 25 Dec. ⚟ 🖥 📷 ♿ phone first. 🌐 **madametussauds.com**

Madame Tussaud began her wax-modelling career rather morbidly, taking death masks of many of the best-known victims of the French Revolution. In 1835 she set up an exhibition of her work in Baker Street, not far from the collection's present site.

The attraction still uses traditional wax-modelling techniques to recreate politicians, royals, film and television actors, rock stars and sporting heroes.

The main sections of the exhibition are "A-List Party", where visitors get to feel what it is like to be at a celebrity party; "Film", devoted to giants of the entertainment world such as Marilyn Monroe and ET; and "World Leaders", including

Traditional wax-modelling at Madame Tussauds

Barack Obama, David Cameron and Martin Luther King.

The "Culture" area has the likes of Shakespeare and Picasso, and the "Music Zone" includes Madonna, Rihanna and The Beatles

"Scream" is the most renowned part of Madame Tussauds, featuring gruesome episodes in the grim catalogue of crime and punishment: the murderer Dr Crippen; Vlad the impaler; and the chill gloom of

an east London Victorian street during Jack the Ripper's time in the late 19th century.

The "Spirit of London" is the finale. Visitors travel in stylized London taxi-cabs and participate in momentous events of the city, from the Great Fire of 1666 to 1960s Swinging London.

Ticket prices also include entry to the Marvel Superheroes 4D Movie Experience – a thrilling cinema show.

There are also educational tours designed for groups and schools – check the website for further information.

Wax figure of Elizabeth II

Tulip time at Queen Mary's Gardens in Regent's Park

❷ Regent's Park

NW1. **Map** 3 C2. **Tel** 0300 061 2300. ⊖ Regent's Park, Baker St, Great Portland St. **Open** 5am–dusk daily. ♿ 🖥 Open air theatre *See Entertainment pp336–7*. Zoo *See p229*. Sports facilities. 🌐 **royalparks.gov.uk**

This area of land became enclosed as a park in 1812. John Nash designed the scheme and originally envisaged a kind of garden suburb, dotted with

56 villas in a variety of Classical styles, with a pleasure palace for the Prince Regent. In the event only eight villas – but no palace – were built inside the park (three survive round the edge of the Inner Circle).

The boating lake, which has many varieties of water birds, is marvellously romantic, especially when music drifts across from the bandstand in the distance. Queen Mary's Gardens are a mass of

wonderful sights and smells in summer, when visitors can enjoy Shakespeare productions at the **Open Air Theatre** nearby.

Nash's master plan for the park continues just beyond its northeastern edge in Park Village East and West. These elegant stucco buildings date from 1828.

The park is also renowned for its excellent sports facilities.

❸ St Marylebone Parish Church

Marylebone Rd NW1. **Map** 4 D5. **Tel** 020 7935 7315. ⊖ Regent's Park. **Open** phone to check. ♿ ✝ 11am Sun. 🖥 🌐 **stmarylebone.org**

This is where the poets Robert Browning and Elizabeth Barrett were married in 1846 after eloping from her strict family home on nearby Wimpole Street. The large, stately church by Thomas Hardwick was consecrated in 1817 after the former church, where Lord Byron was christened in 1778, had become too small.

Hardwick was determined that the same should not happen to his new church – so everything is on a grand scale.

Commemorative window in St Marylebone Parish Church

❹ Harley Street

W1. **Map** 4 E5. 🔵 Regent's Park, Oxford Circus, Bond St, Great Portland St.

The large houses on this late 18th-century street were popular with successful doctors and specialists in the middle of the 19th century when it was a rich residential area. The doctors' practices stayed and lend the street an air of hushed order, unusual in central London. There are very few private houses or apartments here now, but William Gladstone lived at No. 73 from 1876 to 1882.

❺ Portland Place

W1. **Map** 4 E5. 🔵 Regent's Park, Oxford Circus.

The Adam Brothers, Robert and James, laid this street out in 1773. Only a few of the original houses remain, the best being 27 to 47 on the west side, south of Devonshire Street. John Nash added the street to his processional route from Carlton House to Regent's Park and sealed its northern end with Park Crescent.

The building of the Royal Institute of British Architects (1934) at No. 66 is adorned with symbolic statues and reliefs. Its bronze front doors depict London's buildings and the River Thames.

❻ Broadcasting House

Portland Place W1. **Map** 12 E1. 🔵 Oxford Circus. **Open** daily for guided tours only. Pre-booking essential; call 0370 901 1227. 🎫 ♿ 📷 No children under 9. 🅆 **bbc.co.uk**

Broadcasting House was built in 1931 as a suitably modern Art Deco headquarters for the brand-new medium of broadcasting. Its front, curving with the street, is dominated by Eric Gill's stylized relief of Prospero and Ariel. As the invisible spirit of the air, Shakespeare's Ariel was considered an appropriate personification of broadcasting. The character appears in two other sculptures on the western frontage, and again over the eastern entrance in "Ariel Piping to Children".

Broadcasting House is now partly occupied by management, as some radio studios moved to west London in the 1990s. Fascinating tours of Broadcasting House (and also of BBC TV Centre in White City) are available. Each tour is unique, as the itinerary depends on programming and events of the day.

In partnership with English Heritage, a major refurbishment in 2011 opened a public piazza, a BBC shop, a café and an exhibition/interactive area.

Relief on the Royal Institute of British Architects on Portland Place

❼ All Souls, Langham Place

Langham Place W1. **Map** 12 F1. **Tel** 020 7580 3522. 🔵 Oxford Circus. **Open** 9:30am–6pm Mon–Fri, 9am–3pm & 5:30–8:30pm Sun. 🕈 9:30, 11:30am, 6:30pm Sun. ♿ 📷 Sun. 🅆 **allsouls.org**

John Nash designed this church in 1824. Its quirky round frontage is best seen from Regent Street. When it was first built, the spire was ridiculed as it appeared too slender and flimsy.

The only Nash church in London, it had close links with the BBC, based opposite at Broadcasting House, and ten years ago used to double as a recording studio for the daily broadcast church service.

❽ Langham Hotel

1 Portland Place W1. **Map** 12 E1. **Tel** 020 7636 1000. 🔵 Oxford Circus. . 🅆 **langhamhotels.com**

This was London's grandest hotel after opening in 1865. The writers Oscar Wilde and Mark Twain, and composer Antonin Dvořák were among its many distinguished guests. It was, for a time, used by the BBC as a record library and as a venue for recording shows. It has since been restored, bringing it boldly into the 21st century with its luxurious rooms, chic Artesian bar and the exquisite fine-dining restaurant, Roux at the Landau.

All Souls, Langham Place (1824)

❾ Wigmore Hall

36 Wigmore St W1. **Map** 12 E1. **Tel** 020 7258 8200. Box Office: **Tel** 020 7935 2141. ⊖ Bond St, Oxford Circus 🚻 🖉 *See Entertainment p341.* 🅆 **wigmore-hall.org.uk**

This appealing little concert hall for chamber music was designed by T E Collcutt, architect of the Savoy Hotel, in 1900. At first it was called Bechstein Hall because it was attached to the Bechstein piano showroom; the area used to be the heart of London's piano trade. Opposite is the Art Nouveau emporium built in 1907 as Debenham and Freebody's department store – now Debenham's is on Oxford Street.

Late 18th-century Sèvres porcelain vase at the Wallace Collection

❿ Wallace Collection

Hertford House, Manchester Sq W1. **Map** 12 D1. **Tel** 020 7563 9500. ⊖ Bond St, Baker St. **Open** 10am–5pm daily. **Closed** 24–26 Dec. Lectures. 🚻 📷 🖉 📷 🅆 **wallacecollection.org**

This is one of the world's finest private collections of art. It has remained intact since it was bequeathed to the government in 1897 with the stipulation that it should go on permanent public display with nothing added or taken away. The product of passionate collecting for four generations of the

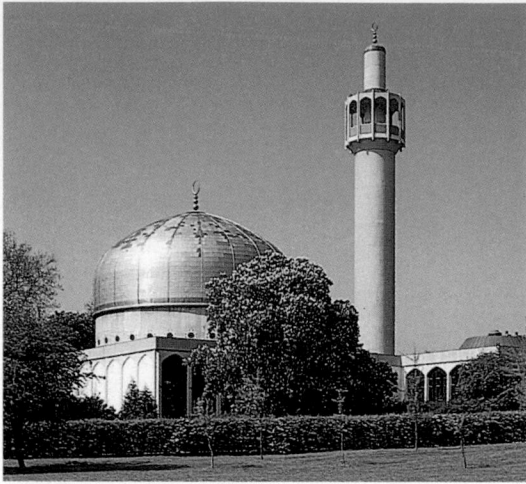

The Mosque on the edge of Regent's Park

Hertford family, it is a must for anyone with even a passing interest in the progress of European art up to the late 19th century. In 2000, four more galleries were opened so that even more of the collection could be shown.

Among the 70 master works are Frans Hals's *The Laughing Cavalier*, Titian's *Perseus and Andromeda* and Rembrandt's *Titus*. There are superb portraits by Reynolds, Gainsborough and Romney. Other highlights include Sèvres porcelain and sculpture by Houdon and Roubiliac. The fine European and Oriental armour collection is the second largest in the UK.

⓫ Sherlock Holmes Museum

221b Baker St NW1. **Map** 3 C4. **Tel** 020 7224 3688. ⊖ Baker St. **Open** 9:30am–6pm daily. **Closed** 25 Dec. 📷 📷 🅆 **sherlock-holmes.co.uk**

Sir Arthur Conan Doyle's fictional detective lived at 221b Baker Street. This building, dating from 1815, has been converted to resemble Holmes's flat, and is furnished exactly as described in the books. Visitors are greeted by Holmes's "housekeeper" and shown to his recreated rooms on the first floor. The shop sells the novels and deerstalker hats.

⓬ London Central Mosque

146 Park Rd NW8. **Map** 3 B3. **Tel** 020 7724 3363. ⊖ Marylebone, St John's Wood, Baker St. **Open** dawn–dusk daily. 🚻 📷 Lectures. 🅆 **iccuk.org**

Surrounded by trees on the edge of Regent's Park, this large, golden-domed mosque was designed by Sir Frederick Gibberd and completed in 1978. Built to cater for the increasing number of Muslim residents and visitors in London, the mosque is capable of holding 1,800 worshippers. The main hall of worship is a plain square chamber with a domed roof and a magnificent carpet. Visitors must remove their shoes before entering the mosque, and women should remember to cover their heads.

Conan Doyle's Sherlock Holmes

A boat trip on Regent's Canal

⑬ Regent's Canal

NW1 & NW8. **Map** 3 C1. **Tel** 020 7482 2660 (waterbus). 🚇 Camden Town, St John's Wood, Warwick Ave. Canal towpaths **Open** dawn–dusk daily. *See Six Guided Walks pp266–7.*
🆆 londonwaterbus.com

John Nash was extremely enthusiastic about this waterway, opened in 1820 to link the Grand Junction Canal, which ended at Little Venice in Paddington in the west, with the London docks at Limehouse in the east. He saw it as an added attraction for his new Regent's Park, and originally wanted the canal to run through the middle of that park. He was persuaded out of that by those who thought that the bargees' bad language would offend the genteel residents of the area. Perhaps this was just as well – the steam tugs that hauled the barges were dirty

and sometimes dangerous. In 1874, a barge carrying gunpowder blew up in the cutting by London Zoo, killing the crew, destroying a bridge and terrifying the populace, and the animals. After an initial period of prosperity for the canal, increasing competition from new railways saw it gradually slip into decline.

Today it has been revived as a leisure amenity; the tow-path is paved as a pleasant walkway and short boat trips are offered between Little Venice and Camden Lock, where there is a thriving crafts market. Visitors to the zoo can use the landing stage that is situated alongside it.

⑭ London Zoo

Regent's Park NW1. **Map** 4 D2.
Tel 0844 225 1826 . 🚇 Camden Town.
Open 10am–5:30pm (4:30pm Nov–Mar) daily. **Closed** 25 Dec. ♿ 📷 📶
🅿 🆆 zsl.org

Opened in 1828, the zoo has been one of London's biggest tourist attractions ever since, and is also a major research and conservation centre. London Zoo has over 600 species of animal, from Sumatran tigers to Mexican red-kneed bird-eating spiders. Exhibits include Penguin Beach, with over 60

London Zoo's aviary designed by Lord Snowdon (1964)

birds, and B.U.G.S! which covers the vast range of life forms found in Earth's major habitats. There are also plenty of interactive activities.

⑮ Cumberland Terrace

NW1. **Map** 4 E2. 🚇 Great Portland St, Regent's Park, Camden Town.

James Thomson is credited with the detailed design of this, the longest and most elaborate of the Nash terraces around Regent's Park. Its imposing central block of raised Ionic columns is topped with a decorated triangular pediment. Completed in 1828, it was designed to be visible from the palace Nash planned for the Prince Regent (later George IV). The palace was never built because the Prince was too busy with his plans for Buckingham Palace (*see pp96–7*).

Nash's Cumberland Terrace, dating from 1828

HAMPSTEAD

Hampstead has always stayed aloof from London, looking down from its site on the high ridge north of the metropolis. Today it is essentially a Georgian village. The heath separating Hampstead from Highgate

reinforces its appeal, isolating it further from the hurly-burly of the modern city. A stroll around the charming village streets, followed by a tramp across the Heath, makes for one of the finest walks in London.

Sights at a Glance

Historic Streets and Buildings
1 Flask Walk and Well Walk
5 Church Row
6 Downshire Hill
13 Vale of Health

Museums and Galleries
2 Burgh House
4 Fenton House
7 Keats House
10 Kenwood House

Parks and Gardens
8 Hampstead Heath
9 Parliament Hill
12 The Hill Garden

Pubs and Bars
3 Old Bull and Bush
11 Spaniards Inn

☐ **Restaurants** see pp301–3
1 Jin-Kichi
2 Gaucho Hampstead
3 The Wells

0 metres   500
0 yards   500

Street Finder, maps 1, 2

◄ Kenwood House on Hampstead Heath

For keys to symbols *see back flap*

Street-by-Street: Hampstead

Perched awkwardly on a hilltop, with its broad heath to the north, Hampstead has kept its villagey atmosphere and sense of being out of the city. This has attracted artists and writers since Georgian times and made it one of London's most desirable residential areas. Its mansions and town houses are perfectly maintained and a stroll through Hampstead's narrow streets is one of London's quieter pleasures.

❸ Old Bull and Bush
This pub on the edge of the Heath was a former haunt for writers and artists.

To Old Bull and Bush

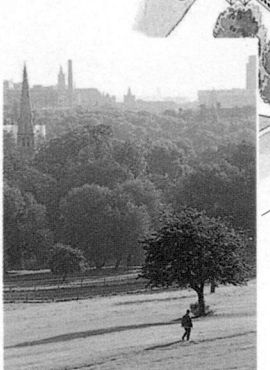

❽ ★ Hampstead Heath
A welcome retreat from the city, its broad open spaces include bathing ponds, meadows and lakes .

Whitestone Pond
takes its name from the old white milestone nearby. It is 4.5 miles (7 km) from Holborn (*see pp134–43*).

Grove Lodge was home to novelist John Galsworthy (1867–1933), author of the *Forsyte Saga*, for the last 15 years of his life.

Admiral's House
dates from about 1700. Built for a sea captain, its name derives from its external maritime motifs. No admiral ever actually lived in it.

Key

— Suggested route

0 metres		100
0 yards		100

❹ ★ Fenton House
Summer visitors should seek out this late 17th-century house and its exquisite walled garden, which are well hidden in the jumble of streets near the Heath.

2 ★ Burgh House
Built in 1702 but much altered since, the house contains an intriguing local history museum and a café overlooking the small garden.

Locator Map
See Central London Map pp16–17

The New End Theatre
produces rare but significant work. The building used to be a morgue.

No. 40 Well Walk
is where artist John Constable lived while working on his many Hampstead pictures.

1 Flask Walk and Well Walk
An alley of charming specialist shops broadens into a residential village street.

Hampstead station

5 ★ Church Row
The tall houses are rich in original detail. Notice the superb ironwork on what is probably London's finest Georgian street .

The Everyman Cinema has been an art cinema since 1933.

Old Bull and Bush in 1900

❶ Flask Walk and Well Walk

NW3. **Map** 1 B5. ⊖ Hampstead.

Flask Walk is named after the Flask pub. Here, in the 18th century, therapeutic spa water from what was then the separate village of Hampstead was put into flasks and sold to visitors or sent to London. The water, rich in iron salts, came from nearby Well Walk where a disused fountain now marks the site of the well. The Wells Tavern, almost opposite the spring, used to be a hostelry that specialized in accommodating those who engaged in the illicit liaisons for which the spa became notorious.

In later times, there have been many notable residents of Well Walk including artist John Constable (at No. 40), novelists D H Lawrence and J B Priestley and the poet John Keats, before he moved to his better-known house in what is now Keats Grove. At the High Street end,

Site of the well on Well Walk

Flask Walk is narrow and lined with old shops. Beyond the pub (note the Victorian tiled panels outside) it broadens into a row of Regency houses, one of which used to belong to the novelist Kingsley Amis.

❷ Burgh House

New End Sq NW3. **Map** 1 B4. **Tel** 020 7431 0144. ⊖ Hampstead. **Open** noon–5pm Wed–Sun (Sat ground floor art gallery & café only), 2–5pm public hols. **Closed** Christmas week. 🖥 📷 Music recitals. 🌐 **burghhouse.org.uk**

The last private tenant of Burgh House was the son-in-law of the writer Rudyard Kipling, who visited here occasionally in the last years of his life until 1936. After a period under the ownership of Hampstead Borough Council, the house was let to the independent Burgh House Trust. Since 1979, the Trust has run it as the Hampstead Museum, which illustrates the history of the area and concentrates on some of its most celebrated residents.

One room is devoted to the life of John Constable, who painted an extraordinary series of studies of clouds from Hampstead Heath. The house also has sections on Lawrence, Keats, the artist Stanley Spencer and others who lived and worked in the area. There is a display about Hampstead as a spa in the 18th and 19th centuries, which is also worth a visit. Burgh House often has exhibitions by contemporary local artists. The house itself was

built in 1703 but is named after a 19th-century resident, the Reverend Allatson Burgh. It has been much altered inside, and today the marvellously carved staircase is a highlight of the interior. Also worth seeing is the music room which was reconstructed in 1920, but contains good 18th-century pine panelling from another house. In the 1720s, Dr William Gibbons, chief physician to the then thriving Hampstead spa, lived here.

A licensed café serves delicious food and has a terrace overlooking the pretty garden.

Burgh House staircase

❸ Old Bull and Bush

North End Rd NW3. **Map** 1 A2. **Tel** 020 8905 5456. ⊖ Golders Green. **Open** 11am–11pm Mon–Sat, 11am–10:30pm Sun. ♿ 🌿 🌐 **thebullandbush.co.uk**

This pub, one of London's oldest and most famous, dates back to 1645, when it was a farmhouse. It received its licence to sell ale in 1721 and quickly became a haunt for artists and literary figures, including the famous artist William Hogarth *(see p261)* and the writer Austin Dobson. It is reputed that Hogarth planted a tree in the pub's garden. Located next to Hampstead Heath, the pub serves food at lunchtime and in the evening, and has barbecues in the summer in the garden. The interior is comfortably furnished.

❹ Fenton House

20 Hampstead Grove NW3. **Map** 1 A4. **Tel** 020 7435 3471. ⊜ Hampstead. **Open** Mar–Oct: 11am–5pm Wed–Sun & public hols (2–5pm some Thu due to lunchtime concerts). 🎦 ♿ ground floor only. 📷 book ahead. 📅 🅦 nationaltrust.org.uk/fentonhouse

Built in 1686, this splendid William and Mary house is the oldest mansion in Hampstead. It contains two specialized exhibitions that are open to the public during the summer: the Benton-Fletcher collection of early keyboard instruments, which includes a harpsichord dating from 1612, said to have been played by Handel; and a fine collection of porcelain. The instruments are kept in full working order and are actually used for concerts held in the house. The porcelain collection was largely accumulated by Lady Binning who, in 1952, bequeathed the house and its contents to the National Trust.

❺ Church Row

NW3. **Map** 1 A5. ⊜ Hampstead.

The row is one of the most complete Georgian streets in London. Much of its original detail has survived, notably the ironwork.

At the west end is St John's, Hampstead's parish church, built in 1745. The iron gates are earlier and come from Canons Park in Edgware. Inside the church is a bust of John Keats. John Constable's grave is in the churchyard, and many Hampstead luminaries are buried in the adjoining cemetery.

❻ Downshire Hill

NW3. **Map** 1 C5. ⊜ Hampstead.

A beautiful street of mainly Regency houses, it lent its name to a group of artists, including Stanley Spencer and Mark Gertler, who would gather at No. 47 between the two World Wars. That same house had

been the meeting-place of Pre-Raphaelite artists, among them Dante Gabriel Rossetti and Edward Burne-Jones. A more recent resident, at No. 5, was the late Jim Henson, the creator of the television show, *The Muppets*.

The church on the corner (the second Hampstead church to be called St John's) was built in 1823 to serve the Hill's residents. Inside, it still has its original box pews.

St John's, Downshire Hill

Lock of Fanny Brawne's hair

❼ Keats House

Keats Grove NW3. **Map** 1 C5. **Tel** 020 7332 3868. ⊜ Hampstead, Belsize Park. **Open** Apr–Oct: 1–5pm Tue–Sun; Nov–Apr: 1–5pm Fri–Sun. **Closed** Good Fri, Christmas week. 🎦 📷 3pm daily. ♿ ground floor only. 📅 Poetry readings, lectures. 🅦 keatshouse.cityoflondon.gov.uk

Originally two semi-detached houses built in 1816, the smaller one became Keats's home in 1818 when a friend persuaded him to move in. Keats spent two

productive years here: *Ode to a Nightingale*, perhaps his most celebrated poem, was written under a plum tree in the garden. The Brawne family moved into the larger house a year later and Keats became engaged to their daughter, Fanny. However, the marriage never took place because Keats died of consumption in Rome before two years had passed. He was only 25 years old.

A copy of one of Keats's love letters to Fanny, the engagement ring he offered her, and a lock of her hair are among the mementos that are exhibited at the house – it was first opened to the public in 1925. Visitors are also able to see facsimiles of some of Keats's manuscripts, part of a collection that serves as an evocative and memorable tribute to his life and work.

Fenton House's 17th-century façade

People relaxing in the open space of Hampstead Heath

❽ Hampstead Heath

NW3. **Map** 1 C2. **Tel** 020 7332 3322.
🚇 Belsize Park, Hampstead.
Open 24 hrs daily. Special walks on
Sundays. ♿ phone for disability
buggies. 🖥 Concerts, some children's
activities in summer. Sports facilities,
bathing ponds. Sports bookings
Tel 020 7332 3773.
W cityoflondon.gov.uk

The best time to stride across
these broad 3 sq miles (8 sq km)
is Sunday afternoon, when the
local residents walk off their roast
beef lunches, discussing the
contents of the Sunday papers.
Separating the hilltop villages
of Hampstead and Highgate

(see p248), the Heath was made
from the grounds of several,
formerly separate, properties
and embraces a variety of
landscapes – woods, meadows,
hills, ponds and lakes. It remains
uncluttered by the haphazard
buildings and statues that
embellish the central London
parks, and its open spaces have
become increasingly precious
to Londoners as the areas
around it get more crowded.
There are ponds for bathing and
fishing and, on three holiday
weekends – Easter, late spring
and late summer – the southern
part of the Heath is taken over
by a funfair (see pp58–61).

❾ Parliament Hill

NW5. **Map** 2 E4. **Tel** 020 7332 3773.
🚇 Belsize Park, Hampstead. ♿
Concerts, children's activities in
summer. Sporting facilities. 🖥

An unlikely but romantic
explanation for the area's name
is that it is where Guy Fawkes's
fellow plotters gathered on
5 November 1605 in the vain
hope of watching the Houses
of Parliament blow up after they
had planted gunpowder there
(see p26). More probably it was
a gun emplacement for the
Parliamentary side during the
Civil War 40 years later. The
gunners would have enjoyed a

❿ Kenwood House

Hampstead Lane NW3. **Map** 1 C1.
Tel 020 8348 1286. 🚇 Golders Green,
Archway, then 210 bus. Estate:
Open 10am–5pm daily. **Closed** 1 Jan,
24–26 Dec. 🅿 Regular events. ♿
ground floor. 🖥 🎭 See Entertainment
pp340–41. W english-heritage.org.uk

This is a magnificent Adam
mansion, filled with Old Master
paintings, including works by
Vermeer, Turner and Romney. It is
situated in landscaped grounds
high on the edge of Hampstead
Heath. There has been a house
here since 1616 – the present one
was remodelled by Robert Adam
in 1764 for the Earl of Mansfield.
Adam refitted existing rooms and

added to the original building.
Most of his work has survived,
the highlight being the library.
A Rembrandt self-portrait is the
star attraction of the collection,
and there are also works by Van
Dyck, Hals and Reynolds. The
2013 movie, Belle, was inspired by
Lord Mansfield's mixed-race niece,
Dido Belle, who also lived here.

The orangery is now
used for occasional
concerts and recitals.

broad view across London; even today, when tall buildings intervene, it provides one of the most spectacular views over the capital. From here the dome of St Paul's is prominent. Parliament Hill is also a popular place for flying kites and sailing model boats on the boating pond.

The historic Spaniards Inn

⓫ Spaniards Inn

Spaniards Rd NW3. **Map** 1 B1.
Tel 020 8731 8406. 🚇 Hampstead, Golders Green. **Open** 11am–11pm Mon–Fri, 10am–11pm Sat, 10am–10:30pm Sun. ♿
🔳 thespaniardshampstead.co.uk

Dick Turpin, the notorious 18th-century highwayman, is said to have frequented this pub. When he wasn't holding up stagecoaches on their way to and from London, he stabled his horse, Black Bess, at the Kenwood stables. The building certainly dates from Turpin's

time and, although the bar downstairs has been altered frequently, the small upstairs Turpin Bar is original. A pair of guns over the bar were reputedly taken from anti-Catholic rioters, who came to Hampstead to burn the Lord Chancellor's house at Kenwood during the Gordon Riots of 1780. The landlord detained them by offering pint after pint of free beer and, when they were drunk, disarmed them.

Among the pub's noted patrons have been the poets Shelley, Keats and Byron, the actor David Garrick and the artist Sir Joshua Reynolds.

The toll house has been restored; it juts into the road so that, in the days when tolls were levied, traffic could not race past without paying.

⓬ The Hill Garden

North End Way NW3. **Map** 1 A2.
🚇 Hampstead, Golders Green.
Open dawn to dusk daily.

This charming garden was created by Edwardian soap manufacturer and patron of the arts Lord Leverhulme. It was originally the grounds to his house, and is now part of Hampstead Heath. It boasts a raised pergola walkway, best seen in summer when the plants are in flower; the garden also has a beautiful formal pond.

Pergola walk at The Hill Garden

⓭ Vale of Health

NW3. **Map** 1 B3. 🚇 Hampstead.

This area was famous as a distinctly unhealthy swamp before it was drained in 1770; until then it was known as Hatches Bottom. Its newer name may derive from people fleeing here from cholera in London at the end of the 18th century. Alternatively, the name could have been the hype of a property developer when it was first recorded in 1801.

The poet James Henry Leigh Hunt put it on the literary map when he moved here in 1815, and played host to Coleridge, Byron, Shelley and Keats.

D H Lawrence lived here briefly and Stanley Spencer painted in a room above the Vale of Health Hotel, demolished in 1964.

Adam redesigned the façade of the old building.

Adam furnished these older rooms.

Lord Mansfield, who lived here from 1754 until 1793, had his dressing room here.

The ante-room was designed at the same time as the library.

The Adam library has a spectacularly curved, painted ceiling.

GREENWICH AND BLACKHEATH

Best known as the place from which the world's time is measured, Greenwich marks the historic eastern approach to London by land and water. Home to the National Maritime Museum and the Queen's House, the Royal Observatory and Cutty Sark, Greenwich has a village feel, with charming shops, markets and museums to explore.

Sights at a Glance

Historic Streets and Buildings
- 2 The Queen's House
- 7 Old Royal Naval College
- 9 Royal Observatory Greenwich
- 12 Croom's Hill

Museums
- 1 National Maritime Museum
- 4 Ranger's House – The Wernher Collection
- 13 The Fan Museum

Churches
- 3 St Alfege Church

Parks and Gardens
- 10 Greenwich Park
- 11 Blackheath

Walkway
- 6 Greenwich Foot Tunnel

Pubs and Bars
- 8 Trafalgar Tavern

Ships
- 5 Cutty Sark

☐ **Restaurants** *see pp301–3*
1 The Greenwich Union
2 Inside

0 metres		500
0 yards		500

Street Finder, maps 23, 24

◄ View of Canary Wharf from Greenwich Park

For keys to symbols *see back flap*

Street-by-Street: Greenwich

This historic town, granted UNESCO World Heritage Site status, marks the eastern approach to London and is best visited by river *(see pp62–7)*. In Tudor times it was the site of a palace much enjoyed by Henry VIII, near a fine hunting ground. The old palace is gone, leaving Inigo Jones's exquisite Queen's House, built for James I's wife. Museums, shops, cafés and markets, Wren's architecture and the magnificent Royal Park all make Greenwich an enjoyable day's excursion.

6 Greenwich Foot Tunnel, leading to the Isle of Dogs, is one of two tunnels built solely for pedestrians.

Greenwich Pier is a boarding point for boats to Westminster, the O2 and the Thames Barrier.

5 Cutty Sark
Clipper ships such as this once traded across the oceans. The impressively restored Cutty Sark has been raised to allow visitors to explore above and below decks.

Greenwich Market
This market, in the heart of Greenwich, sells crafts, antiques and books.

To Cutty Sark DLR

3 St Alfege Church
There has been a church here since 1012.

Spread Eagle Yard
Once a stopping point for horse-drawn carriages. The Guildford Arms is a Georgian gastropub, a hidden treasure in this area.

Locator Map
See Greater London Map pp14–15

Isle of Dogs

Charlton

GREENWICH
AND BLACKHEATH

Lewisham

7 ★ Old Royal Naval College
Wren's stately structure was built
in two halves so that the Queen's
House would keep its river view.

George II Statue
Sculpted by John Rysbrack in
1735, this statue depicts the
king as a Roman emperor.

The Painted Hall
contains 18th-century
murals by Sir James
Thornhill, who painted
the interior of the dome
at St Paul's Cathedral.

ROAD

2 ★ The Queen's House
On his return from Italy, this was
the first building Inigo Jones
designed in the Palladian style.

Key

— Suggested route

0 metres   100
0 yards   100

**1 National Maritime
Museum**
Real and model boats,
paintings and instruments
like this 18th-century compass
illustrate naval history.

❶ National Maritime Museum

Romney Rd SE10. **Map** 23 C2. **Tel** 020 8858 4422. Ⓔ Cutty Sark DLR. ⊜ Greenwich. **Open** 10am–5pm daily. **Closed** 24–26 Dec. 🔲 special exhibitions. 🔲 🔲 🔲 🔲 Lectures. **w** rmg.co.uk

The sea has always played an important role in British history, and this museum – built in the 19th century as a school for sailors' children – celebrates this seafaring heritage, from early British trade and empire to the exploratory expeditions of Captain Cook, and from the Napoleonic Wars through to the modern day.

The Sammy Ofer wing, the biggest development in the museum's history, boasts "the Wave", a 20-m audio-visual installation in which images and films from the museum's vast archives unfurl in dramatic, thematic journeys.

The Nelson gallery looks at the course of British maritime history over the tumultuous 18th century, a period when seafaring heroes were national celebrities. A star exhibit is the uniform that Lord Horatio Nelson was wearing when he was shot at the Battle of Trafalgar in October 1805.

Rather more spectacular is the royal barge built for Prince Frederick in 1732, decorated with gilded mermaids and his Prince of Wales's feathers on the stern. Throughout the museum are scores of finely crafted models of ships and historic paintings.

St Alfege's altar with rails attributed to Jean Tijou

❷ The Queen's House

Romney Rd SE10. **Map** 23 C2. **Tel** 020 8858 4422. Ⓔ Cutty Sark DLR. ⊜ Greenwich. **Open** 10am–5pm daily. Closes early for special events – phone to check. **Closed** 24–26 Dec. 🔲 🔲 🔲 🔲 🔲 **w** rmg.co.uk

The house was designed by Inigo Jones and was completed in 1637. It was originally meant to be the home of Anne of Denmark, wife of James I, but she died while it was still being built and it was finished for Charles I's queen, Henrietta Maria. She fell in love with it and called it her house of delights. After the Civil War it was briefly occupied by Henrietta as dowager queen, but was not much used by the royal family after that.

The building has been refurbished, and now displays the art collection of the National Maritime Museum. In the basement, on the west side,

Prince Frederick's barge at the National Maritime Musueum

visitors can learn about life at The Royal Hospital School, which was Britain's largest school of navigation and seamanship. From 1821 to 1933, it occupied The Queen's House. Visitors can know more about how the students lived and what their days were like. Visitors can also see the spiral "tulip staircase", which curves sinuously upwards without a central support. The staircase is reputed to be haunted.

❸ St Alfege Church

Greenwich Church St SE10. **Map** 23 B2. **Tel** 020 8853 0687. Ⓔ Cutty Sark DLR. **Open** 11am–4pm Mon–Wed, 11am–2pm Thu & Fri, 10am–4pm Sat, noon–4pm Sun. 🔲 8am, 10am Sun. 🔲 if accompanied. Concerts. **w** st-alfege.org

This is one of Nicholas Hawksmoor's most distinctive and powerful designs, with its gigantic columns and pediments topped by urns. It was completed in 1714 on the site of an older church, which marked the martyrdom of St Alfege, the then Archbishop of Canterbury, killed on this spot by Danish invaders in 1012. A second church here was the site of Henry VIII's baptism in 1491 and of 16th-century composer and organist Thomas Tallis's burial in 1585. Today a stained-glass window commemorates Thomas Tallis.

Some of the carved wood inside is by Grinling Gibbons, but much of it was badly damaged by a World War II bomb and has been restored. The wrought iron of the altar and gallery rails is original, attributed to Jean Tijou.

❹ Ranger's House – the Wernher Collection

Chesterfield Walk, Greenwich Park SE10. **Map** 23 C4. **Tel** 020 8294 2548. 🚇 Cutty Sark DLR. 🚉 Blackheath. **Open** See website. 🅿 🅿 guided tours by appointment, call for details. 🅿 🅿 **W** english-heritage.org.uk

The Wernher Collection is located in Ranger's House (1688), an elegant building southeast of Greenwich Park (see p245). It is an enchanting array of over 650 pieces accumulated by South African mine owner Sir Julius Wernher in the late 19th century. The collection is displayed in 12 rooms and includes paintings, jewellery, furniture and porcelain. Highlights include Renaissance masterworks by Hans Memling and Filippo Lippi, over 100 Renaissance jewels, and an opal-set lizard pendant jewel. Other curiosities include enamelled skulls.

Opal-set lizard pendant at the Wernher Collection

The Greenwich Foot Tunnel opened in 1902

❺ Cutty Sark

King William Walk SE10. **Map** 23 B2. **Tel** 020 8858 2698. 🚇 Cutty Sark DLR. 🚢 Greenwich Pier. **Open** 10am–5pm daily (last adm 4:30pm). **Closed** 25 & 26 Dec. 🅿 **Tel** 020 8312 6608. 🅿 🅿 🅿 book ahead. **W** cuttysark.org.uk

This majestic vessel is a survivor of the clippers that crossed the Atlantic and Pacific Oceans in the 19th century. Launched in 1869 as a tea carrier, it was something of a speed machine in its day, winning the annual clippers' race from China to London in 1871 in a time of 107 days. It made its final voyage in 1938 and was put on display here in 1957. In 2006 the Cutty Sark was closed to visitors for renovation work, which suffered a major setback in May 2007 when the ship was severely damaged by fire. It was re-opened by the Queen in spring 2012, fully restored.

❻ Greenwich Foot Tunnel

Between Greenwich Pier SE10 and Isle of Dogs E14. **Map** 23 B1. 🚇 Island Gardens, Cutty Sark DLR. 🚢 Greenwich Pier. **Open** 24hrs daily. Lifts **Open** 7am–7pm Mon–Sat, 10am–5:30pm Sun. 🅿 when lifts open.

This 370-m-(1,200-ft-) long tunnel was opened in 1902 to allow south London labourers to walk to work in Millwall Docks. Today it is

worth crossing for the wonderful views, across the river, of Christopher Wren's Royal Naval College and Inigo Jones's Queen's House.

Matching round red-brick terminals, with glass domes, mark the top of the lift shafts on either side of the river. The tunnel is about 2.5 m (9 ft) high and is lined with 200,000 tiles. Both ends of the tunnel are close to stations on the Docklands Light Railway (DLR), with trains to Canary Wharf (see p251), Limehouse, East London, Tower Hill and Lewisham. Although there are security cameras, the tunnel can be eerie at night.

A late 19th-century figurehead in the Cutty Sark

❼ Old Royal Naval College

King William Walk SE10. **Map** 23 C2. **Tel** 020 8269 4747. ☺ Cutty Sark DLR, Greenwich DLR. ☷ Greenwich, Maze Hill. **Open** 10am–5pm daily. **Closed** 24–26 Dec & some Sat. Grounds: **Open** 8am–6pm daily. Chapel: **Open** 10am–5pm Mon–Sat, 12:30am–5pm Sun. 📞 call 020 8269 1799 to book. ⛔ ♿ 🖥 🏛 **W** ornc.org

These ambitious buildings by Christopher Wren were built on the site of the old 15th-century royal palace, where Henry VIII, Mary I and Elizabeth I were born. The Painted Hall, Chapel, Discover Greenwich Visitor Centre and grounds are open to the public. The west front was completed by Vanbrugh.

Wren's Chapel was destroyed by fire in 1779. The present Greek Revival interior, by James Stuart, is light and airy. The Painted Hall was opulently decorated by Sir James Thornhill in the early 18th century. The ceiling paintings are supported by his illusionistic pillars and friezes.

Next to the visitor centre is a bar-restaurant and Greenwich Tourist Information Centre.

❽ Trafalgar Tavern

Park Row SE10. **Map** 23 C1. **Tel** 020 8858 2909. ☺ Cutty Sark DLR, Greenwich DLR. **Open** noon–11pm Mon–Thu, noon–midnight Fri–Sat, noon–10:30pm Sun. ♿ *See Pubs and Bars pp308–11.* **W** trafalgartavern.co.uk

This charming panelled pub was built in 1837 and quickly became established, along with other waterside inns in

Thornhill's painting of King William III in the Painted Hall of the Old Royal Naval College

Greenwich, as a venue for "whitebait dinners". Government ministers, legal luminaries and the like would arrive from Westminster and Charing Cross by water on celebratory occasions and feast on the tiny fish. The last such meeting of government ministers was held here in 1885. Whitebait still features, when they are in season, on the menu at the pub's restaurant, although they are no longer fished from the Thames.

This was another of Charles Dickens's haunts. He drank here with one of his novels' most famous illustrators, George Cruickshank.

In 1915, the pub became an institution for old merchant seamen. It was restored in 1965 after a spell of being used as a social club for working men.

❾ Royal Observatory Greenwich

Greenwich Park SE10. **Map** 23 C3. **Tel** 020 8858 4422. ☺ Cutty Sark DLR. ☷ Blackheath, Greenwich. **Open** 10am–5pm daily (last adm: 4:30pm). **Closed** 24–26 Dec. 🎦 for Planetarium shows (last show 4pm). 🎦 ♿ 🏛 **W** rmg.co.uk

The meridian (0° longitude) that divides the Earth's eastern and western hemispheres passes through here, and millions of visitors have taken the opportunity of being photographed standing with a foot on either side of it. In 1884, Greenwich Mean Time became the basis of time measurement for most of the world, following the International Meridian Conference in Washington, DC.

The original building, Flamsteed House, was designed by Christopher Wren. Above one of the building's two turrets is a ball on a rod, which has dropped at 1pm every day since 1833 so that sailors on the Thames, and makers of chronometers (navigators' clocks), could set their clocks by it. The house now contains a display of John Harrison's marine timekeepers and an intriguing exhibition about Greenwich Mean Time. Flamsteed was the first Astronomer Royal, appointed by Charles II, and this was the

Trafalgar Tavern viewed from the Thames

official government observatory from 1675 until 1948, when the lights of London became too bright and the astronomers moved to darker Sussex.

A state-of-the-art planetarium, the only one in London, opened here in 2007.

A rare 24-hour clock at the Royal Observatory Greenwich

⑩ Greenwich Park

SE10. **Map** 23 C3. **Tel** 0300 061 2380. 🚇 Cutty Sark DLR, Greenwich DLR. 🚉 Greenwich, Maze Hill, Blackheath. **Open** 6am–7pm daily. 🖥 ♿ Children's shows, playground, boating lake and sports facilities. 🌐 **royalparks.gov.uk** Ranger's House, Chesterfield Walk, Greenwich Park SE10. **Map** 23 C4. 🌐 **english-heritage.co.uk** *See also Wernher Collection, p243.*

Originally the grounds of a royal palace and still a Royal Park, Greenwich Park was enclosed in 1433 and its brick wall built in the reign of James I. Later, in the 17th century, the French royal landscape gardener André Le Nôtre, of Versailles and Fontainebleau fame, was invited to design one at Greenwich. The broad avenue, rising south up the hill, was part of his plan.

There are great river views from the hilltop and on a fine day, most of London can be seen. In 2012, the park played host to the London Olympic equestrian events.

Ranger's House in Greenwich Park

To the southeast of the park, and on the edge of the park's rose garden, is the Ranger's House (1688), which now houses the art collection of Julius Wernher *(see p243).*

From here the walk to the charming village of Blackheath is flat, compared with the steep walk down to the village of Greenwich at the bottom of the hill.

⑪ Blackheath

SE3. **Map** 24 D5. 🚉 Blackheath.

This open heath used to be a rallying point for large groups who were entering London from the east, including Wat Tyler's band of rebels at the time of the Peasants' Revolt in 1381.

Blackheath is also the place where King James I of England (who was also King James VI of Scotland) introduced the game of golf from his native Scotland, to the then largely sceptical English.

Today the heath is well worth exploring for the stately Georgian houses and terraces that surround it. The prettily named Tranquil Vale to the south of the heath is the main shopping strip.

⑫ Croom's Hill

SE10. **Map** 23 C3. 🚇 Cutty Sark DLR, Greenwich DLR. 🚉 Greenwich.

One of the best kept 17th- to early 19th-century streets in London. The oldest buildings are at the Blackheath end: the original Manor House of 1695; No. 68, from about the same date; and No. 66 the oldest of all. Famous Irish actor Daniel Day Lewis grew up here.

⑬ The Fan Museum

12 Croom's Hill SE10. **Map** 23 B3. **Tel** 020 0303 1441. 🚉 Greenwich. **Open** 11am–5pm Tue–Sat, noon–5pm Sun. **Closed** 1 Jan, 24–26 Dec. 📷 no flash. 🎭 by appt. 🏛 🖥 👶 ♿ Lectures, fan-making workshops first Sat of the month. 🌐 **thefanmuseum.org.uk**

One of London's most unlikely museums – the only one of its kind in the UK – opened in 1991. It owes its existence and appeal to the enthusiasm of Helene Alexander MBE, whose personal collection of about 4,000 fans from the 17th century onwards has been augmented by donations, including several fans that were made for the stage. If there, Mrs Alexander will act as a guide.

Stage fan used in a D'Oyly Carte operetta

FURTHER AFIELD

Many of the great houses originally built as country retreats for London's high and mighty were overrun by sprawling suburbs in the Victorian era. Fortunately, several have survived as museums in these now less-rustic surroundings. Most are less than an hour's journey from central London. Richmond Park and Wimbledon Common give a taste of the country, or go on an adventure to explore the Docklands and Thames Barrier.

Sights at a Glance

Historic Streets and Buildings
- ⓫ Sutton House
- ㉑ Charlton House
- ㉒ Eltham Palace
- ㉚ *Hampton Court pp256–9*
- ㉛ Ham House
- ㉜ Orleans House Gallery
- ㉝ Marble Hill House
- ㉟ Syon House
- ㊲ Osterley Park House
- ㊳ PM Gallery and House
- ㊶ Strand on the Green
- ㊷ Chiswick House
- ㊹ Fulham Palace

Churches
- ⓭ St Mary, Rotherhithe
- ⓮ St Anne's, Limehouse
- ㉖ St Mary's, Battersea

Markets
- ❷ Camden Market

0 kilometres 5
0 miles 3

Museums and Galleries
- ❶ Lord's Cricket Ground
- ❸ Freud Museum
- ❻ The Jewish Museum
- ❼ St John's Gate
- ❽ Crafts Council Gallery
- ❿ Geffrye Museum
- ⓬ V&A Museum of Childhood
- ⓯ Museum of London Docklands
- ⓱ William Morris Gallery
- ㉓ Horniman Museum
- ㉔ Dulwich Picture Gallery
- ㉗ Wimbledon Lawn Tennis Museum
- ㉘ Wimbledon Windmill Museum
- ㊱ Musical Museum
- ㊴ Kew Bridge Steam Museum
- ㊸ Hogarth's House

Parks and Gardens
- ㉕ Battersea Park
- ㉙ Richmond Park
- ㊵ *Kew Gardens pp262–3*

Cemeteries
- ❺ Highgate Cemetery

Modern Architecture
- ⓰ Canary Wharf
- ⓴ The O2 Arena
- ㊺ Chelsea Harbour

Historic Districts
- ❹ Highgate
- ❾ Islington
- ㉞ Richmond

Modern Technology
- ⓲ Emirates Air Line Cable Car
- ⓳ Thames Barrier

Key
- ▪ Main sightseeing areas
- ▭ Motorway
- ▬ Main road
- ▭ Minor road

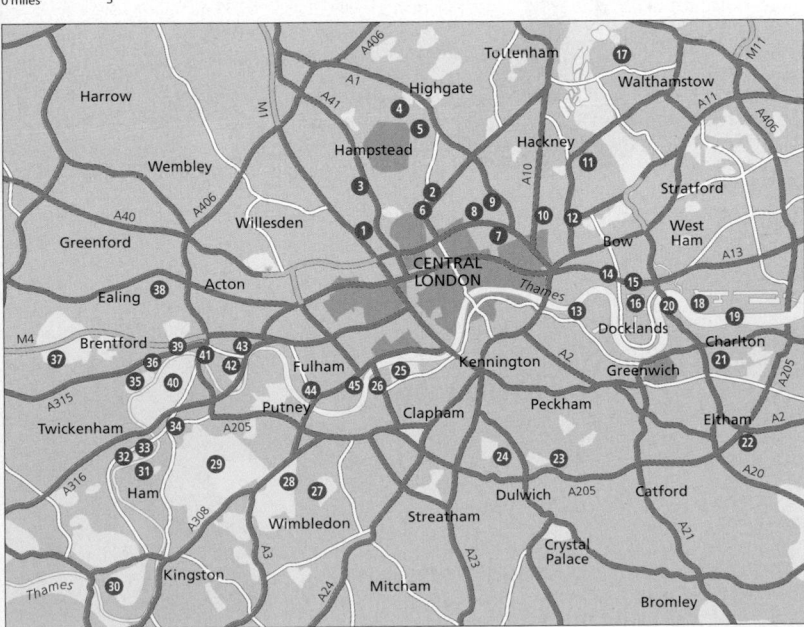

All the sights in this section lie inside the M25 motorway *(see pp14–15)*.

◀ Red deer frequently spotted at Richmond Park

For keys to symbols *see back flap*

North of the Centre

❶ Lord's Cricket Ground

NW8. **Map** 3 A3. **Tel** 020 7616 8595, MCC Museum: 020 7616 8658. 🚇 St John's Wood. Museum: **Open** 10am–4:30pm on non-match days. On match days, museum is open to ticket holders only. **Closed** 1 Jan, 25, 26 & 29 Dec. 🅿️ ♿ 📷 see website; groups call to pre-book. 🎫 *See Entertainment pp346–7.* 🆆 **lords.org**

The headquarters of Britain's chief summer sport contains a museum, including a stuffed sparrow killed by a cricket ball as well as the Ashes (burned wood in an urn), the object of ferocious competition between the English and Australian national teams. The museum explains the history of the game, and mementos of notable cricketers make it a place of pilgrimage for devotees of the sport. Entrance to the museum is included in the tour.

Cricket pioneer Thomas Lord moved his ground here in 1814. The Pavilion (1890), from which women were excluded until 1999, is late Victorian.

❷ Camden Market

NW1. 🚇 Camden Town, Chalk Farm. **Open** 10am–6pm daily.

Camden Market is really six markets located close to each other along Chalk Farm Road and Camden High Street. Packed with shoppers at the weekends, most of the shops and some of the stalls are open on weekdays. Many units are housed in restored Victorian buildings alongside Camden Lock and the canal. The first market here was a crafts market at Camden Lock, in 1975. Today, all the markets sell a wide range of exciting goods, from arts and crafts and street fashion, to new age remedies and body piercing.

Sigmund Freud's famous couch

❸ Freud Museum

20 Maresfield Gdns NW3. **Tel** 020 7435 2002. 🚇 Finchley Rd. **Open** noon–5pm Wed–Sun. **Closed** 24–26 Dec. 📷 no flash. ♿ limited. 🎫 Events. 🆆 **freud.org.uk**

In 1938 Sigmund Freud, the founder of psychoanalysis, fled from Nazi persecution in Vienna to this Hampstead house. Making use of the possessions he brought with him, his family recreated the atmosphere of his Vienna consulting rooms. After Freud died in 1939 his daughter Anna (who was a pioneer of child psychoanalysis) kept the house as it was. In 1986 it was opened as a museum dedicated to Freud. The most famous item is the couch on which patients lay for analysis. A series of 1930s home movies shows cheerful moments with his dog as well as scenes of Nazi attacks on his apartment. The bookshop has a large collection of his works.

The Ashes at Lord's

❹ Highgate

N6. 🚇 Highgate.

There has been a settlement here since at least the early Middle Ages, when an important staging post on the Great North Road from London was established with a gate to control access. Like Hampstead across the Heath *(see pp236–7)*, it soon became fashionable and noblemen built country houses here.

It still has an exclusive feel, with a Georgian High Street and expensive houses. It was on Highgate Hill in medieval times, that Dick Whittington (a poor young lad) and his pet cat were persuaded to turn back, and try their fortune in the city, by the sound of Bow Bells. He went on to become Lord Mayor of London. A statue of a black cat marks the spot of his epiphany *(see p41)*.

❺ Highgate Cemetery

Swain's Lane N6. **Tel** 020 8340 1834. 🚇 Archway. Eastern Cemetery: **Open** 10am–5pm Mon–Fri, 11am–5pm Sat & Sun. 📷 2pm Sat. Western Cemetery: **Open** 📷 only Mar–Nov: 1:45pm Mon–Fri, half-hourly 11am–4pm Sat & Sun; Nov–Feb: half-hourly 11am– 3pm Sat & Sun. No children admitted under 8 years; first come first served. **Closed** 25 & 26 Dec & during funerals (phone to check). 📷 ♿ Eastern only. 🆆 **highgate-cemetery.org**

The western section of this high-Victorian gem opened in 1839. For many years it lay neglected, until a voluntary group, the Friends of Highgate Cemetery, stepped in to save it from further decline. They have restored the Egyptian Avenue, a street of family vaults styled on ancient Egyptian tombs, and the Circle of Lebanon, more vaults in a ring, topped by a cedar tree. In the eastern section lie Karl Marx, Herbert Spencer and novelist George Eliot (real name, Mary Anne Evans).

George Wombwell's memorial at Highgate Cemetery

Jewish Bakers' Union banner, c.1926, Jewish Museum, Camden

❻ The Jewish Museum

129–31 Albert Street, NW1. **Map** 4 E1. **Tel** 020 7284 7384. ⊖ Camden Town. **Open** 10am–5pm Sat–Thu, 10am–2pm Fri. **Closed** Jewish hols, 25 & 26 Dec. 🖼 🔊 🖥 🖼
W jewishmuseum.org.uk

When London's Jewish Museum was founded in 1932 it was split between two sites, in Finchley and Camden. In 2007 the museum celebrated its 75th anniversary with the commencement of works to bring the two collections together in a single building. The project has created enlarged galleries, education facilities and hands-on displays for children.

Celebrating Jewish life in this country from the Middle Ages, the museum is packed with memorabilia. It also has important collections of Jewish ceremonial art, which includes Hanukkah lamps, a collection of Jewish marriage rings and some illuminated marriage contracts. The highlight of this collection is a 16th-century Venetian synagogue ark.

❼ St John's Gate

St John's Lane EC1. **Map** 6 F4. **Tel** 020 7324 4005. ⊖ Farringdon. **Open** 10am–5pm Mon–Sat. **Closed** Christmas week & bank holiday weekends. 📷 11am, 2:30pm Tue, Fri, Sat (donation). 🔊 🔊 limited.
W museumstjohn.org.uk

The Tudor gatehouse and parts of the 12th-century church are all that remain of the priory of the Knights of St John, which flourished here for 400 years and was the precursor of the St John Ambulance. Over the

years, the priory buildings have had many uses, such as offices for Elizabeth I's Master of the Revels, a pub, and a coffee shop run by the artist William Hogarth's father. A museum of the order's history has been renovated, with support from the Heritage Lottery Fund, to create an exhibition space showing hidden parts of the gatehouse and a learning space in the priory church. To see the rest of the building, join a guided tour.

The Crafts Council

❽ Crafts Council

44a Pentonville Rd N1. **Map** 6 D2. **Tel** 020 7806 2500. ⊖ Angel. 📕 library, 10am–5pm Wed & Thu. **Closed** 25 Dec–1 Jan. 🔊 🖼 Lectures. **W** craftscouncil.org.uk

The Crafts Council is the national agency for promoting the creation and appreciation of contemporary crafts in the UK. It has a collection of contemporary British crafts, some of which are loaned to touring exhibitions, and there is a

library. They also organise two large craft fairs – one at the Saatchi Gallery (see *p199*) in May and the other at Somerset House (see *p119*) in September/October.

❾ Islington

N1. **Map** 6 E1. ⊖ Angel, Highbury & Islington.

Islington was once a highly fashionable spa, but the rich began to move out in the late 18th century, and the area deteriorated rapidly. During the 20th century, writers such as Evelyn Waugh, George Orwell and Joe Orton lived here. Now Islington has again returned to fashion as one of London's first areas to become "gentrified", with many young professionals buying and refurbishing old houses.

An older relic is Canonbury Tower, the remains of a medieval manor house converted into apartments in the 18th century. Writers such as Washington Irving and Oliver Goldsmith lived here and today it houses the Tower Theatre. On Islington Green, there is a statue of Sir Hugh Myddleton, who built a canal through Islington in 1613 to bring water to London from Hertfordshire; today a landscaped walk along its banks runs between Essex Road and Canonbury stations. There is a market, Chapel Market close to the Angel station (see *p332*), antique shops at Camden Passage, and a shopping and cinema complex, the N1 Centre.

St John's Priory: today, only the gatehouse remains intact

East of the Centre

⑩ Geffrye Museum

Kingsland Rd E2. **Tel** 020 7739 9893.
🚇 Liverpool St, Old St. **Open** 10am–
5pm Tue–Sun, noon–5pm bank hols.
Closed 1 Jan, Good Fri, 24–26 Dec.
Garden **Open** Apr–Oct. 🚻 🖥 ✏
🎭 Exhibitions & events.
w geffrye-museum.org.uk

This delightful museum is
housed in a set of 18th-century
almshouses. They were built in
1715 on land bequeathed by
Sir Robert Geffrye, a 17th-century
Lord Mayor of London who made
his fortune through trade. Inside,
you take a trip through a series of
11 rooms, chronologically
arranged, which have been
decorated in different period
styles, each one providing an
insight into the domestic interiors
of the urban middle classes.
The historic room settings begin
with Elizabethan (which contains
magnificent panelling) and run
through various major styles,
including High Victorian, while an
attractive extension houses more
modern settings, such as an
example of 1990s "loft living".
Each room contains superb

examples of British furniture of
the period. Outside, there is a
series of garden "rooms" that
show the designs and planting
schemes popular in urban
gardens between the 16th and
20th centuries. There is a good
café, which has a children's menu.

⑪ Sutton House

2–4 Homerton High St E9. **Tel** 020
8986 2264. 🚇 Bethnal Green then
bus 253. **Open** see website for
opening times. 🅿 🚻 limited.
📷 phone first. 🖥 🎭 Regular events.
w nationaltrust.org.uk

One of the few London Tudor
merchants' houses to survive
in something like its original
form. Built in 1535 for Ralph
Sadleir, a courtier to Henry VIII,
it was owned by several wealthy
families before becoming a
girls' school in the 17th century.
In the 18th century the front
was altered, but the Tudor
fabric remains surprisingly
intact, with much original
brickwork, large fireplaces
and linenfold panelling.

⑫ V&A Museum of Childhood

Cambridge Heath Rd E2. **Tel** 020
8983 5200. 🚇 Bethnal Green.
Open 10am–5:45pm daily (to 9pm
1st Thu of month). **Closed** 1 Jan,
25 & 26 Dec. 🚻 🖥 🎭 Workshop,
children's activities.
w vam.ac.uk/moc

This East London branch of the
Victoria and Albert Museum
(see pp212–15) has the largest
collection of childhood-related
objects in the UK. Its array of
toys, games, lavish dolls' houses,
model trains, theatres and
costumes dates from the
16th century to the present day,
and is well explained and
enticingly displayed. The upper
floor has lots of fun activities,
such as dressing up, a playable
jukebox and wobbly mirror.
   The purpose-built museum
building was originally erected
on the V&A site. In 1872, it was
dismantled and reassembled
here to bring the light of learning
to the East End. The toy collection
began in the early 20th century
and became a dedicated
museum of childhood at
Bethnal Green in 1974.

⑬ St Mary, Rotherhithe

St Marychurch St SE16. **Tel** 0207
394 3394. 🚇 Rotherhithe.
Open 9am–6pm daily.
✝ 10am, 6pm Sun. 🚻
w stmaryrotherhithe.org

This church was built in
1715 on the site of a medieval
church. It has nautical
connotations, most notably
a memorial to Christopher
Jones, captain of the *Mayflower*,
on which the Pilgrim Fathers
sailed to North America.
The communion table is
made from the timbers of the
Temeraire, a warship whose
final journey to the breaker's
yard at Rotherhithe was
evocatively recorded in
Turner's painting at the
National Gallery (see pp106–109).
   The church also contains
a fine example of 18th-century
organ building by John Byfield.

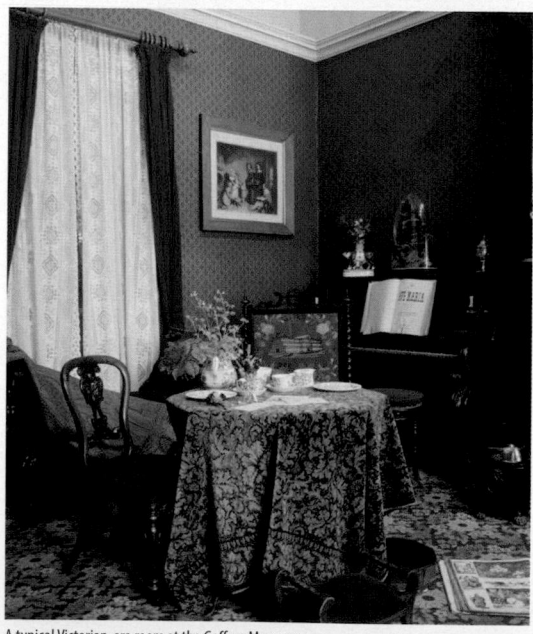

A typical Victorian-era room at the Geffrye Museum

⓮ St Anne's, Limehouse

3 Colt St E14. **Tel** 020 7987 1502. ⊖ Westferry (DLR). **Open** 9:30am–1pm Sun. 🚩 10:30am Sun. 🎵 Concerts, lectures see website for details. Ⓦ **stanneslimehouse.org**

This is one of a group of East End churches designed by Nicholas Hawksmoor, completed in 1724. Its 40-m (130-ft) tower became a landmark for ships using the East End docks – St Anne's still has the highest church clock in London. Damaged by fire in 1850, the church interior was subsequently Victorianized. It was bombed in World War II and is today in need of further restoration.

⓯ Museum of London Docklands

No. 1 Warehouse, West India Quay E14. **Tel** 020 7001 9844. ⊖ Barbican, St Paul's. **Open** 10am–6pm daily. **Closed** 24–26 Dec. 🦽 🚫 🖥 📷 Ⓦ **museumoflondon.org.uk/docklands**

Occupying a late-Georgian warehouse, this museum tells the story of London's docks and their links from Roman times to the present. Recreations let visitors step back in time: notably the dark and dangerous "Sailor-town" of Wapping in the 1850s.

⓰ Canary Wharf

E14. ⊖ Canary Wharf or West India Quay (DLR). 🦽 🚫 🖥 📷 Information centre, concerts.

London's most ambitious commercial development opened in 1991, when the first tenants moved into the 50-storey Canada Tower, designed by Argentine architect César Pelli. At 250 m (800 ft), it dominates the city's eastern skyline. The tower stands on what was the West India Dock, closed, like all the London docks, between the 1960s and the 1980s, when trade moved to the modern port down river at Tilbury. Today, Canary Wharf is thriving. A major shopping complex, as well as offices and restaurants, is located in and around Canada Tower.

⓱ William Morris Gallery

Lloyd Park, Forest Rd E17. **Tel** 020 8496 4390. ⊖ Walthamstow Central. **Open** 10am–5pm Wed–Sun. **Closed** 24–26 Dec and public hols. 🦽 🖥 📷 Lectures. Ⓦ **wmgallery.org.uk**

The most influential designer of the Victorian era, born in 1834, lived in this 18th-century house as a youth from 1848–56. It is now a beguiling and well-presented museum giving a full account of William Morris the artist, designer, writer, craftsman and socialist.

It has examples of his work and that of other members of the Arts and Crafts movement – tiles by William de Morgan, and paintings by members of the Pre-Raphaelite Brotherhood.

Interactive exhibits introduce visitors to techniques such as hand-printing and dyeing.

⓲ Emirates Air Line Cable Car

Western Gateway F16/Edmund Halley Way SE10. ⊖ Royal Victoria (DLR), North Greenwich/The O2 Arena. **Open** 7am–9pm Mon–Fri, 8am–9pm Sat, 9am–9pm Sun. 🚲 Ⓦ **emiratesairline.co.uk**

Connecting the Royal Victoria Dock and The O2, this cable car provides spectacular views over the river during the 5-minute trip.

Intricate detail visible on a William Morris tapestry (1885)

⓳ Thames Barrier

Unity Way SE18. **Tel** 020 8305 4188. 🚢 Charlton, Silvertown. **Open** 10:30am–5pm Thu–Sun (last adm 4:30pm). **Closed** 25 Dec–1 Jan. 🚫 🦽 🖥 📷 exhibition.

In 1236 the Thames rose so high that people rowed across Westminster Hall; London flooded again in 1663, 1928 and in 1953. Something had to be done, and in 1965 the Greater London Council invited proposals. The Thames Barrier was opened in 1984. It is 520 m (1,700 ft) across. Its 10 gates, which pivot from being flat on the river bed, swing up to 1.6 m (6 ft) above the level reached by the tide in 1953. The barrier has been raised over 100 times since 1984, and can be visited by boat in summer.

Unique structure of the O2 Arena

⓴ The O2 Arena

North Greenwich SE10. **Tel** 020 8463 2000 or 0844 856 0202 (to book tickets). ⊖ North Greenwich/The O2 Arena (Jubilee Line). **Open** 9am–late. Ⓦ **theo2.co.uk**

The former Millennium Dome was the focal point of Britain's celebration of the year 2000. Controversial from its earliest days, it is nonetheless a spectacular feat of engineering. Its base is ten times that of St Paul's Cathedral, and Nelson's Column could stand beneath its roof. Its canopy is made from 100,000 sq m (109,000 sq yards) of Teflon-coated spun glass-fibre, and is held by over 70 km (43 miles) of steel cable rigged to twelve 100-m (328-ft) masts.

Now one of London's most popular concert venues, the O2 boasts an entertainment complex with bars, restaurants, a cinema, a sports arena and IndigO2, a smaller venue.

South of the Centre

A Jacobean fireplace at Charlton House

㉑ Charlton House

Charlton Rd SE7. **Tel** 020 8856 3951.
🚉 Charlton. Main house not open
to public. Exhibition area: **Open**
8:30am–6pm Mon–Fri. Peace Garden:
Open 10am–5pm daily. **Closed** public
hols. 🎫 book ahead. ♿ limited.
🖥 9am–4pm Mon–Fri. Concerts; Fri
free.🌐 charlton-house.org

The house was completed in
1612 for Adam Newton, tutor to
Prince Henry. It has good river
views and is the best-preserved
Jacobean mansion in London –
well worth the tricky journey for
enthusiasts of that period. It is
now used as a community centre
and library, but many of the
original ceilings and fireplaces
survive, as does the carved main
staircase. Parts of the wood
panelling, too, are original, and
the ceilings have been restored
using the original moulds. The
summer house in the grounds
was reputedly designed by
Inigo Jones, and a mulberry tree
(probably the oldest in England)
is said to have been planted by
James I in 1608 as part of his
failed attempt to start an
English silk industry.

㉒ Eltham Palace

Court Yard SE9. **Tel** 020 8294 2548.
🚉 Eltham, then a 15-minute walk.
Open Sun–Wed. Apr–Oct: 10am–
6pm; Nov–Dec & Feb–Mar: 10am–
4pm Sun (phone first). **Closed** 31 Dec–
31 Jan. 🅿 ♿ 🚫 🖥 🎫
🌐 english-heritage.org.uk

This unique property lets visitors
relive the grand life of two very
different eras. In the
14th century, English
kings spent
Christmas in a
splendid palace
here. The Tudors
used it as a base
for deer-hunting
but it fell to ruin
after the Civil War
(1642–8). In 1935
Stephen
Courtauld, of
the wealthy
textile family, restored the Great
Hall which, apart from the
bridge over the moat, was the
only part of the medieval palace
to survive. Next to it, he built a
house described as "a wonderful
combination of Hollywood
glamour and Art Deco design".
It has been superbly restored
and is open, along with the
Great Hall, the carp-filled moat
and the 1930s garden.

㉓ Horniman Museum

100 London Rd SE23. **Tel** 020 8699
1872. 🚉 Forest Hill. Gardens:
Open 7:15am–sunset Mon–Sat,
8am–sunset Sun. Museum & Library:
Open 10:30am–5:30pm daily.
Closed 24–26 Dec. 🖥 🎫 ♿ Events
& activities. 🌐 horniman.ac.uk

Frederick Horniman, the tea
merchant, had this museum
built in 1901 to house the curios
he had collected on his travels
around the world in the 1860s. The
museum features a music gallery,
aquarium, world culture displays
and a natural history gallery. There
is a good shop with toys that
represent the popular range of
the museum's collections.

㉔ Dulwich Picture Gallery

College Rd SE21. **Tel** 020 8693 5254.
🚉 West Dulwich, North Dulwich.
Open 10am–5pm Tue–Fri, 11am–5pm
Sat, Sun & bank hol Mon (last adm
4:30pm). **Closed** Mon, 1 Jan, 25 & 26
Dec. 🅿 🎫 3pm Sat & Sun. ♿ 🖥
🏠 🌐 dulwichpicturegallery.org.uk

England's oldest public art
gallery, which was opened in
1817 and designed by Sir John
Soane *(see pp138–9)*.
Its imaginative use of
skylights made it the
prototype of most
art galleries built
since. The gallery
was originally
commissioned to
house the royal
collection for the
King of Poland.
The superb
collection
has works

Rembrandt's *Jacob II de Gheyn* at
Dulwich Picture Gallery

by Rembrandt (his *Jacob II de Gheyn* has been stolen from here four times), Canaletto, Poussin, Watteau, Claude, Murillo and Raphael. The building houses Soane's mausoleum to Desenfans and Bourgeois, who were the original founders of the collection.

㉕ Battersea Park

Albert Bridge Rd SW11. **Map** 19 C5. **Tel** 020 8871 7530. 🔵 Sloane Sq then bus 137. 🚆 Battersea Pk. **Open** 8am–dusk daily. 🚻 📱 Sports facilities. *See Six Guided Walks pp268–9.*
🔲 batterseapark.org

This was the second public park created to relieve the growing urban stresses on Victorian Londoners (the first was Victoria Park in the East End). It opened in 1858 on the former Battersea Fields – a swampy area notorious for every kind of vice, centred around the Old Red House, a disreputable pub.

The new park immediately became popular, especially for its man-made boating lake, with its romantic rocks, gardens and waterfalls.

In 1985, a peace pagoda was opened, a 35-m (100-ft)-high monument built by Buddhist nuns and monks. There are also an excellent children's zoo (entry fee payable), a children's playground, sports activities and an art gallery, the Pumphouse.

Peace Pagoda, Battersea Park

Tennis racket and net from 1888, Wimbledon Lawn Tennis Museum

㉖ St Mary's, Battersea

Battersea Church Rd SW11. **Tel** 020 7228 9648. 🔵 Sloane Sq then bus 19 or 219. **Open** daily by arrangement. ✝ 8:30am Mon–Wed; 8:30am, 11am & 6:30pm Sun. 🚻 Concerts.
🔲 stmarysbattersea.org.uk

There has been a church here since at least the 10th century. The present brick building dates from 1775, but the 17th-century stained glass, commemorating Tudor monarchs, comes from the former church.

In 1782, the poet and artist William Blake was married in the church. Later, J M W Turner painted views of the Thames from the church tower. Benedict Arnold, who served George Washington in the American War of Independence, is buried in the crypt.

㉗ Wimbledon Lawn Tennis Museum

Church Rd SW19. **Tel** 020 8247 3142. 🔵 Southfields. **Open** Apr–Sep: 10am–5:30pm; Oct–Mar: 10am–5pm daily (during championships, ticket holders only). **Closed** 1 Jan, 23 & 30 Jun, 8–9 Jul, 24–26 Dec. 🗼 🚻 📷 📱 📷
🔲 wimbledon.com/museum

Even those with only a passing interest in the sport will find plenty to enjoy at this museum. It traces tennis's development from its invention in the 1860s as a diversion for country house parties, to the sport it is today. Alongside strange 19th-century equipment are film clips showing the great players of the past. More recent matches may be viewed in the video theatre.

㉘ Wimbledon Windmill Museum

Windmill Rd SW19. **Tel** 020 8947 2825. 🔵 🚆 Wimbledon then 30-min walk. **Open** Apr–Oct: 2–5pm Sat, 11am–5pm Sun & pub hols (Nov–Mar: groups only, by arrangement). 🗼 📷 📱 📷
🔲 wimbledonwindmill.org.uk

The mill on Wimbledon Common was built in 1817. The building at its base was turned into cottages in 1864. Boy Scout founder Lord Baden-Powell lived in the mill house. Today the site is a museum housing model windmills.

St Mary's, Battersea

West of the Centre

Ham House

❷❾ Richmond Park

Kingston Vale SW15. **Tel** 0300 061 2200. 🚇 ≋ Richmond then bus 65 or 71. **Open** 7am–dusk (from 7:30 am in winters) daily. 🚻 🚲 🅿 🅆 royalparks.gov.uk

In 1637, Charles I built a wall 8 miles (13 km) round to enclose the royal park as a hunting ground. Today the park is a national nature reserve and deer still graze warily among the chestnuts, birches and oaks, no longer hunted but still discreetly culled. They have learned to co-exist with the thousands of human visitors who stroll here on fine weekends.

In late spring, the highlight is the Isabella Plantation with its spectacular display of azaleas, while the nearby Pen Ponds are very popular with optimistic anglers. (Adam's Pond is for model boats.) The rest of the park is heath, bracken and trees (some of them hundreds of years old). Richmond Gate, in the northwest corner, was designed by the landscape gardener Capability Brown in 1798. Nearby is Henry VIII Mound, where in 1536 the king,

Deer in Richmond Park

staying in Richmond Palace, awaited the signal that his former wife, Anne Boleyn, had been executed. The Palladian White Lodge, built in 1729, is home to the Royal Ballet School.

❸❶ Hampton Court

See pp256–9.

❸❶ Ham House

Ham St, Richmond. **Tel** 020 8940 1950. 🚇 ≋ Richmond then bus 65 or 371. **Open** Apr–Oct: noon–4pm Sat–Thu. **Closed** 1 Jan, 25–26 Dec. 🚫 📷 by appt. 🚲 partial. 🅿 & ☕ 11am–4pm daily (mid-Feb–Oct: to 5pm). Gardens: **Open** Jan–mid-Feb: 11am–4pm daily; mid-Feb–Oct: 11am–5pm daily; Nov–Dec: 11am–4pm daily. 🅆 nationaltrust.org.uk

This magnificent house by the Thames was built in 1610, but its heyday came when it was home to the Duke of Lauderdale, confidant to Charles II and Secretary of State for Scotland. His wife, the Countess of Dysart, inherited it from her father, who had been Charles I's "whipping boy" (punished for the future king's misdemeanours). From 1672, the Duke and Countess modernized the house, and it was regarded as one of Britain's finest. The garden has been restored to its 17th-century form.

On some days in summer, a foot passenger ferry runs from

here to Marble Hill House and Orleans House at Twickenham.

❸❷ Orleans House Gallery

Orleans Rd, Twickenham. **Tel** 020 8831 6000. 🚇 ≋ Richmond then bus 33, 90, 290, R68 or R70. **Open** Apr–Sep: 1–5:30pm Tue–Sat, 2–5:30pm Sun & bank hols; Oct–Mar: 1–4:30pm Tue–Sat, 2–4:30pm Sun & bank hols. **Closed** 1 Jan, Good Fri, 24–26 Dec. Gardens **Open** 9am–dusk daily. 🚲 ground floor. 🅿 📷 🅆 richmond.gov.uk/orleans_house_gallery

This gallery is on the site of the original Orleans House, named after Louis Philippe, Duke of Orleans, who lived there from 1815 to 1817. Adjacent is the Octagon Room, designed by James Gibbs for James Johnson in 1720. The gallery shows exhibitions of local history.

Marble Hill House

❸❸ Marble Hill House

Richmond Rd, Twickenham. **Tel** 020 8892 5115. 🚇 ≋ Richmond then bus 33, 90, 290, R68 or R70. **Open** by guided tour only (phone or access website to check). **Closed** Nov–Mar. 📷 🚲 restricted. 📹 🅿 📷 Fireworks at weekends. *See Entertainment p341.* 🅆 english-heritage.org.uk

Built in 1729 for George II's mistress, Henrietta Howard, the house and its grounds have been open to the public since 1903. It has now been fully restored to its Georgian appearance. There are paintings by William Hogarth and a view of the river and house in 1762 by Richard Wilson, who is regarded as the father of English landscape painting. The café is especially good.

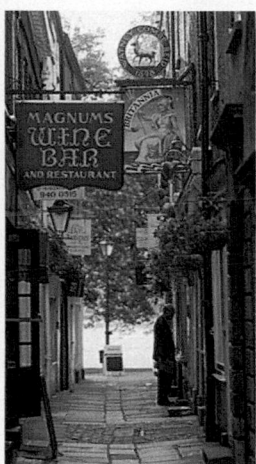

Richmond side street

㉞ Richmond

SW15. 🚇 🚉 Richmond.

This attractive London town took its name from the palace that Henry VII built here in 1500. Many early 18th-century houses survive near the river and off Richmond Hill, notably Maids of Honour Row, which was built in 1724. The beautiful view of the river from the top of the hill has been captured by many artists, and is largely unspoiled.

㉟ Syon House

London Rd, Brentford. **Tel** 020 8560 0882. 🚇 Gunnersbury then bus 237 or 267. House: **Open** mid-Mar–Oct: 11am–5pm Wed–Thu, Sun. House: **Closed** Nov–mid-Mar. Gardens: **Open** mid-Mar–Oct: 10:30am–5pm daily; Nov–mid-Mar: 10:30am–4pm Sat & Sun. 🚻 ♿ 📷 🏛 🖼 📷 ♿ gardens only. 🌐 syonpark.co.uk

The Earls and Dukes of Northumberland have lived here for 400 years – it is the only large mansion in the London area still in its hereditary ownership. The interior was remodelled in

1761 by Robert Adam, and is considered one of his masterpieces. The five Adam rooms house original furnishings and a collection of Old Master paintings.

The 200 acre (80 ha) park was landscaped by Capability Brown, and it includes a lovely 40-acre (16-ha) garden with more than 200 species of rare trees. The park's Great Conservatory inspired Joseph Paxton's designs for the Crystal Palace.

㊱ Musical Museum

399 High St, Brentford. **Tel** 020 8560 8108. 🚇 Gunnersbury, South Ealing then bus 65, 237 or 267. **Open** 11am–5pm Fri–Sun & bank hol Mon. 🚻 ♿ 📷 📷 🏛 🌐 **musicalmuseum.co.uk**

The collection is arranged over three floors and comprises chiefly large instruments, including player (or automatic) pianos and organs, miniature and cinema pianos, and what is thought to be the only surviving self-playing Wurlitzer organ in Europe.

Drawing room: Osterley Park House

㊲ Osterley Park House

Jersey Rd, Isleworth. **Tel** 020 8232 5050. 🚇 Osterley. **Open** Mar–Nov: 11am–5pm Wed–Sun; 1st 2 weeks Dec: noon–3:30pm Sat & Sun. 🚻 📷 🏛 Park **Open** 8am–dusk daily. 🌐 **nationaltrust.org.uk/osterley**

Osterley is ranked among Robert Adam's finest works, and its colonnaded portico and elegant library ceiling are the proof. Much of the furniture is by Adam, the garden and temple are by William Chambers, architect of Somerset House. The garden house is by Adam.

Robert Adam's red drawing room at Syon House

⑳ Hampton Court

Hampton Court was not orginally built as a royal palace but begun in 1514 by Cardinal Wolsey, Henry VIII's Archbishop of York as his riverside country house. Later, in 1528, in the hope of retaining royal favour, Wolsey offered it to the king. After the royal takeover, Hampton Court was twice rebuilt and extended, first by Henry himself and then, in the 1690s, by William and Mary, who employed Christopher Wren as architect.

There is a striking contrast between Wren's Classical royal apartments and the Tudor turrets, gables and chimneys elsewhere. The inspiration for the gardens as they are today comes largely from the time of William and Mary, who created a vast, formal Baroque landscape, with radiating avenues of majestic limes and many collections of exotic plants.

★ The Maze
Lose yourself in one of the garden's most popular features.

Main entrance

★ The Great Vine
The vine was planted in the 1760s, and, in the 19th century, produced up to 910 kg (2,000 lbs) of black grapes.

The Pond Garden
This sunken garden was once a pond to store fresh fish for Henry VIII's Court.

KEY

① River boat pier

② Royal tennis court

③ Privy Garden

④ River Thames

★ The Mantegna Gallery
Andrea Mantegna's nine canvases depicting *The Triumphs of Caesar* (c.1484–1505) are housed here.

Broad Walk
A contemporary print shows the East Front and the Broad Walk during the reign of George II (1727–60).

VISITORS' CHECKLIST

Practical Information
Surrey KT8 9AU.
Tel 0844 482 7777.
[W] **hrp.org.uk**
Open Apr–Oct: 10am–6pm daily;
Nov–Mar: 10am–4:30pm daily
(last adm: 1 hour before closing).
Closed 24–26 Dec.

Transport
R68 from Kew, Richmond or
Twickenham. Hampton Court.
Hampton Court pier.

Long Water
A man-made lake runs parallel to the Thames, from the Fountain Garden across the Home Park.

Fountain Garden
A few of the clipped yews here were planted in the reign of William and Mary.

The East Front
The windows of the Queen's Drawing Room, designed by Wren, overlook the central avenue of the Fountain Garden.

Exploring the Palace

As an historic royal palace, Hampton Court bears traces of many of the kings and queens of England from Henry VIII to the present day. The building itself is a harmonious blend of Tudor and English Baroque architecture. Inside, visitors can see the Great Hall, built by Henry VIII, as well as state apartments of the Tudor court. Many of the Baroque state apartments, including those above Fountain Court by Christopher Wren, are decorated with furniture, tapestries and old masters from the Royal Collection.

Tudor Chimneys
Ornate chimneys, some original, some careful restorations, adorn the roof of the Tudor palace.

★ **Chapel Royal**
The Tudor chapel was re-fitted by Wren except for the carved and gilded vaulted ceiling.

★ **Great Hall**
The stained-glass window in the Tudor Great Hall shows Henry VIII flanked by the coats of arms of his six wives.

KEY

① **Haunted Gallery**

② **Queen's Presence Chamber**

③ **Queen's Guard Chamber**

④ **Wren's east façade**

★ **Clock Court**
Anne Boleyn's Archway is at the entrance to Clock Court. The Astronomical Clock, created for Henry VIII in 1540, is also located here.

King's Great Bedchamber
William III bought the crimson bed from his Lord Chamberlain.

Cardinal Wolsey

Thomas Wolsey (c.1475–1530), simultaneously a cardinal, Archbishop of York and chancellor, was, after the king, the most powerful man in England. However, when he was unable to persuade the pope to allow Henry VIII to divorce his first wife, Catherine of Aragon, Wolsey fell from royal favour. He died while making his way to face trial for treason.

Queen's Gallery
This marble chimneypiece by John Nost was moved from the King's Great Bedchamber to the Queen's Gallery.

★ **Fountain Court**
The windows of state apartments are visible above the cloisters of Fountain Court.

King's Staircase
Leading to the state apartments, the King's Staircase has wall paintings by Antonio Verrio.

1514 Construction of palace begins

1532 Henry starts new hall

1647 Charles I imprisoned by Cromwell

1734 William Kent decorates the Queen's Staircase

1838 Public first admitted to the palace

1986 State apartments partly damaged by fire

1500   1600   1700   1800   1900

1528 Wolsey gives the palace to Henry VIII

1689 William and Mary move to Hampton Court

c.1727 Queen's apartments are finally completed

1773 Great Gatehouse reduced by two storeys

1992 Damaged apartments are reopened

Henry VIII painted by Hans Holbein

⏻ PM Gallery and House

Mattock Lane W5. **Tel** 020 8567 1227.
🚇 Ealing Broadway. **Open** 1–5pm
Tue–Fri, 11am–5pm Sat; Summer:
1–5pm Sun. **Closed** public hols.
♿ Exhibitions. 🌐 **ealing.gov.uk/
pmgalleryandhouse**

Sir John Soane, architect of the
Bank of England *(see p149)*,
designed this house, Pitzhanger
Manor, on the site of an earlier
one. Completed in 1803, it was
to become his own country
residence. There are clear
echoes of his elaborately
constructed town house in
Lincoln's Inn Fields *(see pp138–9)*,
especially in the library,
with its imaginative use
of mirrors, and in the
darkly-painted breakfast
room opposite and in
the "monk's dining
room", which is located
on the basement level.

Soane retained two of
the principal formal rooms:
the drawing room and the
dining room. These were
designed in 1768 by
George Dance the
Younger, with whom
Soane had worked
before establishing his
own reputation.

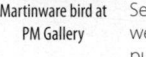

Martinware bird at
PM Gallery

A sympathetic 20th-
century extension has been
refurbished as a gallery offering
a wide range of contemporary
art exhibitions and associated
events. The house also contains
a large exhibition of Martinware,
highly decorated glazed pottery
made in nearby Southall

between 1877 and 1915 and
fashionable in late Victorian
times. The gardens of Pitzhanger
Manor are now a pleasant public
park and offer a welcome contrast
to the bustle of nearby Ealing.

⏻ Kew Bridge Steam Museum

Green Dragon Lane, Brentford.
Tel 020 8568 4757. 🚇 Kew Bridge,
Gunnersbury then bus 65, 237 or 267.
Open 11am–4pm daily (engines
operate at set times – check website
for details). **Closed** Mon (except bank
hols). 🐾 📷 book ahead. 🛗 Sat &
Sun. 🏠 ♿ 🌐 **kbsm.org**

The 19th-century water
pumping station, near the
north end of Kew Bridge,
is now a museum of
steam power and water
in London. Its main
exhibits are five giant
Cornish beam engines
that pumped water here
from the river, to be
distributed in London.
The earliest engines,
dating from 1820, are
similar to those built
to pump water out
of Cornish mines.
See them working at
weekends and on
public holidays.

⏻ Kew Gardens

See pp262–3.

City Barge: Strand on the Green

⏻ Strand on the Green

W4. 🚇 Gunnersbury then bus 237 or
267. 🚆 Kew Bridge.

This charming Thames-side
walk passes some fine
18th-century houses as well as
rows of more modest cottages
once inhabited by fishermen.
The oldest of its three pubs is
the City Barge *(see pp308–11)*,
parts of which date from the
15th century: the name is older
and derives from the time when
the Lord Mayor's barge was
moored on the Thames outside.

⏻ Chiswick House

Burlington Lane W4. **Tel** 020 8995
0508. 🚇 Chiswick. **Open** Apr–Oct:
10am–6pm Sun–Wed & bank hols.
Closed Nov–Mar. 🐾 📷 ♿ phone
ahead. 🛗 9am–5:30pm (to 4pm
winter). 🌳 Gardens **Open** 7am–dusk
daily (free admission). 🌐 **chgt.org.uk**

Completed in 1729 to the
design of its owner, the third
Earl of Burlington, this is a fine
example of a Palladian villa.

Chiswick
House

Burlington revered both Palladio and his disciple Inigo Jones, and their statues stand outside. Built round a central octagonal room, the house is packed with references to ancient Rome and Renaissance Italy, as is the garden.

Chiswick was Burlington's country residence and this house was built as an annexe to a larger, older house (since demolished). It was designed for recreation and entertaining – Lord Hervey, Burlington's enemy, dismissed it as "too little to live in and too big to hang on a watch chain". Some of the ceiling paintings are by William Kent, who also contributed to the garden design.

The house was a private mental home from 1892 until 1928, when a long process of restoration began. The layout of the garden, now a public park, is much as Burlington designed it.

The Belvedere takes centre stage at Chelsea Harbour

Plaque on Hogarth's House

🄴 Hogarth's House

Hogarth Lane, W4. **Tel** 020 8994 6757. 🚇 Turnham Green. **Open** noon–5pm Tue–Sun & bank hol Mon. **Closed** Jan, Good Fri, 25 & 26 Dec. 🎦 🚻 ground floor only. 🚻 🔳 **hounslow.info/ arts/hogarthshouse**

When the painter William Hogarth lived here from 1749 until his death in 1764, he called it "a little country box by the Thames" and painted bucolic views from its windows – he had moved from Leicester Square (see p105). Today, traffic roars by along the Great West Road, on its way to and from Heathrow Airport – rush hour traffic is also notoriously bad here. In an environment as hostile as this, and following

years of neglect and then bombing during World War II, the house has done well to survive. It has now been turned into a small museum and gallery, which is filled mostly with a collection of engraved copies of the moralistic cartoon-style pictures with which Hogarth made his name. Salutary tales, such as *The Rake's Progress* (in Sir John Soane's Museum – see pp138–9), *Marriage à la Mode*, *An Election Entertainment* and many others, can all be seen here.

🄴 Fulham Palace

Bishops Ave SW6. **Tel** 020 7736 3233. 🚇 Putney Bridge. **Open** Summer: 12:30–4:30pm Mon–Thu, noon–5pm Sun & bank hol Mon; Winter: 12:30– 3:30pm Mon–Thu, noon–4pm Sun. **Closed** Good Fri, 25 & 26 Dec. Park **Open** daylight hours daily. 🚻 🎦 2–3 times each month; check website for days and times. 🔳 🚻 Events, concerts, lectures. 🔳 **fulhampalace.org**

The home of the Bishops of London from the 8th century until 1973, the oldest surviving parts of Fulham Palace date from the 15th century. The palace stands in its own landscaped gardens northwest of Putney Bridge. A restoration project completed in 2007 revealed a grand, long-hidden Rococo ceiling.

🄴 Chelsea Harbour

SW10. 🚇 Fulham Broadway. 🎦 Exhibitions. 🔳 🚻

This is an impressive development of modern apartments, shops, offices, restaurants, a hotel and a marina. It is near the site of Cremorne Pleasure Gardens, which closed in 1877 after more than 40 years as a venue for dances and circuses. The centrepiece is the Belvedere, a 20-storey apartment tower with an external glass lift and pyramid roof, topped with a golden ball on a rod that rises and falls with the tide.

Eye-catching entrance to Fulham Palace dating from Tudor times

⓸ Kew Gardens

The Royal Botanic Gardens, Kew, are a World Heritage Site and the most complete public gardens in the world. Their reputation was first established by Sir Joseph Banks, the British naturalist and plant hunter, who worked here in the late 18th century. The former royal gardens were given to the nation in 1841 and now display about 30,000 plants. Garden enthusiasts will want a full day to visit. Kew is also a centre for scientific research.

Princess Augusta
King George III's mother established the first garden on a 9-acre (3.6 ha) site here in 1759.

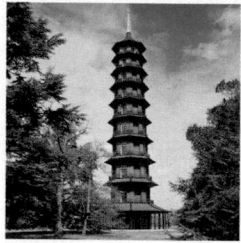

★ **Pagoda**
William Chambers's pagoda, built in 1762, reflects the fashion of the time.

KEY

① Cherry Walk

② The Temperate House

③ Waterlily Pond

④ Queen Charlotte's Cottage

⑤ River Thames

⑥ Sackler Crossing

⑦ Autumn foliage

⑧ Witch hazels

⑨ Azalea Garden

⑩ Climbers and Creepers soft play area

⑪ Kew Palace

⑫ Nash Conservatory

⑬ The Orangery restaurant

⑭ Duke's Garden

⑮ Princess of Wales Conservatory
Encompassing ten climatic zones, this glass-house contains cacti, giant waterlilies and orchids.

⑯ Davies Alpine House

⑰ Rock Garden

⑱ Winter Garden

⑲ Campanile

⑳ Rose Garden

㉑ Crocus carpet

㉒ Temple of Bellona

Lion Gate entrance

★ **Rhizotron and Xstrata Treetop Walkway**
This 200-m (220-yd) walkway meanders through the tree canopy and offers fine views.

Minka House
This minka (traditional wooden Japanese house), built around 1900, was shipped from Japan and reconstructed in the Bamboo Garden in 2001.

Brentford Gate entrance

P

10
11
13
12
20
18
21
15
19
17
16
14

Elizabeth Gate entrance

Victoria Gate entrance

★ Palm House
Designed by Decimus Burton in the 1840s, this famous jewel of Victorian engineering houses exotic plants in tropical conditions.

SIX GUIDED WALKS

London is an excellent city for walkers. Although it is much more spread out than most European capitals, many of the main tourist attractions are fairly close to each other *(see pp16–17)*. Central London is full of parks and gardens *(see pp50–53)*, and there are also several walk routes planned by the tourist board and local history societies. These include footpaths along canals and the Thames, and the Silver Jubilee Walk. Planned in 1977 to commemorate the Queen's Silver Jubilee, the walk runs for 12 miles (19 km) between Lambeth Bridge in the west and Tower Bridge in the east; Visit London *(see p354)* has maps of the route, which is marked by silver-coloured plaques placed at intervals on the pavement.

Each of the 16 areas described in the *Area-by-Area* section of this book has a short walk marked on its *Street-by-Street* map. These walks will take you past many of the most interesting sights in that area. On the following 12 pages are routes for six walks that take you through areas of London not covered in detail elsewhere. These range from the bustling, fashionable King's Road *(see pp268–9)* to the wide open spaces of riverside Richmond and Kew *(see pp270–71)*.

Several companies offer guided walking tours of London *(www.walks.com)*. Most of these have themes, such as ghosts, Jack the Ripper or Shakespeare's London. Look in listings magazines *(see p334)* for details.

The Six Walks

This map shows the location of the six guided walks in relation to the main sightseeing areas of London.

Portobello Road, Notting Hill

Strand on the Green, Kew

0 kilometres _____ 4
0 miles _____ 2

Regent's Canal (pp266–7)

Mayfair (pp272–3)

Notting Hill (pp276–7)

South Bank (pp274–5)

Chelsea and Battersea (pp268–9)

Richmond and Kew (pp270–71)

Key

··· Walk route

◀ Traditional narrow boats on Regent's Canal, Little Venice

A Two-Hour Walk Along the Regent's Canal

Master builder John Nash wanted the Regent's Canal to pass through Regent's Park, but instead it circles north of the park. Opened in 1820, it is long defunct as a commercial waterway but is today a valuable leisure amenity. This walk starts at Little Venice and ends at Camden Lock market, diverting briefly to take in the view from Primrose Hill. For more details on the sights near the Regent's Canal, see pages 222–9.

③ Houseboat on the canal

③ Houseboats moored at Little Venice

From Little Venice to Lisson Grove

At Warwick Avenue station ①, take the left-hand exit and walk straight to the traffic lights by the canal bridge at Blomfield Road. Turn right and descend to the canal through an iron gate ② opposite No. 42, marked "Lady Rose of Regent". The pretty basin with moored narrow boats is Little Venice ③. At the foot of the steps, turn left to walk back beneath the blue iron bridge ④. You soon have to climb up to street level again because this stretch of the towpath is reserved for access to the barges. Cross Edgware Road and walk down Aberdeen

Place. When the road turns to the left by a pub, Crockers ⑤, follow the signposted Canal Way down to the right of some modern flats. Continue your route along the canal towpath, crossing Park Road at street level. The scenery along this stretch is unremarkable, but it is not long before a splash of green to your right announces that you are now walking alongside Regent's Park ⑥.

Regent's Park

Soon you see four mansions ⑦. A bridge on huge pillars marked "Coalbrookdale"

Key

••• Walk route

0 metres   500
0 yards   500

⑧ carries Avenue Road into the park. Cross the next bridge, with London Zoo ⑨ on your right, then turn left up a slope. A few steps later, take the right fork, and turn left to cross Prince Albert Road. Turn right before entering Primrose Hill through a gate ⑩ on your left.

Primrose Hill

From here, there is a view of the zoo aviary ⑪, designed by Lord

⑦ Mansion with riverside gardens

Snowdon and opened in 1965.
Inside the park, keep to the left-hand path that climbs to the top of the hill. Soon you fork right to the summit, which offers a fine view of the city skyline. A viewing panel ⑫ helps identify the landmarks but it does not include the 1990 skyscraper at Canary Wharf, with its pyramid crown, on the left. Descend on the left, making for the park gate at the junction of Regent's Park Road and Primrose Hill Road.

Towards Camden

Almost opposite the gate is the Queens ⑬, a Victorian pub and, just to the left, is No. 122 Regent's Park Road ⑭. This was for 24 years the home of the communist philosopher Friedrich Engels; he was often visited there by his friend Karl Marx.

Turn right and walk down Regent's Park Road for 135 m (150 yd) then turn left up Fitzroy Road. On the right, between Nos. 41 and 39, is the entrance to Primrose Hill Studios ⑮, built

in 1882. Residents have included the musician Sir Henry Wood and illustrator Arthur Rackham, famous for his fairy pictures.

Continue down Fitzroy Road past No. 23 ⑯, once home to the poet W B Yeats, then go right into Chalcot Road and left down Princess Road, past a Victorian board school ⑰. Turn right and rejoin the canal down steps across Gloucester Avenue. Turn left under the railway bridge and past the Pirate Castle ⑱, a water sports centre. Cross a hump bridge and enter Camden Lock Market

⑲ Indoor market, Camden Lock

⑲ *(see p331)* through an arch on your left. After browsing there, you can take the water bus ⑳ back to Little Venice or turn right into Chalk Farm Road and walk up to Camden Town Underground station.

Pedestrian bridge over the canal at Camden Lock ⑲

For keys to symbols *see back flap*

A Three-Hour Walk in Chelsea and Battersea

This delightful circular walk ambles through the grounds of the Royal Hospital and across the river to Battersea Park, with its romantic Victorian landscaping. It then returns to the narrow village streets of Chelsea and the stylish shops on the King's Road. For more details on the sights in Chelsea, see pages 194–9.

③ Royal Hospital

Sloane Square to Battersea Park

From the station ①, turn left and walk down Holbein Place. The Renaissance painter's connection with Chelsea stems from his friendship with Sir Thomas More who lived nearby. Pass the cluster of good antique shops ② as you turn on to Royal Hospital Road. Enter the grounds of the Royal Hospital ③, designed by Christopher Wren, and turn left into the informal Ranelagh Gardens ④. The small pavilion by John Soane ⑤ displays a history of the gardens as a Georgian pleasure resort – it was the most fashionable meeting place for London society. Leave the gardens for fine views of the

⑥ Charles II statue in Royal Hospital

hospital and Grinling Gibbons's bronze of Charles II ⑥. The granite obelisk ⑦ commemorates the 1849 battle at Chilianwalla, in what is now Pakistan, and forms the centre-piece of the main marquee at the Chelsea Flower Show *(see p58)*.

Battersea Park

When crossing the Chelsea Bridge ⑧ (1937), look up at the four gilded galleons on top of the pillars at each end. Turn into Battersea Park ⑨ *(see p253)*, one of London's liveliest, and follow the main path along the river to enjoy the excellent views of Chelsea. Turn left at the exotic Buddhist Peace Pagoda ⑩ to the main part of the park.

Past the bowling greens lies Henry Moore's carving of *Three Standing Figures* ⑪ (1948) and the lake, a favoured spot for wildfowl. (There are boats for hire.) Just beyond the sculpture head northwest and, after crossing the central avenue, fork right and make for the wooden gate into the rustic Old English Garden ⑫. Leave the garden by the metal gate and return to Chelsea via the Victorian Albert Bridge ⑬.

Tips for Walkers

Starting point: Sloane Square. **Length**: 4 miles (6.5 km). **Getting there**: Sloane Square is the nearest tube. There are frequent buses 11, 19, 22 and 349 to Sloane Square and along the King's Road. Royal Hospital Grounds are open only 10am–6pm Mon–Sat, 2–6pm Sun. **Stopping-off points**: There is a café in Battersea Park, by the lake. Cheyne Walk Brasserie, on Cheyne Walk, sells Provençal food and afternoon tea. There are several other pubs, restaurants and sandwich shops to be found along the King's Road. The Chelsea Farmers' Market on Sydney Street has several cafés.

Key

••• Walk route

0 metres 500
0 yards 500

⑫ Old English Garden in Battersea Park

SLOANE ST

SLOANE SQUARE

32

Sloane Square

LOWER SLOANE STREET

30

31

HOLBEIN PLACE

BOURNE STREET

1

PIMLICO RD

CHELTENHAM TERRACE

WALPOLE ST

TERRACE

TURK'S ROW

TURK'S ROW COURT

CHELSEA BRIDGE ROAD

EBURY BRIDGE RD

HOSPITAL ROAD

2

3

4

5

6

RANELAGH GARDENS

7

8

Chelsea Bridge

CHELSEA EMBANKMENT

T h a m e s

9

10

CARRIAGE DRIVE NORTH

QUEENSTOWN ROAD

B A T T E R S E A P A R K

CARRIAGE DRIVE EAST

11

CARRIAGE DRIVE SOUTH

⑬ Albert Bridge

Place ㉒ has retained much of its original character. Where Glebe Place meets the King's Road are three pretty, early 18th-century houses ㉓. Cross Dovehouse Green opposite (it used to be a burial ground), to Chelsea Farmers' Market ㉔, an enclave of cafés and craft shops.

The King's Road

Leave the market on Sydney Street and cross into the garden of St Luke's Church ㉕, where the writer Charles Dickens was married. The walk then winds through pretty back streets until it rejoins the King's Road ㉖ (see p198), which was very fashionable in the 1960s. On the left is The Pheasantry ㉗. Look down the side streets on both left and right to see the squares and terraces: Wellington Square ㉘, then Royal Avenue ㉙, intended as a triumphal way to the Royal Hospital, and Blacklands Terrace ㉚, where book-lovers will want to visit John Sandoe's shop. The Duke of York's Territorial Headquarters ㉛ (1803) on the right – now home to the Saatchi Gallery – marks the approach to Sloane Square ㉜ and the Royal Court Theatre (see Sloane Square p199).

Thomas Carlyle statue ⑮

The Back Streets of Chelsea

Over the bridge is David Wynne's sculpture of a boy and dolphin ⑭ (1975). Pass the sought-after residences on Cheyne Walk and the statues of historian Thomas Carlyle ⑮ and Sir Thomas More ⑯. The area was renowned for gatherings of intellectuals. Past Chelsea Old Church ⑰ is Roper's Gardens ⑱

with its carving by Jacob Epstein. Just beyond these is the old, medieval Crosby Hall ⑲. Justice Walk ⑳ has a nice view of two early Georgian houses – Duke's House and Monmouth House. Turn left to pass the site of the Chelsea porcelain factory ㉑, which used to make highly fashionable (and today very highly collectable) wares in the late 18th century. Glebe

⑬

ROYAL COURT THEATRE

㉜ Royal Court Theatre

A 90-Minute Walk Around Richmond and Kew

This delightful riverside walk begins in historic Richmond by the remains of Henry VII's once-splendid palace and ends at Kew, Britain's premier botanic garden. For more details on the sights in Richmond and Kew, turn to pages 254–63.

The river at low tide

Richmond Green

From Richmond station ①, proceed to Oriel House ②, which is practically opposite. Take the alleyway beneath it, and turn left towards the red-brick and terracotta Richmond Theatre ③, built in 1899. The remarkable Edmund Kean, whose brief, meteoric career in the early 19th century had a lasting impact on English acting, was closely associated with the previous theatre on the site. Opposite is Richmond Green ④. Cross it diagonally and go through the entrance arch ⑤ of the old Tudor palace, which is adorned with the arms of Henry VII.

Richmond

Richmond owes much of its importance – as well as its name – to Henry, victor of the Wars of the Roses and the first Tudor monarch. On becoming king in 1485 he spent a lot of time at an earlier residence on this site, Sheen Palace, dating from the 12th century. The palace burned down in 1499 and Henry had it rebuilt, naming it Richmond after the town in Yorkshire where he held an earldom. In 1603, Henry's granddaughter, Elizabeth I, died here. The houses inside the archway on the left contain remnants, much modified, of the 16th-century buildings. Leave Old Palace Yard at the right-hand corner ⑥, following a sign "To the River", and turn left to pass the White Swan pub ⑦. At the river, go right along the towpath under the iron railway bridge and then the concrete Twickenham Bridge ⑧, completed in 1933, to reach Richmond Lock ⑨, with its cast-iron footbridge built in 1894. The Thames is tidal as far as Teddington, some 3 miles (5 km) upstream, and the lock is used to make the river continuously navigable.

The Riverside

Do not cross the bridge but continue along the wooded path by the river to Isleworth Ait ⑩, a large island where herons may be standing warily on the river bank. Just beyond it, on the far shore, is All Saints' Church ⑪, where the 15th-century tower has survived several rebuildings, most recently in the 1960s. Further round the inlet, Isleworth ⑫, once a small riverside village with a busy harbour, is now a dormitory for central London. Here, there is river traffic to watch: barges, yachts and, in summer, the passenger boats that ply up-river to Hampton Court (see pp256–9). Rowers are out at most times of year, training for races. The most prestigious occasions are the Henley Regatta in July and the Oxford v Cambridge boat race, every spring from Putney to Mortlake (see p58).

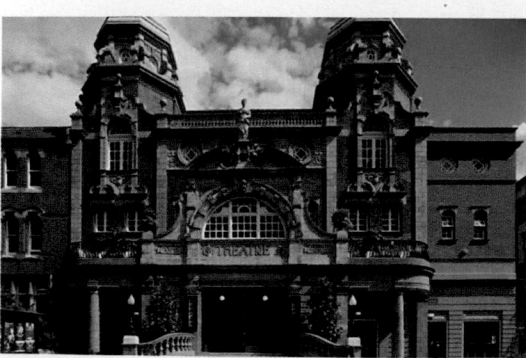

③ Richmond Theatre

Key

••• Walk route

Kew

After a while, the appearance of iron railings on your right marks where Old Deer Park ⑬ turns into Kew Gardens ⑭ (officially known as the Royal Botanic Gardens – see pp262–3). There used to be a riverside entrance for visitors arriving on foot or by water, but the gate ⑮ is now

⑲ Kew Palace in Kew Gardens

out in the 18th century. Just beyond are modern waterside apartments at Brentford ⑰. This was originally an industrial suburb, sited where the Grand Union Canal runs into the Thames, and its residential potential has only recently been exploited. You can pick out the tall chimney of the waterworks ⑱, now a museum dedicated to steam power. On the right, behind the Kew Gardens car park, there is soon a view of Kew Palace ⑲, now fully restored and open to the public.

Beyond the car park, leave the river by Ferry Lane on to Kew Green ⑳. Now you could spend the rest of the day in Kew Gardens or cross Kew Bridge and turn right on to Strand on the Green ㉑, a fine riverside walkway with atmospheric pubs, the oldest of them the City Barge ㉒. Head south down Kew Road if you need to get back, then turn left at Kew Gardens Road to depart from Kew Gardens Underground station (District line).

Tips for Walkers

Starting point: Richmond station, District Line.
Length: 3 miles (5 km).
Getting there: Richmond Underground or railway station. Buses 391 and R68 come here from Kew.
Stopping-off points: There are many cafés, pubs and tearooms in Richmond. The famous Maids of Honour tearoom is at Kew, and Kew Grill is one of several good eateries on Kew Green.

closed and the nearest entrance is to the north, near the car park.
Across the river, there are magnificent views of Syon House ⑯, seat of the Dukes of Northumberland since 1594. Part of the present house dates from the 16th century but it was largely redesigned by Robert Adam in the 1760s. You are looking at it across the garden Capability Brown laid

The river bank between Richmond and Kew

For keys to symbols see back flap

A Two-Hour Walk Through Mayfair to Belgravia

This walk takes you from Green Park to Hyde Park, through the hearts of Mayfair and Belgravia, two of London's most elegant Georgian residential districts. It includes a bracing stroll through Hyde Park and, if you're feeling energetic, a row on the Serpentine.

⑦ L'Artiste Musclé restaurant, Shepherd Market, Mayfair

Green Park to Berkeley Square

Exit Green Park station ① following the signs for Piccadilly North. With Green Park opposite you, turn left. Pass Devonshire House ②, a 1920s office block that replaced the 18th-century mansion designed by William Kent. Only Kent's gates survive, now at the park entrance across Piccadilly. Turn left and walk up Berkeley Street to Berkeley Square ③. To the south, Lansdowne House by Robert Adam has been replaced by an advertising agency ④. There are still a few splendid 18th-century houses to the west, including No. 45 ⑤, home of the soldier and governor, Lord Clive of India.

Mayfair

Keep to the south of the square and turn into Charles Street, noting the evocative lampholders at Nos. 40 and 41 ⑥. Turn left into Queen Street and cross Curzon Street to enter Shepherd Market ⑦ *(see p99)* through Curzonfield House alleyway. Turn right up a pedestrian-only street then right onto Hertford Street, passing the Curzon Cinema ⑧ on the corner of Curzon Street. Here you are almost facing Crewe House ⑨, built in 1730 by Edward Shepherd who also laid out the market.

Turn left and walk up Curzon Street, then turn right onto Chesterfield Street. A left turn at Charles Street brings you to Red Lion Yard ⑩, where a pub stands opposite one of the few weatherboarded buildings in the West End. Turn right into Hay's Mews and left up Chesterfield Hill. Cross Hill Street and South Street and head left until you reach an alley leading to the peaceful haven of Mount Street Gardens ⑪. The gardens back on to the Church of the Immaculate Conception ⑫. Cross the garden and turn left onto Mount Street; then right onto South Audley Street and left at Grosvenor Square ⑬ into Upper Grosvenor Street, passing to the left of the US Embassy. Look out for the statue of Franklin D Roosevelt. Turn right up Park Lane and walk past houses that are the remnants of what used to be

③ Grand Georgian doorway in Berkeley Square

Royal coat of arms above the door of Auckley House

Tips for Walkers

Starting point: Green Park underground station.

Length: 3 miles (5 km).

Getting there: Green Park is on the Victoria, Jubilee and Piccadilly underground lines. Or take bus Nos. 9, 14, 19, 22, 25 or 38 and go to Green Park underground station entrance.

Stopping-off points: There are numerous pubs, cafés and eateries in the area. Serpentine Bar and Kitchen on the Serpentine is open 8am–8pm.

the city's most desirable residential street before the traffic got so heavy ⑭. At the end you can see Marble Arch *(see p211)*.

Hyde Park

Enter the pedestrian subway ⑮ at exit No. 6 and follow signs for Park Lane West Side, exit No. 5. You will emerge at Speakers' Corner ⑯ *(see p211)*, where on Sundays anyone can make a speech on any topic. Cross Hyde Park *(see p211)* south–southwest, enjoying the views on all sides,

⑰ The Serpentine, on a fine day

and make for the boat house ⑰ on the Serpentine (an artificial lake created by Queen Caroline in 1730), where you rent a rowing boat. Turn left and follow the path to Serpentine Bar and Kitchen ⑱ for refreshments. From there, take the stone bridge ⑲ and cross Rotten Row ⑳, where the very fashionable exercise their horses. Leave the park at Edinburgh Gate ㉑.

Knightsbridge

Cross Knightsbridge and, resisting the temptations of two of London's great department stores – Harvey Nichols ㉒ and Harrods ㉓ *(see p211)* on Brompton Road – head down Sloane Street to turn left at Harriet Street. At Lowndes Square, turn right and leave the square on the far side, turning left into Motcomb Street. On your left is the Pantechnicon, an eccentric structure fronted by colossal Doric columns, built in 1830. A path beside it leads to Halkin Arcade ㉔, built in the 1830s and adorned by Geoffrey Wickham's fountain built in 1971.

Belgravia

Turn left out of the arcade onto Kinnerton Street, which boasts one of London's smallest pubs, the Nag's Head ㉕. A street of pretty mews houses runs off to the left of this street at its northern end; look for Ann's Close and Kinnerton Place North. Almost opposite the latter, the street makes a sharp right turn to emerge into Wilton Place opposite St Paul's Church (1843). Turn right here and follow Wilton Crescent round to the left before turning left into Wilton Row, where there is another small pub, the Grenadier ㉖, once the officers' mess of the Guards' barracks and reputedly frequented by the Duke of Wellington. Up Old Barracks Yard to its right there are some old officers' billets and a worn stone said to have been used by the Iron Duke when mounting his horses. The alley leads to a T-junction. To finish the walk, turn right onto Grosvenor Crescent Mews, then left onto Grosvenor Crescent, which leads you to Hyde Park Corner Underground station.

Key

••• Walk route

```
0 metres          400
0 yards           400
```

㉖ Once the officers' mess, now the Grenadier pub, Belgravia

For keys to symbols *see back flap*

A 90-Minute Walk Along the South Bank

The Riverside Walk along the South Bank from Westminster Bridge *(see page 187)* via Bankside to Southwark Cathedral is one of the most entertaining excursions in town. From County Hall to Shakespeare's Globe, the South Bank's well-known music, theatre and film venues, the shops and galleries of Gabriel's Wharf and the Oxo Tower, there's something for everyone. For more details on the sights in Southwark and Bankside, see pages 174–85.

⑭ Cafés and shops at Gabriel's Wharf

on the level above. Moving on along the Riverside Walk, past Waterloo Bridge, you reach BFI Southbank ⑪ *(see p339)* where films are shown throughout the day. Outside its lively café, rows of tables stacked with second-hand books shelter beneath the bridge. The National Theatre ⑫ *(see p190)* also has exhibitions and musical events as well as a good bookshop, while in summer there are free outdoor performances. Several of the theatre's

Westminster

Begin at Westminster station ① by the statue of Queen Boudica (or Boadicea), and walk over Westminster Bridge. Once on the south side ②, there is a fine view back over the river to the Houses of Parliament *(see pp74–5)*. The main building on this side is the former County Hall ③, now offering two hotels, several restaurants and a range of entertainment *(see p190)*, the highlights being the Sea Life London Aquarium ④ to see the vibrant underwater world, and Namco Station, a games

Tips for Walkers

Starting point: Westminster Bridge.
Length: 1.75 miles (2.75 km)
Getting there: Westminster Underground station on the District, Circle and Jubilee lines.
Stopping off points: All the South Bank's art centres have cafés, bars and restaurants. Also: Gourmet Pizza, Gabriel's Wharf; EAT, Riverside House (snacks and sandwiches); Anchor pub with river terrace (bars and restaurant).

hall with computer games, cars and pool tables. For the best city view, the London Eye ⑤ *(see p191)* is beside Jubilee Gardens ⑥, where buskers and mime artists perform. Walk past Hungerford Bridge ⑦ with its modern walkways and trains to Charing Cross Station, on the site of the former Hungerford market. Ahead is the Southbank Centre ⑧ *(see pp188–9)*, the capital's main arts showcase. Music and exhibitions fill the Royal Festival Hall ⑨ *(see p190)*, created for the Festival of Britain in 1951. Check to see what's showing at the Hayward Gallery ⑩ *(see p190)* too, just beyond,

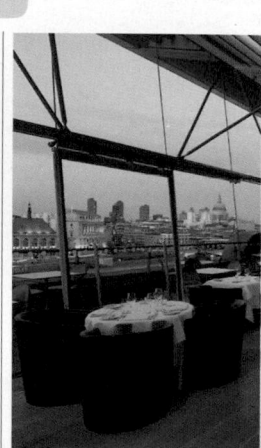

View from the Oxo Tower ⑮

Key

• • • Walk route

⑩ Art at the Hayward Gallery, South Bank

where he had a good view of it. Next door to his house is the exhibition and tour centre for Shakespeare's Globe ㉔ (see p179). A tour around the theatre is the next best thing to attending a performance.

Bankside

Bankside becomes more cramped here, as the historic streets pass The Anchor ㉕ riverside pub and Vinopolis ㉖ to reach the Clink Prison Museum ㉗ (see p184), on the site of one of London's first lock-ups. At St Mary Overie Dock, climb aboard a replica (1973) of Golden Hinde ㉘, in

restaurants, cafés and bars offer outside seating overlooking the South Bank. Past the London Studios (ITV) ⑬ is Gabriel's Wharf ⑭ (see p193), a pleasant diversion of art and craft shops and lively cafés.

The Oxo Tower

The next landmark you come to is the Oxo Tower ⑮, a red-brick industrial building, with contemporary designer shops and galleries, such as gallery@oxo. Take the lift to the top of the tower for an excellent, free view of the city; the Inner Temple and Fleet Street lie opposite. Once down again, the Riverside Walk passes by Sea Containers House ⑯, with gold trimmings (built as a hotel, but now offices) and Doggett's Coat and Badge pub ⑰ (see p65), then continue under Blackfriars Bridge ⑱, emerging by the remaining piers and railway emblem of a former bridge. On the right, opposite the Founders Arms ⑲, is the esteemed Bankside

Gallery ⑳ (see p179), which has regular exhibitions of its members' work. Behind it, opposite Falcon Point Piazza is Marcus Campbell, an excellent art bookshop, a stone's throw from Tate Modern ㉑ (see pp180–83), the best free show on the river. Drop in for a coffee if nothing else. The Millennium Bridge ㉒ leads over to St Paul's (see pp150–53) and the City. Its architect Sir Christopher Wren had a house by Cardinal Cap Alley in Cardinal's Wharf ㉓,

which the Elizabethan buccaneer Sir Francis Drake became the second man to circumnavigate the world. Southwark Cathedral ㉙ (see p178), is a quiet place to end the walk – there is a good tea shop here. Or, if you still feel energetic, browse around Borough Market (see p178) and take a look up at London's new landmark, The Shard (www.the-shard.com), before heading to the tube or train at London Bridge station ㉛.

㉑ Tate Modern: a vast space for contemporary British art

For keys to symbols see back flap

A Two-Hour Walk Around Notting Hill

This walk centres around Portobello Road, the city's most famous antiques and bric-a-brac shopping area in one of the ultra-fashionable parts of London. Great for original souvenirs, the neighbourhood is fascinating at any time, though the streets are busiest on Fridays and Saturdays, when all the shops are open and the market stalls laid out *(see page 333)*. This is the heart of Notting Hill, renowned for its carnival and also favoured as a film setting and a smart address.

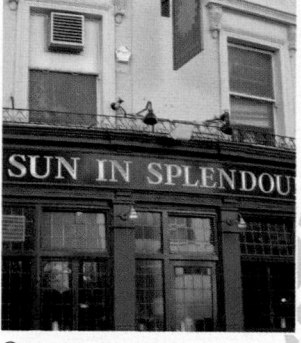

⑤ Sun in Splendour pub frontage

Portobello Road

Leaving Notting Hill Gate tube station ①, follow the signs to Portobello Road *(see p221)*, taking Pembridge Road ②. Intriguing shops here include Retro Woman ③ (Nos. 20 and 32) and Retro Man ④ (No. 34) for period clothes and accessories. At the Sun in Splendour pub ⑤, turn left into Portobello Road. No. 22, among the attractively painted terraced houses on the right, was where George Orwell lived in 1927 before his writing career began ⑥. Cross Chepstow Villas ⑦

and the serious antique shops begin. Near the Portobello Arcade ⑧, signposted with a large teapot, is Portobello Gold (Nos. 95–7), a guest house where Bill, Hillary and Chelsea Clinton dropped in for a beer and a snack in 2000. At No. 115 ⑨ is a plaque to June Aylward who opened the first antique shop in the street. At Colville

Terrace ⑩, the daily fruit and vegetable market begins. On the left is the Electric Cinema ⑪, said to be the oldest working cinema in Britain (1910), and certainly one of the most delightful. If there is not a film showing, you can go in and try the comfortable armchair seats and sofas

The Notting Hill Bookshop

Turn left down Blenheim Crescent to find The Notting Hill Bookshop ⑫, formerly The Travel

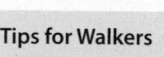

Tips for Walkers

Starting point: Notting Hill Gate underground station.
Length: 1.85 miles (3 km)
Getting there: Notting Hill underground station on Central, District and Circle lines.
Stopping-off points: The area is known for its pubs and restaurants. Try Charlie's Portobello Road Café at 59a Portobello Road; Eve's Market Café at 222 Portobello Road; Tom's Deli at 226 Westbourne Grove (great sandwiches and snacks); Ottolenghi's Patisserie at 63 Ledbury Road (superb pastries).

⑪ The Electric Cinema, the UK's oldest working cinema

Bookshop, a location of the 1999 film *Notting Hill*, in which Hugh Grant was the assistant. Books for Cooks ⑬ (No. 4) is where recipes from the latest books are prepared and sold. Head back to Portobello Road and pass the local Salvation Army centre ⑭. Amble for several blocks to Charlie's Portobello Road Café ⑮ (No. 59a). Relaxed atmosphere and good service, Charlie's offers breakfast, homemade soups and hot specials such as sausage and mash. If you are looking for a traditional Victorian pub, head to Market Bar ⑯. Excitement dwindles once you pass under the Westway flyover, except on Fridays and

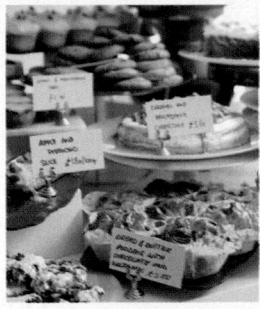
㉓ Ottolenghi Patisserie display

has a glassed-in shrine to Our Lady of Walsingham – an unusual feature in a Protestant church. Just beyond the red-brick Tabernacle Centre for Arts and Education ⑳, where Pink Floyd made their debut in 1966, is My Beautiful Laundrette ㉑, named after the successful 1986 film.

Turn right into Ledbury Road to find high fashion shops, and also, at its end in the still-functioning Westbourne Grove Church ㉒. As you are passing No. 63, try the pastries in Ottolenghi Patisserie ㉓ for a snack to hit the spot. Turn right into Westbourne Grove for more stylish shopping. Dinny Hall ㉔ at No. 200 stocks award-winning jewellery. Detour to Toms deli and café ㉕ at 226, which claims the best toasted sandwiches in town, and is run by Tom Conran, son of the style guru Terence Conran. The Wild at Heart flower stall on Turquoise Island ㉖ opposite, won awards for its designer, Piers Gough, in 1993. On the far side is the Oxfam thrift shop ㉗, where its bargains reflect the good taste of the locals. Head back to Portobello Road ㉘ and Notting Hill Gate tube.

㉖ Award-winning Wild at Heart flower stall

Saturdays when Tent City ⑰ and the Golborne Road Flea Market ⑱ are fully active, and the Portuguese cafés (especially the Lisboa at 55) are bustling. From Golborne Road, turn right into Bevington Road, right along Blagrove Road and right again into Acklam Road to bring you back to Portobello Road. Continue for several blocks, turning left on Talbot Road, where All Saints' Church ⑲

Key

••• Walk route

0 metres   200
0 yards   200

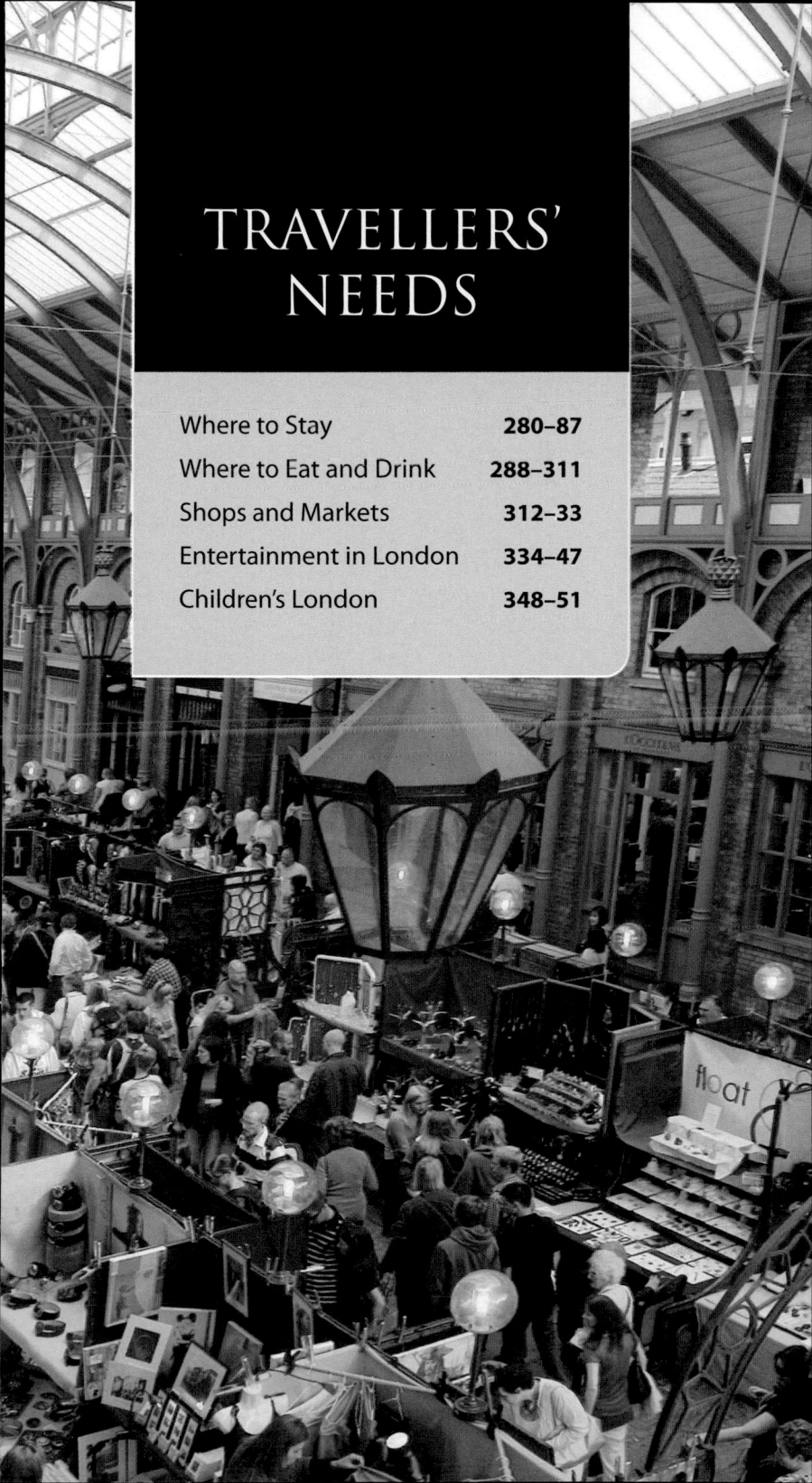

TRAVELLERS' NEEDS

Where to Stay	**280–87**
Where to Eat and Drink	**288–311**
Shops and Markets	**312–33**
Entertainment in London	**334–47**
Children's London	**348–51**

WHERE TO STAY

The high cost of accommodation in London is one of the biggest drawbacks for visitors. At the top end of the market, there is no shortage of expensive pedigree hotels, such as Claridge's and the Ritz. Mid-range hotels, while there are many, tend to be slightly further out of the centre of town. Budget hotels are few and far between thanks to rising property prices. However, there are ways to stay in the capital without breaking the bank. Low-cost hotel chains such as Premier Inn, Novotel and Tune have establishments in convenient locations throughout the city, many concentrated in the centre of town, offering good-quality accommodation at affordable prices. We have inspected more than 250 hotels and apartment complexes across a range of price brackets and localities and chosen 70 of the best of their kind. For further details on these, turn to the listings on pages 284–7. If you don't need a hotel's facilities, consider self-catering apartments and private homes *(see pp282–3)* available at a wide range of prices. Student halls and hostels, and even a few camping sites on London's outskirts, are additional possibilities for those travelling on a budget *(see p283)*.

Where to Look

The most expensive hotels tend to be in smart West End areas such as Mayfair and Belgravia. Often large and opulent, with uniformed staff, they are not always the most relaxing places to stay. For smaller, more personal, but still luxurious hotels, try South Kensington or Holland Park.

The streets off Earl's Court Road are full of hotels at the lower end of the price range. Several of the big railway stations are well served with budget hotels too. Try Ebury Street near Victoria, or Sussex Gardens near Paddington. Close to Euston or Waterloo and in the City and Docklands, well-known hotel chains cater for travellers at a range of prices.

There are also inexpensive hotels in the suburbs, such as Ealing, Hendon, Richmond or Harrow. From here, you can get into town on public transport and by suburban rail line services. Be sure to check the train times for the last train service leaving central London.

If you get stranded at an airport or have to catch an early morning flight, consult the list on page 369. For further information, advice and reservation services, contact visitlondon. com, which publishes several annually updated booklets on the different types of accommodation in Greater London.

Discount Rates

Prices in the capital tend to stay high all year round, but there are bargains. Many hotels, especially the chains, offer reduced rates for weekends and special breaks *(see p282)*. Others work on a more ad hoc basis, depending on how busy they are. If a hotel isn't full, it is always worth trying to negotiate a discount, especially if it is off-season. Older budget hotels may have rooms without showers or private bathrooms. These usually cost less than those with private facilities.

Hidden Extras

Read the small print carefully. Most hotels quote room rates rather than rates per person, but not all. Service charges and VAT are usually included in the quoted price but in some cases they are added on later, which means that the final bill can come as a shock to visitors. Also be aware of high mark-ups on telephone calls made in your hotel room. Breakfast may not be included in room rates, though it generally is in cheaper hotels. Single travellers are usually charged a "supplement" and end up paying about 80 per cent of the double room rate, even if they are occupying a "single" room – so don't accept anything substandard.

Tipping is expected in the more expensive hotels, but

Comfortable foyer area in Charlotte Street Hotel *(see p284)*

◀ Apple Market, Covent Garden Piazza

Attractive façade of the London Bridge Hotel *(see p285)*

there is no need to tip staff other than porters, except perhaps a helpful concierge for arranging theatre tickets or phoning for taxis.

Facilities

Room sizes in London hotels tend to be on the small side whatever the price range, but the majority of hotels provide telephones, televisions and private baths or showers in all their rooms. At the top end of the scale, hotels compete to offer the very latest sound-and-video systems, computer equipment and high-tech gadgetry. Most hotel rooms come equipped with Wi-Fi. Whatever the hotel, you will be expected to vacate your room by noon on the day you leave, sometimes even earlier.

The elegant hallway of The Gore, Kensington *(see p286)*

How to Book

It is always advisable to book your accommodation well in advance, as room availability and prices are likely to fluctuate, with the better quality hotels being more popular. Direct bookings can be made by phone, via the hotel website booking form or by email. This generally entails giving a guarantee: either a credit card number from which a cancellation fee can be deducted, or a one-night deposit (some hotels will expect more for longer stays). Don't forget that if you subsequently cancel, part or all of the room price may be charged unless the hotel can relet the accommodation. Insurance cover is advised.

The visitlondon.com website offers an excellent guide to finding accommodation in London, from self-catered apartments and budget hostels to luxury hotels. To make a booking by phone, call Expedia on 0203 564 5657. Visitors can also book in person upon arrival at the London Visitor Centre at No. 1 Regent Street. There is no booking fee but you will need to give a credit card number. During high season, there may be a one-night deposit to pay. Alternatively, travellers can use a similar booking service at www.superbreak.com or phone or email the service directly on 01904 717 362 or at bookings@superbreak.com. There is no fee if booking online.

Accommodating booking services are also available at the British Hotel Reservation Centre in Victoria railway station. A number of non-LTB booking agencies operate from booths in the major railway stations, charging a small fee to personal callers. You may come across unidentified touts, who often hang around at railway and coach stations offering cheap accommodation, these touts should be avoided.

Online booking is the easiest way to book hotels, with the best prices often only available via the Internet. Many hotels have their own on-line advance

Impeccably stylish interior of the Hotel 41 *(see p286)*

purchase rate while Internet travel sites, holiday retailers and hotel wholesalers such as Expedia (www.expedia.co.uk) and Travelocity (www.travelocity.co.uk) also quote good rates, particularly if you book a hotel and flight together. Increasingly, the Internet demonstrates the fluidity of many hotel "rack rates" (i.e. the prices printed on the tariff sheet), which, far from being fixed in stone, fluctuate widely according to the laws of supply and demand.

Special Breaks

Many travel agencies carry brochures from the major hotel chains listing special offers, which are usually costed on a minimum two-night stay. Some are extraordinarily good value compared to the usual tariff. For most leisure travellers or families with children, this is the best way to get value for money out of London hotels so that you can spend time in the city without breaking the bank.

City-break packages are organized by specialist operators, ferry companies and airlines, and some privately owned hotels too. Sometimes the same hotel may be featured in several brochures at widely differing prices and with different perks. It's worth asking the hotel directly what special rates they offer, and checking their websites too.

Opulent bathroom interiors at the Goring Hotel *(see p286)*

Disabled Travellers

Information about wheelchair access is based largely on hotels' own assessments, so travellers with special needs should always confirm when booking whether an establishment is suitable. If forewarned, many hotels will go out of their way to help disabled visitors. The nationwide Tourism for All scheme provides details on accommodation standards and facilities for elderly visitors or those with mobility problems. For information on hotels that meet the three-tier "National Accessible Standard", contact **DisabledGo** or **Tourism For All**. A guide book for people with access needs, Open Britain, can be obtained from **Disability Rights UK**.

Travelling with Children

London hotels are very welcoming to children and make a concerted effort to cater for the needs of people travelling with children, providing cots, high-chairs, baby-sitting services (always ensure sitters have had a Disclosure and Barring Service, or DBS, check) and special meal arrangements. Ask whether the hotel offers special deals for children – some have special rates, or allow children to stay free of charge in their parents' room.

Self-Catering Flats

Many agencies offer self-catering accommodation in flats, usually for stays of a week or more. Prices, depending on size and location, start at about £300 per week. Some luxury complexes are fully serviced, so you don't need to cook, shop or clean. **Bridge Street Worldwide** has over 550 London apartments in smart locations. It caters mainly for corporate and professional travellers, but its properties can be rented for short-term lets whenever they are available.

The **Landmark Trust** rents apartments in historic or unusual buildings. These include apartments in Hampton Court *(see pp256–9)* and in a pretty 18th-century terrace in the City: one of them was the home of the late poet laureate, Sir John Betjeman. A handbook of Landmark Trust properties is available for a charge via their website.

Staying in Private Homes

A number of agencies organize stays in private homes; several are registered with Visit London. Booking can be made directly with Visit London, with credit card reservations made by telephone.

Several agencies have minimum stays of anything up to a week. Prices depend on location, starting at around £25 per person per night. Sometimes you will enjoy family hospitality, but this isn't guaranteed, so enquire when you book. **Airbnb** offers accommodation for one night's stay or longer in private homes in London and the UK. Deposits may be requested and cancellation fees imposed. The **Bed & Breakfast and Homestay Association** (BBHA) is an umbrella organization for several reputable agencies whose properties are inspected regularly. For details of members, visit the BBHA website *(see box)*.

Uptown Reservations arranges B&B stays in interesting, London homes which have been inspected for their welcome, security and comfort. Prices start at £125 per night for a double room. It works in tandem with **Wolsey Lodges**, a nationwide consortium of distinctive private homes, often of historic or architectural interest, offering individual hospitality. Wolsey Lodges lists charming properties.

Chain Hotels

Chain hotels are an important feature of the London hotel market. Though they can lack character, they offer some of the best value accommodation in town. Some also offer particular facilities; Novotel, for example, caters for both business guests and families. Other good-value chains include Express by Holiday Inn and easyHotel.

Imaginative dining suite, W hotel *(see p284)*

Budget Accommodation

Despite the high cost of many London hotels, budget accommodation does exist, and not only for young travellers.

Dormitory Accommodation and Youth Hostels can be booked through the LTB's information centre at Victoria Station for a small fee plus a refundable deposit. Some private hostels near Earl's Court charge little more than £10 a night for a dormitory bed with breakfast. The **London Hostels Association** has a selection of reasonably priced accommodation throughout central London. **The Youth Hostels Association** (YHA) runs seven hostels in London. There is no age limit, though non-members pay a joining fee. Of the seven, two are located in the heart of London. The Oxford Street hostel is actually in Noel Street, Soho, while the London St Paul's hostel is located near St Paul's Cathedral *(see pp150–53)*. One of the most popular hostels is Holland

City of London Youth Hostel

House, a Jacobean mansion in Holland Park. The easiest way to book a bed online is through the **Hostelling International** (HI) website, which offers a range of global hostels to stay at.

Many student rooms are available at Easter and from July to September. Some of these are in central locations such as South Kensington. **London University Rooms** arranges stays in halls, or, if you need a

room in a hurry, **King's College** or **Imperial College** may be able to find you one.

Recommended Hotels

The hotels on pages 284–87 of this guide are a selection of the best luxury, boutique, character, bed & breakfast and budget hotels in London. They are first listed according to theme, and then alphabetically by area. Most of the hotels are spread across the main tourist areas, although a number that are further afield are included if they offer particularly good value for money, facilities, service or charm.

There are also B&Bs, guest-houses and apartments, as well as pubs and restaurants with rooms. What they all have in common is that, regardless of category and price, they have something special to offer.

Where a hotel has an exceptional feature, such as great-value rates, or spectacular views it has been highlighted as a DK Choice.

DIRECTORY

Reservations and Information

British Hotel Reservation Centre
Victoria Railway Station, East Concourse SW1V 1JU.
Tel 020 7828 1027.
W bhrconline.com
W visitlondon.com
Tel 0203 564 5657.

Disabled Travellers

DisabledGo
Tel 0845 270 4627.
W disabledgo.com

Disability Rights UK
Ground Floor CAN Mezzanine 49-51 East Road N1 6AH. **Tel** 020 7250 8181.
W disabilityrightsuk.org

Tourism For All
7A Pixel Mill, 4 Appleby Road, Kendal, Cumbria LA9 6ES.
Tel 0845 124 9971; 0044 1539 726 111 (overseas).
W tourismforall.org.uk

Self-Catering Agencies

Bridge Street Worldwide
Compass House, 22 Redan Place W2 4SA.
Tel 020 7792 2222.
W bridgestreet.com

Landmark Trust
Shottesbrooke, Maidenhead, Berks SL6 3SW.
Tel 01628 825925.
W landmarktrust.org.uk

Agencies for Stays In Private Homes

Airbnb
W airbnb.com

At Home in London
70 Black Lion Lane W6 9BE. **Tel** 020 8748 2701.
W athomeinlondon.co.uk

Bed & Breakfast & Homestay Assoc.
8 Kelso Place W8 5OP.
Tel 020 7937 2001.
W bbha.org.uk

Uptown Reservations
8 Kelso Place W8 5QD.
Tel 020 7937 2001.
W uptownres.co.uk

Wolsey Lodges
9 Market Place, Hadleigh, Ipswich, Suffolk IP7 5DL.
Tel 01473 822058.
W wolseylodges.com

Hostel Booking

Hostelling International
Tel 01707 324170.
W hihostels.com

London Hostels Association
54 Eccleston Sq SW1V 1PG. **Tel** 020 7727 5665.
W london-hostels.co.uk

Youth Hostels Association
Trevelyan House, Dimple Rd, Matlock, Derbyshire DE4 3YH.
Tel 01629 592700.
W yha.org.uk

Booking Addresses for Residence Halls

Imperial College Summer Accommodation Centre
Sherfield Building, Level 3 SW7 2AZ.
Tel 020 7594 9507.
W imperial.ac.uk/conferenceandevents/accommodation

King's Conference & Vacation Bureau
26–29 Drury Lane, 1st floor WC2B 5RL.
Tel 020 7848 1700.
W kingsvenues.com

London University Rooms
W londonuniversityrooms.co.uk

Where to Stay

Luxury

Westminster and the West End

The Athenaeum ££
116 Piccadilly, W1J 7BJ
Tel *020 7499 3464* **Map** 12 E4
W athenaeumhotel.com
An established hotel, but with up-to-date, airy bedrooms and family-friendly apartments. A great on-site spa.

One Leicester ££
1 Leicester Street, WC2H 7BL
Tel *020 3301 8020* **Map** 13 A2
W oneleicesterstreet.com
Dine at the sumptuous restaurant and stay in one of the calm, white, minimalist rooms.

Claridge's £££
49 Brook Street, W1K 4HR
Tel *020 7629 8860* **Map** 12 E2
W claridges.co.uk
One of London's greats; seamless service and understated luxury in a dazzling Art Deco building. Perfect for a special occasion.

Covent Garden £££
10 Monmouth Street, WC2H 9HB
Tel *020 7806 1000* **Map** 13 B2
W firmdalehotels.com/london/
covent-garden-hotel
A vibrant, sexy and designer-dressed hotel from the Firmdale stable. Combines old-world style with metropolitan chic.

Flemings Hotel and Apartments £££
7–12 Half Moon Street, W1J 7BH
Tel *020 7499 0000* **Map** 12 E4
W flemings-mayfair.co.uk
This tranquil oasis is stylish without being too precious. Choose between charming rooms and apartments.

Four Seasons Hotel London at Park Lane £££
Hamilton Place, W1J 7DR
Tel *020 7499 0888* **Map** 12 E4
W fourseasons.com/london
Sumptuously glossy and in a fantastic location, this hotel boasts immaculate service. It also has a stunning glass-walled rooftop spa.

The Ritz £££
150 Piccadilly, W1J 9BR
Tel *020 7493 8181* **Map** 12 F3
W theritzlondon.com
Perfectly preserved in its original Louis XVI style; glamour and glitz rolled into one. Don't miss the famous afternoon tea.

W £££
10 Wardour Street, W1D 6QF
Tel *020 7758 1000* **Map** 13 A2
W wlondon.co.uk
All glass outside, sleek and bright inside, this luxury global brand hotel is the ultimate in cool.

Bloomsbury and Regent's Park

Charlotte Street £££
15–17 Charlotte Street, W1T 1RJ
Tel *020 7806 2000* **Map** 13 A1
W firmdalehotels.com/london/
charlotte-street-hotel
The groovy favourite of media folk, with lively public areas and a stylish, private cinema.

The Langham £££
1c Portland Place, W1B 1JA
Tel *020 7636 1000* **Map** 12 E1
W london.langhamhotels.co.uk
A grande dame hotel with an Eastern look. Rooms have a relaxing private-home feel.

The City and the East End

DK Choice

Boundary Rooms ££
*2–4 Boundary Street, E2 7DD
(entrance in Redchurch Street)*
Tel *020 7729 1051* **Map** 8 D4
W theboundary.co.uk
A converted Victorian warehouse in trendy Shoreditch is the setting for Terence Conran's hotel. It exudes style, from the retro cellar bar to each perfectly designed bedroom. All rooms are bespoke and decorated with designer objects. Don't miss the spectacular views from the rooftop brasserie, which hums on summer weekends.

Individually designed room at Charlotte Street hotel

Shoreditch Rooms ££
Ebor Street, E1 6AW
Tel *020 7739 5040* **Map** 8 D4
W shoreditchhouse.com
An imaginatively renovated warehouse, home to 26 bright, fresh-looking bedrooms decorated in a New England vintage style.

Kensington and Chelsea

The Capital ££
22–24 Basil Sreet, SW3 1AT
Tel *020 7589 5171* **Map** 11 C5
W capitalhotel.co.uk
All the luxury and service of a grand hotel, but much more intimate and personal. The bedrooms are a good size and traditionally elegant.

Belgraves £££
20 Chesham Place, SW1X 8HQ
Tel *020 7858 0100* **Map** 20 D1
W thompsonhotels.com/hotels/
london/belgraves
New York "boho" in Belgravia, with bold, eclectic design. There's a terrace with a retractable roof, a buzzy lobby and Mark Hix's restaurant.

DK Choice

Mandarin Oriental Hyde Park £££
66 Knightsbridge, SW1X 7LA
Tel *020 7235 2000* **Map** 11 C5
W mandarinoriental.com/london
Mandarin Oriental is a byword for luxury and impeccable Eastern-style service, and this vast Edwardian red-brick pile is no exception. A happy blend of the old and new, it has traditional, swagged bedrooms with mahogany furniture and marble fireplaces, a sleek, contemporary ground floor and a fabulous high-spec granite spa.

Royal Garden £££
2–24 Kensington High Street, W8 4PT
Tel *020 7937 8000* **Map** 10 D5
W royalgardenhotel.co.uk
A 1960s hotel favoured by celebrities and well-suited to families. Go for a room with an unrivalled park view. Service throughout is courteous and very efficient.

The studio suite at the W hotel, Leicester Square

The Halkin by COMO £££
5 Halkin Street, SW1X 7DJ
Tel *020 7333 1059* **Map** 12 D5
w comohotels.com/thehalkin
Welcoming service, fresh flowers,
soft lighting and exquisite beds –
the perfect place to chill out.

The Levin £££
28 Basil Street, SW3 1AS
Tel *020 7589 6286* **Map** 11 C5
w thelevinhotel.co.uk
A little gem; from the pistachio-
coloured reception to the
gorgeous, cosy bedrooms.

Boutique

Westminster and the West End

The Arch ££
*50 Great Cumberland Place,
W1H 7FD*
Tel *020 7724 4700* **Map** 11 C2
w thearchlondon.com
Cleverly converted from a terrace
of townhouses. Popular bar and
laid-back dining.

Bloomsbury and Regent's Park

Megaro, King's Cross ££
Belgrove Street, WC1H 8AB
Tel *020 7843 2222* **Map** 5 C3
w hotelmegaro.co.uk
A buzzing urban hang-out with
striking contemporary rooms.

Montagu Place ££
2–3 Montagu Place, W1H 2ER
Tel *020 7467 2777* **Map** 11 C1
w montagu-place.co.uk
Go for a "Comfy", "Swanky" or
"Fancy" room. An intimate hotel
that stands out from the crowd.
Decorated in neutral shades and
with plentiful facilities.

No. Ten Manchester Street ££
10 Manchester Street, W1U 4DG
Tel *020 7317 5900* **Map** 12 D1
w tenmanchesterstreethotel.com
A handsome Edwardian
townhouse with a gentleman's
club feel. All-weather cigar
terrace and comfy bar.

The City and the East End

The Hoxton ££
81 Great Eastern Street, EC2A 3HU
Tel *020 7550 1000* **Map** 7 C4
w hoxtonhotels.com
The earlier you book this hip
hotel, the less you pay. The vast
open-plan lobby has a real buzz.

**King's Wardrobe by
Bridge Street** ££
6 Wardrobe Place, EC4V 5AF
Tel *020 7792 2222* **Map** 14 F2
w bridgestreet.com/The_Kings_
Wardrobe_by_BridgeStreet_
Worldwide.htm
Flagship building with apartments,
ranging from studios to three
bedrooms, all well equipped.

The Zetter Townhouse ££
49–50 St John's Square, EC1V 4JJ
Tel *020 7324 4567* **Map** 6 E2
w thezettertownhouse.com
Get your toothpaste and
Champagne from the same
vending machine at this hip
hotel with playful touches. Ultra
cool and very welcoming.

Threadneedles £££
5 Threadneedle Street, EC2R 8AY
Tel *020 7657 8080* **Map** 15 B2
w theetoncollection.co.uk/content.
aspx
Immaculate service and luxurious
rooms in a stylish former bank.
A spectacular glass dome
dominates the reception.

Southwark and the South Bank

Bermondsey Square ££
*Bermondsey Square, Tower Bridge
Road, SE1 3UN*
Tel *020 7378 2450* **Map** 16 D4
w bermondseysquarehotel.co.uk
Treat yourself to a loft suite and
hot tub with a view at this wittily
furnished hotel.

DK Choice

London Bridge ££
*8–18 London Bridge Street,
SE1 9SG*
Tel *020 7855 2200* **Map** 15 B4
w londonbridgehotel.com
Through the handsome 19th-
century entrance, a modern
lobby sets the scene for this hip
yet intimate, independently
owned four-star hotel.
Bedrooms are über cool, each
with a black-and-white
bathroom. There's also a well-
equipped gym, three
restaurant/bars and great
weekend rates.

Kensington and Chelsea

The Ampersand ££
10 Harrington Road, SW7 3ER
Tel *020 7589 5895* **Map** 19 A2
w ampersandhotel.com
A whimsical interior inspired by
music, science and nature.

Baby ABode Sydney House ££
9–11 Sydney Street, SW3 6PU
Tel *020 7376 7711* **Map** 19 A3
w abodehotels.co.uk/chelsea
A chic bolthole; pale pistachio
walls, blonde wood floors and
Frette linen sheets.

myhotel Chelsea ££
35 Ixworth Place, SW3 3QX
Tel *020 7225 7500* **Map** 19 B2
w myhotels.com/my-hotel-chelsea
Designed along Feng Shui
principles; you feel a sense of
wellbeing as soon as you arrive.

**Grand Plaza Serviced
Apartments** ££
42 Prince's Square, W2 4AD
Tel *020 7985 8000* **Map** 10 D2
w grand-plaza.co.uk
Snug studios for couples; airy
apartments for groups. Access to
the square's gardens is a big plus.

Space Apart Hotel ££
*36–37 Kensington Gardens Square,
W2 4BQ*
Tel *020 7908 1340* **Map** 10 D2
w aparthotel-london.co.uk
Practical, comfortable
apartments with funky details.

For more information on types of hotel *see page 283*

Further Afield

Avo £
82 Dalston Lane, E8 3AH
Tel *020 3490 5061*
 avohotel.com
DVDs for rent, memory-foam beds and a host of thoughtful extras at this trendy crash pad.

High Road House ££
162–170 Chiswick High Road, W4 1PR
Tel *020 8742 1717*
 highroadhouse.co.uk
Enjoy breakfast in the brasserie, after a night in a chic, Scandinavian-inspired room.

Rafayel on the Left Bank ££
34 Lombard Road, SW11 3RF
Tel *020 7801 3600*
 hotelrafayel.com
Large relaxing rooms, a spa and conscientious staff single out this eco-friendly Battersea hotel.

Town Hall Hotel and Apartments ££
8 Patriot Square, E2 9NF
Tel *020 7871 0460*
 townhallhotel.com
Edwardian architecture, Art Deco interiors and hip furnishings – a winning combination.

Character

Westminster and the West End

Dean Street Townhouse ££
69–71 Dean Street, W1D 3SE
Tel *020 7434 1775*   Map 13 A1
 deanstreettownhouse.com
A dynamic hotel with its Georgian heritage intact. A lively restaurant and charming bedrooms.

The Fox Club ££
46 Clarges Street, W1J 7ER
Tel *020 7495 3656*   Map 12 E3
 foxclublondon.com
Decorated with eye-catching fabrics, this charming hotel is open to non-club members.

Hazlitt's ££
6 Frith Street, W1D 3JA
Tel *020 7434 1771*   Map 13 A2
 hazlittshotel.com
Furnished with antiques, busts and prints, this is a distinctive hotel with bags of charm.

The Orange ££
37 Pimlico Road, SW1W 8NE
Tel *020 7881 9844*   Map 20 D2
 theorange.co.uk
Calls itself a "Public House and Hotel", but really it's a rustic restaurant with four cosy rooms.

The elegant exterior of the Goring Hotel

Hotel 41 £££
41 Buckingham Palace Road, SW1W 0PS
Tel *020 7300 0041*   Map 20 E2
 41hotel.com
A stunning hotel with a clubby atmosphere, black-and-white bedrooms and dark wood.

The Goring £££
Beeston Place, SW1W 0JW
Tel *020 7396 9000*   Map 20 E1
 thegoring.com
There are liveried doormen and a lovely private garden at this great English institution. It's where the Duchess of Cambridge stayed before her wedding.

The Stafford London by Kempinski £££
16–18 St James's Place, SW1A 1NJ
Tel *020 7493 0111*   Map 12 F4
 kempinski.com/en/london/the-stafford-london
A class act. Traditional English country house furnishings and an American Bar.

Bloomsbury and Regent's Park

Durrants ££
26–32 George Street, W1H 5BJ
Tel *020 7935 8131*   Map 12 D1
 durrantshotel.co.uk
An English classic, from the venerable panelled entrance to the tiny snug bar. The uniformed staff and Edwardian lobby set the scene for the rest of the hotel.

Rough Luxe ££
1 Birkenhead Street, WC1H 8BA
Tel *020 7837 5338*   Map 5 C3
 roughluxe.co.uk
Quirky, creative and full of surprises; friendly service, original art and a touch of luxury.

Montague on the Gardens ££
15 Montague Street, WC1B 5BJ
Tel *020 7637 1001*   Map 5 B5
 montaguehotel.com
Full of charm, from the tartan-walled bar to the chintzy rooms.

The City and the East End

DK Choice

The Rookery ££
12 Peter's Lane, Cowcross Street, EC1M 6DS
Tel *020 7336 0931*   Map 6 F5
 rookeryhotel.com
A romantic venue, The Rookery consists of three restored 18th-century houses, crammed with curiosities. Its seductive bedrooms have antique beds and bathrooms with roll-top baths. Downstairs, in the foyer, you'll find an open fire.

Kensington and Chelsea

The Gore ££
190 Queen's Gate, SW7 5EX
Tel *020 7584 6601*   Map 10 F5
 gorehotel.com
A hotel that explodes with character; pictures jostle for wall space; bedrooms are all unique.

Twenty Nevern Square ££
20 Nevern Square, SW5 9PD
Tel *020 7565 9555*   Map 17 C2
 20nevernsquare.com
Some deliciously over-the-top rooms at this calm refuge with colonial and Asian decor.

Vancouver Studios ££
30 Prince's Square, W2 4NJ
Tel *020 7243 1270*   Map 10 D2
 vancouverstudios.co.uk
Elegant modern studios in a stylish townhouse, each has a mini-kitchen with all accessories.

Further Afield

The Alma £
499 Old York Road, SW18 1TF
Tel *020 8870 2537*
 almawandsworth.com
A Victorian tavern, now one of Wandsworth's new-breed pub-restaurants, with 23 rooms.

Bingham ££
61–63 Petersham Road, Richmond Upon Thames, Surrey, TW10 6UT
Tel *020 8940 0902*
 thebingham.co.uk
A Georgian townhouse over-looking the Thames, with a great restaurant. Located close to Richmond's shops.

Fox and Grapes ££
9 Camp Road, SW19 4UN
Tel *020 8619 1300*
W foxandgrapeswimbledon.co.uk
This chic getaway offers small
bedrooms above a gastropub.

The Rose and Crown ££
199 Stoke Newington Church Street,
N16 9ES
Tel *020 7923 3337*
W roseandcrownn16.co.uk
Stay in a king-sized room above
this classic oak-panelled pub.

Bed & Breakfast

Westminster and the West End

Luna Simone £
47–49 Belgrave Road, SW1V 2BB
Tel *020 7834 5897*   **Map** 20 F2
W lunasimonehotel.com
A family-run business since the
1980s. Prices include breakfast.

Lime Tree ££
135–137 Ebury Street, SW1W 9QU
Tel *020 7730 7865*   **Map** 20 E2
W limetreehotel.co.uk
Real value for money at this
established, family-run venture.

The Sumner ££
54 Upper Berkeley Street, W1H 7QR
Tel *020 7723 2244*   **Map** 11 C1
W thesumner.com
A Georgian townhouse full of
warmth and charm. The
decoration is elegant.

Bloomsbury and Regent's Park

Arosfa ££
83 Gower Street, WC1E 6HJ
Tel *020 7636 2115*   **Map** 5 A5
W arosfalondon.com
Guests are made to feel like part
of the family at this simple B&B.

Hart House ££
51 Gloucester Place, W1U 8JF
Tel *020 7935 2288*   **Map** 11 C1
W harthouse.co.uk
Spotless rooms and an excellent
breakfast at this award-winning
townhouse. Rooms are cosy and
appealingly decorated.

Kensington and Chelsea

Hyde Park Rooms £
137 Sussex Gardens, W2 2RX
Tel *020 7723 0225*   **Map** 11 A1
W hydeparkrooms.com
No-frills rooms (some not ensuite), all kept admirably spick
and span. Generous breakfasts.

Rhodes £
195 Sussex Gardens, W2 2RJ
Tel *020 7262 0537*   **Map** 11 A1
W rhodeshotel.com
You are assured of a warm
welcome at this eclectic hotel.

Amsterdam ££
7 Trebovir Road, SW5 9LS
Tel *020 7370 5084*   **Map** 17 C3
W amsterdam-hotel.com
A prize-winning B&B with pastel
rooms and apartments. The
garden is perfect for summer.

Aster House ££
3 Sumner Place, SW7 3EE
Tel *020 7581 5888*   **Map** 19 A2
W asterhouse.com
A peaceful, eco-friendly
sanctuary. Victorian architecture
and traditional furnishings.

Budget

Bloomsbury and Regent's Park

No. 5 Doughty Street ££
5 Doughty Street, WC1N 2PL
Tel *020 7373 9120*   **Map** 6 D4
W blueprintlivingapartments.com/
no-5-doughty-street
Apartments with pizzazz;
Blueprint Living's complex offers
comfort at reasonable rates.

The City and the East End

**Premier Inn London City
(Tower Hill)** £
24 Prescot Street, E1 8BB
Tel *0871 527 8646*   **Map** 16 E2
W premierinn.com/en/hotel/
LONCIT/london-city-tower-hill
Plain but pleasant rooms with
comfortable king-size beds.
Bathrooms have power showers.

DK Choice

Fleet River Bakery Rooms ££
71 Lincolns Inn Fields, WC2A 3JF
Tel *020 7691 1457*   **Map** 14 D1
W fleetriverbakery.com
Above the bustle and graceful
arched windows of this bakery,
these well-appointed, good-
sized studios with their own
kitchen areas are stylish in a
low-key way. Excellent, fresh
breakfast is served every day
by friendly bakery staff – except
for Sundays, when delicious
hampers are provided.
Terrific value for money.

Southwark and the South Bank

Tune – Westminster £
118–120 Westminster Bridge Road,
SE1 7RW
Tel *020 7633 9317*   **Map** 14 D5
W tunehotels.com
London outpost of a modest
Asian chain. Smart, simple,
spotless accommodation.

**Premier Inn London
County Hall** ££
County Hall, Belvedere Road, SE1 7PB
Tel *0871 527 8648*   **Map** 13 C5
W premierinn.com/en/hotel/
LONCOU/london-county-hall
Larger-than-average bedrooms,
some with river views.

Further Afield

Shandon House Hotel £
36-38 Church Road,
Richmond- Upon-Thames,
TW9 1UA
Tel *020 8940 5000*
W shandonhouse.com
Modern, clean and affordable
accommodation in one
of London's more genteel areas.

Self-contained apartment above the Fleet River Bakery

For more information on types of hotel *see page 283*

WHERE TO EAT AND DRINK

Hailed as the world's dining capital, London thrives on an extraordinary culinary diversity. With a long tradition of Indian, Chinese, French and Italian restaurants, eating out in London can nowadays take you on a gastronomic journey around the world, from America to Africa, taking in a pan-European tour, as well as the Middle East, Asia and the Pacific Rim.

London has a dynamic café scene, with good coffee and snacks readily available throughout the day. Good-quality chains have also sprung up all over the capital offering a variety of food options and often seating for large groups. London's pubs have evolved into some of the most popular places to eat. "Gastropubs" are a key part of the London food scene often serving modern British classics, including traditional Sunday lunch. For a selection of mainly informal places to eat and drink, including pubs, see pages 304–11.

Diners at a Leon Restaurant *(see p299)*

London Restaurants

The broadest choice of restaurants can be found in Covent Garden, Piccadilly, Mayfair, Soho and Leicester Square. Knightsbridge, Kensington and Chelsea also offer a good range of restaurants. In Central London, the Southbank, including the area around Butler's Wharf, has a variety of riverside restaurants. Further up the river, there is a cluster along Chelsea Harbour. Chefs such as Fergus Henderson at St John are revitalizing British cooking, combining top notch traditional ingredients with a variety of culinary influences and techniques from around the world. Home-grown British chefs such as Heston Blumenthal, Bruce Poole and Angela Hartnett have been instrumental in helping to elevate London's restaurants to world-class status.

Londoners have long had a tremendously cosmopolitan appetite for Indian, Chinese, French and Italian food, with many restaurants specializing in regional cuisine. Asian food is also increasingly popular, particularly Thai, Korean, Malaysian, Indonesian, Japanese and combinations known as "Asian fusion". Popular Spanish tapas bars have opened up around the capital offering smaller sharing plates.

Most restaurants provide at least one vegetarian option, and some have a separate vegetarian menu. A number of specialist vegetarian restaurants offer more adventurous dishes. Some restaurants exclusively serve fish and seafood.

The range of cuisines offered by London restaurants is matched by the diversity of their location and decor. You'll find all styles from classical ornate and traditional wood-panelled to luxurious contemporary and hard-edged minimalist.

Other Places to Eat

Many hotels have excellent restaurants open to non-residents, which in some cases include a menu devised by, or even actually prepared by, a star chef. These restaurants range from the very formal to the fun and flamboyant, and prices tend to be at the top end of the scale.

In the 1990s, an increasing number of pizza, pasta and brasserie chains sprang up across the city, which continue to serve reliable, good-value food. Gastropubs and wine bars are also still strong London favourites. Both serve anything from standard British dishes to Thai curries and more imaginative International food, complemented by global wine lists. If you're in a hurry, you can grab a quick snack from one of the many popular chain sandwich bars or cafés spread all over the capital.

Commissionaire at the Hard Rock Café *(see p293)*

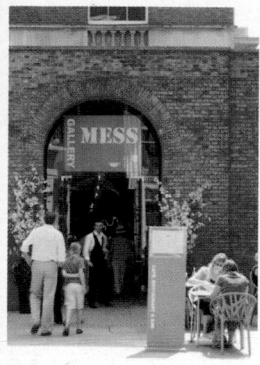

Entrance to the Gallery Mess *(see p296)*

Tips on Eating Out

Most London restaurants serve lunch between noon and 2:30pm, with dinner from 6:30pm until 11pm, which usually means that last orders are taken at 11pm. Even after midnight you can usually find somewhere open to grab a snack. Some restaurants may close for either lunch or dinner during the weekend, so it is always best to check opening times first. Many restaurants and some cafés and brasseries serve alcohol without restriction during licensing hours (11am–11pm).

The traditional British Sunday lunch appears in many pubs and restaurants, although more informal brunches are also very popular. It is worth checking the menu beforehand, however, unless traditional Sunday lunch is what you particularly want, as even high-class restaurants may suspend their normal menu on Sundays.

Most formal restaurants insist on a smart casual dress code (no jeans, trainers or shorts). Some insist on a jacket; a few on jacket and tie. Booking is advisable, especially at gourmet restaurants and between Friday and Sunday.

Smoking is banned in all London pubs and restaurants.

Price and Service

As London is one of the world's most expensive cities, restaurant prices can often seem exorbitant to visitors, with an average three-course meal and a few glasses of house wine at a medium-priced central London restaurant costing around £35–50 per person. Many restaurants have set-price menus which are generally significantly less expensive than ordering à la carte. Similarly, various West End restaurants serve pre-theatre set menus (typically from around 5:30–6pm). Prices may be lower (around £15–25 a head) at smaller, more modest ethnic and vegetarian restaurants, wine bars and pubs.

Before ordering, check the small print on the menu. Prices may include an optional service charge (10–15 per cent).

Be aware that some restaurant staff may leave the "total" box on your credit slip blank, even when service is included in the final bill.

Eating with Children

Many London restaurants, particularly chain restaurants and fast-food establishments, welcome children. A few venues, such as The Rainforest Café on Shaftesbury Avenue, create an unique dining experience especially for kids.

With the growing trend for a more informal style of dining, more restaurants, including those at the top end of the market, have become child-friendly, offering children's menus, smaller portions and high chairs. Some provide colouring books and even put on live entertainment to keep the little diners happy. See page 349 for suggested places that cater particularly for children with a wide range of ages.

Recommended Restaurants

The restaurants on pages 292–303 of this guide cover a comprehensive range of cuisine styles and prices, and are the best of their kind. They are listed by area, mostly in the main tourist districts, although there are a number that merit a special trip further afield. Within these areas, they are listed alphabetically in each of the three price categories.

Some London restaurants have moved away from classic three-course dining towards a tapas or mezze style, offering a selection of numerous small dishes for sharing. Fusion food is ever popular, with chefs borrowing from different cuisines, particularly South East Asian, to produce eclectic menus. Restaurants specializing in British or French cuisine feature either classic or modern dishes. You can choose between places that serve traditional dishes, such as steak and kidney pudding or *coq au vin*, and those where you might find scallop ravioli or seared duck *foie gras*.

Where a restaurant is in some way exceptional – perhaps for its cooking, its good-value menus, or family-friendly facilities – it has been highlighted as a DK Choice.

Bibendum, a popular choice for sophisticated French cuisine *(see p297)*

The Flavours of London

"Modern European cooking" describes much of what's on offer in London, a reflection of the capital's cosmopolitan nature. However, as competitive restaurateurs vie for customers, they often look to traditional foods, from once-unfashionable beetroot to pig's trotters and offal, while increasing concern about what goes into the growing and rearing of food is also reflected on London menus. Even pub food, once limited to Sunday roasts, the ubiquitous "ploughman's lunch" (cheese or ham with bread and pickles) or sandwiches has been a given fresh slant by "gastropubs" and a new breed of sandwich bars offering fresh, top-quality snacks.

Chef and customer at Clerkenwell's St John restaurant

London's Larder

Nowhere better exemplifies the city's love affair with good food than Borough Market *(see p331)*. Its busy stalls of both regional and continental food are a microcosm of what Londoners today like to eat. There is produce from all over Britain – English and Irish cheeses;

Scottish beef; Welsh lamb; Devon cider; Suffolk oysters – as well as from the rest of the world. Visitors can snack as they browse, on anything from Cornish scallops to grilled Spanish chorizo.

Modern British Food

London menus will often detail the provenance of ingredients

with obvious pride. Ancient or "rare" breeds of cattle are name-checked, such as Gloucester Old Spot pork. Once-overlooked, old-fashioned ingredients like rhubarb and black (blood) pudding are being used in creative new ways. Seasonal and organic produce is also taking more of a centre stage. The new breed of "gastropubs" were among

Dorstone (Dorset)   Waterloo (Berkshire)   Blue Stilton

Ashdown (Sussex)   Golden Cross (Sussex)

Selection of superb English farmhouse cheeses

Traditional English Food

You can still find traditional dishes, such as jugged hare, roast beef or brown Windsor soup, but even fish 'n' chips can be harder to hunt down than tapas, pizza or chicken tikka masala. A "full English breakfast" is a fry-up of sausages, eggs, bacon, tomatoes, mushrooms and toast, perhaps with black (blood) pudding. Baked beans and fried potatoes may be included, as can bubble and squeak (re-fried cabbage and potato). There is an English heritage of heavy "nursery" puddings. These are a favourite of gentlemen's clubs and include such treats as treacle tart, jam roly-poly (suet and jam) pudding, spotted dick (suet and currants) and fruit crumbles with custard. Teatime may be a thing of the past but some top hotels still offer "cream teas" with scones, cakes and perhaps cucumber sandwiches.

Celery and Stilton soup The king of English cheeses makes an excellent winter soup when combined with celery.

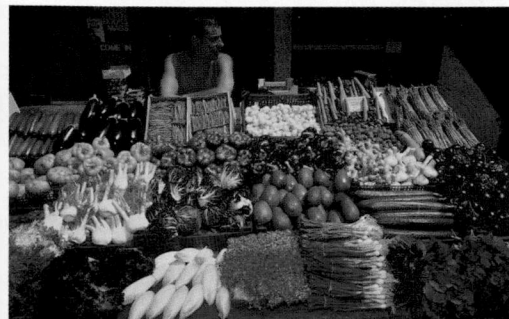
Bountiful vegetable stall at south London's Borough Market

the first to adopt these trends, offering good, imaginative, well-prepared, sensibly-priced food, as well as fine wines and beers, in the relaxed surroundings of the traditional London pub.

Chef Fergus Henderson of St John (see p300) is a pioneer of "head-to-toe" eating, espousing anything from ox cheek and tail to entire roast suckling pig.

London's historic seafood favourites, such as cockles and whelks, are increasingly hard to find at present but, as capital of an island nation, the city offers many fine fish restaurants. Concerns about over-fishing and farmed fish means that you are likely to see more of such local catches as bream, bass, sole and gurnard alongside cod and haddock, as well as salmon being billed as wild, and scallops as diver-caught.

Eastern Flavours

Britain has long had a love affair with both Oriental and Indian food, and some of the best examples of each can be found in London. While chicken tikka masala has been voted the nation's favourite dish (invented here, the legend

A mouthwatering pint of traditional London bitter beer

goes, to satisfy the national passion for gravy by pairing tandoori dry-roasted meat with a mild, creamy sauce), regional Indian food is now to the fore, notably southern cuisine strong on coconut, fish and fruits. The balti is another British take on the food of the subcontinent – named for the bowl-shaped dish in which they are cooked and served, fresh-tasting stews are served alongside vast naan breads for dunking.

In Chinatown, you can enjoy everything from a simple bowl of noodles to gourmet dishes featuring rare ingredients such as razor clams and sea urchins.

WHAT TO DRINK

Beers There are two large brewers in London – Young's and Fuller's – and some micro-brewers, too. The main varieties found in Britain are:
Bitter Brewed from malted barley, hops, yeast and water; drunk at room temperature.
Mild ale Sweeter than bitter.
Lager Hundreds of varieties of this pale carbonated beer are available. Served chilled.
Stout Thick, dark, creamy Guinness is the most famous.
Cider English cider has undergone a revival, with producers often featuring single old English apple varieties and using traditional methods.

Dover sole This is the most tasty flatfish, best served simply grilled with lemon, spinach and new potatoes.

Roast beef Horseradish sauce is a traditional accompaniment, as are crisp Yorkshire puddings made of batter.

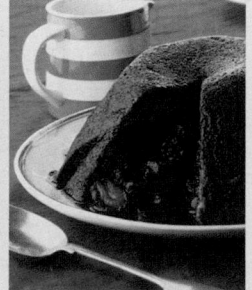
Summer pudding Lightly cooked fruits fill a basin lined with bread, which absorbs the sweet juices.

Where to Eat and Drink

Westminster and the West End

Belgo Centraal   £
Belgian   **Map** 13 B2
50 Earlham Street, WC2H 9LJ
Tel *020 7813 2233*
A bustling branch of a quirky
chain, where staff dress as monks.
Team the excellent lobster or
moules frites with a Trappist beer.

Food for Thought   £
Vegetarian   **Map** 13 B1
31 Neal Street, WC2H 9PR
Tel *020 7836 0239*
Be prepared to queue for tasty
vegetarian dishes, including
perfectly cooked wild mushroom
gnocchi and hearty vegan soups,
at this snug basement café.

Kulu Kulu Sushi   £
Japanese   **Map** 13 A2
76 Brewer Street, W1F 9TU
Tel *020 7734 7316*
Sit on a stool in the bar area and
help yourself to tasty sushi and
sashimi from a conveyor belt.
Perfect for a quick bite.

Princi   £
Italian   **Map** 13 A2
135 Wardour Street, W1F 0UT
Tel *020 7478 8888*
A stylish Milan import. Help
yourself to handmade bread,
wood-fired pizzas and
mouthwatering pastries; eat at
communal tables or at the
gleaming counters.

Regency Café   £
British   **Map** 21 A2
17–19 Regency Street, SW1P 4BY
Tel *020 7821 6596*
A 1950s-style "caff", featured in
the movie *Layer Cake*. Heavenly
hash browns and eggs Benedict
for breakfast or brunch.

DK Choice

Sagar   £
Indian Vegetarian   **Map** 13 C2
31 Catherine Street, WC2B 5JS
Tel *020 7836 6377*
Subtle flavours distinguish a
broad range of dishes from
Southern India at this simple,
canteen-style restaurant. Curries
are freshly made and the lunch
thali (selection of small dishes)
not only tastes good, it's also
great value for money. Don't
overlook the delicious crispy
dosas (potato- filled pancakes).
Efficient, friendly service.

Soho Joe   £
Mediterranean   **Map** 13 A1
22–25 Dean Street, W1D 3RY
Tel *07534 134398*
Thin-crust pizzas are the stars of
the show at this great-value
Italian. Pasta, burgers and toasted
sandwiches also feature.

Tokyo Diner   £
Japanese   **Map** 13 B2
2 Newport Place, WC2H 7JJ
Tel *020 7287 8777*
Authentic food, including *katsu*
curry, sushi and bento boxes, at
this functional three-storey diner.
Strictly no tipping.

Wahaca   £
Mexican   **Map** 13 B3
66 Chandos Place, WC2N 4HG
Tel *020 7240 1883*
Colourful and cool, this is the
original branch of a mini-chain
serving a seasonal menu of tasty
Mexican street food. No bookings.

Al Duca   ££
Italian   **Map** 13 A3
4–5 Duke of York Street, SW1Y 6LA
Tel *020 7839 3090*   **Closed** *Sun*
A reasonably priced and popular

Price Guide
For a three-course meal per person
including tax, service, and half a bottle
of house wine.

£	under £25
££	£25–£60
£££	Over £60

local. Using the freshest of
ingredients, classic Italian dishes
are given a modern twist.

Andrew Edmunds   ££
European   **Map** 13 A2
46 Lexington Street, W1F 0LW
Tel *020 7437 5708*
A tiny, candlelit, romantic retreat.
Imaginative dishes, including
well-balanced seafood and
game, feature on a daily-
changing menu.

Barrafina   ££
Spanish tapas   **Map** 13 A2
54 Frith Street, W1D 4SL
Tel *020 7813 8016*
Take pot luck at this hip joint –
there are just 23 bar stools and
no reservations. Fabulous,
intensely flavoured tapas.

Bocca di Lupo   ££
Italian   **Map** 13 A2
12 Archer Street, W1D 7BB
Tel *020 7734 2223*
A small place (only 14 tables)
with a big Italian heart. Chef
Jacob Kennedy specializes in
robust, little-known traditional
regional recipes.

Chisou   ££
Japanese   **Map** 12 F2
4 Princes Street, W1B 2LE
Tel *020 7629 3931*
Unfussy decor teamed with
delectable sushi at this bona fide
Japanese bistro. There's also a
mind-blowing selection of saké
on offer.

DK Choice

Clos Maggiore   ££
European   **Map** 13 B2
33 King Street, WC2E 8JD
Tel *020 7379 9696*
Try for a table in the courtyard
conservatory at Clos Maggiore,
with its blossom-laden
branches, for a magical
experience. On balmy evenings,
the roof is opened to the stars,
while a fire is lit when it's chilly –
sheer romance. French regional
food inspires the modern
European cooking. Fixed-price
pre- and post-theatre menus are
quite a bargain.

The traditional dining rooms of Clos Maggiore

Dehesa £££
Tapas   Map 12 F2
25 Ganton Street, W1F 9BP
Tel *020 7494 4170*
A buzzy vibe paired with stand-out tapas. Make sure you taste its famous charcuterie and signature dish – stuffed courgette flower.

El Pirata £££
Tapas   Map 12 E4
5–6 Down Street, W1J 7AQ
Tel *020 7491 3810*   **Closed** *Sun*
There's a deft hand in the kitchen at this lively, laid-back restaurant. All the classic Spanish and Portuguese favourites are on offer.

Gopals of Soho £££
Indian   Map 13 A2
12 Bateman Street, W1 5TD
Tel *020 7434 1621*
You don't come to this traditional family-run curry house for the surroundings, but for the intense flavours of the expertly spiced food. Excellent vegetarian *thalis*.

Haozhan £££
Chinese   Map 13 A2
8 Gerrard Street, W1D 5PJ
Tel *020 7434 3838*
A pioneer of superb, inventive cuisine. Try delicate black cod dumplings or wasabi prawns a world away from the standard sweet-and-sour staples.

Hard Rock Café £££
American   Map 12 E4
150 Old Park Lane, W1K 1QZ
Tel *020 7514 1700*
Try American staples at this legend with a fascinating collection of rock memorabilia. Still rocking after more than 40 years.

Inamo £££
Asian fusion   Map 13 A2
134–136 Wardour Street, W1F 8ZP
Tel *020 7851 7051*
An Oriental eatery with a difference. Order your meal on a touch-screen pad and play games while you wait. Fun for groups and large parties.

Le Deuxième £££
French   Map 13 B2
65a Long Acre, WC2E 9JD
Tel *020 7379 0033*
A solid choice, particularly for pre-opera or theatre dining. The bistro-style menu concentrates on interesting combinations and strong flavours.

Mildred's £££
Vegetarian   Map 13 A2
45 Lexington Street, W1F 9AN
Tel *020 7494 1634*   **Closed** *Sun*
Inspired vegetable dishes, fit to

The tables double up as touch-screen menus at Asian-inspired Inamo

convert the most confirmed carnivore. Try the ale and porcini mushroom pie. No bookings.

Nopi £££
Middle Eastern   Map 12 F2
21–22 Warwick Street, W1B 5NE
Tel *020 7494 9584*
Cookery writer Yotam Ottolenghi's grown-up restaurant. A blend of aromatic flavours, bold colours and exciting textures in dishes designed for sharing.

Noura ££
Lebanese   Map 20 E1
16 Hobart Place, SW1W 0HH
Tel *020 7235 9696*
Exceptional *mezzes* and kebabs at the flagship of an award-winning small chain. Classy decor and a tempting brasserie-style menu.

Patara £££
Thai   Map 13 A2
115 Greek Street, W1D 4DP
Tel *020 7437 1071*
An enticing all-rounder, spread over two dimly-lit, soothingly romantic floors. Specialities include several prawn dishes, each an explosion of flavour.

Porter's English Restaurant £££
British   Map 13 C2
17 Henrietta Street, WC2E 8QH
Tel *020 7836 6466*
Fill up on hearty English classics, such as steak and kidney pudding, fish pie and spotted dick. Casual dining and a great choice for families.

Rasa £££
Indian   Map 12 E2
6 Dering Street, W1S 1AD
Tel *020 7629 1346*   **Closed** *Sun*
Unusual and exquisitely fragrant specialities from Kerala, each served on a huge fresh banana leaf. The vegetarian and fish dishes are exceptional.

Refuel £££
British   Map 13 A2
The Soho Hotel, 4 Richmond Mews, W1D 3DH
Tel *020 7559 3007*
Rub shoulders with the glitterati at this stylish media-land hang-out. A diverse menu of modern European cuisine. Great service.

Terroirs £££
Mediterranean   Map 13 B3
5 William IV Street, WC2N 4DW
Tel *020 7036 0660*   **Closed** *Sun*
An impressive selection of biodynamic wines, teamed with wholesome organic food (pork, snails, lentils, mushrooms and charcuterie). Reminiscent of a Parisian wine bar.

Thai Pot £££
Thai   Map 13 B2
1 Bedfordbury, WC2N 4BP
Tel *020 7379 4580*   **Closed** *Sun & bank hol Mon*
Thai staples full of fragrant flavour. Dashes of warm colour jazz up the sleek, contemporary decoration.

DK Choice

The Portrait £££
British   Map 13 B3
National Portrait Gallery, 2 St Martin's Place, WC2H 0HE
Tel *020 7312 2490*
Spot London's famous monuments from a window seat at Searcys' airy top-floor restaurant: they're almost all on view. The excellent food served here is contemporary British: the seabass with marsh samphire stands out. The main dining area is smart and modern, in complete contrast to the historical surroundings. Before or after your meal, be sure to take a turn around the splendid National Portrait Gallery.

For more information on types of restaurants *see page 289*

The elegant afternoon tea at The Wolseley

The Ten Cases ££
British **Map** 13 B1
16 Endell Street, WC2H 9BD
Tel *020 7836 6801*
Outstanding wines – ten reds,
ten whites – plus three choices
per course at this exciting
restaurant. British cooking with
European overtones.

The Wolseley ££
European **Map** 12 F3
160 Piccadilly, W1J 9EB
Tel *020 7499 6996*
The glorious 1920s Wolseley
Motors car showroom makes a
stunning home for this glamorous
café/restaurant. The afternoon
tea is legendary.

Vasco and Piero's Pavilion ££
Italian **Map** 13 A2
15 Poland Street, W1F 8QE
Tel *020 7437 8774* **Closed** *Sun*
Home-made pasta is used in
their own excellent recipes, often
with truffles when in season.
Umbrian specialities, such as pork
and lentils, are favourites.

Yalla Yalla ££
Lebanese **Map** 13 A2
1 Green's Court, W1F 0HA
Tel *020 7287 7663*
Be transported to Beirut at this
little gem, where the spicy street
food packs a punch. Heartier
meals are also on offer.

**Apsleys, a Heinz Beck
Restaurant** £££
Italian **Map** 12 D5
*The Lanesborough Hotel, Hyde Park
Corner, SW1X 7TA*
Tel *020 7333 7254*
If you're celebrating, push the
boat out and order the
impressive seven-course tasting
menu. The Venetian-style dining
room is sumptuous.

Asia de Cuba £££
Fusion (Asian/Cuban) **Map** 13 B2
45 St Martin's Lane, WC2N 4HX
Tel *020 7300 5588*
Combines Asian and Cuban
cuisine, served sharing-style in a
high-energy, sophisticated and
yet relaxed environment.

Atelier de Joël Robuchon £££
French **Map** 13 B2
13–15 West Street, WC2H 9NE
Tel *020 7010 8600*
Try for a front-row seat at the
Japanese-inspired counter in this
contemporary two-Michelin-
starred temple. Flawless modern
French cuisine.

Bellamy's £££
French **Map** 12 E3
18 Bruton Place, W1J 6LY
Tel *020 7491 2727* **Closed** *Sun*
A mews house makes a quietly
traditional dining room and
clubby Oyster Bar. Exclusively
French wines accompany a well-
executed menu.

Bentley's Oyster Bar and Grill £££
Seafood **Map** 12 F3
11 Swallow Street, W1B 4DG
Tel *020 7734 4756* **Closed** *Sun*
A civilized island of calm, in
business since 1916. Chef Richard
Corrigan's inventive creations
keep it firmly on the map. There
are plenty of meat dishes if you're
not in the mood for seafood.

Cecconi's £££
Italian **Map** 12 F3
5A Burlington Gardens, W1S 3EP
Tel *020 7434 1500*
The beautiful people even come
to this captivating Italian for
breakfast. Virtuoso versions of
standard dishes. Gets busy at
peak times, so try to book in
advance if you can.

Cinnamon Club £££
Indian **Map** 21 B1
*The Old Westminster Library,
30–32 Great Smith Street, SW1P 3BU*
Tel *020 7222 2555* **Closed** *Sun*
Delicately spiced North Indian
cuisine, using the freshest
ingredients. Housed in a former
library with an atmosphere of
hushed sophistication.

DK Choice

CUT at 45 Park Lane £££
Steakhouse **Map** 12 D4
45 Park Lane, W1K 1PN
Tel *020 7493 4554*
US celebrity chef Wolfgang
Puck's first European venture is
a paradise for carnivores.
Choose a raw cut from a platter
brought to your table before it
is whisked away and expertly
cooked. The surroundings are as
grand, and the waiters as
courteous and well-informed, as
you'd expect from the price tag.

Hakkasan Mayfair £££
Chinese **Map** 12 E3
17 Bruton Street, W1J 6QB
Tel *020 7907 1888*
Glitzy, adeptly lit showcase for
exquisite Cantonese cuisine,
including some of the finest dim
sum you're likely to taste.

DK Choice

J Sheekey £££
Fish and seafood **Map** 13 B2
*28–32 St Martin's Court, WC2N
4AL*
Tel *020 7240 2565*
London's finest fish restaurant
dates back to the 1890s. It still
occupies a warren of Dickensian
rooms, but now offers a
wonderfully varied menu of
responsibly sourced fish, oysters
and shellfish. Most fun is to sit
on a high stool at the
horseshoe-shaped bar for the
signature oysters and
Champagne. Or dine in the
elegant banquette seating area
and admire the open kitchen.
Perfect for pre- and post-
theatre dining. Friendly and
attentive service.

La Petite Maison £££
French **Map** 12 E2
53–54 Brook's Mews, W1K 4EG
Tel *020 7495 4774*
Come to this exhilarating spot in
a group; the small Mediterranean
dishes and Southern French
flavours combine seasonal
ingredients and are ideal for
sharing. Cutting-edge cuisine.

Le Caprice £££
International **Map** 12 F3
Arlington House, Arlington Street, SW1A 1RJ
Tel *020 7629 2239*
Classy, yet vibrant rendezvous for media types, where everyone is made to feel like a star by the delightful staff. Bistro food.

Le Gavroche £££
French **Map** 12 D2
43 Upper Brook Street, W1K 7QR
Tel *020 7408 0881* **Closed** *Sun*
Come to Michel Roux Jr's flagship restaurant for exceptional *haute cuisine* and supremely professional service. The set lunch is well priced.

Murano £££
European **Map** 12 E3
20 Queen Street, W1J 5PP
Tel *020 7495 1127* **Closed** *Sun*
The clue's in the name. Angela Hartnett's sublime cooking is Venetian influenced. Nothing disappoints, from *amuse-bouches* to *petits fours*.

Nobu £££
Japanese **Map** 12 E4
Metropolitan Hotel W1, 19 Old Park Lane, W1K 1LB
Tel *020 7447 4747*
Sample beautifully prepared sashimi, tempura and many more contemporary, ground-breaking dishes at this Japanese restaurant. The seafood and fish are of the highest quality.

Pollen Street Social £££
British **Map** 12 F2
10 Pollen Street, W1S 1NQ
Tel *020 7290 7600* **Closed** *Sun*
Opened by Gordon Ramsay protégé Jason Atherton in 2011. It's all hard surfaces and cutting-edge art. The food's ravishing too. A well-priced set menu and efficient service.

Rules £££
British **Map** 13 C2
35 Maiden Lane, WC2E 7LB
Tel *020 7836 5314*
Robust British food in an opulent setting – rib of beef, oysters and game from its own country estate – at the capital's oldest restaurant, established in 1798.

Scott's £££
Fish and seafood **Map** 12 D3
20 Mount Street, W1 2HE
Tel *020 7495 7309*
Join the league of celebrities who have dined here, from Winston Churchill to Marilyn Monroe. Its sensational seafood makes it as popular as ever. The roasted shellfish platters are outstanding.

The Ritz Restaurant £££
British **Map** 12 F3
150 Piccadilly, W1J 9BR
Tel *020 7493 8181*
This gilded and frescoed room, with its profusion of chandeliers, is a glamorous setting for impressive cuisine.

The Square £££
French **Map** 12 E3
6–10 Bruton Street, W1J 6PU
Tel *020 7495 7100*
A luxurious haunt of wine-lovers and foodies alike. All down to its encyclopaedic wine list and complex, wonderful food.

Veeraswamy £££
Indian **Map** 12 F3
Victory House, 99 Regent Street, W1B 4RS
Tel *020 7734 1401*
A mix of contemporary and classic cooking at this London institution, opened in 1926.

Yauatcha £££
Chinese **Map** 13 A2
15 Broadwick Street, W1F 0DL
Tel *020 7494 8888*
A reinterpretation of a traditional Chinese teahouse, serving sublime dim sum.

Kensington and Chelsea

DK Choice

Alounak £
Persian **Map** 10 D2
44 Westbourne Grove, W2 5SH
Tel *020 7229 4158*
Queues often snake down the street, so popular is this bazaar-style café. It specializes in deliciously light Middle Eastern food at low prices. Inside, it's all bare wood tables and exposed brick walls. There's no wine on sale, so bring your own. The presence of so many Iranians speaks for itself.

Buona Sera Jam £
Italian **Map** 19 A4
289 King's Road, SW3 5EW
Tel *020 7352 8827*
A lively trattoria that's fun for all the family. Climb miniature ladders to reach the top-tier tables and try the terrific pizzas.

Café Mona Lisa £
French **Map** 18 E5
417 King's Road, SW10 0LR
Tel *020 7376 5447*
A much-loved neighbourhood café with friendly service and a warm feel. Specials chalked up on the blackboards are always a good option.

El Pirata Detapas £
Spanish tapas **Map** 10 D2
115 Westbourne Grove, W2 4UP
Tel *020 7727 5000*
There's a real buzz to this spot, with its on-trend zinc bar and wood floor. The modern tapas offer big flavours for small prices.

Jak's £
Mediterranean **Map** 19 B2
77 Walton Street, SW3 2HT
Tel *020 7584 3441*
Choose from a splendid array of healthy, organic dishes and tempting desserts and eat in the diminutive country-style back room.

Raison d'Etre £
European **Map** 18 F2
18 Bute Street, SW7 3EX
Tel *020 7584 5008* **Closed** *Sun*
They bake their own bread at this very French, very popular café. Sandwiches, made with super fresh ingredients, are delicious. Good selection of fillings.

DK Choice

Assaggi ££
Italian **Map** 9 C2
39 Chepstow Place, W2 4TS
Tel *020 7792 5501* **Closed** *Sun*
Hidden away above a pub, this alluring restaurant feels like a discovery. In fact, it's all the rage and often difficult to book. The bright, simply furnished room reflects the vivid colours of chef Nino Sassu's native Sardinia. Enthusiastic waiting staff.

The sleek interior of Hakkasan Mayfair

For more information on types of restaurants *see page 289*

Bar Boulud ££
French **Map** 11 C5
*Mandarin Oriental Hyde Park, 66
Knightsbridge, SW1X 7LA*
Tel *020 7201 3899*
The look's chic but the mood's
relaxed at US star chef Daniel
Boulud's London venture.
A French-inspired bistro with
unforgettable terrines.

Bluebird ££
European **Map** 19 A4
350 King's Road, SW3 5UU
Tel *020 7559 1000*
This ever-popular restaurant
serves light British dishes made
from seasonal ingredients. It has
a café, bar, food store and also a
wine cellar.

Byron ££
American **Map** 9 C5
222 Kensington High Street, W8 7RG
Tel *020 7361 1717*
The secret is that Byron's burgers
are the best in town; simple and
tasty and made from quality,
freshly minced beef. A stylish
branch with keen staff.

Caraffini ££
Italian **Map** 20 D3
61–63 Lower Sloane Street, SW1 8DH
Tel *020 7259 0235* **Closed** Sun &
bank hol Mon
Service Italian-style at this
old favourite, still hopping at
lunchtimes. Plump for the
lobster taglierini or one of
the specials.

Chez Patrick ££
French **Map** 18 D1
7 Stratford Road, W8 6RF
Tel *020 7937 6388*
Front-of-house owner Patrick gives
excellent advice on ordering at
this intimate restaurant. Classic
French recipes, mostly fish,
flawlessly executed.

E&O ££
Asian fusion **Map** 9 A2
14 Blenheim Crescent, W11 1NN
Tel *020 7229 5454*
Dine on dim sum, tempura, sushi
or sashimi in glossy black
surroundings. Specials might
include pad thai or crispy sea
bass. Dim sum is available all day
at the bar.

Gallery Mess ££
European **Map** 19 C2
*Saatchi Gallery, Duke Of York's HQ,
King's Road, SW3 4RY*
Tel *020 7730 8135*
A desirable lunch spot after an
exhibition. Try for the most
attractive tables, in the airy
cloister, which overlook a leafy
square. Appetizing lunches.

The stylish Asian-fusion restaurant, E&O

Hunan ££
Chinese **Map** 20 D2
51 Pimlico Road, SW1W 8NE
Tel *020 7730 5712* **Closed** Sun
Taiwanese tapas-size portions
keep arriving at your table, as
fiery or mild as you like, until
you're full. Try the signature dish
of hearty broth with minced
pork, mushroom and ginger.

Kensington Place ££
Fish **Map** 9 C4
*201 Kensington Church Street,
W8 7LX*
Tel *020 7727 3184*
Fresh decoration and a classic
menu, including superb beer-
battered fish and chips, game
and steaks at this famous
goldfish bowl brasserie.

Kitchen W8 ££
British **Map** 17 C1
11–13 Abingdon Road, W8 6AH
Tel *020 7937 0120*
A benchmark for quality: Philip
Howard's creative Michelin-
starred cooking in a sleek,
comfortable environment.
And it won't break the bank.

La Poule au Pot ££
French **Map** 20 E2
231 Ebury Street, SW1W 8UT
Tel *020 7730 7763*
Full of romance and rustic French
charm, which complements the
honest cooking. Serves all the
classics, such as *boeuf
bourguignon* and *tarte tatin*.

Le Metro at the Levin Hotel ££
British **Map** 11 C5
28 Basil Street, SW3 1AS
Tel *020 7589 6286*
A basement brasserie with
delectable food and the
ambience of a contemporary
European tearoom. It has comfy
banquettes, and an open kitchen.
Feels like a well-kept secret.

Lucky Seven ££
American **Map** 10 D1
127 Westbourne Park Road, W2 5QI.
Tel *020 7727 6771*
Typical US fare, from burgers to
shakes, at this archetypal East
Coast diner. So tiny, you might
have to share a booth.

Maroush II ££
Lebanese **Map** 19 B1
38 Beauchamp Place, SW3 1NU
Tel *020 7581 5434*
The perfect spot for a late-night
bite; tender, tasty grilled dishes
available till 3am. Fine dining on
the first floor.

The Abingdon ££
International **Map** 17 C1
54 Abingdon Road, W8 6AP
Tel *020 7937 3339*
A converted pub with a refined
feel. Try to secure one of the
comfortable booths for high-end,
brasserie-style food.

The Belvedere ££
French **Map** 9 B5
*Holland Park (off Abbotsbury Road),
W8 6LU*
Tel *020 7602 1238*
Enjoy modern European fare in
a sumptuous former ballroom
overlooking lawns and flower
gardens. A treat, whether you
eat inside or out.

The Enterprise ££
European **Map** 19 B2
35 Walton Street, SW3 2HU
Tel *020 7584 3148*
A humble local pub converted
into a well-groomed restaurant/
bar. Don't miss out on the
impeccably cooked squid and
courgette tempura starter.

The Markham Inn ££
British **Map** 19 B2
2 Elystan Street, SW3 3NS
Tel *020 7581 9139*
In Victorian times, travellers
would congregate in this popular
pub. Now tastefully clubby, with
red Chesterfields and a superior
seasonal menu.

DK Choice

The Painted Heron ££
Indian **Map** 19 A5
112 Cheyne Walk, SW10 0DJ
Tel *020 7351 5232*
Not a run-of-the-mill Indian
restaurant. A smartly modern
room, hung with contemporary
artworks, is the setting for
succulent dishes using
unconventional ingredients,
such as game, wild sea trout,
black cod and soft-shell crab.

Key to prices see page 292

Spicing is complex but not overstated. For the health conscious, there's a vegetarian menu based on Ayurvedic principles.

DK Choice

**Babylon at the
Roof Garden**   £££
British   **Map** 10 D5
*99 Kensington High Street,
W8 5SA*
Tel *020 7368 3993*
The "hanging gardens", overlooked by this fashionable restaurant, sprawl high above the street. Eat here and explore three themed areas filled with trees, flamingos and a fish-stocked stream (phone first to check they're not fully booked). Enjoy the modern British cuisine and the panorama. Best in summer, when you can dine al fresco on the terrace.

Bibendum   £££
French   **Map** 19 A2
*Michelin House, 81 Fulham Road,
SW3 6RD*
Tel *020 7581 5817*
Seasonal food, assiduous service and Michelin House's Art Nouveau stained glass, a stunning backdrop to this airy first-floor dining room. Head chef Matthew Harris produces classic French food with a strong British influence and 21st-century style.

Blakes   £££
Asian   **Map** 18 F3
33 Roland Gardens, SW7 3PF
Tel *020 7370 6701*
Fans, orchids and Oriental touches decorate this seductive sanctuary below stairs. The imaginative menu mingles Mediterranean and Eastern flavours. Specials include the angel-hair pasta with black cod.

**Dinner
by Heston Blumenthal**   £££
British   **Map** 11 C5
*Mandarin Oriental Hyde Park, 66
Knightsbridge, SW1X 7LA*
Tel *020 7201 3833*
London's most hyped restaurant showcases this celebrity chef's inspired take on classic cuisine. Blumenthal is well-known for juxtaposing different flavours. Only for those with deep pockets, but unforgettable.

Launceston Place   £££
British   **Map** 18 E1
1a Launceston Place, W8 5RL
Tel *020 7937 6912*
Imaginative modern cooking in a series of traditional, carpeted rooms. An oasis of calm, where staff pay attention to detail. The menu is designed to complement the setting and features British classics given a flamboyant twist.

**Marcus Wareing at
the Berkeley**   £££
European   **Map** 12 D5
*The Berkeley Hotel, Wilton Place,
SW1X 7RL*
Tel *020 7235 1200*   **Closed** *Sun*
Sample delectable cooking from a superstar chef in the dining room. Sheer genius. Sophisticated fine dining. Has two Michelin stars.

One-0-One   £££
Fish and seafood   **Map** 11 C5
*Sheraton Park Tower Hotel,
101 Knightsbridge, SW1X 7RN*
Tel *020 7290 7101*
Seafood's the thing at this exquisite restaurant. Try Norwegian halibut or crab in stunning recipes from head chef Pascal Proyart, or the signature crab risotto. *Petits plats* make an ideal light lunch. The key to the stand-out menu is the chef's use of the freshest ingredients.

Restaurant Gordon Ramsay £££
French   **Map** 19 C4
68 Royal Hospital Road, SW3 4HP
Tel *020 7352 4441*   **Closed** *Sat & Sun*
Standards remain high at this triple-Michelin-starred shrine to *haute cuisine*. Eye-wateringly expensive, but the menu is truly exciting.

The Ledbury   £££
European   **Map** 9 C2
127 Ledbury Road, W11 2AQ
Tel *020 7792 9090*
Possibly London's most happening restaurant, the realm of thrilling Australian chef Brett Graham. Expect two-Michelin starred culinary fireworks.

Zuma   £££
Japanese   **Map** 11 B5
5 Raphael Street, SW7 1DL
Tel *020 7584 1010*
Spot the celebrities at this cool joint. They're drawn – like everyone – by divine robata-grilled dishes, tempura, nigiri sushi and sashimi.

Bloomsbury and Regent's Park

Golden Hind   £
British   **Map** 12 E1
73 Marylebone Lane, W1U 2PN
Tel *020 7486 3644*   **Closed** *Sun*
Devotees claim its fish and chips are unequalled. A welcoming, no-frills family-run place with no licence, but minimal corkage. The home-made fishcakes make an enticing alternative.

DK Choice

Thai Metro   £
Thai   **Map** 5 A5
38 Charlotte St, W1T 2NN
Tel *020 7436 4201*
The exemplary Thai cooking at this down-to-earth corner café has made it a smash hit. Choose carefully if you can't take your curries too hot: some of the specialities are guaranteed to make you sweat. Service is speedy and efficient, and the bill shouldn't be a nasty shock.

Bam-Bou   ££
Vietnamese   **Map** 13 A1
1 Percy Street, W1T 1DB
Tel *020 7323 9130*   **Closed** *Sun*
Stop off for a drink in the romantic red bar before descending to the candlelit restaurant. Well-crafted French-Vietnamese dishes with Thai and Chinese influences.

Rustic charm and traditional French cuisine at La Poule au Pot

For more information on types of restaurants *see page 289*

Galvin Bistrot de Luxe ££
French **Map** 3 C5
66 Baker Street, W1U 7DJ
Tel *020 7935 4007*
You could be in Paris in the
Galvin brothers' high-class bistro.
Beautifully cooked classics in a
room bristling with happy
customers. Top quality French
cuisine at affordable prices.

Malabar Junction ££
Indian **Map** 13 B1
107 Great Russell Street, WC1B 3NA
Tel *020 7580 5230*
An atrium with wood floors and
wicker chairs. The wide-ranging
menu features specialities from
Kerala, all tender, fragrant and
skilfully prepared.

Ragam ££
Indian **Map** 4 F5
57 Cleveland Street, W1T 4JN
Tel *020 7636 9098*
Not much to look at, but this
veteran offers Keralan specialities
zinging with aromatic flavour.
The filled pancakes are
guaranteed to wow. Choose from
side dishes such as beetroot *baji*
or spinach with lentils.

DK Choice

Salt Yard ££
Tapas **Map** 5 A5
54 Goodge Street, W1T 4NA
Tel *020 7637 0657* **Closed** *Sun*
Fans claim this go-to place
offers the best tapas in London.
What's unique is the
combination of Spanish and
Italian cuisines. Fresh, top-
quality ingredients are centre
stage in such small delights as
duck and spinach *gnocchetti*
and the signature courgette
flowers stuffed with goat's
cheese and drizzled with honey.
Always heaving.

The Chancery ££
European **Map** 14 E1
9 Cursitor Street, EC4A 1LL
Tel *020 7831 4000* **Closed** *Sun*
A small legal-land treasure,
tempting for lazy lunches.
Fabulous hake, muntjac and
slow-cooked pork belly. Well-
priced too.

The White Swan ££
British **Map** 14 E1
108 Fetter Lane, EC4A 1ES
Tel *020 7242 9696* **Closed** *Sat & Sun*
You'll find this place above a
no-nonsense pub. The room's
light and sunny, the cooking
sophisticated, with an innovative
menu with dishes such as braised
octopus *carpaccio*.

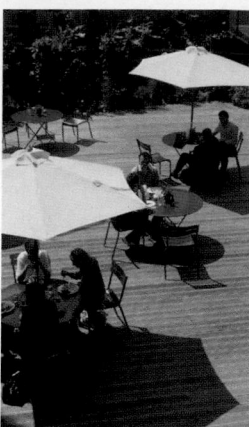
Diners enjoying lunch on the outdoor
decking at Clerkenwell Kitchen

Vanilla Black ££
Vegetarian **Map** 14 E1
17–18 Tooks Court, EC4A 1LB
Tel *020 7242 2622* **Closed** *Sun*
Exciting vegetarian dishes in an
elegant setting. Warm walnut
pannacotta and blue stilton
dumplings – proof positive that
you don't need meat.

Orrery £££
French **Map** 4 D5
*55–57 Marylebone High Street,
W1U 5RB*
Tel *020 7616 8000*
Outstanding modern cuisine
on the first floor of a converted
stable block. Great attention
to detail in both cooking and
service. Ask for a table beside
the arched windows.

Pied à Terre £££
French **Map** 5 A5
34 Charlotte Street, W1T 2NH
Tel *020 7636 1178* **Closed** *Sun*
Adventurous and impeccable
food tops the bill at this discreet
haven. A comfortable dining
room and friendly staff.

Roka £££
Japanese **Map** 5 A5
37 Charlotte Street, W1T 1RR
Tel *020 7580 6464*
Sit at the wood counter in this
goldfish bowl restaurant, graze
on luscious sushi and watch the
chefs at the robata grill. Riveting
and theatrical.

Texture £££
European **Map** 11 C2
34 Portman Street, W1H 7BY
Tel *020 7224 0028* **Closed** *Mon & Sun*
Bold, experimental cookery from
Icelandic chef Agnar Sverrisson.
Expect to find cod, lamb and
herbs from his homeland.

The Providores and Tapa Room £££
International fusion **Map** 4 D5
*109 Marylebone High Street,
W1U 4RX*
Tel *020 7935 6175*
The global fusion food has won
plaudits at this showcase
establishment. For lighter fare,
try the downstairs tapas bar.

The City and the East End

Cây Tre £
Vietnamese **Map** 7 A4
301 Old Street, EC1V 9LA
Tel *020 7729 8662*
The menu's short, but dishes
are authentic and high quality.
Surprises include Cornish
scallops and anchovied chicken
wings plus unusual combinations
like the beef *carpaccio* and
tamarind soup special.

Clerkenwell Kitchen £
British **Map** 6 E4
27–31 Clerkenwell Close, EC1R 0AT
Tel *020 7101 9959* **Closed** *Sat & Sun,
Mon–Fri pm*
A good choice for lunch. Organic
produce, gutsy home cooking
and appealingly modern brick-
and-wood surroundings.

De Palo's £
Italian **Map** 14 F2
8 Bride Court, EC4Y 8DU
Tel *020 7583 8440* **Closed** *Sat & Sun*
Fresh ingredients and authentic
Sicilian flavours are the stars at this
intimate, family-owned restaurant.
Try the amazing *tortiglioni* special.

Kolossi Grill £
Greek **Map** 6 E4
56–60 Rosebery Avenue, EC1R 4RR
Tel *020 7278 5758* **Closed** *Sun*
Home-made Cypriot classics
have been served in this cosy,
unpretentious restaurant for
more than 50 years. Service is
warm and friendly.

The smart interior of Salt Yard, serving
Spanish and Italian tapas

Lahore Kebab House £
Pakistani **Map** 16 E1
2–10 Umberston Street, E1 1PY
Tel *020 7481 9737*
A traditional but spartan Pakistani spot, open late and with the kitchen on view. Spiced curries and kebabs set tastebuds tingling in this warehouse-style space. Bring your own alcohol.

Leon Spitalfields £
European **Map** 8 D5
3 Crispin Place, E1 6DW
Tel *020 7247 4369*
Healthy "superfood" salads and Mediterranean-inspired fast food in a large, bright, colourful space. Open from breakfast to dinner.

Tayyabs £
Punjabi **Map** 16 F1
83 Fieldgate Street, E1 1JU
Tel *020 7247 6400*
A local favourite serving delicious spiced curries and sizzling mixed grills. Don't miss the Kahari Lamb Chops, but be sure to book ahead to avoid the very long queues.

DK Choice

Brawn ££
French **Map** 8 E3
49 Columbia Road, E2 7RG
Tel *020 7729 5692*
Big, bold, full-bodied flavours can be found in abundance in Brawn's seasonal cuisine. Dishes you might find on the daily written menu are venison pie, pig's trotters and ceps with Bordelaise sauce. Accompany your choice with one of the many organic wines. The industrial-rustic dining room has an eclectic charm.

Carnevale ££
Vegetarian **Map** 7 A4
135 Whitecross Street, EC1Y 8JL
Tel *020 7250 3452* **Closed** *Sun*
Stellar culinary creations in a modest little café. Delicious Middle Eastern-inspired risottos, casseroles and curries.

Casa Negra ££
Mexican **Map** 7 C4
54–56 Great Eastern Street, EC2A 3QR
Tel *020 7033 7360* **Closed** *Sun & Mon*
An understated pop-up style Mexican restaurant and bar in Shoreditch. Friendly staff.

Haz Plantation Place ££
Turkish **Map** 15 C2
6 Mincing Lane, EC3M 3BD
Tel *020 7929 3173* **Closed** *Sun*
Order the marvellous *mezze* for a range of authentic dishes, or try the perfectly-cooked tuna steak

Contemporary dining area, L'Anima

with home-made chilli sauce. The set menus are a bargain for the City.

L'Anima ££
Italian **Map** 7 C5
1 Snowden Street, EC2A 2DQ
Tel *020 7422 7000* **Closed** *Sun*
Francesco Mazzei's food is as elegant as the minimalist, glass and white setting. Stunning regional recipes from Sicily and Sardinia.

Le Café du Marché ££
French **Map** 6 F5
22 Charterhouse Square, EC1M 6DX
Tel *020 7608 1609* **Closed** *Sun*
Very French; a hideaway with accomplished classic cooking and a simple, stylish look.

Pham Sushi ££
Japanese **Map** 7 A4
159 Whitecross Street, EC1Y 8JL
Tel *020 7251 6336* **Closed** *Sun*
Exquisite sushi, sashimi, *tempura* and California rolls, all so fresh and full of flavour, you hardly notice the uninspiring interior.

The Peasant ££
British **Map** 6 E2
240 St John Street, EC1V 4PH
Tel *020 7336 7726*
Finely executed brasserie cooking in an agreeable Victorian pub dining room. Enjoy the Chilean chef's first-rate pub food in the cavernous bar below. Splendid Sunday roasts

The Restaurant at St Paul's Cathedral ££
British **Map** 15 A1
St Paul's Cathedral, St Paul's Churchyard, EC4M 8AD
Tel *020 7248 2469*
Have a substantial or a light lunch or a slap-up tea in the beautifully-lit crypt. Imaginative seasonal menus of fine British produce are served daily.

DK Choice

Vinoteca ££
European **Map** 6 E2
7 St John Street, EC1M 4AA
Tel *020 7253 8786* **Closed** *Sun*
Admirers come from far and wide to this Farringdon wine bar. The list of 300 outstanding wines might be the draw, but the excellence of the Modern European food keeps bringing them back. Pairing suggestions are made for every dish. Arrive early for dinner; reservations are only accepted for lunch.

Club Gascon £££
French **Map** 14 F1
57 West Smithfield, EC1A 9DS
Tel *020 7600 6144* **Closed** *Sun*
Dinner here is an experience to savour. Try the creamy signature *foie gras*, paired with a recommended wine.

Galvin La Chapelle £££
French **Map** 8 D5
35 Spital Square, E1 6DY
Tel *020 7299 0400*
A sensitive conversion of a school hall, which certainly has the wow factor, with an elegant menu.

Goodman £££
Steakhouse **Map** 15 B1
11 Old Jewry, EC2R 8DU
Tel *020 7600 8220* **Closed** *Sat & Sun*
Melt-in-the-mouth steaks are the staple at this all-American steak house. You can see the meat dry-ageing in the kitchen.

Hawksmoor £££
Steakhouse **Map** 16 E1
157 Commercial Street, E1 6BJ
Tel *020 7426 4850*
Astonishing, dictionary-thick steaks. They're from traditionally reared Longhorn cattle, dry aged and cooked simply on a charcoal grill – scrumptious.

For more information on types of restaurants *see page 289*

Sauterelle
French   £££
Map 15 C2
The Royal Exchange, EC3V 3LR
Tel *020 7618 2480*   **Closed** *Sat & Sun*
Stylish cuisine in a captivating
setting: on a mezzanine over-
looking the glorious courtyard of
the Grade I-listed Neo-Classical
Royal Exchange.

St John
British   £££
Map 6 E2
26 St John Street, EC1M 4AY
Tel *020 7251 0848*
Not for the squeamish. Fergus
Henderson's celebrated kitchen
makes the most of offal,
including heart, lung, kidney and
more obscure animal parts.

The Boundary
French   £££
Map 8 D4
2 Boundary Street, E2 7DD
Tel *020 7729 1051*
Faultless modern versions of
traditional recipes at style-guru
Terence Conran's sexy, subterranean
hideout. Staff are very attentive.

Southwark and the South Bank

Anchor and Hope
British   £
Map 14 E4
36 The Cut, SE1 8LP
Tel *020 7928 9898*   **Closed** *Sun pm*
Turn up with a good appetite.
Large portions of such gutsy fare
as calves' brains, pumpkin risotto
and braised venison.

Dim T – London Bridge
Asian fusion   £
Map 16 D4
*2 More London Place,
Tooley Street, SE1 2DB*
Tel *020 7403 7000*
Be creative by choosing noodles,
toppings and sauces to make
your own dish. Fun for the family,
plus spectacular river views.

The Laughing Gravy
British   £
Map 14 F3
154–156 Blackfriars Road, SE1 8EN
Tel *020 7998 1707*
A laid-back restaurant, with a
more lively bar, in an old foundry
building. A well-chosen wine list
complements the changing
seasonal menu.

DK Choice

Blueprint Café   ££
European   Map 16 E4
*1st Floor, Design Museum, 28
Shad Thames, SE1 2YD*
Tel *020 7378 7031*
Grab a window seat and enjoy
the view of Tower Bridge to the

Impressive view of St Pauls Cathedral from the Oxo Tower Restaurant

full, using the signature blue
binoculars to zoom in on the
river traffic. With Bentwood
chairs and a sleek wood floor,
the café is right at home on top
of the Design Museum. Chef
Mark Jarvis puts an individual
stamp on classic dishes made
with seasonal produce.

Champor-Champor
Malaysian   ££
Map 15 C4
62–64 Weston Street, SE1 3QJ
Tel *020 7403 4600*
The name means "mix and
match" – a perfect depiction of its
exotic, yet wacky decoration, and
wonderfully eclectic cuisine.

José
Spanish   ££
Map 15 C4
104 Bermondsey Street, SE1 3UB
Tel *020 7403 4902*
Team extraordinarily good
Barcelona-style tapas with a
choice from the varied list of
sherries and wines. The real thing.

Kennington Tandoori
Indian   ££
Map 22 E1
313 Kennington Road, SE11 4QE
Tel *020 7735 9247*
A calm refuge serving some of
the best curries in London,
according to aficionados. Novel
dishes mixed in with classics.

Lobster Pot
French   ££
Map 22 D3
3 Kennington Lane, SE11 4RG
Tel *020 7582 5556* **Closed** *Mon & Sun*
Walk through the door and you're
in Brittany, complete with piped
seagulls. Try the eight-course
"surprise" menu. Book ahead.

Tapas Brindisa
Spanish   ££
Map 15 B4
18–20 Southwark Street, SE1 1TJ
Tel *020 7357 8880*
Hearty flavours steal the show at
this animated tapas bar. Fantastic

Serrano hams, Cantabrian
anchovies and piquillo peppers.

Tito's Peruvian Restaurant
Peruvian   ££
Map 15 B4
4–6 London Bridge Street, SE1 9SG
Tel *020 7407 7787*
Drink a pisco sour while you wait
for robust and spicy regional
dishes, many meat-based, at this
brightly lit local favourite.

Wright Brothers Oyster and Porter House
Seafood   ££
Map 15 B3
11 Stoney Street, SE1 9AD
Tel *020 7403 9554*
Fast food with a difference:
market-fresh fish and shellfish
from Cornwall. The oysters are
sublime. Very informal.

Zucca
Italian   ££
Map 15 C4
184 Bermondsey Street, SE1 3TQ
Tel *020 7378 6809*   **Closed** *Mon*
All white, hard edged and über
cool, with an open kitchen and
mind-blowing menu. Excellent
pasta – including fennel and
lemon tagliatelle – and polenta.

The relaxed dining area of The Laughing
Gravy, in Southwark

DK Choice

Oxo Tower Restaurant, Bar and Brasserie
European   **£££**
Oxo Tower Wharf, Barge House Street, SE1 9GY   **Map** 14 E3
Tel *020 7803 3888*
Whether you're lunching or dining, the eighth-floor view will take your breath away; colourful by day, glittering by night. Eat on the terrace in summer, but when it's cold, the picture windows bring the outside in. Choose between the relaxed brasserie and the sophisticated restaurant, both serving modern British classics.

Roast
British   **£££**
The Floral Hall, Stoney Street, SE1 1TL   **Map** 15 B3
Tel *0845 034 7300*
A smart, light-filled, modern dining room in the eaves of Floral Hall. Come for a whopping breakfast or succulent roasts.

Further Afield

Anarkali
Indian   **£**
303–305 King Street, W6 9NH
Tel *020 8748 1760*
A Hammersmith restaurant in a class of its own. Unique, subtle spicing and a great choice for vegetarians. Delightful service.

DK Choice

Brady's
British   **£**
39 Jew's Row, SW18 1TB
Tel *020 8877 9599*   **Closed** *Sun*
"The best fish and chips in London", assert enthusiasts of this cheerful Wandsworth bistro with a suitably seaside atmosphere. Choose from line-caught, fresh fish, battered or grilled with perfect chips – crunchy outside and fluffy inside – a pint of prawns or smoked salmon. Finish with a traditional English dessert of treacle tart or apple crumble.

Gem
Turkish   **£**
265 Upper Street, N1 2UQ   **Map** 6 F1
Tel *020 7359 0405*
Gem by name and by nature. Fragrant *mezze* at bargain prices in a charming white-painted room decorated with Kurdish farm implements. The speciality is the wonderful

qatme (stuffed Kurdish bread). No bookings.

Mandalay
Burmese   **£**
444 Edgware Road, W2 1EG   **Map** 3 A5
Tel *020 7258 3696*   **Closed** *Sun*
This basic eatery is an ideal introduction to Burmese food. Stir-fries and curries fuse Chinese, Indian and Thai cuisines.

Taiwan Village
Taiwanese   **£**
85 Lillie Road, SW6 1UD   **Map** 17 A5
Tel *020 7381 2900*
If you are hungry, opt for the 13-course "set feast". Dishes draw on regional cuisines, providing a concentration of flavours.

The Greenwich Union
British   **£**
56 Royal Hill, SE10 8RT   **Map** 23 B3
Tel *020 8692 6258*
A local landmark, this pub showcases a unique range of beers. Menus recommend ale pairings for each delicious traditional dish.

Brula
French   **££**
43 Crown Road, St. Margarets TW1
Tel *020 8892 0602*
The best of French bistrot cooking with fresh seasonal ingredients. Set in a charming local establishment, Brula offers great wines and is good value for money.

Buen Ayre
Steakhouse   **££**
50 Broadway Market, E8 4QJ   **Map** 8 F1
Tel *020 7275 9900*
A back-to-basics Hackney hotspot where Argentine steak and grilled

meats are the order of the day. The wine list is huge. Friendly staff.

DK Choice

Canton Arms
British   **££**
177 South Lambeth Road, SW8 1XP   **Map** 21 C4
Tel *020 7582 8710*
In a culinary desert, this stand-out gastropub is worth crossing the river for. Its style is plain and countrified – bar at the front, restaurant at the back – and the food is knock-out: gutsy, meaty flavours, interesting textures and combinations. Don't miss the signature "toasties", unusual but extraordinarily good; try the one filled with haggis.

El Parador
Tapas   **££**
245 Eversholt Street, NW1 1BA   **Map** 4 F2
Tel *020 7387 2789*
Simplicity is key, both in the sunny decoration – yellow walls, terracotta floor, wooden chairs – and market-fresh ingredients.

Emile's
European   **££**
98 Felsham Road, SW15 1DQ
Tel *020 8789 3323*   **Closed** *Sun*
A Putney treasure; good food in an unfussy room. A blackboard, brought to your table, displays the seasonal, monthly changing menu.

Enoteca Turi
Italian   **££**
28 Putney High Street, SW15 1SQ
Tel *020 8785 4449*   **Closed** *Sun*
A convivial restaurant owned and run by a dedicated couple. Main attractions are the relaxed mood and rustic, wholesome cooking.

Argentine grill and steakhouse, Buen Ayre

For more information on types of restaurants *see page 289*

A selection of tempting salads on display at Ottolenghi

Indian Zing ££
Indian
236 King Street,
W6 0RF
Tel *020 8748 5959*
A noteworthy wine list and
contemporary Indian cuisine,
prepared with panache at this
upmarket gem.

Inside ££
European **Map** 23 A4
19 Greenwich South Street,
SE10 8NW
Tel *020 8265 5060* **Closed** *Mon*
A minimalist space where a
constantly changing menu
offers modern European dishes
for fairly reasonable prices.

Jin-Kichi ££
Japanese **Map** 1 A4
73 Heath Street,
NW3 6UG
Tel *020 7794 6158* **Closed** *Mon*
A tiny piece of Tokyo in
Hampstead. With a grill as a
focus, well-spaced tables,
efficient service and sublime
sushi. The food is authentic
and delicious.

Fine dining establishment Chez Bruce,
Wandsworth Common

Khan's ££
Indian
159 Lavender Hill, SW11 5QH
Tel *020 7978 4455*
Low-fat, colour-free authentic
curries with a sufficiently broad
menu to appeal to a range
of palates.

Lamberts ££
British
2 Station Parade, Balham
High Road, SW12 9AZ
Tel *020 8675 2233* **Closed** *Mon*
Harmonious cuisine, top-notch
organic ingredients and
comfortable, easy surroundings.
Classic favourites sit side by side
with modern variations. The wine
list excels and prices are sensible.

Le Sacré Coeur ££
French **Map** 6 E1
18 Theberton Street, N1 0QX
Tel *020 7354 2618*
Montmartre comes to Islington
in this cosy Parisian spot. Classic
French style, with poster-lined
walls, wooden beams, blue-and-
white checked tablecloths and
superior traditional dishes.
Unfailingly friendly service.

Le Vacherin ££
French
76–77 South Parade, W4 5LF
Tel *020 8/42 2121*
A neighbourhood bistro with a
refined, intimate air. It boasts a
sure hand in the kitchen and old-
fashioned service. The set menu
affords good value.

North China ££
Chinese
305 Uxbridge Road, W3 9QU
Tel *020 8992 9183*
A family affair set up in 1976 by
the current owner's father, this
tasteful little restaurant offers
mouthwatering dishes with
specialities from both north and
south China.

Ottolenghi ££
Mediterranean **Map** 6 F1
287 Upper Street, N1 2TZ
Tel *020 7288 1454*
The Islington flagship restaurant
of a popular chain. A designer
space where divine, healthy
dishes are the *raison d'être*.
A chic yet relaxed place serving
daring Mediterranean food.

DK Choice

Sam's Brasserie ££
European
11 Barley Mow Passage, W4 4PH
Tel *020 8987 0555*
Rick Stein protégé Sam Harrison
chose a Chiswick based former
paper factory for his brasserie
and bar. It has a hectic vibe, but
is welcoming to all ages. Menus
offer a welcome range, from
light salads to serious roasts.
There is a special menu for kids
and colouring sheets to keep
them busy.

Singapore Garden ££
Singaporean
83 Fairfax Road, NW6 4DY
Tel *020 7328 5314*
A jovial Swiss Cottage veteran
serving the best soft-shelled
crabs, with chillies and garlic,
you're likely to taste – pure
magic. Also recommended is
the beef *rendang* (slow cooked
beef in thick coconut sauce).

Tatra ££
Polish
24 Goldhawk Road, W12 8DH
Tel *020 8749 8193*
This Shepherd's Bush local blends
the most appetizing tastes from
Eastern Europe. At dinner, be
prepared, as flavoured vodka is
almost compulsory.

The Depot ££
British
Tideway Yard, 125 Mortlake High
Street, SW14 8SN
Tel *084 4288 0726*
A tranquil riverside setting,
informal air and superior
cooking have made this
brasserie a surefire hit. Try for
a window table or enjoy the
outdoor dining terrace in
the summer.

The Glasshouse ££
European
14 Station Parade, Kew, TW9 3PZ
Tel *020 8940 6777*
Asian overtones jazz up
the contemporary European
food at this light, urban, award-
winning restaurant. An alluring
wine list complements the menu.

Key to prices *see page 292*

Comfortable, relaxed and
excellent value for money.

DK Choice

The Wells   ££
British   **Map** 1 B4
30 Well Walk, NW3 1BX
Tel *020 7794 3785*
Take a ramble on Hampstead
Heath before heading to this
splendid gastropub. Either grab
a snack or light bite in the easy-
going bar, or for a smarter affair,
dine in the upstairs room.
Modern European specialities
are on the menu in the warmly
decorated dining room, and
traditional bar snacks in the
downstairs area. Enjoy the
pretty summer terrace when
the weather is good. Busy at
weekends. Friendly staff.

Trinity   ££
British
4 The Polygon, SW4 0JG
Tel *020 7622 1199*
The wonderfully complex
flavours of Adam Byatt's cooking
draw people to this Clapham
staple with handsome looks and
exemplary service. Smoked
rabbit leg, roast cod and
pan-fried sea bream are
satisfying specialities.

Upstairs Bar and Restaurant ££
French
89B Acre Lane, SW2 5TN
Tel *020 7733 8855* **Closed** *Mon & Sun*
Ring a buzzer to get into
this Brixton house that serves
as a restaurant and bar. The
menu is simple and robust
(cod with black cabbage and
smoked garlic, for example).
All food is cooked from market
produce and served on the
top floors.

Bustling atmosphere of Sam's Brasserie

DK Choice

Chez Bruce   £££
British
2 Bellevue Road, SW17 7EG
Tel *020 8672 0114*
Bruce Poole's modern British
food has strong classical
French notes with an emphasis
on offal, fish and remarkable
flavour combinations.
Specialities include home-
made *charcuterie* and bread,
and slow cooked braises.
Overlooking Wandsworth
Common, this light, refined
restaurant has a reputation for
its food, wine and service.

Gaucho – Hampstead   £££
Steakhouse   **Map** 1 A4
64 Heath Street, NW3 1DN
Tel *020 7431 8222*
Hearty steaks are cooked on a
genuine Argentine *asado*
barbecue at this stylish chain
restaurant. Non-meat eaters
might plump for the *ceviche*, a
citrus marinated seafood salad.

The sunny outdoor terrace at the River Café

La Trompette   £££
French
5–7 Devonshire Road, W4 2EU
Tel *020 8747 1836*
Sister of the Chez Bruce outlet,
La Trompette is perfectly
placed close to Kew Gardens.
The menu at Bruce Poole's
Chiswick outpost has roots in
regional France. Defined by
charcuterie and *confits*; rounded
off with comforting desserts.
Relaxed and excellent value for
money. Staff are knowledgeable.

DK Choice

River Café   £££
Italian
*Thames Wharf, Rainville Road,
W6 9HA*
Tel *020 7386 4200*
First-rate seasonal ingredients,
cooked simply, is Ruth Rogers'
ethos at her famous
Hammersmith eatery – one of
the first in London to make the
sourcing of sustainable
ingredients a priority. It is
sophisticated, in a canteen style,
with a wood-burner and open
kitchen. The rustic Italian meals
rarely disappoint and sit
alongside the more refined
dishes on the menu. A pricey
option, but worth every penny.

Zumbura   £
Indian
36 Old Town, SW4 0LB
Tel *020 7720 7902*
Off the beaten tourist track, this
place serves up authentic Punjabi
food in a wonderfully stylish
setting; the owners were
previously interior designers.
Sip top-notch cocktails and
sample a range of delicious
tasting dishes. Don't miss the
Karela (bitter gourd cooked
with lentils).

For more information on types of restaurants *see page 289*

Light Meals and Snacks

When you want to make the most of the available sightseeing time, it doesn't always make sense to sit down for a lengthy restaurant meal. Or, perhaps you don't have the budget or the appetite for a full-course affair. London has several eateries for every taste and occasion – many of them unmissable institutions – from traditional fish-and-chip and pie-and-mash shops to elegant tearooms and cool cafés.

Breakfast

A good breakfast prepares you for a solid day's sightseeing, with the traditional British breakfast including staples such as bacon and eggs, smoked salmon and grilled kippers. Many hotels (see pp284–7) serve traditional breakfasts to non-residents, but to start the day like a 19th-century lord, head for **Simpson's-in-the-Strand**, which on weekdays offers an old-fashioned breakfast menu (as well as classic lunchtime and dinner roasts) in a historic panelled dining room. Porridge, lamb's kidneys, Cumberland sausage and black pudding are just part of the multicourse "10 deadly sins" set breakfast.

Several pubs around Smithfield serve the all-night meat market workers. The most famous of these is the **Cock Tavern**, dishing up good-value fare from 6am onwards. Traditional cafés also fry up artery-clogging working-men's morning meals including egg, sausage, mushrooms and baked beans.

For Continental breakfasts such as pastries and a cappuccino, there are many cafés to choose from. **The Wolseley** serves croissants, brioches and cooked breakfasts in opulent surroundings. Brunch has become increasingly popular in London. The spacious, modern restaurant in the back of popular French grocer/delicatessen, **Villandry**, serves one of the best on Saturday and Sunday. American restaurants such as **Joe Allen** and **Christopher's** also offer brunch, or head for well-heeled Westbourne Grove, where it's a weekend ritual at relaxed eateries such as **202** and **Tom's** delicatessen.

Coffee and Tea

For a cappuccino or espresso at any time of day, step into round-the-clock Soho stalwart **Bar Italia**, which also serves a range of pastries and paninis. It's a legendary late-night pitstop, full of colourful characters (but do keep a hand on your bag/ wallet). There is no shortage of coffee-bar chains, but one of the best is **Caffè Nero**, which dispenses authentic Italian coffee at reasonable prices across town.

If you're out shopping, many of London's department stores have their own cafés; Harvey Nichols' is one of the most stylish, while Selfridges has a branch of the cool Moroccan tearoom **Momo** among its many eating options. Designer stores such as Emporio Armani, Nicole Farhi and Joseph have trendy cafés – from the outside 202 looks like a chic French-style café, but it showcases Nicole Farhi's fashion and home designs downstairs. **Joe's**, surrounded by Joseph's three boutiques at Brompton Cross, is a small yet slick refreshment option; there are a few branches around town. In Portobello Market, quaint tearoom **Still Too Few**, below the antique kitchenalia shop of the same name, serves tea, sandwiches and cakes to bric-a-brac hunters on Saturdays.

Patisseries such as **Maison Bertaux** and **Patisserie Valerie** are a delight, with mouth-watering window displays of French pastries. **Richoux** in Piccadilly is another popular refreshment spot. Smart French bakery/patisserie **Paul** offers delicious tarts and other treats in a Parisian-café atmosphere. The elegantly old-world **The**

Wolseley (see p294) in Piccadilly has an all-day café menu of sandwiches and salads. If you're strolling in picturesque Little Venice, **Café Laville** commands a spectacular view over Regent's Canal. **Bluebird**, Terence Conran's multi-faceted food centre in the converted 1920s Bluebird motor garage on the King's Road, has a café with tables on its cobbled forecourt as well as a more formal restaurant, bar and market.

No visit to London would be complete without taking afternoon tea. Top hotels such as the **Ritz** and **Brown's** offer pots of your choice of tea, scones with jam and cream, delicious, thin cucumber sandwiches and cakes galore. For a relaxed place in beautiful Kensington Gardens, there's nothing to beat **The Orangery**. Its selection of English teas and cakes tastes even better in the elegant surroundings of Sir John Vanbrugh's 18th-century building. Good coffee (and cakes) can also be found at the **Monmouth Coffee House** in Covent Garden. **Fortnum and Mason** (see p313) serves both afternoon and high teas. In Kew, the **Maids of Honour** tearoom offers pastries, reputedly enjoyed by Henry VIII. For a more modern experience, **Sketch** offers exquisite contemporary confections in a restyled Georgian room.

Traditional Cafés

These basic greasy spoons all over the city are a London institution, serving up fried breakfasts and such British staples as sausages, pies and grills. They are usually only open until about 5pm; some close earlier. Granddaddy of them all is East End legend **E Pellicci**, with its wonderful Art Deco interior. A vogue for simple British fare has spawned numerous versions of the "caff", including **River Café** at Putney Bridge station – a quintessential British café with Formica tables and great service.

Museum and Theatre Cafés

Most museums and galleries have cafés, including the Royal Academy, Tate Modern (with wonderful views over the Thames), the National Portrait Gallery and the British Museum. The National Film Theatre on the South Bank has a buzzing bar/café frequented by film fanatics, while St Martin-in-the-Fields church in Trafalgar Square, famous for its concerts, has a capacious self-service café in its vaulted crypt.

Sandwich Bars

A leading sandwich chain in London is **Prêt à Manger**, with branches throughout the centre decked out with metalwork features and serving a range of delicious pre-packed sandwiches, salads, cakes and soft drinks. Another popular sandwich chain is **Eat**, which offers a daily changing menu of innovative soups and salads using seasonal ingredients as well as sandwiches made with home-made breads and tortilla wraps. Quality Italian sandwich fillings in focaccia and ciabatta breads can be had at Soho's **Carlton Coffee House**. For a quick bite, try **Kappacasein**, a popular stall in Borough Market – come here for delicious raclette and toasted cheese sandwiches.

Delis

With Londoners becoming more and more interested in high-quality foods from small producers in Britain and abroad, there has been a boom in stylish delis, many of which provide seating so that you can sample their wares on site. Tom's is a one-stop deli and café. The chic deli **Luigi's** sells delicious Italian fare, from fresh pasta to farmhouse cheeses to freshly roasted vegetables and salads, while deli/cheese shop **La Fromagerie** has a large communal table in the back for light bites. Nearby, is the family-run delicatessen/lunchroom **Paul Rothe & Son**, which

opened in the early 1900s and serves sandwiches and soups among shelves of "British and foreign provisions".

Diners

London is full of American-style fast-food joints, serving burgers, fries, fried chicken, apple pie, milk shakes and cola, particularly around Soho, Leicester Square, Shaftesbury Avenue and Covent Garden. Some time-honoured establishments include family favourite **Maxwell's**, in Covent Garden, the **Hard Rock Café**, and the fun, 1950s-kitsch **Ed's Easy Diner**, but thanks to the continuing vogue for retro burger restaurants, new ones keep popping up. GBK (Gourmet Burger Kitchen) and Byron are some of the best, while **Lucky 7** and The Diner serve up burgers and breakfasts in a dice-and-cards-themed diner, complete with vinyl-seated booths and blaring rock'n'roll.

Pizza and Pasta

Italian food has now become a staple of the British diet. Street-side stands offer variable quality, while there are well-established chains with several branches, including **Ask**. **Pizza Express** offers thin-crust pizzas that are a step up from the norm. Try the elegant Georgian townhouse outlet on Chelsea's King's Road, or the branch in a converted dairy in Soho where there's also live jazz. **Kettners**, also part of the group, offers casual, inexpensive eating in a legendary old dining room (there's also a champagne bar). The **Carluccio's Caffè** chain, which has a branch with al fresco tables in pedestrianized St Christopher's Place, serves good-quality, freshly made pastas and salads. **Marine Ices** near Camden Market serves great pizza and pasta in addition to its famous ice cream (see Street Food p307). Other reliable pasta chains are **Spaghetti House** and **Café Pasta**. Inexpensive pasta is also served at bustling trattorias such as **Pollo** in Soho.

Food in Pubs

Perhaps the biggest – and most popular – change in the London dining scene in the last 15 years has been the transformation in the food found in pubs. Before the early 1990s, most pubs that provided food at all offered a pretty simple range of salads and sandwiches, put together with no great imagination. The last two decades, though, have seen the rapid rise of the "gastropub", in which the food range is treated with as much care as the beer selection. Grilled steaks, fresh fish or English classics like sausage and mash have been reinvigorated by the use of first-rate, organic ingredients and the menus have become increasingly sophisticated, mixing Mediterranean, Oriental and other global influences.

The neighbourhood gastropub has become an essential London institution. Some have separate dining rooms while others have stayed more pub-style, where you order at the bar from a chalked-up menu. All tend to be more relaxed than formal restaurants but they can get busy so book in advance. Among the best are **The Eagle**, **The Engineer**, **The Lansdowne**, **The Queen's Head & Artichoke** and **The Wells** in Hampstead (see also pp308–11).

Fish and Chips

Fish and chips is typically considered the national dish of Britain, with a "chippy" serving a choice of fish (typically cod or plaice) deep-fried in batter, accompanied by chips (thicker cut than French fries). A range of accompaniments includes bread baps (rolls) for a "chip buttie" (a chip sandwich), mushy peas, pickled eggs or onions. Four of the best places for such fare are the **North Sea Fish Restaurant**, **Rock & Sole Plaice**, **Faulkner's** and **Fish Central**. Fish and chips is now considered very "trendy" and is increasingly available on the menu in various smart restaurants and chains such as **Fish!**

Bars and Wine Bars

The range and quality of London's bars has grown over the past five years. There are numerous wine bars in the centre, such as **Café des Amis du Vin** in Covent Garden (downstairs from its ground-floor brasserie), and the legendary **El Vino**, as well as chains such as **Corney & Barrow** and **Balls Bros**, which also serve good food. The cosy **Tapa Room** on the ground floor of acclaimed **The Providores** restaurant serves globally influenced tapas. Good-value food is also part of the success of such chain bars as **All Bar One**. Capitalizing on young Londoners' habit of spending an entire evening out drinking, many style-conscious, modern bars serve food, such as the smart wine bar **28°–50°** in Marylebone, which does French bistrot-style food. **Gordon's Wine Bar** is London's oldest (c.1890), located in an underground cellar (*see also pp308–11*).

Brasseries

Now that informal dining is an integral aspect of life in London, brasseries have become part of the landscape. These are based on the classic French blueprint, with its Parisian ambience and decor, serving such favourites as steak frites and seafood platters – a classic example is long-established **La Brasserie** in South Kensington. Among the chains is **Café Rouge**. **Randall & Aubin** is a buzzy oyster and lobster (plus champagne) bar in a former delicatessen that has retained its period charm and overlooks Soho's lively Brewer Street. Relative newcomer **The Electric Brasserie**, next to Portobello's luxurious arthouse cinema of the same name, is a popular update on the traditional model.

Juice Bars and Organic Cafés

The healthy-diet trend has made juice bars and organic food shops very popular. Longstanding Lebanese favourite **Ranoush Juice** has added outlets to its original Edgware Road location, and chains such as **Crussh** have branches all over London. Organic food chains

DIRECTORY

Breakfast

202
202 Westbourne Grove
W11. **Map** 9 C2.

Christopher's
18 Wellington St WC2.
Map 13 C2.

Cock Tavern
East Poultry Avenue,
Smithfield Market EC1.
Map 6 F5.

Joe Allen
13 Exeter St WC2.
Map 13 C2.

Simpson's-in- the-Strand
100 Strand WC2.
Map 13 C2.

Tom's
226 Westbourne Grove
W11. **Map** 9 B2.

Villandry
170 Great Portland
Street W1.
Map 4 F5.

The Wolseley
160 Piccadilly W1.
Map 12 F3.

Coffee and Tea

Bar Italia
22 Frith St W1.
Map 13 A2.

Bluebird Café
350 King's Rd SW3.
Map 19 A4.

Café Laville
Little Venice Parade, 453
Edgware Rd W2.

Emporio Armani Caffè
191 Brompton Rd SW3.
Map 19 B1.

Joe's
126 Draycott Ave SW3.
Map 19 B2.

Maids of Honour
288 Kew Rd
Richmond, Surrey.

Maison Bertaux
28 Greek St W1.
Map 13 A1.

Monmouth Coffee House
27 Monmouth St WC2.
Map 13 B2.

The Orangery
Kensington Palace,
Kensington Gardens W8.
Map 10 D3.

Patisserie Valerie
17 Motcombe St,
Belgravia SW1.
Map 12 D5.

Paul
29 Bedford St WC2.
Map 13 B2.

Richoux
172 Piccadilly W1.
Map 12 F3.

Sketch
9 Conduit St W1. **Map** 12 F2.

Still Too Few
300 Westbourne Grove
W11. **Map** 9 B2.

Traditional Cafés

E Pellicci
332 Bethnal Green Rd E2.

River Café
Station Approach
South SW6.

Museum and Theatre Cafés

Café in the Crypt
St Martin-in-the-Fields,
Duncannon St WC2.
Map 13 B3.

Riverfront Bar & Kitchen
BFI Southbank, South
Bank SE1. **Map** 14 D3.

Sandwich Bars

Carlton Coffee House
41 Broadwick St W1.
Map 13 A2.

Eat
12 Oxo Tower Wharf,
Barge House St SE1.
Map 14 E3.

Kappacasein
Borough Market SE1.
Map 15 B4.

Prêt à Manger
421 Strand WC2.
Map 13 C3.

Delis

La Fromagerie
2–6 Moxon St W1.
Map 4 D5.

Luigi's
349 Fulham Rd SW6.
Map 18 F4.

Paul Rothe & Son
35 Marylebone Lane W1.
Map 12 D1.

Diners

Ed's Easy Diner
12 Moor St W1.
Map 13 B2.

Hard Rock Café
150 Old Park Lane W1.
Map 12 E4.

Lucky 7
127 Westbourne Park Rd
W2. **Map** 9 C1.

Maxwell's
8 James St WC2.
Map 13 C2.

such as **Planet Organic** and **Whole Foods Market** do a roaring trade in hot and cold fare and freshly squeezed juices alongside their groceries, baked goods and vitamins. With tables on the premises, you can enjoy the freshly prepared food and drinks immediately.

Noodle Bars

Popular chain **Wagamama** still draws queues for its good-value noodles and other Oriental dishes in airy yet basic environs; customers sit at long communal tables. **Dim T Café** serves dim sum and mix-and-match noodles, meat and toppings in a modern café setting. **Taro** is a busy Japanese diner offering cheap sushi, ramen and teriyaki.

Street Food

During summer, many parks have ice-cream vans parked by the entrances, with **Marine Ices** serving some of the town's best ice cream. Hot roasted chestnuts, made on mini-barbecues, are a winter delight found along Oxford Street. Shellfish stalls, selling ready-to-eat potted shrimps, crab, whelks and jellied eels are a feature of many street markets. At Camden Lock and Old Spitalfields Market, you can wander among the stalls choosing from falafel, satay chicken, vegeburgers and honey balls. In the East End, Jewish bakeries such as **Brick Lane Beigel Bake** are open 24 hours a day. Fresh plain bagels as well as ones with

a wide range of fillings are available here. The East End also has the largest number of pie and mash shops, which provide an inexpensive and satisfying "nosh-up" of jellied eels and potatoes, or meat pie with mash and liquor (green parsley sauce). Two classic venues, both on Bethnal Green Road, are **G Kelly** and **S&R Kelly**. Or try **Manze's** on Tower Bridge Road. For the real East End experience, you should drench your food in vinegar and wash it all down with a couple of mugs of strong, hot tea.

Modern pie-maker **The Square Pie Company** sells superior pies with gourmet fillings in Old Spitalfields Market and Selfridges.

DIRECTORY

Pizza and Pasta

Ask
56–60 Wigmore St W1.
Map 12 D1.
One of many branches.

Café Pasta
184 Shaftesbury Ave WC2.
Map 13 2B.

Carluccio's Caffè
St Christopher's Place W1.
Map 12 E2.
One of many branches.

Kettner's
29 Romilly St W1.
Map 13 A2.

Pizza Express
30 Coptic St WC1.
Map 13 B1.
One of many branches.

Pollo
20 Old Compton St W1.
Map 13 A2.

Fish and Chips

Faulkner's
424–426 Kingsland
Rd E8.

Fish!
Borough Mkt SE1.
Map 15 B4.

Fish Central
149–155 Central St EC1.
Map 7 A3.

North Sea Fish Restaurant
7–8 Leigh St WC1. **Map** 5 B4.

Rock & Sole Plaice
47 Endell St WC2.
Map 13 B1.

Wine Bars

28°–50°
15–17 Marylebone Lane
W1. **Map** 12 D1.

All Bar One
103 Cannon St EC4.
Map 15 A2.

Balls Bros
Hays Galleria Tooley St
SE1. **Map** 15 B3.

Café des Amis du Vin
11–14 Hanover Place
WC2. **Map** 13 C2.

Corney & Barrow
19 Broadgate Circle EC2.
Map 7 C5.

Dickens Inn
St Katharine's Dock E1.
Map 16 E3.

Gordon's Wine Bar
47 Villiers St WC2.
Map 13 C3.

Providores Tapa Room
109 Marylebone High St
W1. **Map** 4 D5.

El Vino
1–2 Hare Place, Fleet St
EC4. **Map** 14 E1.

Brasseries

La Brasserie
272 Brompton Rd SW3.
Map 19 B2.

Café Rouge
27 Basil St SW3.
Map 11 C5.
One of many branches.

The Electric Brasserie
191 Portobello Rd W11.
Map 9 B2.

Randall & Aubin
16 Brewer St W1.
Map 13 A2.

Juice Bars and Organic Cafés

Crussh
Unit 1, 1 Curzon
Street W1.
Map 12 E3.

Fluid Juice Bar
208 Fulham Rd SW3.
Map 19 A2.

Planet Organic
22 Torrington Place WC1.
Map 5 A5.

Ranoush Juice
43 Edgware Rd W2.
Map 11 C2.

Whole Foods Market
20 Glasshouse St W1.
Map 13 A3.

Noodle Bars

Dim T Café
32 Charlotte St W1.
Map 13 A1.

Taro
59–61 Brewer St W1.
Map 13 A2.

Wagamama
101 Wigmore St W1.
Map 12 D1.
One of many branches.

Street Food

Brick Lane Beigel Bake
159 Brick Lane E1.
Map 8 E5.

G Kelly
526 Roman Rd E3.
Map 8 D4.

Manze's
87 Tower Bridge Rd SE1.
Map 16 D5.

Marine Ices
8 Haverstock Hill NW3.

S&R Kelly
284 Bethnal Green Rd E2.

London Pubs and Bars

Affectionately known as a "pub" as well as "boozer" and "the local", a public house was originally just that – a house in which the public could eat, drink, and even stay the night. Large inns with courtyards, such as The George Inn, were originally stopping points for horse-drawn coach services. Some pubs stand on historic public house sites, for instance the Ship, the Lamb and Flag and the City Barge. However, many of the finest ones date from the emergence of "gin palaces" in the late 1800s, where Londoners took refuge from the misery of their poverty amid lavish interiors, often with stunning mirrors (The Salisbury) and elaborate decorations. Since the 1990s cocktail-bar boom, the traditional pub has been given an image makeover, restoring the British institution's popularity with a fashionable crowd.

Rules and Conventions

Visitors to London have long been bemused by early pub closing times, which made a night out a bit tricky – an after-theatre nightcap, for example, was usually out of the question outside of your hotel. In theory, reforms to the licensing laws, which came into effect in 2005, mean pubs can now stay open up to 24 hours, as long as they obtain permission from their local authority, and many extend their hours beyond the 11am–11pm standard. Some may close in the afternoon or early evening and also at weekends. You must be at least 18 to buy or drink alcohol, and at least 14 to enter a pub without an adult. Children can be taken into pubs that serve food, or can use outside areas. Order at the bar and pay when you are served; tips are not customary unless you are served food and drink at a table. "Last orders" are usually called 10 minutes before closing, then "time" is called, and a further 20 minutes is then allowed for finishing up drinks. Since July 2007, smoking has been banned from all pubs and clubs.

British Beer

The most traditional beers are available in various different strengths and styles, and are flat (not fizzy), and served only lightly cooled. The spectrum of bottled beers goes from "light" ale, through "pale", "brown", "bitter" and the strong "old". A sweeter, lower alcohol alternative is shandy, a classic mixture of draught beer or lager and lemonade. Many traditional methods of brewing and serving beer have been preserved over the years, and there is a great variety of "real ale" in London pubs. Serious beer drinkers should look for "Free Houses", pubs that are not tied to any particular brewery. The main London brewers are Young's (try their strong "Winter Warmer" beer) and Fuller's. The **Orange Brewery** serves a good pint and excellent food, and offers tours of the brewery.

Other Pub Drinks

Cider is another traditional English drink found in every pub. Made from apples, it comes in a range of strengths and degrees of dryness. Blended Scotch whisky and malt whiskies are also staples, together with gin, usually drunk with tonic water. During the winter, mulled wine (warm and spicy) or hot toddies (brandy or whisky with hot water and sugar) may be served. Non-alcoholic drinks are also always available.

Historic Pubs

Many pubs have a fascinating history and decor, whether it is a beamed medieval snug, a Victorian fantasy, or an extraordinary Arts-and-Crafts interior, as at the **Black Friar**, a must-see temple to imbibing, featuring bronze bas reliefs, and an intimate, marble-and-mosaic chamber at the back. While many of the "gin palaces" of the 19th century have been revamped or abandoned, there are some notable survivors. At the **Prince Alfred** in Maida Vale, the bar is divided by "snobscreens", a feature that enabled the upper set to enjoy a drink without mixing with their servants. The semicircular **Viaduct Tavern**, opposite the Old Bailey, is a suitably stately setting for distinguished barristers and judges, ablaze with mirrors, chandeliers and etched glass, while the **Princess Louise** retains its magnificent central mahogany bar, complete with original clock, moulded ceiling and vivid wall tiles. Less grand but just as lovingly decorated is the tiny, tiled **Dog & Duck** in Soho – but you may have to battle for a seat or (in warm weather) stand outside with its many devotees.

Many pubs have strong literary associations, such as the **Fitzroy Tavern**, a meeting place for writers and artists in the 1930s and 40s, including Dylan Thomas, George Orwell and Augustus John, **Ye Olde Cheshire Cheese** is associated with Dr Johnson, Charles Dickens frequented the **Trafalgar Tavern**, while Oscar Wilde often went to **The Salisbury**. Samuel Pepys witnessed the Great Fire of London from the **Anchor**, on the river at Bankside. The less literary **Old Bull and Bush** in north London was the subject of a well known old music-hall song, while the 17th- century **Lamb and Flag** – one of central London's few surviving timber-framed buildings down an alleyway – was known as the Bucket of Blood because it was the venue for bare-knuckle prize fights. Some pubs have sinister associations, for example some of Jack the Ripper's victims were found near the **Ten Bells**. Dick Turpin, the 18th-century highwayman, took refreshment at the **Spaniards Inn** in north London, and the **French House** in Soho was a meeting point for the French Resistance during World War II.

Pub Names

Signs have hung outside public houses since 1393, when King Richard II decreed they should replace the usual bush outside the door. As most people were illiterate, names that could easily be illustrated were chosen, such as the Rose & Crown, coats of arms (Freemasons' Arms), historical figures (Princess Louise) or heraldic animals (White Lion).

Pub Entertainment

Fringe theatre productions (see p338) are staged at the **King's Head**, the **Latchmere**, and at the **Gate Theatre** above the Prince Albert. Some pubs have live music: there is excellent modern jazz at the **Bull's Head** in Barnes and a wide variety of music styles at the popular **Mean Fiddler**. The diminutive **Golden Eagle**, on a winding backstreet in Marylebone, is a rare central London piano pub with nostalgic singalongs a few nights a week.

Outdoor Drinking

Most pubs with outdoor seating tend to be located slightly outside the city centre. The **Freemason's Arms** for example, near Hampstead Heath, has a very pleasant garden, as does the **Hampshire Hog** in Hammersmith. Some pubs enjoy riverside locations with fine views, from the **Prospect of Whitby** in Wapping and the **Grapes** in Limehouse to the **White Cross** in Richmond.

Microbreweries

Delicious beer is brewed on the premises at microbreweries such as **Mash**, where a space-age interior makes you forget that real ale tends to be the domain of older drinkers.

This bar is frequented by a young and trendy crowd. Huge orange vats indicate where the actual brewing takes place. The **Bünker Bier Hall Bar and Kitchen** in Covent Garden has three signature beers, and a good atmosphere.

Themed Pubs and Bars

Big, brash Irish pubs such as **Filthy McNasty's** and **Waxy O'Connor's** (mocked up like a Catholic church, complete with confessional) attract a young, fun-loving crowd, as does Australian bar chain **Walkabout**. Sports bars are popular as well. The **Sports Café**, near Piccadilly, has three bars, a dance floor – and 120 screens showing global sporting events on satellite TV. More low-key is "footie" bar **Kick** in Shoreditch (there's a smaller sister establishment, **Café Kick**, in Exmouth Market), which features table-soccer games and organic food in a relaxed setting. Pool players can take their cue at a branch of slick pool-bar chain **Elbow Room**.

Gastropubs

Since the early 1990s, many old pubs have been given gleaming makeovers and kitchens turning out superior fare. Among the first "gastropubs" was the **Eagle**, which offers gourmet dishes from the open kitchen that occupies half of the bar. Many, like **The Lansdowne**, have dedicated dining rooms as well as laid-back pub rooms where you can eat, drink or do both. TV foodie Roxy Beaujolais serves simple bistro dishes in tiny, quirky old pub the **Seven Stars** near the Royal Courts of Justice. **The Cow** is known for its oysters and Guinness, while the **Chapel**, the **Fire Station** and the **Dusk** are popular with both drinkers and diners.

Bars

London's bar scene has been gradually transformed since the mid-1990s; up till then, the choice was limited to either

hotel bars, wine bars or pubs. Propelled by a cocktail revival, as well as the fact that eating and drinking out is now deeply ingrained in daily London life, new bars are opening all the time.

Eagerly sought out by style-conscious connoisseurs, the latest watering holes are now as much a talking point as new restaurants. Soho and Covent Garden are brimming with bars, but to sample the hottest nightspots, head either east or west. In the past decade, Shoreditch has been transformed from no-go area to an evening destination, which is spilling into neighbouring Bethnal Green.

One of the earliest pioneers – basement lounge, no-frills **The Shoreditch Electricity Showrooms** – is still hopping. Though slightly further afield, it's since been joined by the gloriously camp **Loungelover**, decorated with crystal chandeliers, vintage handbags and stuffed animals. The hip **Book Club** is an eclectic space in which to eat, drink and enjoy events, from arts and science to crafts and DIY.

Across town in Notting Hill, sip good-value Scorpion Bowls and Zombies in the kitsch tiki-lounge ambience of **Trailer Happiness** or go for classic or more inventive cocktails at the **Lonsdale** with its bronze bubble-studded walls and hazy violet lighting. The area's style bars are in contrast with down-to-earth pubs frequented by the market traders, such as the bustling **Portobello Star**.

If you want to stick to the centre of town, fashionable options include the **Lab Bar**, which serves excellent cocktails, especially Central American drinks such as caprinhas and mojitos, or **Match Bar** an East End lounge bar behind the West End's Oxford Circus. Heading south, the **Fridge Bar** in Brixton has DJs playing decent hip hop and deep house with lots of dancing and drinking.

Many restaurants feature excellent bars. The bar at **Green's Restaurant and Oyster Bar** is a very special place to go, to drink champagne and eat oysters and lobster in elegant surroundings. **Smiths of Smithfield**, opposite the famous meat market, has a large, industrial-style café/bar at ground level, a sleek cocktail and champagne bar on the next floor, topped by two restaurants upstairs; nearby, **St John** *(see p300)* has a stylish bar serving excellent wine and bar food. A drink in the bar is the less-expensive way to experience the **Criterion** brasserie's sumptuous, gilded neo-Byzantine decor. Contemporary Chinese restaurant **Hakkasan** *(see p294)* serves exotic cocktails flavoured with

the likes of ginger and lemongrass in its glamorous Oriental-style bar.

Specialist Bars

Aficionados of particular spirits are well served in London. Scottish restaurant Boisdale's **Macdonald Bar** boasts 170 Scotch malt whiskies (and an impressive selection of Cuban cigars), while the **Rockwell**, an upscale bar in the Trafalgar Hotel, offers London's largest bourbon selection. **Salt** is a slick, modern whisky bar, and **Dollar Grills & Martinis**, in the basement of a glitzed-up former pub, serves a lengthy martini "library". Mexican bar/restaurant

La Perla in Covent Garden has an extensive range of tequilas for your shooting pleasure.

Chain Bars

They may not be the most exciting places to drink, but London's chain bars are a reliable option. Halfway between a bar and a pub, with large windows and white walls, they are also far more female-friendly than dark, smokey pubs. **All Bar One** is very popular, with chunky wood furniture. **Pitcher & Piano** has sofas and blonde wood surrounds, while the **Slug & Lettuce** chain features paintings on the walls and quiet rooms for talking.

DIRECTORY

Soho, Piccadilly

Admiral Duncan
Old Compton St W1.
Map 13 A2.

Balans
60 Old Compton St W1.
Map 13 A2.

Candy Bar
4 Carlisle St W1.
Map 13 A2.

Coach and Horses
29 Greek St WC2.
Map 14 F2.

Compton's of Soho
51–53 Old Compton St W1.
Map 13 A2.

Criterion
224 Piccadilly W1.
Map 13 A3.

Dog & Duck
18 Bateman St W1.
Map 13 A2.

Edge
11 Soho Sq W1.
Map 13 A1.

French House
49 Dean St W1.
Map 13 A2.

Lab Bar
12 Old Compton St W1.
Map 13 A2.

Long Bar
50 Berners Street.
Map 12 F1.

Mash
19–21 Great Portland St W1. **Map** 12 F1.

Match Bar
37–38 Margaret St W1.
Map 12 F1.

Pitcher & Piano
70 Dean St W1.
Map 13 A1.

Rupert Street
50 Rupert St W1.
Map 13 A2.

Sports Café
80 Haymarket SW1.
Map 13 A3.

Waxy O'Connor's
14–16 Rupert St W1.
Map 13 A2.

Mayfair, St James's

Claridge's
Brook St W1.
Map 12 E2.

Rivoli Bar
Ritz Hotel 150 Piccadilly W1.
Map 12 F3.

Salt Whisky Bar
82 Seymour St W2.
Map 11 C2.

Slug & Lettuce
19 Hanover St W1.
Map 12 F2.

Trader Vic's
The London Hilton, 22 Park Lane. **Map** 12 D3.

Covent Garden, Strand

American Bar
The Savoy, Strand WC2.
Map 13 C2.

Bünker Bier Hall Bar and Kitchen
41 Earlham St WC2.
Map 13 B2.

Lamb and Flag
33 Rose St WC2.
Map 13 B2.

La Perla
28 Maiden Lane WC2.
Map 13 C2.

Rockwell Bar
The Trafalgar, 2 Spring Gardens SW1. **Map** 13 B3.

The Salisbury
90 St Martin's Lane WC2.
Map 13 B2.

Seven Stars
53–54 Carey St WC2.
Map 14 D1.

Walkabout
11 Henrietta St WC2.
Map 13 C2.

Bloomsbury, Holborn

Fitzroy Tavern
16 Charlotte St W1.
Map 13 A1.

Princess Louise
208 High Holborn WC1.
Map 13 C1.

The Bar
Rosewood London WC1.
Map 13 C1.

The City, Clerkenwell

All Bar One
103 Cannon St EC4.
Map 15 A2.

Balls Brothers
11 Blomfield St EC2.
Map 15 C1.

The Book Club
100 St Leonard St EC1.
Map 7 C5.

Black Friar
174 Queen Victoria St EC4. **Map** 14 F2.

Corney & Barrow
19 Broadgate Circle EC2.
Map 7 C5.

Dollar Grills & Martinis
2 Exmouth Market EC1.
Map 6 E4.

Eagle
159 Farringdon Rd EC1.
Map 6 E4.

Elbow Room
97–113 Curtain Rd EC2.
Map 7 C4.

Filthy McNasty's
68 Amwell St EC1.
Map 6 E3.

Hotel Bars

London's hotel bars continue to offer an elegant setting for classic and innovative cocktails, with **The Blue Bar** at the Berkeley Hotel and the **Long Bar** at the Sanderson Hotel prime examples. The **American Bar** at The Savoy, decorated in an Art Deco style, has a pianist, a terrific atmosphere and classic cocktails (try the signature White Lady or the Dry Martini, which the bar introduced to Britain), while another Jazz Age gem, the **Rivoli Bar** at the Ritz, has been resplendently restored. **Claridge's Bar** offers excellent champagne cocktails (among other concoctions) in a glamorous, contemporary-classic setting. **Trader Vic's** in the Park Lane Hilton offers an exotically tropical setting in which to enjoy an amazing range of rum cocktails. **The Bar**, in the Rosewood London, is a lively bar with a traditional soul, evoking the atmosphere of a London gentlemen's club with a roaring fire at one end and wooden bar running along the other. Warm, intimate and sophisticated, with plush furniture and handwoven rugs on a parquet floor. **Brasserie Max** in the Covent Garden Hotel is always buzzing and is very popular with theatre and film people.

Gay Bars

Old Compton Street in Soho has a well-established gay scene. Tables spill out on to the pavements and there is a lively atmosphere tolerant of all sexual preferences. **Compton's of Soho**, a busy pub, is across the road from the gay bar and eatery **Balans** and close to the well-known gay pub, **The Admiral Duncan**. The **Edge** is a sprawling bar and club over four floors, while **Rupert Street** is a stylishly low-key option for a relaxed drink. The **Candy Bar** is a popular lesbian bar, while, away from the West End, the **Royal Vauxhall Tavern** hosts Duckie's outrageous cabaret and DJs on Saturday nights.

DIRECTORY

Kick
127 Shoreditch High St E1.
Map 8 D3.

Loungelover
1 Whitby St E1.
Map 8 D4.

Ship Tavern
23 Lime St EC3.
Map 15 C2.

The Shoreditch Electricity Showrooms
39a Hoxton Sq N1.
Map 7 C3.

Smiths of Smithfield
67–77 Charterhouse St EC1.
Map 6 F5.

Ten Bells
84 Commercial St E1.
Map 8 D5.

Viaduct Tavern
126 Newgate St EC1.
Map 14 F1.

Ye Olde Cheshire Cheese
145 Fleet St EC4.
Map 14 E1.

Southwark and South Bank

Anchor
34 Park Street SE1.
Map 15 A3.

Fire Station
150 Waterloo Rd SE1.
Map 14 E4.

George Inn
77 Borough High St SE1.
Map 15 B4.

Hampstead

Freemasons Arms
32 Downshire Hill NW3.
Map 1 C5.

Old Bull and Bush
North End Way NW3.
Map 1 A3.

Spaniards Inn
Spaniards Rd NW3.
Map 1 A3.

Knightsbridge, Belgravia

Blue Bar
The Berkeley, Wilton Pl
SW1. **Map** 12 D5.

Boisdale
15 Eccleston St SW1.
Map 20 E1.

The Lansdowne
90 Gloucester Ave NW1.
Map 4 D1.

Primrose Hill, Marylebone

Chapel
48 Chapel St NW1.
Map 3 B5.

Coco Momo
79 Marylebone High
St W1. **Map** 4 D5.

Golden Eagle
59 Marylebone Lane W1.
Map 12 D1.

Bayswater, Notting Hill

The Cow
89 Westbourne
Park Rd W11.
Map 9 B1.

Lonsdale
44–48 Lonsdale Rd W11.
Map 9 B2.

Portobello Star
171 Portobello Rd W11.
Map 9 B2.

Prince Albert
11 Pembridge Rd W11.
Map 9 C3.

Trailer Happiness
177 Portobello Rd W11.
Map 9 B2.

Further Afield

Bull's Head
373 Lonsdale Rd SW13.

City Barge
27 Strand-on-the-
Green W4.

Fridge Bar
1 Town Hill Parade SW2.

Grapes
76 Narrow St E14.

Hampshire Hog
227 King St W6.

King's Head
115 Upper St N1.
Map 6 F1.

Latchmere
503 Battersea
Pk Rd SW11.

Prince Alfred
5a Formosa St W9.

Prospect of Whitby
57 Wapping Wall E1.

Royal Vauxhall Tavern
372 Kennington
Lane SE11.
Map 22 D3.

Trafalgar Tavern
Park Row SE10.

White Cross
Water Lane, Richmond,
Surrey.

SHOPS AND MARKETS

London is still one of the most lively shopping cities in the world. Ultramodern stores sit comfortably alongside the old-fashioned emporia presided over by tailcoated staff. You can buy anything here, as long as you're prepared to pay. Luxury goods are expensive, although bargain-hunters will find a wealth of cheap goods in the thriving markets, which often exude a carnival atmosphere. Explore the famous department stores, which encompass a huge breadth of merchandise, or seek out specialist shops. In general, you'll find upmarket designer stores around Knightsbridge, Knightsbridge, Chelsea, Regent Street and Bond Street, while Oxford Street is the frenetic centre for mid-priced labels as well as mainstream department stores. Notting Hill, Islington, Soho and Covent Garden are all rich in small, independent shops and specialist shops. Merchandise found in these areas include clothes, from raincoats and traditional tweeds to cutting-edge design and catwalk copies; books and records; perfumes; art and antiques; and craft goods such as jewellery, ceramics and leather.

When to Shop

In central London, most shops open from 10am and close between 5:30–6pm from Monday to Saturday, and are also open 11am–4pm Sunday. Many department stores have longer hours. The "late night" shopping until 7 or 8pm is on Thursdays and Fridays in Oxford Street and the rest of the West End, and on Wednesdays in Knightsbridge and Chelsea. Some shops in tourist areas, such as Covent Garden *(see pp112–21)* are open until 7pm or later every day and on Sundays. Some street markets *(see pp331–3)* are usually open on Sundays as well.

Bags from two of the most famous West End shops

How to Pay

Most shops accept all major credit cards, including MasterCard, American Express, Diners Club, Japanese Credit Bureau and Visa. However, smaller shops and street markets do not. A few of the stores also accept traveller's cheques, especially if they're in sterling; for other currencies, the rate of exchange is less favourable than in a bank. You need your passport.

Most shops no longer accept payment by personal cheque, and their use is likely to be phased out completely by 2018. Debit cards are accepted in many major stores, as are Euros.

Rights and Services

On a defective purchase, you usually get a refund, if proof of purchase is produced and the goods are returned. This isn't always the case with sales goods, so inspect them carefully. Most large stores, and some small ones, will pack goods up for you and send them anywhere in the world.

VAT Exemption

VAT (Value Added Tax) is a sales tax of 20%, which is charged on virtually all goods sold in Britain. The exceptions are books, food and children's clothes. VAT is mostly included in the advertised or marked price, although business suppliers, including some stationers and electrical goods shops, often charge separately.

Non-European Union visitors to Britain who stay no longer than three months may claim back VAT. If you plan to do so, carry your passport when shopping. You must complete a form in the store when you buy the goods and then give a copy to Customs while leaving the country. The tax refund may be returned by cheque or attributed to your credit card, but then a service charge will be deducted and most stores have a minimum purchase threshold (often £50 or £75). If you arrange to have your goods shipped directly home from the store, VAT should be deducted before you pay.

Harrods' elaborate Edwardian tiled food halls

Twice-Yearly Sales

The traditional sale season starts after Christmas to February and again in June to July, when shops slash their prices and sell off unwanted stock. The department stores have some of the best reductions; for the famous **Harrods** *(see p211)*, queues start to form outside long before opening.

Best of the Department Stores

The king of London's department stores, by tradition is **Harrods**, with over 300 departments and a staff of 5,000. The spectacular food hall with Edwardian tiles displays fish, cheese, fruit and vegetables. The specialities also include fashions for all ages, china and glass, kitchenware and electronics. **Harvey Nichols** aims to stock the best of everything. Clothes are particularly strong on high fashion, with emphasis on talented British, European as well as American names. There's also an impressive menswear section. The food hall, opened in 1992, is one of London's most stylish.

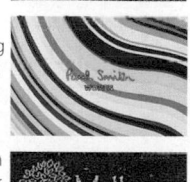
Some well-known names in British clothes design

    Selfridges, on Oxford Street, has a wide choice of labels, a great lingerie department and a section devoted to emerging designers. A melange of high-street concessions on the ground-floor caters to young women. It also has a food hall featuring global delicacies.

    The original **John Lewis** was a draper, and even today his shop has a good selection of fabrics and haberdashery. Its china, glass and household items make John Lewis, and its popular Sloane Square partner, Peter Jones, equally popular with Londoners. **Liberty** *(see p111)* near Carnaby Street still sells beautiful silks and other Oriental goods, for which it was famed after opening in 1875.

Look out for the famous scarf department. **Fortnum and Mason's** ground-floor food department is so engrossing that the upper floors of classic fashion and luxury items often remain free of crowds. The food section has everything from Fortnum's tins of biscuits and tea to the lovely wicker hampers. The latest addition to the retail scene is **Westfield London**, an impressive, up-market shopping destination with over 250 retailers, as well as several restaurants.

Marks and Spencer

Marks and Spencer has come a long way since 1882, when the Russian emigré, Michael Marks had a single stall in Leeds' Kirkgate market with the sign, "Don't ask the price – it's a penny!" It now has more than 690 stores worldwide and most stock is "own label" – Marks and Spencer's underwear in particular is a staple of the British wardrobe. The food department mostly stores convenience foods. The main Oxford Street branches at the Pantheon (near Oxford Circus) and Marble Arch are best for clothes and household goods.

Shopping Areas

As well as offering a wealth of delights for the discerning bargain hunter, London's thriving markets also provide an atmospheric glimpse into the past, with many dating back to Medieval times.

    Soak up the rich colours, aromas and flavours at specialist food stalls, browse quaint antique shops for curios or pick up a retro bargain at one of the many vintage clothes outlets that spill on to the streets. Early risers have a better chance of finding a bargain *(see also pp331–3)*.

Doorman at Fortnum and Mason

DIRECTORY
Department Stores

Fortnum and Mason
181 Piccadilly W1.
Map 12 F3. **Tel** 020 7734 8040.

Harrods
87–135 Brompton Rd SW1.
Map 11 C5. **Tel** 020 7730 1234.

Harvey Nichols
109–125 Knightsbridge SW1.
Map 11 C5. **Tel** 020 7235 5000.

John Lewis
300 Oxford St W1.
Map 12 E1. **Tel** 020 7629 7711.

Liberty
210–220 Regent St W1.
Map 12 F2. **Tel** 020 7734 1234.

Selfridges
400 Oxford St W1.
Map 12 D2. **Tel** 0870 837 7377.

Westfield London
W uk.westfield.com/london

Penhaligon's for scents *(see p325)*

London's Best: Shopping Streets and Markets

London's best shopping areas range from the elegance of Knightsbridge, where porcelain, jewellery and *couture* clothes come at the highest prices, to colourful markets such as Brick Lane, Spitalfields and Portobello. Meccas for those who enjoy searching for a bargain, London's markets also reflect the vibrant street life engendered by its enterprising multicultural community. The city is fertile ground for specialist shoppers; there are streets crammed with antique shops, antiquarian booksellers and art galleries. Turn to pages 316–30 for more details of shops, grouped according to category.

Kensington Church Street
Home to over 60 antique dealers with one of the largest selections of art and antiques in London (*see p217*).

Regent's Park and Marylebone

See inset map

Portobello Road Market
Over 1,000 stalls sell *objets d'art*, jewellery, medals, paintings and silverware – plus fresh fruit and vegetables (*see p333*).

0 kilometres   1
0 miles   0.5

Kensington and Holland Park

South Kensington and Knightsbridge

Picca and Jam

Chelsea

Knightsbridge
Exclusive designer-wear is on sale here, at Harrods as well as smaller stores (*see p211*).

King's Road
Once a centre for avant-garde fashion in the 1960s and 1970s, the street is now home to chain-stores and designer shops. This area also has upmarket antique shops (*see p198*).

PORTMAN SQUARE

WIGMORE ST

House of Fraser

John Lewis

BHS

OXFORD STREET

ORCHARD ST

Debenhams

Oxford Circus

SEYMOUR ST

Selfridges

Bond Street

OXFORD STREET

Marks & Spencer

Marble Arch

OXFORD

SOUTH MOLTON ST

NEW BOND STREET

HANOVER SQUARE

HANOVER STREET

REGENT STREET

GREAT MARLBOROUGH ST

POLAND ST

WARDOUR STREET

Liberty

CARNABY ST

BROADWICK ST

MADDOX ST

CONDUIT ST

SAVILE ROW

Hamleys

BEAK STREET

GOLDEN SQUARE

BREWER ST

OLD BOND STREET

BURLINGTON ARCADE

PICCADILLY

Piccadilly Circus

JERMYN ST

Fortnum & Mason

London's West End Shops

Oxford Street is sometimes called London's High Street and many of the shops that line it are branches of national or international chains. The big department stores such as Selfridges and John Lewis also loom along this street, as do smaller shops selling clothes and tourist souvenirs. On Regent Street, Piccadilly and Bond Street, prices rise and shoppers search for specialized purchases among the designer clothes shops, jewellers and art and antique dealers, while Carnaby Street has a more eclectic vibe.

Brick Lane Market
In this East End street, everything from old books to new trainers is on sale *(see p331)*.

Bloomsbury and Fitzrovia

Smithfield and Spitalfields

Covent Garden and the Strand

Holborn and the Inns of Court

The City

RIVER THAMES

South Bank

Southwark and Bankside

ehall
nd
inster

Petticoat Lane
London's most famous market has leather, clothes, watches, jewellery and toys *(see p333)*.

Gabriel's Wharf
The wharf has been converted into small shops selling art, jewellery and crafts *(see p193)*.

Covent Garden and Neal Street
Street entertainers perform in this lively and historic market. The specialist shops of Neal Street are nearby *(see p117)*.

Charing Cross Road
Shops selling old and new books line this street and the nearby Cecil Court *(see p322)*.

Clothes

London has never been better for clothes shopping, offering a virtually inexhaustible range of styles, price levels and quality, across a far-reaching and varied geographical area. Besides the traditional British-style famous the world over, you'll also find international designers, global and home-grown chains and an ever increasing number of independent boutiques catering to every taste. While old-fashioned tailors, shirt-makers and cobblers still thrive, often in their original premises, shops are increasingly design-led. The hugely popular high-street chains have perfected the art of producing good-quality catwalk knock-offs, while a new generation of British design talent has revitalized the fashion scene.

Traditional Clothing

British tailoring and fabrics are world-renowned for their high quality. In Savile Row, you can follow in the sartorial footsteps of Winston Churchill and the Duke of Windsor, among other dapper luminaries, and have a suit made to measure or buy one off the peg. Established in 1806, **Henry Poole** was the first tailor in the Row. At **H Huntsman & Sons**, you can choose from three options – bespoke, custom-made, and ready-to-wear. The bespoke suits are painstakingly hand-stitched on the premises, which partly explains the exorbitant £3,000-plus price tag. In addition to making suits to order, **Gieves & Hawkes** has two ready-to-wear lines.

A new generation of fashion-conscious tailors, known for modern cuts and vibrant fabrics, has joined the distinguished and traditional line-up, including **Ozwald Boateng** and **Richard James**. Jermyn Street is famous for smart shirts. At venerable shops such as **Turnbull & Asser** or the family-run **Harvie & Hudson**, you can either have them custom-made or choose the less expensive standard-sized options. Many manufacturers, including the popular shirt chain **Pink**, now also sell a wide variety of classic women's blouses.

In the past few years, several bastions of classic British style have completely reinvented themselves as fashion labels. **Burberry** is the best example of this, although it still does a brisk trade in its famous trenchcoats,

checked clothing (for children too) and distinctive accessories. **Daks** is also a good choice for classic raincoats, suits and accessories for both sexes, which produces high-fashion takes on traditional British looks. **Dunhill** specializes in immaculate, if expensive, menswear and accessories, while at the **Crombie**

outlet, you can buy the famous fitted overcoat which came to be known by the company's name. The famous menswear emporium, **Hackett**, caters to a younger, yet still conservative, clientele. Designers **Margaret Howell** and **Nicole Farhi** create updated versions of relaxed British country garments for men and women, such as knitwear, tweeds and sheepskin coats. You can still find a more traditional, smart country look in the Regent Street, Piccadilly or Knightsbridge areas. Waxed Barbour jackets are on sale at Harrods (see p313). **Cordings**, established 1839, is good for country-gent/-lady gear, such as check shirts, moleskin trousers and Covert coats.

While **Liberty** (see p313) now has a good selection of contemporary designers, it still uses its famous patterned prints to make blouses and stylish men's shirts as well as scarves and ties. Floral

Size Chart

For Australian sizes follow British and American convention

Children's clothing

British	2–3	4–5	6–7	8–9	10–11	12	14	14+ (years)
American	2–3	4–5	6–6X	7–8	10–12	14	16 (size)	
Continental	2–3	4–5	6–7	8–9	10–11	12		
14	14+ (years)							

Children's shoes

British	7½	8	9	10	11	12	13	1	2
American	7½	8½	9½	10½	11½	12½	13½	1½	2½
Continental	24	25½	27	28	29	30	32	33	34

Women's dresses, coats and skirts

British	6	8	10	12	14	16	18	20
American	4	6	8	10	12	14	16	18
Continental	32	34	36	38	40	42	44	46

Women's blouses and sweaters

British	30	32	34	36	38	40	42
American	6	8	10	12	14	16	18
Continental	34	36	38	40	42	44	46

Women's shoes

British	3	4	5	6	7	8
American	5	6	7	8	9	10
Continental	36	37	38	39	40	41

Men's suits

British	34	36	38	40	42	44	46	48
American	34	36	38	40	42	44	46	48
Continental	44	46	48	50	52	54	56	58

Men's shirts

British	14	15	15½	16	16½	17	17½	18
American	14	15	15½	16	16½	17	17½	18
Continental	36	38	39	41	42	43	44	45

Men's shoes

British	7	7½	8	9	10	11	12
American	7½	8	8½	9½	10½	11	11½
Continental	40	41	42	43	44	45	46

print "English rose" dresses and feminine blouses can be found at **Laura Ashley**, although the store has introduced more contemporary looks as well.

Modern British Design and Street Fashion

London designers are known for their eclectic, irreverent style. Grand dames Vivienne Westwood and Zandra Rhodes have been on the scene since the 1970s – the latter opened the **Fashion and Textile Museum** in south-east London in 2003. It features 3,000 of her own garments as well as examples by other influential fashion figures. Many British designers of international stature have their flagship stores in the capital, including the popular **Paul Smith** and **Stella McCartney**, both of whom showcase their collections in fabulous townhouses. **Matthew Williamson** and the late **Alexander McQueen** also have stand-alone stores. Young homegrown talent such as Alice Temperley, whose feminine frocks are beloved of the London party set, Eley Kishimoto, characterized by bold prints, and avant-garde design duo Boudicca, can be found in most of the capital's boutiques.

Selfridges (see p313) also has an impressive selection of emerging designers. **Dover Street Market**, conceived by Comme des Garçons' Rei Kawakubo, revives the age-old London tradition of the covered clothes market, but in a much more upmarket milieu. Its four minimalist floors showcase a varied array of goods, from glitzy shoes by king of the platform, Terry de Havilland to cool art books and vintage and contemporary designer clothes.

If you want to take home a bit of British design, but can't afford the high prices, it's worth visiting **Debenhams**, which has harnessed the talents of numerous leading designers, including Jasper Conran, Julien Macdonald and Ben De Lisi, to create cheaper clothes exclusive to the store. Young designers often start out with a

stall on Portobello Road or Old Spitalfields Market (see p333), both good sources of interesting clothing. There are also a few good designer sale shops: **Paul Smith Sale Shop** is located in central London. While those looking for **Burberry** bargains at its factory outlet will have to travel a bit further afield to the East End. For those willing to travel further, **Bicester Village** is an excellent discount shopping centre with mid- to high-end stores.

Boutiques

London is home to an extensive variety of boutiques – hot new shops crop up and, it must be said, close down with dizzying regularity. The mother of them all is **Browns**. Established in the 1970s, it occupies several storefronts in South Molton Street and stocks a wide selection of international labels. But the highest concentration of boutiques is in Notting Hill, near the intersection of Westbourne Grove and Ledbury Road. Because of the numerous cafés in the area, and the relaxed, affluent atmosphere away from the crowded West End shopping districts, it's an extremely pleasant place to browse.

JW Beeton embodies quirky British style, while **Matches**, which also has outposts in Richmond and Wimbledon, dominates Ledbury Road with three separate shops – one for both sexes, another just for women plus one specializing in frocks by Diane von Furstenberg. Like Browns in the West End, Matches stocks international designer labels, including Balenciaga, Prada and Chloé, interspersed with a variety of British talent such as Temperley, Bella Freud, Matthew Williamson and Georgina Goodman. **Question Air** and **Feathers** also stock designer labels, while **Aimé** specializes in French clothes and homewares. A short walk away in a quiet residential street, celebrity favourite, **The Cross** is a delightfully understated little shop, packed with women's fashion, cute children's clothes and toys, toiletries and

varied displays of unusual accessories. **Cross The Road**, located opposite, caters to chic interiors while **The Dispensary** in Kensington Park Road is much loved by locals for its Notting Hill style. Primrose Hill, Islington, Soho and the streets radiating off Seven Dials near Covent Garden are also dotted with independent fashion shops. Some, such as **Labour of Love** in Islington, combine clothes with a careful selection of interior items, art books and CDs. **Diverse**, also in Islington, caters for both sexes with a great selection of labels.

Chain Stores and Street Fashion

In Britain, designer looks are no longer, as they once were, the exclusive preserve of the rich. National fashion chains – or "high-street" stores – have never been better, both in terms of quality and design. Moreover, the cheaper versions of all the latest styles appear in the shops, almost as soon as they have been sashayed down the catwalk. **Oasis** and **Topshop** have both won celebrity fans for their up-to-the-minute, young womenswear. The latter, which proudly claims to be "the world's largest fashion store", is a complete mine of inexpensive clothes and beautiful accessories; there is even an in-store "boutique" with latest collections by hip designers, and a vintage section as well.

Vintage fashion (see p318) has become so popular, many high-street chains either sell it or feature collections which recreate the style.

The upmarket chains, **Jigsaw** and **Whistles** are more expensive with the emphasis on beautiful fabrics and shapes which, while stylish, don't slavishly copy the catwalk. **Jigsaw Junior**, available in larger branches, offers delectable mini versions of its designs for little girls. **Reiss** and **Ted Baker** are more popular with the trend-conscious young men, though they also have good women's collections. More streetwise shops can be found in and around Newburgh Street, behind Carnaby Street. **Cecil Gee** in Covent Garden is among the trailblazers for men.

Vintage Fashion

The city offers a vast hunting ground for the aficionados of vintage style, from market stalls to the exclusive shops showcasing immaculately preserved designer-wear. Head east for funky emporia such as **Rokit**, which also has other branches in Camden and Covent Garden, in addition to the huge warehouse, **Beyond Retro**. Grays Antique Market (see p332) covers all the bases with the award-winning Vintage Modes, spanning the styles of the past century as well as fashion-conscious Advintage, run by a former department-store personal shopper. Glamorous evening gowns and pin-up lingerie for the girls, flashy Hawaiian shirts and novelty bar accessories for the guys, can be found at Sparkle Moore's gloriously kitsch string of stalls, **The Girl Can't Help It** in Alfies Antique Market, which also houses excellent vintage shop **Persiflage**.

For mint-condition 1930s bias-cut silk slips and 1920s flapper dresses, head to **Annie's Vintage Clothes** in Camden Passage. **Absolute Vintage**'s flagship store, on Hanbury Street, has great vintage items; fresh and unique, it has something vintage for everyone. Be warned, neither of these shops is cheap, they both charge quite handsomely.

Knitwear

From the sought-after Fair Isle jumpers to Aran knits, the traditional British knitwear is famous. The best places for these are in Piccadilly, Regent Street and Knightsbridge. Heritage label **Pringle** has been revitalized with more contemporary shapes and vivid colours. Luxurious, casual labels **Joseph** and **The White Company** feature modern chunky knits, while **John Smedley** concentrates on more simple designs in fine-gauge wool and sea island cotton. For cashmere,

N Peal, which has both men's and women's shops at opposite ends of the Burlington Arcade, has a great selection – including a fairly cheaper, fashion-conscious line, npealworks. While the popular chain, **Brora** offers an affordable range of contemporary, Scottish cashmere for the entire family. **Marilyn Moore**, designs hip interpretations of classic knitwear.

Underwear and Lingerie

Marks & Spencer (see p313) is the most popular source of reasonably priced basics; it now has several fashionable lingerie lines as well. **Agent Provocateur**, owned by the famous designer, Vivienne Westwood's son and his wife, oozes retro pin-up glamour, from the slightly kinky, pink-uniforms worn by the staff to its nostalgically seductive bra sets. **Tallulah Lingerie** sells wispy negligées, hand-made silk under-garments and sumptuous bridal lingerie. For top quality bra sets head to **Rigby and Peller**. This British institution holds a Royal Warrant of Appointment and has experts on hand to help you find the perfect lingerie for your shape.

Children's Clothes

You can get traditional hand-smocked dresses and romper suits from Liberty, **Young England** and **Rachel Riley**, which stock smocks, gowns and tweed coats. Burberry's New Bond Street store has a children's section showcasing adorable mini macs, kilts and other items featuring the famous check. **Trotters** offers everything from shoes and clothes to haircuts, while **Their Nibs** sells eclectic designer children's clothing. The **Little White Company** makes soft, comfortable and traditional clothes for boys and girls in pure cotton and wool. They also sell delightful bedding and sleepwear.

Shoes

Some of the most famous names in the footwear industry are based in Britain. If you have a few thousand pounds to spare, you can have a pair custom-made by

the Royal Family's shoemaker, **John Lobb**. Ready-made, traditional brogues and Oxfords are the mainstay of **Church's Shoes**, while **Oliver Sweeney** gives classics a contemporary edge. For traditional, bench-made shoes at bargain prices, it's worth travelling further afield to Battersea, and splurge at the **Shipton & Heneage** outlet. It offers an exceptionally wide range of Oxfords, Derbys, loafers and boots crafted in the same Northamptonshire factories as some of the most celebrated names, for considerably lower prices, the out-of-the-way location keeps costs down.

Fans of the Fab Four can step into their idols' shoes; **Anello & Davide** designed the original Beatle Boot and still sells bespoke shoes in a range of materials. **The British Boot Company** in funky Camden has the widest range of Dr Martens, which were originally designed as hard-wearing work boots and appropriated by the rock 'n' rollers.

Jimmy Choo and **Manolo Blahnik** are two celebrated shoe designers, popular with some of most fashionable women worldwide. Their sophisticated high heels and cutting-edge designs are much sought-after.

While **French Soles** produces stunning, quality ballet flats and pumps in numerous colours and materials, **Emma Hope** in Sloane Square is best known for simple, timeless shapes embellished with embroidery or beadwork. Less expensive, yet good quality designs can be found in **Hobbs** or **Pied à Terre**, while **Faith** and **Office** turn out young fashion-led styles, the latter also sells men's shoes.

If you are on a look out for something that's a bit different, it's worth visiting London designer **Georgina Goodman's** shop in the picturesque Shepherd Market, where she showcases her unique ready-to-wear range.

The Natural Shoe Store, a Covent Garden institution of more than 30 years' standing, sells what its name says – shoes crafted from natural products. Vegan shoes and Birkenstocks are among its top sellers.

DIRECTORY

Traditional Clothing

Burberry
21–23 New Bond St W1.
Map 12 F2.
Tel 020 7930 3343.

Cordings
19–20 Piccadilly W1.
Map 13 A3.
Tel 020 7734 0830.

Crombie
48 Conduit St W1.
Map 12 F2.
Tel 020 7434 2886.
One of two branches.

Daks
10 Old Bond St W1.
Map 12 F3.
Tel 020 7409 4000.

Dunhill
48 Jermyn St W1.
Map 12 F3.
Tel 0845 458 0779.

Gieves & Hawkes
1 Savile Row W1.
Map 12 E3.
Tel 020 7432 6403.

H Huntsman & Sons
11 Savile Row W1.
Map 12 F3.
Tel 020 7734 7441.

Hackett
87 Jermyn St SW1.
Map 13 A3.
Tel 020 7930 1300.
One of several branches.

Harvie & Hudson
77 Jermyn St SW1.
Map 12 F3.
Tel 020 7930 3949.
One of three branches.

Henry Poole & Co
15 Savile Row W1.
Map 12 F3.
Tel 020 7734 5985.

Jaeger
200–206 Regent St W1.
Map 12 F2.
Tel 020 7979 1100.

Laura Ashley
House of Fraser, 318
Oxford St W1.
Map 12 F1.
Tel 0844 800 3752.
One of several branches.

Liberty
Regent St W1.
Map 12 F2.
Tel 020 7734 1234.

Margaret Howell
34 Wigmore St W1.
Map 12 E1.
Tel 020 7009 9009.

Nicole Farhi
25 Conduit St W1.
Map 10 F2.
Tel 020 7499 8368.
One of several branches.

Ozwald Boateng
30 Savile Row &
9 Vigo St W1.
Map 12 F3.
Tel 020 7437 2030.

Pink
85 Jermyn St SW1.
Map 12 F3.
Tel 020 7930 6364.
One of several branches.

Richard James
29 Savile Row W1.
Map 12 F2.
Tel 020 7434 0605.

Turnbull & Asser
71–72 Jermyn St SW1.
Map 12 F3.
Tel 020 7808 3000.

Modern British Design and Street Fashion

Alexander McQueen
4–5 Old Bond St W1.
Map 12 F3.
Tel 020 7355 0088.

Bicester Village
50 Pingle Drive, Bicester,
Oxfordshire OX26 6WD.
Tel 1869 366266.

Burberry Factory Shop
29–53 Chatham Place E9.
Tel 020 8985 3344.

Debenhams
334–348 Oxford St W1.
Map 12 E2.
Tel 08445 616 161.

Dover Street Market
17–18 Dover Street W1.
Map 12 F3.
Tel 020 7518 0680.

Fashion and Textile Museum
83 Bermondsey St SE1.
Map 15 C4.
Tel 020 7407 8664.

Matthew Williamson
28 Bruton St W1.
Map 12 E3.
Tel 020 7629 6200.

Paul Smith
Westbourne House 120 &
122 Kensington Park Rd
W11. **Map** 9 B2.
Tel 020 7727 3553.
One of several branches.

Paul Smith Sale Shop
23 Avery Row W1.
Map 12 E2.
Tel 020 7493 1287.

Stella McCartney
30 Bruton St W1.
Map 12 E3.
Tel 020 7518 3100.

Vivienne Westwood
44 Conduit St W1
Map 12 F2.
Tel 020 7439 1109.

Boutiques

Aimé
32 Ledbury Rd W11.
Map 9 C2.
Tel 020 7221 7070.

Anna
126 Regent's Park Rd
NW1. **Tel** 020 7483 0411.

Browns
23–27 South Molton St
W1. **Map** 12 E2.
Tel 020 7514 0039.

The Cross
141 Portland Rd W11.
Map 9 A3.
Tel 020 7727 6760.

Diverse
286 & 294 Upper St,
Islington N1. **Map** 6 F1.
Tel 020 7359 8877.

Feather & Stitch
16 King St TW9.
Tel 020 8332 2717.

Feathers
176 Westbourne Grove
W11. **Map** 9 C2.
Tel 020 7243 8800.

JW Beeton
48–50 Ledbury Road W11.
Map 9 C2.
Tel 020 7229 8874.

Matches
60–64, 83 & 85 Ledbury
Rd W11. **Map** 9 C2.
Tel 020 7221 0255.

Question Air
28 Rosslyn Hill NW3.
Map 1 C5.
Tel 020 7435 9921.

Chain Stores and Street Fashion

Cecil Gee
36 Long Acre WC2.
Map 13 B2.
Tel 020 7379 0061.

The Dispensary
200 Kensington Park Rd
W11. **Map** 9 B2.
Tel 020 7727 8797.

Hobbs
84–88 King's Rd SW3.
Map 19 C2.
Tel 020 7581 2914.
One of many branches.

Jigsaw
6 Duke of York Sq, Kings
Rd SW3. **Map** 19 C2.
Tel 020 7730 4404.
One of many branches.

Karen Millen
247 Regent St W1. **Map**
12 F1. **Tel** 020 7629 1901.
One of several branches.

Oasis
12–14 Argyll St W1.
Map 12 F2.
Tel 020 7434 1799.
One of several branches.

Reiss
Kent House, 14-17 Market
Place W1.
Map 12 F1.
Tel 020 7637 9112.
One of several branches.

DIRECTORY

Ted Baker
9–10 Floral St WC2.
Map 13 C2.
Tel 020 7836 7808.
One of several branches.

Topshop
Oxford Circus W1.
Map 12 F1.
Tel 0844 848 7487.
One of several branches.

Whistles
12–14 St Christopher's Pl
W1. **Map** 12 D1.
Tel 020 7487 4484.
One of several branches.

Vintage Fashion

Absolute Vintage
15 Hanbury Street E1.
Map 8 E5.
Tel 020 7247 3883.

Annie's Vintage Clothes
12 Camden Passage N1.
Map 6 F1.
Tel 020 7359 0796.

Beyond Retro
110–112 Cheshire St E2.
Map 8 E4.
Tel 020 7613 3636.

The Girl Can't Help It
Alfies Antiques Market,
13–25 Church
Street NW8. **Map** 3 A5.
Tel 020 7724 8984.

Persiflage
Alfies Antiques Market,
13–25 Church
St NW8. **Map** 3 A5.
Tel 020 7724 7366.

Rokit
101 & 107 Brick
Lane E1. **Map** 8 E4.
Tel 020 7247 3777.
One of three branches.

Knitwear

Brora
81 Marylebone High St
W1. **Map** 4 D5.
Tel 020 7224 5040.
One of several branches.

John Smedley
24 Brook St W1.
Map 12 E2.
Tel 020 7495 2222.

Joseph
299 Fulham Rd SW10.
Map 18 F3.
Tel 020 7352 6776.
One of several branches.

Marilyn Moore
7 Elgin Crescent W11.
Map 9 B2.
Tel 020 7727 5577.

N Peal
Burlington Arcade,
Piccadilly, W1.
Map 12 F3.
Tel 020 7499 6485.

Pringle Scotland
112 New Bond St W1.
Map 12 E2. **Tel** 020 7297
4580.

The White Company
Unit 5, Slingsby Pl, St
Martin's Courtyard
WC2. **Map** 13 B2.
Tel 020 8166 0200.

Underwear and Lingerie

Agent Provocateur
6 Broadwick St W1.
Map 13 A2.
Tel 020 7439 0229.
One of several branches.

Myla
77 Lonsdale Rd W11.
Map 9 B2.
Tel 020 7221 9222.
One of several branches.

Rigby & Peller
22A Conduit St W1.
Map 12 F2.
Tel 020 7491 2200.

Tallulah Lingerie
65 Cross St, Islington N1.
Map 6 F1.
Tel 020 7704 0066.

Children's Clothes

Little White Company
90 Marylebone High St W1.
Map 4D5.
Tel 020 7486 7550.

Rachel Riley
82 Marylebone High St
W1. **Map** 4 D5.
Tel 020 7935 7007.

Their Nibs
46–47 Upper Berkeley
Street, London, W1H
5QW. **Map** 11 C1.
Tel 020 7101 0351.

Trotters
34 King's Rd SW3.
Map 19 C2.
Tel 020 7259 9620.

Young England
The Old Imperial Laundry,
71 Warrior Gardens SW11.
Tel 07960 698 269.
By appointment only.

Shoes

Anello & Davide
15 St Alban's Grove,
Kensington W8.
Map 10 E5.
Tel 020 7938 2255.

The British Boot Company
5 Kentish Town Rd NW1.
Map 4 F1.
Tel 020 7485 8505.

Church's Shoes
108–10 Jermyn St SW1.
Map 12 F3.
Tel 020 7930 8210.

Emma Hope
53 Sloane Sq SW1.
Map 19 C2.
Tel 020 7259 9566.
One of three branches.

Faith
192–194 Oxford St W1.
Map 12 F1.
Tel 020 7580 9561.
One of several branches.

French Soles
6 Ellis St SW1.
Map 19 C2.
Tel 020 7730 3771.

Georgina Goodman
12–14 Shepherd St W1.
Map 12 E4.
Tel 020 7499 8599.

Gina
189 Sloane St SW1.
Map 19 C1.
Tel 020 7235 2932.

Hobbs
124 Long Acre WC2.
Map 13 B2.
Tel 020 7836 0625.
One of several branches.

Jimmy Choo
27 New Bond St W1.
Map 12 F2.
Tel 020 7493 5858.

John Lobb
88 Jermyn St SW1.
Map 12 F3.
Tel 020 7930 8089.

Kate Kuba
Unit 3, Cabot Pl,
Canary Wharf E14.
Tel 020 7715 5305.

Manolo Blahnik
49–51 Old Church St,
Kings Road SW3.
Map 19 A4.
Tel 020 7352 3863.

Office
57 Neal St WC2.
Map 13 B1.
Tel 020 7379 1896.
One of several branches.

Oliver Sweeney
5 Conduit St W1.
Map 12 F2.
Tel 020 7491 9126.

Pied à Terre
19 South Molton St W1.
Map 12 E2.
Tel 020 7629 1362.

Shelly's
12 The Broadway SW19.
Tel 020 8947 6162.
One of several branches.

Shipton & Heneage
117 Queenstown Rd SW8.
Map 20 E5.
Tel 020 7738 8484.

The Natural Shoe Store
13 Neal St WC2.
Map 13 B1.
Tel 020 7836 5254.

Specialist Shops

London may be famed for grand department stores such as Harrods, but there are many specialist shops which should also figure on the visitor's itinerary. Some have expertise built up over a century or more, while others are new and fashionable or cater to the whims of eccentric collectors. Whether you are looking for traditional British products and food, high-tech gadgets, or the latest trends in music, London has a wide range of stores to suite everyone's tastes.

Food

Britain's reputation for terrible food is proving hard to shake off, but over the past decade, not only has the national cuisine improved immeasurably, London has become one of the culinary capitals of the world. There is an unprecedented interest in local and organic produce as well as delicacies imported from all over Europe. This is reflected in the growing number of food markets, the main one being Borough Market *(see p331)*. Specialities that are well worth sampling include a variety of chocolates, biscuits, preserves, cheeses and teas *(see pp290–91)*.

The food halls of Fortnum & Mason, Harrods and Harvey Nichols *(see p313)* are good outlets for all of these, but it's also worth visiting the gastro-nomic gems dotted around town. Of these, **A Gold**, housed in an atmospheric old milliner's shop near Spitalfields Market, specializes in traditional foods from across Britain. Its wares, including cheeses, sausages, jams, baked goods, English wines and mead, are advertised on chalkboards. **Paxton & Whitfield**, a delightful shop dating from 1797, stocks more than 300 cheeses, including baby Stiltons and Cheshire truckles, along with pork pies, biscuits, oils and preserves.

The shelves of tiny **Neal's Yard Dairy** groan with huge British farmhouse cheeses. **Paul Rothe & Son** is a family-run deli that has hardly changed since it opened more than a century ago. Besides selling "British and foreign provisions", such as preserves, old-fashioned sweets and biscuits, the white-coated proprietors also serve morning toast and sandwiches on proper china. For traditional English chocolates, such as violet or rose creams and after-dinner mints in beautiful gift boxes, head for **Charbonnel et Walker** in Royal Arcade off Old Bond Street. It has been in business for more than 100 years, and holds Royal warrants. True chocoholics will be in their element at **The Chocolate Society**'s shop/café, where only the finest pure chocolate is available. Also committed to "real" chocolate, **Rococo** is well-known for its unique blue-and-white Victorian-esque packaging.

Drinks

Tea, the most British of drinks, comes in all kinds of flavours. Fortnum & Mason's traditional teas come in appealingly refined gift selections. **The Tea House** is packed with myriad varieties from classic to creative (such as "summer pudding"), colourful tourist-oriented tins and teapots. **Postcard Teas** is another specialist retailer of high-quality teas.

The quaint 19th-century **Algerian Coffee Stores** manages to pack more than 140 varieties of coffee and 200 teas into its small shop. Family business **HR Higgins**, sells fine coffees and teas from around the world. There are many attractive gift boxes and you can try before you buy in the coffee room downstairs.

For whisky lovers, **The Vintage House** displays the widest array of single malts in England, including some very old bottles. **Berry Bros & Rudd** is one of the oldest wine merchants in the world, still trading in wines, fortified wines and spirits from its ancient, panelled shop in St James's. In contrast, **Vinopolis** *(see p184)*, Bankside's "wine city", which charges admission, has a vast range of wines to choose from once you been on their interactive world wine tour and enjoyed five tastings. You can continue to imbibe in the restaurant or wine bar.

One-Offs

Sadly, many of London's quirky old specialist shops have closed, but there are still some fascinating anachronisms, as well as interesting newcomers, to be found across the city. A large number of specialist traders operate from stalls in antiques markets such as Alfies and Portobello Road *(see p333)*, where you can find everything from old military medals to commemorative china and vintage luggage. A notable survivor is **James Smith & Sons**, the largest and oldest umbrella shop in Europe. It first opened for business in 1830. Behind its mahogany and glass-panelled façade lies an array of high-quality umbrellas and walking sticks, including the once ubiquitous city gent brolly.

Halcyon Days specializes in little enamelled copper boxes, the delightful products of a revived English 18th-century craft. Top-quality wooden chess sets and boards, including an ornamental design featuring Sherlock Holmes characters, are available at **Chess & Bridge Ltd**. **VV Rouleaux**, on the other hand, is festooned with every imaginable type of ribbon and flamboyant trimming.

For serious collectors of model-making kits and historic TV character dolls and toys, **Comet Miniatures** has the largest selection in London. **Honeyjam** sells traditional toys and games for all ages. Without a Gameboy in sight, **Benjamin Pollock's Toyshop** does a nifty line in miniature self-assembly paper theatres as well as other traditional toys and antique teddies. **Flower Space** specializes in 1960s and 1970s furniture and classic movie prints.

At **The Bead Shop** in Covent Garden, you will find two floors stocked with everything from Swarovski crystals to semi-precious beads and sterling silver. The tasteful erotic boutique **Coco de Mer**, banishes the seedy sex shop cliché with its exquisite handmade lingerie and aesthetically pleasing sex toys.

Fans of Doctor Who and all things science fiction will love **ScifiCollector** on the Strand. It stocks a huge range of Doctor Who, Red Dwarf and other collectable toys and merchandise. There is also a section for first day covers, stamp sheets and signed items. Special events held at the store include appearances by science fiction authors, artists and actors.

Books and Magazines

Bookshops are high among London's specialities. Charing Cross Road (see p110) is undoubtedly the focal point for those searching for new, antiquarian and second-hand volumes. Although film buffs won't be able to browse in the shop that inspired the book and film, *84 Charing Cross Road*, they will be consoled by a commemorative plaque marking the site of the now defunct Marks & Co, which bore the celebrated address.

On the strip there are plenty of other antiquarian booksellers, shelves groaning with dusty finds. **Francis Edwards** here has a good selection covering travel, natural history, naval and military history and art and literature. Many shops offer a book-finding service if the title you want is no longer in print.

Charing Cross Road is famously the home of **Foyles**, known for its massive but notoriously badly organized stock; however, it was given a facelift and is now much easier to navigate. Here, you'll find everything from the latest bestsellers to academic tomes.

London's largest women's interest bookshop, **Silver Moon**, is on the third floor, there's a jazz shop and a cool café *(see below)*, plus an art gallery and real live piranhas in the children's department. As well as large branches of chains **Waterstone's** and **Blackwell**, many specialist bookshops are based here. A popular one is **Magma**, which is excellent for design subjects and avant-garde illustrated books.

Stanfords *(see p114)*, which stocks maps and guides to cover the globe, is in Long Acre; more travel books can be found at the **Travel Bookshop** in Notting Hill. Nearby is **Books for Cooks**, complete with café and test kitchen.

The beautiful Edwardian **Daunt Books** in Marylebone has a soaring, galleried back room devoted entirely to travel titles and, unusually, related fiction organized by country. Graphic novels and American and European comics are the speciality at **Gosh!** and **Orbital Comics**, while fantasy and science fiction abound at **Forbidden Planet**. For gay writing, visit the pioneering **Gay's The Word**, near Russell Square. The best selection of books on movies is found at the **Cinema Store**.

London's oldest bookshop, **Hatchards** in Piccadilly, is also one of the best, offering a well-organized and extensive choice. **Grant & Cutler** is an unrivalled source of foreign books and videos, while **Watkins Books**, located alongside other antiquarian bookshops in Cecil Court, specializes in all manner of esoteric subjects.

Cecil Court *(see p103)* is a charming pedestrian alleyway lined with dealers specializing in everything from illustrated children's books to modern first editions. There are also shops selling old prints covering every theme – great for gifts – and especially theatrical memorabilia.

The French Bookshop in South Kensington is stocked full of best-selling French titles. If you are looking for newspapers and magazines from abroad, **Capital Newsagents** stocks among others, American, Italian, French, Spanish and Middle Eastern publications. **Gray's Inn News** is also worth a visit for European press. For those with a keen interest in vintage magazines, there are more than 200,000 in the basement of **Vintage Magazines** in Soho, dating from the early 1900s all the way through to the present day. There are also all manner of movie and popular-culture memorabilia and gifts on the ground floor of the shop.

CDs and Records

As one of the world's greatest centres of recorded music, London has a huge and excellent selection of record shops catering to fans of all musical styles. **Fopp** sells a wide range of music from pop to punk to peaceful easy listening, and their Covent Garden branch stocks a comprehensive range.

Small specialist shops tend to cater to the more esoteric tastes. **Rough Trade** was at the centre of the emerging punk scene and still sniffs out interesting indie talent today, found in both East and West London. For jazz, check out **Ray's Jazz**, which is now housed in Foyle's bookshop along with a cool café where you can chill out to the vibe.

For a shop that has specialized in jazz since 1974, **Honest Jon's** also offers various types of music in both vinyl and CD form. In particular, it carries an extensive selection of soul and reggae. **Haggle Vinyl** sells rare, hard to find music and collectable records, from reggae to pop.

EGEA UK: Alternative Music Shop is based in North London, specializing in world, folk and international jazz music. Mainly CDs, as well as books and DVDs.

There is a high concentration of indie vinyl and CD shops in and around Berwick Street. **Sister Ray** is the largest indie record store in the West End. For 12-inch singles, the medium of club and dance music, one of the top places to go is **BM Music**.

DIRECTORY

Foods

A Gold
42 Brushfield St E1.
Map 8 D5.
Tel 020 7247 2487.

Charbonnel et Walker
1 Royal Arcade, 28 Old
Bond St W1. **Map** 12 F3.
Tel 020 7318 2075.

The Chocolate Society
36 Elizabeth St SW1.
Map 20 E2.
Tel 020 7259 9222.

Neal's Yard Dairy
17 Short's Gardens WC2.
Map 13 B2.
Tel 020 7240 5700.

Paul Rothe & Son
35 Marylebone
Lane W1. **Map** 12 E1.
Tel 020 7935 6783.

Paxton & Whitfield
93 Jermyn St SW1.
Map 12 F3.
Tel 020 7930 0259.

Rococo
321 King's Rd SW3.
Map 19 A4.
Tel 020 7352 5857.

Drinks

Algerian Coffee Stores
52 Old Compton St W1.
Map 13 A2.
Tel 020 7437 2480.

Berry Bros & Rudd
3 St James's St SW1.
Map 12 F4.
Tel 020 7396 9600.

HR Higgins
79 Duke St W1.
Map 12 D2.
Tel 020 7629 3913.

Postcard Teas
9 Dering St W1.
Map 12 E2.
Tel 020 7629 3654.

The Tea House
15A Neal St WC2.
Map 13 B2.
Tel 020 7240 7539.

Vinopolis
1 Bank End SE1.
Map 15 B3.
Tel 020 7940 8333.

The Vintage House
42 Old Compton St W1.
Map 13 A2.
Tel 020 7437 5112.

One-Offs

Benjamin Pollock's Toyshop
44 The Market, Covent
Garden Piazza WC2.
Map 13 C2.
Tel 020 7379 7866.

Chess & Bridge Ltd
44 Baker St W1.
Map 12 D1.
Tel 020 7486 7015.

Coco de Mer
23 Monmouth St WC2.
Map 13 B2.
Tel 020 7836 8882.

Comet Miniatures
44–48 Lavender Hill SW11.
Tel 020 7228 3702.

Flower Space
301 Portobello Rd W10.
Map 9 A1.
Tel 020 8968 9966.

Halcyon Days
14 Brook St W1.
Map 12 E2.
Tel 020 7629 8811.

Honeyjam
267 Portobello Rd W11.
Map 9 A1.
Tel 020 7243 0449.

James Smith & Son
53 New Oxford St W1.
Map 13 B1.
Tel 020 7836 4731.

ScifiCollector
79 Strand WC2.
Map 13 C3.
Tel 020 7836 2341.

The Bead Shop
21a Tower St WC2.
Map 13 B2.
Tel 020 7240 0931.

VV Rouleaux
102 Marylebone Lane W1.
Map 4 D5.
Tel 020 7224 5179.

Books and Magazines

Blackwell
100 Charing Cross Rd
WC2. **Map** 13 B2.
Tel 020 7292 5100.

Books for Cooks
4 Blenheim Crescent W11.
Map 9 B2.
Tel 020 7221 1992.

Capital Newsagents
48 Old Compton St W1.
Map 13 A2.
Tel 020 7437 2479.

Cinema Store
Unit 4B, Upper St Martin's
Lane WC1. **Map** 13 B2.
Tel 020 7379 7838.

Daunt Books
83–84 Marylebone High
St W1. **Map** 4 D5.
Tel 020 7224 2295.

Forbidden Planet
179 Shaftesbury Ave W1.
Map 13 A2.
Tel 020 7420 3666.

Foyles
113–119 Charing Cross
Rd WC2. **Map** 13 B1.
Tel 020 7437 5660.

Francis Edwards
72 Charing Cross Rd WC2.
Map 13 B1.
Tel 020 7379 7669.

The French Bookshop
28 Bute St SW7.
Map 18 F2.
Tel 020 7584 2840.

Gay's The Word
66 Marchmont St WC1.
Map 5 B4.
Tel 020 7278 7654.

Gosh!
1 Berwick St W1.
Map 13 B1.
Tel 020 7636 1011.

Gray's Inn News
50 Theobalds Rd WC1.
Map 6 D5.
Tel 020 7405 5241.

Hatchards
187 Piccadilly W1.
Map 12 F3.
Tel 020 7439 9921.

Magma
8 Earlham St WC2.
Map 13 B2.
Tel 020 7240 8498.

Orbital Comics
8 Great Newport St WC2.
Map 13 B2.
Tel 020 7240 0591.

Stanfords
12–14 Long Acre WC2.
Map 13 B2.
Tel 020 7836 1321.

Waterstone's
421 Oxford St W1.
Map 11 D2.
Tel 020 7495 8507.

Watkins Books
19–21 Cecil Court WC2.
Map 13 B2.
Tel 020 7836 2182.

Vintage Magazines
39–43 Brewer St W1.
Map 13 A2.
Tel 020 7439 8525.

CDs and Records

BM Music
25 D'Arblay St W1.
Map 13 A2.
Tel 020 7437 0478.

EGEA UK: Alternative Music Shop
267 Archway Rd N6.
Tel 020 8347 5555.

Fopp
1 Earlham St WC2.
Map 13 B2.
Tel 020 7379 0883.

Haggle Vinyl
114 Essex Rd N1.
Map 6 F1.
Tel 020 7704 3101.

Honest Jon's
278 Portobello Rd W10.
Map 9 B2.
Tel 020 8969 9822.

Ray's Jazz
(See Foyles).
Tel 020 7437 5660.

Rough Trade West
130 Talbot Rd W11.
Map 9 C1.
Tel 020 7229 8541.

Rough Trade East
91 Brick Lane E1.
Map 8 E5.
Tel 020 7392 7788.

Sister Ray
34–35 Berwick St W1.
Map 13 A1.
Tel 020 7734 3297.

Gifts and Souvenirs

London is a wonderful place to shop for gifts. It presents an impressive array of original ceramics, jewellery, perfume and glassware, exotic merchandise from around the world including jewellery from India and Africa, stationery from Europe and kitchenware from France and Italy. The elegant, Regency-period Burlington Arcade (see p93), the largest of several covered shopping arcades in the area, is popular for its high-quality clothes, antique and new jewellery, leather goods and other items, many of which are made in the UK. It is also a real boon when the famously unpredictable weather turns nasty.

The shops at big museums, such as the Victoria and Albert (see pp212–15), the Natural History (see pp204–5) and the Science Museum (see pp208–9) often have unusual items to take home as mementoes, while Contemporary Applied Arts and the market in Covent Garden Piazza (see p116) sell a range of British pottery, knitwear, pictures, clothing and other crafts. To buy all your gifts under one roof, go to Liberty (see p111), where beautiful stock from the world over fills every department, and the classic Liberty print features on many goods.

Gift Shops

If the phrase "gift shop" conjures up images of tacky tourist souvenirs, think again. A number of interesting shops bringing together a variety of present-friendly goods under one roof, has sprung up in the capital. **Eightsq** is a delightful store with an irresistible collection covering everything from elegant furniture to interesting plaques and impressive accessories. Bestsellers include hand-painted furniture, organic cotton baby clothes and bags for life. There are several other quirky, small shops in this street good for gift-hunting, including **Labour & Wait**.

A short walk away, **Story**, in a beautifully preserved 18th-century residential street, looks more like a gallery space than a shop. The fascinating mix of wares unites vintage dresses, organic bath products and modern and classic furnishings.

Across town in Notting Hill, **Brissi** is a lovely emporium kitted out with beautifully crafted household items, including elegant furniture and lamps, stylish mirrors and lighting. It also stocks summer fashion accessories for women, such as sun hats, tote bags and flip-flops.

The **Design Museum Shop** is a museum gift shop with a difference. It displays postmodern toys, games and innovative – and in some cases surprisingly affordable – accessories for home and office by big design names such as Arne Jacobsen, Tord Boontje and Eames. There are some wonderfully witty items, such as shoe-shaped shoe brushes and a doorstop in the form of a figure holding it open. Boutiques, **Saloon** and **Labour of Love** (see p317) also sell an eclectic range of items.

Jewellery

There are styles to suit every taste, from the fine, traditional jewellery found in the exclusive shops of Bond Street to unusual pieces by independent designers in areas like Covent Garden (see pp112–21), Gabriel's Wharf (see p193), and Camden Lock (see p331). Antique jewellery can be found in Hatton Garden and the Silver Vaults (see p143). The Crown Jeweller, **Garrard** in Albemarle Street, has been brought bang up-to-date under creative director Jade Jagger. Be warned, the spectacular creations have pricetags to match. Its former

business partner, **Asprey** sells updated classics, while **Butler & Wilson** specializes in reproductions of vintage jewellery and accessories. **Nude Jewellery London**, tucked away in Mayfair's Shepherd Market, deals mainly in handmade pieces, and **Kabiri**, with stores in Covent Garden and Marylebone and a concession in Selfridges, aims to bring works of previously unseen jewellery designers to London. **Assya** is a boutique jewellery store selling precious and semi-precious pieces. It is designed as a *boudoir* so customers can try on a gorgeous array of jewellery, have a drink and relax. The husband and wife duo, **Wright & Teague** design covetable modern silver and gold charm bracelets and necklaces, among other things.

The **Victoria & Albert shop** sells modern replicas of ancient British designs, as does the shop at the British Museum (see pp126–9). The **Lesley Craze Gallery**, which also deals in other handmade accessories and crafts, sells jewellery by designers from around the globe. Liberty (see p111) stocks a wide range of attractive jewellery as well.

Hats

Traditional men's headgear, from flat caps to trilbies and toppers, can be found at **Edward Bates**. Venerable hatter **Lock & Co**, established in 1672, caters for both men and women, while Swaine Adeney Brigg sells hats for both sexes by well-known name **Herbert Johnson**.

Philip Treacy is Britain's most celebrated milliner and his fabulous creations are on display at his shop on Elizabeth Street and in upmarket department stores. Established name **Stephen Jones** also has some very eye-catching looks, while **Rachel Skinner**'s beautifully made, slightly nostalgic designs range from cute cloches to extravagant Ascot confections, which are less expensive than more famous names. **Fred Bare**'s funky, affordable designs can be bought from the shop in Columbia Road on Sundays when the weekly flower market is in bloom, or from high-end department stores.

Bags and Leather Goods

Traditional British luggage, bags and small leather goods can be found in the streets and arcades off Piccadilly. **Swaine Adeney Brigg** sells umbrellas, hats, classic bridle-leather bags, old-fashioned walking sticks and other accoutrements for the country gent and lady. Well known for its classic, hardwearing bags and luggage is upmarket **Mulberry**. Established in 1971, its modern interpretations of English country clothes and accessories are sought after by fashion folk as well as anyone who appreciates fine quality.

The ultimate luxury is **Connolly**, a name famous for crafting sleek leather interiors for Rolls-Royce. Its two swish shops sell items that hark back to the golden age of motoring, such as leather driving jackets and shoes, magnificent tool cases and smart luggage, bound diaries and other extravagant home accessories and clothes.

J&M Davidson, owned by an Anglo-French couple, produces beautifully crafted, slightly retro bags, belts and small leather goods, often in unusual colours or skins. The shop in Notting Hill also stocks a line of clothes and interior items. In Piccadilly, **Bill Amberg**'s shop sells simple, contemporary bags in various types of leather, suede and other skins, plus gloves, wallets, leather boxes and unusual items such as a stylish leather and sheepskin baby "papoose".

Lulu Guinness and **Anya Hindmarch** both bring British wit and eccentricity to their handbags. Guinness's elaborate designs include a bag in the shape of a flowerpot topped with red roses and a circular purse resembling an old fashioned rotary telephone dial and there are also many London-themed items.

Hindmarch is famous for personalised, digitally printed photo bags, but also produces classic leather ones. For less expensive but high quality unique bags, try **Radley**.

Scarves

The luxury French designer store, **Hermès**, sells beautiful silk and cashmere scarves, often using vibrant colours. Of course, Liberty's famous print scarves are perennially popular. Small, stylish **Fenwick** is also known for its accessories department, which includes a wide array of interesting scarves by the likes of Pucci and Missoni, as well as bags, hats and a huge range of hair decorations. The **V&A Museum** shop has a good selection of scarves, including William Morris print silk scarves and stunning replica scarves inspired by V&A collections. N Peal *(see p318)* has an extensive choice of cashmere scarves and shawls.

Perfumes and Toiletries

Many British perfumeries use recipes that are hundreds of years old. **Floris** and **Penhaligon's**, for example, still manufacture the same flower-based scents and toiletries for men and women that they sold in the 19th century. The same goes for men's specialists **Truefitt & Hill** and **George F Trumper**, where you can buy some wonderful reproductions of antique shaving equipment as well. Chemist and perfumer **DR Harris** has been making its own range of toiletries for over two centuries; it's worth stopping in just to see the old-fashioned shop.

Neal's Yard Remedies employs traditional herbal and floral remedies as bases for its natural, therapeutic products. Former facialist **Jo Malone** uses such delicious aromas as herbs, fruit, even coffee, as well as traditional floral essences in her fragrances, skincare and candles, which come in simple yet sophisticated packaging. If you're looking for an unusual scent, head for **Miller Harris**;

young Grasse-trained perfumer Lyn Harris creates fragrances with remarkable depth, which come in boxes decorated with botanical prints. **Content** is an organic skincare boutique store that sells an advanced range of beauty products, cherry-picked from around the globe. It also has a naturopathic clinic and beauty salon, making it one of London's leading organic and natural apothecaries.

Space NK stocks the best and the most up-to-date collection of beauty products from around the world, along with its popular own-brand range. **The Body Shop** uses recyclable plastic packaging for its affordable natural cosmetics and toiletries, and encourages staff and customers alike to take an interest in environmental issues. **Molton Brown** sells a range of natural cosmetics, body and haircare products in branches throughout London. **Kiehl's** American luxury toiletries and skincare brand has its own store in Covent Garden.

Stationery

For luxurious writing paper and desk accessories, try the Queen's stationer, **Smythson** of Bond Street. The little bound notebooks and address books embossed with a wide selection of amusing and practical titles, such as "Travel Notes" and "Blondes, Brunettes, Redheads" make great gifts and souvenirs. Fortnum and Mason *(see p313)* does handsome leather-bound diaries, blotters and pencil holders, while Liberty *(see p111)* embellishes desk accessories with its famous Art Nouveau prints. **The Wren Press** is known for its high quality and prestigious stationery. They create bespoke letterheads, timeless stationery designs and unique invitations. It also holds two Royal Warrants.

Aspinal of London, known for its fine leather goods, such as hand-crafted wallets and purses, handbags and travel bags, also produces leather-bound high-end stationery. Beautiful photo albums, diaries, iPad and iPhone cases and sleeves, pencil cases and even leather-encased tape measures are sold out of their Marylebone store alongside all manner of other leather and non-leather gift ideas, such as silk and cashmere scarves.

Shepherd's Bookbinders stocks a range of handmade and decorative papers. Its marbled paper can make a glorious giftwrap for that very special present. Finally, for greeting cards, pens, gift wrapping paper and general stationery, pop into one of the branches of **Paperchase**.

Interiors

Wedgwood still makes the famous pale blue Jasper china that Josiah Wedgwood designed in the 18th century. You can buy this and the Irish Waterford crystal, at **Waterford Wedgwood** on Piccadilly. For a fine variety of original pottery, visit **Contemporary Ceramics**, the gallery of the Craft Potters Association, or go to **Contemporary Applied Arts**. **Mint's** hand-picked selection of unique furniture, home accessories, china and glassware by established names and up-and-coming design talent is a pleasure to browse. Large interior stores, **Heal's** and the

Conran Shop have a great display of stylish, modern accessories for the home. Those with more traditional tastes may prefer **Thomas Goode**, presided over by courteous tail-coated staff, which sells exquisite china, glassware, crystal, linen and gifts, including some antique pieces. The **Nicole Farhi Home** line exudes the same laid-back luxury as her clothes. If you're on a tighter budget, check out **Graham & Green**, which stocks a huge array of attractive items from around the globe, ranging from Moroccan tea glasses to Mongolian cushions and pretty nightwear.

Labour & Wait is a wonderful source of solid, functional British

DIRECTORY

Gift Shops

Brissi
196 Westbourne Grove W11. **Map** 10 B2.
Tel 020 7727 2159.

Design Museum Shop
Shad Thames SE1.
Map 16 E4.
Tel 020 7940 8787.

Eightsq
Market Street, Spitalfields E1. **Map** 8 D5.
Tel 020 7375 0060.

Labour & Wait
85 Redchurch St E2.
Map 8 E4.
Tel 020 7729 6253.

Story
4 Wilkes St E1. **Map** 8 E5.
Tel 020 7377 0313.

Jewellery

Asprey
167 New Bond St W1.
Map 12 F3.
Tel 020 7493 6767.

Assya London
53 Ledbury Road W11.
Map 9 C2.
Tel 020 7243 1687.

Butler & Wilson
20 South Molton St W1.
Map 12 E2.
Tel 020 7409 2955.

Garrard
24 Albemarle St W1.
Map 12 F3.
Tel 0870 871 8888.

Kabiri
37 Marylebone High St W1. **Map** 4 D5.
Tel 020 7317 2150.

Lesley Craze Gallery
33–35a Clerkenwell Green EC1. **Map** 6 E4.
Tel 020 7608 0393.

Nude Jewellery
36 Shepherd Market, Mayfair W1. **Map** 12 E4.
Tel 020 7629 8999.

Wright & Teague
35 Dover St W1.
Map 12 F3.
Tel 020 7629 2777.

Hats

Edward Bates
73 Jermyn St SW1.
Map 13 A3.
Tel 020 7734 2722.

Fred Bare
118 Columbia Rd E2.
Map 8 E3.
Tel 020 7229 6962.

Herbert Johnson
54 St James's Street SW1.
Map 12 F3.
Tel 020 7409 7277.

Lock & Co
6 St James's St SW1.
Map 12 F4.
Tel 020 7930 8874.

Philip Treacy
69 Elizabeth Street SW1.
Map 20 E2.
Tel 020 7730 3992.

Rachel Skinner
13 Princess Rd NW1.
Map 4 D1.
Tel 020 7209 0066.

Stephen Jones
36 Great Queen St WC2.
Map 13 C1.
Tel 020 7242 0770.

Bags and Leather Goods

Anya Hindmarch
15–17 Pont St SW1.
Map 20 D1.
Tel 020 7838 9177.

Bill Amberg
9 Shepherd Market W1.
Map 12 E4.
Tel 020 7499 0962.

Connolly
41 Conduit St W1.
Map 12 F2.
Tel 020 7439 2510.

J&M Davidson
97 Golborne Rd W10.
Tel 020 8969 2244.

Lulu Guinness
3 Ellis St SW1.
Map 19 C2.
Tel 020 7823 4828.

Mulberry
50 New Bond St W1. **Map** 12 E2.
Tel 020 7491 3900.

Radley
37 Floral St WC2. **Map** 13 B2. **Tel** 020 7379 9709.

Swaine Adeney Brigg
7 Piccadilly Arcade (at St James) SW1. **Map** 12 F3.
Tel 020 7409 7277.

Scarves

Fenwick
63 New Bond St W1.
Map 12 E2.
Tel 020 7629 9161.

Hermès
179 Sloane St SW1.
Map 11 C3.
Tel 020 7823 1014.
One of several branches.

V&A Enterprises
V&A Museum, Cromwell Rd SW7. **Map** 19 A1.
Tel 020 7942 2696.

Perfumes and Toiletries

The Body Shop
64, 360 & 374, Oxford St W1. **Map** 12 D2–F1.
Tel 020 7631 0027.

Content
14 Bulstrode St W1.
Map 12 D1.
Tel 020 3075 1006.

DR Harris
52 Piccadilly W1.
Map 12 F3.
Tel 020 7930 3915.

items for home and garden, such as old-fashioned stainless steel kettles, Welsh blankets and Guernsey sweaters. **David Mellor** is famous for his streamlined modern cutlery designs, while **Divertimenti** sells all manner of kitchen equipment and has a pleasant café at the back.

Bridgewater Pottery has chunky mugs, crockery and tea towels, which are decorated with traditional motifs and amusing mottoes. The Cloth Shop in Notting Hill stocks beautiful new and antique British wool and cashmere blankets and throws, as well as cottons, velvets and soft

furnishings. **Cath Kidston** designs fresh, nostalgic, English-style prints which adorn everything from humble household items to fashion accessories. There's a huge range of pretty, giftable goods such as toiletries, ironing-board covers, laundry bags, eiderdowns, clothes for women and children, bags, china and stationery.

Several interiors stores on Upper Street in the affluent Islington offer an impressive cache of gifts. **After Noah** is a big warehouse-like space bursting with vintage and retro-look items which also include, Bakelite rotary telephones,

nostalgic toiletries, old metal tins and street signs, classic board games and a huge assortment of children's toys. There is another branch in King's Road and a concession in Harvey Nichols (see p313).

The modern interiors emporium **Aria** has two stores in the same vicinity. One of these concentrates entirely on furniture and housewares by designers such as Alessi and Philippe Starck, while its satellite across the street sells gifts, including stationery, frames, bags and jewellery. Also on the same stretch is the contemporary-design heavy-weight **twentytwentyone**.

DIRECTORY

Floris
89 Jermyn St SW1.
Map 13 A3.
Tel 020 7930 2885.

George F Trumper
9 Curzon St W1.
Map 12 E3.
Tel 020 7499 1850.

Jo Malone
23 Brook St W1.
Map 12 E2.
Tel 0870 192 5181.

Kiehl's
29 Monmouth St WC2.
Map 13 B1.
Tel 020 7240 2411.

Miller Harris
21 Bruton St W1.
Map 12 E3.
Tel 020 7629 7750.

Molton Brown
58 South Molton St W1.
Map 12 E2.
Tel 020 7493 7319.

Neal's Yard Remedies
15 Neal's Yard WC2.
Map 13 B1.
Tel 020 7379 7222.

Penhaligon's
13 Market Building,
Covent Garden
Piazza WC2.
Map 13 C2.
Tel 020 3040 3030.

Space NK
131 Westbourne Grove
W2. **Map** 9 C2.
Tel 020 7727 8063.

Truefitt & Hill
71 St James's St SW1.
Map 12 F3.
Tel 020 7493 2961.

Stationery

Aspinal of London
46 Marylebone High St W1.
Map 4 D5.
Tel 020 7224 0413.

Asprey
167 New Bond St W1.
Map 12 F3.
Tel 020 7493 6767.

Paperchase
213 Tottenham Court Rd
W1. **Map** 5 A5.
Tel 020 7467 6200.

Shepherd's Bookbinders
30 Gillingham Street SW1.
Map 20 F2.
Tel 020 7233 9999.

Smythson
40 New Bond St W1.
Map 12 E2.
Tel 020 7629 8558.

The Wren Press
1 Curzon St W1J.
Map 12 D2.
Tel 020 7351 5887.

Interiors

After Noah
121 Upper Street N1.
Map 6 F1.
Tel 020 7359 4281.

Aria
Barnsbury Hall, Barnsbury
St N1. **Map** 6 F1.
Tel 020 7704 6222.

Cath Kidston
51 Marylebone High St W1.
Map 4 D5.
Tel 020 7935 6555.

The Cloth Shop
290 Portobello Rd W10.
Map 9 A1.
Tel 020 8968 6001.

Conran Shop
Michelin House, 81
Fulham Rd SW3.
Map 19 A2.
Tel 020 7589 7401.

Contemporary Applied Arts
89 Southwark St SE1.
Map 14 F3.
Tel 020 7436 2344.

Contemporary Ceramics
63 Great Russell St WC1.
Map 13 B1.
Tel 020 7845 4600.

David Mellor
4 Sloane Sq SW1.
Map 20 D2.
Tel 020 7730 4259.

Divertimenti
33–34 Marylebone High
St W1. **Map** 4 D5.
Tel 020 7935 0689.

Emma Bridgewater
81a Marylebone High St.
Map 4 D5. **Tel** 020 7486
6897. Also: 739 Fulham
Road. **Map** 17 C5.
Tel 020 7371 5264.

Graham & Green
4 Elgin Crescent W11.
Map 9 B2.
Tel 020 7243 8908.

Heal's
196 Tottenham Court Rd
W1. **Map** 5 A5.
Tel 020 7636 1666.

Mint
2 North Terrace SW3. **Map**
19 A1. **Tel** 020 7225 2228.

Nicole Farhi Home
115 Fulham Rd SW3.
Tel 020 7838 0937.

Thomas Goode
19 South Audley St W1.
Map 12 D3.
Tel 020 7499 2823.

twentytwentyone
274 Upper St N1. **Map** 6
F1. **Tel** 020 7288 1996.

Waterford Wedgwood
Sold at John Lewis, 300
Oxford St W1.
Map 12 E1.
Tel 0844 693 1765.

Art and Antiques

London's art and antique shops are spread across the length and breadth of the capital city. While the more fashionable and more expensive dealers are mainly concentrated in a relatively small area bounded by Mayfair and St James's, other shops and galleries catering to a relatively modest budget are scattered over the rest of the city. Whether your taste is for Old Masters or young modern artists, Boule or Bauhaus, you are bound to find something of beauty in London that is within your financial means.

Mayfair

Cork Street is the centre of the British contemporary art world. The huge line-up of galleries offers work in varying degrees of the avant-garde. The biggest name to look out for is **Waddington Custot Galleries**, and if you want to discover the flavour of the month, a stop here is a must. However, purchasing is only for the serious and rich collector. The **Mayor Gallery**, famous for Dada and Surrealism, was the first gallery to open in the street. **Redfern Gallery** shows mainstream modern art while **Flowers Central**, part of a growing modern gallery chain, has some unusual British pieces. A couple of doors down, **Browse and Darby Gallery** sells 19th- and 20th-century British and French paintings as well as contemporary works.

Also look into Clifford Street, where **Maas Gallery** excels in Victorian masters, and Sackville Street for **Henry Sotheran**'s rare books and prints. On Albemarle Street, the **Albemarle Gallery** specializes in contemporary prints and sculptures, show-casing the works of international and British artists. Established and up-and-coming talents are featured in the gallery's frequent, stunning installations.

Nearby, New Bond Street is the centre of the fine antiques trade in London. If it's Turner watercolours or Louis XV furniture you're after, this is the place. A walk up from Piccadilly takes you past the lush portals of **Richard Green** (which also has a gallery in Dover Street) and the **Fine Art Society**, among other extremely smart galleries. For jewellery and *objets d'art* visit **David Aaron Ancient Art** and **Grays Antique Market**; for silver, go to **S J Phillips**; and for 18th-century British furniture and art, try **Mallett Antiques**.

Even if you are not a buyer, these galleries are fascinating places to visit, so don't be afraid to walk in – you can learn more from an hour spent here than you can from weeks of studying text books. Also on New Bond Street are two of the big London auction houses, Bonhams and Sotheby's.

St James's

South of Piccadilly lies a maze of 18th-century streets. This is gentlemen's club country *(see Pall Mall p94)* and the galleries mostly reflect the traditional nature of the area. The centre is Duke Street, home of Old Master dealers, **Johnny van Haeften** and **Derek Johns**. Nearby, on King Street, you will find the main salerooms of **Christie's**, the well-known auction house where Van Goghs and Picassos change hands for millions. On the corner of Bury Street, celebrating past masculine pleasures is the sophisticated **Pullman Gallery**, which specializes in automobile art and collectables, vintage cocktail shakers, racy cigarette cases and other bar accessories.

Walk back up Bury Street past several interesting galleries, including the **Tryon Gallery** for traditional British sporting pictures and fine sculptures. Also duck into Ryder Street to take in **Chris Beetle**'s gallery of works by illustrators and caricaturists.

Knightsbridge

If you walk around to the back of **Harrods** *(see p313)*, you'll find the beginning of pretty Walton Street, which is lined with art galleries, traditional interior shops and boutiques. As you would expect in this exclusive area, prices are high. On nearby Brompton Road, the **Crane Kalman** gallery shows an enticing variety of contemporary art. Not far away is **Harvey Nichols** *(see p313)*, Knightsbridge's other swish department store. Motcomb Street houses some notable galleries, including the fascinating **Mathaf Gallery**, which features 19th-century British and European paintings of the Arab world.

Pimlico Road

The antique shops that line this road tend to cater predominantly for the pricey requirements of the interior decorator. This is where to come if you are searching for an Italian leather screen or a silver-encrusted ram's skull. Of particular fascination is **Westenholz**. While he doesn't deal in antiques, the Queen's nephew, furniture designer **Viscount Linley** produces some beautiful pieces that could pass as such, as well as contemporary designs. The finely crafted accessories, such as inlaid wooden boxes and frames, make great gifts.

East and West

London's East End is a growth area for contemporary art. In addition to the famous **White Cube Gallery** in Hoxton Square and **Flowers East** in Kingsland Road, there is a cluster of art dealers and galleries in **The Tea Building** on nearby Shoreditch High Street. **The Approach** combines an upstairs gallery with a good pub, frequented by local artists.

On the other side of the river in south east London, **Purdy Hicks**, based in a converted warehouse near Tate Modern, is great for contemporary British painting. Over in Mayfair, **Eyestorm** is a gallery that shows the work of both leading and emerging artists.

The **Oxo Tower Wharf**, in a landmark Thameside building topped by a good restaurant, is a hive of creativity, housing over 30 design and craft studios. You can find everything from hand-woven textiles and jewellery to homewares and fashion. Among the highlights are Black + Blum's innovative, affordable interior designs – for example, a lamp in the shape of a reading figure, made up of a lightbulb "holding" a book shade. Bodo Sperlain's delicate modern china and Studio Fusion's striking enamel pieces are also a draw for the visitors.

There are also some very interesting contemporary galleries in the vicinity of Portobello Road and Westbourne Grove. Some of the popular names include **East West Gallery** for contemporary art, **Themes & Variations**, which combines striking post-war and contemporary furniture and decorative art, and **Gallery 85**, smartly refurbished and boasting a range of the finest antiques, including some exceptional Meissen porcelain.

A browse along Kensington Church Street in west London will reveal everything from Arts and Crafts furniture to Staffordshire dogs in a concentration of small antiques emporia.

North

High-profile American dealer Larry Gagosian has been at the forefront of the regeneration of famously sleazy King's Cross by opening his second gallery here, in a capacious former garage. Expect world-class contemporary names as well as lesser-known artists at **Gagosian Gallery**. **Victoria Miro**'s massive Victorian warehouse in Islington is a showcase for British as well as young international talent. At its two spaces in the same quiet Marylebone Street, the **Lisson Gallery** often features cutting-edge installations.

Thompson's Gallery has locations in Marylebone and the City, selling a diverse mix of appealing if somewhat mainstream current British art.

Affordable Art

For the chance to acquire a work by what could become one of the big names of the future, visit the **Contemporary Art Society**. Its annual ARTFutures market showcases the work of more than 100 artists, their prices run from £100 into the thousands.

Open seven days a week all year round, **Will's Art Warehouse** in Putney sells pieces from £50–£3,000. This friendly gallery offers a wide variety of art to choose from and holds a new exhibition every six weeks. The owner founded the aptly named Affordable Art Fair, which takes place twice a year in Battersea Park.

Photography

The largest collection of original photographs for sale in the country is to be found in the print sales room of the **Photographers' Gallery**. The gallery displays work from emerging global talent and established artists, as well as works from its historical archives over its three floors of exhibition space. There are also talks, events, workshops and courses, as well as a bookshop and a café.

Atlas Gallery is one of the foremost galleries in London, dealing exclusively with fine art photography. It is also the official gallery for Magnum photographs. **Hamiltons Gallery** is worth visiting, especially during its major exhibitions.

Michael Hoppen's three-floor space in Chelsea shows both vintage and current works. If you want to take home a piece of London's rock n' roll heritage, the **Rock Archive**, near Camden Passage in Islington, is a great source of limited-edition prints of British music legends such as Paul Weller posing with Pete Townshend or Mick Jagger jamming with Ronnie Wood.

Bric-a-Brac and Collectables

For smaller, more affordable pieces, it's worth going to one of the established London markets, such as Portobello Road, Camden Passage (see p332) or Bermondsey (see p331), which is the main antiques market, catering to the trade. Conveniently situated in the city's main shopping district, Grays Antique Markets (see p332) have some great specialist dealers, but the prices are a bit higher than elsewhere given the location, while further afield, Greenwich Market (see p332) is well worth a rummage and may throw up some bargains. Many high streets out of the centre of town have covered markets of specialist stalls.

Alfies Antique Market is London's largest indoor market for antiques and collectables. The dealers are experienced specialists, and anyone interested in 20th-century design and vintage fashion especially will enjoy browsing amongst the eclectic mix on sale.

Auctions

If you are confident enough, auctions are a much cheaper way to buy art or antiques, but be sure to read the small print in the catalogue, which usually costs around £15. Bidding is simple – you need to register, take a number, then raise your hand when the lot you want comes up. The auctioneer will see your bid. It's as easy as that, and can be great fun.

The main auction houses in London are **Christie's Fine Art Auctioneers**, **Sotheby's Auctioneers** and **Bonhams**. Don't forget Christie's saleroom in Kensington, and Sotheby's premises in Olympia, which both offer art and antiques for the modest budget. Bonhams' second London saleroom in Knightsbridge holds weekly auctions of affordable antiques and collectables.

DIRECTORY

Mayfair

Albemarle Gallery
49 Albemarle St W1.
Map 12 F3.
Tel 020 7499 1616.

Browse and Darby Gallery
19 Cork St W1.
Map 12 F3.
Tel 020 7734 7984.

David Aaron Ancient Art
22 Berkeley Square W1.
Map 12 E3.
Tel 020 7491 9588.

Fine Art Society
148 New Bond St W1.
Map 12 E2.
Tel 020 7629 5116.

Flowers Central
21 Cork St W1. **Map** 12 F3.
Tel 020 7439 7766.

Grays Antique Markets
58 Davies St & 1-7 Davies Mews W1. **Map** 12 E2.
Tel 020 7629 7034.

Henry Sotheran
2 Sackville St W1.
Map 12 F3.
Tel 020 7439 6151.

Maas Gallery
15a Clifford St W1.
Map 12 F3.
Tel 020 7734 2302.

Mallett Antiques
37 Dover Street W1S.
Map 12 F3.
Tel 020 7499 7411.

Mayor Gallery
22a Cork St W1.
Map 12 F3.
Tel 020 7734 3558.

Redfern Gallery
20 Cork St W1. **Map** 12 F3.
Tel 020 7734 1732.

Richard Green
33 & 147 New Bond St.
Also: 39 Dover St W1.
Map 12 E2.
Tel 020 7493 3939.

S J Phillips
139 New Bond St W1.
Map 12 E2.
Tel 020 7629 6261.

Waddington Custot Galleries
11, 12, 34 Cork St W1.
Map 12 F3.
Tel 020 7851 2200.

St James's

Chris Beetle
8 & 10 Ryder St SW1.
Map 12 F3.
Tel 020 7839 7551.

Derek Johns
12 Duke St SW1.
Map 12 F3.
Tel 020 7839 7671.

Johnny van Haeften
13 Duke St SW1.
Map 12 F3.
Tel 020 7930 3062.

Pullman Gallery
14 King St SW1.
Map 12 F4.
Tel 020 7930 9595.

Tryon Gallery
7 Bury St SW1. **Map** 12 F3.
Tel 020 7839 8083.

Knightsbridge

Crane Kalman
178 Brompton Rd SW3.
Map 19 B1.
Tel 020 7584 7566.

Mathaf Gallery
24 Motcomb St SW1.
Map 12 D5.
Tel 020 7584 2396.

Pimlico Road

Linley
60 Pimlico Rd SW1. **Map** 20 D2. **Tel** 020 7730 7300.

Westenholz
80–82 Pimlico Rd SW1.
Map 20 D2.
Tel 020 7824 8090.

East and West

The Approach
1st Floor, 47 Approach Rd E2. **Tel** 020 8983 3878.

East West Gallery
8 Blenheim Cres W11.
Map 8 D4.
Tel 020 7229 7981.

Eyestorm
27 Hill St W1. **Map** 12 E3.
Tel 0845 643 2001.

Flowers East
82 Kingsland Rd E2.
Tel 020 7920 7777.

Gallery 85
85 Portobello Rd W11.
Map 9 A1.
Tel 020 7243 6365.

Oxo Tower Wharf
Bargehouse St SE1.
Map 14 E3.
Tel 020 7021 1600.

Purdy Hicks
65 Hopton St SE1. **Map** 14 F3. **Tel** 020 7401 9229.

The Tea Building
56 Shoreditch High St E1.
Map 8 D4.
Tel 020 7729 2973.

Themes & Variations
231 Westbourne Grove W11. **Map** 9 B2.
Tel 020 7727 5531.

White Cube Gallery
Hoxton Square N1.
Map 7 C3.
Tel 020 7930 5373.

North

Gagosian Gallery
6–24 Britannia St WC1.
Map 5 C3.
Tel 020 7841 9960.

Lisson Gallery
29 & 52-54 Bell St NW1.
Map 3 B5.
Tel 020 7724 2739.

Thompson's Gallery
15 New Cavendish St W1.
Map 4 E5.
Tel 020 7935 3595.

Victoria Miro
16 Wharf Rd N1.
Map 7 A2.
Tel 020 7336 8109.

Affordable Art

Contemporary Art Society
59 Central Street EC1.
Map 7 A3.
Tel 020 7017 8400.

Will's Art Warehouse
180 Lower Richmond Rd SW15. **Tel** 020 8246 4840.

Photography

Atlas Gallery
49 Dorset St W1.
Map 3 C5.
Tel 020 7224 4192.

Hamiltons Gallery
13 Carlos Place London W1. **Map** 12 E3.
Tel 020 7499 9493.

Michael Hoppen
3 Jubilee Place SW3.
Map 19 B3.
Tel 020 7352 3649.

Photographers' Gallery
16–18 Ramilies St W1.
Map 12 F1.
Tel 020 7087 9300.

Rock Archive
Image Space Gallery, 199 Bishopsgate EC2M.
Map 8 D5.
Tel 020 7267 4716.

Bric-a-Brac and Collectables

Alfies Antique Market
13–25 Church St NW8.
Map 3 A5.
Tel 020 7723 6066.

Auctions

Bonhams, W & FC, Auctioneers
Montpelier St SW7.
Map 11 B5.
Tel 020 7393 3900. Also: 101 New Bond St W1.
Map 12 E2.
Tel 020 7447 7447.

Christie's Fine Art Auctioneers
8 King St SW1.
Map 12 F4.
Tel 020 7839 9060. Also: 85 Old Brompton Road SW7.
Map 18 F2.
Tel 020 7930 6074.

Sotheby's Auctioneers
34–35 New Bond St W1.
Map 12 E2.
Tel 020 7293 5000. Also: Hammersmith Rd W14.
Map 17 A1.
Tel 020 7293 5555.

Markets

Even if you're not looking for cut-priced cabbages or a silk sari, it's worth paying a visit to one of London's crowded, colourful markets. Many mix English traditions with those of more recent immigrants, creating an exotic atmosphere and a fascinating patchwork quilt of merchandise. At some, the seasoned cockney hawkers have honed their sales patter to an entertaining art, which reaches fever pitch just before closing time as they advertise ever-plummeting prices. Keep your wits about you and your hand on your purse and join in the fun. For details, go to www.visitlondon.com.

Archway Market

Holloway Rd N19. 🚇 *Archway.* 🚌 *4, 17, 41, 43, 143, 271.* **Open** *11am–7pm Thu, 10am–5pm Sat.*

This young and growing market is one of North London's best kept secrets. Its speciality traders are committed to offering shoppers things that can't be bought anywhere else, including organic cheeses, breads and cakes, gourmet pickles and chutneys, farm-pressed juices and much more. Tasty lunch options include Breton crêpes, spicy curries and organic hot dogs. Several craft stalls sell unusual objects and gifts.

Bermondsey Market (New Caledonian Market)

Long Lane and Bermondsey St SE1. **Map** *15 C5.* 🚇 *London Bridge, Borough.* **Open** *4am–1pm Fri. Starts closing midday. See p184.*

Bermondsey is the gathering point for London's antique traders every Friday. Serious collectors start early and scrutinize the paintings, the silver and the vast array of old jewellery. Browsers might uncover some interesting curiosities but most bargains go before 9am.

Berwick Street Market

Berwick St W1. **Map** *13 A1.* 🚇 *Piccadilly Circus, Leicester Sq.* **Open** *9am–6pm Mon–Sat. See p110.*

The spirited costermongers of Soho's Berwick Street sell some of the cheapest and most attractive fruit and vegetables in the West End. Spanish black radish, star fruit and Italian plum tomatoes are among the produce you might find here, in addition to the various nuts and sweets. The market is good for fabrics and cheap household goods too, as well as for leather handbags and delicatessen. Separated from Berwick Street by a seedy passageway is the quieter Rupert Street market, where stallholders sell cheap street fashion.

Borough Market

Southwark St SE1. **Map** *15 B4.* 🚇 *London Bridge.* **Open** *11am–5pm Thu, noon–6pm Fri, 8am–5pm Sat, (for lunch: 10am–3pm Mon–Wed). See p178.*

On one of London's most ancient trading sites, Borough has for many years been a wholesale market catering to the restaurant and hotel trade. Now open to the public from Wednesday to Saturday, the award-winning market has a reputation as London's premier centre for fine foods, selling a vast array of British and international foodstuffs. Among the cornucopia is organic meat, fish and produce, top-quality handmade cheeses, breads, sweets, chocolates, coffees and teas and also soaps. It's a favourite foraging ground for the city's celebrity chefs.

Brick Lane Market

Brick Lane E1. **Map** *8 E5.* 🚇 *Shoreditch, Liverpool St, Aldgate East.* **Open** *11am–6pm Sat, 9am–5pm Sun. See pp172–73.*

This massively popular East End jamboree is at its best around its gloriously frayed edges. Pick through the mish-mash of junk sold on Bethnal Green Road or head east on Cheshire Street, past the new outcrop of fashionable home-design and gift shops, to explore the indoor stalls, packed with tatty furniture and old books. Much of the action takes place in cobbled Sclater Street and the lots on either side. Here, you'll find everything from fresh shellfish and trainers to old power tools and new bicycles. Further south on Brick Lane itself, the trendy boutiques and cafés give way to spice shops and curry restaurants in this centre for London's Bangladeshi community.

Brixton Market

Electric Ave SW9. 🚇 *Brixton.* **Open** *8am–6pm Mon, Tue, Thu–Sat; 8am–3pm Wed.*

This market offers a wonderful assortment of Afro-Caribbean food, from goats' meat, pigs' feet and salt fish to plantain, yams and breadfruit. There is an abundance of produce in the large Brixton Village and Market Row arcades, where exotic fish are a highlight. You'll also find Afro-style wigs, strange herbs and potions, traditional African ensembles and fabrics, and children's toys. From record stalls, the bass of raw reggae pounds through this cosmopolitan market like a heartbeat.

Broadway Market

Broadway Market, between Andrews Rd & Westgate St E8. 🚌 *386.* **Open** *8am–6pm Sat.*

Although this market is a bit tricky to get to because it's not served by the tube, it's worth getting a bus from Islington or walking from Bethnal Green tube. One of London's oldest, Broadway Market had gone into decline until its rebirth as a popular organic farmers' market. On Saturdays, the historic street running between London Fields and the Regent's Canal, comes alive with around 40 stalls selling fruit and vegetables, cheeses, baked goods, meats and confectionery. Also lining Broadway Market are some interesting, arty shops, catering to the young creative types who have been colonizing this part of Hackney over the past couple of decades. Black Truffle (No. 74), owned by shoemaker Melissa Needham, stocks a range of accessories made by independent designers – both local and international – while textile designer Barley Massey sells her own unusual designs and those of others at Fabrications (No. 7). L'Eau à la Bouche (No. 49) is a superior deli offering everthing from charcuterie to fruit tarts. There are also a couple of contemporary galleries such as Flaca (No. 69) and Seven Seven (No. 75–77). When it's time to refuel, duck into the Dove pub (No. 24–28) for a choice of Belgian beers.

Camden Lock Market

Chalk Farm Road NW1. 🚇 *Camden Town.* **Open** *9:30am–6pm daily.*

Camden Lock Market has grown swiftly since its opening in 1974, spreading along Chalk Farm Road and Camden High Street. Crafts, new and second-hand street fashion, wholefoods, books, records and antiques, form the bulk of the goods that a shopper can choose from. Its setting alongside the Regent's Canal is a bonus, too. Often, thousands of young people come here simply to enjoy the vibrant atmosphere, especially at weekends when Camden Lock is abuzz with activity (see p248).

Camden Passage Market

Camden Passage N1. **Map** *6 F1.*
🚇 *Angel.* **Open** *9am–6pm Wed, Sat.*
Camden Passage is a quiet walkway where cafés nestle among bijou antique shops. Prints, silverware, 19th-century magazines, jewellery and toys are among the many collectables that are on show. Don't miss the tiny shops tucked away in the atmospherically poky Pierrepont Arcade; one is precariously stacked with 18th and 19th-century porcelain; another specializes in antique puzzles and games. Jubilee Photographica deals in photographs from the 19th century onwards. The passage is also lined with shops – Annie's Vintage Clothes is known for pristine 1920s–40s frocks, while Origin sells classic 20th-century furniture. There's a specialist book market on Thursdays.

Chapel Market

Chapel Market N1. **Map** *6 E2.*
🚇 *Angel.* **Open** *9am–6pm Tue–Sat, 8:30am–4pm Sun.*
This is one of London's most traditional and exuberant street markets. Weekends are best; the fruit and vegetables are varied and cheap, the fish stalls are the finest in the area, there are also stalls selling European delicacies and cheeses and a wealth of bargain household goods.

Church Street Market

Church St NW8 and Bell St NW1. **Map** *3 A5.* 🚇 *Edgware Rd.* **Open** *8am–6pm Mon–Sat.*
Like many of London's markets, Church Street reaches a crescendo at the weekend. On Friday and Saturday, stalls selling cheap clothes, household goods, fish, cheese and antiques join the everyday fruit and vegetable stalls. Alfies Antique Market (No. 13–25) houses around 100 dealers selling everything from jewellery to furniture. There is also a cluster of interesting stand-alone antique furniture shops, plus the fascinating Gallery of Antique Costume and Textiles (No. 2), showcasing 17th century garments.

Columbia Road Market

Columbia Rd E2. **Map** *8 D3.*
🚇 *Shoreditch, Old St.*
Open *8am–3pm Sun. See p173.*

This is the perfect place to come to buy greenery and blossoms, or just to enjoy the fragrances and colours. Cut flowers, plants, shrubs, seedlings and pots are all sold at about half their normal prices on a Sunday morning in this charming Victorian street. (During December, as you might expect, there's a brisk trade in Christmas trees.) There are also some lovely shops that keep market hours, such as Angela Flanders' pretty perfumerie (No. 96), Salon for vintage jewellery and cufflinks (No. 142) and hip hatter, Fred Bare (No. 118). When you're shopped out, take tea at Treacle (No. 160), which turns out cute retro cupcakes and classic jam sponge cakes, plus cups of proper tea to wash them down. There is also a selection of vintage and modern china for sale. People with a sweet tooth can snack on deep-fried prawns from hole in the wall, Lee's Seafoods (No. 134).

Earlham Street Market

Earlham St WC2. **Map** *13 B2.*
🚇 *Covent Garden.* **Open** *10am–4pm Mon–Sat.*
Situated on a short road just off Shaftesbury Avenue, this market is a small affair. Several stalls sell a range of items from second-hand clothes to fashion jewellery and accessories.

East Street Market

East St SE17. 🚇 *Elephant and Castle.* **Open** *8am–5pm Tue–Fri, 8am–6:30pm Sat, 8am–2pm, Sun.*
East Street Market's high spot is Sunday, when more than 250 stalls fill the narrow street and a small plant and flower market is set up on Blackwood Street. The majority of traders sell clothes, accessories and household goods, although there is plenty of British and Afro-Caribbean produce, fish and other delicacies. Charlie Chaplin (see p33) was born in this street and sought inspiration for his characters in the area.

Gabriel's Wharf and Riverside Walk Markets

56 Upper Ground and Riverside Walk SE1. **Map** *14 E3.* 🚇 *Waterloo. Gabriel's Wharf* **Open** *11am–6pm Tue–Sun; Riverside Walk* **Open** *noon–7pm Sat, Sun. See p193.*

Little shops filled with ceramics, paintings and jewellery surround a bandstand in Gabriel's Wharf where jazz groups sometimes play in the summer. A few stalls are set up around the courtyard, selling ethnic

clothing and handmade jewellery and pottery. The book market under Waterloo Bridge includes a good selection of new and old Penguin paperbacks.

Grays Antique Markets

58 Davies St & 1–7 Davies Mews W1. **Map** *12 E2.* 🚇 *Bond Street.* **Open** *10am–6pm Mon–Fri, 11am–5pm Sat.*
Conveniently placed in the West End, Grays probably isn't the place to bag a bargain – the liveried doorman is a tip-off that this place is posh – but it makes a pleasant place to browse. There are some lovely pieces here, from costume jewellery and fabulous vintage fashion to enamel boxes and modern first editions from Biblion bookseller.

Greenwich Market

College Approach SE10. **Map** *23 B2.*
🚆 *Greenwich.* 🚇 *Cutty Sark DLR.*
Open *10am–5:30pm Wed–Sun.*
At weekends, the area west of Hotel Ibis accommodates dozens of trestle tables piled with coins, medals, banknotes, second-hand books, Art Deco furniture, assorted bric-a-brac and vintage clothing. The covered crafts market specializes in wooden toys, clothes made by young designers, handmade jewellery and accessories.

Jubilee and Apple Markets

Covent Gdn Piazza WC2. **Map** *13 C2.*
🚆 *Covent Gdn.* **Open** *9am–5pm daily.*
Covent Garden has become the centre of London streetlife, with some of the capital's best busking. Both these markets sell crafts and designs. The Apple Market, inside the Piazza where the famous fruit and vegetable market was housed (see p116), has knitwear, jewellery and novelty goods. Jubilee Hall sells antiques on Monday, crafts at the weekend, and a large selection of clothes, handbags, cosmetics and tacky mementoes in between. The East Colonnade Market also does a variety of stalls, from handmade soaps to hand-knitted children's clothing. Every Thursday on the East Piazza, the Real Food Market, aka the "Larder of London", trades in sustainably and ethically produced gourmet delicacies, including ready-made meals and street food.

Leadenhall Market

Whittington Ave EC3. **Map** *15 C2.*
🚇 *Bank, Monument.* **Open** *10am–6pm Mon–Fri. See p161.*

There has been a marketplace on this site since medieval times, but the present spectacular, glass-roofed structure was built in 1881. Leadenhall Market was traditionally famous for fish, meat and poultry, but only fishmonger HS Linwood & Sons remains. The smart, red and green façades now bear the names of upmarket clothing chains, restaurants, pubs and gift shops. Leadenhall does, however, retain something of its reputation as a centre of fine food. More than a dozen stalls set up shop on the cobblestones beneath this dramatic structure Monday to Friday from 10am to 6pm. Wares include European cheeses, cured meats, baked goods, condiments and other gourmet goods as well.

Leather Lane Market

Leather Lane EC1. **Map** *6 E5.* 🚇 *Farringdon, Chancery Lane.* **Open** *10am–2pm Mon–Fri.*
This ancient street, originally called Leveroun Lane, has played host to a market for over 300 years. The history of the Lane, however, has nothing to do with leather. Stalls here sell cut-price high-street clothes, plus shoes, bags, jewellery and accessories. All are well worth a browse.

Marylebone Farmers' Market

Cramer St car park, behind Marylebone High St W1. **Map** *4 D5.* 🚇 *Baker Street, Bond Street.* **Open** *10am–2pm Sun.*
In response to Britain's interest in local organic produce, weekly markets have sprung up all over the city. This enables farmers and other producers to sell directly to the public. Locations include Islington Green and the car park behind Waterstone's, Notting Hill, but Marylebone is the largest and most central, offering seasonal fruit and veg, dairy products, fish, meat, breads, preserves and sauces. There is also a line-up of excellent gourmet shops in adjacent Moxon Street, including a renowned rare-breed pork butcher, the Ginger Pig, and La Fromagerie delicatessen with its extensive cheese cave.

Old Spitalfields Market

Commercial St E1. **Map** *8 D5.* 🚇 *Aldgate East, Liverpool Street.* **Open** *10am–5pm Mon–Fri, 9am–5pm Sun. See p172.*
The main market is on a Sunday, and is a mecca for those interested in the latest street fashion trends. Many young designers have stalls, and prices are also reasonable. The stalls

are of mixed quality, so you have to really search for the gems. The organic food stalls and a selection of cafés make it a good brunch venue any day. A varying number of stalls are open during the week.

Petticoat Lane Market

Middlesex St E1. **Map** *16 D1.* 🚇 *Liverpool St, Aldgate, Aldgate East.* **Open** *9am–2pm Sun (Wentworth St 10am–2:30pm Mon–Fri). See p171.*
Probably the most famous of all London's street markets, Petticoat Lane continues to attract many thousands of visitors and locals every Sunday. The prices may not be as cheap as some of those to be found elsewhere, but the sheer volume of leather goods, clothes (the Lane's traditional strong point), watches, cheap jewellery and toys more than make up for that. A variety of fast-food sellers do a brisk trade catering for the bustling crowds that throng the market on a weekend.

Piccadilly Crafts Market

St James's Church, Piccadilly W1. **Map** *13 A3.* 🚇 *Piccadilly Circus, Green Park.* **Open** *antiques: 10am–6pm Tue. Arts and crafts: 10am–6pm Wed–Sat.*
Many of the markets in the Middle Ages were held in churchyards and Piccadilly Crafts Market is rekindling that ancient tradition. It is aimed mostly at visitors rather than locals, and the merchandise on display ranges from tacky T-shirts to wooden toys. All are spread out in the shadow of Wren's beautiful church *(see p92)*.

Portobello Road Market

Portobello Rd W10. **Map** *9 C3.* 🚇 *Notting Hill Gate, Ladbroke Grove.* **Open** *antiques and junk: 5:30am–5:30pm Sat. General market: 9am–6pm Mon–Wed, 9am–1pm Thu, 9am–7pm Fri & Sat. See p221.*
Portobello Road is really three or four markets rolled into one. The Notting Hill end has more than 1,000 stalls in numerous arcades and on the street, displaying a compendium of *objets d'art*, jewellery, old medals, paintings and silverware. Most stalls are managed by experts, so bargains are very rare. Further down the gentle hill, antiques give way to fruit and vegetables. The next transformation comes under the Westway flyover, where young fashion designers sell inexpensive creations alongside second-hand clothes, record and food stalls on Fridays and Saturdays. It's also worth venturing into the covered Portobello Green market,

which has an interesting mix of small shops selling everything from avant-garde fashion to kitsch cushions and lingerie. From this point on, the market becomes increasingly shabby.

Ridley Road Market

Ridley Rd E8. 🚆 *Dalston.* **Open** *6am–6pm Mon–Thu, 6am–7pm Fri & Sat.*
Early last century, Ridley Road was a centre of the Jewish community. Since then, Asians, Greeks, Turks and West Indians have also settled in the area and the market is a lively celebration of this cultural mix. Highlights include the 24-hour bagel bakery, shanty-town shacks selling green bananas and reggae records, colourful drapery stalls and cheap fruit and vegetables.

Roman Road Market

Roman Rd, between Parnell Rd and St Stephen's Rd E3. 🚇 *Bethnal Green.* 🚌 *8.* **Open** *10am–3pm Tue & Thu, 9am–4pm Sat. Farmers' market 1st Sat of month.*
This lively market established in the 19th century has a real East End flavour and traditionally sells everything from cheap bedding and fashion to cut-price cleaning products and fruit and veg. Chances are that you'll be treated to some colourful cockney patter from the stallholders trying to drum up custom. As well as the standard market traders, some more unusual vendors, street entertainers and special events add variety to the mix. When you pay a visit to the Roman Road Market, you may just be tempted to buy some of the handmade jewellery, vintage clothes or antiques being sold at the stalls.

Shepherd's Bush Market

Goldhawk Rd W12. 🚇 *Goldhawk Road, Shepherd's Bush.* **Open** *9am–6pm Mon–Sat.*
A focal point for many of the local ethnic communities, this rambling market contains an impressive volume of eclectic wares. West Indian food, Afro wigs, Asian spices, exotic fish, rugs and other household goods are just some of the major attractions. There are acres of cheap clothing for every occasion, from floral flannel nighties and men's suits to clubwear and elaborately beaded wedding gowns. Cheap fabric stalls are a highlight of the Shepherd's Bush Market, and there is even an on-site tailor and barber.

ENTERTAINMENT IN LONDON

London has the enormous, multi-layered variety of entertainment that only the great cities of the world can provide, and, as always, the city's historical backdrop adds depth to the experience. While few things could be more contemporary than dancing the night away in style at a famed nightclub such as Café de Paris or Heaven, you could also choose to spend the evening picturing the ghosts of long-dead Hamlets pacing ancient boards in the shadow of one of the living legends that grace the West End theatres today. There's a healthy, innovative fringe theatre scene too, plus world-class ballet and opera in fabled venues such as Sadler's Wells, the Royal Opera House and the Coliseum. In London you'll be able to hear the best music,

ranging from classical, jazz and rock to rhythm and blues, while dedicated movie buffs can choose from hundreds of different films each night, both in large, multi-screen complexes and excellent small independent cinemas. Sports fans can watch a game of cricket at Lords, cheer on oarsmen on the Thames or eat strawberries and cream at Wimbledon. Should you be feeling adventurous and sporty yourself, you could try going for a horse ride along Rotten Row in Hyde Park. There are festivals, celebrations and sports to attend, and there's plenty for children to do, too – in fact, there's plenty for everyone to do. Whatever you want, you'll be sure to find it on offer in London; it's just a question of knowing where to look.

Top; Cultural classics: a concert at Kenwood House; Above left; open-air theatre at Regent's Park; Above right; performers at the Coliseum

Information Sources

For details of events in London, check the comprehensive weekly listings and review magazine *Time Out* (published every Tuesday), sold at most newsagents and many bookshops. The commuter newspaper *Metro* (week days) and London's evening newspaper, the *Evening Standard*, are both free and

give brief daily listings. The *Independent* has daily listings and also reviews a different arts sector every day, plus a weekly round-up section, "The Information"; the *Guardian* has arts reviews in its G2 section every day and weekly listings in "The Guide" on

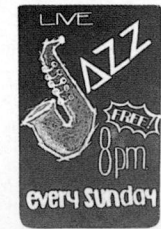

Café sign advertising free live music

Saturday. The *Independent, Guardian* and *The Times* all have lists of ticket availability.

Specialized news sheets, brochures and advance listings are distributed free in the foyers of theatres, concert halls, cinemas and arts complexes such as the South Bank and Barbican. Tourist information offices and hotel foyers often have the same publications. Fly posters advertise forthcoming events on billboards everywhere.

The Society of London Theatre (SOLT) publishes an informative free broadsheet every fortnight, available in many theatre foyers. It tends to concentrate on mainstream theatres, but does provide invaluable information about what's on. The National Theatre and the Royal Shakespeare Company also publish free broadsheets detailing future performances, distributed at the theatres. SOLT's website (www.officiallondontheatre.co.uk) provides full details of current productions. It also has news, interviews, access information and online ticket booking. Many theatres operate a faxback service which enables you to see a seating plan showing the unsold seats for any performance.

Booking Tickets

Some of the more popular shows and plays in London's West End – the latest Lloyd Webber musical for instance – can be totally booked out for weeks and even months ahead and you will find it impossible to purchase any tickets. This is not the norm, though, and most tickets will be available on the night, especially if you would be prepared to queue in front of the theatre for returns. However, for a stress-free holiday, it helps to book tickets in advance; this will ensure that you get the day, time and seats that you want. You can book tickets from the box office in person, by telephone, online or by post. Quite a few hotels have concierges or porters who will give advice on where to go and arrange tickets for you.

Box offices are usually open from about 10am–8pm, and accept payment by cash, credit card, traveller's cheque or else a personal UK cheque when supported by a cheque

Line-up from the Royal Ballet, on stage at Covent Garden

guarantee card. Many venues will now sell unclaimed or returned tickets just before the performance; ask at the box office for the queuing times. To reserve seats by telephone, call the box office and either pay on arrival or send payment – seats are usually held for three days.

Some venues now have separate phone numbers for your credit card bookings – check before you call. Reserve your seat, and always take your credit card with you when you collect your ticket. Some smaller venues do not accept credit cards.

Palace Theatre plaque

Disabled Visitors

Many London venues are old buildings and were not originally designed with disabled visitors in mind, but a lot of facilities have been

updated, particularly to give access to those using wheelchairs, or for those with hearing difficulties.

Telephone the box office prior to your visit to reserve the special seating places or equipment, which are often limited. Special discounts may be available; for details and information on facilities, visit Artsline's website, www.artsline. org.uk.

Transport

Night buses (see p375) are now the preferred late-night mode of transport, or phone for a cab from the venue. If you find yourself outside the city centre late at night, do not rely on being able to hail a black taxi quickly in the street. Never take an unlicensed mini-cab. The Underground usually runs until just after midnight, but check the timetables in the stations (see pp372–73).

Booking Agencies

Tickets are also available from agencies. Try the theatre box office first; if no seats are available there, find out the standard prices before going to an agency. Most, but not all, are reputable. Agencies advertising top show tickets for "tonight" may really have them, and they may be a fair price. If you order by phone, tickets will be posted to you or sent to the theatre for you to collect. Commission should be a standard 22%. Some shows waive the agency fee by paying the commission themselves; this is usually advertised, and agencies should then charge standard box office prices. Always compare prices, try to avoid agencies in bureaux de change, and do not be tempted to buy from ticket touts or unofficial Internet sources.

Ticket booth in Leicester Square

London's Theatres

London offers an extraordinary range of theatrical entertainment – this is one of the world's great stages, and, at its best, standards of quality are extremely high. Despite their legendary reputation for reserve, the British are passionate about theatre and London's theatres reflect every nuance of this passion. You can stroll along a street of West End theatres and find a sombre Samuel Beckett, Brecht or Chekhov play showing next door to some absurdly frothy farce like *No Sex Please, We're British!* Amid such diversity there is always something to appeal to everyone.

West End Theatre

There is a distinct glamour to the West End theatres. Perhaps it is the glittering lights of the foyer and the impressively ornate interiors, or maybe it is their hallowed reputations – but whatever it is, the old theatres retain a magic all of their own.

The West End billboards always feature a generous sprinkling of world-famous performers such as Judi Dench, Kenneth Branagh, John Malkovich and Kevin Spacey.

The major commercial theatres cluster along Shaftesbury Avenue and the Haymarket and around Covent Garden and Charing Cross Road. Unlike the national theatres, most West End theatres survive only on profits; they do not receive any state subsidy. They rely on an army of ever-hopeful "angels" (financial backers) and producers to keep the old traditions alive.

Many theatres are historical landmarks, such as the classic **Theatre Royal Drury Lane**, established in 1663 *(see p117)*, and the elegant **Theatre Royal Haymarket** – both superb examples of early 19th-century buildings. Another to note is the **Palace** *(see p110)*, with its terracotta exterior and imposing position right on Cambridge Circus.

National Theatre

The **National Theatre** is based in the Southbank Centre *(see p190)*. Here, the large, open-staged Olivier, the proscenium-staged Lyttelton and the small, flexible Cottesloe offer a range of size and style, making it possible to produce every kind of theatre from large, extravagant works to miniature masterpieces. The complex is also a lively social centre. Enjoy a drink with your friends before your play begins; watch the crowds and the river drift by; wander around the many free art exhibitions; relax during the free early evening concerts in the foyer or browse through the theatre bookshop.

The **Royal Shakespeare Company** is Britain's national theatre company, one of the world's great theatre ensembles, with an unparalleled reputation for its dramatic interpretation of Shakespeare and other leading dramatists. Although its official home since the 19th century has been in Stratford-upon-Avon, the company has maintained a regular London presence since the 1960s. Its London base used to be the Barbican Centre, but now the RSC enjoys regular London seasons in the West End, at the Novello Theatre and other smaller venues. If you want to find out where the RSC is performing in London call their ticket hotline.

National Theatre Bookings

National Theatre
(Lyttelton, Cottesloe, Olivier) South Bank SE1. **Map** 14 D3. **Tel** 020 7452 3000.
W nationaltheatre.org.uk

Royal Shakespeare Company
Tel 0844 800 1110 (tickets, information).

Pantomime

Should you happen to be visiting London between December and February, one unmissable experience for the whole family is pantomime. "Panto" is an absurd tradition in which major female characters are played by men and male characters by women, and the audience has to participate, shouting encouragement according to a set formula. Whatever adults may think of it, children love the experience.

Open Air Theatre

A performance of one of Shakespeare's airier creations, such as *A Midsummer Night's Dream*, takes on an atmosphere of pure enchantment among the green vistas of **Regent's Park** *(see p226)*. Lavish opera productions are staged during the summer months in **Holland Park** *(see p220)*. Wear warm clothing, take a blanket and, to be safe, an umbrella. Refreshments are available, or you can take a picnic.

Open-air performances of a different kind can be experienced at **Shakespeare's Globe** on Bankside *(see p179)*. This authentic reproduction of an Elizabethan playhouse, open to the skies – but with protected seating – is open to visitors all year round but only puts on performances in the summer months.

Open Air Theatre Bookings

Holland Park Theatre
Holland Park. **Map** 9 B4.
Tel 020 7361 3570. **Open** Jun–Aug.
W operahollandpark.com

Open Air Theatre
Inner Circle, Regent's Park NW1.
Map 4 D3. **Tel** 0844 826 4242.
Open Jun–Sep.
W openairtheatre.org

Shakespeare's Globe
New Globe Walk SE1. **Map** 15 A3.
Tel 020 7401 9919. **Performances** Apr–Oct. W shakespearesglobe.com

DIRECTORY

West End Theatres

Adelphi ⑬
Strand WC2.
Tel 0844 412 4651.

Aldwych ⑱
Aldwych WC2.
Tel 0844 453 9025.

Ambassadors ㉖
West St WC2.
Tel 0844 811 2334.

Apollo ㉜
Shaftesbury Ave W1.
Tel 0844 482 9671.

Cambridge ㉔
Earlham St WC2.
Tel 0844 412 4652.

Criterion ⑦
Piccadilly Circus W1.
Tel 020 7839 8811.

Dominion ㉓
Tottenham Court Rd.
Tel 0844 847 1775.

Duchess ⑯
Catherine St WC2.
Tel 0844 482 9672.

Duke of York's ③
St Martin's Lane WC2.
Tel 0844 871 7623.

Fortune ⑳
Russell St WC2.
Tel 0844 871 7626.

Garrick ④
Charing Cross Rd WC2.
Tel 0844 482 9673.

Gielgud ㉛
Shaftesbury Ave W1.
Tel 0844 482 5141.

Harold Pinter ⑧
Panton St SW1.
Tel 0844 871 7627.

Her Majesty's ⑩
Haymarket SW1.
Tel 0844 412 4653.

Lyceum ⑮
Wellington St WC2.
Tel 0844 844 0005.

Lyric ㉝
Shaftesbury Ave W1.
Tel 0844 482 9674.

New Leicester Square Theatre ⑤
Leicester Pl W1.
Tel 0844 873 3433.

New London ㉑
Drury Lane WC2.
Tel 0844 412 4654.

Noel Coward ①
St Martin's Lane WC2.
Tel 0844 482 5120.

Novello ⑰
Aldwych WC2.
Tel 0844 482 5170.

Palace ㉘
Shaftesbury Ave W1.
Tel 0844 482 9676.

Phoenix ㉗
Charing Cross Rd WC2.
Tel 0844 871 7629.

Piccadilly ㉞
Denman St W1.
Tel 0844 412 6666.

Playhouse ⑫
Northumberland Ave WC2.
Tel 0844 871 7631.

Prince Edward ㉙
Old Compton St W1.
Tel 0844 482 5151.

Prince of Wales ⑥
Coventry St W1.
Tel 0844 482 5115.

Queen's ㉚
Shaftesbury Ave W1.
Tel 0844 482 5160.

Shaftesbury ㉒
Shaftesbury Ave WC2.
Tel 020 7379 5399.

St Martin's ㉕
West St WC2.
Tel 0844 499 1515.

Theatre Royal Drury Lane ⑲
Catherine St WC2.
Tel 0844 412 4660.

Theatre Royal Haymarket ⑨
Haymarket SW1.
Tel 020 7930 8800.

Trafalgar Studios ⑪
Whitehall SW1.
Tel 0844 871 7632.

Vaudeville ⑭
Strand WC2.
Tel 0844 482 9675.

Wyndham's ②
Charing Cross Rd WC2.
Tel 0844 482 5138.

Fringe Theatre

London's fringe theatre acts as an outlet for new, adventurous writing and for writers from other cultures and lifestyles – works by Irish writers appear regularly, as do plays by Caribbean and Latin American authors and feminist and gay writers.

The plays are usually staged in tiny theatres based in pubs, such as the **Gate Theatre** above the Prince Albert pub in Notting Hill, the **King's Head** in Islington and the **Latchmere** pub in Battersea, or in warehouses and spare space in larger theatres, such as the **Donmar Warehouse** and the **Lyric**.

Venues like the **Bush Theatre**, the **Almeida** and the **Jerwood Theatre Upstairs** at the Royal Court have earned their reputations for discovering outstanding new works, some of which have subsequently transferred successfully to the West End.

Foreign-language plays are sometimes performed at national cultural institutes; for example, you might be able to catch Molière at the **Institut Français** or Brecht at the **Goethe Institute**; check the listings magazines.

For alternative stand-up comedy and cabaret, where you can encounter the sharp edge of satire with its brash, newsy style, try the **Comedy Store**, the birthplace of so-called "alternative" comedy, or the **Hackney Empire**, a former Victorian music hall that showcases local talent and hosts theatre, music and comedy events.

Budget Tickets

There is a wide range of prices for seats in London theatres. The cheaper West End tickets, for example, can cost under £10, whereas the best seats for musicals hover around £35–50. However, it is usually quite possible to obtain cheaper tickets.

"tkts" (see p335) is the only official discount theatre ticket shop in London, and sells tickets on the day of the performance for a wide range of mainstream shows. Located on the south side of Leicester Square, the booth is open Monday to Saturday (10am– 7pm) for matinee and evening shows, and Sunday (noon– 3:30pm) for matinees only. Payment is by cash or credit card, and there is a strict limit of up to four tickets per purchase, and a small service charge.

You can sometimes get reduced price seats for matinee performances, press and preview nights – it is always worth checking with the box office to see what they currently have on offer.

Choosing Seats

If you go to the theatre in person, you will be able to see its seating plan and note where you can get a good view at an affordable price. If you book by telephone, you should note the following: stalls are in front of the stage and expensive. The back stalls are slightly cheaper; dress, grand or royal circles are above the stalls and cheaper again; the upper circle or balcony are the cheapest seats but you will have to climb several flights of stairs; the slips are seats that run along the edges of the theatre; boxes are the most expensive option.

It is also wise to bear in mind that some of the cheap seats have a restricted view.

Theatre-Related Activities

If you are curious about how the mechanics of the theatre work, you would probably enjoy a back-stage tour. The National Theatre organizes tours (see p336). The tour includes the Lyttleton, Olivier and Cottesloe auditoria, as well as the workshops and dressing rooms. The London Palladium also offers a backstage guided tour of the theatre's history.

Irate Ghosts

Many of London's oldest theatres are reputed to have ghosts; however, the two most famous spectres haunt the environs of the Garrick and the Duke of York's (see p337). The Garrick is heavily atmospheric and the ghost of Arthur Bourchier, a manager at the turn of the 20th century, is reputed to make fairly regular appearances. He hated critics and many believe he is still trying to frighten them away. The ghost occupying the Duke of York's theatre was Violet Melnotte, an actress manager during the 1890s, who was famed for her extremely fiery temper.

Fringe Theatre

Almeida
Almeida St N1.
Tel 020 7359 4404.

Bush Theatre
Shepherds Bush Green W12.
Tel 020 8743 5050.

Comedy Store
1a Oxendon St WC2.
Map 13 B3.
Tel 0844 871 7699.

Donmar Warehouse
41 Earlham St WC2.
Map 13 B2.
Tel 0844 871 7624.

Gate Theatre
The Prince Albert Pub,
11 Pembridge Rd W11.
Map 9 C3.
Tel 020 7229 0706.

Goethe Institute
50 Prince's Gate,
Exhibition Rd SW7.
Map 11 A5.
Tel 020 7596 4000.

Hackney Empire
291 Mare St E8.
Tel 020 8985 2424.

Institut Français
17 Queensberry Pl SW7.
Map 18 F2.
Tel 020 7871 3515.

King's Head
115 Upper St N1. Map 6
F1. Tel 020 7478 0160.

Lyric
King St, Hammersmith
W6. Tel 020 8741 6850.

Theatre 503
The Latchmere Pub, 503
Battersea Park Rd SW11.
Tel 020 7978 7040.

Royal Court
Sloane Sq SW1.
Map 19 C2.
Tel 020 7565 5000.

Cinemas

If you can't find a movie you like in London, then you don't like movies. The huge choice of British, American, foreign-language, new, classic, popular and special-interest films makes London a major international film centre, with about 250 different films showing at any one time. There are about 50 cinemas in the central district of London alone, many of them ultra-modern multi-screened complexes. The big commercial chains show current smash-hits and a healthy number of independent cinemas offer some inventive programmes drawing on the whole history of film. London's listings magazines carry full details of what's on where.

West End Cinemas

"West End" is a loose term for the main cinemas in the West End of London, which show new releases, such as the **Odeon Leicester Square**, but it also includes the cinemas found in Chelsea, Fulham and Notting Hill. Programmes begin around midday and are then repeated every two or three hours, with the last show around 8:30pm; there are often late-night screenings on Fridays and Saturdays.

West End cinemas are very expensive, but admission is often cheaper for afternoon performances or on Mondays. Reserve your seats well in advance for screenings of the more popular films on Friday and Saturday evenings and Sunday afternoon.

BFI London Imax

The largest IMAX screen in Britain shows specially created movies accompanied by surround sound. Subjects like spaceflight or the undersea world suit this breathtaking format well, as do animations.

Repertory Cinemas

These cinemas often show foreign-language and slightly more "off-beat" art films and sometimes change programmes daily or even several times each day. Some cinemas show two or three films, often on the same theme, for one entrance charge.

These include the **Prince Charles**, which is situated centrally, close to Leicester Square, the **Everyman** in locations across north London, the ICA in the Mall, the **Ritzy** in Brixton, South London and the BFI Southbank.

BFI Southbank

Formerly known as the National Film Theatre, BFI Southbank is located in the Southbank Centre, near Waterloo Station. It has two cinemas of its own, which together offer a huge and diverse selection of films, both British and international. The BFI Southbank also holds regular screenings of rare and restored films and television programmes. It is absolutely essential for movie buffs to pay a visit.

Foreign-Language Films

These are screened at a number of repertory and independent cinemas, including the **Renoir**, the **Prince Charles**, the **Curzon Soho** in Shaftesbury Avenue, the **Screen** cinemas chain and the **Ciné Lumière**. Films are shown in the original language, with English subtitles.

Film Certificates

Children are allowed to go to a cinema unaccompanied by an adult to films which have been awarded either a U (universal) or a PG (parental guidance advised) certificate for viewing. Children must be accompanied by an adult to view a film rated 12A.

With other films, the numbers 12, 15 or 18 quite simply denote the minimum ages allowed for admission to the cinema.

London Film Festival

The most important cinema event in Britain is held every November, when over 100 films – some of which will have already won awards abroad – from a number of countries are screened. The BFI Southbank, several of the repertory cinemas and some of the big West End cinemas have special showings of these films. Details are published in the listings magazines. Tickets are quite hard to come by but some "standby" tickets will generally be available to the public 30 minutes before a screening.

Cinema Addresses

BFI London IMAX
Waterloo Rd SE1.
Map 14 D4.
Tel 0330 333 7878.

BFI Southbank
Southbank Centre, SE1.
Map 14 D3.
Tel 020 7928 3232.

Ciné Lumière
Institut Français, 17 Queensberry Pl SW7. **Map** 18 F2. **Tel** 020 7871 3515.

Curzon Soho
93–107 Shaftesbury Ave W1. **Map** 13 B2.
Tel 0330 500 1331.

Everyman
Hollybush Vale NW3.
Map 1 A5.
Tel 0871 906 9060.

Odeon Leicester Sq
Leicester Sq, WC2.
Map 13 B2.
Tel 0871 224 4007.

Prince Charles
Leicester Pl, WC2.
Map 13 B2.
Tel 020 7494 3654.

Renoir
Brunswick Sq WC1.
Map 5 C4.
Tel 0330 500 1331.

Ritzy
Coldharbour Lane SW2.
Tel 0871 902 5739.

Screen Cinemas
96 Baker St NW1.
Map 3 C5.
Tel 0871 906 9060.

Opera, Classical and Contemporary Music

Opera has always been tarred with a somewhat elitist reputation in Britain. However, televised concerts and free outdoor concerts in Hyde Park and the Piazza, Covent Garden, have greatly increased its popularity. London is home to five world-class orchestras and a veritable host of smaller music companies and contemporary music ensembles; it also houses three permanent opera companies and numerous smaller opera groups and leads the world with its period orchestras. It is a major centre for the classical recording industry, which helps to support a large community of musicians and singers. Mainstream, obscure, traditional and innovative music are all to be found in profusion. *Time Out* magazine *(see p334)* has the most comprehensive listings of the classical music on offer around the capital.

London Music Festivals

The BBC-run Promenade concerts are mostly held at the Royal Albert Hall *(see p341)* between July and September. More than 70 concerts feature soloists, orchestras and conductors from around the world, performing a wide repertoire, from much-loved classics to newly commissioned pieces. Every concert is broadcast live both on the radio and online. Tickets are best bought in advance, but 500 standing or 'promming' places are sold on the day, one and a half hours before the performance. The City of London Festival is held annually in June and July, when churches and public buildings in the City host a range of varied musical events. Venues such as the Tower of London *(see p156)* and Goldsmiths' Hall lend a special atmosphere to the events. Many concerts are free. For more details, apply to the information office (0845 401 5040) from May onwards.

Royal Opera House

Floral Street WC2. **Map** 13 C2. **Tel** 020 7304 4000. *See p117.* W roh.org.uk
The building, with its elaborate red, white and gold interior, is opulent; it looks, and is, expensive. It is the home of the Royal Opera and the Royal Ballet, but visiting opera and ballet companies also perform here. Many productions are shared with foreign opera houses, so check that you haven't already seen the same production at home. Works are always performed in the original language, but English translations are flashed up above the stage.

Seats are usually booked well in advance, particularly if major stars such as Placido Domingo or Anna Netrebko are performing. Tickets range from about £5 to £200 or more for a world-class star. The cheapest seats tend to go first, although a number of these tickets are reserved for sale on the day. Some of the cheaper seats have extremely restricted views. Standing passes can often be obtained right up to the time of a performance. Standby information is available on the day, and there are often concessions on tickets.

London Coliseum

St Martin's Lane WC2. **Map** 13 B3. **Tel** 0871 911 0200 (24 hrs), 020 7845 9300 (booking). *See p121.* W **eno.org**
The Coliseum, home of the English National Opera (ENO), was founded in 1961. The company's hallmarks are performances in English, high musical standards and a permanent ensemble

complemented by guest appearances. Productions range from the classic to the adventurous. For weekday performances, there are 500 prebookable seats at £10 and under.

Southbank Centre

Southbank Centre SE1. **Map** 14 D4. **Tel** 0844 875 0073. *See pp188–9.* W **southbankcentre.co.uk**
The Southbank Centre includes the **Royal Festival Hall (RFH)**, the **Queen Elizabeth Hall**, the **Purcell Room** and the **Hayward Gallery**. There are nightly performances, mostly of classical music, interspersed with opera, jazz, ballet and modern dance seasons, as well as festivals of contemporary and ethnic music. The largest concert hall on the South Bank is the RFH. Built in the 1950s, it is now considered one of the best modernist structures in London. The RFH is ideal for major orchestras and large-scale choral works. The airy halls outside the auditorium are also used to house exhibitions, a number of cafés, a book and music shop, and the occasional free performance.

The Purcell Room is comparatively small and tends to host chamber and contemporary music in addition to many debut recitals of young artists. The Queen Elizabeth Hall lies somewhere in between. It stages medium-sized ensembles whose audiences, while too large for the Purcell Room, would not fill the Festival Hall. Jazz and ethnic music are performed here

and the innovative and often controversial Opera Factory makes several appearances throughout the year. It performs a range of modern interpretations of the classics, and often commissions new works. The London Philharmonic Orchestra and the Philharmonia are resident at the South Bank. The Royal Philharmonic and the BBC Symphony Orchestra are frequent visitors, along with leading ensembles and soloists such as Angela Gheorghiu, Mitsuko Uchida, Stephen Kovacevich and Anne-Sofie von Mutter. World-class conductors who have played here include Daniel Barenboim, Kurt Masur and Simon Rattle.

The Academy of St Martin-in-the-Fields, the London Festival Orchestra, Opera Factory, the London Classical Players and the London Mozart Players all have regular seasons. There are also frequent free foyer concerts, and throughout the summer the centre is well worth visiting.

Barbican Concert Hall

Silk Street EC2. **Map** 7 A5. **Tel** 020 7638 8891. *See p167.* W **barbican.org.uk**
The Barbican is the home of the London Symphony Orchestra (LSO). Classical concerts are performed by the resident LSO and the BBC Symphony Orchestra, as well as many other visiting orchestras and ensembles, as part of the Barbican's own international concert seasons. The concert hall is also renowned for its performances of contemporary music, including jazz, blues and world music.

Royal Albert Hall

Kensington Gore SW7. **Map** 10 F5. **Tel** 020 7589 8212. *See p207.* W **royalalberthall.com**
Each year the Royal Albert Hall hosts over 300 concerts, from ballet to rock, pop, opera and national events. From mid-July to mid-September, it is devoted to the Henry Wood Promenade Concerts, the "Proms". Organized by the BBC, the season features the BBC Symphony Orchestra performing modern symphonies and other works as well as classics. Tickets for the Proms can be bought on the day of performance or booked in advance, but long queues build up early in the day, so Promenaders take cushions to sit on. Tickets sell out weeks ahead for the "Last Night of the Proms", which has become a national institution.
    The hall is also open for tours that take you on a journey of its extraordinary history.

Handel House Museum

25 Brook St W1. **Map** 12 E2. **Tel** 020 7495 1685. **Open** 10am–6pm Tue–Sat (until 8pm Thu), noon–6pm Sun. W **handelhouse.org**
Located in the finely restored Georgian house where George Frideric Handel lived from 1723 until his death in 1759, the Handel House Museum provides an intimate venue for performances. Thursday night recitals of Baroque music on period instruments are held in the panelled rehearsal and performance room, where Handel himself would have entertained his guests. Concert tickets include access to the museum. Check the website for more details.

Outdoor Music

London has many outdoor musical events in summer. Many royal parks, palaces, stately homes, National Trust properties and council parks host a range of music festivals and performances throughout summer. Arrive early as the concerts are popular, particularly if fireworks are to accompany the music. Take a sweater and a picnic. Purists beware – people walk around, eat and talk throughout and the music is amplified so it can be a little distorted. You don't get your money back if it rains, as they have never abandoned a performance yet. These events sell out fast and it's best to book tickets in advance.
    Other venues include Marble Hill House in Twickenham *(see p254)*, with practices similar to Kenwood, Crystal Palace Park and Holland Park.

Wigmore Hall

36 Wigmore St W1. **Map** 12 E1. **Tel** 020 7935 2141. *See p228.* W **wigmore-hall.org.uk**
Because of its excellent acoustics, the Wigmore Hall is a favourite with visiting artists, and attracts international names such as Andreas Scholl and András Schiff for a wide-ranging programme of events. It presents seven evening concerts a week, BBC Monday lunchtime concerts, and a Sunday morning concert from September to July.

St Martin-in-the-Fields

Trafalgar Sq WC2. **Map** 13 B3. **Tel** 020 7766 1100. *See p104.* W **smitf.org**
This elegant Gibbs church is where the famous Academy of St Martin-in-the-Fields and the famous choir of the same name began life. Orchestras as disparate as the Delmont Ensemble and the London Oriana Choir provide evening concerts. The choice of each programme is partly dictated by the religious year; for example, Bach's *St John Passion* is played at Ascensiontide. Free lunchtime concerts are held on Mondays, Tuesdays and Fridays by young artists.

St John's, Smith Square

Smith Sq SW1. **Map** 21 B1. **Tel** 020 7222 1061. *See p83.* W **sjss.org.uk**
This converted Baroque church has good acoustics and seating. It hosts concerts by groups such as the Academy of Ancient Music, the London Mozart Players, the Monteverdi Choir and Polyphony. The concert period runs from September to mid-July.

Broadgate Arena

3 Broadgate EC2. **Map** 7 C5. W **broadgateinfo.net**
This open-air venue in the City offers a summer season of lunchtime concerts, with varied programmes from up-and-coming musicians.

Music Venues

Orchestral

Barbican Concert Hall
Broadgate Arena
Queen Elizabeth Hall
Royal Albert Hall
Royal Festival Hall
St Martin-in-the-Fields
St John's, Smith Square

Chamber and Ensemble

Barbican Concert Hall
Broadgate Arena
Handel House Museum
LSO St Luke's
Purcell Room
Royal Festival Hall foyer
St Martin-in-the-Fields
St John's, Smith Square
Wigmore Hall

Soloists and Recitals

Barbican Concert Hall
Handel House Museum
Purcell Room
Royal Albert Hall
St Martin-in-the-Fields
St John's, Smith Square
Wigmore Hall

Children's

Barbican Concert Hall
Royal Festival Hall

Free

Barbican Concert Hall
Royal Festival Hall foyer
Royal National Theatre foyer
St Martin-in-the-Fields (lunchtime)

Early Music

Purcell Room
Wigmore Hall

Contemporary Music

Barbican Concert Hall
Southbank Centre

Dance

London-based dance companies present a range of styles from classical ballet to mime, jazz, experimental and ethnic dance. London is also host to visiting companies as diverse as the classic Bolshoi Ballet and the innovative Jaleo Flamenco. Most dance companies (with the exception of the resident ballets) have short seasons that seldom last longer than a fortnight and often less than a week – check the listings magazines for details *(see p334)*. Theatres that regularly feature dance are the Royal Opera House, the London Coliseum, Sadler's Wells and The Place Theatre. There are also performances at the Southbank Centre and other arts centres throughout the city.

a number of visiting dancers. A purpose-built space in Deptford, south London, the **Bonnie Bird Theatre**, presents a rich and diverse mix of dance, music and physical theatre. Other venues include the **Institute of Contemporary Arts** (ICA) *(see p94)* and the **Chisenhale Dance Space**, a centre for small companies currently regarded as being on the experimental fringes.

Ballet

The **Royal Opera House** *(see p117)* and the **London Coliseum** in St Martin's Lane are by far the best venues for classical ballet, providing the stage for foreign companies when they visit London. The Opera House is home to the Royal Ballet, which usually invites major international guest artists to take up residence. Book well in advance for classics such as *Swan Lake* and *Giselle*. The company also has an unusual repertoire of modern ballet; triple bills provide a mixture of new and old and seats are normally quite readily available.

The English National Ballet holds its summer season at the **London Coliseum**. It has a similar repertoire to the Royal Ballet and stages some very popular productions.

Visiting companies also perform at **Sadler's Wells**, which, although it is London's premier venue for contemporary dance, also hosts a few companies with a classical repertoire.

Contemporary

A plethora of new and young companies is flourishing in London, each one with a distinctive style. **Sadler's Wells** in Islington, near Angel, has a proud reputation as the host of contemporary dance companies from around the world. There are regular visits from such luminaries of dance as the Nederlands Dance Theatre and the Alvin Ailey Company from New York. The innovative English ensemble, the Rambert Dance Company, have a regular, twice-a-year slot at the theatre – usually in May and November. A stunning modern theatre was built on the historic site of the Sadler's Wells Ballet in 1998. The **Peacock Theatre** (the West End home of Sadler's Wells) also features contemporary dance as part of its programme.

The Place is the home of contemporary and ethnic dance companies and has a year-round programme of performances from these and

Ethnic

There is a constant stream of visiting groups coming to perform traditional dance from all over the world. Both **Sadler's Wells** and the **Riverside Studios** are major venues, while classical ethnic dance companies, including Indian and Far Eastern, have seasons at the Southbank Centre, often in the **Queen Elizabeth Hall**. Check the listings magazines for details.

Dance Festivals

There are two major contemporary dance festivals each year in London, featuring many different companies. Spring Loaded runs from February to April, while Dance Umbrella runs from early October to early November. The listings magazines carry all details.

Other smaller festivals include Almeida Dance, from the end of April to the first week of May at the **Almeida Theatre**, and The Turning World, a festival running in April and May offering dance from all over the world.

Dance Venues

Almeida Theatre
Almeida St N1.
Tel 020 7359 4404.

Bonnie Bird Theatre
Creekside SE8.
Map 23 A2.
Tel 020 8691 8600.

Chisenhale Dance Space
64 Chisenhale Rd E3.
Tel 020 8981 6617.

ICA
Nash House, Carlton House Terrace, The Mall SW1.
Map 13 A4.
Tel 020 7930 3647.

London Coliseum
St Martin's Lane WC2.
Map 13 B3.
Tel 020 7845 9300.

Peacock Theatre
Portugal St WC2.

Map 14 D1.
Tel 020 7863 8198.

The Place
17 Duke's Rd WC1.
Map 5 B3.
Tel 020 7121 1100.

Queen Elizabeth Hall
Southbank Centre SE1.
Map 14 D4.
Tel 0844 875 0073.

Riverside Studios
Crisp Rd W6.
Tel 020 8237 1111.

Royal Opera House
Floral St WC2. **Map** 13 C2.
Tel 020 7304 4000.

Sadler's Wells
Rosebery Ave EC1.
Map 6 E3.
Tel 020 7863 8198.

Rock, Pop, Jazz, Reggae and World Music

You will find the whole range of popular music being strummed and hummed, howled, growled or synthesized in London. There may be as many as 80 listed concerts on an ordinary weeknight, featuring rock, reggae, soul, folk, country, jazz, Latin and world music. In addition to the gigs, there are music festivals in the summer at parks, pubs, halls and stadiums throughout the capital (see p345). Check the listings magazines and keep your eyes open for publicity posters (see p334).

Major Venues

The largest venues in London are host to an extraordinary variety of music.

Places where pop idols hope to draw enormous crowds of adoring fans include the **O2 Arena** in Greenwich, the indoor **Wembley Arena**, the **Eventim Apollo**, or, if they take themselves seriously, the grand **Royal Albert Hall**.

The **O2 Academy Brixton** and the **Town and Country Club** are next in prominence and size. Each can take well over 1,000 people, and for many Londoners these former cinemas are the capital's best venues, with seating upstairs, large dance-floors downstairs and accessible bars.

Rock and Pop

Indie music is one of the mainstays of London's live music output. Following the leads of Manchester and Bristol, the capital has a healthy, cross-fertilized rock scene; venues all over town offer Britpop, bratpop, hip-hop, trip-hop and the many other variations on pop which have yet to be labelled for the mass market. The **Union Chapel** in Islington hosts a variety of bands. Kentish Town's **Bull and Gate** is good for goth, and rock is the order of the day at venues such as **The Bullet Bar** and **O2 Shepherd's Bush Empire** among others.

The **Underworld** in Camden is a famous live venue for up and coming bands as well as big name artists such as Sheryl Crow, Radiohead and The Darkness. The venue is also

home to two nightclubs. London is the home of pub-rock, which is a vibrant blend of rhythm and blues, rock and punk that has been evolving since the 1960s as a genre in which bands frequently develop before finding their real musical identity. Such diverse bands as the Clash, Dr Feelgood and Dire Straits all started as pub rockers. While there's usually no entrance fee to pub gigs, drinks tend to be surcharged.

New bands have a popular showcase at the **Betsey Trotwood** in Clerkenwell most week nights, while **Borderline**, near to Leicester Square, is frequented by record company talent scouts.

The **Barfly** in Chalk Farm delivers a good range of indie acts. **Koko** in Camden is a great intimate venue in a restored theatre dating from 1900. Here you can listen to the finest established artists such as Madonna or Coldplay and live performances from up-and-coming indie bands. Another good venue for stimulating rock bands in North London is **The Garage** at Highbury Corner.

Jazz

The number of jazz venues in London continues to grow – both the music and the lifestyle which are romantically imagined to go with it are officially hip once again. **Ronnie Scott's** in the West End is still the pick of the vintage crop, and since the 1950s, many of the finest performers in the world have come to play here. The **100 Club** in Oxford Street is

another very popular venue for confirmed jazzniks. Jazz and food have formed a partnership at venues such as the **Palookaville** in Covent Garden, the **Dover Street Restaurant and Bar** and the largely vegetarian **Jazz Café**. Others include the **Pizza Express** on Dean Street and the **Mau Mau Bar**, on Portobello Road.

The **Southbank Centre** (see pp188–9) and also the **Barbican** (see p167) feature formal jazz concerts and free jazz in the foyers.

Reggae

London's large West Indian community has made the city the European reggae capital. At the **Notting Hill Carnival** (see p59), late in August, many top bands perform free.

Reggae has now become integrated with the mainstream rock music scene, and bands appear at most of London's rock venues.

World Music

Musicians from every corner of the globe live in London. "World music" includes African, Latin, South American, anything exotic, and its popularity has sparked a revitalization of British and Irish folk music. **Cecil Sharp House** has regular shows for folk purists, while the **ICA** (see p94) hosts innovative acts. **Cargo** in Shoreditch has an eclectic programme of live music that includes African beats and Latin funk. Hot Latin nights can be found at **Cuba Libre** in Islington, and laid-back vibes pervade the **Notting Hill Arts Club**. For all French Caribbean and African sounds, you could check **Le Café de Piaf** inside Waterloo Station; and for the widest selection of African sounds and food in town, try visiting the **Africa Centre** in Covent Garden. The **Barbican Centre**, the **Royal Festival Hall** and the **Queen Elizabeth Hall** at the Southbank Centre all offer plenty of world music.

Clubs

The old cliché that London dies when the pubs shut no longer holds true. Europe has long scoffed at Londoners going to bed at 11pm when the night is only just beginning in Paris, Madrid and Rome, but London has caught on at last and you can revel all night if you want to. The best clubs are not all confined to the city's centre – initial disappointment that your hotel is a half-hour tube-ride from Leicester Square can be offset by the discovery of a trendy club right on your doorstep.

Etiquette

Fashions and club nights change very rapidly and nightspots open and close down all the time. Some of the best club nights are one-nighters – check the listings magazines (see p334). Be aware that there are sometimes bouncers on the door, enforcing a variety of dress or other appearance codes for a particular club. If you are set on visiting one of these, do some research before you go.

A few clubs require that you arrange membership 48 hours in advance, and you may also find that you have to be introduced by a member. Again, check these details in the listings magazines. Groups of men may not be welcome, so split up and find a woman to go in with; expect to queue to get in. Entrance fees may seem reasonable, but drinks tend to be over-priced.

Opening times are usually 10pm–3am Monday to Saturday, although many clubs stay open until 6am at the weekend and some open on Sunday from about 8pm to midnight.

Mainstream

London offers a broad selection of nightclubs that cater for all musical tastes and budgets.

Most of the more upmarket nightclubs in London, for example **Annabel's**, have a strict members-only policy; they require nominations by current members and have long waiting lists, so unless you mix in privileged circles you are unlikely to get in.

Traditional disco-type clubs which are easier to enter include the **Café de Paris**, where you can dine and boogie the night away. For those with a lust for samba and Latin beats **Guanabara** in Covent Garden is friendly, unpretentious and fun.

Further north, the **Forum** hosts popular club nights, which feature classic soul, funk and rhythm and blues. Similar clubs are **East Village** in Shoreditch and the **Tattershall Castle**, a disco boat moored on the bank of the Thames.

Fashionable Venues and Club Nights

Over the last few years London has become one of the most innovative and sought-after club capitals in the world. It is now a major stage where trends are set. **Heaven** hosts England's premier "house" night. With its huge dance floor, excellent lasers, sound systems and lightshows it's very popular, so start queuing early. **The Roxy** in Soho is a relaxed club and bar playing a mixture of indie, electronic, and pop (students get discounts). The **Ministry of Sound** is a New York-style club that set the pattern for others to follow, hosting some of the world's best-known DJs. If you are feeling energetic, club nights are also run at the **Queen of Hoxton** in Shoreditch. Try **Envy Nightclub** for funky house, electro and old skool, and for die-hard clubbers there's always **Fabric**. **Electric Brixton**, formely the much-loved Fridge, hosts club events and live music.

As with many clubs, **Bar Rumba** has different themes on different evenings, but if you like your dancing with a dash of spice and a lot of sauce, sashay along to its salsa night with dance classes also available. **Cargo**, the pioneering live/ mixed music venue, features some of London's funkiest sounds. **93 Feet East** showcases a variety of live music and club nights from indie and rock to techno beats. Dress in uniform for the "School Disco Night" with 70s, 80s and 90s sounds. It takes place on Saturdays in the **HMV Forum**, but check listings – it moves sometimes.

In Kensington, **The Roof Gardens** is London's only rooftop private members club. It opens on Friday and Saturday nights, admits over 21s only and has a "no effort, no entry" dress code. Apply for entry via the website, at www.roofgardensclub.com.

Gay

London has a number of gay nightclubs. The best-known and most popular is **Heaven**, with its huge dance floor and bar and video lounge under the arches of Charing Cross station. The **Queen of Hoxton** hosts mixed gay nights.

Transvestite

Watch for the occasional "Kinky Gerlinky" night in the listings magazines, an outrageously kitsch collection of drag queens and assorted exotica. In Soho, **Madame Jojo's** revue is a fabulous whirl of glittering colour and extreme high camp.

Casinos

To gamble in London, you must be a member, or at least the guest of a member, of a licensed gaming club. Most clubs are happy to let you join but membership must be arranged 48 hours in advance. Many will let you in to use facilities other than the gambling tables until about 4am, when most close. Try the excellent restaurants and bars, which are often subject to the usual licensing laws (see p308). Many clubs also have "hostesses" – beware the cost of their company.

DIRECTORY

Major Music Venues

Eventim Apollo
Queen Caroline St W6.
Tel 0844 249 4300 (tickets),
020 8563 3800 (venue).

The Forum
9–17 Highgate Rd NW5.
Tel 020 7428 4099.

O2 Academy Brixton
211 Stockwell Rd SW9.
Tel 0844 477 2000.

Royal Albert Hall
See p207.

SSE Arena, Wembley
Empire Way, Wembley,
Middlesex HA9.
Tel 0844 815 0815, 0844
824 4824.

Rock and Pop Venues

Barfly
49 Chalk Farm Rd NW1.
Map 4 F1.
Tel 020 7424 0800.

Betsey Trotwood
56 Farringdon Rd EC1.
Map 6 E4.
Tel 020 7253 4285.

Borderline
Orange Yard, Manette St
WC2. **Map** 13 B1.
Tel 020 7734 5547.

Hoxton Square Bar and Kitchen
2–4 Hoxton Sq N1.
Tel 020 7613 0709.

Koko
1a Camden High St NW1.
Map 4 F2.
Tel 0870 432 5527.

The Garage
20–22 Highbury Corner,
N5. **Tel** 0844 847 1678.

O2 Shepherd's Bush Empire
Shepherd's Bush Green
W12. **Tel** 0844 477 2000.

The Underworld
174 Camden High St
NW1. **Map** 4 F1.
Tel 020 7482 1932.

Union Chapel
The Vestry, Compton Ave
N1. **Tel** 020 7226 1686.

Jazz Venues

100 Club
100 Oxford St W1.
Map 13 A1.
Tel 020 7636 0933.

Barbican Hall
See p167.

Dover Street Restaurant and Bar
8–10 Dover St W1.
Map 12 F3.
Tel 020 7629 9813.

Jazz Café
5 Parkway NW1.
Map 4 E1.
Tel 020 7485 6834.

Mau Mau Bar
265 Portbello Rd W11.
Map 9 A1.
Tel 020 7229 8528.

Pizza Express
10 Dean St W1.
Map 13 A1.
Tel 0845 602 7017

Ronnie Scott's
47 Frith St W1.
Map 13 A2.
Tel 020 7439 0747.
w ronniescotts.co.uk

Royal Festival Hall
See p190.

Vortex Jazz Club
Dalston Culture House
Gillett St, N16.
Map 8 1D.
Tel 020 7245 4097.

World Music

Africa Centre
38 King St WC2.
Map 13 C2.
Tel 020 7836 1973.

Barbican Centre
See p167.

Cargo
83 Rivington St EC2.
Map 7 C3.
Tel 020 7739 3440.

Cecil Sharp House
2 Regent's Park Rd NW1.
Map 4 D1.
Tel 020 7485 2206.

Cuba Libre
72 Upper St N1.
Map 6 F1.
Tel 020 7354 9998.

ICA
See p94.

Notting Hill Arts Club
21 Notting Hill Gate W11.
Map 9 C3.
Tel 020 7460 4459.

Queen Elizabeth Hall
Southbank Centre SE1.
Map 14 D4.
Tel 020 7960 4200.

Royal Festival Hall
See p190.

Clubs

93 Feet East
150 Brick Lane,
Shoreditch E1.
Map 8 E4.
Tel 020 7770 6006.

Annabel's
44 Berkeley Sq W1.
Map 12 E3.
Tel 020 7629 1096.

Bar Rumba
36 Shaftesbury Ave WC2.
Map 6 E2.
Tel 020 7287 6933.

Café de Paris
3 Coventry St W1.
Map 13 A3.
Tel 020 7734 7700.

Cargo
89 Rivington St EC2.
Map 7 C3.
Tel 020 7749 7840.

East Village
89 Great Eastern St EC2.
Map 7 C4.
Tel 020 7739 5173.

Electric Brixton
Town Hall Parade, Brixton
Hill SW2.
Tel 020 7274 2290.

Fabric
77a Charterhouse St EC1.
Map 6 F5.
Tel 020 7336 8898.

Gate Restaurant, Bar and Club
87 Notting Hill Gate W11.
Tel 020 7727 9007.

Guanabara
Drury Lane WC2. **Map** 13
C1. **Tel** 020 7242 8600.

Heaven
Under the Arches, Villiers
St WC2. **Map** 13 C3.
Tel 020 7930 2020.

Madame Jojo's
8–10 Brewer St W1. **Map**
13 A2. **Tel** 020 7734 3040.

Ministry of Sound
103 Gaunt St SE1.
Tel 020 7740 8600.

Queen of Hoxton
1 Curtain Rd EC2.
Map 7 C3.
Tel 020 7422 0958.

Tattershall Castle
Victoria Embankment,
SW1. **Map** 13 C3.
Tel 07584 680 186.

The Roof Gardens
99 Kensington High St
W8. **Map** 10 D5.
Tel 020 7937 7994.

The Roxy
3–5 Rathbone Place W1.
Map 13 A1.
Tel 020 7255 1098.

Sport

The range of sports on offer in London is quite phenomenal. Should you feel the urge to watch a game of medieval tennis or go scuba-diving in the city centre, you've come to the right place. More likely, you'll just want to watch a football or rugby match, or play a set of tennis in a park. With far more public facilities than most European capitals, London is the place to enjoy cheap, accessible sport. Wembley Stadium, the national stadium for football, is located in north-west London. The Olympic Stadium, Aquatics Centre and other venues were built in Stratford for the 2012 Olympic Games. Events were also held at venues across the city.

Athletics

Athletes will find a good choice of running tracks, often with free admission. **Linford Christie Stadium** has good facilities; **Regent's Park** is free; try also **Parliament Hill Fields**. For a sociable jog, meet the Bow Street Runners at **Jubilee Hall** on Tuesdays at 6pm.

Cricket

Five-day test matches and one-day internationals are played in summer at **Lord's** (see p248) and the **Kia Oval**, near Vauxhall. Tickets for the first four days of tests and for one-day games are hard to get, but you may get in on the last day and see a thrilling finish. When Middlesex and Surrey play county games at these grounds, there are always seats.

Football (Soccer)

This is the most popular spectator sport in Britain, its season running from August to May, with matches on weekends and weekday evenings. It is the most common topic of conversation in pubs, where games are often shown live on TV. Premier League and FA Cup games are frequently sold out in advance. London's top clubs include **Arsenal, Chelsea, West Ham** and **Tottenham Hotspur**.

Golf

There are no golf courses in central London, but a few are scattered around the outskirts. The most accessible public courses are **Hounslow Heath, Chessington** (nine holes, train from Waterloo) and **Richmond Park** (two courses, computerized indoor teaching room). If you didn't pack your clubs, sets can be hired at a reasonable price.

Greyhound Racing

At a night "down the dogs", you can follow the races on a screen in the bar, stand by the track or watch from the comfort of the restaurant (book in advance) at **Romford Stadium** or **Wimbledon Stadium**.

Horse Racing

High class flat racing in summer and steeplechasing in winter can be seen at **Ascot, Kempton Park** and **Sandown Park**, which are all less than an hour from central London by train. Britain's most famous flat race, the Derby, is run at **Epsom** in June.

Horse-Riding

For centuries, fashionable riders have exercised their steeds in Hyde Park; **Ross Nye** will provide you with a horse so that you can follow a long tradition.

Ice-Skating

Ice-skaters should head for London's best-known rink, **Queens**. The most attractive ice rinks, open only in winter, are at **Somerset House** (see p119) and at the **Tower of London** (see pp156–9).

Rugby Football

Rugby union, or rugger, is a 15-a-side game, once played only by amateurs, but now a professional sport. International matches are played at **Twickenham Rugby Football Ground**. The season runs from September to April and you can watch "friendly" weekend games at local grounds. Top London teams **Saracens** and **Rosslyn Park** can be seen at their own grounds outside the centre of town.

Squash

Squash courts tend to be busy, so try to book at least two days ahead. Many sports centres have squash facilities and will hire out equipment, including **Swiss Cottage Sports Centre** and the **Oasis Sports Centre**.

Swimming

Best indoor pools include **Chelsea Sports Centre**, the **Oasis** and **Porchester Baths**; for outdoor swimming, try **Highgate and Hampstead Ponds** (two separate ponds for men and women and one mixed) and the **Oasis**.

Tennis

There are hundreds of tennis courts in London's public parks, most of them cheap to hire and easily reserved. It can be busy in the summer, so book your court two or three days ahead. You must supply your own racquet and balls. Good public tennis courts include **Holland Park** and **Parliament Hill**.

Tickets for the Centre Court of the **All England Lawn Tennis Club** at Wimbledon are hard to obtain – it is possibly easier to enter the tournament as a player than to obtain tickets for Centre Court; try queueing overnight, or queue for return tickets after lunch on the day – for a bargain price, you can still enjoy a good four hours of tennis (see p59).

Traditional Sports

An old London tradition is the University Boat Race, held in March or April, when teams from Oxford and Cambridge row from Putney to Mortlake *(see p58)*; a newer tradition is the London Marathon, which is run from Greenwich to The Mall at Westminster *(see p58)* on an April Sunday. You can watch croquet at **Dulwich Croquet Club** and medieval (real) tennis at **Queen's Club**.

Water Sports

There are facilities for a wide variety of water sports at the **Docklands Sailing & Water Sports Centre**. You can choose from sports such as windsurfing, dinghy sailing, powerboating, waterskiing and canoeing. Rowing boats are also available for hire by the hour on the calmer, central London waters of the **Serpentine** in Hyde Park and **Regent's Park Lake**.

Working Out

Most sports centres have gymnasiums, work-out studios and health clubs. If you are a member of the YMCA, you'll be able to use the excellent facilities at the **Central YMCA**. **Jubilee Hall Clubs** and the **Oasis Sports Centre** both offer a variety of aerobic classes, keep-fit and weight training. For those who have overdone it, the **Chelsea Sports Centre** has a sports injury clinic.

DIRECTORY

All England Lawn Tennis and Croquet Club
Church Rd, Wimbledon SW19. **Tel** 020 8944 1066.

Arsenal (Emirates) Stadium
Ashburton Grove N7.
Tel 020 7619 5000.

Ascot Racecourse
Ascot, Berkshire.
Tel 0844 346 3000.

Central YMCA
112 Great Russell St WC1.
Map 13 B1.
Tel 020 7343 1844.

Chelsea Football Club
Stamford Bridge SW6.
Tel 0871 984 1955.

Chelsea Sports Centre
Chelsea Manor St SW3.
Map 19 B3.
Tel 020 7352 6985, 020 7352 9006.

Chessington Golf Course
Garrison Lane, Surrey.
Tel 020 8391 0948.

Docklands Sailing & Watersports Centre
235a Westferry Rd, E14.
Tel 020 7537 2626.
w dswc.org

Dulwich Croquet Club
Giant Arches Rd, Off Burbage Rd SE24.
w dulwichcroquet.com

Epsom Racecourse
Epsom Downs, Surrey.
Tel 01372 726 311.

Hampstead and Highgate Ponds
Mixed: off East Heath Rd NW3. **Map** 1 C4. Men's and Women's: Millfield Lane N6. **Map** 2 E3.
Tel 020 7485 3873.

Holland Park Public Tennis Courts
1 Ilchester Place W8. **Map** 9 B5. **Tel** 020 7602 2226.

Hounslow Heath Golf Course
Staines Rd, Middlesex TW4.
Tel 020 8570 5271.

Jubilee Hall Clubs
30 The Piazza, Covent Garden WC2. **Map** 13 C2.
Tel 020 7836 4007.

Kempton Park
Sunbury on Thames, Middx.
Tel 01932 753 518.

Kia Oval
Kennington Oval SE11.
Map 22 D4.
Tel 0844 375 1845.

Linford Christie Stadium
Du Cane Rd W12.
Tel 07908 788 739.

Lord's Cricket Ground
St John's Wood NW8.
Map 3 A3.
Tel 020 7616 8500.

Oasis Swimming Pool & Sports Centre
32 Endell St WC2. **Map** 13 B1. **Tel** 020 7831 1804.

Parliament Hill
Highgate Rd NW5. **Map** 2 E5. **Tel** 020 7332 3773.

Porchester Centre
Queensway W2. **Map** 10 D1. **Tel** 020 7792 2919.

Queen's Club (Real Tennis)
Palliser Rd W14. **Map** 17 A3. **Tel** 020 7385 3400.

Queens Ice Skating Club
17 Queensway W2.
Map 10 E2.
Tel 020 7229 0172.

Regent's Park and Lake
Regent's Park NW1.
Map 3 C3. **Tel** 0300 061 2300, 020 7724 4069 (boat hire).

Richmond Park Golf
Roehampton Gate, Priory Lane SW15.
Tel 020 8876 3205.

Romford Stadium
London Road, Essex RM7.
Tel 01708 762 345.

Rosslyn Park Rugby
Priory Lane, Upper Richmond Rd SW15.
Tel 020 8876 1879.

Ross Nye Stables
8 Bathurst Mews W2. **Map** 11 A2. **Tel** 020 7262 3791.

Sandown Park Racecourse
Esher, Surrey.
Tel 01372 464 348.

Saracens Rugby Football Club
5 Vicarage Rd, Watford, Hertfordshire, WD1.
Tel 01727 792 800.

Serpentine
Hyde Park W2. **Map** 11 B4.
Tel 020 7262 1330 (boat hire).

Somerset House Ice Rink
Strand WC2. **Map** 14 D2.
Tel 0844 847 1520.

Tottenham Hotspur FC
White Hart Lane, 748 High Rd N17.
Tel 0844 499 5000.

Twickenham Rugby Ground
Whitton Rd, Twickenham, Middlesex.
Tel 020 8892 8877.

West Ham United
Boleyn Ground, Green St, Upton Park E13.
Tel 0871 529 1966.

CHILDREN'S LONDON

London offers children a potential goldmine of fun, excitement and adventure. Each year there are new attractions and sights opening up and older ones being updated.

First-time visitors may want to watch traditional ceremonies *(see pp54–7)* or visit famous buildings, but these are merely the tip of the iceberg. While London's parks, zoos and adventure playgrounds provide outdoor activities there are also loads of workshops, activity centres and museums providing quizzes, hands-on experiments and interactive displays. A day out need not be costly; children under 11 are entitled to free tube, bus and DLR travel provided they are travelling with an adult who has a valid ticket or Oyster Card, and most museums are free to everyone anyway.

Practical Advice

A little planning is the key to a successful outing with children. You may want to check the opening hours of the places you plan to visit in advance, by telephone or online via the venue's website. Work out your journey carefully using the tube map at the end of this book.

If you are travelling with very young children, remember that there are very likely to be queues at the Underground stations or bus stops near popular sights. These will be long during peak hours, so buy your tickets, Travelcard or Oyster Card in advance *(see p370)*.

Children under 11 can travel free on buses and tubes and child fares operate for all children between the ages of 11 and 15. Children very often enjoy using public transport, especially when it's a novelty, so plan your outing carefully using one form of transport for the outward journey and another for the journey home. You can get

Punch and Judy show in the Piazza, Covent Garden

around London easily by bus, Underground, taxi, train and riverboat *(see pp370–77)*.

Visiting all the exhibitions and museums as a family doesn't have to be as expensive as it sounds. The majority of London's principal museums have no entry charge. For those where you do have to pay, an annual family season ticket, usually for two adults and up to four children, is available. This often costs only marginally more than the initial visit. In some cases you can buy a family ticket that covers a group of museums. Being able to visit a sight more than once means that you won't exhaust your children and put them off museums for life by trying to see absolutely everything over one long, tiring day.

If your children want a break from sightseeing, most borough councils provide information on activities for children such as playgroups, theatres, fun-fairs and activity centres in their area. Leaflets are usually available from libraries and leisure centres, as well as local town halls. During the long summer school holidays (July to the beginning of September) there are organized activity programmes all over London.

Children and the Law

Children under 14 are not allowed into British pubs and wine bars (unless there is a special family room or garden) and only people over 18 can drink or buy any alcohol. In restaurants, the law is a little more relaxed. Those over 16 can drink wine or beer with their meal, but you still have to be over 18 to be served spirits. In general, young children are rarely welcome anywhere they might create a nuisance. Some films are classed as unsuitable for children *(see p339)*.

If you want to take your children by car, you must use seat belts wherever they are

Covent Garden clowns

Eating Out with Children

Restaurants are becoming more welcoming of tiny patrons. Italian eateries, such as Ask and Pizza Express, are often the most friendly, but even the traditional British pub, once resolutely child-free, has relented, with beer gardens and family rooms. As long as your offspring are reasonably well-behaved, most informal restaurants will be happy to serve a family. Some can also provide highchairs and booster cushions, as well as colouring mats to keep children entertained while waiting for their food to arrive. Many will also offer special children's menus with small helpings, which will cut the cost of your meal.

Over the weekend, some restaurants (such as **Smollensky's** and **Sticky Fingers**) provide live entertainment for children in the form of clowns, face painters and magicians. It is always worth trying to book in advance (especially for Sunday lunch), so that you don't have to hang around waiting with tired and hungry children.

Coming up for air at Smollensky's

London has a number of restaurants ideal for older children. Among these are the **Jamie's Italian** and the **Leon**, both of which have many branches across the city.

For budget eating, try the Café in the Crypt, St Martin-in-the-Fields (*see p104*).

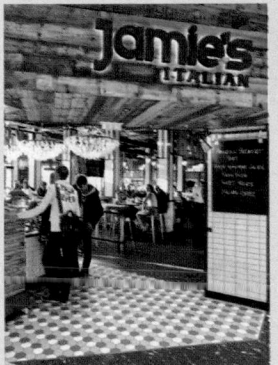
Dine at Jamie's Italian restaurant

Useful Addresses

Jamie's Italian
11 Upper St Martin's Lane WC2. **Map** 13 B2. **Tel** 020 3326 6390.

Leon
73–76 Strand WC2. **Map** 13 C3. **Tel** 020 7240 3070.

Smollensky's
105 Strand WC2. **Map** 14 D2. **Tel** 020 7497 2101.

Sticky Fingers
1a Phillimore Gdns, W8. **Map** 9 C5. **Tel** 020 7938 5338.

provided. Children below 135 cm (4ft 5 inches) or under 12 years need a special car seat.

Family Fun

Many London museums (*see pp42–5*) and theatres (*see pp336–8*) provide brilliant activities and workshops; crafts sessions, story times, child-friendly trails around museums or historic sites, or themed events specifically designed to get children engaged in and interacting with the exhibits and information on display. Some activities are educational; others purely for the fun of it. The children's theatres are also a great way to spend a rainy afternoon. A day at the fair is always a success – try Hampstead fair on summer bank holidays. London has a great many sports centres (*see pp346–7*), which often have special clubs to occupy

children of every age. For more family-friendly ideas, see DK's *Family Guide to London*.

If you need childcare or babysitting facilities, call **Nannies Unlimited, Sitters, Kensington Nannies**, or **Pippa Pop-Ins**, a nursery school offering childcare. Childminders are verified by the DBS check.

Childminding

Kensington Nannies
3 Hornton Place W8. **Map** 10 D5. **Tel** 020 7937 2333.
W kensington-nannies.com

Nannies Unlimited
64 The Moores, Redhill, Surrey, RH1 2PE. **Tel** 01737 643918.

Pippa Pop-Ins
430 Fulham Road SW6. **Map** 18 D5. **Tel** 020 7731 1445.
Also at 233 New King's Rd SW6.

Sitters
Tel 08447 367367.
W sitters.co.uk

Airborne at the Hampstead fair

Holiday fun at Pippa Pop-Ins

Shopping

All children love a visit to **Hamleys** toy shop or Harrods toy department *(see p313)*. **Davenport's Magic Shop** and **Victoria Park Books** are smaller and more specialized.

Both the **Early Learning Centre** (many branches) and **Children's Bookshop** have good selections of books. Some shops organize readings and signings by children's authors, especially during Children's Book Week, held in October.

Useful Numbers & Websites
Children's Bookshop **Tel** 020 8444 5500; Davenport's Magic Shop **Tel** 020 7836 0408; Victoria Park Books **Tel** 020 8986 1124; Early Learning Centre **W** elc.com; Hamleys **Tel** 0870 333 2455.

Bears at Hamleys toy shop

Museums and Galleries

London has a wealth of museums, exhibitions and galleries; more information on those listed here is to be found on pages 42–45. Most have been updated over the last few years to incorporate some exciting modern display techniques. It's unlikely that you'll have to drag reluctant children around an assortment of lifeless, stuffy exhibits.

The British Museum *(pp126–9)* has fabulous treasures from all over the world, and the Horniman Museum *(p252)* has interactive displays from many different cultures. The Science Museum *(pp208–9)*, with over 600 working exhibits, is one of London's best attractions for children – its hands-on galleries in the basement, including the much-loved Launch Pad, will help keep them amused for hours. The interactive displays in the high-tech Wellcome Wing are also entertaining. Popular with families, the Natural History Museum *(pp204–5)* next door contains hundreds of amazing objects and animals from the world of nature. Included is a Dinosaur Exhibition. Suits of armour built for knights and monarchs can be seen at the Tower of London *(pp156–9)*. More up-to-date armoury and weapons, including aircraft and the tools of modern warfare, can be seen at the National Army Museum *(p199)* and the Imperial War Museum *(pp192–3)*. Also worth a visit is the Guards' Museum *(p83)* located on Birdcage Walk. London's colourful past is brought alive at the Museum of London. The superb, but expensive, London Aquarium *(p190)*, on the bank of the

Shirley Temple doll at Bethnal Green Museum

Thames, offers close-up encounters with sea life from starfish to sharks.

The V&A Museum of Childhood *(p250)*, the children's branch of the V&A in East London, and Pollock's Toy Museum *(p133)* are both especially good for young children.

For older children, try one of London's Brass Rubbing Centres: the great Brass Rubbing Centre in the Crypt of St Martin-in-the-Fields *(p104)* or at St James's Church on Piccadilly *(p92)*. Madame Tussauds *(p226)* and Tower Bridge *(p155)* are firm favourites with children.

The Great Outdoors

London is fortunate in having many parks and open spaces *(see pp50–53)*. Most local parks contain conventional playgrounds for children, many with modern, safe equipment. Some parks also have One O'Clock Clubs (enclosed areas for children under five with activities supervised by play-workers) as well as adventure playgrounds, nature trails, boating ponds and athletic tracks for older children and energetic adults. A delightful

Puppets at the Little Angel Theatre, Islington

Playground at Gunnersbury Park

children's park in Bloomsbury is Coram's Fields (p131), where grassy areas, sand-pits and playgrounds make it perfect for picnics. Kite-flying on Blackheath (p245), Hampstead Heath or Parliament Hill can be fun, as can boating in Regent's Park. A trip to Primrose Hill (pp266–7) can be combined with a visit to the Zoo and Regent's Canal (p229). The large parks are one of London's greatest assets for parents who have energetic children.

For a good walk or cycle ride, there are parks all over London. For instance, there's Hyde Park in the city centre; Hampstead Heath up in the north; Wimbledon Common in southwest London; and Gunnersbury Park in west London. Cyclists should be sure to watch out for pedestrians and remember that some paths may be out of bounds.

Battersea Park has a children's zoo and Crystal Palace Park (Penge SE20) has a dinosaur park. Richmond Park has a deer herd. For a relaxing trip, go and feed the ducks in St James's Park.

Children's Theatre

Introducing children to the theatre can be great fun for adults too. Get involved at the **Little Angel Theatre,** or the **Puppet Theatre Barge** in Little Venice. The **Unicorn Theatre** offers the best range of children's theatre and the **Polka Children's Theatre** has some good shows.

Useful Numbers

Little Angel Theatre
Tel 020 7226 1787.

Polka Children's Theatre
Tel 020 8543 4888.
W polkatheatre.com

**Puppet Theatre Barge
Marionette Performers**
Tel 020 7249 6876.
W puppetbarge.com

Unicorn Theatre
Tel 020 7645 0560.
W unicorntheatre.com

Deer in Richmond Park

Sightseeing

For seeing the sights of London, you can't beat the top of a double-decker bus (see pp374–5). It's a cheap and easy way of entertaining children, and if they get restless, you can always jump off the bus at the next stop.

London's colourful ceremonies are detailed on pages 54–7. Children will also enjoy such spectacles as the summer fun-fairs in

Boating lake near Winfield House in Regent's Park

London's parks, the firework displays throughout London on Guy Fawkes Night (every 5 November) and the Christmas decorations in Oxford Street and Regent Street and Trafalgar Square's Christmas tree.

Behind the Scenes

Older children in particular will love the opportunity to look "behind the scenes" and see how famous events or institutions are run.

If you have a brood of sports enthusiasts, you should visit Twickenham Rugby Football Ground (see p347), Lord's Cricket Ground (p248), the Wimbledon Lawn Tennis Museum (p253), and Chelsea Football Stadium (p347).

For budding theatre buffs, the Royal National Theatre (p190), the Royal Opera House (p117), Sadler's Wells (p342), and the Theatre Royal Drury Lane (p117) all offer tours.

Other good buildings for children to visit include the Tower of London (pp156–9), the Old Bailey law courts (p149) and the Houses of Parliament (pp74–5).

If none of the above satisfies the children, the London Fire Brigade (020 7587 4063) offers more unusual guided tours.

Tuojiangasaurus skeleton at the Natural History Museum

SURVIVAL
GUIDE

Practical Information   354–63

Getting to London   364–69

Getting Around London   370–77

PRACTICAL INFORMATION

London has responded well to the demands of modern tourism. The range of facilities on offer to travellers, from ATMs and medical clinics to boutique hotels and late-night transport, continues to expand. Whether you find London an expensive city will depend on the exchange rate between the pound and your own currency. It is known for high hotel prices, but even here there are good mid-range and budget options *(see pp280–3)*. You need not spend a lot on food, if you choose carefully and make the most of the range London has to offer; for the price of a single meal at some West End restaurants you could eat enjoyably for several days *(see pp304–7)*. The following tips will help you make the most of your visit.

Crossing the Millennium Bridge

When to Go

London's weather is famously changeable, but in general it is chilly from November to February, and warmest from June to August *(see p61)*. It can rain at any time of year, so pack accordingly. Extremes of temperature – whether of cold in winter or heat in summer – are rare, so there is no time of year when London "closes down" and everyone goes on holiday. Events and cultural programmes run throughout the year. Many major concert series and exhibitions take place in winter and spring, but there are plenty of cultural events during the summer too, such as the BBC Proms season of classical concerts, and open-air theatre seasons. In short, there's plenty to see all year round *(see pp58–61)*.

Visas and Passports

Citizens of European Union countries may enter the UK for an unlimited period with a passport or national identity card. Visitors from the United States, Canada, Australia and New Zealand need only a full passport for tourist and business stays of up to six months, but on arrival they must fill in an Immigration Card, which is given out on incoming flights. Citizens of some countries may require a visa; details can be found in the "Visa Services" section of the **UK Border Agency** (UKBA) website. The UK is not signed up to the Schengen open-borders agreement operated by most EU countries. Hence, visitors arriving from France or any other Schengen country must still pass through immigration checks when entering the UK.

The UKBA has a strict points-based visa system under which anyone from any non-EU country (including the USA, Canada, Australia and New Zealand) entering Britain for any purpose other than pure tourism or short business trips (this includes students on short study-abroad programmes) must obtain a visa before travelling. The visa system is complicated and detailed, so check well in advance; details are on the UKBA website.

Signposted directions

Customs Information

EU residents may carry any amount of goods between EU countries without paying duty, as long as the goods are for their personal use. Customs officers can still question whether large amounts of any item are genuinely for your own use. Examples of amounts usually accepted are: up to 3,200 cigarettes and up to 90 litres of wine. For travellers arriving from outside the EU, stricter allowances apply – for example, 200 cigarettes. Visitors not resident in the EU can reclaim the Value Added Tax (VAT) on many goods when they leave Britain, but note that the items must have been bought from a shop operating the VAT Retail Export Scheme (which should be indicated in the shop window). Ask the retailer for the correct form, which has details on how to obtain your refund; these can also be found on the UKBA website under "Travel and Customs".

Tourist Information and Tours

Visit London is the city's central tourism service and is a key source of information. Tourist Information Centres can be found all over London (visit www.london.com has a full list). The City of London Information Centre, located by St Paul's Cathedral, provides leaflets on attractions, tours, museums, walks and public transport. Others can be found at main rail stations. The centres sell travel-cards and **London Pass** *(see p355)* discount cards, provide currency exchange and distribute Visit London's handy free monthly magazine, *London Planner*.

For comprehensive listings information – including art, cinema, music, theatre and nightlife – visit the websites of **LondonNet** and *Time Out London*, London's leading listings magazine.

Double-decker sightseeing boat on the Thames

Guided tours are an effective way to explore the city; a trip in an open-topped double-decker bus makes a good introduction. **Original London Sightseeing Tours** and **Big Bus Tours** are the main companies offering hop-on, hop-off services, with tickets valid for 24 or 48 hours. Other tour companies include **London Walks**, which offers over 40 different routes, and **London Duck Tours**, for tours in a World-War II era vehicle. To find a private tour guide to suit your interests, contact the **Association of Professional Tourist Guides**. For river cruises and commuter services, see page 63.

Major sights in London are often crowded with long queues. Museums and galleries get particularly busy at weekends and on late-opening nights, so try to visit midweek.

Admission Prices

Admission to the main collections of London's major public museums and galleries is free, but you will pay to see temporary exhibits. Private museums and other attractions have admission charges; they vary greatly, but for adults most are between £5 and £15. There are often reduced prices for seniors, students and children.

If you aim to do lots of sightseeing, you can cut costs with a **London Pass**, a card that gives you free entry and fast-track admission at many attractions. Cards are valid for 1, 2, 3 or 6 days and can be combined with a bus and Underground travelcard. A London Pass can be bought in advance from www.visitlondon.com and mailed to your home or collected from a tourist centre.

Opening Hours

Opening times for individual sights are listed in the *Area by Area* section of this book. Core visiting times are 10am to 5pm or 6pm daily; last admission is usually 1 hour before closing time. Most of the big museums have at least one late-opening day each week. Opening hours are often shorter on Sundays and public holidays. Some smaller attractions are closed on Mondays.

Social Customs and Etiquette

Londoners are traditionally renowned for queueing – whether for theatre tickets, taxis or takeaways. Things aren't quite as genteel as they used to be, but in general, anyone barging in will still encounter frosty glares.

Casual clothing is accepted in most restaurants, and only a few upscale establishments still require men to wear a jacket and tie.

The religious pattern of London reflects the city's huge ethnic diversity; all of the world's major faiths are represented here.

Smoking is forbidden in all public indoor spaces. Some hotels still designate bedrooms for smokers, but it's best to double check when booking.

Tipping

It is usual to tip in restaurants, hotels, hairdressers, taxis and minicabs, but not for bar service in pubs. Many restaurants add a service charge – usually 12.5 per cent – to the bill, in which case an extra tip is not necessary. Be wary of places that add a service charge, then encourage you to add a "gratuity" when you pay by credit card. In taxis and cabs, tip around 10 per cent; for hotel porters, £1 is usually sufficient.

Travellers with Special Needs

Access to transport and attractions, and services for wheelchair users and others with mobility problems is continually improving. The Visit London website has a guide to access and services. **Transport for London** (TfL) produces a *Getting around London* guide, which can be downloaded from the TfL or Visit London websites, and is available free from Underground stations. **Artsline** gives information on facilities at cultural events and venues.

Nearly all London buses have wheelchair-access ramps, and all licensed taxis and some mini-cabs are wheelchair-accessible. The huge task of improving access to the entire Underground network is ongoing. Underground maps show accessible stations. Most museums and theatres have access facilities, but hotels with fully adapted rooms are scarce.

Disabled drivers with a blue badge allowing free parking should note that in four London boroughs – the City, Westminster, Kensington & Chelsea, and Camden – it allows you to park only in designated blue-badge bays.

London bus with ramp for easy wheelchair access

The Natural History Museum, a great day out for the whole family

Travelling with Children

Under Transport for London's "Kids Go Free" scheme, travel is free on buses, the Underground, DLR and trains within London for all children aged under 11 accompanied by an adult (up to four children per adult). Children aged 11–15 can also travel free, with or without an adult, on all buses, and for reduced prices on the Underground and DLR (see p370); also available is a Zip Oyster 11–15 Identity Card, which can be ordered online and collected at a tourist information centre on arrival in London; see the Visit London and Transport for London websites.

Most museums and attractions have reduced prices for children under 11; at several, entry is free for under-5s. Many also offer good-value family tickets. Plenty of restaurants welcome children, and a number of hotels have family rooms; the Novotel chain represents particularly good value for families.

London is a child-friendly city. A huge variety of entertainment and activities are laid on for children, and many museums have special kids' programmes. There are dozens of parks, many of them with playground facilities. The Visit London website's "Family" pages are a useful source of information. *Time Out London's* "Kids" pages are good for current attractions.

Senior Travellers

Older visitors enjoy fewer special benefits than younger ones, but there are reduced admission prices for over-60s at most museums and other attractions. You may be asked to show photo ID. Free travel on public transport is only available to residents.

Gay and Lesbian Travellers

London has a huge and diverse gay scene. Its core is Soho – it even has a (non-official) **LGBT Tourist Office**, which offers advice on everything from the best gay bars to accommodation. It's hard to keep track of everything going on, but the **Pink Paper** and **Gay London** websites, as well as the gay pages of *Time Out London*, have up-to-date information.

Travelling on a Budget

London can be a very expensive city, but sightseeing costs can be cut with the London Pass (see p355), and remember that admission to London's largest museums is free. To get around town by public transport, always buy a travelcard rather than single tickets; for trips out of town, coach is much cheaper than train, especially when booked in advance. Discounted theatre tickets can be bought at the **tkts** booth in Leicester Square, and many theatres have cheap-ticket nights.

London has plenty of budget restaurants and cafés, and even quite grand restaurants offer accessibly priced lunch menus. As well as dorm- style hostels, there are no-frills budget hotels with private rooms, some ensuite, for under £50 (see p283). There's also a growing trend for spare-room lets and "couch surfing" via the **Airbnb** website.

Students pay lower admission to many exhibitions, and holders of an **ISIC** (International Student Identity Card) or IYTC (International Youth Travel Card) are eligible for a range of other discounts. A **Hostelling International** card is also handy for lower rates at hostels and other discounts.

Electricity

The voltage in London is 240V AC, and plugs have three square pins. Visitors will need plug adaptors for appliances, and with any older North American 110V equipment you may also need a current transformer.

Conversion Chart

Officially the metric system is used, but imperial measures are still common.

Imperial to metric
1 inch = 2.5 centimetres
1 foot = 30 centimetres
1 mile = 1.6 kilometres
1 ounce = 28 grams
1 pound = 454 grams
1 pint = 0.6 litre
1 gallon = 4.6 litres

Metric to imperial
1 millimetre = 0.04 inch
1 centimetre = 0.4 inch
1 metre = 3 feet 3 inches
1 kilometre = 0.6 mile
1 gram = 0.04 ounce
1 kilogram = 2.2 pounds

International Student Identity Card (ISIC)

Time

London is on Greenwich Mean Time (GMT) during the winter months, five hours ahead of Eastern Standard Time and ten hours behind Sydney. From late March to late October, clocks are set forward 1 hour to British Summer Time (equivalent to Central European Time). At any time of year, you can check the correct time by dialing 123 on a BT landline to contact the 24-hour automated Speaking Clock service (note that there is a charge for this service).

Responsible tourism

London has set itself ambitious targets for improving the urban environment and reducing energy use. **Thames 21**, for example, is an environmental charity which involves the local community in schemes to help keep the river Thames clean and clear.

The **Green Tourism Business Scheme** awards "Green Tourism" badges to businesses in the UK that meet the highest

Green Tourism badge

environmental standards. These standards ensure that each business is committed to sustainable tourism and dedicated to minimising its damage to the environment. See the website for green accommodation details.

Recycling bins, which separate paper and plastic are widely available and many shoppers carry reusable cloth bags to avoid using plastic bags.

DIRECTORY

Visas and Passports

UK Border Agency
W ukba.homeoffice. gov.uk

Embassies and Consulates

Australian High Commission
Australia House, The Strand, WC2.
Map 13 C2.
Tel 020 7379 4334.
W uk.embassy.gov.au

Canadian High Commission
1 Grosvenor Square, W1.
Map 12 D2. Tel 020 7258 6600. W unitedking dom.gc.ca

New Zealand High Commission
80 Haymarket, SW1.
Map 13 A3.
Tel 020 7930 8422.
W nzembassy.com/ united-kingdom

United States Embassy
24 Grosvenor Square, W1.
Map 12 D2.
Tel 020 7499 9000.
W usembassy.org.uk

Tourist Information

Association of Professional Tour Guides
Tel 020 7611 2545.
W guidelondon.org.uk

Big Bus Tours
Tel 020 7808 6753.
W eng.bigbustours.com

City of London Information Centre
St. Paul's Churchyard EC4M 8BX. **Map** 15 A2.
Open Daily.

London Duck Tours
Tel 020 7928 3132.
W londonducktours. co.uk

LondonNet
W londonnet.co.uk

London Pass
W londonpass.com

London Walks
Tel 020 7624 3978.
W walks.com

Original London Sightseeing Tour
Tel 020 8877 1722.
W theoriginaltour.com

Time Out London
W timeout.com/ london

Transport for London
W tfl.gov.uk

Visit London
W visitlondon.com

Religious Services

Anglican (Episcopalian)
St. Paul's Cathedral EC4.
Map 15 A2.
Tel 020 246 8350.
W stpauls.co.uk

Catholic
Westminster Cathedral, Victoria St SW1. **Map** 20 F1. Tel 020 7798 9055.
W westminster cathedral.org.uk

Evangelical Alliance
UK Resource Centre, 176 Copenhagen St N1.
Map 6 D1.
Tel 020 7520 3830.
W eauk.org

Jewish
Liberal Jewish Synagogue, 28 St John's Wood Rd NW8.
Map 3 A3. Tel 020 7286 5181. W ljs.org

United Synagogue (Orthodox)
735 High Rd, N12.
Tel 020 8343 8989.
W theus.org.uk

Muslim
Islamic Cultural Centre, 146 Park Rd NW8.
Map 3 B3.
Tel 020 7724 3363.
W iccuk.org

Travellers with Special Needs

Artsline
W artsline.org.uk

Transport for London
Tel 0843 222 1234 (24 hours).
W tfl.gov.uk

Gay & Lesbian Travellers

Diva
W divamag.co.uk

Gay London
W gaylondon.com

Gay Times
W gaytimes.co.uk

LGBT Tourist Information Office
25 Frith St, W1.
Map 13 B2.
Tel 020 7437 0003.
W gaytouristoffice. co.uk

Travelling on a Budget

Airbnb
W airbnb.com

Hostelling International
W hihostels.com

ISIC (International Student Identity Card)
W isiccard.com

tkts (Discount Theatre Tickets)
Leicester Square, WC2.
Map 13 B2. W tkts.co.uk

Responsible Tourism

Thames 21
W thames21.org.uk

Tourism Business Scheme
Tel 01738 632 162.
W greenbusiness.co.uk

Personal Security and Health

London is a large city which, like any other, has had its share of urban problems. It has also been a terrorist target, and London life is sometimes disrupted by security alerts. Nearly all of these turn out to be false alarms, but they should always still be taken seriously. Never hesitate to approach one of London's many police constables for assistance – they are trained to help the public with problems.

Mounted police

Police

If you are robbed, or are the victim of any other kind of crime, report it to the police as soon as possible. Patrolling police officers are generally fairly easy to find in central London, but if you cannot find one, call or go to the nearest police station – these are listed on the **Metropolitan Police** website; alternatively, your hotel should be able to advise. Note that the **City of London Police** is a separate force, with its own website. Police stations are also shown on the Street Finder maps towards the end of this book (*pp378–415*).

When you report a crime, police will take a statement from you, and you will need to list any lost or stolen items.

What to be Aware of

It is unlikely that your stay in London will be blighted by crime. Even in run-down parts of town, the risk of having your pocket picked or bag stolen is not particularly great. It is actually more likely to happen in the middle of heaving shopping crowds in areas like Oxford Street or Camden Lock, or perhaps on a packed Underground platform.

As in any big city, the risk of being a victim of street crime can be further reduced by following a few sensible precautions. Make sure your possessions are adequately insured before you travel.

Do not carry all your valuables around with you, but take only as much cash as you need, and leave the rest in a hotel safe or a locked suitcase.

Avoid poorly lit or isolated places like backstreets, parks and unmanned railway stations at night, and don't use ATMs after dark. To be extra careful, try to travel around in a group at night.

In crowds, be aware of anyone standing especially close. Keep bags zipped up; keep a hand on your bag when walking along; and never leave bags unattended in any public place – they may be stolen or considered a security threat. When you sit at a table, especially outdoors, always keep your bag within reach and in sight – preferably on your lap or on the table – and never leave it on the ground or hanging on the back of a chair.

In an Emergency

In a serious emergency, you can call 999 – or the European emergency number 112 – to summon police, fire or ambulance services. Note that this is only for genuine emergencies, so if you

Traffic police officer

have a lesser problem, it is better to contact a police station or hospital directly.

Lost and Stolen Property

Although you should report thefts, or loss of any property, to the police, be warned that it's unlikely that they will be able to recover any of it for you. However, they will give you a copy of your police statement, which you will need to make an insurance claim.

If you lose anything on buses, Underground and DLR trains or in taxis (black cabs), it should eventually reach the **Transport for London Lost Property Office** in Baker Street. You can also enquire about lost items online, through the TfL website (under "Help & Contact" or "Useful Contacts"). It will usually take a few days for items to reach the office, so if you notice the loss the same day, try to enquire about it at the station nearest to where you lost it, or at the nearest police station. Items lost on river boats or in minicabs should be held by the individual companies.

Hospitals and Pharmacies

All European Union nationals with a European Health Insurance Card (EHIC), as well as citizens of some other countries with special agreements with the UK (Australia and New Zealand among them), can obtain free treatment from the British **National Health Service (NHS)**. Visitors from other non-EU countries should have full medical cover as part of their travel insurance, and if necessary make use of an NHS or private hospital (such as **Medical Express**) on a paying basis.

Pharmacy sign

Typical London police car

London ambulance

London fire engine

In case of emergency, anyone – EU or non-EU – will be treated free of charge.

If you have an accident or other problem needing medical attention, ask your hotel to recommend a doctor, or go to the nearest NHS health centre (doctor's surgery) or hospital Accident & Emergency (A&E) department. Not all hospitals have A&E departments, but those that do are listed on the NHS and Visit London websites, and in local phone books. In many cases, the simplest thing may be to call **NHS Direct**, a free advice service that will give you immediate health advice and also direct you to the nearest hospital A&E department.

If you have a dental problem, you can also call NHS Direct for addresses of emergency dentists. Dental treatment through the NHS is not entirely free, so it may make more sense to arrange private treatment (again, hotels should be able to recommend a dentist) and claim on your insurance policy.

Pharmacies (also known as chemists) are plentiful around London, and pharmacists are trained to dispense and advise on a wide range of medications. Some medicines are only available with a prescription. It is worth noting that prescription drugs are not free even if you are entitled to NHS treatment; if you are not, you will be charged the full price, and so will need to make an insurance claim. **Boots** is the largest chain of pharmacies in the UK. Most pharmacies are closed on Sundays, but those listed in the Directory, below, have extended hours.

Travel and Health Insurance

All visitors to London should have a comprehensive travel insurance policy providing adequate cover for all eventualities including potential legal expenses, theft, lost luggage or other property, accidents, cancellations, travel delays and medical cover. Even if you are entitled to use the NHS for medical needs, it can be a good idea to have private medical insurance included too, as a backup, since this may allow you to get quicker treatment with fewer formalities. Your insurance company should provide you with a 24-hour emergency number in case of need.

DIRECTORY

Emergencies

Police, Fire & Ambulance services
Tel 999 or 112.
Calls are free.

Police

City of London Police
Tel 101 (non-emergencies).
w cityoflondon.
police.uk

Metropolitan Police
Tel 0300 123 1212.
w met.police.uk

West End Central Police Station
27 Saville Row, W1.
Map 12 F2.
Tel 020 7437 1212.

Lost Property

Transport for London Lost Property Office
200 Baker St, NW1.
Map 3 C5.
Tel 0343 222 1234.
Open 9am–5pm daily.
w tfl.gov.uk

Health Services

Medical Express (Private)
117A Harley St, W1.
Tel 0800 9800 700.
w medicalexpress
clinic.com

NHS
w nhs.uk
To locate a hospital, look under "Find and choose services".

NHS Direct
Tel 0845 4647.
w nhsdirect.nhs.uk
(24-hr health information and nurse-led advice).

University College Hospital
Accident and Emergency,
235 Euston Road NW1.
Map 5 A4.
Tel 0845 155 5000.

Dentists

24-Hour Emergency Dental Clinic
8F Gilbert Place WC1.
Map 13 B1.
Tel 020 3199 0178.
w 24hour-london-emergencydentist.co.uk

Late-opening Pharmacies

Bliss Chemist
5–6 Marble Arch W1.
Map 11 C2.
Tel 020 7723 6116. Open 9am until midnight daily.

Boots the Chemist
302 Regent St, W1.
Map 13 A3.
Tel 020 7637 9418.
Open 7:45am–8pm Mon–Fri, 9am–7pm Sat, noon–6pm Sun.
w boots.com

Superdrug
508–520 Oxford St, W1.
Map 11 C2. Tel 020 7629 1649. Open 7am–11pm Mon–Fri, 8am–10pm Sat, 12:30–6:30pm Sun.
w superdrug.com

Banking and Local Currency

Visitors to London will find that banks usually offer the best rates of exchange, but care should be taken to check the small-print details relating to commission and other charges before completing any transaction. Privately owned bureaux de change have variable exchange rates and commissions – some, in particular, charge more for changing smaller amounts of money – but they do stay open long after the banks have closed.

Cashpoint machine

Banks and Bureaux de Change

Banking hours vary. The minimum opening hours for all banks are 9:30am–3:30pm Mon–Fri, but many branches now stay open till 5 or 5:30pm, especially in central London; some also open on Saturdays from about 10am–4pm. All banks are closed on Sundays and public holidays (see p61). The commission charged on currency exchange will vary from bank to bank.

When banks are closed, there are plenty of other facilities for changing cash and traveller's cheques across the city. You will find bureaux de change at airports, main rail stations, in large stores, and at many other locations. **Chequepoint**, **Thomas Cook** and **Travelex** are some of the largest companies. The central London (Piccadilly) branch of **Money Corporation** is open 24 hours daily.

Credit Cards and Traveller's Cheques

Major credit cards such as Visa and MasterCard, and debit cards such as Delta, Maestro and Cirrus, are widely accepted all over London. Fewer businesses accept the American Express card, because of their high charges.

British credit and debit cards operate on a chip-and-PIN security system; you must enter your PIN number into a card reader to validate the purchase. If you have a North American or other card that does not use chip-and-pin technology, your card will have to be swiped in the more traditional way.

It may also be useful to have some currency with you in traveller's cheques, in case you lose your cards. Traveller's cheques cannot be used to pay for goods

DIRECTORY

Bureaux de Change

All have branches across London.

Chequepoint
Tel 1 800 528 4800.
W americanexpress.com

Money Corporation
18 Piccadilly, W1.
Map 13 A3.
Tel 08456 210 210.
Open 24-hrs daily.
W moneycorp.com

Thomas Cook
Tel 0845 246 4353.
W thomascook.com/money

Travelex
Tel 0845 872 7627.
W travelex.co.uk

Lost Credit Cards

American Express
Tel 01273 696 933.

MasterCard
Tel 0800 964 767.

Visa
Tel 0800 891 725.

directly in shops in the UK, but must be exchanged for cash at a bank or bureau de change. US dollar and Euro traveller's cheques are easily exchanged at all banks and change desks. Again, check the latest commission rates and conditions before cashing your cheques.

ATMs

There are ATM cash machines (also known as cashpoints), from which you can obtain cash with any of the major credit or debit cards, at all bank branches, many post offices and many other locations such as stations. The cards accepted by each ATM are indicated on the machine, which usually gives instructions in several languages. Given the high commission rates sometimes charged by banks and bureaux de change for exchanging traveller's cheques, the most economical, as well as most convenient, way to get cash can be to withdraw it from an ATM with a debit card.

Main High Street Banks

These are some of the high-street banks found all over London. Many will also offer currency-exchange facilities, but proof of identity may be required.

Santander logo

National Westminster logo

HSBC

HSBC logo

Barclays Bank logo

Lloyds TSB logo

Avoid using the independent ATMs found in some small shops, as they often carry expensive extra charges. There is also a certain risk of crime at some ATMs. Avoid using any in dark streets at night, and don't use an ATM if any part of it looks damaged or as if it has been tampered with, especially the card slot. Be aware of anyone standing close to you when

using an ATM, and shield the numbered keypad with your hand as you enter your PIN.

Currency

Britain's currency is the pound sterling (£), which is divided into 100 pence (p). Since there are no exchange controls in Britain, there is no limit to how much cash you may import or export. Many

large stores in London accept payments in US dollars and Euros, but often at a poor exchange rate.

English bank notes of all denominations always feature the Queen's head on one side

Bank Notes

English notes used in the UK are £5, £10, £20 and £50. Scotland has its own notes which, despite being legal tender throughout the UK, are often accepted with reluctance.

£50 note

£20 note

£10 note

£5 note

Coins of the Realm

Coins in circulation are £2, £1, 50p, 20p, 10p, 5p, 2p and 1p (they are shown here slightly smaller than actual size). They all have the Queen's head on the other side.

2 pounds (£2)

1 pound (£1)

50 pence (50p)

20 pence (20p)

10 pence (10p)

5 pence (5p)

2 pence (2p)

1 penny (1p)

Communication and Media

The telecommunications systems in Britain are efficient and inexpensive. Most static landline phones and public phoneboxes are operated by British Telecom (BT), and there are many other mobile phone operators and Internet service providers. Charges on BT lines depend on when, where and for how long you talk. National calls are most expensive from 9am to 1pm on weekdays. A cheap rate applies before 7am or after 7pm on weekdays, and all day at weekends. Cheap times for overseas calls vary, but tend to be at weekends and in the evening.

International and Local Telephone Calls

All London landline telephone numbers have 11 digits and begin with the code 020. Phone numbers in central London continue with 7 and in outer London with 8, although some business numbers continue with 3. If you are calling from another London number, you do not need to dial the 020, but only the remaining eight digits. Every other part of Britain has its own area code, beginning with 01 or 02.

Whenever possible, avoid making calls from hotels – above all, long-distance – as most add hefty surcharges, and some even charge for freephone lines. There are several special-rate numbers within the UK. Phone numbers beginning 03 are low-cost numbers used mostly by public bodies, such as the police. All 0800 or 0808 numbers are free to call from UK landlines (but not from mobile phones). 0844, 0845, 0870 and 0871 numbers are reduced-rate lines that are used by many companies and organizations for information services. Numbers beginning 09 are premium-rate and so particularly expensive.

To call Britain from abroad, dial 00 44, but then omit the initial zero from the UK area code. So to call the London number 020 7123 4567 from abroad, you would dial 00 44 20 7123 4567. To call abroad from London, dial 00 and then the usual country code (for example, Australia: 61; USA and Canada: 1).

Mobile Phones

All UK mobile phone numbers begin with 07. Calling a mobile from a landline is considerably more expensive than calling another landline.

There is a very high level of mobile ownership in London and signal coverage is good all over the city. UK mobiles use the European-standard 900 and 1900 MHz frequencies, so mobiles from other European countries work easily here so long as they have their roaming facility enabled. North American and Asian cell phones will not operate here unless they have a tri- or quad-band facility (which is increasingly standard on current phones). Before using a mobile while travelling, always check with your own service provider on the current level of roaming charges, which can be high. Many companies offer "packages" of foreign calls to cut costs.

If you anticipate using the phone a great deal, it may well be more economical to buy a cheap "pay-as-you-go" British mobile (a basic phone can cost as little as £10, or less) from one of the main local providers such as **O2**, **EE** or **Vodafone**, all of which have shops all over the city.

Public Telephones

You will find a **BT** phonebox on many streets in central London, and in every railway station. Some are the old-style red ones, others are much more modern in appearance; but whichever type,

British Telecom logo

they generally have the same technology inside. Some have multimedia terminals allowing Internet and email access. You can pay with coins, or by credit or debit card. Payphones accept 10p, 20p, 50p, £1 and £2 coins; some also accept Euro coins (50c, €1 and €2). The minimum call cost is 60p for the first 30 minutes to a UK landline; and 10p for each 10 minutes after that. For a short call, use 10p or 20p pieces, as payphones only return unused coins. For credit-card calls, the minimum charge can be anything from £1.20 to £6.50.

Old BT phonebox	Modern BT phonebox

Useful Dialling Codes

- The area code for London is 020.
- Phone numbers in central London start with 7 or 3, and in outer areas with 8. The 020 prefix must be used if dialling from outside these two areas.
- British Telecom directory enquiries is 118 500.
- If you have any problems contacting a number, call the operator on 100.
- To make an international call, dial 00 followed by the country code (USA and Canada: 1; Australia: 61; New Zealand: 64), the area code and the number. The international operator number is 155 (freephone).
- A phonecard needs at least £2 credit for an international call.
- In an emergency, dial 999 or 112. All emergency calls are free.

Internet and Email

Internet access is very easy to find in London. Public libraries, tourist information centres and some other public buildings have free terminals. Internet cafés are common in every part of the city, and rates per hour are often very low.

Many hotels and a growing number of budget B&Bs and hostels offer Wi-Fi access. Some hotels charge, but this is increasingly rare. There are also many free Wi-Fi hotspots across London, in public libraries, arts centres, cafés, restaurants and pubs.

Postal Services

Standard post in the UK is handled by the **Royal Mail**. There are main post offices providing all postal services in every London district, as well as many smaller sub-post offices attached to newsagents and other small shops – these can handle all normal mail. Main post offices are usually open from 9am to 5:30pm Monday to Friday, and to 12:30pm on Saturday. **Trafalgar Square Post Office** has extended hours: 8am–8pm Monday to Saturday. Post offices also exchange money and handle international money transfers.

Post within the UK can be sent by first- or second-class mail. First-class costs a little more and is quicker. Stamps can be bought from post offices or any shop with a "Stamps sold here" sign. Newsagents usually sell them, but may only have UK first- and second-class stamps, so for international mail you may need to find a post office. Hotels nearly always sell stamps, and

larger ones may have mail boxes. Public post boxes come in different shapes and sizes – some are sunk into walls – but are always red, and can be found throughout the city. There

Old-style pillar box

Newsagent stocking a range of international newspapers

are several collections a day (Mon–Sat); collection times are indicated on the box.

International letters and cards sent from London take about three days to reach European destinations, and four to six days to North America, Japan or Australasia. A competitively priced Airsure service is available for express deliveries (2–4 days worldwide), as well as a much slower but cheaper surface mail option.

Newspapers and Magazines

London's main local paper is the *Evening Standard*, distributed free in the centre of town from noon on weekdays. *Time Out London* magazine, published each Thursday, is London's most comprehensive listings guide.

A range of international newspapers and magazines, including *USA Today*, *International Herald Tribune* and major European papers, is on sale at many newsstands and newsagents around central London. For more specialist foreign press, one of the best places to go is Old Compton Street in Soho, where newsagents regularly carry an extraordinary global variety.

TV and Radio

The UK's analogue signal has been turned off; all radio and TV is digital. The publicly owned BBC operates several television stations, including BBC One,

BBC Two and BBC News. Other free-to-air channels are the independent ITV, Channel 4 and Five. Extra channels available include BBC3 (youth-oriented), BBC4 (arts-oriented), and various movie, shopping and music channels. In addition, many hotels also have satellite systems. If you want to be able to view a wide range of US and other international channels (such as ESPN), ask whether a hotel has Sky Plus or an enhanced Freeview package.

The BBC also has a large number of radio stations, of which Radios 1 (97–99 FM) and 2 (88–91 FM) focus on pop music of different kinds, Radio 3 (90.2 FM) on classical and jazz, Radio 4 (92–96 FM) on speech and drama, and Radio 5 (909/693 AM) on news and sport. BBC London (94.9 FM) is good for keeping up with local issues and interests.

DIRECTORY

Telephone Services

British Telecom (BT)
Tel 150 or 0800 800 150.
W bt.com

O2
Tel 0344 809 0222.
W o2.co.uk

Orange
Tel 07973 100 150.
W orange.co.uk

EE
Tel 0800 956 6000.
W ee.co.uk

Vodafone
Tel 0808 408 408.
W vodafone.co.uk

Postal Services

Royal Mail
Tel 0845 7740 740.
W royalmail.com

Trafalgar Square PO
24 William IV St, WC2.
Map 13 B3. **Tel** 020 7930 9580.

Newspapers and Magazines

Evening Standard
W standard.co.uk

Time Out
W timeout.com/london

GETTING TO LONDON

London is one of Europe's central hubs for international air and rail travel. By air, travellers face a bewildering choice of carriers from Europe, North America, Australasia, the Far East and every other part of the globe. Stiff competition on some routes, especially from major European countries and North America, means that low-fare deals can often be found, so it's always worth shopping around. Since 1995, the Channel Tunnel has provided an efficient high-speed train link –

Eurostar – between France and Belgium and the UK, as well as a fast, weatherproof Channel crossing for drivers. Eurostar trains depart from St Pancras International Station in London's King's Cross. Many European cruises sail from or finish at ports not far from London, such as Southampton, Dover or Tilbury, and there are efficient passenger and car ferry services from Europe, using large ferries and faster jetfoils and catamarans, across the North Sea and the English Channel.

Station concourse at St Pancras International

Arriving by Rail

Eurostar runs frequent daily trains to London from Paris, Brussels and Lille, where the Paris and Brussels lines meet. Non-stop trains from Paris (Gare du Nord) take 2 hours 15 minutes; from Brussels, 1 hour 50 minutes. Some trains also stop at Calais before entering the Channel Tunnel on the French side, and at Ashford and Ebbsfleet on the English. If you travel by train from any other part of Europe and want to connect with Eurostar, it's best to do so at Lille, as you change trains in the same station – quicker and far easier than doing so in Paris. Check-in on Eurostar is only 30 minutes before departure, so it's generally far quicker than flying.

Eurostar trains arrive in London at St Pancras International, on the northern edge of central London, next to King's Cross Underground station. The station is a junction of six Underground lines, so is well connected with every part of

the city. Eurostar fares vary a good deal according to flexibility and the time of day you travel (early morning trains are often the cheapest), so check current rates on the website when booking. Information and bookings for connecting trains from other parts of Europe can be found on the **Voyages–sncf** website.

London has eight mainline rail stations at which trains from different parts of Britain terminate: Paddington serves the West Country, Wales and the South Midlands; Liverpool Street serves East Anglia and Essex; King's Cross, St Pancras and Euston cover northern Britain; and Charing Cross, Victoria and Waterloo cover southern England, and also the main Channel ferry ports.

The current UK railway system is complicated and can be confusing. Lines are run by several different companies, but they are coordinated by **National Rail**, which operates a joint information service.

Fare structures are especially complex: tickets can be very expensive or surprisingly cheap, depending on whether you grasp how the system operates. Going to a station the same day you want to travel and buying a ticket over the counter is always the most expensive way to travel. Whenever possible, book trains in advance and check alternative fares, bearing in mind that the best fares may only be available online. The National Rail website has a useful "cheapest fare finder" feature, which then links you to the relevant company site to make the booking. Also helpful is **Trainline**, an independent booking agency which often has discounted tickets. Tickets booked online can usually be collected at the station.

Fares on suburban rail services around London are less complex, so there is no need to book ahead. Rail lines within London accept the Oyster Card (see p370).

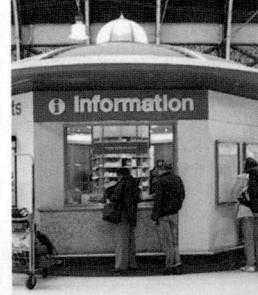

Rail information point at a London station, for help and advice

Cross-Channel ferry heading to Calais

Arriving by Coach

International and national coach services from every part of Europe and the UK arrive in London at Victoria Coach Station on Buckingham Palace Road, about five minutes' walk from Victoria rail and Under-ground stations, and with several local bus stops outside. If you're planning to travel to any UK destinations outside of the London area, it's slower but nearly always cheaper to do it by coach than by train, with fares as low as £1 on some London–Oxford services (although some train compan-ies try to offer lower fares on the same routes).

National Express operates the most extensive UK coach network, with around 1,000 destinations covered, and is also associated with Eurolines international coach services. **Megabus** has especially low fares to many UK destinations, and also discount train offers. **Green Line** runs buses between London and the surrounding counties, and has a service to Luton Airport (see p369).

Arriving by Sea and Tunnel

The **Eurotunnel** shuttle – the other train service using the Channel Tunnel – is a drive-on, drive-off service for cars between Calais and Folkestone, where the Tunnel connects with the M20 motorway to London. There are usually four shuttles per hour, with a journey time of about 35 minutes.

If you prefer to brave the elements, there are still plenty of ferry services between southeast England and Continental ports. Harwich in Essex has ferries from Esbjerg in Denmark, with **DFDS Seaways**; and from Hook of Holland in the Netherlands, with **Stena Line**. Dover is the busiest port, with frequent services from France: from Dunkerque and Boulogne with DFDS; from Calais with **P&O Ferries** and DFDS. Newhaven–Dieppe ferries are also operated by DFDS.

There are also several routes in the western Channel, which take longer, but may leave you better located for the west of England: to Portsmouth from Caen, Cherbourg, Le Havre and St Malo with **Brittany Ferries**, or from Le Havre with DFDS; to Poole from Cherbourg with Brittany Ferries; or to Poole or Weymouth from St Malo and the Channel Islands with **Condor Ferries**.

Crossing times to Dover are around 1 hour 15 minutes; in the western Channel, it takes more like 5-6 hours, although in summer, fast jetfoils and cat-amarans cut this to 2–3 hours.

There are also ferry services from Spain: from Santander to Plymouth or Portsmouth with Brittany Ferries; and from Bilbao to Portsmouth with P&O. Crossings take around 24 hours, on comfortable "mini-cruise-ships".

Driving time from Dover or the Channel Tunnel to central London is usually around 2 hours; from Portsmouth, 2–2½ hours. If you bring a car to London, always try to arrange a place to stay with free parking, otherwise this can become extremely expensive.

DIRECTORY

Rail Services

Eurostar
London St Pancras International.
Tel 0344 8224 777.
w eurostar.com

National Rail
Tel 0845 748 4950.
w nationalrail.co.uk

Rail Europe
Tel 1 800 622 8600 (USA),
0844 848 5848 (UK).
w uk.voyages-sncf.com

Trainline
Tel 0871 244 1545.
w thetrainline.com

Coach Services

Green Line
Tel 0844 801 7261.
w greenline.co.uk

Megabus
Tel 0900 160 0900.
w megabus.com/uk

National Express
Tel 08717 818 181.
w nationalexpress.com

Tunnel and Ferries

Brittany Ferries
Tel 0871 244 0744.
w brittany-ferries.com

Condor Ferries
Tel 01202 207 216.
w condorferries.co.uk

DFDS Seaways
w dfdsseaways.co.uk

Eurotunnel
Tel 08443 353 535.
w eurotunnel.com

P&O Ferries
Tel 0871 664 2121.
w poferries.com

Stena Line
Tel 0844 770 7070.
w stenaline.co.uk

Arriving by Air

London's two main airports, Heathrow and Gatwick, are augmented by smaller facilities at Luton, Stansted and London City *(see pp368–9)*. Check which airport you will land at, and plan your journey from there. All the airports have train or coach links; Heathrow is also connected to central London by Underground. Because the airports are so far apart from each other, travelling between them is best avoided. Further details can be found online.

Access to the underground in the arrival terminal at Heathrow

British Airways passenger jet at Heathrow airport

Airlines and Fares

Heathrow and Gatwick have long-haul connections with every part of the world, on scores of airlines. The main United States airlines offering scheduled flights to London include **Delta**, **United**, **American Airlines** and **US Airways**, while from Canada there are frequent services with **Air Canada**. **British Airways** and **Virgin Atlantic** also fly from many North American cities. The flight time from New York is about 6½ hours; from Los Angeles, about 10 hours. The choice of carriers from Australasia and Asia is enormous too: **Qantas**, **Air New Zealand** and British Airways may be the obvious first choices, but operators such as **Singapore Airlines** and **Emirates** offer interesting alternatives.

All the main carrier airlines, such as British Airways, Air France, **Iberia** and **Lufthansa**, offer frequent European connections, mostly to Heathrow or Gatwick, but they now carry less traffic than the low-cost airlines. **Ryanair** has budget flights to all of Europe, Ireland and the UK, mostly from Stansted, while **easyJet** runs almost as extensive a European and British network from Stansted, Luton and Gatwick.

Very few airlines now offer reduced prices for children. Low-cost flights can normally be booked only through each airline's own website. Note that low-cost airlines regularly add "extra" charges on top of the fare – such as one for checking in luggage. Ryanair in particular, charges £70 if you cannot download and print your own boarding card, and need one issued by ground staff at the airport.

Security

Security is tighter than ever at London airports. Allow at least two hours to check in and get through security before your flight, especially – because of its size – at Heathrow. Allow ample time also (2 hours again) to catch low-cost flights if you are checking in a bag, since in the interests of keeping costs down there are not many check-in staff, so lines move slowly.

Heathrow (LHR)

Heathrow in west London is one of the world's busiest airports. It has five terminals, so it's important to know which one your flight will arrive at or depart from. Terminals 1, 2 and 3, the oldest, share an Underground station and Heathrow Central rail station; Terminal 4 has its own Underground station; Terminal 5, which opened in 2008, has Underground and rail stations. A free shuttle bus runs between the Terminals. Most British Airways flights use Terminal 5; most other long-haul airlines use Terminals 3 or 4. There are shops and other facilities in every terminal.

There are several ways into London from Heathrow. The fastest rail service is the **Heathrow Express**, with trains every 15 minutes from around 5am to 11:30pm daily to Paddington station on the west side of central London. Journey time is about 15 minutes, and trains also stop at Terminal 5. To get to Terminals 1, 2 and 3, take the shuttle bus from Terminal 4. Fares are quite high, at around £25 single, £39 return (slightly less if you buy online). **Heathrow Connect** trains run

Heathrow Terminal 5, used exclusively by British Airways

on the same lines but with several stops, and take 25–30 minutes to reach Paddington. Fares are around £9.50 single.

The Underground (tube) offers a much cheaper way of getting into London, but is also much slower. Trains run frequently, calling at all Heathrow Terminals from around 5am to midnight Monday to Saturday; 5:50am–11:30pm Sunday. Unlike the Heathrow Express, the tube runs right into the city centre; allow about 45 minutes to get to Leicester Square. As on all London public transport, it's cheaper with an Oyster Card *(see p370)*; the adult fare from Heathrow into the city centre is £5.50.

National Express and other companies run a number of bus routes from Heathrow to Oxford, London, other London airports and other destinations. The main bus station is at Terminals 1, 2 and 3, but buses also stop at 4 and 5. A taxi to central London costs about £50. Driving time is from 30 minutes to 1 hour. It's worth noting that local minicab companies offer much cheaper rates *(see p377)*.

London City Airport, within sight of the city's Docklands area

London City Airport (LCY)

London City is the closest airport to central London, in the Docklands business area just east of London's financial district (the City). Unlike the low-cost airports, it was created primarily for business travellers, so flights are quite expensive. It offers flights to many European destinations, and a luxury service to New York.

London City has its own station on the Docklands Light Railway (DLR), which connects with the Underground network at Tower Hill and Bank. An Express Shuttle Bus runs every 30 minutes to Canary Wharf, for £7 single fare. A taxi to the City costs about £28 and takes 30 minutes; to the West End £40, taking around 45 minutes.

London Airports

Luton
Stevenage
Stansted Airport
A120
A1(M)
Luton Airport
A5
Welwyn Garden City
Harlow
M11
Chelmsford
A41
M1
St Albans
Lea
M25
Roding
A12
High Wycombe
Watford
Enfield
Brentwood
Basildon
M40
Harrow
Tottenham Hale
Thames
Romford
Kings Cross
Liverpool Street
London City Airport
A13
Thames
Slough
Paddington
Canning Town
M4
Victoria
M4
London Bridge
Dartford
Gravesend
Heathrow Airport
Clapham Junction
Beckenham
A2
Bracknell
M25
Kingston upon Thames
M3
Croydon
Bromley
M2
Woking
Sutton
Epsom
A3
M20
A23
M25
Maidstone
Redhill
A24
A21
Tonbridge
Medway
A22
Gatwick Airport
Royal Tunbridge Wells
Crawley

Key

- ▦ Motorway
- ▬ 'A' road
- — Railway

0 kilometres   15
0 miles   10

Gatwick (LGW)

Gatwick airport lies due south of central London, and handles long-haul, European and low-cost flights. There are two terminals – North and South – so as at Heathrow, you need to be clear on which you need. The train station and main bus stops are at the South Terminal, from where there is a free shuttle train to the North. Allow around 20 minutes to transfer between terminals. There are banks, shops, cafés and other facilities at both.

There is a choice of three rail services from Gatwick into London, all from the same station. The **Gatwick Express** is the fastest, with trains every 15 minutes to Victoria Station. It runs from around 4.30am to midnight daily and takes about 30 minutes (a little longer on Sundays), but it isn't cheap; the fare is around £20 single, £35 return. Cheaper tickets can be bought online. **First Capital Connect** runs around four trains per hour over the same period to St Pancras International via several stops including East Croydon and London Bridge. Journey time is about an hour, and single fare around £10. **Southern Railway** has several trains each hour to London Victoria, with a journey time of 30–50 minutes and a single fare of around £11.

Entrance to Stansted's spacious modern passenger terminal

National Express and other companies run buses from the South Terminal to Heathrow and many towns in southern England (including central London), and **easyBus** runs frequently from the North and South terminals to Earl's Court/West Brompton in London. Buses are not limited to easyJet passengers, and fares begin at £2. A taxi into central London will set you back around £90, and can take 1–2 hours. As at Heathrow, minicab companies offer better rates to Gatwick.

Stansted (STN)

Around 40 miles northeast of London, Stansted is the airport in southeast England most popular with the low-cost airlines, and so has a huge number of flights to destinations in every part of Europe.

The rail link into London is the **Stansted Express** train, which runs every 15 minutes from around 6am to 12:30am, with variations at weekends. Trains run to Liverpool Street, on the east side of central London, with a stop at Tottenham Hale (where you can transfer to the Victoria Underground line). Trains from Liverpool Street to Stansted run from approximately 4:40am to 11:30pm daily. The full journey takes 45 minutes. Adult fares to Liverpool Street are £23.40 single, £33.20 return (cheaper online). **National Express East Anglia** trains also run roughly once an hour to London Stratford station in East London's Olympic Park, with several stops, taking one hour for a fare of about £23.50.

Several bus services run from Stansted to London. National Express runs to Victoria Coach Station (prices start at £5, book ahead) and many other destinations around the region, but easyBus is again the cheapest, with tickets to Baker Street Underground station

Gatwick's free monorail service linking the two terminals

Airport	From city centre	Average journey time	Average taxi fare
London City	10 km (6 miles)	Tube and DLR: 40 minutes	£28
Heathrow	23 km (14 miles)	Rail: 15 minutes Tube: 45 minutes	£50
Gatwick	45 km (28 miles)	Rail: 30 minutes Bus: 70 minutes	£90
Luton	51 km (32 miles)	Rail: 35 minutes Bus: 70 minutes	£60
Stansted	55 km (34 miles)	Rail: 45 minutes Bus: 75 minutes	£90

from £2. A taxi to central London can take 1 hour 30 minutes and cost £90–100.

Luton (LTN)

Luton airport lies northwest of London near the M1 motorway, and is used almost exclusively by charter flights and low-cost airlines, especially easyJet. A shuttle bus connects the terminal with Luton Airport Parkway train station (about a five-minute drive), from around 5am to midnight daily. First Capital Connect has about four trains each hour to London St Pancras – a journey of around 25–40 minutes for an adult single fare of £14. **East Midlands Trains** operate on the same route, and are a little cheaper, at £12. Green Line buses (route 757) run every 15 minutes almost 24 hours

daily between the airport and London Victoria Coach station, with adult fares around £10 (see p365); easyBus has frequent services to Victoria via Baker Street, with tickets from £2. National Express runs from Luton to Heathrow, Gatwick, Stansted and other destinations. A taxi into London will cost around £60, and take about 45 minutes.

Airport Hotels

Given the long check-in times at the main airports, it can be a good idea – or even necessary – to stay nearby the night before departure, especially if you have an early-morning flight. There is a large number of hotels in the vicinity of Heathrow and Gatwick; many of these frequently have discount offers. All of them provide shuttle

Relaxing bar of the popular Sheraton Skyline hotel

buses to the airport terminals – in budget hotels this may be charged extra. The **Premier Inn**, **Travelodge** and **Holiday Inn** chains have cheap, functional, rooms close to the airports. A selection of airport hotels is listed below, but there are many more to choose from.

DIRECTORY

Major Airlines

Air Canada
w aircanada.com

Air New Zealand
w airnewzealand.com

American Airlines
w aa.com

British Airways
w britishairways.com

Delta Airlines
w delta.com

easyJet
w easyjet.com

Emirates
w emirates.com

Iberia
w iberia.com

Lufthansa
w lufthansa.com

Qantas
w qantas.com.au

Ryanair
w ryanair.com

Singapore Airlines
w singaporeair.com

United Airlines
w united.com

US Airways
w usairways.com

Virgin Atlantic
w virgin-atlantic.com

Travel Websites
w bestfares.com
w cheapflights.com
w ebookers.com
w expedia.com
w flights.com
w orbitz.com
w priceline.com
w travelnow.com
w travelocity.com

Airport Information

Gatwick
Tel 0844 892 0322.
w gatwickairport.com

Heathrow
Tel 0844 335 1801.
w heathrowairport.com

London City Airport
Tel 020 7646 0088.
w londoncityairport.com

Luton
Tel 01582 405 100,
0906 211 500 00 (flight information).
w london-luton.co.uk

Stansted
Tel 0844 335 1803.
w stanstedairport.com

Airport Transport

easyBus
w easybus.co.uk

East Midlands Trains
Tel 08457 125 678.
w eastmidlandstrains.co.uk

First Capital Connect
Tel 0845 026 4700.
w firstcapitalconnect.co.uk

Gatwick Express
Tel 0845 850 1530.
w gatwickexpress.com

Heathrow Connect
Tel 0845 678 6975.
w heathrowconnect.com

Heathrow Express
Tel 0845 600 1515.
w heathrowexpress.com

National Express East Anglia
Tel 0845 600 7245.
w nationalexpress eastanglia.com

Southern Railway
Tel 0845 127 2920.
w southernrailway.com

Stansted Express
Tel 0845 600 7245.
w stanstedexpress.com

Hotels

Holiday Inn London Heathrow Ariel
Tel 0871 423 4901.
w ihg.com

Premier Inn Heathrow (Bath Road)
Tel 0871 527 8508.
w premierinn.com

Sofitel London Gatwick
Tel 01293 567 070.
w sofitel.com

Travelodge Gatwick Airport
Tel 0871 984 6031.
w travelodge.co.uk

GETTING AROUND LONDON

London has one of the busiest and most extensive public transport systems in Europe; it also has all the problems of overcrowding to match. A programme is underway to upgrade the Underground train system (the Tube). Within London and its suburbs, most of the public transport systems – the Underground, city buses, overground rail lines, river buses – are coordinated by Transport for London (TfL), which operates a common ticketing system centred on the pay-as-you-go Oyster Card, which commuters use to "touch in" each time they go on public transport. Oyster Cards are rapidly replacing the need for paper tickets.

Green Travel

Travelling around London by foot, tube, bus, train or river bus is more energy-efficient than taking your own vehicle or a taxi. The Congestion Charge helps to discourage driving in the city centre (see p371). London continues to invest in improved conditions for cyclists, and this can be the fastest way to get around the city – **Transport for London's** website has a dedicated cycling page. Several "green" minicab companies use hybrid or alternative-fuel vehicles to reduce their carbon footprint, such as **Gogreencar** and **Climatecars**.

The Transport System

The Underground railway – or "tube", as Londoners call it – is generally the fastest, most convenient way to get around the city. The Docklands business district and some other areas of east London and Greenwich are served by the Dock-lands Light Railway (DLR), which connects with the tube network principally at Bank, Tower Hill, Canary Wharf and Stratford. Tube and DLR lines do not run to every part of the city, however; in particular, large parts of south London are reliant on over-ground rail connections. Bus routes cover every part of London. There are also several riverbus boat services (see pp62–63).

Avoid travelling on public transport during morning and evening "rush hour" – 7–10am and 4–7pm Monday to Friday – if at all possible.

"Heritage" bus

For detailed information on every aspect of transport in London, check the TfL website, which has an invaluable "Journey Planner" feature. TfL also has several Travel Information Centres. Those at Heathrow and Piccadilly Circus Underground stations and Euston, King's Cross, Liverpool Street and Victoria mainline stations are particularly helpful, and provide free maps and other information.

Oyster Cards and Travelcards

London's public transport is relatively expensive compared to that of many European cities, but if you use one of the multi-journey cards available to visitors you will cut your costs considerably. For tube, DLR and local train fares, London is divided into six main fare zones radiating out from Zone 1 in the centre (on buses, there is a flat fare for each trip, no matter how far you travel). If you aim to pack all your sightseeing into one or two days, the best ticket to get will be a one-day off-peak Travelcard, which gives unlimited travel on all systems after 9:30am on weekdays (or any time on Saturday and Sunday) within your chosen zones for a flat fee (£8.80 for an adult card for Zones 1 and 2,

A London Underground sign outside a station

which covers most of the main sights in London). If you expect to travel more freely, it will be better to get a pay-as-you-go Oyster Card, which you can charge up with as much credit as you wish. Whenever you use public transport, you "touch in" with your card on a yellow Oyster Card reader, and the corresponding amount is deducted. On Underground, DLR and overground trains you must also remember to "touch out" at the station where you finish your journey, or you will be charged the maximum fare for the line.

Travelcards and Oyster Cards can be bought at tube and local rail stations, Travel Information Centres and hundreds of small shops that have the TfL "Ticket Stop" sticker in the window. You can also obtain them before arriving in London, on Eurostar, Gatwick Express or Stansted Express trains, or online, with advance delivery to 63 countries, through the Visit London and TfL websites.

Travel is free on all buses for under-16s; the Under-ground and DLR are free for under-11s, and have reduced fares for 11–15-year-olds. A one-day Travelcard for 11–15s costs only £3.40 for main fare zones, 1 to 6. Details of all current fares and tickets can be found on www.tfl.gov.uk.

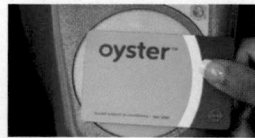

Pre-paid Oyster card being placed on a card reader

A pedestrian zebra crossing

Walking

Once you get used to traffic driving on the left, London can be enjoyably explored on foot, but take care crossing the road. There are two types of pedestrian crossing in London: striped "zebra" crossings, marked by beacons; and push-button crossings at traffic lights. Traffic should stop if you wait at a zebra crossing, but at push-button crossings, cars will not stop until they have a red light. Look out for instructions printed on the road, which tell you from which direction you can expect traffic to appear.

Driving in London

For visitors, driving is usually the worst way of getting around town. Traffic moves at an average of 11 mph (18 kmh) for much of the day, parking is scarce and expensive, and in the city centre there is the added cost of the Congestion Charge – a £10-a-day fee (pay in advance) for private vehicles entering the central charging zone (roughly: the City, the West End, and Mayfair in the west; and south as far as Elephant & Castle) between 7am and 6pm Monday to Friday. If you are determined to drive, remember to drive on the left.

All the well-known car-rental firms are represented in London. Renting a car in advance through a site such as **Auto Europe**, or as an add-on with your flight, will get the best rates. To drive right out of London from the centre takes about 1 hour in any direction; if you want to tour the countryside, it can be less tiring to take a train to a city like Oxford and rent there.

Parking

Parking is prohibited at all times wherever the street is marked with red or there are double yellow lines by the kerb. If there is a single yellow line, parking is normally allowed from 6:30pm–8am Monday to Saturday and all day Sunday, but exact hours vary, so always check the signs along each street. Where there is no line at all, parking is free at all times, but this is rare in central London. Note that rental car drivers are still liable for parking fines.

Cycling

The TfL "Cycling" page is an invaluable source of information on cycling around the city. Cycle routes – sometimes even separate cycle lanes – are signposted around the city.

Barclays Cycle Hire, London's bike hire scheme, has 6,000 bikes available at docking terminals across the city. Visit the website for details of how to access the bikes. The **London Bicycle Tour Company** delivers and collects bikes to and from your location. With your rented bike you should be given a helmet, lock and other accessories.

DIRECTORY

Transport for London
Tel 0843 222 1234 (info), 0845 900 1234 (Congestion Charge).
W tfl.gov.uk

Green travel

Climatecars
Tel 020 7350 5960.
W climatecars.com

Gogreencar
Tel 020 7502 3670.
W gogreencar.co.uk

Driving

Auto Europe
Tel 1 888 223 5555 (USA), 0800 358 1229 (UK).
W autoeurope.com

Europecar
Tel 0871 384 9847 (UK).
W europecar.com

Hertz Rent a Car
Tel 1 800 654 3001 (USA), 0870 841 5161 (UK).
W hertz.com

Parking

National Car Parks
Tel 0845 050 7080.
W ncp.co.uk

Cycling

Barclays Cycle Hire
Tel 0845 026 3630.
W tfl.gov.uk

London Bicycle Tour Company
Tel 020 7928 6838.
W londonbicycle.com

London Cycling Campaign
Tel 020 7234 9310.
W lcc.org.uk

A cycle path in one of London's parks

Travelling by Underground

The underground system, known as the "tube" to Londoners, has some 270 stations, each identified by the Underground logo. Trains run every day except Christmas Day, from about 5:30am till midnight Monday to Thursday; 5:30am till 1am on Friday and Saturday; and 6:30am to 11:30pm on Sunday. Exact times of first and last trains are posted at stations and on the Transport for London website: www.tfl.gov.uk. The Docklands Light Railway (DLR), with some 40 stations in east and southeast London, connects with the tube and also runs to London City Airport. For schedules and all other information, call 0843-222 1234 or check the TfL website.

London Underground train

Planning Your Journey

There are 12 tube lines, all named and colour-coded (red for Central, blue for Victoria, and so on), which intersect at various stations. Some lines, like the Jubilee, have a single branch; others, like the Northern, have more than one, so it's important to check the digital boards on the platform and the destination on the front of the train. The Circle Line is a continuous loop around central London but now extends to Hammersmith. Maps of the entire Tube system (see

inside back cover) are posted at each station. Note that the tube map is topological, not geographical; it isn't to scale, nor can it be relied upon for directions. From it, you can work out where to change lines to travel to any station on the system. All eight of London's mainline rail stations (see p364) have associated Tube stations. Due to the ongoing tube improvement programme, services are sometimes suspended, usually at weekends. When this happens, replacement buses are provided. Check for line closures before travelling.

Buying a Ticket

All tube and DLR stations fall within one of six main fare zones (see p370). The zones you travel through determine the cost of your journey. Unless you plan on making very few journeys by tube, it will usually be best to travel with a multi-journey Travelcard or an Oyster Card (see p370). However, you can also buy single or return tickets from ticket offices and ticket machines. All Underground and DLR stations have touch-screen machines that give step-by-step instructions in a variety of languages. They accept coins, notes and credit and debit cards, and you can also use them to top up your credit on an Oyster Card. To check on current fares, select the ticket type you need, choose the station you wish to travel to, and the fare will be displayed on screen.

How to read the Journey Planner Maps
(see inside back cover)

Station for changing between lines or to British Rail train

Double circle, meaning two stations are linked

Station serving two lines

Tube Architecture

The Underground's reputation for exciting architecture was established in the 1930s. In 1999 the Jubilee Line Extension opened to great acclaim, with six imposing and elegant stations designed by a group of top architects including Will Alsop (North Greenwich), Norman Foster (Canary Wharf) and Matthew Hopkins (Westminster). A similarly light, spacious style has been adopted in the impressive tube, DLR, bus and mainline rail hub at Stratford, which is the gateway to the Olympic Park.

Concourse at Canary Wharf Station, Jubilee Line

Making a Journey by Underground

1 When you first enter the station, check which line, or lines, you need to take. If you have any difficulty planning your route, ask the clerk at the ticket office for help.

⊖ **Journey planner**

Feed your ticket into the slot at the front of the machine; retrieve it from the slot at the top.

2 Buy your ticket, Travelcard or Oyster Card from a ticket office or ticket machine at the station. Keep your ticket; you will need it to exit at your destination. For return trips, you will usually be given one ticket that you must keep for both journeys. Oyster Cards can be topped up for later trips.

If you have an Oyster Card, just touch it on the yellow card reader.

Central line →

3 The platforms are on the other side of the ticket barriers. These are easy to use if you follow the instructions above.

The ticket office is near the ticket barriers in most stations.

Central line
Westbound platform 5 →

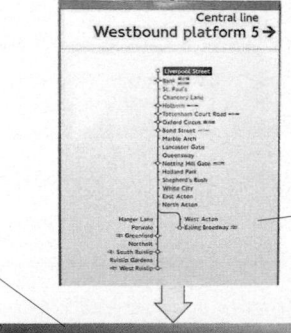

4 Follow the directions to the line on which you need to travel. In some cases this can be a complicated route, but it will be well sign-posted.

5 You will eventually find yourself with a choice of platforms for the line you want. Look at the list of stations if you are not sure which direction to take.

6 All platforms have electronic indicators displaying the final destination of the next two or three trains and how long you will have to wait before they arrive. On lines with branches, they also indicate the route of each train.

1 HAINAULT via Newbury Park
2 EPPING   5 mins

On all DLR and some tubes, push a button to open the carriage doors.

7 Once you have begun your journey, you can check on your progress using the line chart displayed in every carriage. On many trains, the name of the next station is announced before you arrive, and as you pull into each station you will see its name posted along the walls.

Way out →

≥ British Rail

Hammersmith & City →
Metropolitan and Circle lines

8 After leaving the train, look for signs giving directions to exits or to platforms for any connecting lines.

Travelling by Bus and Boat

The red double-decker bus is one of London's most recognizable symbols, but the design of London buses has changed a great deal over the years. The old, classic open-backed Routemaster buses have been withdrawn (with the exception of two "heritage" routes), and in their place there are modern, square-sided double-deckers, single-deckers for less busy routes and a modernized Routemaster bus allowing passengers to hop on and hop off. Travelling by bus is an enjoyable, easy way to see London, especially in the middle of the day, and much cheaper than going by tube or DLR if you have an Oyster Card. On the minus side, bus journeys can be slow, especially during rush hour (7–10am and 4–7pm Monday to Friday).

Finding the Right Bus

Bus maps showing all the main routes are available free from Travel Information Centres, or can be downloaded from the Visit London and Transport for London websites. All London bus stops have bus route signs displaying the routes that run from that stop, with lists of their main destinations. On streets that are used by several bus routes – notably Oxford Street in the West End – routes are bunched together at different stops near each other, so make sure you find the right one. Stops also have local area maps showing which of the adjacent bus stops, identified by a letter, you need for buses to a particular area. If in doubt, check with the bus driver when boarding.

Using the London Buses

Buses halt at stops marked with the London bus logo. Some stops are "request" stops, where drivers will not stop unless they are waved down by a passenger. Destinations are displayed clearly on the front of the bus, and on many buses, the next upcoming stop is indicated on electronic information boards, or announced by an automatic voice system. However, if you are unsure which stop you need, ask the driver to alert you, and stay on the lower deck.

Board buses at the front, so that you can touch in your Oyster Card on the yellow Oyster reader by the driver's cab, show your Travelcard or buy a single ticket. In central London, single tickets cannot be bought on board the bus, but must be bought in advance from ticket machines at the bus stop, and then shown to the driver. Fares are the same for each bus trip no matter how far you travel, at £2.40 for a single ticket or £1.40 with an Oyster Card – so the Oyster saving is considerable. Inspectors often check whether passengers have valid tickets or passes.

Bus Stops

If you are boarding a bus at a yellow stop (below), you must buy a ticket at the adjacent machine before boarding. At some stops, called request stops, the driver will not halt unless asked. If you want to board, raise your arm as the bus approaches the stop; when you want to get off, ring the bell once before your stop.

Useful Bus Routes

Several of London's bus routes are particularly convenient for the capital's main sights and shops. If you arm yourself with an Oyster Card or Travelcard and are in no particular hurry, sightseeing or shopping by bus can be great fun. The cost of a journey by public transport is far less than any of the charges levied by tour operators, although you won't have the commentary that tour companies give you as you pass sights (*see p354–5*). There are also some sights or areas in London that are either hard to get to by Underground, or can be reached much more directly by bus. Buses run regularly from the city centre to, for instance, the Albert Hall (*see p207*) and Chelsea (*see pp194–9*).

Thames Clipper boat on the river heading towards Waterloo Bridge

Night Buses

Some main bus routes run 24 hours daily. Night bus services (indicated by the letter "N" added before the route number) also run on many popular routes from 11pm until 6am, generally 3–4 times per hour up to 2–3am, but often only once an hour after that. Many night bus routes originate in or pass through Trafalgar Square, then run out into the suburbs. In the centre they are often very crowded, especially at weekends, but empty out quickly as they move further out. Plan your journey carefully;

London is so big that even if you board a bus going in the right direction, you can still be a long walk from your accommodation. As always, be aware of your personal security when travelling at night.

Riverboats

Some of London's most spectacular views can only be seen from the River Thames. River trips have also been integrated into London's general transport service. **Thames Clippers** has a riverbus service with catamarans running every

20 minutes from 6am to 1am daily in both directions, on a route between Waterloo and Woolwich, via the London Eye, Tower Bridge, Greenwich and other stops at the various river piers. They also operate the **Tate Boat**, a direct boat between the Tate Britain and Tate Modern museums (every 40 minutes in each direction, 10am to 5pm), as well as special services for events at the O2 Arena. Oyster Cards can be used on board, and Travelcard holders get discounted tickets. For all details, check with Thames Clippers or www.tfl.gov.uk.

DIRECTORY

Riverboat Services

Tate Boat
Tel 020 7887 8888.
W tate.org.uk/tatetotate

Thames Clippers
Tel 020 7001 2222.
W thamesclippers.com

For more information on river cruises see "Cruise Highlights" on p63.

Tottenham Court Road, British Museum, Aldgate, Oxford Circus (Liberty), Covent Garden, Cambridge Circus, The Strand, Aldwych, St Paul's, Cannon Street, Tower of London, Piccadilly Circus, Charing Cross (National Gallery), London Bridge, Victoria (Buckingham Palace), Waterloo, OXO Tower, Westminster (Westminster Abbey), Tate Britain

KEY
Route 7
Route 14
Route 11
Route 15
Route 87
Route RV1
Underground station
Railway station

Travelling by Rail

London's local and suburban train lines (also known as the "overground") are used by hundreds of thousands of commuters every day. For visitors, rail services are most useful for trips to the outskirts of London and areas of the city without nearby Underground connections (especially in south London). If you are planning to travel outside of the capital, always try to book rail tickets in advance, and check to see what alternative fares are available; for more on rail tickets see p364.

Useful Routes

Two of the most popular rail lines for visitors to London are those from Charing Cross (via London Bridge) and, on weekdays, Cannon Street to Greenwich *(see pp238–45)*; and Waterloo to Hampton Court *(see pp256–9)*. A First Capital Connect line runs right through London, north to south, from Luton via St Pancras International to Gatwick. The North London line makes a loop around north London all the way from the East End to Kew *(see pp262–3)* and Richmond.

Using the Trains

London has eight main railway terminuses serving different parts of Britain. Each terminus is also the start-point for local and suburban lines that cover the whole of southeast England. There are over one hundred smaller London stations. Rail services travel overground and vary between trains that stop at every station, faster suburban trains, and express trains that run non-stop to major destinations. Some train doors will open automatically, others at the touch of a button.

Rail Tickets

Travelcards and Oyster Cards are valid on nearly all overground rail services that fall entirely within the London area (defined as Transport for London fare zones 1–6, plus three more suburban zones), so using one or the other will generally be much more economical, and a lot quicker, than buying individual tickets. Be aware, though, that on most overground trains, peak travel times include the evening rush hour (4–7pm Monday–Friday) as well as the morning one (before 9:30am), so with an Oyster you will be charged more during these times. Many small stations do not have staffed ticket counters, just machines.

Return tickets for rail travel

Day Trips

Southern England has a lot to offer visitors besides London. By rail or by bus *(see p365)*, getting out of the city is fast and easy. For details of sights, contact Visit Britain (www.visitbritain.com; 020 7578 1000). National Rail (0845 748 4950) has details of all rail services.

Boating on the River Thames at Windsor Castle

Audley End
Village with a stunning Jacobean mansion nearby.
🚆 from Liverpool Street.
40 miles (64 km); 1 hr.

Bath
Beautiful Georgian city, with Roman baths.
🚆 from Paddington.
107 miles (172 km); 1 hr 25 mins.

Brighton
Lively and attractive seaside resort. See the Royal Pavilion.
🚆 from Victoria or London Bridge.
53 miles (85 km); 1 hr.

Cambridge
University city with fine art gallery and ancient colleges.
🚆 from Liverpool Street or King's Cross.
54 miles (86 km); 1 hr.

Canterbury
Its cathedral is one of England's oldest and greatest sights.
🚆 from Victoria.
62 miles (100 km); 1 hr 25 mins.

Hatfield House
Elizabethan palace with remarkable contents.
🚆 from King's Cross or Moorgate to Hatfield station.
21 miles (33 km); 20 mins.

Oxford
Like Cambridge, famous for its ancient university.
🚆 from Paddington.
56 miles (90 km); 1 hr.

St Albans
Cathedral and Roman theatre.
🚆 from King's Cross or Moorgate.
25 miles (40 km); 30 mins.

Salisbury
Famous for its cathedral, and close to Stonehenge.
🚆 from Waterloo.
84 miles (135 km); 1 hr 40 mins.

Windsor
Riverside town with Britain's grandest royal castle.
🚆 from Paddington, change Slough.
20 miles (32 km); approx. 30 mins.

Travelling by Taxi

London's black cabs are as much of an institution as its red buses. Black cabs (some of which, it should be pointed out, are not actually black – you will often see blue, green, red or even white cabs) are the only cabs licensed to pick up passengers who hail a cab on the street, and their drivers have to take a stringent test on their knowledge of London and its traffic routes before they are awarded a licence. Minicabs, which by law must be booked in advance, not hailed, are a cheaper alternative for specific journeys.

London taxi rank

Finding a Cab

Licensed London taxis, or "black cabs", are large, distinctive vehicles – of which there are now several models – whose yellow "Taxi" sign is lit up whenever the taxi is free. You can hail them on the street, phone for them, or find them at taxi ranks, especially at airports, main rail stations and major hotels. Raise your arm and wave purposefully. If a cab stops, it must take you anywhere within a radius of 6 miles (9.6 km), as long as it is in the Metropolitan Police district, which includes most of the Greater London area and Heathrow Airport.

Taxi Fares

All black cabs have meters that start ticking at around £2.20 as soon as the driver accepts your custom. The fare then increases by the minute, or for each 311 m (340 yds) travelled. There are also three tariff time bands: the cheapest is 6am–8pm Monday–Friday; the next-most expensive, 8–10pm Monday–Friday and 6–10pm Saturday–Sunday; the most expensive, 10pm–6am nightly. The meter must be clearly visible in the vehicle. It is usual to tip taxi and minicab drivers. If you lose anything in a licensed taxi, contact Transport for London's lost property office *(see p359)*. You will need the driver's cab licence number, displayed in the back of the taxi.

Minicabs

Licensed minicabs are badged with a blue-and-white Transport for London sticker, usually on the back window. Do not use the unlicensed cabs that sometimes cruise for business in the street. Transport for London's Cabwise service is a good way of finding a safe cab: text "CAB" to 60835 and you will be sent phone numbers for one black cab office and two reliable minicab companies in the area. If your mobile is international, text your location (street name and postal district) to 00-44-7797 800 000 to access the same service (international charges will apply).

DIRECTORY

Complaints (Transport for London)
Tel 0343 222 1234.
🌐 tfl.gov.uk

Computer Cabs
Tel 020 7908 0271.
🌐 computercab.co.uk

Dial-a-Minicab
Tel 0800 019 6768.
🌐 dialaminicab.com

Lady Minicabs (women-only drivers)
Tel 020 7272 3300.

Radio Taxis
Tel 020 7272 0272.
🌐 radiotaxis.co.uk

The light, when lit, shows the cab is available.

The meter displays your fare as it increases, and surcharges for extra passengers, luggage or unsocial hours. Fares are the same in all licensed black cabs.

Fare   Surcharges

Licensed Taxi Cabs

London's cabs are a safe way of travelling around the city. They can carry a maximum of five passengers, are all accessible for wheelchair users and have ample luggage space.

STREET FINDER

The map references given with all sights, hotels, restaurants, shops and entertainment venues described in this book refer to the maps in this section only *(see* How Map References Work *opposite)*. A complete index of street names and all the places of interest marked on the maps can be found on the following pages.

The key map shows the area of London covered by the Street Finder, with the postal codes of all the various districts. The maps include the sightseeing areas (which are colour-coded), as well as the whole of central London with all the districts important for hotels, restaurants, pubs and entertainment venues.

Postal districts are labelled and outlined in green.

Key

– – Postal district boundary

How the Map References Work

The first figure tells you which *Street Finder* map to turn to.

⓬ Wesley's Chapel–Leysian Mission

49 City Rd EC1. **Map** 7 B4. **Tel** 020 7253 2262 ⊖ Old St. House **Open** 10am–4pm Mon–Sat, 12:30–1:45pm Sun. ♿ not house. ✝ 9:45am (not 1st Sun of month), 11am Sun, 12:45pm Thu. 📷 groups book ahead. 🎧 🅆 wesleyschapel.org

The letter and number give the grid reference. Letters go across the map's top and bottom; figures on its sides.

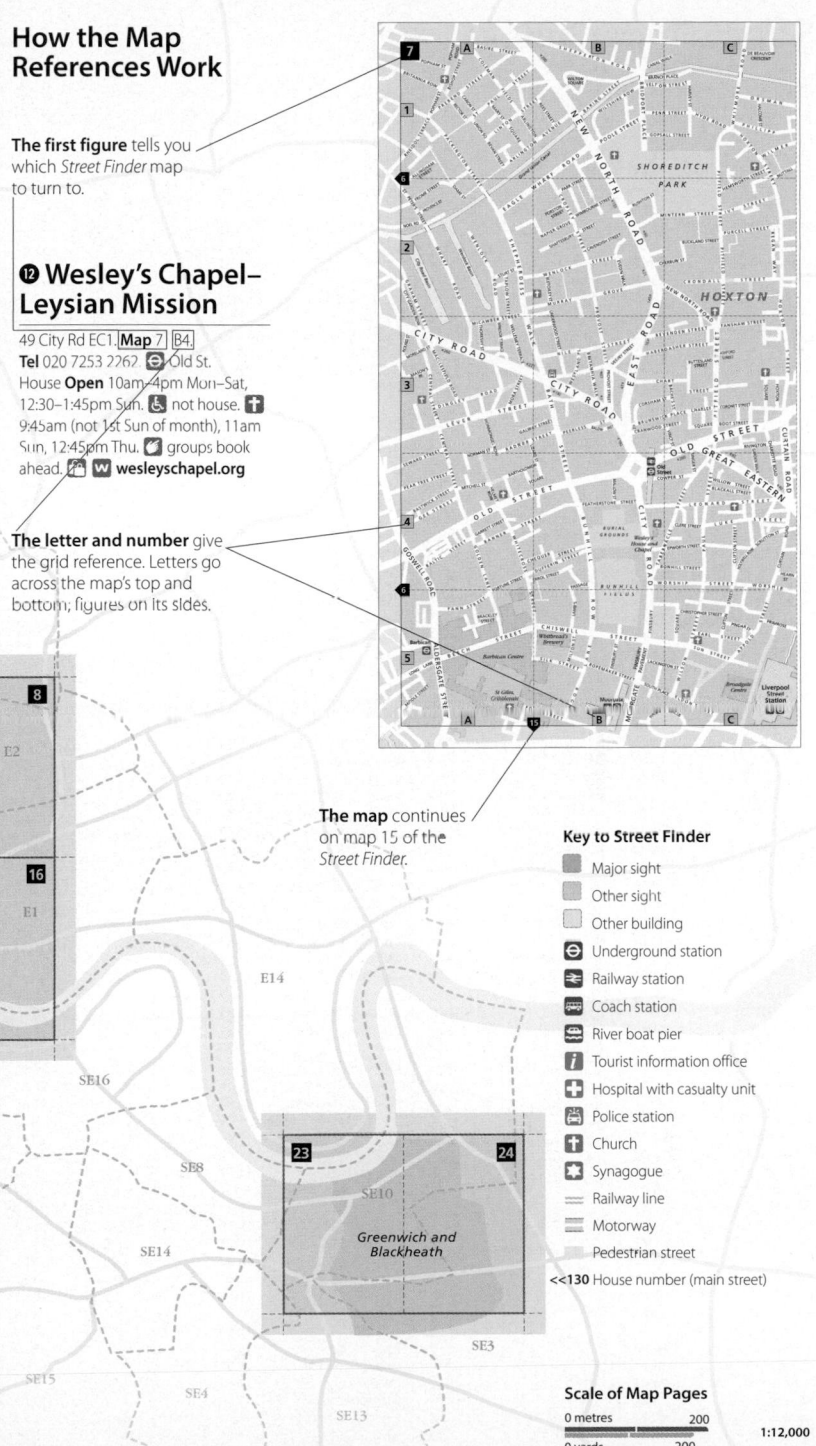

The map continues on map 15 of the *Street Finder*.

Key to Street Finder

▪ Major sight
▪ Other sight
▪ Other building
⊖ Underground station
🚉 Railway station
🚌 Coach station
⛴ River boat pier
ℹ Tourist information office
➕ Hospital with casualty unit
🔲 Police station
✝ Church
✡ Synagogue
═ Railway line
═ Motorway
▪ Pedestrian street
<<130 House number (main street)

Scale of Map Pages

0 metres 200
0 yards 200

1:12,000

Street Finder Index

A

A102 (M) SE10	24 F1
A40 (M) Flyover W2	3 A5
Abbey Gdns W6	17 A4
Abbey Orchard St SW1	13 B5
Abbey St SE1	16 D5
Abbot's La SE1	15 C4
Abbotsbury Clo W14	9 B5
Abbotsbury Rd W14	9 B5
Abchurch La EC4	15 B2
Aberdeen Ter SE3	23 C5
Abingdon Rd W8	17 C1
Abingdon St SW1	21 B1
Abingdon Vlls W8	17 C1
	18 D1
Acacia Rd NW8	3 A1
Acklam Rd W10	9 A1
Acton Ms E8	8 D1
Acton St WC1	5 C3
	6 D3
Ada Pl E2	8 F1
Ada St E8	8 F1
Adam St WC2	13 C3
Adam's Row W1	12 D3
Addington St SE1	14 D5
Addison Ave W11	9 A4
Addison Cres W14	9 A5
Addison Rd W14	9 A5
Addle Street EC2	15 A1
Adelphi Theatre WC2	13 C3
Adler St E1	16 E1
Admiral's Wlk NW3	1 A4
Admiralty Arch SW1	13 B3
Admiralty, The SW1	13 B4
Agincourt Rd NW3	2 D5
Aintree St SW6	17 A5
Airlie Gdns W8	9 C4
Air St W1	13 A2
Aisgill Ave W14	17 C3
Albany Courtyard W1	12 F3
Albany St NW1	4 E2
Albemarle St W1	12 F3
Albert Bridge SW3	19 B4
Albert Bridge SW11	19 B5
Albert Bridge Rd SW11	19 B5
Albert Ct SW7	10 F5
Albert Embankment SE1	13 C5
Albert Embankment SE1	21 C2
Albert Memorial SW7	10 F5
Albert St NW1	4 E1
Alberta St SE17	22 F3
Albion Pl EC1	6 F5
Albion St W2	11 B2
Aldenham St NW1	5 A2
Aldermanbury EC2	15 A1
Aldermanbury Sq EC2	15 A1
Alderney St SW1	20 E2
Aldersgate St EC1	7 A5
Aldersgate St EC1	15 A1
Aldford St W1	12 D3
Aldgate EC3	16 D2
Aldgate High St EC3	16 D1
Aldridge Rd Vlls W11	9 B1
Aldwych WC2	14 D2
Alexander Pl SW7	19 A1
Alexander Sq SW3	19 B1
Alexander St W2	10 D1
Alfred Pl WC1	5 A5
Alie St E1	16 E1
All Hallows by the Tower EC3	16 D3
All Saint's Dri SE3	24 E5
All Saint's Rd W11	9 B1
All Saint's St N1	5 C2
All Souls Church W1	12 F1
Allen St W8	18 D1
Allestree Rd SW6	17 A5
Allhallows La EC4	15 B3
Allingham St N1	7 A1
Allington St SW1	20 F1
Allitsen Rd NW8	3 A2
Allsop Pl NW1	3 C4
Alpha Pl SW3	19 B4
Ambergate St SE17	22 F3
Ambrosden Ave SW1	20 F1
Ampton St WC1	6 D3
Amwell St EC1	6 E3
Anderson St SW3	19 C2
Andrew's Rd E8	8 F1
Angel Ct EC2	15 B1
Angel Pas EC4	15 B3
Angel St EC1	15 A1
Angerstein La SE3	24 F4
Anhalt Rd SW11	19 B5
Ann La SW10	18 F5
Annandale Rd SE10	24 E1
Anselm Rd SW6	17 C4
Apothecaries' Hall EC4	14 F2
Appleby St E2	8 D2
Appold St EC2	7 C5
Apsley House W1	12 D4
Aquinas St SE1	14 E4
Archbishop's Pk SE1	22 D1
Archel Rd W14	17 B4
Argyle Sq WC1	5 C3
Argyle St WC1	5 C3
Argyll Rd W8	9 C5
Argyll St W1	12 F2
Arlington Ave N1	7 A1
Arlington Rd NW1	4 E1
Arlington Sq N1	7 A1
Arlington St W1	12 F3
Armadale Rd SW6	17 C5
Armitage Rd SE10	24 E1
Arnold Circus E2	8 D3
Artesian Rd W2	9 C2
Arthur St EC4	15 B2
Artillery La E1	8 D5
Artillery Row SW1	21 A1
Arundel Gdns W11	9 B2
Arundel St WC2	14 D2
Ashbridge St NW8	3 A4
Ashburn Gdns SW7	18 E2
Ashburn Pl SW7	18 E2
Ashburnham Gro SE10	23 A4
Ashburnham Pl SE10	23 A3
Ashburnham Rd SW10	18 F5
Ashby St EC1	6 F3
Asher Way E1	16 F3
Ashford St N1	7 C3
Ashley Pl SW1	20 F1
Ashmill St NW1	3 B5
Astell St SW3	19 B3
Atherstone Ms SW7	18 F1
Atterbury St SW1	21 B2
Attneave St WC1	6 D4
Aubrey Rd W8	9 B4
Aubrey Wlk W8	9 B4
Audley Sq W1	12 D3
Audrey St E2	8 F2
Augustus St NW1	4 F2
Auriol Rd W14	17 A2
Austin St E2	8 D3
Australia House WC2	14 D2
Austral St SE11	22 F1
Aveline St SE11	22 D3
Avenue Rd NW8	3 A1
Avenue, The SE10	23 C3
Avery Row W1	12 E2
Avonmore Rd W14	17 A1
Aybrook St W1	12 D1
Aylesbury St EC1	6 F4
Aylesford St SW1	21 A3
Ayres St SE1	15 A4

B

Babmaes St SW1	13 A3
Bache's St N1	7 C3
Back Church La E1	16 F2
Back Hill EC1	6 E4
Back La NW3	1 B5
Bacon St E1, E2	8 E4
Bainbridge St WC1	13 B1
Baker St NW1, W1	3 C5
	12 D1
Balcombe St NW1	3 B4
Balderton St W1	12 D2
Baldwin St EC1	7 B3
Baldwin's Gdns EC1	6 E5
Balfe St N1	5 C2
Ballast Quay SE10	23 C1
Ballast Quay SE10	24 D1
Balniel Gate SW1	21 B3
Baltic St EC1	7 A4
Bank End SE1	15 3B
Bank of England EC2	15 B1
Bankside SE1	15 A3
Bankside Gallery SE1	14 F3
Banner St EC1	7 A4
Banning St SE10	24 D1
Banqueting House SW1	13 B4
Barbican Centre EC2	7 A5
Barclay Rd SW6	17 C5
Bardsley La SE10	23 A2
Barford St N1	6 E1
Barge House St SE1	14 E3
Baring St N1	7 B1
Bark Pl W2	10 D2
Barkston Gdns SW5	18 D2
Barnby St NW1	5 A2
Barnet Gro E2	8 E3
Barnham St E1	16 D4
Barnsbury Rd N1	6 E1
Baron St N1	6 E2
Baroness Rd E2	8 E3
Baron's Ct Rd W14	17 A3
Baron's Keep W14	17 A2
Baron's Pl SE1	14 E5
Barrow Hill Rd NW8	3 A2
Barter St WC1	13 C1
Bartholomew Clo EC1	7 A5
Bartholomew La EC2	15 B1
Bartholomew Sq EC1	7 A4
Barton Rd W14	17 A3
Basil St SW3	11 C5
Basing St W11	9 B1
Basinghall Ave EC2	15 B1
Basinghall St EC2	15 B1
Basire St N1	7 A1
Bassett Rd W10	9 A1
Bastwick St EC1	7 A4
Batchelor St N1	6 E1
Bateman's Row EC2	8 D4
Bath St EC1	7 B3
Bathurst Ms W2	11 A2
Bathurst St W2	11 A2
Battersea Bridge SW3, SW11	19 A5
Battersea Bridge Rd SW11	19 A5
Battersea Park SW11	19 C5
	20 D5
Battersea Pk Rd SW8, SW11	20 F5
Battersea Power Station SW8	20 F4
Battle Bridge La SE1	15 C4
Battle Bridge Rd NW1	5 B2
Batty St E1	16 F1
Baxendale St E2	8 E3
Bayham St NW1	4 F1
Baylis Rd SE1	14 E5
Bayswater Rd W2	10 E3
Bayswater Rd W2	11 A2

B (continued)

Beaconsfield Clo SE3	24 F2
Beaconsfield Rd SE3	24 F2
Beak St W1	12 F2
Bear Gdns SE1	15 A3
Bear La SE1	14 F4
Beauchamp Pl SW3	19 B1
Beaufort Gdns SW3	19 B1
Beaufort St SW3	18 F3
	19 A4
Beaufoy Wlk SE11	22 D2
Beaumont Ave W14	17 B3
Beaumont Cres W14	17 B3
Beaumont Pl W1	5 A4
Beaumont St W1	4 D5
Beck Clo SE13	23 A5
Bedale St SE1	15 B4
Bedford Ave WC1	13 B1
Bedford Gdns W8	9 C4
Bedford Pl WC1	5 B5
Bedford Row WC1	6 D5
Bedford Sq WC1	5 B5
Bedford St WC2	13 C3
Bedford Way WC1	5 B4
Bedfordbury WC2	13 B2
Beech St EC2	7 A5
Belfast Gdns SE3	24 E2
Belgrave Ms North SW1	12 D5
Belgrave Ms West SW1	20 D1
Belgrave Pl SW1	20 D1
Belgrave Rd SW1	20 F2
	21 A3
Belgrave Sq SW1	12 D5
Belgrove St WC1	5 C3
Bell La E1	16 D1
Bell St NW1	3 A5
Bell Wharf La EC4	15 B2
Bell Yd WC2	14 D1
Bellot St SE10	24 D1
Belvedere Rd SE1	14 D4
Bemerton St N1	5 C1
Bennett Gro SE13	23 A5
Bentinck St W1	12 D1
Berkeley Sq W1	12 E3
Berkeley St W1	12 E3
Bermondsey Antiques Mkt SE1	15 C5
Bermondsey St SE1	15 C4
Bermondsey Wall East SE16	16 F5
Bermondsey Wall West SE16	16 E4
Bernard St WC1	5 C4
Berners St W1	12 F1
	13 A1
Berry St EC1	6 F4
Berwick St W1	13 A1
Bessborough Pl SW1	21 A3
Bessborough St SW1	21 A3
Bethnal Grn Rd E1	8 D4
Bethnal Grn Rd E2	8 F3
Bethwin Rd SE5	22 F5
Bevan St N1	7 A1
Bevenden St N1	7 C3
Bevington St SE16	16 F5
Bevis Marks EC3	16 D1
BFI Southbank SE1	14 D3
Bickenhall St W1	3 C5
Bidborough St WC1	5 B3
Big Ben SW1	13 C5
Billing Rd SW10	18 E5
Billingsgate EC3	15 C3
Bina Gdns SW5	18 E2
Binney St W1	12 D2
Birdcage Wlk SW1	12 F5
	13 A5
Birkenhead St WC1	5 C3
Bisham Gdns N6	2 F1
Bishop King's Rd W14	17 A2
Bishop St N1	7 A1

Bishops Ave, The NW2   1 B1
Bishop's Bridge Rd W2   10 E1
Bishop's Rd SW11   19 B5
Bishopsgate EC2   8 D5
  15 C1
Bishopsgate Church
  Yard EC2   15 C1
Bishopswood Rd N6   2 D1
Black Prince Rd SE1   21 C2
Black Prince Rd SE11   22 D2
Blackall St EC2   7 C4
Blackfriars Bridge EC4   14 F2
Blackfriars La EC4   14 F2
Blackfriars Rd SE1   14 F3
Blackfriars Underpass EC4   14 F2
Blackheath SE3   24 D5
Blackheath Ave SE10   24 D3
Blackheath Hill SE10   23 B4
Blackheath Rise SE3   23 B5
Blackheath Rd SE10   23 A4
Blackheath Vale SE3   24 D5
Blackwall La SE10   24 E1
Blagrove Rd W10   9 A1
Blandford Sq NW1   3 B5
Blandford St W1   12 D1
Blantyre St SW10   18 F5
Blenheim Cres W11   9 A2
Bletchley St N1   7 B2
Blewcoat School SW1   13 A5
Bliss Cres SE13   23 A5
Blisset St SE10   23 A4
Blomfield St EC2   15 C1
Bloomfield Terr SW1   20 D3
Bloomsbury Pl WC1   5 C5
Bloomsbury Sq WC1   5 C5
Bloomsbury St WC1   13 B1
Bloomsbury Way WC1   13 C1
Blue Anchor Yrd E1   16 E2
Blythe Rd W14   17 A1
Boadicea St N1   5 C1
Boating Lake NW1   3 C3
Boating Lake SW11   20 D5
Bolney St SW8   21 C5
Bolsover St W1   4 F5
Bolton Gdns SW5   18 D3
Bolton St W1   12 E3
Boltons, The SW10   18 E3
Bond Way SW8   21 C4
Bonhill St EC2   7 C4
Bonnington Sq SW8   21 C4
Boot St N1   7 C3
Borough High St SE1   15 B4
Borough Mkt SE1   15 B4
Borough Rd SE1   14 F5
Borough Rd SE1   15 A5
Boscobel St NW8   3 A5
Boston Pl NW1   3 B4
Boswell St WC1   5 C5
Boundary St E2   8 D4
Bourdon St W1   12 E2
Bourne St SW1   20 D2
Bouverie Pl W2   11 A1
Bouverie St EC4   14 E2
Bow La EC4   15 A2
Bow St WC2   13 C2
Bower Ave SE10   24 D3
Bowling Grn La EC1   6 E4
Bowling Grn St SE11   22 E4
Boyfield St SE1   14 F5
Brackley St EC1   7 A5
Brad St SE1   14 E4
Braganza St SE17   22 F3
Braham St E1   16 E1
Braidwood St SE1   15 C4
Bramber Rd W14   17 B4
Bramerton St SW3   19 A4
Bramham Gdns SW5   18 D2
Branch Hill NW3   1 A4
Branch Pl N1   7 B1
Brand St SE10   23 B3
Bray Pl SW3   19 C2
Bread St EC4   15 A2

Bream's Bldgs EC4   14 E1
Brechin Pl SW7   18 F2
Brecon Rd W6   17 A4
Bremner Rd SW7   10 F5
Brendon St W1   11 B1
Bressenden Pl SW1   20 F1
Brewer St W1   13 A2
Brick La E1, E2   8 E5
  8 E3
Brick St W1   12 E4
Bridge Pl SW1   20 F2
Bridge St SW1   13 C5
Bridgefoot SE1   21 C3
Bridgeman St NW8   3 A2
Bridgeway St NW1   5 A2
Bridport Pl N1   7 B1
Bridstow Pl W2   9 C1
Brill Pl NW1   5 B2
Britannia Row N1   7 A1
Britannia St WC1   5 C3
Britannia Wlk N1   7 B3
British Library WC1   5 B3
British Museum WC1   5 B5
British Telecom
  Tower W1   4 F5
Brittania Rd SW6   18 D5
Britten St SW3   19 A3
Britton St EC1   6 F5
Brixton Rd SW9   22 E5
Broad Sanctuary SW1   13 B5
Broad Wlk NW1   4 D2
Broad Wlk, The W8   10 E4
Broadbridge Clo SE3   24 F3
Broadcasting House W1   12 E1
Broadgate Centre EC2   7 C5
Broadley St NW8   3 A5
Broadley Terr NW1   3 B4
Broadwall SE1   14 E3
Broadway SW1   13 A5
Broadway Mkt E8   8 F1
Broadwick St W1   12 F2
  13 A2
Broken Wharf EC4   15 A2
Brompton Cemetery
  SW10   18 D4
Brompton Oratory SW7   19 A1
Brompton Pk Cres SW6   18 D4
Brompton Pl SW3   19 B1
Brompton Rd SW3   11 B5
  19 B1
Brompton Sq SW3   19 B1
Bromwich Ave N6   2 F3
Bronsart Rd SW6   17 A5
Brook Dri SE11   22 E1
Brook Gate W1   11 C3
Brook Ms North W2   10 F2
Brook St W1   12 E2
Brook St W2   11 A2
Brooke St EC1   6 E5
Brookmill Rd SE8   23 A5
Brook's Ms W1   12 E2
Brougham Rd E8   8 F1
Brown St W1   11 B1
Brownlow Ms WC1   6 D4
Brownlow St WC1   6 D5
Brunswick Ct SE1   16 D5
Brunswick Gdns W8   10 D4
Brunswick Pl N1   7 B3
Brunswick Sq WC1   5 C4
Brushfield St E1   8 D5
Bruton La W1   12 E3
Bruton Pl W1   12 E3
Bruton St W1   12 E3
Buck Hill Wlk W2   11 A3
Buckingham Gate SW1   12 F5
Buckingham Gate SW1   13 A5
Buckingham Palace SW1   12 F5

Buckingham Palace
  Gardens SW1   12 E5
Buckingham Palace
  Rd SW1   20 E2
Buckingham St WC2   13 C3
Buckland St N1   7 C2
Bull Wharf La EC4   15 A2
Bulls Gdns SW3   19 B2
Bulmer Pl W11   9 C3
Bunhill Fields EC1   7 B4
Bunhill Row EC1   7 B4
Burdett Ms W2   10 D1
Burgh House NW3   1 B4
Burgh St N1   6 F2
Burial Grounds EC1   7 B4
Burlington Arcade W1   12 F3
Burlington Gdns W1   12 F3
Burnaby St SW10   18 F5
Burney St SE10   23 B3
Burnsall St SW3   19 B3
Burnthwaite Rd SW6   17 C5
Burrell St SE1   14 F3
Burslem St E1   16 F2
Burton St WC1   5 B4
Burton's Ct SW3   19 C3
Bury Pl WC1   13 C1
Bury St EC3   16 D1
Bury St SW1   12 F3
Bush House WC2   14 D2
Buttesland St N1   7 C3
Buxton St E1   8 E4
Byward St EC3   16 D2

C

Cabinet War Rooms and
  Churchill Museum SW1   13 B4
Cable St E1   16 F2
Cade Rd SE10   23 C1
Cadogan Gate SW1   19 C2
Cadogan Gdns SW3   19 C2
Cadogan La SW1   20 D1
Cadogan Pier SW3   19 B4
Cadogan Pl SW1   19 C1
Cadogan Sq SW1   19 C1
Cadogan St SW3   19 C2
Cale St SW3   19 A3
Caledonian Rd N1   5 C2
  6 D1
Callender Rd SW7   10 F5
Callow St SW3   18 F4
Calshot St N1   6 D2
Calthorpe St WC1   6 D4
Calvert Ave E2   8 D3
Calvert Rd SE10   24 E1
Calvin St E1   8 D5
Camberwell New Rd SE5   22 E5
Cambridge Circus WC2   13 B2
Cambridge Gdns W10   9 A1
Cambridge Pl W8   10 E5
Cambridge Sq W2   11 A1
Cambridge St SW1   20 F3
Camden High St NW1   4 F1
Camden St NW1   4 F1
  5 A1
Camden Wlk N1   6 F1
Camera Pl SW10   18 F4
Camlet St E2   8 D4
Camley St NW1   5 A1
Campden Gro W8   9 C4
Campden Hill W8   9 C4
Campden Hill Rd W11   9 C4
Campden Hill Sq W8   9 B4
Campden St W8   9 C4
Canadian Embassy SW1   13 B3
Canal Wlk N1   7 B1
Canning Pl W8   10 E5
Cannon La NW3   1 B4
Cannon Pl NW3   1 B4
Cannon Row SW1   13 B5
Cannon St EC4   15 A2
Cannon St Rd E1   16 F1

Canon St N1   7 A1
Canrobert St E2   8 F2
Canterbury Pl SE17   22 F2
Capland St NW8   3 A4
Caradoc Clo W2   9 C1
Caradoc St SE10   24 D1
Cardigan St SE11   22 D3
Cardinal's Wharf SE1   15 A3
Cardington St NW1   5 A3
Carey St WC2   14 D1
Carlingford Rd NW3   1 B5
Carlisle La SE1   14 D5
  22 D1
Carlisle Pl SW1   20 F1
Carlos Pl W1   12 E3
Carlow St NW1   4 F1
Carlton House Terr SW1   13 A4
Carlyle Sq SW3   19 A3
Carlyle's House SW3   19 B4
Carmelite St EC4   14 E2
Carnaby St W1   12 F2
Carnegie St N1   6 D1
Carol St NW1   4 F1
Caroline Gdns E2   8 D3
Caroline Pl W2   10 D2
Caroline Terr SW1   20 D2
Carriage Dri East SW11   20 D5
Carriage Dri North SW11   19 C5
  20 D4
Carriage Dri West SW11   19 C5
Carroun Rd SW8   22 D5
Carter La EC4   14 F2
Cartwright Gdns WC1   5 B3
Cartwright St E1   16 E2
Casson St E1   8 E5
Castle Baynard St EC4   14 F2
  15 A2
Castle La SW1   12 F5
Castletown Rd W14   17 A3
Cathcart Rd SW10   18 E4
Cathedral St SE1   15 B3
Catherine Gro SE10   23 A4
Catherine St WC2   13 C2
Catton St WC1   13 C1
Causton St SW1   21 B2
Cavendish Ave NW8   3 A2
Cavendish Pl W1   12 E1
Cavendish Sq W1   12 E1
Cavendish St N1   7 B2
Caversham St SW3   19 C4
Caxton St SW1   13 A5
Cedarne Rd SW6   18 D5
Cenotaph SW1   13 B4
Central Criminal
  Court EC4   14 F1
Central Mkt WC2   13 C2
Central St EC1   7 A3
Chadwell St EC1   6 E3
Chadwick St SW1   21 A1
Chagford St NW1   3 C4
Chaldon Rd SW6   17 A5
Challoner St W14   17 B3
Chalton St NW1   5 A2
Chamber St E1   16 E2
Chambers St SE16   16 F5
Chambord St E2   8 E3
Chance St E1,E2   8 D4
Chancel St SE1   14 F4
Chancery La WC2   14 D1
Chandos Pl WC2   13 B3
Chandos St W1   12 E1
Chapel Mkt N1   6 E2
Chapel Side W2   10 D2
Chapel St NW1   3 B5
Chapel St SW1   12 D5
Chapter Rd SE17   22 F3
Chapter St SW1   21 A2
Charing Cross Pier WC2   13 C3
Charing Cross Rd WC2   13 B1
Charlbert St NW8   3 A2
Charles Dickens
  Museum WC1   6 D4

Each place name is followed by its postal district number and then by its Street Finder reference

Street	Ref
Charles La NW8	3 A2
Charles Sq N1	7 C3
Charles St W1	12 E3
Charles II St SW1	13 A3
Charleville Rd W14	17 A3
Charlotte Rd EC2	7 C3
Charlotte St W1	4 F5
	5 A5
	13 A1
Charlotte Terr N1	6 D1
Charlton Pl N1	6 F1
Charlton Way SE3	24 D4
Charlwood St SW1	20 F3
	21 A2
Charrington St NW1	5 A2
Chart St N1	7 C3
Charterhouse Sq EC1	6 F5
Charterhouse St EC1	6 F5
Cheapside EC2	15 A1
Chelsea Bridge SW1	20 E4
Chelsea Bridge Rd SW1, SW8	20 D3
Chelsea Embankment SW3	19 B4
	20 D4
Chelsea Manor St SW3	19 B3
Chelsea Old Church SW3	19 A4
Chelsea Physic Garden SW3	19 C4
Chelsea Pk Gdns SW3	18 F4
Chelsea Royal Hospital SW3	20 D3
Chelsea Sq SW3	19 A3
Cheltenham Terr SW3	19 C3
Chenies Ms WC1	5 A4
Chenies St WC1	5 A5
Cheniston Gdns W8	18 D1
Chepstow Cres W11	9 C2
Chepstow Pl W2	9 C2
Chepstow Rd W2	9 C1
Chepstow Vlls W11	9 C2
Chequer St EC1	7 B4
Cherbury St N1	7 C2
Chesham Pl SW1	20 D1
Chesham St SW1	20 D1
Cheshire St E2	8 E4
Chesson Rd W14	17 B4
Chester Gate NW1	4 E3
Chester Ms SW1	12 E5
Chester Rd NW1	4 D3
Chester Row SW1	20 D2
Chester Sq SW1	20 E1
Chester St SW1	12 E5
Chester Terr NW1	4 E3
Chester Way SE11	22 E2
Chesterfield Wlk SE10	23 C4
Cheval Pl SW7	19 B1
Chevening Rd SE10	24 F1
Cheyne Gdns SW3	19 B4
Cheyne Wlk SW3, SW10	19 A5
Chicheley St SE1	14 D4
Chichester St SW1	21 A3
Chicksand St E1	8 E5
Chiltern St W1	4 D5
	12 D1
Chilton St E2	8 E4
Chilver St SE10	24 F1
Chilworth Ms W2	10 F1
Chilworth St W2	10 F2
Chiswell St EC1	7 B5
Christ Church, Spitalfields E1	8 E5
Christchurch Hill NW3	1 B4
Christchurch St SW3	19 C4
Christchurch Way SE10	24 D1
Christian St E1	16 F1
Christopher St EC2	7 C5
Chryssell Rd SW9	22 E5
Church Row NW3	1 A5
Church St NW8	3 A5
Churchill Gardens SW1	20 F3
Churchill Gardens Rd SW1	20 F3
Churchway NW1	5 A3
Churchyard Row SE11	22 F2
Churton St SW1	20 F2
Circus St SE10	23 B3
City Garden Row N1	6 F2
	7 A2
City Rd EC1	6 F2
	7 B3
City Rd Basin N1	7 A2
Clabon Ms SW1	19 C1
Clanricarde Gdns W2	10 D3
Clapham Rd SW9	22 D5
Claredale St E2	8 F2
Claremont Clo N1	6 E2
Claremont Sq N1	6 E2
Claremont St SE10	23 A2
Clarence Gdns NW1	4 F3
Clarence House SW1	12 F4
Clarendon Pl W2	11 A2
Clarendon Rd W11	9 A2
Clarendon St SW1	20 F3
Clareville Gro SW7	18 F2
Clareville St SW7	18 F2
Clarges St W1	12 E3
Clarissa St E8	8 D1
Claverton St SW1	21 A3
Claylands Rd SW8	22 D4
Clayton St SE11	22 E4
Cleaver Sq SE11	22 E3
Cleaver St SE11	22 E3
Clem Attlee Ct SW6	17 B4
Clement's La EC4	15 C2
Cleopatra's Needle WC2	13 C3
Clere St EC2	7 C4
Clerkenwell Green EC1	6 E4
Clerkenwell Rd EC1	6 E5
Cleveland Gdns W2	10 E2
Cleveland Sq W2	10 E2
Cleveland St W1	4 F5
Cleveland Terr W2	10 F1
Clifford St W1	12 F2
Clifton St EC2	7 C4
Clink Exhibition SE1	15 B3
Clink St EC1	15 B3
Clipstone St W1	4 F5
Cliveden Pl SW1	20 D2
Cloth Fair EC1	6 F5
Cloudesley Pl N1	6 E1
Cloudesley Rd N1	6 E1
Cloudesley Sq N1	6 E1
Cloudesley St N1	6 E1
Club Row E1,E2	8 D4
Cluny Ms SW5	17 C2
Coate St E2	8 F2
Cochrane St NW8	3 A2
Cock La EC1	14 F1
Cockspur St SW1	13 B3
Coin St SE1	14 E3
Colbeck Ms SW7	18 E2
Coldbath St SE13	23 A5
Cole St SE1	15 B5
Colebrooke Row N1	6 F2
Coleherne Ct SW5	18 E3
Coleherne Rd SW10	18 D3
Coleman Fields N1	7 A1
Coleman St EC2	15 B1
Coleraine Rd SE3	24 E2
Coley St WC1	6 D4
College Pl NW1	5 A1
College St EC4	15 B2
Collier St N1	5 C2
	6 D2
Collingham Gdns SW5	18 E2
Collingham Pl SW5	18 D2
Collingham Rd SW5	18 E2
Colnbrook St SE1	22 F1
Colomb St SE10	24 E1
Colonnade WC1	5 C4
Columbia Rd E2	8 D3
Colville Gdns W11	9 B2
Colville Ms W11	9 B2
Colville Rd W11	9 B2
Colville Terr W11	9 B2
Combe Ave SE3	24 E3
Combe Ms SE3	24 E3
Combedale Rd SE10	24 F1
Comeragh Rd W14	17 A3
Commercial Rd E1	16 E1
Commercial St E1	8 D5
Commerell St SE10	24 D1
Compton Ave N6	1 C1
Compton St EC1	6 F4
Concert Hall Approach SE1	14 D4
Conduit Ms W2	10 F2
Conduit St W1	12 F2
Conington Rd SE13	23 A5
Conley St SE10	24 E1
Connaught Pl W2	11 C2
Connaught Sq W2	11 B2
Connaught St W2	11 B2
Constantine Rd NW3	2 D5
Constitution Hill SW1	12 E5
Cook's Rd SE17	22 F4
Coomer Pl SW6	17 C4
Coopers La NW1	5 B2
Cooper's Row EC3	16 D2
Cope Pl W8	17 C1
Copenhagen St N1	5 C1
Copenhagen St N1	6 D1
Copperas St SE8	23 A2
Copperfield St SE1	14 F4
	15 A4
Copthall Ave EC2	15 B1
Coptic St WC1	13 B1
Coral St SE1	14 E5
Corams' Fields WC1	5 C4
Cork St W1	12 F3
Cornhill EC3	15 C2
Cornwall Cres W11	9 A2
Cornwall Gdns SW7	18 E1
Cornwall Rd SE1	14 E4
Cornwall Terr NW1	3 C4
Coronet St N1	7 C3
Corporation Row EC1	6 E4
Corsham St N1	7 B3
Cosmo Pl WC1	5 C5
Cosser St SE1	22 D1
Cosway St NW1	3 B5
Cottage Pl SW3	19 A1
Cottesmore Gdns W8	18 E1
Cottington Clo SE11	22 F2
Cottington St SE11	22 E2
Coulson St SW3	19 C2
Counter St SE1	15 C4
County Hall SE1	13 C5
Courtauld Gallery WC2	14 D2
Courtenay St SE11	22 D3
Courtfield Gdns SW5	18 E2
Courtfield Rd SW7	18 E2
Courthope Rd NW3	2 E5
Courtnell St W2	9 C1
Cousin La EC4	15 B3
Coutt's Cres NW5	2 F3
Covent Garden WC2	13 C2
Coventry St WC1	13 A3
Cowcross St EC1	6 F5
Cowper St EC2	7 B4
Cramer St W1	4 D5
Crane St SE10	23 C1
Cranleigh St NW1	5 A2
Cranley Gdns SW7	18 F3
Cranley Ms SW7	18 F3
Cranley Pl SW7	18 F2
Cranmer Rd SW9	22 E5
Cranwood St EC1	7 B3
Craven Hill W2	10 F2
Craven Hill Gdns W2	10 E2
Craven Hill Rd W2	10 F2
Craven St WC2	13 B3
Craven Terr W2	10 F2
Crawford Pas EC1	6 E4
Crawford Pl W1	11 B1
Crawford St W1	3 C5
Creechurch La EC3	16 D1
Creed St EC4	14 F2
Creek Rd SE8	23 A2
Cremer St E2	8 D2
Cremorne Rd SW10	18 F5
Cresswell Gdns SW5	18 E3
Cresswell Pl SW10	18 E3
Cressy Rd NW3	2 D5
Crestfield St WC1	5 C3
Crewdson Rd SW9	22 D5
Crimsworth Rd SW8	21 B5
Crinan St N1	5 C2
Cringle St SW8	20 F5
Crispin St E1	8 D5
Croftdown Rd NW5	2 F4
Cromer St WC1	5 C3
Cromwell Cres SW5	17 C2
Cromwell Gdns SW7	19 A1
Cromwell Pl SW7	19 A1
Cromwell Rd SW5, SW7	18 D2
	18 F1
Crondall St N1	7 C2
Croom's Hill SE10	23 C3
Croom's Hill Gro SE10	23 B3
Cropley St N1	7 B2
Crosby Row SE1	15 B5
Croston St E8	8 F1
Crown Office Row EC4	14 E2
Crowndale Rd NW1	4 F2
	5 A1
Crucifix La SE1	15 C4
Cruden St N1	6 F1
Crutched Friars EC3	16 D2
Cubitt St WC1	6 D3
Culford Gdns SW3	19 C2
Culross St W1	12 D3
Culworth St NW8	3 B2
Cumberland Cres W14	17 A2
Cumberland Gate W1	11 C2
Cumberland Mkt NW1	4 F3
Cumberland Place NW1	11 C2
Cumberland St SW1	20 F3
Cumberland Terr NW1	4 E2
Cumberland Terr Ms NW1	4 E2
Cumming St N1	6 D2
Cundy St SW1	20 D2
Cureton St SW1	21 B2
Curlew St SE1	16 E4
Cursitor St EC4	14 E1
Curtain Rd EC2	7 C3
Curzon St W1	12 E3
Cut, The SE1	14 E4
Cutlers Gdns E1	16 D1
Cutty Sark SE10	23 B2
Cynthia St N1	6 D2
Cyrus St EC1	6 F4

D

Street	Ref
D'Arblay St W1	13 A2
Dabin Cres SE10	23 A4
Dacre St SW1	13 A5
Dallington St EC1	6 F4
Dame St N1	7 A2
Danbury St N1	6 F2
Dante Rd SE11	22 F2
Danube St SW3	19 B3
Danvers St SW3	19 A4
Dartmouth Clo W11	9 C1
Dartmouth Gro SE10	23 B5
Dartmouth Hill SE10	23 B4
Dartmouth Row SE10	23 B5
Dartmouth St SW1	13 A5
Davidson Gdns SW8	21 B5
Davies St W1	12 E2
Dawes Rd SW6	17 A5
Dawson Pl W2	9 C2
Dawson St E2	8 E2
De Beauvoir Cres N1	7 C1
De Laune St SE17	22 F3
De Vere Gdns W8	10 E5

Deal St E1	8 5F	
Dean Ryle St SW1	21 B1	
Dean St W1	13 A1	
Dean's Yd SW1	13 B5	
Decima St SE1	15 C5	
Delaford St SW6	17 A5	
Delancey St NW1	4 E1	
Delverton Rd SE17	22 F3	
Denbigh Pl SW1	20 F3	
Denbigh Rd W11	9 B2	
Denbigh St SW1	20 F2	
Denbigh Terr W11	9 B2	
Denham St SE10	24 F1	
Denman St W1	13 A2	
Denning Rd NW3	1 B5	
Dennis Severs House E1	8 D5	
Denny St SE11	22 E2	
Denyer St SW3	19 B2	
Derbyshire St E2	8 F3	
Dereham Pl EC2	8 D4	
Dericote St E8	8 F1	
Derry St W8	10 D5	
Design Museum SE1	16 E4	
Devonshire Clo W1	4 E5	
Devonshire Dri SE10	23 A4	
Devonshire Pl W1	4 D5	
Devonshire Sq EC2	16 D1	
Devonshire St W1	4 E5	
Devonshire Terr W2	10 F2	
Dewey Rd N1	6 E1	
Diamond Terr SE10	23 B4	
Diana, Princess of Wales Memorial Playground W2	10 D3	
Dilke St SW3	19 C4	
Dingley Rd EC1	7 A3	
Dinsdale Rd SE3	24 E2	
Disbrowe Rd W6	17 A4	
Disney Pl SE1	15 A4	
Diss St E2	8 E2	
Ditch Alley SE10	23 A4	
Dock St E1	16 E2	
Dockhead SE1	16 E5	
Dr Johnson's House EC4	14 E1	
Doddington Gro SE17	22 F3	
Doddington Pl SE17	22 F4	
Dodson St SE1	14 E5	
Dolben St SE1	14 F4	
Dolphin Sq SW1	21 A3	
Dombey St WC1	5 C5	
Donegal St N1	6 D2	
Donne Pl SW3	19 B2	
Doon St SE1	14 E3	
Doric Way NW1	5 A3	
Dorset Rd SW8	21 C5	
	22 D5	
Dorset St NW1, W1	3 C5	
Doughty Ms WC1	6 D4	
Doughty St WC1	6 D4	
Douglas St SW1	21 A2	
Douro Pl W8	10 E5	
Dove House St SW3	19 A3	
Dove Row E2	8 F1	
Dover St W1	12 F3	
Down St W1	12 E4	
Downing St SW1	13 B4	
Downshire Hill NW3	1 C5	
Draycott Ave SW3	19 B2	
Draycott Pl SW3	19 C2	
Draycott Terr SW3	19 C2	
Drayton Gdns SW10	18 F3	
Druid St SE1	16 D4	
Drummond Cres NW1	5 A3	
Drummond Gate SW1	21 B3	
Drummond St NW1	4 F4	
	5 A4	
Drury La WC2	13 C1	
Drysdale St N1	8 D3	
Duchess of Bedford's Wlk W8	9 C5	
Duchess St W1	4 E5	
Duchy St SE1	14 E3	
Dufferin St EC1	7 B4	
Duke Humphery Rd SE3	24 D5	
Duke of Wellington Pl SW1	12 D5	
Duke of York St SW1	13 A3	
Duke St SW1	12 F3	
Duke St W1	12 D2	
Duke St Hill SE1	15 B3	
Duke's La W8	10 D4	
Duke's Rd WC1	5 B3	
Duke's Pl EC3	16 D1	
Dunbridge St E2	8 F4	
Duncan Rd E8	8 F1	
Duncan St N1	6 F2	
Duncan Terr N1	6 F2	
Dunloe St E2	8 E2	
Dunraven St W1	11 C2	
Dunston Rd E8	8 D1	
Dunston St E8	8 D1	
Durant St E2	8 F2	
Durham St SE11	22 D3	
Durham Terr W2	10 D1	
Durward St E1	8 F5	
Dutton St SE10	23 B4	
Dyott St WC1	13 B1	
E		
Eagle Ct EC1	6 F5	
Eagle St WC1	13 C1	
Eagle Wharf Rd N1	7 A2	
Eamont St NW8	3 B2	
Earl St EC2	7 C5	
Earlham St WC2	13 B2	
Earl's Court Exhibition Centre SW5	17 C3	
Earl's Court Gdns SW5	18 D2	
Earl's Court Rd SW5, W8	18 D2	
	17 C1	
Earl's Court Sq SW5	18 D3	
Earl's Terr W8	17 B1	
Earl's Wlk W8	17 C1	
Earlswood St SE10	24 D1	
Earsby St W14	17 A2	
East Ferry Rd E14	23 A1	
East Heath NW3	1 B3	
East Heath Rd NW3	1 B4	
East Pier E1	16 F4	
East Rd N1	7 B3	
East Smithfield E1	16 E3	
East Tenter St E1	16 E2	
Eastbourne Ms W2	10 F1	
Eastbourne Terr W2	10 F1	
Eastcastle St W1	12 F1	
	13 A1	
Eastcheap EC3	15 C2	
Eastney St SE10	23 C1	
Eaton Gate SW1	20 D2	
Eaton La SW1	20 E1	
Eaton Ms SW1	20 D1	
Eaton Ms North SW1	20 D1	
Eaton Ms West SW1	20 D2	
Eaton Pl SW1	20 D1	
Eaton Sq SW1	20 D1	
Eaton Terr SW1	20 D2	
Ebbisham Dri SW8	22 D4	
Ebor St E1	8 D4	
Ebury Bridge SW1	20 E2	
Ebury Bridge Rd SW1	20 E3	
Ebury Ms SW1	20 E1	
Ebury Sq SW1	20 E2	
Ebury St SW1	20 E2	
Eccleston Bridge SW1	20 E2	
Eccleston Ms SW1	20 D1	
Eccleston Pl SW1	20 E2	
Eccleston Sq SW1	20 F2	
Eccleston St SW1	20 E1	
Edge St W8	9 C4	
Edgware Rd W2	3 A5	
	11 B1	
Edith Gro SW10	18 E4	
Edith Rd W14	17 A2	
Edith Terr SW10	18 E5	
Edith Vlls W14	17 B2	
Edwardes Sq W8	17 C1	
Effie Rd SW6	17 C5	
Egerton Cres SW3	19 B1	
Egerton Dri SE10	23 A4	
Egerton Gdns SW3	19 B1	
Egerton Pl SW3	19 B1	
Egerton Terr SW3	19 B1	
Elaine Gro NW5	2 E5	
Elcho St SW11	19 B5	
Elder St E1	8 D5	
Eldon Gro NW3	1 B5	
Eldon Rd W8	18 E1	
Eldon St EC2	7 C5	
Elgin Cres W11	9 A2	
Elia St N1	6 F2	
Eliot Hill SE13	23 B5	
Eliot Pl SE3	24 D5	
Eliot Vale SE3	23 C5	
Elizabeth Bridge SW1	20 E2	
Elizabeth St SW1	20 E2	
Ellen St E1	16 F2	
Ellerdale Clo NW3	1 A5	
Ellerdale Rd NW3	1 A5	
Elliott's Row SE11	22 F1	
Elm Pk Gdns SW10	18 F3	
	19 A3	
Elm Pk Rd SW3	18 F4	
Elm Pl SW7	18 F3	
Elm St WC1	6 D4	
Elsham Rd W14	9 A5	
Elvaston Pl SW7	18 E1	
Elverson Rd SE8	23 A5	
Elverton St SW1	21 A1	
Elwin St E2	8 E3	
Elystan Pl SW3	19 B2	
Elystan St SW3	19 B2	
Emba St SE16	16 F5	
Embankment Gdns SW3	19 C4	
Emerald St WC1	6 D5	
Emerson St SE1	15 A3	
Emma St E2	8 F2	
Emperor's Gate SW7	18 E1	
Endell St WC2	13 B1	
Enderby St SE10	24 D1	
Endsleigh Gdns WC1	5 A4	
Endsleigh St WC1	5 A4	
Enford St W1	3 B5	
English Grounds SE1	15 C4	
Enid St SE16	16 E5	
Ennismore Gdns SW7	11 A5	
Ennismore Gdns Ms SW7	11 A5	
Ensign St E1	16 F2	
Epirus Rd SW6	17 C5	
Epworth St EC2	7 C4	
Erasmus St SW1	21 B2	
Errol St EC1	7 B4	
Essex Rd N1	6 F1	
Essex St WC2	14 D2	
Essex Vlls W8	9 C5	
Estcourt Rd SW6	17 B5	
Estelle Rd NW3	2 E5	
Esterbrooke St SW1	21 A2	
Eustace Rd SW6	17 C5	
Euston Rd NW1	4 F4	
	5 A4	
Euston Sq NW1	5 A3	
Euston St NW1	5 A4	
Evelyn Gdns SW7	18 F3	
Evelyn Wlk N1	7 B2	
Eversholt St NW1	4 F2	
Eversholt St NW1	5 A3	
Ewer St SE1	15 A4	
Exeter St WC2	13 C2	
Exhibition Rd SW7	11 A5	
	19 A1	
Exton St SE1	14 E4	
Eyre St Hill EC1	6 E4	
Ezra St E2	8 E3	
F		
Fabian Rd SW6	17 B5	
Fair St SE1	16 D4	
Fairclough St E1	16 F1	
Fairholme Rd W14	17 A3	
Fakruddin St E1	8 F4	
Falconwood Ct SE3	24 E5	
Falkirk St N1	8 D2	
Fan Museum SE10	23 B3	
Fane St W14	17 B4	
Fann St EC1	7 A5	
Fanshaw St N1	7 C3	
Faraday Museum W1	12 F3	
Farm La SW6	17 C5	
Farm St W1	12 E3	
Farmer's Rd SE5	22 F5	
Farncombe St SE16	16 F5	
Farnham Royal SE11	22 D3	
Farringdon La EC1	6 E4	
Farringdon Rd EC1	6 E4	
Farringdon St EC4	14 F1	
Fashion and Textile Museum SE1	15 C4	
Fashion St E1	8 E5	
Faunce St SE17	22 F3	
Fawcett St SW10	18 E4	
Feathers Pl SE10	23 C2	
Featherstone St EC1	7 B4	
Felton St N1	7 B1	
Fenchurch Ave EC3	15 C2	
Fenchurch Bldgs EC3	16 D2	
Fenchurch St EC3	15 C2	
	16 D2	
Fentiman Rd SW8	21 C4	
	22 D5	
Fenton House NW3	1 A4	
Fernshaw Rd SW10	18 E4	
Ferry St E14	23 B1	
Festival/South Bank Pier SE1	14 D3	
Fetter La EC4	14 E1	
Field Rd W6	17 A4	
Fieldgate St E1	16 F1	
Filmer Rd SW6	17 B5	
Finborough Rd SW10	18 E4	
Fingal St SE10	24 F1	
Finsbury Circus EC2	7 B5	
	15 B1	
Finsbury Mkt EC2	7 C5	
Finsbury Pavement EC2	7 B5	
Finsbury Sq EC2	7 B5	
Finsbury St EC2	7 B5	
First St SW3	19 B1	
Fisherton St NW8	3 A4	
Fishmongers' Hall EC3	15 B2	
Fitzalan St SE11	22 D2	
Fitzgeorge Ave W14	17 A2	
Fitzjames Ave W14	17 A2	
Fitzjohn's Ave NW3	1 B5	
Fitzroy Pk N6	2 E1	
Fitzroy Sq W1	4 F4	
Fitzroy St W1	4 F5	
Flask Wlk NW3	1 B5	
Flaxman Terr WC1	5 B3	
Fleet Rd NW3	2 D5	
Fleet St EC4	14 E1	
Fleming Rd SE17	22 F4	
Fleur de Lis St E1	8 D5	
Flitcroft St WC2	13 B1	
Flood St SW3	19 B3	
Flood Wlk SW3	19 B3	
Floral St WC2	13 C2	
Florence Nightingale Museum SE1	14 D5	
Florida St E2	8 F3	
Flower Wlk, The SW7	10 F5	
Foley St W1	4 F5	
Folgate St E1	8 D5	
Forbes St E1	16 F2	
Fordham St E1	16 F1	
Fore St EC2	7 B5	

Each place name is followed by its postal district number and then by its Street Finder reference

Foreign & Common-	
wealth Office SW1	13 B4
Forset St W1	11 B1
Forston St N1	7 B2
Forsyth Gdns SE17	22 F4
Fortune St EC1	7 A4
Foster La EC2	15 A1
Foubert's Pl W1	12 F2
Foulis Terr SW7	19 A2
Fount St SW8	21 B5
Fountains, The W2	10 F3
Fournier St E1	8 E5
Foxley Rd SW9	22 E5
Foyle Rd SE3	24 E2
Frampton St NW8	3 A4
Francis St SW1	20 F1
	21 A1
Franklins Row SW3	19 C3
Frazier St SE1	14 E5
Frederick St WC1	6 D3
Friend St EC1	6 F3
Frith St W1	13 A2
Frognal NW3	1 A5
Frognal Gdns NW3	1 A5
Frognal La NW3	1 A5
Frognal Rise NW3	1 A4
Frognal Way NW3	1 A5
Frome St N1	7 A2
Fulham Broadway SW6	17 C5
Fulham Rd SW6	17 C5
Fulham Rd SW10	18 F4
Fulham Rd SW3	19 A2
Fulthorp Rd SE3	24 F5
Fulwood Pl WC1	6 D5
Furnival St EC4	14 E1

G

Gabriel's Wharf SE1	14 E3
Gainsborough	
Gdns NW3	1 B4
Gainsford St SE1	16 D4
Galway St EC1	7 A3
Gambia St SE1	14 F4
Ganton St W1	12 F2
Garden History,	
Museum of SE1	21 C1
Garden Ms W2	11 A2
Garden Row SE1	22 F1
Garden Wlk EC2	7 C4
Gardners La EC4	15 A2
Garlick Hill EC4	15 A2
Garrett St EC1	7 A4
Garrick St WC2	13 B2
Garway Rd W2	10 D2
Gascoigne Pl E2	8 D3
Gasholder Pl SE11	22 D3
Gaskin St N1	6 F1
Gatliff Rd SW1	20 E3
Gayfere St SW1	21 B1
Gayton Cres NW3	1 B5
Gayton Rd NW3	1 B5
Gaza St SE17	22 F3
Gee St EC1	7 A4
Geffrye Museum E2	8 D2
Geffrye St E2	8 D2
General Wolfe Rd SE10	23 C4
George Row SE16	16 E5
George St W1	12 D1
Georgette Pl SE10	23 B3
Gerald Rd SW1	20 D2
Geraldine Mary	
Harmsworth Park	
SE11	22 E1
Geraldine St SE11	22 F1
Gerrard Pl WC2	13 B2
Gerrard Rd N1	6 F2
Gerrard St W1	13 A2
Gerridge St SE1	14 E5
Gertrude St SW10	18 F4
Gibbs Grn W14	17 B3
Gibson Rd SE11	22 D2

Gibson Sq N1	6 E1
Gibson St SE10	24 D1
Gilbert Rd SE11	22 E2
Gilbert St W1	12 D2
Gillingham St SW1	20 F2
Gilston Rd SW10	18 F3
Giltspur St EC1	14 F1
Gipsy Moth IV SE10	23 B2
GLA Headquarters SE1	16 D4
Gladstone St SE1	22 F1
Glasgow Terr SW1	20 F3
Glasshill St SE1	14 F4
Glasshouse St W1	13 A3
Glasshouse Wlk SE11	21 C3
Glaz'bury Rd W14	17 A2
Glebe Pl SW3	19 B4
Gledhow Gdns SW5	18 E2
Gledstanes Rd W14	17 A3
Glenhurst Ave NW5	2 F5
Glenister Rd SE10	24 E1
Glentworth St NW1	3 C4
Gliddon Rd W14	17 A2
Globe St SE1	15 B5
Gloucester Ave NW1	4 D1
Gloucester Circus SE10	23 B3
Gloucester Cres NW1	4 E1
Gloucester Gate NW1	4 E2
Gloucester Ms W2	10 F2
Gloucester Ms West	
W2	10 E1
Gloucester Pl NW1	3 C4
Gloucester Pl W1	11 C1
Gloucester Pl Ms W1	11 C1
Gloucester Rd SW7	18 E1
Gloucester Sq W2	11 A2
Gloucester St SW1	20 F3
Gloucester Terr W2	10 E1
Gloucester Wlk W8	9 C4
Godfrey St SW3	19 B3
Goding St SE11	21 C3
Godson St N1	6 E2
Goffers Rd SE3	24 D5
Golden La EC1	7 A4
Goldington Cres NW1	5 A1
Goldington St NW1	5 A2
Goldsmith's Row E2	8 F2
Goldsmith's Sq E2	8 F2
Goodge Pl W1	5 A5
Goodge St W1	5 A5
Goodmans Yd E1	16 E2
Goods Way NW1	5 B2
Gopsall St N1	7 B1
Gordon House Rd NW5	2 F5
Gordon Sq WC1	5 A4
Gordon St WC1	5 A4
Gorleston St W14	17 A2
Gorsuch St E2	8 D2
Gosfield St W1	4 F5
Gosset St E2	8 E3
Goswell Rd EC1	6 F3
	7 A4
Gough St WC1	6 D4
Goulston St E1	16 D1
Gower Pl WC1	5 A4
Gower St WC1	5 A4
Gower's Wlk E1	16 E1
Gracechurch St EC3	15 C2
Grafton Pl NW1	5 A3
Grafton St W1	12 F3
Grafton Way W1	4 F4
Grafton Way WC1	5 A4
Graham St N1	6 F2
	7 A2
Graham Terr SW1	20 D2
Granary St NW1	5 A1
Granby St E2	8 E4
Granby Terr NW1	4 F2
Grand Union Canal N1	7 A1
Grand Union Canal NW1	
Grant St N1	6 E2
Grantbridge St N1	6 F1
Granville Pk SE13	23 C5

Granville Sq WC1	6 D3
Gratton Rd W14	17 A1
Gravel La E1	16 D1
Gray St SE1	14 E5
Gray's Inn WC1	6 D5
Gray's Inn Gardens WC1	6 D5
Gray's Inn Rd WC1	5 C3
	6 D4
Great Castle St W1	12 F1
Great College St SW1	21 B1
Great Cumberland Pl W1	11 C2
Great Dover St SE1	15 B5
Great Eastern St EC2	7 C4
Great George St SW1	13 B5
Great Guildford St SE1	15 A4
Great James St WC1	6 D5
Great Malborough St W1	12 F2
Great Maze Pond SE1	15 B4
Great Newport St WC2	13 B2
Great Ormond St WC1	5 C5
Great Percy St WC1	6 D3
Great Peter St SW1	21 B1
Great Portland St W1	4 F5
	12 F1
Great Pulteney St W1	13 A2
Great Queen St WC2	13 C1
Great Russell St WC1	13 B1
Great Scotland Yd SW1	13 B3
Great Smith St SW1	13 B5
	21 B1
Great St Helen's EC3	15 C1
Great Suffolk St SE1	14 F4
	15 A5
Great Sutton St EC1	6 F4
Great Titchfield St W1	4 F5
	12 F1
Great Tower St EC3	15 C2
Great Western Rd W11	9 C1
Great Winchester St EC2	15 C1
Great Windmill St W1	13 A2
Greatorex St E1	8 E5
Greek St W1	13 A2
Green Hill NW3	1 B5
Green Park SW1	12 E4
Green St W1	12 D2
Greencoat Pl SW1	21 A1
Greenfield Rd E1	16 F1
Greenwell St W1	4 F5
Greenwich Church St	
SE10	23 B2
Greenwich District	
Hospital SE10	24 E1
Greenwich Foot	
Tunnel E14, SE10	23 B1
Greenwich High Rd SE10	23 A3
Greenwich Park SE10	23 C3
	24 D3
Greenwich Pier SE10	23 B1
Greenwich South St SE10	23 A4
Greet St SE1	14 E4
Grendon St NW8	3 A4
Grenville Pl SW7	18 E1
Grenville St WC1	5 C4
Gresham St EC2	15 A1
Greville St EC1	6 E5
Grey Eagle St E1	8 D5
Greycoat Pl SW1	21 A1
Greycoat St SW1	21 A1
Greyhound Rd W14	17 A4
Grosvenor Cres SW1	12 D5
Grosvenor Cres Ms SW1	12 D5
Grosvenor Gdns SW1	20 E1
Grosvenor Gate W1	11 C3
Grosvenor Pl SW1	12 D5
Grosvenor Rd SW1	20 E4
	21 A4
Grosvenor Sq W1	12 D2
Grosvenor St W1	12 E2
Grote's Pl SE3	24 D5
Grove Terr NW5	2 F4
Grove, The N6	2 F1

Guards' Museum SW1	13 A5
Guildford Gro SE10	23 A4
Guildhall EC2	15 B1
Guildhouse St SW1	20 F2
Guilford St WC1	5 C4
Gunter Gro SW10	18 E4
Gunterstone Rd W14	17 A2
Gunthorpe St E1	16 E1
Gutter La EC2	15 A1
Guy St SE1	15 C4
Guy's Hospital EC1	15 B4
Gwendwr Rd W14	17 A3

H

Haberdasher St N1	7 B3
Hackford Rd SW9	22 D5
Hackney Rd E2	8 E2
Haddo St SE10	23 A2
Hadrian St SE10	24 D1
Haggerston Park E2	8 E2
Haggerston Rd E8	8 E1
Halcome St N1	7 C1
Haldane Rd SW6	17 B5
Half Moon St W1	12 E4
Halfmoon Cres N1	6 D1
Halford Rd SW6	17 C4
Halkin St SW1	12 D5
Hall Pl W2	3 A5
Hall St EC1	6 F3
Hallam St W1	4 E5
Hallfield Estate W2	10 E1
Halsey St SW3	19 C2
Halstow Rd SE10	24 F1
Hamilton Pl W1	12 D4
Hammersmith Rd W14	17 A2
Hampstead Gro NW3	1 A4
Hampstead Heath N6	1 C1
Hampstead High St NW3	1 B5
Hampstead Hill Gdns NW3	1 C5
Hampstead La NW3	1 B1
Hampstead La N6	2 D1
Hampstead Ponds NW3	1 C4
Hampstead Rd NW1	4 F2
Hampstead Way NW11	1 A1
Hanbury St E1	8 E5
Handel St WC1	5 C4
Handforth Rd SW9	22 D5
Hankey Pl EC1	15 B5
Hannell Rd SW6	17 A5
Hanover Gate NW1	3 B3
Hanover Pl WC2	13 C2
Hanover Sq W1	12 E2
Hanover St W1	12 F2
Hanover Terr NW1	3 B3
Hans Cres SW1	11 C5
Hans Pl SW1	19 C1
Hans Rd SW3	11 C5
	19 C1
Hans St SW1	19 C1
Hanson St W1	4 F5
Hanway Pl W1	13 A1
Hanway St W1	13 A1
Harcourt St W1	3 B5
Harcourt Ter SW10	18 E3
Hardwick St EC1	6 E3
Hardwidge St SE1	15 C4
Hardy Rd SE3	24 F2
Hare & Billet Rd SE3	23 C5
	24 D5
Hare Wlk N1	8 D2
Harewood Ave NW1	3 B4
Harley Gdns SW10	18 F3
Harley Pl W1	12 E1
Harley St W1	4 E5
	12 E1
Harleyford Rd SE11	21 C3
	22 D4
Harmsworth St SE17	22 F3
Harper Rd SE1	15 A5
Harpur St WC1	5 C5
Harriet Wlk SW1	11 C5

Harrington Gdns SW7 **18 E2**
Harrington Rd SW7 **18 F2**
 19 A2
Harrington Sq NW1 **4 F2**
Harrington St NW1 **4 F3**
Harrison St WC1 **5 C3**
Harrow Rd W2 **3 A5**
Harrowby St W1 **11 B1**
Hart St EC3 **16 D2**
Hartington Rd SW8 **21 B5**
Hartismere Rd SW6 **17 B5**
Harvey St N1 **7 C1**
Harwood Rd SW6 **18 D5**
Hasker St SW3 **19 B1**
Hastings St WC1 **5 B3**
Hatfields SE1 **14 E3**
Hatton Pl EC1 **6 E5**
Havelock St N1 **5 C1**
Hay Hill W1 **12 F3**
Hay St E2 **8 F1**
Haydon St EC3 **16 D2**
Hayles St SE11 **22 F1**
Haymarket SW1 **13 A3**
Hay's La SE1 **15 C3**
Hay's Ms W1 **12 E3**
Hayward, The SE1 **14 D3**
Hazlitt Rd W14 **17 A1**
Headfort Pl SW1 **12 D5**
Hearn St EC2 **7 C4**
Heath Brow NW3 **1 A3**
Heath Hurst Rd NW3 **1 C5**
Heath Side NW3 **1 C4**
Heath St NW3 **1 A4**
Heath Way SE3 **24 F3**
Heathcote St WC1 **5 C4**
Heddon St W1 **12 F2**
Helmet Row EC1 **7 A4**
Hemans St SW8 **21 B5**
Hemingford Rd N1 **6 D1**
Hemming St E1 **8 F4**
Hemsworth St N1 **7 C2**
Heneage St E1 **8 E5**
Henrietta Pl W1 **s12 E1**
Henrietta St WC2 **13 C2**
Henriques St E1 **16 F1**
Herbal Hill EC1 **6 E5**
Herbrand St WC1 **5 B4**
Hercules Rd SE1 **14 D5**
Hercules Rd SE1 **22 D1**
Hereford Rd W2 **9 C1**
 10 D2
Hereford St E2 **8 F4**
Hermit St EC1 **6 F3**
Herrick St SW1 **21 B2**
Hertford St W1 **12 E4**
Hesper Ms SW5 **18 D2**
Hessel St E1 **16 F1**
Hester Rd SW11 **19 B5**
Hewett St EC2 **8 D4**
Hexagon, The N6 **2 E2**
Heyford Ave SW8 **21 C5**
Heysham La NW3 **1 A4**
Hide Pl SW1 **21 A2**
High Bridge SE10 **23 C1**
High Holborn WC1 **6 D5**
 13 B1
 14 D1
High Timber St EC4 **14 F2**
Highfields Grn N6 **2 E2**
Highgate Cemetery N6 **2 F2**
Highgate Clo N6 **2 E1**
Highgate High St N6 **2 F1**
Highgate Ponds N6 **2 E3**
Highgate Rd NW5 **2 F4**
Highgate West Hill N6 **2 E2**
Highmore Rd SE3 **24 E3**
Highway, The E1 **16 F2**
Hilary Clo SW6 **18 D5**
Hill St W1 **12 E3**
Hill, The NW3 **1 A2**
Hillgate Pl W8 **9 C3**
Hillgate St W8 **9 C3**

Hillingdon St SE5 **22 F5**
Hillsleigh Rd W8 **9 B4**
Hillway N6 **2 F2**
Hindmarsh Clo E1 **16 F2**
HMS Belfast SE1 **16 D3**
Hobart Pl SW1 **20 E1**
Hobury St SW10 **18 F4**
Hogarth Rd SW5 **18 D2**
Holbein Pl SW1 **20 D2**
Holborn EC1 **14 E1**
Holborn Circus E4 **14 E1**
Holford Rd NW3 **1 B4**
Holford St WC1 **6 D3**
Holland Gdns W14 **17 A1**
Holland Gro SW9 **22 E5**
Holland House W8 **9 B5**
Holland Park W8 **9 B4**
Holland Pk W11 **9 A4**
Holland Pk Ave W11 **9 A4**
Holland Pk Gdns W14 **9 A4**
Holland Pk Ms W11 **9 B4**
Holland Pk Rd W14 **17 B1**
Holland Rd W14 **9 A5**
 17 A1
Holland St SE1 **14 F3**
Holland St W8 **10 D5**
Holland Vlls Rd W14 **9 A5**
Holland Wlk W8 **9 B4**
Holles St W1 **12 E1**
Holly Bush Vale NW3 **1 A5**
Holly Hill NW3 **1 A4**
Holly Lodge Gdns N6 **2 E2**
Holly Wlk NW3 **1 A5**
Hollymount Clo SE10 **23 B4**
Hollywood Rd SW10 **18 E4**
Holmead Rd SW6 **18 E5**
Holywell La EC2 **8 D4**
Holywell Rd SE11 **22 F2**
Holyrood St SE1 **15 C4**
Homer Row W1 **11 B1**
Homestead Rd SW6 **17 B5**
Hooper St E1 **16 E2**
Hop Exchange EC1 **15 B4**
Hopetown St E1 **8 E5**
Hopton St SE1 **14 F3**
Horatio St E2 **8 E2**
Horbury Cres W11 **9 C3**
Hornton St W8 **10 D5**
Horse Guards SW1 **13 B4**
Horse Guards Rd SW1 **13 B4**
Horseferry Pl SE10 **23 A2**
Horseferry Rd SW1 **21 B1**
Horseguards Ave SW1 **13 B4**
Hortensia Rd SW10 **18 E5**
Hosier La EC1 **14 F1**
Hoskins St SE10 **23 C1**
Houghton St WC2 **14 D2**
Houndsditch EC3 **16 D1**
Houses of Parliament
 SW1 **13 C5**
Howick Pl SW1 **21 A1**
Howie St SW11 **19 B5**
Howland St W1 **4 F5**
Hows St E2 **8 D2**
Hoxton Sq N1 **7 C3**
Hoxton St N1 **7 C1**
Hugh St SW1 **20 E2**
Humber Rd SE3 **24 E2**
Humbolt Rd W6 **17 A4**
Hungerford Foot
 Bridge SE1 **13 C3**
Hunter St WC1 **5 C4**
Huntley St WC1 **5 A4**
Hunton St E1 **8 E5**
Hyde Park W2 **11 B3**
Hyde Pk Corner W1 **12 D4**
Hyde Pk Cres W2 **11 A1**
Hyde Pk Gate SW7 **10 E5**
Hyde Pk Gdns W2 **11 A2**
Hyde Pk Sq W2 **11 A2**
Hyde Pk St W2 **11 B2**

Hyde Rd N1 **7 C1**
Hyde Vale SE10 **23 C4**

I

Ifield Rd SW10 **18 E4**
Ilchester Gdns W2 **10 D2**
Ilchester Pl W14 **9 B5**
Imperial College Rd SW7 **18 F1**
Imperial War
 Museum SE11 **22 E1**
Inglebert St EC1 **6 E3**
Ingleside Gro SE3 **24 F2**
Ingram Ave NW11 **1 B1**
Inner Circle NW1 **4 D3**
Inner Temple Gdns EC4 **14 E2**
Institute of
 Contemporary Arts
 SW1 **13 B3**
Instruments,
 Museum of SW7 **10 F5**
Inverforth Clo NW3 **1 A3**
Inverness Ms W2 **10 E2**
Inverness Pl W2 **10 E2**
Inverness Terr W2 **10 E2**
Ironmonger La EC2 **15 B1**
Ironmonger Row EC1 **7 A3**
Island Gardens E14 **23 B1**
Islington Grn Gdns N1 **6 F1**
Islington High St N1 **6 E2**
Iverna Ct W8 **10 D5**
Iverna Gdns W8 **18 D1**
Ives St SW3 **19 B2**
Ivor Pl NW1 **3 B4**
Ivy St N1 **7 C2**
Ixworth Pl SW3 **19 B2**

J

Jackman St E8 **8 F1**
Jacob St SE1 **16 E5**
Jamaica Rd SE1 **16 E5**
Jamaica Rd SE16 **16 F5**
James St W1 **12 D1**
James St WC2 **13 C2**
Jameson St W8 **9 C3**
Jamme Masjid E1 **8 E5**
Janeway St SE16 **16 F5**
Jay Ms SW7 **10 F5**
Jermyn St SW1 **12 F3**
 13 A3
Jewel Tower SW1 **13 B5**
Jewish Museum NW1 **4 E1**
Jewry St EC3 **16 D2**
Joan St SE1 **14 F4**
Jockey's Fields WC1 **6 D5**
John Adam St WC2 **13 C3**
John Carpenter St EC4 **14 E2**
John Fisher St E1 **16 E2**
John Islip St SW1 **21 B2**
John Penn St SE13 **23 A4**
John Ruskin St SE5 **22 F5**
John's Ms WC1 **6 D5**
John's St WC1 **6 D5**
Johnson's Pl SW1 **20 F3**
Jonathan St SE11 **22 D2**
Jubilee Footbridges SE1 **13 C3**
Jubilee Gardens SE1 **14 D4**
Jubilee Pl SW3 **19 B3**
Judd St WC1 **5 B3**
Judges Wlk NW3 **1 A4**
Juer St SW11 **19 B5**
Juxon St SE11 **22 D1**

K

Kay St E2 **8 F2**
Kean St WC2 **13 C2**
Keat's Gro NW3 **1 C5**
Keat's House NW3 **1 C5**
Keep, The SE3 **24 F5**
Keeton's Rd SE16 **16 F5**

Kelsey St E2 **8 F4**
Kelso Pl W8 **18 D1**
Kemble St WC2 **13 C2**
Kemplay Rd NW3 **1 B5**
Kempsford Gdns SW5 **18 D3**
Kempsford Rd SE11 **22 E2**
Kemsing Rd SE10 **24 F1**
Kenchester Clo SW8 **21 C5**
Kendal Clo SW9 **22 F5**
Kendal St W2 **11 B2**
Kenley Wlk W11 **9 A3**
Kennet St E1 **16 F3**
Kennington Gro SE11 **22 D4**
Kennington La SE11 **22 D3**
Kennington Oval SE11 **22 D4**
Kennington Park SE11 **22 E4**
Kennington Pk
 Gdns SE11 **22 F4**
Kennington Pk Rd SE11 **22 E4**
Kennington Rd SE1 **22 E1**
Kensington Church
 St W8 **10 D4**
Kensington Ct Pl W8 **10 E5**
Kensington Ct W8 **10 E5**
Kensington Gardens W2 **10 E4**
Kensington Gdns Sq W2 **10 D2**
Kensington Gate W8 **10 E5**
Kensington Gore SW7 **10 F5**
Kensington High St W8 **9 C5**
 10 D5
Kensington High St W14 **17 B1**
Kensington Palace W8 **10 D4**
Kensington Palace
 Gdns W8 **10 D3**
Kensington Pk Gdns W11 **9 B3**
Kensington Pk Rd W11 **9 B2**
Kensington Pl W8 **9 C4**
Kensington Rd W7, W8 **10 E5**
 11 A5
Kensington Roof
 Gardens W8 **10 D5**
Kensington Sq W8 **10 D5**
Kent Pas NW1 **3 B4**
Kent St E2 **8 E2**
Kentish Bldgs SE1 **15 B4**
Kenton St WC1 **5 B4**
Kenway Rd SW5 **18 D2**
Kenwood Clo NW3 **1 B1**
Kenwood House N6 **1 C1**
Keyworth St SE1 **14 F5**
Kidbrooke Gdns SE3 **24 F5**
Kildare Gdns W2 **10 D1**
Kildare Terr W2 **10 D1**
Killick St N1 **5 C2**
Kiln Pl NW5 **2 F5**
King St EC2 **15 B1**
King St SW1 **12 F4**
 13 A3
King St WC2 **13 B2**
King Charles St SW1 **13 B5**
King Edward St EC1 **15 A1**
King Edward Wlk SE1 **22 E1**
King George St SE10 **23 B3**
King James St SE1 **14 F5**
King William St EC4 **15 B2**
King William Wlk SE10 **23 B2**
Kingly St W1 **12 F2**
King's Bench Wlk EC4 **14 E2**
King's Head Yd SE1 **15 B4**
Kings Rd SW3 **19 A4**
King's Rd SW6, SW10 **18 E5**
King's Scholars Pas SW1 **20 F1**
King's Terr NW1 **4 F1**
King's Cross Rd WC1 **5 C2**
 6 D3
Kingsland Basin N1 **8 D1**
Kingsland Rd E2 **8 D1**
Kingsmill Ter NW8 **3 A2**
Kingstown St NW1 **4 D1**
Kingsway WC2 **13 C1**
Kinnerton St SW1 **11 C5**
Kinnoul Rd W6 **17 A4**

Kipling St SE1	15 C5
Kirby Gro SE1	15 C4
Kirby St EC1	6 E5
Kirtling St SW8	20 F4
Kirton Gdns E2	8 E3
Knaresborough Pl SW5	18 D2
Knighten St E1	16 F4
Knightrider St EC4	14 F2
Knightsbridge SW1	12 D5
Knivet Rd SW6	17 C4
Knox St W1	3 C5
Kynance Pl SW7	18 E1

L

Laburnum St E2	8 D1
Lackington St EC2	7 B5
Ladbroke Cres W11	9 A1
Ladbroke Gdns W11	9 B2
Ladbroke Gro W11	9 A1
Ladbroke Rd W11	9 B3
Ladbroke Sq W1	19 B3
Ladbroke Terr W11	9 B3
Ladbroke Wlk W11	9 B3
Lafone St SE1	16 D4
Lamb St E1	8 D5
Lamb Wlk SE1	15 C5
Lamb's Conduit St WC1	5 C4
Lamb's Pas EC1	7 B5
Lambeth Bridge SE1	21 C1
Lambeth High St SE1	21 C2
Lambeth Palace Rd SE1	14 D5
	21 C1
Lambeth Palace SE1	21 C1
Lambeth Rd SE1	22 D1
Lambeth Wlk SE11	22 D1
Lamble St NW5	2 F5
Lamlash St SE11	22 F1
Lamont Rd SW10	18 F4
Lancaster Ct SW6	17 C5
Lancaster Gate W2	10 F2
Lancaster House SW1	12 F4
Lancaster Ms W2	10 F2
Lancaster Pl WC2	13 C2
Lancaster Rd W11	9 A1
Lancaster St SE1	14 F5
Lancaster Terr W2	10 F2
Lancaster Wlk W2	10 F3
Lancelot Pl SW7	11 B5
Langbourne Ave N6	2 F3
Langdale Rd SE10	23 A3
Langham Hotel W1	12 E1
Langham Pl W1	12 E1
Langham St W1	12 F1
Langley La SW8	21 C4
Langley St WC2	13 B2
Langton Rd SW9	22 F5
Langton St SW10	18 F4
Langton Way SE3	24 F4
Lansdowne Cres W11	9 A3
Lansdowne Rd W11	9 A2
Lansdowne Rise W11	9 A3
Lansdowne Terr WC1	5 C4
Lansdowne Wlk W11	9 B3
Lant St SE1	15 A5
Lassell St SE10	23 C1
	24 D1
Launceston Pl W8	18 E1
Laundry Rd W6	17 A4
Laurence Poutney La EC4	15 B2
Laverton Pl SW5	18 D2
Lavington St SE1	14 F4
Law Society WC2	14 E1
Lawn La SW8	21 C4
Lawrence St SW3	19 A4
Laystall St EC1	6 D4
Leadenhall Mkt EC3	15 C2
Leadenhall St EC3	15 C2
	16 D2
Leake St SE1	14 D4
Leamington Rd Vlls W11	9 B1
Leather La EC1	6 E5

Leathermarket St SE1	15 C5
Leathwell Rd SE13	23 A5
Ledbury Rd W11	9 C2
Leeke St WC1	5 C3
Lees Pl W1	12 D2
Leicester Pl WC2	13 B2
Leicester Sq WC2	13 B3
Leicester St WC2	13 A2
Leigh St WC1	5 B4
Leighton House W14	17 B1
Leinster Gdns W2	10 E2
Leinster Pl W2	10 E2
Leinster Sq W2	10 D2
Leinster Terr W2	10 E2
Leman St E1	16 E1
Lennox Gdns Ms SW1	19 B1
Lennox Gdns SW1	19 C1
Leonard St EC2	7 C4
Lethbridge Clo SE13	23 A5
Letterstone Rd SW6	17 B5
Lever St EC1	7 A3
Lewisham Hill SE13	23 B5
Lewisham Rd SE13	23 A4
Lexham Gdns W8	18 D1
Lexington St W1	13 A2
Leyden St E1	16 D1
Library St SE1	14 F5
Lidlington Pl NW1	4 F2
Lilestone St NW8	3 B4
Lillie Rd SW6	17 A5
Lime St EC3	15 C2
Limerston St SW10	18 F4
Lincoln's Inn Fields WC2	14 D1
Lincoln's Inn WC2	14 D1
Linden Gdns W2	9 C3
Linhope St NW1	3 B4
Linley Sambourne House W8	9 C5
Linton St N1	7 A1
Lisburne Rd NW3	2 E5
Lisgar Terr W14	17 B2
Lisle St WC2	13 A2
Lissenden Gdns NW5	2 F5
Lisson Gro NW1	3 B5
Lisson Gro NW8	3 A4
Lisson St NW1	3 A5
Little Boltons, The SW10	18 E3
Little Britain EC1	15 A1
Little Chester St SW1	12 E5
Little College St SW1	21 B1
Little Dorrit Ct SE1	15 A4
Little Portland St W1	12 F1
Liverpool Rd N1	6 E1
Liverpool St EC2	15 C1
Lizard St EC1	7 A3
Lloyd Baker St WC1	6 D3
Lloyd St WC1	6 D3
Lloyd's of London EC3	15 C2
Lloyd's Ave EC3	16 D2
Lloyd's Row EC1	6 E3
Lodge Rd NW8	3 A3
Logan Ms W8	17 C2
Logan Pl W8	17 C2
Lollard St SE11	22 D2
Loman St SE1	14 F4
Lombard St EC3	15 B2
London Aquarium SE1	14 C4
London Bridge SE1	15 B3
London Bridge City Pier SE1	15 C3
London Bridge St EC1	15 B4
London Central Mosque NW1	3 B3
London Coliseum WC2	13 B3
London Dungeon SE1	13 C4
London Eye SE1	13 C4
London Rd SE1	14 F5
	22 F1

London St W2	10 F1
	11 A1
London Transport Museum WC2	13 C2
London Wall EC2	15 A1
London Zoo NW1	4 D2
London, Museum of EC2	15 A1
Long Acre WC2	13 B2
Long La EC1	6 F5
	7 A5
Long La SE1	15 B5
Long Pond Rd SE3	24 D4
Long St E2	8 D3
Longford St NW1	4 F4
Longridge Rd SW5	17 C2
Longville Rd SE11	22 F2
Lonsdale Rd W11	9 B2
Lord Hill Bridge W2	10 D1
Lord's Cricket Ground NW8	3 A3
Lorrimore Rd SE17	22 F4
Lorrimore Sq SE17	22 F4
Lot's Rd SW10	18 E5
Lothbury EC2	15 B1
Loughborough St SE11	22 D3
Lovat La EC3	15 C2
Love La EC2	15 A1
Lower Addison Gdns W14	9 A5
Lower Belgrave St SW1	20 E1
Lower Grosvenor Pl SW1	20 E1
Lower Marsh SE1	14 D5
Lower Sloane St SW1	20 D3
Lower Terr NW3	1 A4
Lower Thames St EC3	15 C3
	16 D3
Lowndes Pl SW1	20 D1
Lowndes Sq SW1	11 C5
Lowndes St SW1	20 D1
Lucan Pl SW3	19 B2
Ludgate Circus EC4	14 F1
Ludgate Hill EC4	14 F1
Luke St EC2	7 C4
Lupus St SW1	20 F3
	21 A3
Luscombe Way SW8	21 B5
Luton Pl SE10	23 B3
Luton St NW8	3 A4
Luxborough St W1	4 D5
Lyall St SW1	20 D1
Lyndale Clo SE3	24 E2

M

Mabledon Pl WC1	5 B3
Mablethorpe Rd SW6	17 A5
Macclesfield Rd EC1	7 A3
McGregor Rd W11	9 B1
Mackennal St NW8	3 B2
Mackeson Rd NW3	2 D5
Macklin St WC2	13 C1
Mackworth St NW1	4 F3
McLeod's Ms SW7	18 E1
Maclise Rd W14	17 A1
Madame Tussauds' NW1	4 D5
Maddox St W1	12 F2
Maiden La WC2	13 C2
Maidenstone Hill SE10	23 B4
Makepeace Ave N6	2 F3
Malet St WC1	5 A5
Mall, The SW1	12 F4
	13 A4
Mallord St SW3	19 A4
Mallow St EC1	7 B4
Malta St EC1	6 F4
Maltby St SE1	16 D5
Malton Rd W10	9 A1
Manchester Rd E14	23 B1
Manchester Sq W1	12 D1
Manchester St W1	12 D1
Manciple St SE1	15 B5
Mandela St NW1	4 F1

Mandela St SW9	22 E5
Mandeville Clo SE3	24 F3
Mandeville Pl W1	12 D1
Manette St W1	13 B1
Manor Pl SE17	22 F3
Manresa Rd SW3	19 A3
Mansell St E1	16 E2
Mansfield Rd NW3	2 E5
Mansford St E2	8 F2
Mansion House EC4	15 B2
Manson Pl SW7	18 F2
Maple St E2	8 F4
Maple St W1	4 F5
Marble Arch W1	11 C2
Marchbank Rd W14	17 B4
Marchmont St WC1	5 B4
Margaret St W1	12 F1
Margaretta Terr SW3	19 B4
Margery St WC1	6 D3
Marigold St SE16	16 F5
Marine St SE16	16 E5
Mark St EC2	7 C4
Market Entrance SW8	21 A5
Market Ms W1	12 E4
Markham Sq SW3	19 B3
Markham St SW3	19 B3
Marlborough Bldgs SW3	19 B2
Marlborough House SW1	13 A4
Marlborough Rd SW1	13 A4
Marlborough St SW3	19 B2
Marloes Rd W8	18 D1
Marshall St W1	12 F2
Marshalsea Rd SE1	15 A4
Marsham St SW1	21 B1
Mary Pl W11	9 A3
Mary St N1	7 A1
Marylebone High St W1	4 D5
Marylebone La W1	12 E1
Marylebone Rd NW1	3 B5
	4 D5
Marylebone St W1	4 D5
Marylee Way SE11	22 D2
Maryon Ms NW3	1 C5
Mason's Pl EC1	7 A3
Matheson Rd W14	17 B2
Matilda St N1	6 D1
Maunsel St SW1	21 A1
Mawbey St SW8	21 B5
Maxwell Rd SW6	18 D5
Maygood St N1	6 D2
Maze Hill SE10	24 D2
Meadow Rd SW8	21 C5
	22 D4
Mecklenburgh Gardens WC1	5 C4
Medway St SW1	21 A1
Melbury Rd W14	17 B1
Mendora Rd SW6	17 A5
Mercer St WC2	13 B2
Meredith St EC1	6 F3
Mermaid Ct SE1	15 B4
Merryfield SE3	24 F5
Merton La N6	2 E2
Methley St SE11	22 E3
Mews St E1	16 E3
Meymott St SE1	14 E4
Micawber St N1	7 A3
Middle St EC1	7 A5
Middle Temple La EC4	14 E2
Middlesex St E1	16 D1
Midland Pl E14	23 B1
Midland Rd NW1	5 B2
Milborne Gro SW10	18 F3
Miles St SW8	21 B4
Milford La WC2	14 D2
Milk St EC2	15 A1
Mill Row N1	8 D1
Mill St SE1	16 E5
Millbank SW1	21 B1
Millfield La N6	1 C1
Millfield La N6	2 D1
Millfield Pl N6	2 E3

Place	Ref
Millman St WC1	5 C4
Milmans St SW10	19 A4
Milner St SW3	19 C1
Milson Rd W14	17 A1
Milton St EC2	7 B5
Milverton St SE11	22 E3
Mincing La EC3	15 C2
Minera Ms SW1	20 D2
Ministry of Defence SW1	13 C4
Minories EC3	16 D2
Minories Hill EC3	16 D2
Mint St SE1	15 A4
Mintern St N1	7 C2
Mirabel Rd SW6	17 B5
Mitchell St EC1	7 A4
Mitre Rd SE1	14 E4
Mitre St EC3	16 D2
Molyneux St W1	11 B1
Monck St SW1	21 B1
Monkton St SE11	22 E2
Monmouth Rd W2	10 D2
Monmouth St WC2	13 B2
Montpelier St SW7	11 B1
Montagu Mansions W1	3 C5
Montagu Pl W1	4 D5
	11 C1
Montagu Sq W1	11 C1
Montagu St W1	11 C1
Montague Pl WC1	5 B5
Montague St WC1	5 B5
Montclare St E2	8 D4
Montford Pl SE11	22 D3
Montpelier Pl SW7	11 B5
Montpelier Row SE3	24 E5
Montpelier Sq SW7	11 B5
Montpelier Wlk SW7	11 B5
Montrose Ct SW7	11 A5
Montrose Pl SW1	12 D5
Monument EC3	15 C2
Monument St EC3	15 C2
Moorhouse Rd W2	9 C1
Moor La EC2	7 B5
Moore Pk Rd SW6	18 D5
Moore St SW3	19 C2
Moorfields EC2	7 B5
Moorgate EC2	7 B5
	15 B1
Mora St EC1	7 A3
Moravian Pl SW10	19 A4
Morden Clo SE13	23 B5
Morden Hill SE13	23 B5
Morden Rd SE3	24 F5
Morden Rd Ms SE3	24 F5
Morden St SE13	23 A4
Moreland St EC1	6 F3
	7 A3
Moreton Pl SW1	21 A3
Moreton St SW1	21 A3
Morgan's La SE1	15 C4
Morley St SE1	14 E5
Mornington Ave W14	17 B2
Mornington Cres NW1	4 F2
Mornington Pl NW1	4 F2
Mornington Terr NW1	4 E1
Morocco St SE1	15 C5
Morpeth Terr SW1	20 F1
Mortimer St W1	12 F1
Morwell St WC1	13 A1
Moscow Rd W2	10 D2
Mossop St SW3	19 B2
Motcomb St SW1	12 D5
Mount Pleasant WC1	6 D4
Mount Row W1	12 E3
Mount St W1	12 D3
Mount, The NW3	1 A4
Mounts Pond Rd SE3	23 C5
	24 D5
Mowll St SW9	22 D5
Moylan Rd W6	17 A4
Mulberry St E1	16 F1
Mulberry Wlk SW3	19 A4
Mulgrave Rd SW6	17 B4
Mulvaney Way SE1	15 C5
Mund St W14	17 B3
Munden St W14	17 A2
Munster Rd SW6	17 A5
Munster Sq NW1	4 F4
Muriel St N1	6 D1
Murphy St SE1	14 E5
Murray Gro N1	7 B2
Musard Rd W6	17 A4
Muscal Rd SW1	13 B1
Mycenae Rd SE3	24 F2
Myddelton Pas EC1	6 E3
Myddelton Sq EC1	6 E3
Myddelton St EC1	6 E4
Myrdle St E1	16 F1

N

Napier Gro N1	7 B2
Napier Pl W14	17 B1
Napier Rd W14	17 A1
Nash St NW1	4 E3
Nassington Rd NW3	2 D5
National Gallery WC2	13 B3
National Maritime Museum SE10	23 C2
National Portrait Gallery WC2	13 B3
National Theatre SE1	14 D3
Natural History Museum SW7	18 F1
	19 A1
Navarre St E2	8 D4
Nazrul St E2	8 D2
Neal St WC2	13 B1
Neal's Yd WC2	13 B1
Neckinger St SE1	16 E5
Nectarine Way SE13	23 A5
Nelson Gdns E2	8 F3
Nelson Pl N1	6 F2
Nelson Rd SE10	23 B2
Nelson Sq SE1	14 F4
Nelson's Column WC2	13 B3
Nesham St E1	16 F3
Netherton Gro SW10	18 F4
Nevada St SE10	23 B3
Nevern Pl SW5	17 C2
Nevern Rd SW5	17 C2
Nevern Sq SW5	17 C2
Neville St SW7	19 A3
New Bond St W1	12 E2
New Bridge St EC4	14 F2
New British Library NW1	5 B3
New Broad St EC2	15 C1
New Cavendish St W1	4 E5
New Change EC4	15 A2
New Compton St WC2	13 B1
New Covent Garden Mkt SW8	21 A5
New End NW3	1 B4
New End Sq NW3	1 B4
New Fetter La EC4	14 E1
New Inn Yd EC2	8 D4
New North Rd N1	7 B1
New North St WC1	5 C5
New Oxford St WC1	13 B1
New Palace Yd SW1	13 B5
New Rd E1	8 F5
	16 F1
New Row WC2	13 B2
New Scotland Yd SW1	13 A5
New Sq WC2	14 D1
New St EC2	16 D1
New Wharf Rd N1	5 C2
New Zealand House SW1	13 A3
Newburn St SE11	22 D3
Newcomen St SE1	15 B4
Newcourt St NW8	3 A2
Newgate St EC1	14 F1
	15 A1
Newington Butts SE11	22 F2
Newington Causeway SE11	5 A5
Newman St W1	13 A1
Newport St SE11	22 D2
Newton Rd W2	10 D1
Newton St WC2	13 C1
Nicholas La EC4	15 B2
Nile St N1	7 B3
Nine Elms La SW8	21 A4
Noble St EC2	15 A1
Noel Rd N1	6 F2
	7 A2
Noel St W1	13 A1
Norfolk Cres W2	11 B1
Norfolk Pl W2	11 A1
Norfolk Rd NW8	3 A1
Norfolk Sq W2	11 A1
Norland Sq W11	9 A4
Norman Rd SE10	23 A3
Norman St EC1	7 A4
Normand Rd W14	17 B4
North Audley St W1	12 D2
North East Pier E1	16 F4
North End Ave NW3	1 A2
North End NW3	1 A2
North End Rd NW6	17 C3
North End Rd W14	17 A2
North End Way NW3	1 A2
North Gower St NW1	4 F3
North Gro N6	2 F1
North Rd N6	2 F1
North Row W1	11 C2
North Tenter St E1	16 E2
North Terr SW3	19 A1
North West Pier E1	16 F4
North Wharf Rd W2	10 F1
Northampton Rd EC1	6 E4
Northampton Sq EC1	6 F3
Northburgh St EC1	6 F4
Northdown St N1	5 C2
Northington St WC1	6 D5
Northumberland Ave WC2	13 B3
Northumberland Pl W2	9 C1
Norton Folgate E1	8 D5
Norway St SE10	23 A2
Notting Hill Gate W11	9 C3
	10 D3
Nottingham Pl W1	4 D5
Nottingham St W1	4 D5
Nutford Pl W1	11 B1
Nuttall St N1	7 C1
	8 D1

O

Oak Hill Pk NW3	1 A5
Oak Hill Way NW3	1 A4
Oak Tree Rd NW8	3 A3
Oak Village NW5	2 F5
Oakcroft Rd SE13	23 C5
Oakden St SE11	22 E2
Oakeshott Ave N6	2 F2
Oakley Gdns SW3	19 B4
Oakley Sq NW1	5 A2
Oakley St SW3	19 B4
Oakwood Ct W14	9 B5
Oat La EC2	15 A1
Observatory Gdns W8	9 C4
Offley Rd SW9	22 E5
Old Bailey EC4	14 F1
Old Bethnal Grn Rd E2	8 F3
Old Bond St W1	12 F3
Old Brewery Ms NW3	1 B5
Old Broad St EC2	15 C1
Old Brompton Rd SW5	18 D3
Old Brompton Rd SW7	19 A2
Old Castle St E1	16 D1
Old Cavendish St W1	12 E1
Old Church St SW3	19 A3
Old Compton St W1	13 A2
Old Ct Pl W8	10 D5
Old Gloucester St WC1	5 C5
Old Jamaica Rd SE16	16 E5
Old Jewry EC2	15 B1
Old Marylebone Rd NW1	3 B5
	11 B1
Old Montague St E1	8 E5
Old Nichol St E2	8 D4
Old Orchard, The NW3	2 D5
Old Palace Yd SW1	13 B5
Old Paradise St SE11	22 D2
Old Pk La W1	12 E4
Old Pye St SW1	21 A1
Old Quebec St W1	11 C2
Old Queen St SW1	13 B5
Old Royal Observatory SE10	23 C3
Old St EC1	7 A4
Old St Thomas's Operating Theatre EC1	15 B4
Old Vic SE1	14 E5
Old Woolwich Rd SE10	23 C1
	24 D1
Olympia W14	17 A1
Olympia Way W14	17 A1
Ongar Rd SW6	17 C4
Onslow Gdns SW7	18 F2
Onslow Sq SW7	19 A2
Ontario St SE1	22 F1
Opal St SE11	22 F2
Orange St WC2	13 B3
Orbain Rd SW6	17 A5
Orchard Dri SE3	24 D5
Orchard Hill SE13	23 A5
Orchard Rd SE3	24 D5
Orchard St W1	12 D2
Orchard, The SE3	23 C5
Orchardson St NW8	3 A1
Orde Hall St WC1	5 C5
Ordnance Hill NW8	3 A1
Orlop St SE10	24 D1
Orme Ct W2	10 D3
Orme La W2	10 D3
Ormiston Rd SE10	24 F1
Ormonde Gate SW3	19 C3
Ormonde Terr NW8	3 C1
Ormsby St E2	8 D2
Orsett St SE11	22 D3
Orsett Terr W2	10 E1
Orsman Rd N1	7 C1
	8 D1
Osborn St E1	16 E1
Osnaburgh St NW1	4 E4
Ossington St W2	10 D3
Ossulston St NW1	5 A2
Oswin St SE11	22 F1
Otto St SE17	22 F4
Outer Circle NW1	3 B2
	4 D2
Oval Pl SW8	22 D5
Oval Rd NW1	4 E1
Oval, The SE11	22 D4
Oval Way SE11	22 D3
Ovington Gdns SW3	19 B1
Ovington Sq SW3	19 B1
Ovington St SW3	19 B1
Owen St EC1	6 E2
Oxford Gdns W10	9 A1
Oxford Sq W2	11 B1
Oxford St W1	12 D2
	13 A1

P

Pakenham St WC1	6 D4
Packington Sq N1	7 A1
Packington St N1	6 F1
	7 A1
Paddington Basin W2	11 A1
Paddington Garden W2	3 A5

Paddington St W1	4 D5	Pembroke Gdns W8	17 C1	Poole St N1	7 B1	Queen Victoria St EC4	14 F2

Paddington St W1 — 4 D5
Page St SW1 — 21 B2
Paget St EC1 — 6 F3
Pagoda Gdns SE3 — 23 C5
Palace Ave W8 — 10 D4
Palace Ct W2 — 10 D3
Palace Gate W8 — 10 E5
Palace Gdns Ms W8 — 10 D3
Palace Gdns Terr W8 — 10 D3
Palace Grn W8 — 10 D4
Palace St SW1 — 12 F5
Palace Theatre WC2 — 13 B2
Palfrey Pl SW8 — 22 D5
Pall Mall SW1 — 13 A3
Pall Mall East SW1 — 13 B3
Palliser Rd W14 — 17 A3
Palmer St SW1 — 13 A5
Pancras Rd NW1 — 5 B2
Panton St SW1 — 13 A3
Parade, The SW11 — 19 C5
Paradise Wlk SW3 — 19 C4
Paragon Pl SE3 — 24 E5
Paragon, The SE3 — 24 F5
Pardoner St SE1 — 15 B5
Paris Garden SE1 — 14 E3
Park Cres W1 — 4 E5
Park La W1 — 11 C2
                 12 D3
Park Pl SW1 — 12 F4
Park Rd NW1, NW8 — 3 B3
Park Row SE10 — 23 C1
Park Sq East NW1 — 4 E4
Park Sq Gdns NW1 — 4 E4
Park Sq West NW1 — 4 E4
Park St SE1 — 15 A3
Park St W1 — 12 D2
Park Village East NW1 — 4 E2
Park Vista SE10 — 23 C2
                   24 D2
Park West Pl W2 — 11 B1
Park Wlk SW10 — 18 F4
Parker St WC2 — 13 C1
Parkfield St N1 — 6 E2
Parkgate Rd SW11 — 19 B5
Parkville Rd SW6 — 17 B5
Parkway NW1 — 4 E1
Parliament Hill N6 — 2 D4
                      2 E4
Parliament Sq SW1 — 13 B5
Parliament St SW1 — 13 B4
Parr St N1 — 7 B2
Parry St SW8 — 21 C4
Pascal St SW8 — 21 B5
Pater St W8 — 17 C1
Paul St EC2 — 7 C4
Paultons Sq SW3 — 19 A4
Paultons St SW3 — 19 A4
Paveley Dri SW11 — 19 A5
Paveley St NW8 — 3 B4
Pavilion Rd SW1 — 11 C5
                   19 C1
Peabody Ave SW1 — 20 E3
Peace Pagoda SW11 — 19 C5
Peachum Rd SE3 — 24 F2
Pear Tree St EC1 — 7 A4
Pearman St SE1 — 14 E5
Pearson St E2 — 8 D2
Pedley St E1 — 8 E4
Peel St W8 — 9 C4
Peerless St EC1 — 7 B3
Pelham Cres SW7 — 19 A2
Pelham Pl SW7 — 19 A2
Pelham St SW7 — 19 A2
Pellant Rd SW6 — 17 A5
Pelter St E2 — 8 D3
Pelton Rd SE10 — 24 D1
Pembridge Cres W11 — 9 C2
Pembridge Gdns W2 — 9 C3
Pembridge Pl W2 — 9 C2
Pembridge Rd W11 — 9 C3
Pembridge Sq W2 — 9 C3
Pembridge Vlls W11 — 9 C2

Pembroke Gdns W8 — 17 C1
Pembroke Gdns Clo W8 — 17 C1
Pembroke Rd W8 — 17 C1
Pembroke Sq W8 — 17 C1
Pembroke Vlls W8 — 17 C1
Penfold St NW1, NW8 — 3 A4
Penn St N1 — 7 B1
Pennant Ms W8 — 18 D1
Pennington St E1 — 16 F3
Penryn St NW1 — 5 A2
Penton Pl SE17 — 22 F2
Penton Rise WC1 — 6 D3
Penton St N1 — 6 D2
Pentonville Rd N1 — 6 D2
Penywern Rd SW5 — 18 D3
Penzance Pl W11 — 9 A3
Penzance St W11 — 9 A3
Pepper St SE1 — 15 A4
Pepys St EC3 — 16 D2
Percival St EC1 — 6 F4
Percy Circus WC1 — 6 D3
Percy St W1 — 13 A1
Perham Rd W14 — 17 A3
Perrin's La NW3 — 1 B5
Perrin's Wlk NW3 — 1 A5
Peter Jones SW3 — 19 C2
Peter Pan Statue W2 — 10 F3
Petersham La SW7 — 18 E1
Petersham Pl SW7 — 18 E1
Peto Pl NW1 — 4 E4
Petticoat La E1 — 16 D1
Petticoat Sq E1 — 16 D1
Petty France SW1 — 13 A5
Petyward SW3 — 19 B2
Phene St SW3 — 19 B4
Philbeach Gdns SW5 — 17 C2
Phillimore Gdns W8 — 9 C5
Phillimore Pl W8 — 9 C5
Phillimore Wlk W8 — 9 C5
Phillipp St N1 — 7 C1
                  8 D1
Philpot La EC3 — 15 C2
Phoenix Pl WC1 — 6 D4
Phoenix Rd NW1 — 5 A3
Photographer's
     Gallery WC2 — 13 B2
Piccadilly Circus W1 — 13 A3
Piccadilly W1 — 12 E4
                 13 A3
Pickard St EC1 — 7 A3
Pilgrim St EC4 — 14 F2
Pilgrim's La NW3 — 1 C5
Pilgrimage St EC1 — 15 B5
Pimlico Rd SW1 — 20 D2
Pinchin St E1 — 16 F2
Pindar St EC2 — 7 C5
Pitfield St N1 — 7 C2
Pitt St W8 — 10 D4
Pitt's Head Ms W1 — 12 E4
Platt St NW1 — 5 A1
Playing Fields SE11 — 22 F2
Plender St NW1 — 4 F1
                  5 A1
Plough Yd EC2 — 8 D4
Plumber's Row E1 — 16 F1
Pocock St SE1 — 14 F4
Point Hill SE10 — 23 B4
Pointers Clo E14 — 23 A1
Poland St W1 — 12 F1
Poland St W1 — 13 A2
Pollard Row E2 — 8 F3
Pollock's Toy Museum W1 — 5 A5
Polygon Rd NW1 — 5 A2
Pond Pl SW3 — 19 A2
Pond Rd SE3 — 24 F5
Pond St NW3 — 1 C5
Ponler St E1 — 16 F2
Ponsonby Pl SW1 — 21 B3
Ponsonby Terr SW1 — 21 B3
Pont St SW1 — 19 C1
                20 D1
Ponton Rd SW8 — 21 A4

Poole St N1 — 7 B1
Pope Rd SE1 — 16 D5
Popham Rd N1 — 7 A1
Popham St N1 — 7 A1
Porchester Gdns W2 — 10 D2
Porchester Pl W2 — 11 B1
Porchester Rd W2 — 10 D1
Porchester Sq W2 — 10 D1
Porchester Terr W2 — 10 E2
Porlock St SE1 — 15 B5
Portland Pl W1 — 4 E5
Portland Rd W11 — 9 A3
Portman Clo W1 — 11 C1
Portman Ms South W1 — 2 D2
Portman Sq W1 — 12 D1
Portobello Rd W10 — 9 A1
Portobello Rd W11 — 9 B2
Portpool La EC1 — 6 D5
Portsmouth St WC2 — 14 D1
Portsoken St E1 — 16 D2
Portugal St WC2 — 14 D1
Pottery La W11 — 9 A3
Poultry EC2 — 15 B2
Powis Gdns W11 — 9 B1
Powis Sq W11 — 9 B1
Powis Terr W11 — 9 B1
Pownall Rd E8 — 8 E1
Praed St W2 — 10 F1
              11 A1
Pratt St NW1 — 4 F1
Pratt Wlk SE11 — 22 D1
Prebend St N1 — 7 A1
Prescot St E1 — 16 E2
Price's Yd N1 — 6 D1
Prideaux Pl WC1 — 6 D3
Prima Rd SW9 — 22 E5
Primrose Hill NW3, NW8 — 3 B1
Primrose St EC2 — 7 C5
Prince Albert Rd
     NW1, NW8 — 3 B2
                  4 D1
Prince Arthur Rd NW3 — 1 B5
Prince Charles Rd SE3 — 24 E4
Prince Consort Rd SW7 — 10 F5
Prince of Wales Rd SE3 — 24 F4
Prince's Gate SW7 — 11 A5
Prince's Gate Ms SW7 — 19 A1
Prince's Gdns SW7 — 11 A5
Prince's Rise SE13 — 23 B5
Prince's Sq W2 — 10 D2
Prince's St EC2 — 15 B1
Princedale Rd W11 — 9 A3
Princelet St E1 — 8 E5
Princes Pl W11 — 9 A3
Princes St W1 — 12 F2
Princess Rd NW1 — 4 D1
Princeton St WC1 — 6 D5
Printer Sq EC4 — 14 E1
Prior St SE10 — 23 B3
Priory Wlk SW10 — 18 F3
Pritchard's Rd E2 — 8 F1
Protheroe Rd SW6 — 17 A5
Provence St N1 — 7 A2
Provost St N1 — 7 B3
Public Gardens W1 — 4 D5
Puddle Dock EC4 — 14 F2
Purbrook St SE1 — 16 D5
Purcell St N1 — 7 C2
Purchese St NW1 — 5 A2

Q

Quaker St E1 — 8 D4
Queen Anne St W1 — 12 E1
Queen Anne's
     Gate SW1 — 13 A5
Queen Elizabeth St SE1 — 16 D4
Queen Mary's
     Gardens NW1 — 4 D3
Queen Sq WC1 — 5 C5
Queen St EC4 — 15 B2
Queen St Pl EC4 — 15 A2

Queen Victoria St EC4 — 14 F2
                         15 A2
Queen's Chapel SW1 — 13 A4
Queen's Club Gdns W14 — 17 A4
Queen's Gallery SW1 — 12 F5
Queen's Gdns SW1 — 12 F5
Queen's Gdns W2 — 10 E2
Queen's Gate SW7 — 10 F5
                    18 F1
Queen's Gate Gdns SW7 — 18 F1
Queen's Gate Ms SW7 — 10 F5
Queen's Gate Pl SW7 — 18 F1
Queen's Gate Pl Ms SW7 — 18 F1
Queen's Gate Terr SW7 — 18 E1
Queen's Gro NW8 — 3 A1
Queen's House SE10 — 23 C2
Queen's Wlk SW1 — 12 F4
Queen's Wlk SE1 — 14 E3
                   16 E4
Queenhithe EC4 — 15 A2
Queensberry Pl SW7 — 18 F1
Queensborough Ms W2 — 10 E2
Queensborough Terr W2 — 10 E2
Queensbridge Rd E2, E8 — 8 E1
Queensdale Rd W11 — 9 A4
Queenstown Rd SW8 — 20 E4
Queensway W2 — 10 D2
Quilter St E2 — 8 E3

R

Racton Rd SW6 — 17 C4
Radnor Ms W2 — 11 A2
Radnor Pl W2 — 11 A1
Radnor St EC1 — 7 A3
Radnor Terr W14 — 17 B1
Radnor Wlk SW3 — 19 B3
Radstock St SW11 — 19 B5
Railway Approach SE1 — 15 B3
Railway St N1 — 5 C2
Raleigh St N1 — 6 F1
Rampayne St SW1 — 21 A3
Randall Pl SE10 — 23 A3
Randall Rd SE11 — 21 C2
Ranelagh Gardens SW3 — 20 D3
Ranelagh Gro SW1 — 20 D3
Ranger's House SE10 — 23 C4
Raphael St SW7 — 11 B5
Rathbone Pl W1 — 13 A1
Rathbone St W1 — 13 A1
Ravensbourne Pl SE13 — 23 A5
Ravenscroft St E2 — 8 E2
Ravensdon St SE11 — 22 E3
Ravent Rd SE11 — 22 D2
Rawlings St SW3 — 19 B2
Rawstorne St EC — 16 F3
Ray St EC1 — 6 E4
Raymond Bldgs WC1 — 6 D5
Rector St N1 — 7 A1
Red Lion Sq WC1 — 5 C5
Red Lion St WC1 — 6 D5
Redan Pl W2 — 10 D2
Redburn St SW3 — 19 B4
Redchurch St E2 — 8 D4
Redcliffe Gdns SW10 — 18 E3
Redcliffe Ms SW10 — 18 E3
Redcliffe Pl SW10 — 18 E4
Redcliffe Rd SW10 — 18 4F
Redcliffe Sq SW10 — 18 D3
Redcross Way SE1 — 15 A4
Redesdale St SW3 — 19 B3
Redfield La SW5 — 18 D2
Redhill St NW1 — 4 E3
Redington Rd NW3 — 1 A5
Redvers St N1 — 8 D2
Reedworth St SE11 — 22 E2
Rees St N1 — 7 B1
Reeves Ms W1 — 12 D3
Regan Way N1 — 7 C2
Regency St SW1 — 21 A2
Regent Sq WC1 — 5 C3

Regent St W1, SW1	12 F1	
	13 A3	
Regent's Park NW1	3 C2	
	4 D2	
Regent's Pk Terr NW1	4 E1	
Regent's Pl SE3	24 F5	
Regent's Pk Rd NW1	3 C1	
	4 D1	
Regent's Row E8	8 E1	
Renfrew Rd SE11	22 F2	
Rennie St SE1	14 F3	
Restell Clo SE3	24 E2	
Rheidol Terr N1	7 A1	
Richard's Pl SW3	19 B2	
Richborne Terr SW8	22 D5	
Richmond Terr SW1	13 B4	
Rick La SW5	18 D3	
Rickett St SW6	17 C4	
Ridgmount Gdns WC1	5 A5	
Ridgmount St WC1	5 A5	
Riding House St W1	12 F1	
Riley Rd SE1	16 D5	
Ring, The W2	11 A3	
Risinghill St N1	6 D2	
Rita Rd SW8	21 C5	
Ritz Hotel SW1	12 F3	
River St EC1	6 E3	
Rivington St EC2	7 C3	
Roan St SE10	23 A2	
Robert St NW1	4 F3	
Robert Adam St W1	12 D1	
Roberta St E2	8 F3	
Robin Gro N6	2 F2	
Rochester Row SW1	21 A2	
Roderick Rd NW3	2 E5	
Rodmarton St W1	11 C1	
Rodmere St SE10	24 E1	
Rodney St N1	6 D2	
Roger St WC1	6 D4	
Roland Gdns SW7	18 F3	
Roland Way SW7	18 F3	
Romilly St W1	13 A2	
Romney Clo NW11	1 A1	
Romney Rd SE10	23 B2	
Romney St SW1	21 B1	
Rona Rd NW3	2 E5	
Rood La EC3	15 C2	
Ropemaker St EC2	7 B5	
Roper's Garden SW3	19 A4	
Rosaline Rd SW6	17 A5	
Rosary Gdns SW7	18 E2	
Rosaville Rd SW6	17 B5	
Rose Alley SE1	15 A3	
Rose St WC2	13 B2	
Rose Theatre SE1	15 A3	
Rosebery Ave EC1	6 E4	
Rosemoor St SW3	19 B2	
Rosewood Gdns SE13	23 A5	
Rosmead Rd W11	9 A2	
Rosslyn Hill NW3	1 C5	
Rossmore Rd NW1	3 B4	
Rotary St SE1	14 F5	
Rotten Row SW7	11 A4	
Roupell St SE1	14 E4	
Rowallan Rd SW6	17 A5	
Royal Academy of Arts W1	12 F3	
Royal Academy of Music NW1	4 D4	
Royal Albert Hall SW7	10 F5	
Royal Ave SW3	19 C3	
Royal College of Art SW7	10 F5	
Royal College of Music SW7	10 F5	
Royal College St NW1	5 A1	
Royal Courts of Justice WC2	14 D2	
Royal Exchange EC4	15 C2	
Royal Festival Hall SE1	14 D4	
Royal Free Hospital NW3	2 D5	
Royal Hill SE10	23 B3	
Royal Hospital Cemetery SE10	24 F1	
Royal Hospital Rd SW3	19 C3	
Royal Hospital Rd SW3	20 D3	
Royal Mint St E1	16 E2	
Royal Ms SW1	12 E5	
Royal Naval College (Old) SE10	23 C2	
Royal Opera House WC2	13 C2	
Royal Parade SE3	24 E5	
Royal Rd SE17	22 F4	
Royal St SE1	14 D5	
Rudall Cres NW3	1 B5	
Rumbold Rd SW6	18 E5	
Rupert St W1	13 A2	
Rushton St N1	7 B2	
Rushworth St SE1	14 F4	
Russell Gdns W14	9 A5	
Russell Gdns Ms W14	9 A5	
Russell Rd W14	17 A1	
Russell Sq WC1	5 B5	
Russell St WC2	13 C2	
Russett Way SE13	23 A5	
Ruston Ms W11	9 A1	
Rutherford St SW1	21 A2	
Ruthin Rd SE3	24 F2	
Rutland Gdns SW7	11 B5	
Rutland Gate SW7	11 B5	
Ryculf Sq SE3	24 F5	
Ryder St SW1	12 F4	
Rylston Rd SW6	17 B4	

S		
Saatchi Gallery SW3	19 C2	
Shard	15 C4	
St Agnes Pl SE11	22 E4	
St Alban's Rd NW5	2 F3	
St Alban's St SW1	13 A3	
St Alfege Passage SE10	23 B2	
St Andrew's EC4	14 E1	
St Andrew's Gdns WC1	6 D4	
St Andrew's Pl NW1	4 E4	
St Andrews St EC4	14 E1	
St Anne's Clo N6	2 F3	
St Ann's St SW1	21 B1	
St Ann's Terr NW8	3 A2	
St Austell Rd SE13	23 B5	
St Barnabas St SW1	20 D2	
St Bartholomew's Hospital EC1	14 F1	
St Bartholomews-the-Great EC1	6 F5	
St Botolph Church EC1	15 A1	
St Botolph St EC3	16 D1	
St Bride St EC4	14 E1	
St Bride's EC4	14 F2	
St Chad's Pl WC1	5 C3	
St Chad's St WC1	5 C3	
St Clement Danes WC2	14 D2	
St Crispin Clo NW3	2 D5	
St Cross St EC1	6 E5	
St Edmund's Terr NW8	3 B1	
St Ethelreda's EC1	6 E5	
St George's Bloomsbury WC1	13 B1	
St George's Cathedral SE1	14 E5	
St George's Circus SE1	14 F5	
St George's Dri SW1	20 F2	
St George's Fields W2	11 B2	
St George's Gdn W1	12 D3	
St George's Gdns WC1	5 C4	
St George's Rd SE1	22 F1	
St George's Sq SW1	21 A3	
St German's Pl SE3	24 F4	
St Giles EC2	7 A5	
St Giles, Cripplegate High St WC2	13 B1	
St Helen's Bishopsgate EC3	15 C1	
St James's Church SW1	13 A3	
St James's Palace SW1	12 F4	
St James's Park SW1	13 A4	
St James's Pk Lake SW1	13 A4	
St James's Pl SW1	12 F4	
St James's Rd SE16	16 F5	
St James's Sq SW1	13 A3	
St James's St SW1	12 F3	
St John St EC1	6 E2	
St John's SE1	14 E4	
St John's Gdns SW1	21 B1	
St John's Gdns W11	9 A3	
St John's High St NW8	3 A2	
St John's La EC1	6 F5	
St John's Pk SE3	24 F3	
St John's Smith Sq SW1	21 B1	
St John's Sq EC1	6 F4	
St John's Wood Church Gdns NW8	3 A3	
St John's Wood High St NW8	3 A2	
St John's Wood Rd NW8	3 A3	
St John's Wood Terr NW8	3 A2	
St Katherines Dock E1	16 E3	
St Katherines Pier E1	16 E3	
St Katharine's Way E1	16 E3	
St Lawrence Terr W10	9 A1	
St Leonard's Terr SW3	19 C3	
St Loo Ave SW3	19 B4	
St Luke's Ms W11	9 B1	
St Luke's Rd W11	9 B1	
St Luke's St SW3	19 B3	
St Magnus the Martyr EC3	15 C3	
St Margaret Pattens EC3	15 C2	
St Margaret's Church SW1	13 B5	
St Margaret St SW1	13 B5	
St Mark St E1	16 E2	
St Mark's Cres NW1	4 D1	
St Mark's Rd W11	9 A2	
St Martin's La WC2	13 B2	
St Martin's Le Grand EC1	15 A1	
St Martin's Pl WC2	13 B3	
St Martin's St WC2	13 B3	
St Martin-in-the-Fields WC2	13 B3	
St Mary Abbots Terr W14	17 B1	
St Mary at Hill EC3	15 C2	
St Mary Axe EC3	15 C1	
St Mary's Hospital W2	11 A1	
St Mary Le Strand WC2	14 D2	
St Mary's Path N1	6 F1	
St Mary's Wlk SE11	22 E2	
St Mary-le-Bow EC4	15 A2	
St Marylebone Parish Church W1	4 D5	
St Matthew's Row E2	8 E4	
St Michael's St W2	11 A1	
St Olaf's Rd SW6	17 A5	
St Oswald's Pl SE11	22 D3	
St Pancras Church WC1	5 B3	
St Pancras Way NW1	5 A1	
St Paul St N1	7 A1	
St Paul's Cathedral EC4	15 A2	
St Paul's Church WC2	13 C2	
St Paul's Churchyard EC4	15 A1	
St Peter's Clo E2	8 F2	
St Peter's St N1	6 F1	
	7 A2	
St Petersburgh Pl W2	10 D3	
St Stephen Walbrook EC4	15 B2	
St Stephen's Gdns W2	9 C1	
St Stephen's Terr SW8	21 C5	
St Swithin's La EC4	15 B2	
St Thomas St SE1	15 B4	
St Thomas' Hospital SE1	13 C5	
St Thomas' Way SW6	17 B5	
Sackville St W1	12 F3	
Saffron Hill EC1	6 E5	
Sail St SE11	22 D1	
Salamanca St SE1, SE11	21 C2	
Sale Pl W2	11 A1	
Salem Rd W2	10 D2	
Salisbury Ct EC4	14 E2	
Salisbury St NW8	3 A4	
Sampson St E1	16 F4	
Sancroft St SE11	22 D2	
Sandwich St WC1	5 B3	
Sandys Row E1	8 D5	
Sans Wlk EC1	6 E4	
Saunders Ness Rd E14	23 B1	
Savernake Rd NW3	2 E5	
Savile Row W1	12 F2	
Savona St SW8	20 F5	
Savoy Chapel WC2	13 C2	
Savoy Hill WC2	13 C3	
Savoy Pl WC2	13 C3	
Savoy Row WC2	13 C3	
Savoy St WC2	13 C2	
Savoy, The WC2	13 C2	
Scala St W1	5 A5	
Scarborough St E1	16 E2	
Scarsdale Vlls W8	17 C1	
	18 D1	
Science Museum SW7	18 F1	
	19 A1	
Sclater St E1	8 E4	
Scott Lidgett Cres SE16	16 F5	
Scott St E1	8 F4	
Scovell Cresent SE1	15 A5	
Scrutton St EC2	7 C4	
Seagrave Rd SW6	17 C4	
	18 D4	
Sebastian St EC1	6 F3	
Sedlescombe Rd SW6	17 C4	
Seething La EC3	16 D2	
Selby St E1	8 F4	
Selfridge's W1	12 D2	
Selwood Pl SW7	18 F3	
Selwood Terr SW7	18 F3	
Semley Pl SW1	20 E2	
Serle St WC2	14 D1	
Serpentine Gallery W2	11 A4	
Serpentine Rd W2	11 C4	
	12 D4	
Serpentine, The W2	11 B4	
Settles St E1	16 F1	
Seven Dials WC2	13 B2	
Seville St SW1	11 C5	
Seward St EC1	7 A4	
Seymour Ms W1	12 D1	
Seymour Pl W1	3 B5	
	11 B1	
Seymour St W1,W2	11 C2	
Seymour Wlk SW10	18 E4	
Shad Thames SE1	16 E4	
Shaftesbury Ave W1	13 A2	
Shaftesbury Ave WC2	13 B1	
Shaftesbury St N1	7 B2	
Shafto Ms SW1	19 C1	
Shafts Ct EC3	15 C1	
Shakespeare's Globe SE1	15 A3	
Shalcomb St SW10	18 F4	
Sharsted St SE17	22 F3	
Shawfield St SW3	19 B3	
Sheffield Ter W8	9 C4	
Sheldon Ave N6	2 D1	
Sheldrake Pl W8	9 C5	
Shelton St WC2	13 B2	
Shenfield St N1	8 D2	
Shepherd Mkt W1	12 E4	
Shepherd St W1	12 E4	
Shepherdess Wlk N1	7 A2	
Shepherd's Wlk NW3	1 B5	
Shepperton Rd N1	7 B1	
Sherbourne La EC4	15 B2	
Sherbrooke Rd SW6	18 D5	
Sherlock Holmes Museum1	3 C4	
Sherwood St W1	13 A2	
Shipton St E2	8 E2	
Shirlock Rd NW3	2 E5	
Shoe La EC4	14 E1	
Shooters Hill Rd SE3	24 D4	
Shooters Hill Rd SE18	23 C4	

Each place name is followed by its postal district number and then by its Street Finder reference

Shoreditch High St EC2	8 D3
Shoreditch Park E2	7 B1
Shorrold's Rd SW6	17 C5
Short St SE1	14 E4
Shouldham St W1	11 B1
Shroton St NW1	3 B5
Sidmouth St WC1	5 C3
Silk St EC2	7 B5
Sinclair Rd W14	17 A1
Singer St EC2	7 C4
Sir John Soane's Museum WC2	14 D1
Skinner St EC1	6 E4
Slaidburn St SW10	18 F4
Sleaford St SW8	20 F5
Sloane Ave SW3	19 B2
Sloane Ct East SW3	20 D3
Sloane Gdns SW1	20 D2
Sloane Sq SW1	19 C2
	20 D2
Sloane St SW1	11 C5
	19 C1
Smith Sq SW1	21 B1
Smith St SW3	19 C3
Smith Terr SW3	19 C3
Smithfield Mkt EC1	6 F5
Snow Hill EC1	14 F1
Snowfields SE1	15 B4
Soho Sq W1	13 A1
Soho St W1	13 A1
Somers Cres W2	11 A1
South Audley St W1	12 D3
South Eaton Pl SW1	20 D2
South Edwardes Sq W8	17 C1
South End Clo NW3	2 D5
South End Rd NW3	1 C5
South Gro N6	2 F1
South Hill Pk NW3	2 D5
South Hill Pk Gdns NW3	2 D4
South Island Pl SW9	22 D5
South Lambeth Pl SW8	21 C4
South Lambeth Rd SW8	21 C4
South Molton La W1	12 E2
South Molton St W1	12 E2
South Parade SW3	19 A3
South Pl EC2	7 B5
South Row SE3	24 E5
South St W1	12 D3
South Tenter St E1	16 E2
South Terr SW7	19 A2
South Wharf Rd W2	11 A1
Southampton Pl WC1	13 C1
Southampton Row WC1	5 C5
Southampton St WC2	13 C2
Southern St N1	5 C2
Southwark Bridge SE1	15 A3
Southwark Bridge Rd SE1	15 A4
Southwark Cathedral EC1	15 B3
Southwark St SE1	14 F3
	15 A4
Southwell Gdns SW7	18 E1
Southwick St W2	11 A1
Southwood La N6	2 F1
Spa Fields EC1	6 E4
Spaniards Clo NW11	1 B1
Spaniards End NW3	1 B1
Spaniards Rd NW3	1 A3
Sparta St SE10	23 A4
Speakers' Corner W2	11 C2
Spedan Clo NW3	1 A4
Spelman St E1	8 E5
Spencer House SW1	12 F4
Spencer St EC1	6 F3
Spenser St SW1	20 F1
Spital Sq E1	8 D5
Spital St E1	8 E5
Spitalfields Centre Museum of Immigration E1	8 E5
Spitalfields Market	8 D5
Spring St W2	10 F2
Spur Rd SW1	12 F5
Squires Mount NW3	1 B4
Squirries St E2	8 F3
Stable Yd Rd SW1	12 F4
Stafford Terr W8	9 C5
Stag Pl SW1	20 F1
Stamford St SE1	14 E3
Stanford Rd W8	18 E1
Stanhope Gdns SW7	18 F2
Stanhope Gate W1	12 D4
Stanhope Ms East SW7	18 F2
Stanhope Ms West SW7	18 F2
Stanhope Pl W2	11 B2
Stanhope St NW1	4 F3
Stanhope Terr W2	11 A2
Stanley Cres W11	9 B2
Stanley Gdns W11	9 B2
Stannary St SE11	22 E3
Stanway St N1	8 D2
Stanwick Rd W14	17 B2
Staple Inn WC1	14 E1
Staple St SE1	15 B5
Stardome NW1	4 D5
Star Rd W14	17 B4
Star St W2	11 A1
Starcross St NW1	4 F3
Stean St E8	8 D1
Stephen St W1	13 A1
Stephenson Way NW1	5 A4
Steward St E1	8 D5
Stewart's Rd SW8	20 F5
Stock Exchange (Old) EC4	15 C1
Stockwell St SE10	23 B2
Stone Bldgs WC2	14 D1
Stonefield St N1	6 E1
Stones End St SE1	15 A5
Stoney La E1	16 D1
Stoney St SE1	15 B3
Stonor Rd W14	17 B2
Store St WC1	5 A5
Storey's Gate SW1	13 B5
Stormont Rd N6	2 D1
Stowage SE8	23 A2
Straightsmouth St SE10	23 B3
Strand WC2	13 B3
Strand La WC2	14 D2
Stratford Rd W8	18 D1
Stratheden Rd SE3	24 F4
Stratton St W1	12 E3
Streatham St WC1	13 B1
Streatley Pl NW3	1 B4
Strode Rd SW6	17 A5
Strutton Ground SW1	21 A1
Sturt St N1	7 A2
Stutfield St E1	16 F2
Sudeley St N1	6 F2
Suffolk La EC4	15 B2
Suffolk Pl SW1	13 A3
Suffolk St SW1	13 B3
Sumner Pl SW7	19 A2
Sumner St SE1	15 A3
Sun Rd W14	17 B3
Sun St EC2	7 C5
Sunderland Terr W2	10 D1
Surrey Row SE1	14 F4
Surrey St WC2	14 D2
Sussex Gdns W2	11 A1
Sussex Pl NW1	3 C4
Sussex Pl W2	11 A2
Sussex Sq W2	11 A2
Sussex St SW1	20 F3
Sutherland Pl W2	9 C1
Sutherland St SW1	20 E3
Sutton Row W1	13 A1
Swain's La N6	2 F1
Swallow St W1	12 F3
Swan La EC4	15 B3
Swan La Pier SE1	15 B3
Swan St SE1	15 A5
Swan Wlk SW3	19 C4
Swanfield St E2	8 E3
Swinton St WC1	5 C3
Sydney Pl SW3	19 A2
Sydney St SW3	19 A3
Symons St SW3	19 C2

T

Tabard St SE1	15 B5
Tabernacle St EC2	7 C4
Tachbrook St SW1	21 A2
Tadema Rd SW10	18 F5
Talbot Pl SE3	24 D5
Talbot Rd W2,W11	9 C1
Talbot Sq W2	11 A2
Talgarth Rd W6,W14	17 A3
Tallis St EC4	14 E2
Tanner St SE1	16 D5
Tamworth St SW6	17 C4
Tanza Rd NW3	2 D4
Taplow St N1	7 A2
Tarves Way SE10	23 A3
Tasso Rd W6	17 A4
Tate Britain SW1	21 B2
Tate Modern SE1	14 F3
	15 A3
Tavistock Cres W11	9 B1
Tavistock Pl WC1	5 B4
Tavistock Rd W11	9 B1
Tavistock Sq WC1	5 B4
Tavistock St WC2	13 C2
Taviton St WC1	5 A4
Teale St E2	8 F2
Tedworth Sq SW3	19 C3
Teesdale Clo E2	8 F2
Teesdale St E2	8 F2
Telegraph St EC2	15 B1
Temple EC4	14 E2
Temple Ave EC4	14 E2
Temple Bar Memorial WC2	14 D2
Temple La EC4	14 E2
Temple Pl WC2	14 D2
Temple St E2	8 F2
Templeton Pl SW5	17 C2
Tent St E1	8 F4
Tenterden St W1	12 E2
Terminus Pl SW1	20 F1
Tetcott Rd SW10	18 E5
Thames St SE10	23 A2
Thanet St WC1	5 B3
Thaxton Rd W14	17 B4
Thayer St W1	12 D1
Theatre Royal WC2	13 C2
Theatre Royal Haymarket WC2	13 A3
Theberton St N1	6 E1
Theed St SE1	14 E4
Theobald's Rd WC1	5 C5
	6 D5
Thessaly Rd SW8	20 F5
Thirleby Rd SW1	20 F1
Thistle Gro SW7	18 F3
Thomas More St E1	16 E3
Thoresby St N1	7 A3
Thorncroft St SW8	21 B5
Thorney St SW1	21 B1
Thornham St SE10	23 A2
Thornhaugh St WC1	5 B5
Thrale St SE1	15 A4
Thrawl St E1	8 E5
Threadneedle St EC4	15 B2
Throgmorton Ave EC2	15 C1
Throgmorton St EC2	15 B1
Thurloe Pl SW7	19 A1
Thurloe Sq SW7	19 A1
Thurloe St SW7	19 A2
Thurlow Rd NW3	1 B5
Tiber Gdns N1	5 C1
Tilney St W1	12 D3
Tilton St SW6	17 B4
Tinworth St SE11	21 C3
Titchborne Row W2	11 B2
Titchfield Rd NW8	3 B1
Tite St SW3	19 C4
Tolpuddle St N1	6 E2
Tom Smith Clo SE3	24 D2
Tompion St EC1	6 F3
Tonbridge St WC1	5 B3
Tooley St EC1	15 B3
Tooley St SE1	16 D4
Tor Gdns W8	9 C4
Torrington Pl WC1	5 A5
Torrington Sq WC1	5 A4
Tothill St SW1	13 B5
Tottenham Ct Rd W1	4 F4
	5 A5
	13 A1
Tottenham St W1	5 A5
Toulmin St SE1	15 A5
Tournay Rd SW6	17 C5
Tower Bridge E1	16 D3
Tower Bridge E1	16 D4
Tower Bridge Approach E1	16 E3
Tower Bridge Rd SE1	16 D4
Tower Clo NW3	1 C5
Tower Hill EC3	16 D2
Tower of London EC3	16 D3
Townshend Rd NW8	3 B1
Toynbee St E1	16 D1
Tradescant Rd SW8	21 C5
Trafalgar Rd SE10	24 D1
Trafalgar Sq SW1	13 B3
Trafalgar Sq W1	13 B3
Trafalgar Studios SW1	13 B3
Tranquil Vale SE3	24 D5
Treasury, The SW1	13 B5
Treaty St N1	5 C1
Trebovir Rd SW5	17 C3
Tregunter Rd SW10	18 E4
Trevanion Rd W14	17 A2
Trevor Pl SW7	11 B5
Trevor Sq SW7	11 B5
Trevor St SW7	11 B5
Trinity Church Sq SE1	15 A5
Trinity Sq EC3	16 D2
Trinity St SE1	15 A5
Triton Sq NW1	4 F4
Tudor St EC4	14 E2
Tufton St SW1	21 B1
Turin St E2	8 E3
Turk's Row SW3	19 C3
	20 D3
Turners Wood NW11	1 A1
Turneville Rd W14	17 B4
Turnmill St EC1	6 E5
Turpentine La SW1	20 E3
Thurtle Rd E2	8 E1
Tuskar St SE10	24 D1
Twyford St N1	5 C1
Tyers Gate SE1	15 C5
Tyers St SE11	22 D2
Tyers Terr SE11	22 D3
Tyler St SE10	24 E

U

Ufford St SE1	14 E4
Ulundi Rd SE3	24 E2
Underwood Rd E1	8 F5
Underwood St N1	7 B3
Unicorn Pass SE1	16 D3
Union Sq N1	7 A1
Union St SE1	14 F4
	15 A4
Union Wlk E2	8 D3
University St WC1	5 A4
University College WC1	5 A4
University College Hospital WC1	5 A4
Upcerne Rd SW10	18 E5
Upper St N1	6 F1
Upper Terr NW3	1 A4
Upper Belgrave Street SW1	20 E1
Upper Berkeley St W1	11 C1

Upper Brook St W1   12 D2
Upper Cheyne Row SW3   19 B4
Upper Grosvenor St W1   12 D3
Upper Ground SE1   14 E3
Upper Marsh SE1   14 D5
Upper Montagu St W1   3 C5
Upper Phillimore Gdns W8   9 C5
Upper St Martin's La WC2   13 B2
Upper Thames St EC4   15 A2
Upper Wimpole St W1   4 D5
Upper Woburn Pl WC1   5 B4
US Embassy W1   12 D2
Uxbridge St W8   9 C3

V

Vale,The SW3   19 A4
Vale of Health NW3   1 B3
Valentine Pl SE1   14 F5
Vallance Rd E1,E2   8 F4
Vanbrugh Fields SE3   24 E3
Vanbrugh Hill SE3   24 E2
Vanbrugh Hill SE10   24 E1
Vanbrugh Pk SE3   24 E3
Vanbrugh Pk Rd SE3   24 F3
Vanbrugh Pk Rd West SE3   24 E3
Vanbrugh Terr SE3   24 F4
Vane Clo NW3   1 B5
Vanston Pl SW6   17 C5
Varndell St NW1   4 F3
Vassall Rd SW9   22 E5
Vaughan May E1
Vauxhall Bridge SW1   21 B3
Vauxhall Bridge Rd
SW1, SE1   20 F1
  21 A2
Vauxhall Bus Station SW8   21 C4
Vauxhall Gro SW8   21 C4
Vauxhall Park SW8   21 C4
Vauxhall St SE11   22 D3
Vauxhall Wlk SE11   21 C3
Vere St W1   12 E1
Vereker Rd W14   17 A3
Vernon Rise WC1   6 D3
Vernon St W14   17 A2
Vestry St N1   7 B3
Vicarage Gate W8   10 D4
Victoria & Albert
Museum SW7   19 A1
Victoria
Embankment EC4   14 E2
Victoria
Embankment SW1   13 C4
Victoria Embankment
WC2   13 C3
Victoria Embankment
Gdns WC2   13 C3
Victoria Gro W8   18 E1
Victoria Rd W8   10 E5
  18 E1
Victoria St SW1   13 B5
  20 F1
  21 A1
Victoria Tower
Gardens SW1   21 C1
Villiers St WC2   13 C3
Vince St EC1   7 C3
Vincent Sq SW1   21 A2
Vincent St SW1   21 A2
Vincent Terr N1   6 F2
Vine La SE1   16 D4
Vine St EC3   16 D2
Vintner's Pl EC4   15 A2
Virginia Rd E2   8 D3
Voss St E2   8 F3

W

Wakefield St WC1   5 C4
Wakley St EC1   6 F3
Walbrook EC4   15 B2
Walcot Sq SE11   22 E1

Waldorf Hotel WC2   13 C2
Walham Gro SW6   17 C5
Wallace Collection W1   12 D1
Walmer Rd W11   9 A3
Walnut Tree Rd SE10   24 E1
Walnut Tree Wlk SE11   22 D1
Walpole St SW3   19 C3
Walton Pl SW3   19 C1
Walton St SW3   19 B2
Wandon Rd SW6   18 E5
Wandsworth Rd SW8   21 B5
Wansdown Pl SW6   18 D5
Wapping High St E1   16 F4
Wardour St W1   13 A2
Warham St SE5   22 F5
Warner Pl E2   8 F2
Warner St EC1   6 E4
Warren St W1   4 F4
Warwick Gdns W14   17 B1
Warwick La EC4   14 F1
Warwick Rd SW5   18 D3
Warwick Rd W14   17 B1
Warwick Sq SW1   20 F2
Warwick St W1   12 F2
Warwick Way SW1   20 F2
Wat Tyler Rd SE10   23 B5
Waterford Rd SW6   18 D5
Waterloo Bridge
SE1,WC2   14 D3
Waterloo Pl SW1   13 A3
Waterloo Rd SE1   14 E4
Waterson St E2   8 D3
Watling St EC4   15 A2
Weaver St E1   8 E4
Weavers La SE1   16 D4
Webb Rd SE3   24 E2
Webber Row SE1   14 E5
Webber St SE1   14 E4
  15 A5
Weighouse St W1   12 D2
Welbeck St W1   12 D1
Well Rd NW3   1 B4
Well Wlk NW3   1 B4
Welland St SE10   23 B2
Wellcome Collection NW1   5 A4
Weller St SE1   15 A5
Wellesley Terr N1   7 A3
Wellington Arch W1   12 D4
Wellington Bldgs SW1   20 E3
Wellington Pl NW8   3 A3
Wellington Rd NW8   3 A2
Wellington Row E2   8 E3
Wellington Sq SW3   19 C3
Wellington St WC2   13 C2
Wells Rise NW8   3 C1
Wells St W1   12 F1
Wenlock Basin N1   7 A2
Wenlock Rd N1   7 A2
Wenlock St N1   7 B2
Wentworth St E1   16 D1
Werrington St NW1   5 A2
Wesley's House &
Chapel EC1   7 B4
West Sq SE11   22 F1
West St WC2   13 B2
West Cromwell Rd
SW5,W14   17 B3
West Eaton Pl SW1   20 D1
West Ferry Rd E14   23 A1
West Gro SE10   23 B4
West Harding St EC4   14 E1
West Heath NW3   1 A3
West Heath Rd NW3   1 A4
West Hill Ct N6   2 E3
West Hill Pk N6   2 E2
West Pier E1   16 F4
West Smithfield EC1   14 F1
West Tenter St E1   16 E2
Westbourne Cres W2   10 F2
Westbourne Gdns W2   10 D1
Westbourne Gro W2   10 D2
Westbourne Gro W11   9 B2

Westbourne Pk Rd W2   10 D1
Westbourne Pk Rd W11   9 B1
Westbourne Pk Vlls W2   10 D1
Westbourne St W2   11 A2
Westbourne Terr W2   10 E1
Westcombe Hill SE10   24 F1
Westcombe Pk Rd SE3   24 E2
Westcott Rd SE17   22 F4
Westerdale Rd SE10   24 F1
Westgate Terr SW10   18 D3
Westgrove La SE10   23 B4
Westland Pl N1   7 B3
Westminster Abbey SW1   13 B5
Westminster Bridge
SE1, SW1   13 C5
Westminster Bridge
Rd SE1   14 D5
Westminster Cathedral
SW1   20 F1
Westminster Hospital
SW1   21 B1
Westminster School
Playing Fields SW1   21 A2
Westmoreland Pl SW1   20 E3
Westmoreland St W1   4 D5
Westmoreland Terr SW1   20 E3
Weston Rise WC1   6 D3
Weston St SE1   15 C4
Westway A40(M) W10   9 A1
Wetherby Gdns SW5   18 E2
Wetherby Pl SW7   18 E2
Weymouth Ms W1   4 E5
Weymouth St W1   4 E5
Weymouth Terr E2   8 E2
Wharf Pl E2   8 F1
Wharf Rd N1   7 A2
Wharfdale Rd N1   5 C2
Wharton St WC1   6 D3
Wheatsheaf La SW8   21 C5
Wheler St E1   8 D4
Whetstone Pk WC2   14 D1
Whiston Rd E2   8 D1
Whitbread Brewery EC2   7 B5
Whitcomb St WC2   13 A3
White Lion St N1   6 E2
White's Row E1   8 D5
Whitechapel Art
Gallery E1   16 E1
Whitechapel High St E1   16 E1
Whitechapel Rd E1   8 F5
  16 E1
  16 E1
Whitchurch La E1   16 E1
Whitecross St EC1,EC2   7 A4
Whitfield St W1   4 F4
Whitefriars St EC4   14 E2
Whitehall SW1   13 B3
Whitehall Ct SW1   13 C4
Whitehall Pl SW1   13 B4
Whitehead's Gro SW3   19 B2
White's Grounds SE1   16 D4
Whitfield Rd SE3   23 C5
Whitfield St W1   5 A5
Whitgift St SE11   21 C2
Whitmore Rd N1   7 C1
Whitworth St SE10   24 D1
Wicker St E1   16 F2
Wickham St SE11   22 D3
Wicklow St WC1   5 C3
Wigmore Hall W1   12 E1
Wigmore St W1   12 D1
Wilcox Rd SW8   21 B5
Wild Ct WC2   13 C1
Wild St WC2   13 C1
Wild's Rents SE1   15 C5
Wildwood Gro NW3   1 A2
Wildwood Rise NW11   1 A1
Wildwood Rd NW11   1 A1
Wilfred St SW1   12 F5
Wilkinson St SW8   21 C5
William St SW1   11 C5
William IV St WC2   13 B3
William Rd NW1   4 F3

Willoughby Rd NW3   1 B5
Willow Pl SW1   20 F2
Willow Rd NW3   1 C4
Willow St EC2   7 C4
Wilmer Gdns N1   7 C1
Wilmer Gdns N1   8 D1
Wilmington Ms SW1   11 C5
Wilmington Sq WC1   6 E3
Wilsham St W11   9 A3
Wilkes St E1   8 E5
Wilson Gro SE16   16 F5
Wilson St EC2   7 C5
Wilton Cres SW1   12 D5
Wilton Pl SW1   12 D5
Wilton Rd SW1   20 F1
Wilton Row SW1   12 D5
Wilton Sq N1   7 B1
Wiltshire Row N1   7 B1
Wimborne St N1   7 B2
Wimpole Ms W1   4 E5
Wimpole St W1   4 E5
  12 E1
Winchester Clo SE17   22 F2
Winchester St SW1   20 E3
Wincott St SE11   22 E2
Windmill Hill NW3   1 A4
Windmill Wlk SE1   14 E4
Windsor Terr N1   7 A3
Winfield House NW1   3 B3
Winforton St SE10   23 B4
Winnington Rd N2   1 B1
Winsland St W2   10 F1
  11 A1
Woburn Pl WC1   5 B4
Woburn Sq WC1   5 B4
Woburn Wlk WC1   5 B4
Wolseley St SE1   16 E5
Wood Clo E2   8 F4
Wood St EC2   15 A1
Woodbridge St EC1   6 F4
Woodland Gro SE10   24 D1
Woodlands Pk Rd SE10   24 D2
Woods Ms W1   12 D2
Woodseer St E1   8 E5
Woodsford Sq W14   9 A4
Woodsome Rd NW5   2 F4
Woodstock St W1   12 E2
Woolwich Rd SE10   24 E1
Wootton St SE1   14 E4
Worfield St SW11   19 B5
World's End Pas SW10   18 F5
Wormwood St EC2   15 C1
Woronzow Rd NW8   3 A1
Worship St EC2   7 C4
Wren St WC1   6 D4
Wright's La W8   10 D5
Wycherley Clo SE3   24 E3
Wyclif St EC1   6 F3
Wyldes Clo NW11   1 A2
Wynan Rd E14   23 A1
Wyndham Rd SE5   22 F5
Wyndham St W1   3 C5
Wynford Rd N1   6 D2
Wynyatt St EC1   6 F3
Wyvil Rd SW8   21 B5

Y

Yardley St WC1   6 E4
Yeoman's Row SW3   19 B1
York Gate NW1   4 D4
York House Pl W8   10 D4
York Rd SE1   14 D4
York St W1   3 B5
York Ter East NW1   4 D4
York Ter West NW1   4 D4
York Way N1   5 C1
Yorkton St E2   8 E2
Young St W8   10 D5

Each place name is followed by its postal district number and then by its Street Finder reference

D **E** **F** **4**

KINGSTOWN STREET
PRINCESS RD
ST MARK'S CRESCENT
GLOUCESTER AVENUE
REGENT'S PARK TERR
OVAL ROAD
GLOUCESTER CRESCENT
ARLINGTON ROAD
BAYHAM STREET
CAROL STREET
CAMDEN ST
MANDELA ST

1

K ROAD
PRINCE ALBERT ROAD
PARKWAY
Jewish Museum
DELANCEY STREET
CAMDEN HIGH STREET
CAMDEN STREET
CAMDEN TOWN
BAYHAM STREET
PLENDER STREET
KING'S TERRACE

(Canal)
CIRCLE

5

GLOUCESTER GATE
PARK VILLAGE EAST
MORNINGTON STREET
ARLINGTON
MORNINGTON CRESCENT
CARLOW ST
MORNINGTON CRESCENT
CROWNDALE RD
EVERSHOLT ST
HARRINGTON SQUARE

2

London Zoo
BROAD WALK
GLOUCESTER GATE
ALBANY STREET
CUMBERLAND TERRACE
OUTER CIRCLE
PARK VILLAGE EAST
AUGUSTUS
STANHOPE STREET
GRANBY TERR
HARRINGTON STREET
MACKWORTH STREET
HAMPSTEAD ROAD
LIDLINGTON PL
HAMPSTEAD ROAD

PARK

CUMBERLAND TERRACE MEWS
REDHILL STREET
CHESTER TERRACE
NASH STREET
CUMBERLAND MARKET
ROBERT STREET
VARNDELL STREET

3

CHESTER ROAD
BROAD WALK
CHESTER GATE
ALBANY STREET
CLARENCE GARDENS
WILLIAM ROAD
STANHOPE STREET
NORTH GOWER ST
STARCROSS STREET
GOWER ST

QUEEN MARY'S GARDENS
INNER CIRCLE
MUNSTER SQUARE
LONGFORD STREET
DRUMMOND
TRITON SQUARE
STANHOPE STREET

4

CIRCLE
ST ANDREW'S PLACE
PARK SQUARE EAST
PETO PLACE
OSNABURGH STREET
EUSTON ROAD
WARREN STREET
WARREN STREET
TOTTENHAM COURT ROAD
₩282

OUTER CIRCLE
YORK GATE
PARK SQUARE GARDENS
PARK SQUARE WEST
ROAD
PARK CRESCENT
Great Portland Street
₩3
WARREN STREET
WHITFIELD STREET
FITZROY
GRAFTON WAY

5

YORK TERRACE EAST
Royal Academy of Music
MARYLEBONE
Regent's Park
₩1
BOLSOVER STREET
GREENWELL STREET
CLEVELAND
FITZROY STREET
MAPLE STREET
₩★

YORK TERRACE WEST
LUXBOROUGH STREET
Madame Tussauds'
The Stardome
St Marylebone Parish Church
DEVONSHIRE STREET
DEVONSHIRE PLACE
HARLEY STREET
HALLAM STREET
GREAT PORTLAND STREET
British Telecom Tower
HOWLAND STREET

5

MARYLEBONE
PADDINGTON STREET
NOTTINGHAM ST
MARYLEBONE HIGH ST
BEAUMONT STREET
UPPER WIMPOLE STREET
DEVONSHIRE STREET
WEYMOUTH STREET
PORTLAND PLACE
CLIPSTONE STREET
NEW CAVENDISH STREET
TITCHFIELD STREET
HANSON STREET
₩★

PADDINGTON STREET GARDENS
CHILTERN STREET
CRAMER ST
MARYLEBONE HIGH ST
MARY'S BONE STREET
WIMPOLE MEWS
WEYMOUTH STREET
WESTMORELAND STREET
WIMPOLE STREET
NEW CAVENDISH STREET
WEYMOUTH MEWS
DUCHESS STREET
GOSFIELD STREET
FOLEY STREET

D **E** **12** **F**

A BASIRE STREET **B** SHEPPERTON ROAD **C** DE BEAUVOIR CRESCENT

POPHAM ST
POPHAM ST
BRITANNIA ROW
CANAL WALK
BRANCH PLACE
ORSMA
HALCOMBE

COLEMAN
BISHOP STREET
PREBEND STREET
RECTOR ST
PAUL FIELDS
ARLINGTON
MARY ST
CANON ST
UNION SQ
REES STREET
ARLINGTON AVENUE
WILTON SQUARE
BARING STREET
WILTSHIRE ROW
BRIDPORT PLACE
FELTON STREET
HARVEY ST
PENN STREET
GOPSALL STREET
HYDE ROAD
WHITMORE
HOXTON STREET
PHILLIPP
WILM

RHEIDOL TERRACE
ALLINGHAM STREET
ST FROME STREET
ST PETER'S STREET
PROVENCE ST
NOEL RD
DAMES ST
WHARF ROAD
EAGLE WHARF ROAD
Grand Union Canal

POOLE STREET
SHOREDITCH
PARK

PARR STREET
FORSTON STREET
CROPLEY
WIMBOURNE STREET
RUSHTON ST
MINTERN STREET
IVY STREET
PURCELL STREET
REGAN WAY
PITFIELD

NAPIER GROVE
SHAFTESBURY STREET
CAVENDISH STREET
BUCKLAND STREET
CHERBURY ST

2

City Road Basin
GRAHAM STREET
CITY GARDEN ROW
WHARF ROAD
Wenlock Basin
WENLOCK
SHEPHERDESS
STURT ST
TAPLOW STREET
WALK
WENLOCK
MURRAY
BLETCHLEY ST
GROVE
STREET
EVELYN WALK
NEW NORTH ROAD
CRONDALL STREET
HOXTON

MICAWBER STREET
WINDSOR TERRACE
WELLESLEY TERRACE
UNDERWOOD STREET
PROVOST STREET
BEVENDEN STREET
FANSHAW STREET
PITFIELD STREET

CITY ROAD
PICARD ST
MORELAND ST
MASON'S PL
MACCLESFIELD ROAD
CENTRAL STREET
DINGLEY ROAD
MORA STREET
BATH STREET
NILE STREET
BRITANNIA WALK
WESTLAND
VESTRY STREET
STREET
HABERDASHER STREET
BUTTESLAND STREET
ASHFORD STREET
HOXTON SQUARE

3

LEVER STREET
IRONMONGER ROW
GALWAY STREET
CITY ROAD
PROVOST STREET
CHART STREET
CORSHAM STREET
BACHE'S STREET
CORONET STREET
HOXTON

NORMAN ST
RADNOR STREET
LIZARD ST
PEERLESS STREET
BALDW INST
BRUNSWICK PLACE
CRANWOOD STREET
VINCES ST
SQUARE
BOOT STREET
OLD GREAT EASTERN STREET

SEWARD STREET
BARTHOLOMEW SQUARE
RIVINGTON
GARDEN WALK
CHARLOTTE RD

PEAR TREE STREET
MITCHELL ST
HELMET ROW
Old Street
COWPER ST
SINGER ST
WILLOW STREET
BLACKALL STREET

4

BASTWICK STREET
GEE STREET
GARRETT STREET
OLD STREET
FEATHERSTONE STREET
MALLOW ST
CITY ROAD
CLERE STREET
LEONARD STREET
PAUL
LUKE
STREET
SCRUTTON ST
CLIFTON STREET
HOLYWELL ROW

BANNER STREET
WHITECROSS STREET
BUNHILL
BURIAL GROUNDS
Wesley's House and Chapel
TABERNACLE
EPWORTH STREET

BALTIC STREET
GOLDEN LANE
CHEQUER STREET
DIFFERIN STREET
ERROL STREET
ROW
BONHILL STREET

GOSWELL ROAD
FANN STREET
FORTUNE STREET
PASSAGE
BUNHILL FIELDS
WORSHIP STREET
STREET
WORSHIP

BRACKLEY STREET
LAMB'S
CHISWELL STREET
FINSBURY SQUARE
CHRISTOPHER STREET
CLIFTON STREET
PINDAR ST
APPOLD ST
PRIMRO

Barbican
BEECH STREET
Whitbread's Brewery
STREET
EARL STREET
SUN STREET

LONG LANE
ALDERSGATE STREET
Barbican Centre
SILK STREET
MILTON ST
NAYNE
FINSBURY ST
ROPEMAKER STREET
FINSBURY PAVEMENT
LACKINGTON ST
WILSON
STREET

MIDDLE STREET
St Giles, Cripplegate
FORE STREET
MOOR
Moorgate
MOORGATE
SOUTH PLACE
ELDON STREET
FINSBURY CIRCUS
Broadgate Centre
Liverpool Street Station

A **B** **C**

D E F

12

43b
31b

BRESSENDEN PLACE

STAG PLACE

ALLINGTON STREET

VICTORIA STREET

1

LOWER GROSVENOR PLACE

BELGRAVE MEWS WEST

CHESHAM PLACE

LYNDES ST

BELGRAVE PLACE

UPPER BELGRAVE ST

HOBART PL

LOWER BELGRAVE STREET

GROSVENOR GARDENS

BEESTON PL

EATON LANE

WILTON ROAD

ASHLEY
Westminster
Cathedral
CARLISLE PLACE
KING'S SCHOLAR'S PASSAGE
MORPETH TERRACE
AMBROSDEN AVENUE
FRANCES STREET
WILLOW PLACE
THIRLBY ROAD

21

1168

Victoria
TERMINUS PL

Victoria

EATON SQUARE

LOWNDES PLACE

EATON MEWS NORTH

ECCLESTON MEWS

GROSVENOR GARDENS

Victoria

ECCLESTON BRIDGE

BRIDGE PLACE

GILLINGHAM STREET

GUILDHOUSE STREET
37b

WILTON ROAD

VAUXHALL BRIDGE ROAD

WARWICK WAY

2

CHESHAM STREET

LYALL

EATON MEWS

EATON STREET

EATON SQUARE

CHESTER SQUARE

EBURY MEWS

EBURY

ELIZABETH STREET

ECCLESTON STREET

PALACE STREET

BELGRAVE ROAD

ECCLESTON SQUARE

DENBIGH STREET

CHURTON STREET

CLIVEDEN PL

WEST EATON PLACE

EATON TERR

EATON GATE

SOUTH EATON PLACE

GERALD ROAD

CHESTER MEWS WEST

MINERA MEWS

Sloane Square

CAROLINE TERRACE

CHESTER ROW

TERRACE

Victoria Coach Station

BUCKINGHAM PALACE ROAD

Elizabeth Bridge

HUGH STREET

ECCLESTON SQUARE

CAMBRIDGE STREET

ALDERNEY STREET

GEORGE'S SQUARE

WARWICK SQUARE

DRIVE

52b

3

SLOANE GARDENS

HOLBEIN PLACE

GRAHAM STREET

BOURNE STREET

EBURY STREET

CUNDY ST

SEMLEY PLACE

EBURY SQUARE

PIMLICO ROAD

STRABANAE ST

GROVE

EBURY BRIDGE ROAD

EBURY BRIDGE

WINCHESTER STREET

SUTHERLAND STREET

WESTMORELAND TERRACE

CLARENDON STREET

CAMBRIDGE STREET

WARWICK SQUARE

SUSSEX STREET

ALDERNEY STREET

GLOUCESTER STREET

CHELWOOD STREET

DENBIGH PLACE

DENBIGH STREET

LOWER SLOANE ST

SLOANE COURT

CHELSEA BRIDGE ROAD

Chelsea Royal Hospital

BLOOMFIELD TERR

RANELAGH GROVE

GATLIFF ROAD

WELLINGTON BUILDINGS

PEABODY AVENUE

TURPENTINE LANE

WESTMORELAND PL

SUTHERLAND STREET

LUPUS STREET

CUMBERLAND STREET

GLASGOW TERRACE

LUPUS STREET

JOHNSON'S PLACE

RANELAGH GARDENS

CHURCHILL GARDENS

CHURCHILL GARDENS ROAD

#124

GROSVENOR ROAD

CHELSEA EMBANKMENT

Chelsea Bridge

Grosvenor Bridge

4

KIRTLING STREET

21

Thames

CARRIAGE DRIVE NORTH

Battersea Power Station

CRINGLE ST

QUEENSTOWN ROAD

CARRIAGE DRIVE EAST

CARRIAGE DRIVE EAST

BATTERSEA PARK ROAD

SLEAFORD STREET

THESSALY ROAD

SAVONA STREET

5

PARK

Boating Lake

Battersea Park

STEWART'S ROAD

D E F

23

POINTERS CLOSE

WEST FERRY RD

A

EAST FERRY ROAD

MANCHESTER ROAD

Island Gardens DLR

B

FERRY STREET

FERRY ST

MIDLAND PLACE

SAUNDERS NESS ROAD

ISLAND GARDENS

C

HIGH BRIDGE

HOSKINS ST

Thames

River

Greenwich Foot Tunnel

CRANE STREET

EASTNEY STREET

PARK

OLD WOOLWICH RD

1

Greenwich Pier

Gipsy Moth IV

Cutty Sark

GREENWICH CHURCH STREET

i

Old Royal Naval College

ROMNEY ROAD

PARK

FEATHERS PLACE

ROW

Queen's House

ROW

THAMES STREET

NORWAY ST

HORSEFERRY PLACE

Cutty Sark DLR

KING WILLIAM

WALK

2

STOWAGE

COPPERAS ST STREET

C R E E K   R O A D

39»

BARDSLEY   LANE

G R E E N W I C H

ROAD

CLAREMONT STREET

HASDO STREET

STREET

RANDALL PL

St Alfege

NELSON ROAD

STOCKWELL ST

NEVADA ST

«15

National Maritime Museum

G R E E N W I C H

Old Royal Observatory

ROAN

STRAIGHTSMOUTH STREET

HIGH

BURNEY STREET

ROYAL

Fan Museum

GLOUCESTER CIRCUS

CROOM'S HILL GROVE

C R O O M ' S

THE

AVENU

3

NORMAN

TARVES

WAY

ROAD

Greenwich

«61

STREET

CIRCUS STREET

HILL

R O A D

STREET

HILL

GEORGETTE PLACE

GEORGE

HILL

Rang Hot

GREENWICH

DRIVE

«133

«86

LANGDALE ROAD

ASHBURNHAM   PLACE

SOUTH   STREET

BRAND   STREET

PRIOR STREET

ROYAL

KING

LUTON PL

HYDE

CHESTERFIELD ROAD

4

CATHERINE GROVE

EGERTON

ASHBURNHAM   GROVE

DEVONSHIRE   DRIVE

GUILDFORD GROVE

«116

GREENWICH

DABIN CRESCENT

BLISSET   STREET

WINFORTON STREET

MAIDENSTONE HILL

STREET

DILTON   STREET

HILL

POINT HILL

DIAMOND TERRACE

WESTGROVE LANE

WEST GROVE

VALE

CADE ROAD

GENERAL WOLFE ROAD

BLACKHEATH RD

«2

5»

B L A C K H E A T H   H I L L

HOLLYMOUNT CLOSE

DARTMOUTH ROW

DARTMOUTH HILL

S H O O T E R S   H I L L   R O A D

HARE AND BILLET ROAD

WHITFIELD ROAD

WALK

5

DITCH ALLEY

JOHN PENN STREET

BECK CLOSE

COLDBATH

BENNETT GROVE

MORDEN STREET

SPARTA STREET

LEWISHAM

LETHBRIDGE CLOSE

DARTMOUTH GROVE

ORCHARD HILL

NECTARINE WAY

BLISS CRESCENT

STREET

RAVENSBOURNE PLACE

RUSSETT WAY

ROAD

MORDEN HILL

MORDEN CLOSE

BLACKHEATH RISE

PRINCE'S RISE

LEWISHAM HILL

WAT TYLER ROAD

ST AUSTELL ROAD

POND

MOUNTS

GRANVILLE PARK

DEEN TERRACE

THE ORCHARD

PAGODA GARDENS

ELIOT

VA

BROOKMILL ROAD

ELVERSON ROAD

LEATHWELL ROAD

Elverson Road DLR

ROSEWOOD GARDENS

CONINGTON RD

«159»

ELIOT HILL ROAD

OAKCROFT ROAD

ABER

ROAD

A

B

C

D   E   F

A102 (M)

BELLOT ST

COMMERELL ST
CONLEY STREET
BLACKWALL LANE

GLENISTER RD

FINGAL STREET

CHILVER ST

DENHAM ST

COMBEDALE

WESTCOMBE HILL

KGP&9 STREET

PELTON

CHRISTCHURCH WAY

WHITWORTH ST

213b

379

WOOLWICH   ROAD

112b

1

BANNING STREET

HADRIAN STREET
CARADOC ROAD

TRAFALGAR   ROAD

COLOMB STREET

RODMERE STREET

VANBRUGH HILL

ANNANDALE   ROAD

HALSTOW   ROAD

KEMSING   ROAD

WESTERDALE   ROAD

Greenwich
District
Hospital

CHEVENING ROAD

ROYAL
HOSPITAL
CEMETERY

BSON ST
STREET

OLD WOOLWICH ROAD
ORLOP STREET

WOODLAND GROVE

EARLSWOOD STREET

TYLER STREET

CALVERT   ROAD

ORMISTON ROAD

Westcombe Park

TUSKAR STREET

WOODLANDS

WALNUT TREE ROAD

COLOMB STREET

ANNANDALE   ROAD

HUMBER   ROAD

RUTHIN ROAD

VISTA

PARK   ROAD

RESTELL CLOSE

DINSDALE ROAD

HUMBER   ROAD

PEACHUM   ROAD

COLERAINE ROAD

MYCENAE   ROAD

BEACONSFIELD   ROAD

Maze Hill

TOM SMITH CLOSE

MAZE

HILL

ULUNDI ROAD

FOYLE   ROAD

WEBB   ROAD

BELFAST GARDENS

COLERAINE   ROAD

HARDY   ROAD

INGLESIDE GROVE

BEACONSFIELD

BEACONSFIELD   ROAD

MYCENAE   ROAD

2

PARK

WESTCOMBE

VANBRUGH   HILL

LYNDALE CLOSE

PARK

HIGHCOMBE ROAD

MAZE   HILL

VANBRUGH FIELDS

WYCKERLEY CLOSE

VANBRUGH PARK ROAD WEST

COMBE AVE

COMBE MEWS

VANBRUGH PARK R RD

WESTCOMBE   PARK   ROAD

WOODBRIDGE CLOSE

3

VANBRUGH   PARK

VANBRUGH   ST

MANDEVILLE CLOSE

HEATH   WAY

JOHN'S

PARK

CHARLTON   WAY

MAZE   HILL

VANBRUGH TERRACE

ANGERSTEIN LANE

LANGTON   WAY

STRATHEDEN   ROAD

BLACKHEATH   AVENUE

BOWER   AVENUE

SHOOTERS   HILL   ROAD

CHARLTON   WAY

CHARLES   ROAD

PRINCE   OF   WALES   ROAD

ST   GERMAN'S   PLACE

37b

4

DUKE   HUMPHREY   ROAD

LONG   POND   ROAD

BLACKHEATH

GOFFS

TALBOT   PLACE

MOUNTS POND ROAD

BLACKHEATH VALE

ROAD

TRANQUIL VALE

ALL SAINTS DRIVE

ROYAL   PARADE

MONTPELIER   ROW

PRINCE   OF   WALES   ROAD

SOUTH   PARAGON

PARAGON   SQUARE

FALCONWOOD COURT

ROW

POND   ROAD

THE PARAGON

RYCULFF   ROAD

FULTHORP   ROAD

MERRIDALE

MORDEN   ROAD

KIDBROOKE GARDENS

REGENT'S PLACE

5

HARE   AND   BILLET   ROAD

ORCHARD DRIVE
ORCHARD ROAD

ELIOT PLACE

GROTE'S PLACE

D   E   F

BLACKHEATH

THE KEEP

General Index

Page numbers in **bold** type refer to main entries

A

Abakanowicz, Magdalena 183
Abbey, Westminster 46, 48, 72, **78–81**
Actors **41**
Adam, James 28, 40
  Portland Place 227
Adam, John 121
Adam, Robert 28, 40
  Adelphi 121
  Apsley House 99
  Fitzroy Square 132–3
  Kenwood House 236–7
  Lansdowne House 272
  Osterley Park House 255
  Portland Place 227
  Syon House 255, 271
Adams, John Quincy 155 Adelphi **121**
Adelphi Theatre **118**, 337
Admiral's House
  Street-by-Street map 232
Admiralty Arch **104**
  Street-by-Street map 103
The Adoration of the Kings
  (Bruegel) 108
Affordable art galleries
  (commercial) **329**, 330
Africa Centre 345
Agencies, booking tickets 335
Ai Weiwei 183
Air Canada 366
Air New Zealand 366
Air travel **366**
Airbnb 282, 356
Airports **366–9**
  map 367
Airsure 363
Albany **92**
  Street-by-Street map 90
Albert, Prince Consort 30
  Albert Memorial 200, **207**
  Lancaster House 98
  Royal Albert Hall 207
  Victoria and Albert Museum 212
Albert Bridge
  Chelsea and Battersea walk 268
  Street-by-Street map 197
Albert Hall Mansions
  Street-by-Street map 203
Albert Memorial 201, 207
  Street-by-Street map 203
Aldwych Theatre 337
Alexander, Helene 245
Alexandra, Queen 95
Alfege, St, Archbishop of
  Canterbury 243
Alfred the Great, King of Wessex
  21, 140

Algerian Coffee House 111
Ali, Monica 41
All England Lawn Tennis and
  Croquet Club 346
All Hallows by the Tower **155**
All Saints' Church
  Isleworth, Richmond and Kew
  walk 270
All Souls, Langham Place **227**
  London's Best: Churches 46, 49
Almeida Theatre 338, 342
Alsop, Will 372
Altdorfer, Albrecht 108
The Ambassadors (Holbein) **107**, 108
Ambassadors Theatre 337
Ambulances 358
American Airlines 366
American Express 360
The Anchor 177, **184, 275**
Andre, Carl 183
Annabel's 344, 345
Anne, Princess Royal 97
Anne, Queen 37
  Kensington Palace 210
  Queen Square 130
  statues of 82, 150
Anne of Denmark 242
The Annunciation (Lippi) 108
Antiques
  Archway Market **331**
  Bermondsey Antiques Market
  184, 331
  Chelsea Antiques Fair 58
  shops **328–30**
Antiquities
  London's Best: Museums and
  Galleries 44
Antonello da Messina
  St Jerome in his Study 108
Apollo Theatre 337
Apothecaries' Hall **154**
Apple Market **332**
Apsley, Baron 99
Apsley House **99**
Aquarium, London 64, 189, **190**, 350
Archaeology
  London's Best: Museums and
  Galleries **44**
Archbishops of Canterbury 192
Archer, Thomas 83
Architecture
  architects and engineers **40**
  Post-Modern architecture 35
  Tube Architecture 372
Arnolfini Portrait (van Eyck) 108
Arsenal Stadium 345
Art Antiques London 59
Art shops **328–30**
Arte Povera 183
Artists **40–41**
Artsline 355

Ascot Racecourse 347
Ashcroft, Dame Peggy 41
Association of Professional Tourist
  Guides 355
At the Theatre (Renoir) 107
Athletics **346**
ATMs 360–61
Auctions and auction houses
  329, 330
Audley End 376
Auerbach, Frank 87
August Bank Holiday 61
Augusta, Princess 262
Austen, Jane 41
Auto Europe 371
Autumn in London **60**

B

Bacon, Francis
  Tate Britain 86
  Tate Modern 182
  *Three Studies for Figures at the
  Base of a Crucifixion* 84, 86
Baden-Powell, Lord 166, 253
Baer, Jo 183
Bag shops **325**, 326
Baird, John Logie 111
Ballet **342**
  Royal Opera House 117
Bank of England 27, 28
Bank of England Museum **149**
  Street-by-Street map 147
Bank notes **361**
Banking **360–61**
Banks, Sir Joseph 262
Bankside
  walks 274–5
  see also Southwark and
  Bankside
Bankside Gallery **179,** 275
Bankside Pier 12
Bankside Power Station 182
Banqueting House 27, **82**
  Great Days in London 10
  A River View of London 64
  Street-by-Street map 73
Baptism of Christ (Piero della
  Francesca) 106
Bar at the Folies Bergère (Manet)
  43
Barbican **167**
  Street-by-Street map 165
Barbican Centre 52, 167
Barbican Concert Hall **341**
Barclays Cycle Hire 371
Barfly 343, 345
Barrie, J M 210, 221
Barry, Sir Charles 40
  Houses of Parliament 74
  Reform Club 94
  Royal College of Surgeons 136
  Travellers' Club 94
Barry, E M

Barry E M (cont.)
  Charing Cross 121
  Royal Opera House 117
Bars **306**, **308–11**
Bath 376
Bathers at Asnières (Seurat) 109
Battersea Park 52, 53, 253
  London's Best: Parks and
    Gardens 51
  walks **268–9**
Battersea Power Station 191
Baylis, Lilian 193
Bazalgette, Sir Joseph 30, 40
BBC 32
  All Souls, Langham Place 227
  Broadcasting House **227**
  Bush House 120
  TV channels 363
Beating the Bounds 58
Beating the Retreat 56, 59
The Beatles 34
Beauchamp Tower 156
Becket, St Thomas à, Archbishop
  of Canterbury 22
Beckman, Max 182
Bed and Breakfast **287**
Bed & Breakfast and Homestay
  Association 282, 283
Bedford, 5th Duke of
  statue of 125
Bedford, Earl of 113
Bedford Square 124
  Street-by-Street map 124
Beefeaters 156
Beer 291
  microbreweries **309**
  pubs **308–11**
  Whitbread's Brewery **170**
Behind the scenes tours 338, **351**
Belfast, HMS **185**
  Great Days in London 12, 13
  A River View of London 67
Belgravia
  walks **272–3**
Bell, Larry 183
Bell, Vanessa 41, 130
Bellini, Giovanni 108
  Courtauld Institute 119
  Doge Leonardo Loredan 106
  National Gallery 108
Bengalis 173
Bentley, John Francis 83
Berkeley Square 29, 52
  walks 272
Bermondsey Antique Market
  184, **331**
Berwick Street Market **110**, **331**
Betjeman, John 132, 167
Beuys, Joseph 182
Bevis, L Cubitt 196
BFI London IMAX 187, **339**
BFI Southbank 187, **339**
  Street-by-Street map 188

Bicester Village 317
Bicycle hire 13, 371
Bicycles 371
Big Ben 70, 74, **76**
  Great Days in London 12, 13
  Street-by-Street map 73
Big Bus Tours 355
Billingsgate (Old) **154**
  A River View of London 66
Binning, Lady 235
Bird, Francis 150
Black Death (1348) 22, 23
Blackfriars Bridge
  A River View of London 65
Blackheath **245**
  see also Greenwich and
    Blackheath
Blacklands Terrace
  Chelsea and Battersea walk
    269
Blake, Sir Peter
  Royal College of Art 202, 207
  Tate Britain 86
Blake, William 86
  St James's Church, Piccadilly 92
  St Mary's, Battersea 253
  tomb of 170
Blewcoat School **83**
Bligh, William
  tomb of 192
Blitz 33, 34
Blomfield, Sir Arthur 206
"Blood, Colonel" 157
Bloody Tower 156
Bloomsbury and Fitzrovia **123–33**
  area map 123
  bed and breakfast **287**
  British Museum **126–9**
  hotels 284–6
  pubs 310
  restaurants 297–8
  Street-by-Street map 124–5
Bloomsbury Group 41, 123, 130
Bloomsbury Square **130**
  Street-by-Street map 125
Blue Posts
  Street-by-Street map 102
Boats
  Cutty Sark 240, **243**
  HMS Belfast 67, **185**
  National Maritime Museum
    241, **242**
  Oxford v Cambridge boat race
    58
Boer War 31
Boetti, Alighiero 183
Boleyn, Anne
  execution 24, 157, 254
  Hampton Court 258
Bombings (July 2005) 35
Bond Street
  Great Days in London 11

Bookshops **322**, 323
  Charing Cross Road 110
Boots the Chemist 359
Borderline 343, 345
Borough Market **178**, **331**
  Great Days in London 12
  Street-by-Street map 177
Bosch, Hieronymus
  Christ Mocked 108
Boswell, James 115, 142
Boswells
  Street-by-Street map 115
Botticelli, Sandro
  Courtauld Institute 119
  National Gallery 108
Boucher, François 109
Boudicca, Queen 20
  statue of 73
Bourchier, Arthur 338
Bourchier, Elizabeth 170
Bourgeois 253
Bourgeois, Louise 182, 183
Boutique **hotels 285–6**
Bow Street Police Station
  Street-by-Street map 115
Boy and Dolphin (Wynne) **197**, 269
Brancusi, Constantin
  Fish 181, 183
Brasseries **306**, 307
Brawne, Fanny 235
Breakfast **304**, 306
  in hotels 280
Brentford
  Richmond and Kew walk 271
Breweries
  microbreweries **309**, 310
  Whitbread's Brewery **170**
Bric-à-brac shops **329**, 330
Brick Lane **172–3**
Brick Lane Market 173, **331**
  London's Best: Shopping Streets
    and Markets 315
Bridge Street Worldwide 282
Bridges
  Albert Bridge 197
  Blackfriars Bridge 65
  Holborn Viaduct **142**
  Hungerford Bridge 188
  London Bridge18, 22–3, 26, 177
  Millennium Bridge 175
  New London Bridge 34
  Southwark Bridge 176
  Tower Bridge 67, **155**
  Waterloo Bridge 189
Brighton 376
British Airways 366
British Hotel Reservation Centre
  283
British Library **131**
British Museum 38, 122, **126–9**
  floorplan 126–7
  Great Court and the Old
    Reading Room 129

British Museum (cont.)
Great Days in London 13
London's Best: Museums and Galleries 42, 44
Street-by-Street map 124
Visitors' checklist 127
British Summer Time 357
British Telecom 362
Brittany Ferries 365
Britten, Benjamin 206
Brixton Market **331**
Broadcasting House **227**
Broadgate Arena **341**
Broadway Market **331**
Brompton Cemetery 53
Brompton Oratory **206**
London's Best: Churches 46, 49
Street-by-Street map 203
Brompton Square
Street-by-Street map 203
Brougham, Lord 138
Brown, Lancelot 'Capability'
Richmond Park 254
Syon House 255, 271
Browning, Elizabeth Barrett 224, 226
Browning, Robert 224, 226
Bruegel, Pieter the Elder
The Adoration of the Kings 108
Courtauld Institute 119
Buckingham, Duke of 120
Buckingham Palace 17, **96–7**, 191
Great Days in London 10
London's Best: Ceremonies 54, 56
The Mall **95**
Buddhist Peace Pagoda
Chelsea and Battersea walk 268
Budget hotels **287**
Budget travel 356, 357
The Bullet Bar (music venue) 343
Bunhill Fields 53, **170**
Bunyan, John
tomb of 170
Bureaux de change 360
Burgh, Rev Allatson 234
Burgh House **234**
Street-by-Street map 233
The Burghers of Calais (Rodin) 72
Burlington, 3rd Earl of 260–61
Burlington Arcade **93**
Great Days in London 11
Street-by-Street map 90
Burne-Jones, Edward 23
Downshire Hill 235
Kensington Square 221
Leighton House 220
Burns, Robert 120
Burton, Decimus 40
Athenaeum 94
Palm House, Kew Gardens 263
Wellington Arch 99
Buses 31, 370, **374–5**
Bush, Irving T 120
Bush House **120**
Bush Theatre 338

Byfield, John 250
Byron, Lord
Albany 92
Holland House 220
St Marylebone Parish Church 226
Spaniards Inn 237
Vale of Health 237

C

Cabs *see* Taxis
Cabwise 377
Caesar, Julius 19, 20
Café de Paris 344, 345
Cafés **304–5**
Organic **306**, 307
Tate Britain 85
Cakes and Ale Sermon
London's Best: Ceremonies 57
Cambridge 376
Cambridge Theatre 337
Camden
Regent's Canal walk 267
Camden Lock Market **331**
Camden Market **248**
Camden Passage Market **332**
Camping 280
Canada Tower 35, 251
Canaletto
Dulwich Picture Gallery 253
National Gallery 109
Rome: The Pantheon 96
Canal, Regent's **229**, 264, **266–7**
Canary Wharf 35, **251**, 372
Canova, Antonio 99
Canterbury 376
Canute, King 71
Capon, William 141
Car hire 371
Car travel **371**
children 348–9
Caracci, Annibale 95
Caravaggio 109
Cardinal's Wharf **179**
Carlyle, Thomas
Carlyle's House 40, **198**
Chelsea 195
London Library 94
statue of 269
Carlyle's House 40, **198**
Street-by-Street map 196
Carnaby Street **111**, 315
Caro, Anthony 171
Carol services 61
Caroline, Queen 211, 273
Carracci, Annibale 95, 109
Carrington, Dora 130
Carter, Gilbert 198
Casinos **344**
Casson, Sir Hugh 83, 207
Cathedrals
St Paul's Cathedral 26, 47, 65, 144, 146, **150–53**
Southwark Cathedral 47, 48, 66, 177, **178**
Westminster Cathedral 46, 49, **83**

Catherine, Duchess of Cambridge 37, 79
Catherine of Aragon 76, 259
Catholic Church
Brompton Oratory **206**
Westminster Cathedral **83**
Cavendish, Lord 93
Caxton, William 23, 140
CD shops **322**, 323
Cecil Court
Street-by-Street map 103
Cecil Sharp House 343, 345
Cemeteries **53**
Bunhill Fields **170**
Highgate Cemetery **248**
Cenotaph **76–7**
London's Best: Ceremonies 55, 56
Street-by-Street map 73
Central Hall
Street-by-Street map 72
Ceremonies, London's Best **54–7**
Certificates, films 339
Cézanne, Paul 119
Chain bars **310**
Chamberlain, Neville 77
Chambers, Sir William
Osterley Park House 255
Pagoda, Kew Gardens 262
Somerset House 119
Changing of the Guard 96
London's Best: Ceremonies 56
Channel ferries **365**
Channel Tunnel 365
Chapel Market **332**
Chapel of St Thomas 22
Chaplin, Charlie 33, 41
statue of 105
Character hotels **286–7**
Chardin, Jean-Baptiste-Siméon 109
Charing Cross 35, **121**
A River View of London 64
Charing Cross Road **110**
London's Best: Shopping Streets and Markets 315
Street-by-Street map 102
Charles, Prince of Wales 35, 109
Clarence House 98
Crown Jewels 158
St Paul's Cathedral 151, 152
Charles I, King 37, 109
Banqueting House 82
Charles I Commemoration 61
Crown Jewels 158
execution 26
Hampton Court 259
Houses of Parliament 75
Richmond Park 254
Tower of London 159
Charles II, King 37, 117
Banqueting House 82
Crown Jewels 158
Green Park 99
Greenwich Royal Observatory 244

Charles II, King (cont.)
The Mall 95
Monument 154
and Nell Gwynne 41
Oak Apple Day 54, 57
Restoration 26–7
Royal Hospital 199
St James's Park 95
Soho Square 110
statue of 199, 268
Tower of London 159
Charles Dickens Museum 40, 131
Charles Street, Piccadilly 272
Charlotte, Queen
Queen's Chapel 95
statue of 130
Whitbread's Brewery 170
Charlotte Street **133**
Charlton House **252**
Charterhouse **166**
Street-by-Street map 165
Chaucer, Geoffrey 23, 41
Chelsea **195–9**
area map 195
pubs 311
Street-by-Street map 196–7
walks **268–9**
Chelsea Farmers' Market
Chelsea and Battersea walk 269
Chelsea Flower Show 58
Chelsea Football Club 347, 351
Chelsea Harbour **261**
Chelsea Hospital 58
London's Best: Ceremonies 54,
57
Chelsea Old Church **198**
Chelsea and Battersea walk 269
London's Best: Churches 48
Street-by-Street map 196
Chelsea Old Town Hall
Street-by-Street map 197
Chelsea Pensioners 199
Chelsea Physic Garden 52, **199**
Street-by-Street map 197
Chelsea porcelain factory 269
Chelsea Sports Centre 347
Chemists 359
Chequepoint 360
Chessington Golf Course 347
Chesterfield Street, Mayfair 272
Chevalier, Maurice 111
Cheyne, Lady Jane 198
Cheyne Walk **198**
Street-by-Street map 197
Childminders 349
Children **348–51**
clothes shops **318**, 320
in hotels 282
in restaurants 289, **349**
Tate Britain 87
travelling with 356
Chinatown **110**
Great Days in London 11, 12, 13
Street-by-Street map 102
Chinese New Year 61
Ching Court 114

Chisenhale Dance Space 342
Chiswick House 52, **260–61**
The Cholmondeley Ladies (British
School) 86
Christ Church, Spitalfields 172
London's Best: Churches 49
Street-by-Street map 165
Christ Mocked (Bosch) 108
Christmas 60, 61
Church of England 357
Church Row **235**
Street-by-Street map 233
Church Street Market **332**
Church Walk
Street-by-Street map 219
Churches
All Hallows by the Tower **155**
All Saints' Church, Isleworth 270
All Souls, Langham Place 46, 49,
227
Brompton Oratory 46, 49, 203,
206
Chelsea Old Church 48, 196,
198, 269
Christ Church, Spitalfields 49,
165, **172**
Holy Trinity 203
Immaculate Conception,
Mayfair 272
London's Best **46–9**
Notre Dame 102
Queen's Chapel 48, **95**
St Alfege 49, 240, **242–3**
St Andrew, Holborn **142**
St Anne's, Limehouse 49, **251**
St Bartholomew-the-Great 48,
167
St Bartholomew-the-Less 164
St Botolph, Aldersgate **166**
St Bride's 48, 49, **141**
St Clement Danes 49, 137, **140**
St Etheldreda's Chapel **142–3**
St George's, Bloomsbury 48, 49,
125, **130**
St Giles, Cripplegate **170**
St Helen's Bishopsgate **160**
St James Garlickhythe 49, 146
St James's, Piccadilly 49, 91, **92**
St John's, Smith Square **83**
St Katherine Cree **160**
St Leonard's **171**
St Luke's 269
St Magnus the Martyr 49, **154**
St Margaret Pattens **155**
St Margaret's 72, **76**
St Martin-in-the-Fields 46, 48,
49, 103, **104**
St Mary, Rotherhithe **250**
St Mary Abchurch 147
St Mary-at-Hill **154–5**
St Mary-le-Bow 48, 49, 146, **149**
St Mary-le-Strand 47, 49, **120**
St Mary Woolnoth 47, 49, 147
St Marylebone Parish Church
224, **226–7**
St Mary's, Battersea **253**

Churches (cont.)
St Nicholas Cole 146
St Pancras 49, **132**
St Paul's, Belgravia 273
St Paul's, Covent Garden 46, 48,
115, **116**
St Stephen Walbrook 47, 49,
147, **148**
Savoy Chapel **118**
spires 48
Temple Church 47, 48
Wesley's Chapel-Leysian
Mission **170–71**
see also Cathedrals
Churchill, Clementine 76
Churchill, Winston 33
Churchill Museum and Cabinet
War Rooms 72, 77
St Margaret's Church 76
St Paul's Cathedral 152
statue of 73, 76
Churchill Museum and Cabinet
War Rooms **77**
Street-by-Street map 72,
Ciné Lumière **339**
Cinema **339**
Cineworld 339
Cipriani, Giovanni 98
The City **145–61**
area map 145
Beating the Bounds 58
Great Days in London 12
hotels 284–6
London's Best: Ceremonies 55,
57
pubs 310–311
restaurants 298–300
St Paul's Cathedral **150–53**
Street-by-Street map 146–7
Tower of London **156–9**
City Hall 67
City of London Festival 59
City of London Information
Centre 354
Civil War 26
Clarence House **98**
Claude Lorrain 109, 253
Claudius, Emperor 20
Cleopatra's Needle **120**
A River View of London 64
Clerkenwell
pubs 310–11
Climate **58–61**
Clink Prison Museum **184** 275
Street-by-Street map 177
Clive of India 272
Clore Galleries, Tate Britain 84, **87**
Cloth Fair **167**
Street-by-Street map 165
Clothes
boutiques **317**, 319
chain stores 317–8, 319–20
children's clothes **318**, 320
knitwear **318**, 320
lingerie **318**, 320
modern British fashion **317**, 319

Clothes (cont.)
shoes **318**, 320
shops **316–19**
size chart **316**
street fashion **317**, 319
traditional **316**, 319
underwear **318**, 320
Clowns' Service 61
London's Best: Ceremonies 57
Clubs **344**, 345
Pall Mall 94
Coach and Horses 111, 310
Coach travel **365**
Cocteau, Jean 102, 215
Coffee **304**, 306
Coins **361**
Coleridge, Sir John Taylor 137
Coleridge, Samuel Taylor 237
Collcutt, T E 228
Collectables shops **329**, 330
College of Arms
Street-by-Street map 146
Columbia Road Market **173**, **332**
Comedy Store 338
Commonwealth 26, 37
Company of Watermen
London's Best: Ceremonies 57
Computer Cabs 377
Condor Ferries 365
Congestion Charge 371
Constable, John 41
Burgh House 234
Charlotte Street 133
grave of 235
The Hay-Wain **107**, 109
National Gallery 109
Well Walk 233, 234
Contemporary dance **342**
Conversion chart, measurements
356
Cook, Captain James 29, 242
Copley, John Singleton 161
Coram, Thomas 131
Coram's Fields 131, 351
Coronations
Coronation Day gun salutes 59
Crown Jewels **158**
Westminster Abbey **81**
Corot, Jean-Baptiste Camille 109
Costume and jewellery
London's Best: Museums and
Galleries **44**
Couch surfing 356
County Hall **190**, 274
Great Days in London 11
A River View of London 64
Street-by-Street map 189
Courtauld Institute of Art Gallery
119
London's Best: Museums and
Galleries 43, 45
Courtauld, Samuel 119
Courtauld, Stephen 252
Covent Garden and the Strand
113–21
area map 113

Covent Garden and the Strand
(cont.)
Great Days in London 11, 13
London's Best: Shopping Streets
and Markets 315
May Fayre and Puppet Festival
58
pubs 311
Street-by-Street map 114–15
Crafts Council Gallery **249**
London's Best: Museums and
Galleries 44
Crafts and design
London's Best: Museums and
Galleries **44**
shops 326–7
Cragg, Tony 87
Credit cards **360**
in restaurants 289
in shops 312
Crewe House, Mayfair 272
Cricket **346**
Kia Oval Cricket Ground 346
Lord's Cricket Ground **248**
test matches 59
Crime 358
Crippen, Dr 226
Criterion Theatre 337
Cromwell, Oliver 37
Apothecaries' Hall 154
Banqueting House 82
Commonwealth 26
Hampton Court 259
Lincoln's Inn 138
Museum of London 168
Oak Apple Day 57
St Giles, Cripplegate 170
Croom's Hill **245**
Crosby Hall
Chelsea and Battersea walk 269
Crowds, avoiding 355
Crown Jewels 156, **158**
Cruickshank, George 244
Crystal Palace **30–31**
open-air concerts 59
Cubitt, Thomas 132
Cumberland Terrace **229**
Currency **361**
Curzon Cinema 272
Curzon Street, Mayfair 272
Curzonfield House 272
Custom House
A River View of London 66
Customs and immigration **354**
Cutty Sark **243**
Street-by-Street map 240
Cycling 371

D
Dalí, Salvador 43, 182, 190
Dance **342**
Dance, George the Elder 148
Dance, George the Younger 260
Darwin, Charles 198
Daubigny, Charles-François 109

Davenport's Magic Shop 350
Davison, Emily 130
Day Lewis, Daniel 245
Day trips **376**
Deacon, Richard 87
Dean, Tacita 87
Dean's Yard **76**
Street-by-Street map 72
Defoe, Daniel
tomb of 170
Degas, Edgar 119
Delacroix, Eugène 109
Delis **305**, 306
Dennis Severs House **173**
Dentists 359
Department stores **313**
Depression 32, 33
Derain, André 182
Desenfans 253
Design Museum **185**
Great Days in London 12
London's Best: Museums and
Galleries 43, 44
A River View of London 67
Devonshire House
Piccadilly walks 272
DFDS 365
Dialling codes 362
Diana, Princess of Wales 35, 210
Diana, Princess of Wales
Memorial Fountain 11, 211
Kensington Gardens 210
Kensington Palace 210
Memorial Playground **221**
St Paul's Cathedral 151, 152
Spencer House 93
Dickens, Charles
Carlyle's House 198
Charles Dickens Museum 40,
131
Gray's Inn 143
Old Curiosity Shop 139
St Luke's Church 269
Trafalgar Tavern 244
Westminster Abbey 81
Ye Olde Cheshire Cheese 142
Diners **305**, 306
Disability Rights UK 277
Disabled visitors **355**, 357
entertainment 335
in hotels **282**, 283
Discounts
air travel 366
in hotels 280
museum tickets 348
student travellers 356
theatre tickets 338
Disraeli, Benjamin
St Andrew, Holborn 142
statue of 72
Docklands Light Railway (DLR)
35, 367
Docklands Sailing and
Watersports Centre 347
Docks 28
St Katharine's Dock **160**

Dr Johnson's House **142**
Doge Leonardo Loredan (Bellini) 106
Doggett's Coat and Badge
  A River View of London 65
Doggett's Coat and Badge Race 59
  London's Best: Ceremonies 57
Doll, Charles 130
Domesday Book 22
Dominion Theatre 337
Donmar Warehouse 118, 338
Donne, John 41
  Lincoln's Inn 138
  tomb of 153
Dormitory accommodation 283
Dover House
  Street-by-Street map 73
Downey, Juan 183
Downing, Sir George 77
Downing Street **77**
  Great Days in London 10
  Street-by-Street map 73
Downshire Hill **235**
Doyle, Sir Arthur Conan 40
  Sherlock Holmes Museum **228**
Drake, Sir Francis 25
Drayson Mews
  Street-by-Street map 219
Drink *see* Food and drink
Dryden, John
  Lamb and Flag 117
  Westminster School 76
Duccio 108
Duchess Theatre 337
Duke of York's Headquarters
  Chelsea and Battersea walk 269
Duke of York's Theatre 337
Dulwich Croquet Club 347
Dulwich Picture Gallery **252–3**
  London's Best: Museums and
  Galleries 45
Dunstan, St 80
Durham, Joseph 207
Dvořák, Antonin 227
Dynamic Suprematism (Malevich)
  183
Dysart, Countess of 254

E

Earlham Street Market 332
East End
  art galleries **328–9**, 330
  hotels 284–6
  restaurants 298–300
East Street Market **332**
East Village 344, 345
Easter 58, 61
EasyBus 368
EasyJet 366
Edinburgh, Duke of
  Buckingham Palace 97
  Duke of Edinburgh's Birthday
  gun salutes 59
Edward, Prince 97
Edward I, King 36
  Charing Cross 121

Edward I, King (cont.)
  Tower of London 157
Edward II, King 36
Edward III, King 36, 76
Edward IV, King 36, 159
Edward V, King 36
Edward VI, King 24, 36
Edward VII, King 31, 32, 37
  Crown Jewels 158
  Marlborough House 95
Edward VIII, King 33, 37
Edward the Confessor, King 22
  coronation 158
  Crown Jewels 158
  Houses of Parliament 75
  Westminster Abbey 71, 79, 81
Egg, Augustus 86
Eisenhower, Dwight 94
El Vino 141
  Street-by-Street map 137
Eleanor of Castile 121
Electrical adaptors **356**
Elgin, Lord 126, 129
Eliasson, Olafur 183
Eliot, George
  Cheyne Walk 198
  grave of 248
Eliot, T S
  Cheyne Walk 198
  Russell Square 130
Elizabeth, Queen Mother
  Crown Jewels 158
Elizabeth I, Queen 24, 37
  Greenwich 244
  National Portrait Gallery 105
  portrait of 25
  Richmond Palace 270
  Royal Exchange 149
  St James's Palace 93
  tomb of 81
Elizabeth II, Queen 34, 37
  Albert Memorial 207
  Buckingham Palace 97
  Celebrations 58, 59
  Ceremonies 54, 55, **56**, 61
  Coronation 79, 81, 158
  Jubilee Gardens 189
  Madame Tussauds 226
  Queen's Gallery 98
  St James's Palace 93
  Silver Jubilee 34
Elizabethan London **24–5**
Eltham Palace **252**
Email 363
Embankment 55
Embankment Galleries 119
Embankment Gardens
  A River View of London 64
Embassies and consulates 357
Embassy, US 272
Emergencies **358**, 359
Emin, Tracey 87
Emirates Air Line Cable Car 251
Engels, Friedrich 267
Engineers **40**
English National Opera 121

Entertainment **334–47**
  booking tickets 335
  cinema **339**
  clubs **344**, 345
  dance **342**
  disabled visitors 335
  information sources 334–5
  opera, classical and
    contemporary music **340–41**
  in pubs **309**
  rock, pop, jazz, reggae and
    world music **343**, 345
  sport **346–7**
  theatres 336–8
Envy Nightclub 344
Epsom Racecourse 347
Epstein, Sir Jacob 40
  Imperial War Museum 192
  Rima 210
  Roper's Garden 196, 198, 269
  St James's Park Station 83
  Tate Britain 86
Eros, statue of 92, 105
Ethelbert, King 21
Ethnic dance **342**
Etiquette **355**
  in clubs 344
Eton College
  London's Best: Ceremonies 57
Etty, William 86
Eurolines 365
Europcar 371
Europe
  map 14
European Health Insurance Card
  358
Eurostar 364
  St Pancras International 132
Eurotunnel 365
Evangelical services 357
Eventim Apollo 345
Everyman Cinema 339
  Street-by-Street map 233

F

FA Cup Final 58
Faber, Father Frederick William
  206
Fabric 344, 345
Fabro, Luciano 183
Fan Museum, the **245**
Faraday, Michael 99
Faraday Museum **99**
  London's Best: Museums and
  Galleries 45
Farrell, Terry 35
  Charing Cross 35, 121
  Ching Court 114
Fashion *see* Clothes
Fashion and Textile Museum 184
Fawkes, Guy
  Gunpowder Plot 26, 75
  Parliament Hill 236
Fenton House 52, **235**
  Street-by-Street map 232
Ferries, cross-channel **365**

Festival of Britain (1951) 34, 187, 190
Festivals **58–61**
  dance **342**
  music **340**
Film **339**
Fine art galleries (commercial) **328–30**
Fire services 358, 359
Fireworks 60
First Capital Connect 368, 369
Fischli, Peter 183
Fish (Brancusi) 181, 183
Fish and chips 305, **307**
Fishmongers' Hall **154**
  A River View of London 66
Fitzalwin, Henry 22
Fitzrovia see Bloomsbury and Fitzrovia
Fitzroy Square **132–3**
Fitzroy Tavern **133**
Flamsteed, John 244
Flamsteed House 244
Flask Walk **234**
  Street-by-Street map 233
Flats, self-catering **282**, 283
Flaxman, John 117
Fleet Street **140–41**
  Street-by-Street map 137
Fleming, Ian 198
Florence Nightingale Museum **192**
  London's Best: Museums and Galleries 45
Foley, John 207
Food and drink
  light meals and snacks 304–7
  pubs **308–11**
  shops **321**, 323
  What to Eat in London **290–91**
  see also Restaurants
Football **346**
Fopp 323
Foreign-language films **339**
Forster, E M 41
Fortnum and Mason 313
  Great Days in London 10
  Street-by-Street map 90
Fortune Theatre 337
Foster, Sir Norman
  British Museum 129
  Canary Wharf Underground Station 372
  the Gherkin 35, 40
  Sackler Galleries 92
Foundling Museum **131**
Fournier Street **172**
Fowke, Francis 207
Fowler, Charles 116
Fox, Charles James
  statue of 125
Fox and Anchor pub
  Street-by-Street map 164
Frampton, Sir George 210
Franklin, Benjamin 167
Frederick, Prince of Wales 242

French House 111, 310
Freud, Anna 248
Freud, Lucien 86
Freud, Sigmund 40
  Freud Museum 44, **248**
Fringe theatre **338**
Fry, Roger 41, 133
Fulham Palace **261**
Funfairs 59
Furniture and interiors
  London's Best: Museums and Galleries **44**

G

Gabriel's Wharf **193**, 275, **332**
  Great Days in London 13
  London's Best: Shopping Streets and Markets 315
  A River View of London 65
Gainsborough, Thomas 40
  Dulwich Picture Gallery 45
  Kenwood House 45
  National Gallery 109
  Tate Britain 86
  Wallace Collection 228
Galleries, commercial **328–30**
  see also Museums and galleries
Galsworthy, John 232
Gandhi, Mahatma 129
Gardens see Parks and gardens
Garnet, Henry 161
Garrick, David 237
Garrick Club
  Street-by-Street map 114
Garrick Theatre 337
Gastropubs 309
Gate Theatre 338
Gatwick Airport **368**
  hotels 369
Gatwick Express 368
Gauguin, Paul 119
De Gaulle, Charles
  The French House 111
  St James's Square 94
Gay bars 311
Gay clubs **344**
Gay and lesbian travellers 356, 357
Geffrye, Sir Robert 250
Geffrye Museum **250**
  London's Best: Museums and Galleries 44
Gentile da Fabriano 108
George, Prince 35
George I, King 28, 37
  St George's Bloomsbury 48, 49, 130
George II, King 28, 37
  Downing Street 77
  Foundling Museum 131
  Hampton Court 257
  Henrietta Howard (mistress) 254
  Marble Hill House 254
  statue of 241

George II, King (cont.)
  White Lodge 254
George III, King 28, 37
  British Library 131
  Queen Square 130
  Queen's Chapel 95
  Royal Mews 98
  Whitbread's Brewery 170
George IV, King (Prince Regent) 29, 37
  Buckingham Palace 96
  Cumberland Terrace 229
  National Gallery 106
George V, King 32, 37
George VI, King 34, 37
  Crown Jewels 158
  portrait of 33
George Inn **178**, 311
  Street-by-Street map 177
Georgian London **28–9**
Géricault, Théodore 109
Gertler, Mark 235
Ghosts, in theatres **338**
Gibberd, Sir Frederick 228
Gibbons, Grinling
  All Hallows by the Tower 155
  St Alfege Church 243
  St James's Church, Piccadilly 92
  St Mary Abchurch 147
  St Paul's Cathedral 153
  St Paul's Church 116
  statue of Charles II 199, 268
  Tower of London 159
Gibbons, Dr William 234
Gibbs, James 40
  churches **49**
  Orleans House 254
  St Martin-in-the-Fields 46, 48, 103, 104
  St Mary-le-Strand 47, 120
Gielgud, Sir John 41
Gielgud Theatre 105, 337
Gift shops **324**, 326
Gilbert, Alfred
  statue of Eros 92
Gilbert Collection (V&A) 215
Gilbert & George 86–7
Gill, Eric
  Broadcasting House 227
  St James's Park Station 83
  Westminster Cathedral 83
Gladstone, William
  Albany 92
  Harley Street 227
  statue of 136
Glebe Place
  Chelsea and Battersea walk 269
Globe Theatre see Shakespeare's Globe
Goethe Institute 338
Goldsmith, Oliver 249
Golf **346**
Good Friday 58, 61
Goodwin's Court
  Street-by-Street map 114
Gordon, Douglas 87

Gormley, Antony 87
Grable, Betty 161
Grahame, Kenneth 219
Des Granges, David
   The Saltonstall Family 85
Grant, Duncan 41, 130
Gray's Antique Markets **332**
Gray's Inn 52, **143**
Great Bed of Ware **214**
Great Cumberland Place 28
Great Exhibition (1851) **30–31**,
   202, 207, 211
Great Days in London 10–13
Great Fire of London (1666) 19,
   26–7
   Monument **154**
Great River Race 60
Great Stink (1858) 30
Greater London
   map 15
Greater London Council (GLC) 35
Green Park 52, **99**
   London's Best: Parks and
   Gardens 51
   walks 272
Green Tourism Business Scheme
   357
Green travel 370
Greene, Graham 92
Greenline Buses 365, 369
Greenwich and Blackheath **239–
   45**
   area map 239
   cruise highlights 63
   Great Days in London 11
   Street-by-Street map 240–41
Greenwich Foot Tunnel **243**
   Street-by-Street map 240
Greenwich Market **332**
   Street-by-Street map 240
Greenwich Mean Time 244
Greenwich Park 53, **245**
   London's Best: Parks and
   Gardens 51
Greenwich Royal Observatory
   244–5
Greiflenhagen, Maurice
   A London Street Scene 32
Grenadier pub, Belgravia 273
Gresham, Sir Thomas 41, 149
   tomb of 160
Grey, Lady Jane 157
Greyhound racing **346**
Gribble, Herbert 206
Grimaldi, Joseph 57
Grosvenor Square 28
Grove, George 206
Grove Lodge
   Street-by-Street map 232
Guanabara 344
Guards Museum **83**
   London's Best: Museums and
   Galleries 44
Guided tours 355
Guildhall 161
   London's Best: Ceremonies 57

Guildhall Art Gallery **161**
Guildhall School of Music and
   Drama 167
Gunpowder Plot (1605) 26, 75,
   161, 236
Guy Fawkes Night 60
Guy's & St Thomas' Hospital
   Old Operating Theatre 178–9
Gwynne, Nell 41
   Theatre Royal 117
   tomb of 104
Gyms **347**

H

Hackney Empire 338
Haig, Earl
   statue of 73
Hall, Sir Benjamin 76
Hals, Frans 236
   Laughing Cavalier **42**, 228
Ham House 27, 52, **254**
Hamilton, Richard 86
Hamleys 350
Hammersmith Apollo 343, 345
Hampstead **231–7**
   area map 231
   pubs 311
   Street-by-Street map 232–3
Hampstead Heath 53, 231, **236**
   London's Best: Parks and
   Gardens 50
   open-air concerts 59
   Street-by-Street map 232
Hampstead Ponds 347
Hampton Court 52, **256–9**
   cruise highlights 63
   park **256–7**
   timeline 259
   Visitors' checklist 257
Hampton Court Flower Show 59
Handel, George Frideric
   Fenton House 232, 235
   Foundling Museum 131
   Handel House Museum 40, **341**
   Museum of Musical
   Instruments 206
   Royal Opera House 117
   St Katharine Cree 160
Hanover, House of 37
Hanover Square 28
Hard Rock Café 305, 349
Hardiman, Alfred 73 Hardwick,
   Thomas 226–7
Harley Street **227**
   Street-by-Street map 225
Harold Pinter Theatre 337
Harrison, John 244
Harrod, Henry Charles 211
Harrods **211**, 312, 313
Harvard, John 178
Harvest of the Sea 60
Harvey Nichols 313
Hat shops 324–5, 326
Hatfield House 376
Hatton, Sir Christopher 143

Hatton Garden **143**
Hawksmoor, Nicholas 40
   Christ Church, Spitalfields 172
   churches **48–9**
   St Alfege 242–3
   St Anne's, Limehouse 251
   St George's, Bloomsbury 48, 130
   St Mary Woolnoth 47, 147
   Westminster Abbey 78
The Hay-Wain (Constable) **107**,
   109
Haydn, Joseph 206
Hay's Galleria
   A River View of London 66
Hay's Mews, Mayfair 272
Hayward Gallery 187, **190**
   Great Days in London 12
   London's Best: Museums and
   Galleries 45
   Street-by-Street map 188
Health care **358–9**
Heathrow Airport **366–7**
   hotels 369
Heathrow Connect (train service)
   366–7
Heathrow Express (train service)
   366
Henrietta Maria, Queen
   Queen's Chapel 48, 95
   Queen's House, the 242
Henry, Prince of Wales 141
Henry I, King 36
Henry II, King 22, 36
Henry III, King 36
   Tower of London 157
   Westminster Abbey 80
Henry IV, King 36
Henry V, King 36
Henry VI, King 36
   Ceremonies 57
Henry VII, King 36
   Richmond 255
   Richmond Palace 270
Henry VIII, King 24, 36
   Charterhouse 166
   Chelsea 195
   execution of Anne Boleyn 24,
   254
   Green Park 99
   Greenwich 244
   Hampton Court 256–9
   Horse Guards 82
   Hyde Park 211
   Lincoln's Inn 138
   National Portrait Gallery 105
   portrait of 259
   Richmond Park 254
   St Alfege 243
   St Bartholomew-the-Great 167
   St James's Palace 90, 93
   St James's Park 95
   and Sir Thomas More 41
   Tower of London 159
   Victoria and Albert Museum
   212
   Westminster Abbey 80

Henry of Reyns 79
Henry Wood Promenade
    Concerts (The Proms) 59, 60,
    340, 341
Henson, Jim 235
Hepworth, Barbara 86
Her Majesty's Theatre 337
Hertford family 228
Hertz Rent a Car 371
Herzog and de Meuron 182
Hess, Rudolph 157
Highgate **248**
Highgate Cemetery 53, **248**
Hill, Rowland 30
The Hill Garden 52, **237**
Hiller, Susan 182
The Hippodrome 103
Hiring cars 371
Hirst, Damien 87
History **19–37**
HMS Belfast 12, **185**
HMV Forum 344
Hockney, David 173
    Royal College of Art 202, 207
    Tate Britain 86
    Whitechapel Art Gallery 171
Hodgkin, Howard 87
Hogarth, William 40
    Foundling Museum 131
    Hogarth's House **261**
    Leicester Square 105
    Marble Hill House 255
    Old Bull and Bush 234
    Portrait of Captain Coram 131
    St Bartholomew-the-Great 167
    St John's Gate 249
    Sir John Soane's Museum 138
    Tate Britain 86
    tomb of 104
Holbein, Hans
    The Ambassadors **107**, 108
    Henry VIII 259
    National Portrait Gallery 105
Holborn and the Inns of Court
    135–43
    area map 135
    Lincoln's Inn: Street-by-Street
    map 136–7
    pubs 310
Holborn Viaduct **142**
Holden, Charles 83, 139
Holidays, public 61
Holland, Henry 92
Holland House **220**
    Street-by-Street map 218
Holland Park 52, **220**
    London's Best: Parks and
    Gardens 50
    open-air theatre season 59
    Street-by-Street map 218
    see also Kensington and
    Holland Park
Holland Park Public Tennis Courts
    347
Holmes, Sherlock 40
    Sherlock Holmes Museum **228**

Holy Trinity, Dalston
    Clowns' Service 57
Holy Trinity, South Kensington
    Street-by-Street map 203
Hop Exchange **178**
Hopkins, Matthew 372
Horniman, Frederick 252
Horniman Museum **252**
Horse Guards **82**
    Great Days in London 12
    London's Best: Ceremonies 54,
    56
    Street-by-Street map 73
    Trooping the Colour 59
Horses
    London International Horse
    Show 61
    racing **346**
    riding **346**
    Royal Mews **98**
Hospitals 358–9
    St Bartholomew's Hospital 164
Hostelling International 356, 357
Hostels 283
Hotels **280–87**
    airport hotels 369
    bars **310**, 311
    bed and breakfast **287**
    Bloomsbury and Regent's Park
    284–6
    booking on-line 281
    boutique hotels **285–6**
    budget accommodation 283,
    287
    chain hotels 282
    character hotels **286–7**
    children in 282
    City and the East End **284–7**
    disabled travellers **282**, 283
    discount rates 280
    facilities 281
    Further afield **286–7**
    hidden extras 280–81
    how to book 281
    Kensington and Chelsea **284–6**
    luxury hotels **284–5**
    Ritz Hotel **93**
    Savoy Hotel **118**
    self-catering flats **282**, 283
    special breaks 281
    Westminster and the West End
    284–6
    where to look 280
Houdon, Jean-Antoine 228
Hounslow Heath Golf Course 347
Houses, historic
    Apsley House **99**
    Burgh House 233, **234**
    Charlton House 252
    Chiswick House **260–61**
    Clarence House **98**
    Fenton House 232, **235**
    Ham House **254**
    Hogarth's House **261**
    Holland House 218, **220**
    Keats House **235**

Houses, historic (cont.)
    Kenwood House **236–7**
    Lancaster House **98**
    Leighton House 218, **220**
    Linley Sambourne House 219,
    220
    Marble Hill House **254–5**
    Marlborough House **95**
    Orleans House Gallery **254**
    Osterley Park House **255**
    Pitzhanger Manor **260**
    Queen's House 241, **242**
    Ranger's House 243, 245
    Spencer House **93**
    Sutton House **250**
    Syon House **255**
    see also Palaces
Houses of Parliament 17, **74–5**,
    191
    Great Days in London 10, 12,
    13
    London's Best: Ceremonies 55,
    56
    State Opening of Parliament 56,
    60
    Street-by-Street map 73
Hoyland, John 171
Huguenots 163, 172
Hungerford Bridge
    Street-by-Street map 188
Hunt, Leigh 195, 237
Hunt, William Holman 86
Hyde Park 52, 53, **211**
    Great Exhibition (1851) 31
    London's Best: Ceremonies 54,
    56
    London's Best: Parks and
    Gardens 50
    walks 273

I

Ice-skating 61, **346**
IMAX cinema 187, **339**
Immigration **354**
Imperial College
    Street-by-Street map 203
    Summer Accommodation
    Centre 283
Imperial War Museum **192–3**
    Great Days in London 13
    London's Best: Museums and
    Galleries 43, 45
Ingres, Jean-Auguste-Dominique
    109
Inns of Court
    A River View of London 65
    see also Holborn and the Inns of
    Court
Institut Français 338
Institute of Contemporary Arts
    (ICA) **94**, 342
Insurance **359**
Interiors shops **326**, 327
International Student Identity
    Card 356

International Youth Travel Card
356
Internet services **363**
booking hotel rooms 281
Inwood, Henry and William
132
Irving, Henry 41
Irving, Washington 249
Isleworth
Richmond and Kew walk 270
Islington **249**

J

Jacob II de Gheyn (Rembrandt)
252, 253
Jamie's Italian 349
James, Henry 198
James I, King 25, 26, 37, 141
Banqueting House 82
Blackheath 245
Charlton House 252
Greenwich Park 245
Hyde Park 211
James II, King 27, 37, 214
Jazz **343**, 345
Jazz Café 343, 345
Jermyn Street 91
Jewel Tower **76**
Street-by-Street map 72
Jewellery
Crown Jewels 156, **158**
Hatton Garden **143**
London's Best: Museums and
Galleries **44**
shops **324**, 326
Jews
Jewish Museum **249**
religious services 357
John, Augustus 40, 133
John, King 22, 36
John Lewis 313
Johnson, James 254
Johnson, Dr Samuel 40, 184
Boswells 115
Dr Johnson's House **142**
Memorial service 57
statue of 140
Ye Olde Cheshire Cheese 142
Jones, Adrian 99
Jones, Christopher 250
Jones, Sir Horace
Leadenhall Market 161
Smithfield Market 164, 166
Jones, Inigo 40, 261
Banqueting House 27, 64, 73,
82
Charlton House 252
churches **48**
Piazza and Central Market
(Covent Garden) 113, 116
Queen's Chapel 95
Queen's House 241, **242**, 243
St Paul's Church 46, 115, **116**
Jonson, Ben
Fleet Street 141

Jonson, Ben (cont.)
Lincoln's Inn 138
Westminster School 76
Jubilee Footbridge 64
Jubilee Gardens
Street-by-Street map 189
Jubilee Hall Clubs 347
Jubilee Line 34
Jubilee Line Architecture 372
Jubilee Market **332**
Street-by-Street map 115
Juice bars 306–7
Justice Walk
Chelsea and Battersea walk 269

K

Kandinsky, Wassily 183
Kauffer, E McKnight 116
Kean, Edmund 41, 270
Keats, John 40
Apothecaries' Hall 154
Keats House **235**
St John's, Hampstead 235
Spaniards Inn 237
Vale of Health 237
Well Walk 234
Kempton Park Racecourse 347
Kensal Green Cemetery 53
Kensington and Chelsea
bed and breakfast **287**
hotels **284–6**
restaurants **295–7**
Kensington Church Street
London's Best: Shopping Streets
and Markets 314
Kensington Civic Centre
Street-by-Street map 219
Kensington Gardens 52, **210–11**
Great Days in London 11, 13
London's Best: Parks and
Gardens 50
Kensington and Holland Park
217–21
area map 217
Street-by-Street map 218–19
see also South Kensington and
Knightsbridge
Kensington Palace 52, **210**
Great Days in London 11
London's Best: Museums and
Galleries 44
Kensington Palace Gardens **221**
Kensington Roof Gardens **220–21**
Kensington Square **221**
Kent, William 272
Chiswick House 261
Hampton Court 259
Horse Guards 82
Kensington Gardens 210
Kenwood House 52, **236–7**
London's Best: Museums and
Galleries 45
open-air concerts 59
Kew
cruise highlights 63
walks 271

Kew Bridge Steam Museum **260**
London's Best: Museums and
Galleries 45
Kew Gardens 28, 52, 53, **262–3**
London's Best: Parks and
Gardens 50
Visitors' checklist 263
Kew Palace
Richmond and Kew walk 271
Keynes, John Maynard 41
Kia Oval Cricket Ground 346, 347
Kids Go Free 356
King, Martin Luther 226
King Street
Street-by-Street map 91
King's College, Cambridge 57
King's Conference Vacation
Bureau 283
King's Head 309, 338
Kings and queens 36–7
King's Road **198**
Chelsea and Battersea walk 269
London's Best: Shopping Streets
and Markets 314
Street-by-Street map 196
Kipling, Rudyard 234
Kitaj, R B 87
Knights Templar
Temple 137, 141
Temple Church 47, 48
Knightsbridge
art and antique shops **328**, 330
London's Best: Shopping Streets
and Markets 314
see also South Kensington and
Knightsbridge
Knitwear shops **318**, 320
Koko 343, 345
De Kooning, Wilhelm 182

L

Lady Minicabs 377
Laing, Gerald 86
Skydiver VI 86
Lamb and Flag 117, 308
Street-by-Street map 114
Lambeth Palace **192**
Lancaster, House of 36
Lancaster House **98**
Landmark Trust 282, 283
Landseer, Edwin 104
Lane, Danny 215
Langham Hotel **227**
Lansdowne House 272
Lasdun, Sir Denys 190
Last Night of the Proms 60
Latimer, Bishop 24
Lauderdale, Duke of 254
Laughing Cavalier (Hals) **42**, 228
Law Courts *see* Royal Courts of
Justice
Law Society **139**
Street-by-Street map 137
Lawrence, D H 234, 237
Lawrence, T E 153

Lawrence, Thomas 86
Lawrence, Sir Thomas 198
LD Lines 365
Leadenhall Market **161**, 332–3
Leaders **41**
Leather goods shops **325**, 326
Leather Lane Market **333**
Legislation, children 348–9
Leicester Square **105**
　Great Days in London 12, 13
　Street-by-Street map 102
Leigh, Vivien 43
Leighton, Lord 218, 220
Leighton House **220**
　Street-by-Street map 218
Leon 349
Leonardo da Vinci
　Queen's Gallery 98
　Victoria and Albert Museum 215
　Virgin and Child (Burlington
　　House Cartoon) 106, 108
Leverhulme, Lord 237
Lewis, Wyndham 86
Liberty **111**, 313
Liberty, Arthur Lasenby 111
Library, British **131**
Light meals and snacks 304–7
Lincoln, Abraham
　statue of 76
Lincoln's Inn 138–9
　Street-by-Street map 136–7
Lincoln's Inn Fields 52, **139**
　Street-by-Street map 136
Linford Christie Stadium 347
Linley Sambourne House **220**
　London's Best: Museums and
　　Galleries 44
　Street-by-Street map 219
Lippi, Filippo
　The Annunciation 108
Lisson Grove
　Regent's Canal walk 266
Little Angel Theatre 351
Little Venice 229, **264**
　Regent's Canal walk 266
Live Aid 35
Livery Companies
　London's Best: Ceremonies 57
Livingstone, David 203
Livingstone, Ken 35
Lloyd Webber, Andrew 110
Lloyd's of London 12, 27, 34, **161**
Lombard Street 147
London Aquarium *see* Sea Life
　London Aquarium
London Bicycle Tour Company
　371
London Boat Show 61
London Bridge 18, 22–3, 26
　Street-by-Street map 177
London to Brighton veteran car
　rally 60
London Central Mosque **228**
London City Airport **367**
London Clinic
　Street-by-Street map 225

London Coliseum **121**, **340**, 342
London County Council (LCC) 31
London Cycling Campaign 371
London Docklands Museum 251
London Duck Tours 355
London Dungeon **190**
London Eye 35, 186, 191
　Great Days in London 11, 12, 13
　A River View of London 64
　Street-by-Street map 188
London Festival of Railway
　Modelling 58
London Film Festival **339**
London Hostel Association 283
London International Horse
　Show 61
London Jamme Masjid **172**
London Marathon 58
London Palladium 338
London Pass 354, 355
London Silver Vaults **143**
A London Street Scene
　(Greiflenhagen) 32
London Symphony Orchestra
　(LSO) 341
London Transport Lost Property
　Office 358, 359
London Travel Information 370–
　71
London Walks 355
London Zoo 53, **229**
　Regent's Canal walk 266, 267
London's Transport Museum
　116–17
　Great Days in London 11, 13
　London's Best: Museums and
　　Galleries 45
　Street-by-Street map 115
Long, Richard 87
Longhi, Pietro 109
Lord, Thomas 248
Lord Mayor
　Lord Mayor's Show 55, 57, 60,
　　169
　Mansion House **148**
Lords, House of *see* Houses of
　Parliament
Lord's Cricket Ground 248, 347
Loredan, Doge Leonardo 106
Lost property 358, 359
Louis Philippe, Duke of Orleans
　254
Lovat, Lord 159
Lucas, Sarah 87
Luton Airport **369**
Lutyens, Sir Edwin
　Cenotaph 73, 76
Luxury hotels **284–5**
Lyceum Theatre 337
Lyric (Hammersmith) 338
Lyric Theatre 105, 338

M

McBean, Angus 43
Mackmurdo, A H 251

McQueen, Steve 87
Madame Jojo 344, 345
Madame Tussauds **226**
　Street-by-Street map 224
Madonna and Child
　(Michelangelo) 92
Magazine shops **322**, 323
Magnus, St 154
Magritte, René 182
Mahler, Gustav 117
Maida Vale
　pubs 311
Maison Bertaux 111, 304, 306
Makerius, Sameer 183
Malevich, Kasimir 182
　Dynamic Suprematism 183
The Mall **95**
Manchester Square 28
Mandela, Nelson
　statue of 189
Manet, Édouard
　Bar at the Folies Bergère 43
　Courtauld Institute 119
Mansfield, Earl of 236, 237
Mansion House **148**
　Street-by-Street map 147
Mantegna, Andrea 108
　The Triumphs of Caesar 256
Mantz, Werner 183
Maps
　Bloomsbury and Fitzrovia 123,
　　124–5
　bus routes 374–5
　Central London 16–17
　Ceremonies: London's Best
　　54–5
　Chelsea 195, 196–7
　Churches: London's Best 46–7
　The City 145, 146–7
　Covent Garden 114–15
　Covent Garden and the Strand
　　113
　Elizabethan London 24
　Georgian London 28
　Greater London 15
　Greenwich 240–41
　Greenwich and Blackheath 239
　Hampstead 231, 232–3
　Holborn and the Inns of Court
　　135
　Kensington and Holland Park
　　217, 218–19
　Lincoln's Inn 136–7
　London between the World
　　Wars 32
　Marylebone 224–5
　Medieval London 22
　Museums and Galleries:
　　London's Best 42–3
　Parks and Gardens: London's
　　Best 50–51
　Piccadilly and St James's 89,
　　90–91
　Postwar London 34
　Regent's Park and Marylebone
　　223

Maps (cont.)
Restoration London 26
Roman London 20
Shopping Streets and Markets:
London's Best 314–15
Smithfield 164–5
Smithfield and Spitalfields 163
Soho and Trafalgar Square 101
South Bank 187, 188–9
South Kensington and
Knightsbridge 201, 202–3
Southwark and Bankside 175,
176–7
Trafalgar Square 102–3
Victorian London 30
Walks in London 265–77
West End theatres 337
Western Europe 14
Whitehall and Westminster 71,
72–3
Marble Arch **211**
Marble Hill House **254–5**
open-air concerts 59
Markets **331–3**
Alfies Antique Market **329**
Archway Market **331**
Apple Market **332**
Bermondsey Antique Market
184, **331**
Berwick Street Market **110**, **331**
Billingsgate **154**
Borough Market 177, **178**, **331**
Brick Lane Market 173, **331**
Brixton Market **331**
Camden Lock Market **331**
Camden Market **248**
Camden Passage Market **332**
Chapel Market **332**
Church Street Market **332**
Columbia Road Market **173**,
332
Covent Garden 116, 315
Earlham Street Market **332**
East Street Market **332**
Gabriel's Wharf Market **332**
Greenwich Market 240, **332**
Jubilee Market **332**
Leadenhall Market **161**, **332**
Leather Lane Market **333**
London's Best **314–15**
Marylebone Farmers' Market
333
New Caledonian Market **331**
Old Spitalfields Market **172**,
333
Petticoat Lane **171**, **333**
Piccadilly Crafts Market **333**
Portobello Road **221**, **333**
Ridley Road Market **333**
Riverside Walk Market **332**
Roman Road **333**
Shepherd's Bush Market **333**
Smithfield Market 164, **166**
Marks and Spencer **313**
Marlborough, Duchess of 95
Marlborough House **95**

Marlowe, Christopher 41
Marochetti, Carlo 72
Martin, John 86
Martin, Sir Leslie 190
Marx, Karl 267
British Museum 129
grave of 248
Mary I, Queen 24, 25, 36–7
Greenwich 244
tomb of 81
Mary II, Queen 37
Hampton Court 256, 257, 259
Kensington Palace 210
Marylebone
Street-by-Street map 224–5
see also Regent's Park and
Marylebone
Marylebone Farmers' Market **333**
Masaccio 108
Matcham, Frank 121
Matisse, Henri
The Snail 183
Matthew, Sir Robert 190
Maurice, Bishop of London 151
May Day 61
Mayfair
art and antiques shops **328**,
330
walks **272–3**
Mayor Thames Festival 60
Maze, Hampton Court 256
Measurements, conversion chart
356
Medical Express 358
Medical treatment **358–9**
Medicines 359
Medieval London **22–3**
churches **48**
Megabus 365
Melbury Road
Street-by-Street map 218
Mendieta, Ana 183
Meridian 244
Merz, Marisa 183
Metropolitan Railway 30, 32
Michelangelo
Madonna and Child 92
National Gallery 108
Microbreweries **309**
Middle Temple 52–3
Military
London's Best: Ceremonies **56**
London's Best: Museums and
Galleries **44–5**
Mill, John Stuart 221
Millais, John Everett 220
Ophelia 84, 86
Millennium Bridge 175
Milton, John 41
Bunhill Fields 170
tomb of 170
Minicabs 377
Ministry of Defence
A River View of London 64
Ministry of Sound 344, 345
Mobile phones 362

Modigliani, Amedeo 119
Mohammed Ali, Viceroy of Egypt
120
Monet, Claude 61
Courtauld Institute 119
National Gallery 109
Money **360–61**
Monuments
Cenotaph **76–7**
The Monument 12, 66, **154**
Nelson's Column 104
Temple Bar Memorial 137, **140**
Victoria Monument 98
War Memorial 177
Moody, F W 202
Moore, Henry
Imperial War Museum 192–3
St James's Park Station 83
St Stephen Walbrook 47, 148
Tate Britain 86
Three Standing Figures 268
More, Sir Thomas 24, **41**, 268
Chelsea 196
Chelsea Old Church 198
statues of 196, 198, 269
Tower of London 157
De Morgan, William 251
Morris, William
Liberty 111
Linley Sambourne House 220
Victoria and Albert Museum
214
William Morris Gallery 44, **251**
Mosques
London Central Mosque **228**
London Jamme Masjid **172**
Mount Street, Mayfair 272
Mount Street Gardens 272
Mozart, Wolfgang Amadeus 111
Murillo, Bartolomé Esteban 109,
253
Museum Street
Street-by-Street map 124
Museums and galleries (general)
admission charges 355
avoiding crowds 355
cafés **305**, 306
children in 348, **350**
London's Best **42–5**
Museums and galleries
(individual)
Apsley House 99
Bank of England Museum 147,
149
Bankside Gallery **179**
British Museum 42, 44, 122,
126–9
Broadcasting House 227
Burgh House 233, **234**
Carlyle's House **198**
Charles Dickens Museum **131**
Charlton House **252**
Chiswick House **260–61**
Clink Prison Museum 177, **184**
Courtauld Institute of Art
Gallery 43, 45, 119

Museums and galleries (cont.)
Crafts Council Gallery 44, **249**
Cutty Sark 240, **243**
Dennis Severs House **173**
Design Museum 43, 44, 67, **185**
Dr Johnson's House **142**
Dulwich Picture Gallery 45, **252–3**
Eltham Palace **252**
Embankment Galleries 119
Fan Museum, the **245**
Faraday Museum 45, **99**
Fashion and Textiles Museum 184
Fenton House **235**
Florence Nightingale Museum 45, **192**
Foundling Museum **131**
Freud Museum 44, **248**
Geffrye Museum 44, **250**
Greenwich Royal Observatory **244–5**
Guards Museum 44, **83**
Guildhall Art Gallery **161**
Ham House **254**
Handel House Museum 40, **341**
Hayward Gallery 45, 187, 188, **190**
HMS Belfast **185**
Hogarth's House **261**
Horniman Museum **252**
Imperial War Museum 43, 45, **192–3**
Institute of Contemporary Arts **94**
Jewel Tower 76
Jewish Museum **249**
Keats House **235**
Kensington Palace 44
Kenwood House 45, **236–7**
Kew Bridge Steam Museum 45, **260**
Leighton House **220**
Linley Sambourne House 44, 219, **220**
London Dungeon **190**
London's Transport Museum 45, 115, 116–17
Lord's Cricket Ground 248
Madame Tussauds 224, **226**
Marble Hill House **254–5**
Museum of Garden History 45, 52, **192**
Museum of London 17, 43, 44, 45, 148, 165, **168–9**
Museum of London Docklands 251
Museum of Musical Instruments 206
Musical Museum **255**
National Army Museum 44, **199**
National Gallery 43, 45, 103, **106–9**
National Maritime Museum 45, 241, **242**
National Portrait Gallery 43, 103, **104–5**

Museums and galleries (cont.)
Natural History Museum 42, 45, 202, **204–5**
Old Operating Theatre **178–9**
Osterley Park House **255**
Photographers' Gallery **111**
PM Gallery and House **260**
Pollock's Toy Museum 45, **133**
Prince Henry's Room 141
The Queen's Gallery **98**
Queen's House 241, **242**
Ranger's House, Greenwich 245
Royal Academy of Arts 42, 45, 90, **92**
Royal College of Surgeons 136
Royal Mews **98**
Royal Observatory 45
Saatchi Gallery 45, 249, 269
St John's Gate 249
Science Museum 42, 45, 202, **208–9**
Serpentine Gallery **210**
Shakespeare's Globe **179**
Sherlock Holmes Museum **228**
Sir John Soane's Museum 44, 136, **138–9**   Somerset House 119
Spitalfields Centre Museum of Immigration & Diversity **172**
Syon House **255**
Tate Britain 43, 45, **84–7**
Tate Modern 43, 45, 65, **180–83**
Tower Bridge Exhibition 155
Tower of London 43, 44–5, **156–9**
Victoria and Albert Museum 42, 44, 45
Victoria and Albert Museum of Childhood 45, **250**
Wallace Collection 45
Music
dance **342**
festivals **341**
Henry Wood Promenade Concerts 59, 60
Museum of Musical Instruments 206
Musical Museum **255**
open-air concerts **53**, 59
opera, classical and contemporary music 340–41
rock, pop, jazz, reggae and world music **343**, 345
Royal College of Music 202, **206**
shops **322–3**
Muslims
London Central Mosque **228**
London Jamme Masjid **172**
religious services 357
Myddleton, Sir Hugh 249

N

Nag's Head pub, Belgravia 273
Name-day Ceremonies **57**

Napoleon I, Emperor 99, 104
Nash, John 28, 40
All Souls, Langham Place 46, 49, **227**
Buckingham Palace 96
Carlton House Terrace 94
Clarence House 98
Cumberland Terrace 29, 229
Marble Arch 211
Park Crescent 225
Piccadilly Circus 92
Portland Place 227
Regent's Canal 229, 266
Regent's Park 223, 224, 226
Royal Mews 98
Royal Opera Arcade 94
Theatre Royal 40, 102, 105
Trafalgar Square 104
United Services Club 94
Nash, Paul
Imperial War Museum 192
London's Transport Museum 116–17
National Army Museum **199**
London's Best: Museums and Galleries 44
National Express 365, 368, 369
National Film Theatre (BFI Southbank) 187, **339**
Street-by-Street map 188
National Gallery 16, **106–9**
floorplan 106–7
Great Days in London 10, 12, 13
London's Best: Museums and Galleries 43, 45
Sainsbury Wing 106, **109**
Street-by-Street map 103
Visitors' checklist 107
National Maritime Museum **242**
London's Best: Museums and Galleries 45
Street-by-Street map 241
National Portrait Gallery **104–5**
Great Days in London 10, 13
London's Best: Museums and Galleries 43
Street-by-Street map 103
National Rail 364
National Theatre 34, 187, 190, 336
National Trust
Blewcoat School 83
Fenton House 235
George Inn 178
Natural History Museum **204–5**
floorplan 204–5
Great Days in London 13
London's Best: Museums and Galleries 42, 45
Street-by-Street map 202
Visitors' checklist 205
Navy Day 56, 60
Neal Street **117**
Great Days in London 13
London's Best: Shopping Streets and Markets 315
Street-by-Street map 114

Neal's Yard **117**
  Great Days in London 11, 13
  Street-by-Street map 114
Neal's Yard Dairy 117
Nelson, Admiral Lord
  National Maritime Museum 242
  Nelson's Column 104
  St Paul's Cathedral 153
Neri, St Philip 206
New Caledonian Market 331
New End Theatre
  Street-by-Street map 233
New London Bridge 34
New London Theatre 337
New Row
  Street-by-Street map 114
New Year's Day 61
New Year's Parade 61
Newcomen, Thomas 42
Newman, John Henry 206
Newspapers 363
Newton, Adam 252
Newton, Sir Isaac 27, 105
Newton, William 139
NHS (National Health Service)
  358, 359
NHS Direct 358–9
Night buses 375
Nightingale, Florence
  Florence Nightingale Museum
  45, **192**
  tomb of 152
Nightingale, Lady
  Lady Nightingale's Memorial 81
93 Feet East 344, 345
Noel Coward Theatre 337
Nogueira, Lucia 183
Noodle bars 307
Norman kings 36
North London
  art and antique shops **329**, 330
North London Line 376
Northumberland, Dukes of 255,
  271
Northumberland, Earls of 255
Nost, John 259
Le Nôtre, André 245
Notting Hill **221**
  Great Days in London 13
  pubs 311
  walks 276–7
Notting Hill Arts Club 343, 345
Notting Hill Carnival 59
Novello Theatre 337

O

O2 Academy Brixton 343, **345**
O2 Arena **251**
O2 Shepherd's Bush Empire 345
  Oasis Sports Centre 346, 347
Observatory, Greenwich Royal
  244–5
Odeon Leicester Square 339
Olaf II Haraldsson, King of Norway
  21
Old Bailey **149**

Old Billingsgate **154**
  A River View of London 66
Old Bull and Bush 232, **234**
Old Compton Street 111
Old Curiosity Shop **139**
  Street-by-Street map 136
Old Dairy
  Street-by-Street map 196
Old Deer Park
  Richmond and Kew walk 271
Old English Garden
  Chelsea and Battersea walk 268
Old Operating Theatre 12, 13,
  178–9
Old Spitalfields Market **172, 333**
Old Vic 34, 41, 187, **193**
Olivier, Laurence 41
  National Theatre 190
Olympic Games (1948) 34
Olympic Games (2012) 35, 245,
  346, 370, 372
100 Club 345
One-off shops 321–2, 323
Ono, Yoko 87
Open air concerts **53**, 59, **341**
Open air theatre 59, 226, **336**
Opening hours **355**
  banks 360
  pubs 308
  restaurants 289
  shops 312
Opera **340–41**
  English National Opera 121
  Royal Opera House **117**
Ophelia (Millais) 84, 86
The Orangery 218
Oranges and Lemons service 58
  London's Best: Ceremonies 57
Oriel House
  Richmond and Kew walk 270
Original London Sightseeing
  Tours 355
Orleans House Gallery **254**
Orton, Joe 249
Orwell, George 133, 249, 276
Osterley Park 52
Osterley Park House **255**
Outdoor drinking, pubs **309**
Outdoor music **53**, 59, **341**
Oval Cricket Ground 346, 347
Oxford 376
Oxford, Robert Harley, Earl of 223
Oxford v Cambridge boat race 58
Oxford v Cambridge rugby union
  match 61
OXO Tower **193**, 275
  A River View of London 65
Oyster card (bus & tube ticket)
  370, 373, 374

P

P&O Ferries 365
Painted Hall 244
Palace Theatre **110**, 111, 337
Palace of Westminster *see* Houses

  of Parliament
Palaces
  Buckingham Palace **96–7**, 191
  Eltham Palace **252**
  Fulham Palace **261**
  Kensington Palace 44, 52, **210**
  Kew Palace 271
  Lambeth Palace **192**
  Richmond Palace 270
  St James's Palace 90, **93**
  Whitehall Palace 82
  Winchester Palace 23
  see also Houses, historic
Pall Mall **94**
  Street-by-Street map 91
Palladio, Andrea 260–61
Palmerston, Lord
  Holland House 220
  Queen Anne's Gate 82
Pankhurst, Emmeline 148
Pantomime 30, **336**
Paolozzi, Eduardo
  Royal College of Art 207
Paris, Matthew 36
Park Crescent
  Street-by-Street map 225
Parking 371
Parks and gardens
  Barbican Centre 52
  Battersea Park 51, 52, 53, **253**,
  268
  Berkeley Square 32
  Blackheath **245**
  Chelsea Flower Show 58
  Chelsea Physic Garden 52, 197,
  199
  children in **350–51**
  Chiswick House 52
  Coram's Fields 131, 351
  Diana, Princess of Wales
  Memorial Playground **221**
  Embankment Gardens 64
  Fenton House 52, 232
  Gray's Inn 52
  Green Park 51, 52, **99**
  Greenwich Park 51, 53, **245**
  Ham House 52, 254
  Hampstead Heath 50, 53, 231,
  232, **236**
  Hampton Court 52, **256–7**
  Hampton Court Flower Show
  59
  The Hill Garden 52, **237**
  Holland Park 50, 52, 218, **220**
  Hyde Park 50, 52, 53, **211**
  Jubilee Gardens 189
  Kensington Gardens 13, 50, 52,
  210–11
  Kensington Palace Gardens 52,
  221
  Kensington Roof Gardens **220–
  21**
  Kenwood 52
  Kew Gardens 28, 50, 52, 53,
  262–3
  Lincoln's Inn Fields 52, 139

Parks and gardens (cont.)
London Zoo 53
London's Best **50–53**
Middle Temple 52–3
Museum of Garden History 45,
52, **192**
Osterley Park 52
Parliament Hill 53, **236–7**
PM Gallery and House 260
Ranelagh Gardens 268
Regent's Park 51, 52, 53, 224,
226
Richmond Park 50, 53, **254**
Roper's Garden 196, **198**, 269
Russell Square 52
St James's Park 51, 52, 53, 95
Soho Square 53
Syon House 53, 271
Victoria Embankment Gardens
120
Parliament see Houses of
Parliament
Parliament Hill 53, **236–7**, 347
Parliament Square 12, **76**
Street-by-Street map 72
Parmigianino 108
Passports 354
Pasta 305, **307**
Paterson, William 27
Patisserie Valerie 111, 304, 306
Pavlova, Anna 110
Paxton, Joseph 31
Peabody Buildings 31
Peace – Burial at Sea (Turner) 85
Peacock Theatre 342
Pearly Kings and Queens
London's Best: Ceremonies 57
Pearly Harvest Festival 60
Peasants' Revolt (1381) 23, 245
Peel, Sir Robert 41
Pelli, César 251
Penn, William 139, 155
Pepys, Samuel 27, 41
All Hallows by the Tower 155
Piazza and Central Market
(Covent Garden) 116
Ye Olde Cheshire Cheese 142,
311
Perfume shops **325**, 326–7
Peter Pan
statue of 210, 221
Petticoat Lane **171**, **333**
London's Best: Shopping Streets
and Markets 315
Pharmacies 359
The Pheasantry 198
Chelsea and Battersea walk 269
Phillimore Place
Street-by-Street map 219
Phoenix Theatre 337
Phoneboxes **362**
Photographers' Gallery 111, 329,
330
Photography shops **329**, 330
Piano, Renzo 185
Piazotta, Enzo

The Young Dancer 112
Piazza and Central Market
(Covent Garden) **116**
Great Days in London 12, 13
Street-by-Street map 115
Picasso, Pablo
Tate Modern 182
Piccadilly Arcade 89
Piccadilly Circus **92**
Street-by-Street map 91
Piccadilly Crafts Market **333**
Piccadilly and St James's **89–99**
area map 89
art and antiques shops **328**,
330
Buckingham Palace **96–7**
pubs 310
Street-by-Street map 90–91
walks 272–3
Piccadilly Theatre 337
Pickpockets 358
Piero di Cosimo 108
Piero della Francesca 108
Baptism of Christ 106
Pimlico
art and antiques shops **328**,
330
Piombo, Sebastiano del 108
Pippa Pop-Ins 349
Pisanello 108
Pissarro, Camille 119
Pistoletto, Michelangelo 183
Pitt, William the Elder 92
Pitzhanger Manor and Gallery **260**
Pizza Express 343, 345
Street-by-Street map 124
Pizzas **305**, 307
The Place 342
Plague (1665) 26, 27
Plantagenets 36
Plaques, famous Londoners 41
Playhouse Theatre 337
Poets' Corner, Westminster Abbey
81
Police **358**, 359
Polka Children's Theatre 351
Pollock, Benjamin 133
Pollock, Jackson
Whitechapel Art Gallery 171
Pollock's Toy Museum **133**
London's Best: Museums and
Galleries 45
Pop music **343**, 345
Porchester Centre 347
Portcullis House 73
Portland Place **227**
Street-by-Street map 225
Portman Square 28
Portobello Road **221**
Great Days in London 13
walks 276–7
Portobello Road Market **333**
London's Best: Shopping Streets
and Markets 314
Portrait of Captain Coram
(Hogarth) 131

Portsmouth, Duchess of 117
Post-Modern architecture 35
Postal services **363**
Postwar London **34–5**
Poussin, Nicolas
Dulwich Picture Gallery 45, 253
Pre-Raphaelite Brotherhood 86,
251
Priestley, J B 234
Prime Ministers
Downing Street **77**
Houses of Parliament 74
Primrose Hill
Regent's Canal walk 267
Prince Charles Cinema 339
Prince Edward Theatre 337
Prince Henry's Room **141**
Street-by-Street map 137
Prince of Wales Theatre 337
Princes in the Tower **159**
Private homes, staying in 282
Promenade Concerts 59, 60, 340,
341
Public holidays 61
Public Record Office 31
Public telephones 362
Pubs **308–11**
The Anchor 177, **184**
children in 348
Fitzroy Tavern **133**
food in **305**, 307, 309
Fox and Anchor 164
George Inn 177, **178**
Lamb and Flag 118
Old Bull and Bush 232, **234**
Prospect of Whitby 63
Saracen's Head 164
Spaniards Inn **237**
Trafalgar Tavern **244**
Ye Olde Cheshire Cheese **142**
Puppet Theatre Barge 351
Purcell, Henry 160
Purcell Room 340
Puritans 26

Q

Qantas 366
Quattro Stagioni (Twombly) 181
Queen Anne's Gate 82
Queen Elizabeth Hall 340, 342,
345
Street-by-Street map 188
Queen Mary's Gardens, Regent's
Park 226
Queen Square **130**
Queens **36–7**
Queen's Chapel **95**
London's Best: Churches 48
Queen's Club (Real Tennis) 347
The Queen's Gallery **98**
Queen's House, Greenwich 239,
242, 243
Street-by-Street map 241
Tower of London 156
Queens Ice Skating Club 347

Queen's Theatre 337
Queensway **221**
Queues 355

R

Racing
greyhound **346**
horse **346**
Rackham, Arthur 267
Radio 363
Radio Taxis 377
Rail travel **364, 376**
Railway stations 364
Charing Cross Station 121
St Pancras Station **132**
Waterloo Station **193**
Railways see Trains
Rainfall 60
Raleigh, Sir Walter 25, 157
Ranelagh Gardens
Chelsea and Battersea walk 268
Ranger's House, Greenwich 243, 245
Raphael
Dulwich Picture Gallery 253
National Gallery 106, 108
Rauschenberg, Robert 171
Ravens
Tower of London 156
Record shops **322**, 323
Red Lion Yard, Mayfair 272
Regency churches **49**
Regent's Canal 229, 264
walks **266–7**
Regent's Park **226**
London's Best: Parks and Gardens 51, 52, 53
open-air theatre season 59
Regent's Canal walk 266
Street-by-Street map 224
Regent's Park Lake 347
Regent's Park and Marylebone **223–9**
area map 223
bed and breakfast **287**
hotels **284–6**
restaurants **297–8**
Street-by-Street map: Marylebone 224–5
Reggae **343**
Religious services 357
Rembrandt
Dulwich Picture Gallery 45
Jacob II de Gheyn 252–3
Kenwood House 236
National Gallery 109
Wallace Collection 228
Remembrance Sunday 60
London's Best: Ceremonies 55, 56
Rennie, John 189
Renoir, Pierre Auguste
At the Theatre 107
Courtauld Institute 119
Renoir Cinema 339
Repertory cinemas **339**

Responsible Tourism **357**
Restaurants **288–307**
Bloomsbury and Regent's Park **297–300**
children in 289
The City and East End 298–300
Further afield **301–3**
Kensington and Chelsea **295–7**
price and service 289
Southwark and the South Bank **300–301**
Westminster and the West End **292–5**
What to Eat in London **290–91**
see also Food and drink
Restoration London **26–7**
Reynolds, Sir Joshua 40
Kenwood House 45, 236
Leicester Square 105
National Gallery 109
Royal Academy of Arts 90
Spaniards Inn 237
Tate Britain 86
tomb of 104
Wallace Collection 228
Richard I, King 36
Great Seal 23
statue of 72
Richard II, King 36, 108
Richard III, King 36
College of Arms 146
Princes in the Tower 159
Richardson, Sir Ralph 41
Richelieu, Cardinal 109
Richier, Germaine 182
Richmond 62, **255**
walks **270–71**
Richmond, William 152
Richmond House
Street-by-Street map 73
Richmond Palace 270
Richmond Park 53, **254**
London's Best: Parks and Gardens 50
Richmond Park Golf 347
Richmond Theatre 270
Ridley, Bishop 24
Ridley Road Market **333**
Riley, Bridget 183
Ritz, César 90, 93
Ritz Hotel **93**
Great Days in London 10
Street-by-Street map 90
Ritzy Cinema 339
River Cruises 62–3
A River View of London **62–7**
Rivera, Diego 182
Riverboats 375
Riverside Studios 342
Riverside Walk Market **332**
Rock music **343**, 345
Rodin, Auguste
The Burghers of Calais 72
Rogers, Richard 35
Lloyd's of London 34, 161

Rokeby Venus (Velázquez) 107
Roman Amphitheatre 21, 161
Roman Bath **120**
Roman Catholic Church 357
Roman London 19, **20–21**
Amphitheatre 161
Museum of London 168
Roman Road Market **333**
Rome: The Pantheon (Canaletto) 96
Romford Stadium 347
Romney, George 228, 236
Ronnie Scott's 111, 343, 345
Roosevelt, Franklin D. 272
Roper, Margaret 198
Roper, William 198
Roper's Garden **198**
Chelsea and Battersea walk 269
Street-by-Street map 196
Rose Theatre 179
Ross Nye Stables 347
Rossetti, Dante Gabriel
Cheyne Walk 195, 196
Downshire Hill 235
Liberty 111
Venus Venticordia 40
Rosslyn Park Rugby 347
Rothko, Mark 182
Rothschild, Baron Ferdinand 128
Rotten Row, Hyde Park 273
Roubiliac, Louis François
Lady Nightingale's Memorial 81
Wallace Collection 228
Rousseau, Henri (Le Douanier) 109
Roxy 345
Royal Academy of Art 28, **92**
Great Days in London 11
London's Best: Museums and Galleries 42, 45
Street-by-Street map 90
Summer Exhibition 59
Royal Academy of Music
Street-by-Street map 224
Royal Albert Hall **207**
concerts **341**, 345
Henry Wood Promenade Concerts 59, 60, 340, 341
Street-by-Street map 202
Royal Avenue
Chelsea and Battersea walk 269
Royal Botanic Gardens see Kew Gardens
Royal College of Art **207**
Street-by-Street map 202
Royal College of Music **206**
Street-by-Street map 202
Royal College of Organists
Street-by-Street map 202
Royal College of Surgeons
Street-by-Street map 136
Royal Court Theatre 199
Royal Courts of Justice (the Law Courts) 135, **140**
Street-by-Street map 137
Royal Exchange **149**
Street-by-Street map 147

Royal Festival Hall 34, 187, **190**
  concerts 340
  Great Days in London 12
  Street-by-Street map 188
Royal Geographical Society
  Street-by-Street map 203
Royal Hospital **199**
  Chelsea and Battersea walk 268
Royal Institute of British
  Architects (RIBA) 227
  Street-by-Street map 225
  Victoria and Albert 212, 214–15
Royal Mail 363
Royal Mews **98**
Royal Naval College, Old 243, **244**
  Street-by-Street map 241
Royal Observatory Greenwich
  London's Best: Museums and
  Galleries 45
Royal Opera Arcade **94**
Royal Opera House **117**
  ballet 342
  Great Days in London 13
  opera **340**
  Street-by-Street map 115
Royal Salutes
  London's Best: Ceremonies 56
Royal Shakespeare Company **336**
Royal Society of Painter-
  Printmakers 179
Royal Watercolour Society 179
Royalty **36–7**
  Buckingham Palace **96–7**
  coronations **81**
  London's Best: Ceremonies **56**
  Royal Mews **98**
Rubens, Peter Paul
  Banqueting House 27, 73, 82
  Courtauld Institute 119
  Dulwich Picture Gallery 45
  Kenwood House 45
  National Gallery 106, 109
Rugby **346**
Rules (restaurant)
  Street-by-Street map 115
Ruskin, John 111
Russell Square 52, **130**
  Street-by-Street map 125
Ryanair 366
Rysbrack, John Michael
  George II Statue 241

S

SSE Arena Wembley 345
Saatchi Gallery 199, 249
  London's Best: Museums and
  Galleries 45
Sackler Galleries 92
Sadleir, Ralph 250
Sadler's Wells **342**
Safety **358–9**
St Albans 376
St Alfege **242–3**
  London's Best: Churches 49
  Street-by-Street map 240

St Andrew, Holborn **142**
St Anne's, Limehouse **251**
  London's Best: Churches 49
St Anne's Church Tower, Soho
  111
St Bartholomew-the-Great **167**
  London's Best: Churches 48
  Street-by-Street map 165
St Bartholomew-the-Less
  Street-by-Street map 164
St Bartholomew's Hospital
  Street-by-Street map 164
St Botolph, Aldersgate **166**
St Bride's **141**
  London's Best: Churches 48, 49
St Clement Danes **140**
  London's Best: Churches 49
  Oranges and Lemons service
  57, 58
  Street-by-Street map 137
St Etheldreda's Chapel **142–3**
St George's, Bloomsbury **130**
  London's Best: Churches 49
  spire 48
  Street-by-Street map 125
St Giles, Cripplegate **170**
St Helen's Bishopsgate **160**
St James Garlickhythe
  London's Best: Churches 49
  Street-by-Street map 146
St James's *see* Piccadilly and St
  James's
St James's, Piccadilly **92**
  London's Best: Churches 49
  Street-by-Street map 91
St James's Palace **93**
  London's Best: Ceremonies 54
  Street-by-Street map 90
St James's Park 52, 53, **95**
  Great Days in London 10, 12, 13
  London's Best: Parks and
  Gardens 51
  open-air concerts 59
St James's Park Station **83**
St James's Square **94**
  Street-by-Street map 91
St James's Street
  Great Days in London 10
St Jerome in his Study (Antonello
  da Messina) 108
St John's, Smith Square **83**
  concerts **341**
St John's Gate **249**
St Katharine's Dock **160**
  Great Days in London 11, 12,
  13
  A River View of London 67
St Katherine Cree **160**
St Leonard's Church **171**
St Luke's Church
  Chelsea and Battersea walk 269
St Magnus the Martyr **154**
  London's Best: Churches 49
St Margaret Pattens **155**
St Margaret's, Westminster **76**
  Street-by-Street map 72

St Martin-in-the-Fields **104**
  concerts **341**
  London's Best: Churches 46, 49
  spire 48
  Street-by-Street map 103
St Martin's Theatre 337
  Street-by-Street map 114
St Mary, Battersea **253**
St Mary, Rotherhithe **250**
St Mary Abchurch
  Street-by-Street map 147
St Mary-le-Bow **149**
  London's Best: Churches 49
  Pearly Harvest Festival 60
  Pearly Kings and Queens 57
  spire 48
  Street-by-Street map 146
St Mary-at-Hill **154–5**
  Harvest of the Sea 60
St Mary of Lambeth (Museum of
  Garden History) **192**
St Mary Overie Dock 275
St Mary-le-Strand **120**
  London's Best: Churches 47, 49
St Mary Woolnoth
  London's Best: Churches 47, 49
  Street-by-Street map 147
St Marylebone Parish Church
  226–7
  Street-by-Street map 224
St Nicholas Cole
  Street-by-Street map 146
St Olave's House
  A River View of London 66
St Pancras International Station
  132, 364
St Pancras Parish Church **132**
  London's Best: Churches 49
St Paul's Cathedral 144, **150–53**
  Cakes and Ale Sermon 57
  floorplan 152–3
  Great Days in London 12, 13
  Great Fire 26
  London's Best: Churches 47
  A River View of London 65
  Street-by-Street map 146
  timeline 151
  views of 179
  Visitors' checklist 151
St Paul's Church **116**
  London's Best: Churches 46, 48
  Street-by-Street map 115
St Stephen Walbrook **148**
  London's Best: Churches 47, 49
  Street-by-Street map 147
Sales 59, 61, **313**
Salisbury 376
The Saltonstall Family (des
  Granges) 85
Samson and Delilah (Van Dyck) 45
The Sanctuary 72
Sandoe, John 269
Sandown Park Racecourse 347
Sandwich bars **305**, 307
Saracen's Head 164
Saracens Rugby Football Club 347

Sargent, John Singer 41, 86, 192
Saunders, Nicholas 117
Savoy Chapel **118**
Savoy Hotel **118**
   A River View of London 64
The Scale of Love (Watteau) 109
Scarf shops **325**, 327
Schaufelburg, Ernest 118
Schengen agreement 354
School of London painters 87
Schools
   Blewcoat School **83**
   Charterhouse **166**
   Westminster 76
Science
   London's Best: Museums and
      Galleries **45**
Science Museum **208–9**
   floorplan 208–9
   Great Days in London 13
   London's Best: Museums and
      Galleries 42, 45
   Street-by-Street map 202
   Visitors' checklist 209
Scott, Sir George Gilbert 40
   Albert Memorial 207
   Hereford Screen 215
Scott, Sir Giles Gilbert
   Bankside Power Station 182
   Waterloo Bridge 189
Scott, John 118
Screen Cinemas 339
Sea Life London Aquarium **190**,
   350
   Street-by-Street map 189
Security **358–9**
   at airports 366
Sehgal, Tino 183
Self-catering flats **282**, 283
Self-Portrait with Bandaged Ear
   (Van Gogh) 119
Selfridges 313
   Great Days in London 11
Senate House
   Street-by-Street map 124
The Serpentine 211
Serpentine Gallery **210**
   Great Days in London 11
Serra, Richard 183
Seurat, Georges
   Bathers at Asnières 109
Seven Dials **118**
   Street-by-Street map 114
Severs, Dennis
   Dennis Severs House **173**
Shaftesbury, Earl of 92, 105
Shaftesbury Avenue **105**
   Street-by-Street map 102
Shaftesbury Theatre 337
Shakespeare, William 26, 41, 226
   British Library 131
   Fleet Street 141
   Gray's Inn 143
   Great Bed of Ware 214
   Madame Tussauds 226
   National Portrait Gallery 104, 105

Shakespeare, William (cont.)
   Old Vic 193
   Southwark Cathedral 178
   statue of 102
   Temple 141
   Twelfth Night 25
   Westminster Abbey 81
Shakespeare's Globe **24–5**, 66,
   179
   Great Days in London 12, 13
   A River View of London 66
   Street-by-Street map 176
The Shard 35, 66, 185, 275
Shaw, George Bernard 41
   British Museum 129
   Fitzroy Square 133
Shaw, Norman 40
   Albert Hall Mansions 203
Sheen Palace 270
Shell Building
   Street-by-Street map 189
Shell Mex House
   A River View of London 64
Shelley, Harriet 210
Shelley, Percy Bysshe 210, 237
Shepherd, Edward 99, 272
Shepherd Market **99**, 272
Shepherd's Bush Market **333**
Sherlock Holmes Museum **228**
Sherman, Cindy 182
*Shipping at the Mouth of the
   Thames* (Turner) 87
Shoe shops 318
Shopping **312–33**
   art and antiques **314**
   bags and leather goods **325**,
      326
   books **322**, 323
   CDs **322**, 323
   children **318**, 320, **350**
   clothes **316–19**
   drinks **321**, 323
   food **321**, 323
   gifts **324**, 326
   hats **324–5**, 326
   interiors **326**, 327
   jewellery **324**, 326
   London's Best **314–15**
   magazines **322**, 323
   one-offs **321**, 323
   perfumes & toiletries **325**, 326–7
   records **322**, 323
   scarves **325**, 326
   souvenirs **324–7**
   specialist shops **321–3**
   stationery **325–6**, 327
Shoreditch Electricity Rooms 309
Sicilian Avenue
   Street-by-Street map 125
Siddons, Sarah 41
Silent Change, Guildhall 60
   London's Best: Ceremonies 57
Silver
   London Silver Vaults **143**
Simpson, Wallis 33
Singapore Airlines 366

Sir John Soane's Museum **138–9**
   London's Best: Museums and
      Galleries 44
   Street-by-Street map 136
Skating **346**
Skinners' Hall
   Street-by-Street map 147
Skydiver VI (Laing) 86
Sloane, Sir Hans
   British Museum 126
   Chelsea Physic Garden 199
   Sloane Square 199
   statue of 197, 199
Sloane Square **199**
   Chelsea and Battersea walk 268,
      269
Smirke, Robert 126
Smith, Sir Matthew 161
Smith, Zadie 41
Smithfield Market **166**
   Street-by-Street map 164
   turkey auction 61
Smithfield and Spitalfields **163–
   73**
   area map 163
   Museum of London **168–9**
   restaurants **298–300**
   Smithfield: Street-by-Street
      map 164–5
Smoking 308, 355
Smollensky's 349
Snacks **304–7**
The Snail (Matisse) 183
Soane, Sir John 28, 40
   Bank of England 149
   Dulwich Picture Gallery 252–3
   Pitzhanger Manor and Gallery
      260
   Ranelagh Gardens 268
   Sir John Soane's Museum 136,
      138–9
Soho and Trafalgar Square **101–
   11**
   area map 101
   The Heart of Soho **111**
   National Gallery **106–9**
   pubs 311
   Trafalgar Square: Street-by-
      Street map 102–3
Soho Square 53, **110**
Somerset, Duke of 119
Somerset House **119**
   ice rink 346, 347
   A River View of London 64
South Bank **187–93**
   area map 187
   pubs 311
   A River View of London 64
   Street-by-Street map 188–9
South Kensington and
   Knightsbridge **201–15**
   area map 201
   pubs 311
   Street-by-Street map 202–3
   Victoria and Albert Museum
      212–15

Southbank Centre **340**
  Great Days in London 12, 13
  Street-by-Street map 188–9
Southern Railway 368
Southwark and Bankside **175–85**
  area map 175
  Great Days in London 12, 13
  pubs 311
  restaurants **300–301**
  Street-by-Street map 176–7
  Tate Modern **180–83**
Southwark Bridge
  A River View of London 66
  Street-by-Street map 176
Southwark Cathedral **178, 275**
  London's Best: Churches 47, 48
  A River View of London 66
  Street-by-Street map 177
Southwark Wharves
  A River View of London 67
Souvenir shops **324–7**
Spacey, Kevin 193
Spaniards Inn **237**, 311
Speakers' Corner **211**, 273
Specialist shops **321–3**
Spence, Sir Basil 82, 219
Spencer, Earl 93
Spencer, Herbert
  grave of 248
Spencer, Stanley
  Burgh House 234
  Downshire Hill 235
  Vale of Health 237
Spencer House **93**
  Street-by-Street map 90
Spires, churches 48
Spitalfields *see* Smithfield and
  Spitalfields
Spitalfields Centre Museum of
  Immigration & Diversity **172**
Spitalfields Market *see* Old
  Spitalfields Market
Sports **346–7**
  for children 349
  in parks **53**
Sports Cafe 309
Sprague, William 118
Spread Eagle Yard
  Street-by-Street map 240
Spring Equinox celebration 58
Spring in London **58**
Squares
  Bedford Square 124
  Berkeley Square 29, 52
  Bloomsbury Square 125, **130**
  Brompton Square 203
  Fitzroy Square **132–3**
  Grosvenor Square 28
  Hanover Square 28
  Kensington Square **221**
  Leicester Square **105**
  Manchester Square 28
  Parliament Square 72, **76**
  Piazza and Central Market
    (Covent Garden) 116
  Portman Square 28

Squares (cont.)
  Queen Square **130**
  Russell Square 52, 125, **130**
  St James's Square 91, **94**
  Sloane Square **199**
  Soho Square 53, **110**
  Trafalgar Square **104**
Squash **346**
Stamps, postage 363
Stanfords 322, 323
  Street-by-Street map 114
Stansted Airport **368**
  hotels 369
  Stansted Express (rail) 368
Staple Inn **143**
State Opening of Parliament 60
  London's Best: Ceremonies 56
Stationery shops 325–6, 327
Statues
  Abraham Lincoln 76
  Albert Memorial 207
  Benjamin Disraeli 72
  Boadicea 73
  Charles II 199, 268
  Charles James Fox 125
  Charlie Chaplin 105
  Duke of Bedford 125
  Earl Haig 73
  Eros 92, 105
  Field Marshal Sir George Stuart
    White 225
  Franklin D. Roosevelt 272
  George I 130
  George II 241
  Sir Hans Sloane 197, 199
  John Betjeman 132
  Nelson Mandela 72, 189
  Peter Pan 210, 221
  Queen Anne 82, 150
  Queen Charlotte 130
  Queen Victoria 210
  Richard I 72
  Dr Samuel Johnson 140
  Thomas Carlyle 269
  Thomas More 196, 198, 269
  William III 91, 94
  William Gladstone 136
  William Shakespeare 102
  Winston Churchill 72, 76
  see also Monuments
Steer, Philip Wilson 40
Stephen, King 36
Stevenson, Robert Louis 133
Sticky Fingers 349
  Street-by-Street map 219
Stirling, Sir James 84
Stock Exchange 29, **160**
Strachey, Lytton 130
Strand *see* Covent Garden and
  the Strand
Strand on the Green **260**
Street food 307
The Struggle is My Life (Walters)
  189
Stuart, House of 37
Stuart, James 244

Student travel 356, 357
Summer in London **59**
Sunflowers (Van Gogh) 109
Sunshine 59
Surrealists 182
Sutherland, Graham
  Imperial War Museum 192
  London's Transport Museum
    116–17
Sutton House **250**
Swimming **346**
Swinburne, Algernon 195
Syon House 53, **255**
  Richmond and Kew walk 271

T

Tallis, Thomas
  tomb of 243
Tate Britain **84–7**
  Clore Galleries 84, **87**
  floorplan 84–5
  London's Best: Museums and
    Galleries 43, 45
  Visitors' checklist 85
Tate Modern **180–83**
  Bankside Power Station 182
  floorplan 180–81
  Great Days in London 12, 13
  London's Best: Museums and
    Galleries 43, 45
  A River View of London 65
  Street-by-Street map 176
  Visitors' checklist 181
  walks 274–5
Tattershall Castle 344
Taxes
  VAT (Value Added Tax) 312, 354
Taxis **377**
Taylor-Wood, Sam 87
Tea **304**, 306
Telecom Tower 34, 133
Telephones **362**
Television 363
Telford, Thomas 160
Temperatures 61
Temple **141**
  A River View of London 65
  Street-by-Street map 137
Temple Bar Memorial **140**
  Street-by-Street map 137
Temple Church
  London's Best: Churches 47, 48
Temple of Mithras 20
Tennis **346**
  Wimbledon Lawn Tennis
    Championships 59
  Wimbledon Lawn Tennis
    Museum **253**
Tennyson, Alfred Lord 198
Terry, Ellen 41
Thackeray, William
  Carlyle's House 198
  Charterhouse 166
Thames, River
  Great River Race 60
  Great Stink (1858) 30

Thames, River (cont.)
Richmond and Kew walk 270
A River View of London **62–7**
Thames Barrier 35, 63, **251**
Thatcher, Margaret 34
Wesley's Chapel-Leysian
Mission 171
Theatre **336–8**
actors **41**
Adelphi Theatre **118**
cafés **305**, 306
children in **351**
London Coliseum **121**
London Palladium **338**
National Theatre **190**
Old Vic **193**
open air theatre season 59, 226
Palace Theatre **110**
Royal Opera House **117**
Shakespeare's Globe **24–5**, 66,
176, **179**
tkts half-price ticket booth 338
Wyndham's Theatre **118**
Theatre Royal Drury Lane 117,
337, 351
Street-by-Street map 115
Theatre Royal Haymarket 40, **105**,
337
Street-by-Street map 102
Theatre Upstairs 338
Theft 350
Themed pubs and bars **309**
Thomas, Dylan 123, 133
Thomas Neal's **118**
Street-by-Street map 114
Thomson, James 229
Thornhill, Sir James
Painted Hall 241, 244
St Paul's Cathedral 153
Thornycroft, Thomas 73
Thrale, Henry 184
Thrale, Mrs 142
Three Standing Figures (Moore)
268
*Three Studies for Figures at the Base
of a Crucifixion* (Bacon) 84, 86
Tiepolo, Giovanni Battista 109
Tijou, Jean
St Alfege Church 243
St Paul's Cathedral 153
Time **357**
Time Out London 354
Tipping
in hotels 280–81
Tite, William 149
Titian
National Gallery 108
Wallace Collection 228
Toiletry shops **325**, 326–7
Tottenham Hotspur FC 347
Tourist Information 357
Tourist information centres **354**
Tours and tour guides **355**, 357
Tower Bridge **155**
Great Days in London 12, 13
A River View of London 67

Tower Green 156
Tower of London 16, 18, 23, 27,
156–9
Crown Jewels **158**
Great Days in London 11, 12, 13
Line of Kings **159**
London's Best: Ceremonies 55,
56
London's Best: Museums and
Galleries 43, 44–5
Ordnance Gallery **159**
The Princes in the Tower **159**
A River View of London 67
Royal Castle and Armour
Gallery **159**
Small Armoury and Crypt **159**
timeline 157
Visitors' checklist 157
White Tower 157, **159**
Townsend, C Harrison 171
Toys
London's Best: Museums and
Galleries **45**
Pollock's Toy Museum 45, **133**
V&A Museum of Childhood **250**
Tradescant, John 192
Trafalgar Square **104**
Great Days in London 10, 12, 13
Street-by-Street map 102–3
see also Soho and Trafalgar
Square
Trafalgar Studios **82**, 337
Trafalgar Tavern 11, **244**, 311
Trainline 364
Traitors' Gate, Tower of London
157
Transmanche 365
Transport for London (TfL) 358,
370, 371, 372
Transvestite clubs **344**
Travel **364–77**
air **366–9**
Bloomsbury and Fitzrovia 123
buses **370**, **374–5**
cars **371**
Chelsea 195
children 348
The City 145
coaches **365**
Covent Garden and the Strand
113
cycling 371
Greenwich and Blackheath 239
Hampstead 231
Holborn and the Inns of Court
135
Kensington and Holland Park
217
late-night 335
London's Transport Museum 45,
116–17
Piccadilly and St James's 89
rail **364**, **376**
Regent's Park and Marylebone
223
Smithfield and Spitalfields 163

Travel (cont.)
Soho and Trafalgar Square 101
South Bank 187
South Kensington and
Knightsbridge 201
Southwark and Bankside 175
taxis **377**
Underground 370, **372–3**
walking 371
Whitehall and Westminster 71
Travelcards 370, 372
Travelex 360
Traveller's cheques **360**
Treasury
Street-by-Street map 72
Trees
Green London **52–3**
Trent, N A 121
The Triumphs of Caesar
(Mantegna) 256
Trooping the Colour 59
London's Best: Ceremonies 54,
56
"Tube" *see* Underground
Tudor kings and Queens 36–7
Turkey auction 61
Turner, J M W 40, 250
Cheyne Walk 195, 196, **198**
Clore Galleries 84, **87**
Kenwood House 236
National Gallery 109
Peace – Burial at Sea 85
St Mary's, Battersea 253
*Shipping at the Mouth of the
Thames* 87
Tate Britain 43
Turpin, Dick 237
Tussaud, Madame *see* Madame
Tussauds
Twain, Mark
Langham Hotel 227
Ye Olde Cheshire Cheese 142
Twickenham Bridge
Richmond and Kew walk 270
Twickenham Rugby Ground 347
Twinings 136
Twombly, Cy 182
Quattro Staglioni 181
Tyler, Wat
Blackheath 245
death 154
Smithfield 164

U

Uccello, Paolo 108
Underground 31, 370, **372–3**
The Underworld (music venue)
343, 345
Unicorn Theatre 351
Union Chapel 343, 345
United Airlines 366
Universities, accommodation in
283
University College Hospital 359
Uptown Reservations 282

V

Vale of Health **237**
Van Dyck, Sir Anthony
 Kenwood House 236
 National Gallery 109
 Samson and Delilah 45
Van Eyck, Jan
 Arnolfini Portrait 108
Van Gogh, Vincent
 National Gallery 109
 Self-Portrait with Bandaged Ear
 119
 Sunflowers 109
Vanbrugh, Sir John 244
Varah, Rev Chad 148
VAT (Value Added Tax) 312, 354
Vaudeville Theatre 337
Vaughan Williams, Ralph 206
Velázquez, Diego
 Apsley House 99
 National Gallery 109
 Rokeby Venus 107
Venturi, Robert 109
Venus Venticordia (Rossetti) 40
Vermeer, Jan
 Kenwood House 236
 Queen's Gallery 98
 *Young Woman Standing at a
 Virginal* 109
Verrio, Antonio 259
Victoria, Queen 30, 31, 37, 104
 Albert Memorial 207
 Buckingham Palace 96
 Crown Jewels 158
 Kensington Palace 210
 Lancaster House 98
 Old Vic 193
 Queensway 221
 Royal Albert Hall 207
 Royal Mews 98
 statue of 210
 Victoria and Albert Museum 212
 Victoria Monument 98
 Westminster Abbey 79
Victoria and Albert Museum 42,
 44, 203, **212–15**
 floorplan 212–13
 Great Days in London 13
 London's Best: Museums and
 Galleries 42, 44, 45
 Museum of Childhood 250
 Street-by-Street map 203
 Victoria and Albert Museum of
 Childhood 45, **250**
 Visitors' checklist **213**
Victoria Embankment Gardens **120**
Victorian London **30–31**
 churches 49
Vinopolis **184, 275**
 Street-by-Street map 177
Victoria Park Books 350
Vintage fashion 318, 320
Vintners' and Distillers' Wine
 Harvest 60
 London's Best: Ceremonies 57

Virgin Atlantic 366
Virgin and Child (Burlington
 House Cartoon) (Leonardo da
 Vinci) **106**, 108
Visas 354, 357
Visit Britain 376
Visit London 58, 59, 281, 282, 354,
 355
 Accommodation Booking
 Service 281
Visual arts
 London's Best: Museums and
 Galleries **45**
Vortex Jazz Club 345
Vorticist group 86

W

W Hotel
 Street-by-Street map 102
Wagner, Richard 117
Walks **264–77**, 371
 Chelsea and Battersea **268–9**
 Mayfair to Belgravia **272–3**
 Portobello **276–7**
 Regent's Canal **266–7**
 Richmond and Kew **270–71**
 South Bank **274–5**
Wallace Collection **228**
 London's Best: Museums and
 Galleries 42, 45
Walpole, Sir Robert 77
Walters, Ian
 The Struggle is My Life 189
Walton Street
 art and antiques shops 328
War Memorial
 Street-by-Street map 177
Water sports **347**
Waterhouse, Alfred 40
 Natural History Museum 204
Waterloo Bridge
 Street-by-Street map 189
Waterloo Station **193**
Watteau, Jean Antoine
 Dulwich Picture Gallery 253
 The Scale of Love 109
Watts, George Frederick
 Kensington Gardens 210
 St Botolph, Aldersgate 166
Waugh, Evelyn 249
Weather **58–61**
Webb, Sir Aston
 Admiralty Arch 104
 The Mall 95
 Victoria and Albert Museum
 213
Weiss, David 183
Well Walk **234**
 Street-by-Street map 233
Wellcome Collection 132
Wellington, Duke of 40, 94, 273
 Apsley House 99
 Lancaster House 98
Wellington Arch **99**
Wellington Square
 Chelsea and Battersea walk 269

Wernher, Sir Julius 243, 245
Wernher Collection at Ranger's
 House **243**, 245
Wesley, John 28
 Charterhouse 165, 166
Wesley's Chapel-Leysian Mission
 170–71
West, Benjamin 86
West End
 art and antiques **328–9**, 330
 cinemas 339
 London's Best: Shopping Streets
 and Markets 315
 theatres **336–7**
West Ham United 347
Westfield London 313
Westminster Abbey 22, **78–81**
 ceremonies 58
 Coronation ceremony 158
 Easter procession and hymns
 58
 floorplan 80–81
 Great Days in London 10, 12, 13
 Dr Johnson memorial service
 57
 London's Best: Churches 46, 48
 Street-by-Street map 72
 Visitors' checklist 79
Westminster Cathedral **83**
 London's Best: Churches 46, 49
Westminster Hall 23, 74
Westminster Pier 73
Westminster School 76
 Street-by-Street map 72
Westminster and the West End
 bed and breakfast 287
 hotels **284–6**
 restaurants **292–5**
 see also Whitehall and
 Westminster
Westwood, Vivienne 35, 215
Weyden, Rogier van der 108
Wheelchair access *see* Disabled
 travellers
Whistler, James McNeill 40
 Cheyne Walk 195, 196
Whistler, Rex 85
Whit Monday 61
Whitbread, Samuel 170
Whitbread's Brewery **170**
White, Field Marshal Sir George
 Stuart
 statue of 225
White Tower, Tower of
 London157, **159**
Whitechapel Art Gallery **171**
Whitehall and Westminster
 71–87
 area map 71
 Houses of Parliament **74–5**
 Street-by-Street map 72–3
 Tate Britain **84–7**
 Westminster Abbey **78–81**
Whiteleys 221
Whitestone Pond
 Street-by-Street map 232

Whitfield, William 73
Whittington, Richard (Dick) 22, 23, **41**, 248
Wickham, Geoffrey fountain, Halkin Arcade 273
Wigmore Hall **228**, **341**
Wilde, Oscar 41, 227
Wildlife, in parks **53**
Wilkie, David 85, 86
Wilkins, William 106
William, Prince 35, 79
William I the Conqueror, King 22, 36
  Tower of London 157, 159
William II, King 36
William III, King 27, 37, 244
  Hampton Court 256, 257, 259
  Kensington Palace 210
  statue of 91, 94
  Tower of London 159
William IV, King 29, 37, 210
  Buckingham Palace 96
  Clarence House 98
William Morris Gallery **251**
Wilson, Sir Colin St John 131
Wilson, Jane and Louise 87
Wilson, Richard 255
Wimbledon Lawn Tennis Championships 59
Wimbledon Lawn Tennis Museum **253**
Wimbledon Windmill Museum 253
Winchester, Bishops of 184
Winchester Palace 23
Windsor 376
Windsor, House of 37
Wine
  Vinopolis **184**
Winter in London **61**
Woburn Walk **132**

Wolsey, Cardinal **259**
  Cardinal's Wharf 179
  Hampton Court 256
Wolsey Lodges 282, 283
Wombwell, George 248
Wood, Sir Henry 267
Woolf, Virginia 41
  Bloomsbury Square 130
  Fitzroy Square 133
World music **343**, 345
World War I 32
  Cenotaph 76–7
World War II 19, 32
  Blitz 33, 34
  Cabinet War Rooms 77
Wornum, Grey 225
Wren, Sir Christopher 40, 120
  Cardinal's Wharf 179, 275
  Christ Church 165
  churches **49**
  Flamsteed House 244
  Hampton Court 256–8
  Kensington Palace 210
  Marlborough House 95
  The Monument 12, 154
  Royal Hospital 199, 268
  Royal Naval College 241, 243, **244**
  St Andrew, Holborn 142
  St Bride's 48, 141
  St Clement Danes 137, 140
  St James Garlickhythe 146
  St James's, Piccadilly 91, 92
  St Magnus the Martyr 154
  St Margaret Pattens 155
  St Mary Abchurch 147
  St Mary-le-Bow 48, 146, 149
  St Mary-at-Hill 154–5
  St Nicholas Cole 146
  St Paul's Cathedral 12, 47, 65, **150–53**

Wren, Sir Christopher (cont.)
  St Stephen Walbrook 47, 147, 148
  Theatre Royal 117
  tomb of 152
Writers **41**
Wyatt, Benjamin Dean
  Apsley House 99
  Lancaster House 98
  Theatre Royal 117
Wyman, Bill 219
Wyndham's Theatre **118**, 337
Wynne, David
  Boy and Dolphin **197**, 269

Y

Ye Olde Cheshire Cheese **142**, 311
Yeats, W B 132
YMCA, Central 347
York, Prince Andrew, Duke of 97
York, Frederick, Duke of 98
York, House of 36
Young British Artists (YBAs) 87
The Young Dancer (Piazotta) 112
Young Woman Standing at a Virginal (Vermeer) 109
Youth culture 35
Youth hostels 283
Youth Hostels Association 283

Z

Zoo 53, **229**

Acknowledgments

Dorling Kindersley would like to thank the following people whose help and assistance contributed to the preparation of this book.

Main Contributor

Michael Leapman was born in London in 1938 and has been a journalist since he was 20. He has worked for most British national newspapers and writes about travel and other subjects for several publications, among them *The Independent, Independent on Sunday, The Economist* and *Country Life*. He has written ten books, including *London's River* (1991) and the award-winning *Companion Guide to New York* (1983, revised 1991). In 1989 he edited the acclaimed *Book of London*.

Contributors

James Aufenast, Yvonne Deutch, Guy Dimond, George Foster, Iain Gale, Fiona Holman, Phil Harriss, Lindsay Hunt, Christopher Middleton, Steven Parissien, Christopher Pick, Bazyli Solowij, Matthew Tanner, Mark Wareham, Jude Welton, Ian Wisniewski. Dorling Kindersley wishes to thank the following editors and researchers at Webster's International Publishers: Sandy Carr, Matthew Barrell, Siobhan Bremner, Serena Cross, Annie Galpin, Miriam Lloyd, Ava-Lee Tanner.

Additional Photography

Max Alexander, Peter Anderson, Stephen Bere, June Buck, Peter Chadwick, Michael Dent, Philip Dowell, Mike Dunning, Philip Enticknap, Andreas Einsiedel, Rhiannon Furbear, Steve Gorton, Christi Graham, Alison Harris, Peter Hayman, Stephen Hayward, John Heseltine, Roger Hilton, Sean Hunter, Ed Ironside, Colin Keates, Dave King, Bob Langrish, Neil Lukas, Neil Mersh, Nick Nichols, Sofía Nieto, Robert O'Dea, Ian O'Leary, Vincent Oliver, John Parker, Tim Ridley, Ellen Root, Rough Guides/Viktor Borg, Rough Guides/Roger Norum, Rough Guides/Suzanne Porter, Rough Guides/Natascha Sturny, Rough Guides/Mark Thomas, Kim Sayer, Chris Stevens, James Stevenson, James Strachan, Doug Traverso, David Ward, Mathew Ward, Steven Wooster, Nick Wright.

Additional Illustrations

Ann Child, Gary Cross, Tim Hayward, Arghya Jyoti Hore, Fiona M Macpherson, Janos Marffy, David More, Chris D Orr, Richard Phipps, Rockit Design, Michelle Ross, John Woodcock.

Cartography

Andrew Heritage, James Mills-Hicks, Chez Picthall, John Plumer (DK Cartography). Advanced Illustration (Cheshire), Contour Publishing (Derby), Euromap Ltd (Berkshire). Street Finder maps: ERA Maptec Ltd (Dublin) adapted with permission from original survey and mapping from Shobunsha (Japan).

Cartographic Research

James Anderson, Roger Bullen, Tony Chambers, Ruth Duxbury, Jason Gough, Ailsa Heritage, Jayne Parsons, Donna Rispoli, Jill Tinsley, Andrew Thompson, Lorwerth Watkins.

Design and Editorial

Managing Editor Douglas Amrine
Managing Art Editor Geoff Manders
Senior Editor Georgina Matthews
Series Design Consultant David Lamb
Art Director Anne-Marie Bulat
Production Controller Hilary Stephens
Picture Research Ellen Root, Rhiannon Furbear, Susie Peachey
DTP Editor Siri Lowe
Revisions Team Keith Addison, Namrata Adhwaryu, Ashwin Adimari, Emma Anacootee, Elizabeth Atherton, Sam Atkinson, Lydia Baillie, Chris Barstow, Oliver Bennett, Kate Berens, Julie Bowles, Chloe Carleton, Michelle Clark, Carey Combe, Vanessa Courtier, Lorna Damms, Hannah Dolan, Jessica Doyle, Caroline Elliker, Nicola Erdpresser, Jane Ewart, Simon Farbrother, Gadi Farfour, Fay Franklin, Leonie Glass, Simon Hall, Marcus Hardy, Kaberi Hazarika, Sasha Heseltine, Paul Hines, Phil Hunt, Stephanie Jackson, Gail Jones, Laura Jones, Nancy Jones, Bharti Karakoti, Stephen Knowlden, Priya Kukadia, Esther Labi, Maite Lantaron, Michelle de Larrabeiti, Chris Lascelles, Jude Ledger, Jeanette Leung, Darren Longley Carly Madden, Tanya Mahendru, Hayley Maher, Ferdie McDonald, Alison McGill, Caroline Mead, Jane Middleton, Rebecca Milner, Sonal Modha, Fiona Morgan, Hassan Muhammad, Claire Naylor, George Nimmo, Catherine Palmi, Louise Parsons, Marianne Petrou, Andrea Powell, Leigh Priest, Rada Radojicic, Mani Ramaswamy, Marisa Renzullo, Erin Richards, Nick Rider, Ellen Root, Liz Rowe, Simon Ryder, Tracy Smith, Sadie Smith, Susannah Steel, Kathryn Steve, Anna Streiffert, Rachel Symons, Andrew Szudek, Hugh Thompson, Ajay Verma, Karen Villabona, Diana Vowles, Matthew Walder, Andy Wilkinson, Sophie Wright.

Special Assistance

Christine Brandt at Kew Gardens, Sheila Brown at The Bank of England, John Cattermole at London Buses Northern, the DK picture department, especially Jenny Rayner, Pippa Grimes at the V&A, Emma Healy at the V&A Museum of Childhood, Alan Hills at the British Museum, Emma Hutton and Cooling Brown Partnership, Gavin Morgan at the Museum of London, Clare Murphy at Historic Royal Palaces, Ali Naqei at the Science Museum, Patrizio Semproni, Caroline Shaw at the Natural History Museum, Gary Smith at National Rail, Monica Thurnauer at Tate, Simon Wilson at Tate, Alastair Wardle.

Photographic Reference

The London Aerial Photo Library, and P and P F James.

Photography Permissions

Dorling Kindersley would like to thank all the museums, galleries, churches and other sights that allowed us to photograph at their establishments.

Picture Credits

a = above; b = below/bottom; c = centre; f = far; l = left;
r = right; t = top.

Works of art have been reproduced with the permission of
the following copyright holders:
Three Studies for Figures at the Base of the Crucifixion, (1944,
detail), Francis Bacon © Estate of Francis Bacon/DACS,
London 2011 84cl; *Untitled* (1964) © Larry Bell Larry Bell
Studio Annex / TAOS 233 Ranchitos Road Taos, New Mexico
United States 183tc; Fish 1926, Constantin Brancusi ©
ADAGP, Paris and DACS, London 2008 181bl; *From the Freud
Museum* (1991-6) © Susan Hiller 182cr; Bust of *Lawrence of
Arabia* © The Family of Eric H. Kennington, RA 153bl; *Self-
Portait with Knickers* Sarah Lucas 2000 Copyright the artist,
courtesy Sadie Coles HQ, London; *Quattro Stagioni* 1993–4,
© Cy Twombly 181crb.

The Publishers are grateful to the following individuals,
companies and picture libraries for permission to reproduce
their photographs:

123RF.com: William Perugini 265cr; **41 Hotel:** 281tr.
Alamy Images: Mike Booth 156cla; Paul Brown 58bc; Paul
Carstairs 60br; Construction Photography 222; Cliff Hide
Travel 243tc; Martyn Goddard 359tl; Scott Hortop Travel
225crb; Richard Green 125br; lynn hilton 162; Eric Nathan
138tl, 330tl, Picturebank 167br; Maurice Savage 257br;
Tribaleye Images/J Marshall 180cla; SuperStock 108c; Steve
Vidler 72tr, Tony Watson 98tr; **The Albermarle Connection:**
93tr; L'ANIMA RESTAURANT: 299tr; **Arcaid:** Richard Bryant,
Architect Foster and Partners 126t; Richard Bryant 251cr;
Arcblue: Peter Durant 191clh; **The Art Archive:** 23bl, 30cla,
30bc, 31bl, 32br, 32clb, 33cra, 37tc, 37crb; British Library,
London 22crb; Imperial War Museum, London 34bc;
Museum of London 19b, 31br, 32bl; Science Museum,
London 31crb; Stoke Museum Staffordshire Polytechnic
27bl, 29crb, 37bc; Victoria and Albert Museum, London
24clb, 25bc, 29tr; **AWL Images:** Rex Butcher 186; **Axiom:**
James Morris 166tl.
Governor and Company of the Bank of England: 147tc;
Bibendum Restaurant Ltd: 289br; **Bridgeman Art Library,
London:** 25t; British Library, London 18, 23ca, (detail) 25br,
28cb, (detail) 36c, 36bl; © Coram in the care of the Foundling
Museum 131tc; Courtesy of the Institute of Directors,
London 33ca; Guildhall Library, Corporation of London 28br,
78cl; ML Holmes Jamestown – Yorktown Educational Trust,
VA (detail) 21bc; Master and Fellows, Magdalene College,
Cambridge (detail) 27clb; Marylebone Cricket Club, London
248c; William Morris Gallery, Walthamstow 23tl, 251bc;
Museum of London 26–7; O'Shea Gallery, London (detail)
26crb; Royal Holloway & Bedford New College 159bc; Russell
Cotes Art Gallery and Museum, Bournemouth 40tr; Thyssen-
Bornemisza Collection, Lugano Casta 259bl; Westminster
Abbey, London (detail) 36bc; White House, Bond Street,
London 32c. **British Airways:** Adrian Meredith Photography:
366cla; reproduced with permission of the British Library
Board: 131br; © The British Museum: 20ca, 21ca, 42tr, 126–7
all pics except 126t, 128–9 all pics; **Brittany Ferries:** 365tl;
BT Group plc: 362c. **Buen Ayre Restaurant:** 301br.

Camera Press: London: Cecil Beaton 81tl; Charles Dickens
Museum: 131c; **Charlotte Street Hotel:** 280bl, 284bc; **Chez
Bruce:** 302bl; **The Clerkenwell Kitchen:** 298tc; **Clos
Maggiore:** 292bl; **Collections:** Oliver Benn 62br; Philip
Craven 262cla; Julie Hamilton 232tr; John Miller 165bl; Liz
Stares 263bl; **Colorific!:** Steve Benbow 57tl; **Conran
Restaurants:** 314bc; **Corbis:** 88, Bettmann 6-7; Bruce
Burkhardt 291c; Paul Cunningham 37cra, Demotix/Angus
Mordant 35crb, Sarah J Duncan 130clb; 97tc; Jason Hawkes
68-69; Angelo Hornak 63c, 185br; JAI/Alan Copson 38, 171bl,
185tl; London Aerial Photo Library 191bl, 191cla; Kim Sayer
10bl; Patrick Ward 63tl; **Courtesy of the Corporation of
London:** 57c, 148tr; **Courtauld Institute, London:** 43br,
119bl; **Cutty Sark Trust:** 240cla.
Copyright Dean and Chapter of Westminster: 80bl, 81br;
Dewynters Ltd.: David Crosswaite 115cra; **Dr Johnson's
House: Dorling Kindersley:** Jamie Marshall /6tl; The Science
Museum, London 202bc; **Dreamstime.com:** Basphoto 261tr;
Beaucroft 319tr; Lowerkase 64cla; **Courtesy of the
Governors and the Directors Dulwich Picture Gallery:** 45tr,
252bl.
E&O, Ricker Restaurants: 296tc; **Francis Edwards:** 315bl;
English Heritage: 254cr, 260b; Jonathon Bailey 243bl;
English Life Publications Ltd: 255br, **Mary Evans Picture
Library:** 20bl, 20bc, 21bl, 21br, 24bl, 26bl, 29bc, 29br, 31tl,
31ca, 31bc, 34bl, 36br, 37tl, 37clb, 37bl, 37br, 41bl, 74bc,
74clb, 92b, 114bl, 116bl, 137tl, 141tl, 161tc, 179cl, 207br,
218tr, 228br.
Courtesy of Fan Museum: Hélène Alexander Collection
245b; **Fleet River Bakery Rooms:** 287br; **Fotolia:** Balliolman
112; **Freud Museum, London:** 248t.
Gore Hotel, London: 281bl; **The Goring Hotel, London:**
282tl; **Geffrye Museum, London:** 250tl; **Getty Images:** 35br;
Gregory Bajor 246; Walter Bibikow 122; Miguel Carminati 70;
Alan Copson 352-3; Flickr/Richard Newstead 2-3; Heritage
Images 107tl, Peter Macdiarmid 183br; Eric Nathan 144;
SuperStock 109br; **Green Tourism Business Scheme:** 357tr;
greenwichmarket.net 240clb.
Hakkasan Mayfair: 295bc; **Robert Harding Picture Library:**
35cra, 44cra, 54cla, 60cr, 244tr, 335tr, 359cl, 376bl; Philip
Craven 210t; Nigel Francis 368tr; Sylvain Gradadam 291tl;
Brian Hawkes 25cb; Michael Jenner 25cra, 229tr; Nick Wood
65bl; **Harrods:** (printed by kind permission of Mohamed al
Fayed): 312bl; **Hayes-Davidson (computer generated
images):** 176clb; **Hayward Gallery:** Richard Haughton 275tl;
Jonty Wilde 190tl; **Reproduced with permission of Her
Majesty's Stationery Office (Crown Copyright):** 158 all pics;
John Heseltine: 53tr, 65br, 130b; **Friends of Highgate
Cemetery:** 248b; **Historic Royal Palaces (Crown Copyright):**
5ca, 5tr, 7t, 39c, 156tr, 157clb, 256–7 all except 256br and
257br, 258–9 all except 259bl; **The Hulton Getty:** 28bl, 130tl,
234tl.
The Image Bank, London: Gio Barto 57b; Derek Berwin 35tl;
Romilly Lockyer 17tl, 17br, 74cla; Leo Mason 58cr; Terry
Williams 141bl; **Inamo Restaurant:** 293tr; **iStockphoto.com:**
Alan Crawford 366br; peterspiro 371br.
Peter Jackson Collection: 28–9; **Jewish Museum, London:**
249tl. **The Laughing Gravy:** 300br; **Leon Restaurants:**
288cla; **Leighton House:** 218bl; **Little Angel Marionette
Theatre:** 351tl; **London Ambulance Service:** Tim Saunders

359cla; **London Aquarium:** 11tr, 190cr; **London Bridge Hotel:** 281tl; **London City Airport:** 367tr; **London Palladium:** 105br; **London Transport Museum:** 32cla, Madame Tussauds: 224cla, 226cra, 226t; **Mansell Collection:** 23br, 24cl, 24br, 25bl, 26cl, 26clb, 27br, 31cla; **Rob Moore:** 117tr; **Museum of London:** 17crb, 20clb, 21tc, 21crb, 22tl, 25crb, 43tc, 165crb, 168–9; **Reproduced by courtesy of the Trustees, The National Gallery, London:** (detail) 39tc, 106–7 all except 106t, 108tr, 108b, 109ca, 109bl; **National Portrait Gallery, London:** 4t, 43tl, 103cra, 104br; **National Postal Museum, London:** 30bl; **By permission of the Keeper of the National Railway Museum, York:** 32–3; **National Trust Photographic Library:** Wendy Aldiss 27cra; John Bethell 254tl, 255tr; Michael Boys 40br; **Natural History Museum, London:** 204tr, 205crb; John Downs 16clb, 205tc, Derek Adams 204b, 204cl; **New Shakespeare Theatre co:** 334clb; Ottolenghi: 277tc, 302tl; **OXO Tower Restaurant/Harvey Nichols:** 300tr.
Palace Theatre Archive:110tc; **Parliamentary Copyright House of Lords 2012:** Photography by Chris Moyse 75crb; **Pictor International, London:** 62cl, 176br; **Pictures Colour Library:** 56br; **Pippa Pop-ins Children's Nursery, London:** 349br; **Pitzhanger Manor Museum:** 260c; **Popperfoto:** 33tl, 33crb, 34tl, 34tr, 34cl, 37tr, 41br; **Post House Heathrow:** Tim Young 369tr; **La Poule au Pot:** 297bl; **Press Association Ltd:** 33bl, 33br; **Public Record Office (Crown Copyright):** 22b.
Bill Rafferty: 334cb; **RBS Group:** 360bl, 360cb; **Rex Features Ltd:** 55tl; Andrew Laenen 56crb; Jonathon Player 290cla; **The Ritz, London:** 93bl; **The River Cafe:** 303bl; **Royal Academy of Arts, London:** 92tr; **The Board of Trustees of The Royal Armouries:** 43tr, 159t, 159br; **Trustees of the Royal Botanic Gardens,
Kew:** Andrew McRob 50cl, 262–3 all pics except 262cla, 263bl; **The Royal Collection © 2013 Her Majesty Queen Elizabeth II:** 1c, 8–9, 55bl, 95tr, 96tr, 96cla, 96ca, 97bl, 97br, 256br; Derry Moore 97cra; **Royal College of Music, London:** 206c.
Image Courtesy of the Saatchi Gallery, London: Matthew Booth 289tl; **St Paul's Cathedral:** Sampson Lloyd 150cb, 152cla, 153tr; **Salt Yard:** 298br; **Sam's Brasserie:** 303tr; **The Savoy Group:** 118cr; **Science Museum, London:** 208–9

all pics; **Society of London Theatre/tkts:** 335br; **Somerset House:** Peter Durant/arcblue.com 119tr; **Spencer House Ltd:** 90bl; **Southbank Press Office:** 188clb; Stephen Cummiskey 188cla; Graeme Duddridge 274cla; **STA Travel Group:** 356bc; **Superstock:** Loop Images/ Tom Hanslien 200 , /Alex Hare 174, /Ricky Leaver 230, 238; Londonstills.com 264; Nomad 194; Prisma 216; Travelshots 278-79; **Syndication International:** 39tr, 54clb, 55crb, 60bl, 61c; Library of Congress; 29bl.
Tate London 2001: 84–5 all pics, 86 all pics, 87br, 180–81, 182–3, 275br. **Transport for London:** 355br, 370br, 372tr, 372–73 all maps and tickets, 374bl, 375tl; **Travel Pictures:** Stuart Black 100; **Courtesy of the Board of Trustees of The Victoria and Albert Museum:** 39br, 42br; 212–13 all pics; purchased with the assistance of the NACF and the Goldsmith's Company 213cra; 214–15 all pics, 350tc; **View Pictures:** Dennis Gilbert 372br. **W Hotel London:** 282br, 285tl; **By kind permission of the trustees of The Wallace Collection, London:** 42cla, 228cl; **Philip Way Photography:** 66clb, 152bl, 179br; **Courtesy of the Trustees of the Wedgwood Museum, Barlaston, Stoke-on-Trent, Staffs, England:** 30br; **Vivienne Westwood:** Patrick Fetherstonhaugh 35bl; **The Wimbledon Lawn Tennis Museum:** Micky White 253tr; **The Wolseley:** 294tl; Photo © Woodmansterne: Jeremy Marks 39tl, 151cra; **Youth Hostel Association:** 283tc.
Zefa: 54br, 334cl; Bob Croxford 59c; Clive Sawyer 59br.

Front Endpaper: **Alamy:** Construction Photography Ltr; lynn hilton Rcra; **AWL Images:** Rex Butcher Rbr; **Corbis:** Rbl; **Fotolia:** Balliolman Rtr; **Getty Images:** Walter Bibikow Rtl; Miguel Carminati Rfbl; Eric Nathan Rcrb; **Superstock:** age fotostock/Charles Bowman Ltc; Loop Images/Tom Hanslien Lbl, /Alex Hare Rfbr, /Ricky Leaver Ltl; Nomad Lbc; Prisma Lclb; Travel Pictures: Stuart Black Rftl.

Jacket: Front main and Spine top –
4Corners: Massimo Ripani.
Map Cover – **4Corners:** Massimo Ripani.
All other images © Dorling Kindersley
For further information see www.DKimages.com

Special Editions of DK Travel Guides

The London Underground

Chesham · Chalfont & Latimer ≷
Amersham
Watford Junction ≷
Watford High Street ≷
Edgware
Burnt Oak
Chorleywood
Watford
Bushey ≷
Stanmore
Canons Park
Colindale
Hendon Central
Rickmansworth
Croxley
Carpenders Park ≷
Moor Park
Hatch End ≷
Queensbury
Brent Cross
West Ruislip ≷
Northwood
Headstone Lane ≷
Kingsbury
Golders Green
Ma
Hillingdon
Northwood Hills
Harrow & Wealdstone ≷
Kenton
Neasden
Hampste
Ruislip
Pinner
Preston Road
Finchley Road & Frognal
Heath
Uxbridge · Ickenham
Ruislip Manor
North Harrow
Wembley Park
Dollis Hill
Hampstead
Eastcote
Harrow-on-the-Hill
Ruislip Gardens
Rayners Lane
Northwick Park
South Kenton
North Wembley
Willesden Green
Belsize Park
South Ruislip ≷
West Harrow
Wembley Central ≷
Brondesbury Park
Kilburn †
West Hampstead ≷
Chalk Farr
South Harrow
Stonebridge Park
Harlesden
Willesden Junction
Kensal Rise
Brondesbury
Finchley Road
Camden To
Northolt
Sudbury Hill
Kensal Green
Queen's Park
Kilburn High Road
South Hampstead
Swiss Cottage
St. John's Wood
Mornington Crescer
Greenford
Sudbury Town
Alperton
Kilburn Park
Maida Vale
Warwick Avenue
Royal Oak
Westbourne Park
Paddington
Edgware Road
Marylebone ≷
Baker Street
Great Portland Street
Euston
Perivale
Warren Street
Regent's Park
Hanger Lane
Ladbroke Grove
Latimer Road
Shepherd's Bush
Edgware Road
Bayswater
Park Royal
East Acton
White City
Notting Hill Gate
Lancaster Gate
†Bond Street
Oxford Circus
Goodge Street
North Ealing
≷ Ealing Broadway
West Acton
North Acton
Wood Lane
Holland Park
Queensway
Marble Arch
Green Park
Tottenham Court Road
Ealing Common
Acton Central
Shepherd's Bush Market
Kensington (Olympia) ≷
High Street Kensington
Hyde Park Corner
Piccadilly Circus
South Acton
Goldhawk Road
Barons Court
Knightsbridge
Gloucester Road †
Sloane Square
St. James's Park
Acton Town
Hammersmith
Earl's Court
South Kensington
Victoria
Westminster
South Ealing
Northfields
Boston Manor
Chiswick Park
Turnham Green
Stamford Brook
Ravenscourt Park
West Kensington
≷ West Brompton
Pimlico
† Waterloo
Osterley
Hounslow East
Hounslow Central
Gunnersbury
Fulham Broadway
Heathrow Terminals 1, 2, 3
Hounslow West
Hatton Cross
Parsons Green
Kew Gardens
Putney Bridge
Imperial Wharf ≷
River Thames
Heathrow Terminal 4
Richmond ≷
East Putney
Vauxhall
Heathrow Terminal 5
Southfields
Oval
Ke
Wimbledon Park
Clapham Junction ≷
Wandsworth Road
Stockw
Wimbledon
Clapham High Street
Clapham North

Legend

Clapham Common
Clapham South
Balham
Tooting Bec
Tooting Broadway
Colliers Wood
South Wimbledon
Morden

MAYOR OF LONDON

tfl.gov.uk

24 hour travel information
0343 222 1234*

*Service and network charges may apply. See tfl.gov.uk/terms for details.

✉ Sig
tf